The Outbreak of the English Civil War

Anthony Fletcher
Professor of History, University of Durham

Edward Arnold

A division of Hodder & Stoughton
LONDON   MELBOURNE   AUCKLAND

First published in Great Britain 1981
First published in paperback 1985 (with corrections)
Reprinted 1989, 1993

British Library Cataloguing in Publication Data

Fletcher, Anthony
  The outbreak of the English Civil War.
  1. Great Britain — History — Civil War,
  1642–1649
  I. Title
  942.06'2   DA415

  ISBN 0 7131 6454 9

Typeset in 11/12 Plantin by Colset Private Limited, Singapore.
Printed and bound in Great Britain for Edward Arnold, a division of Hodder and Stoughton Limited, Mill Road, Dunton Green, Sevenoaks, Kent TN13 2YA, by Athenaeum Press Ltd, Newcastle upon Tyne

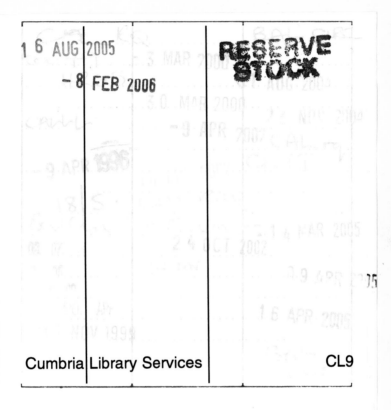

For my students at Sheffield 1970–1979

That great God who is the searcher of my heart knows with what a sad sense I go on upon this service and with what a perfect hatred I detest this war without an enemy, but I look upon it as *opus Dei,* which is enough to silence all passion in me. The God of peace in his good time send us the blessing of peace and, in the meantime, fit us to receive it. We are both upon the stage and must act the parts that are assigned to us in this tragedy; let us do it in a way of honour and without personal animosities.

Sir William Waller to Sir Ralph Hopton,
16 July 1643.

Contents

Preface and Acknowledgements

Many thanks are due at the end of writing this book. I begin with my students because if it had not been for their insistent questioning in the first years that I taught a special subject on the origins of the civil war I might not have undertaken the task. Members of my special subject group between 1970 and 1979 had the arguments that appear here tried out on them in a succession of different forms. Their responses were often stimulating, just as their questions were worrying. But above all their enthusiasm for the subject was a constant encouragement. It is a pleasure to dedicate the book collectively to them.

My numerous debts to those who have written about this period are acknowledged in the footnotes. The authoritative account, now almost 100 years old, remains that of S.R. Gardiner. His was a staggering achievement. His narrative only needs correction on a few points of detail. Although this book contains a new narrative it is in no sense an attempt to replace Gardiner's. Certain events which he treated fully have deliberately been passed over lightly, in order to allow space for discussion of aspects of the political process which seem to me to have received too little attention in the past.

I am grateful to the Twenty-Seven Foundation and to the University of Sheffield Research Fund for grants towards the costs of research. Archivists in county records offices and town halls too numerous to mention by name have been unfailingly helpful in answering my queries and making available documents in their care. So have the staffs of the Bodleian Library and the British Library. I am also deeply grateful to the Yale Center for Parliamentary Research for the loan of their transcripts of the diaries of Sir Simonds D'Ewes, Framlingham Gawdy, Roger Hill, John Moore and Sir Thomas Peyton for the period 11 January–31 August 1642. These transcripts are the work of Mrs Anne Young, who has given unstinting help with checking the wording of my quotations and my references to the originals. Anne Young's meticulous work on the diaries has saved me many months of labour.

Another profound debt is to those who have deposited their theses in university libraries and made them available to readers. I have profited from consulting the following:

L. Beats, 'Politics and Government in Derbyshire 1640–1660', University of Sheffield PhD thesis (1978)

J.B. Crummett, 'The Lay Peers in Parliament 1640–1644', University of Manchester PhD thesis (1970)

C.G. Durston, 'Berkshire and its County Gentry 1625–1649', University of Reading PhD thesis (1977)

G.A. Harrison, 'Royalist Organisation in Gloucestershire and Bristol', University of Manchester MA thesis (1961)

G.A. Harrison, 'Royalist Organisation in Wiltshire 1642–1646', University of London PhD thesis (1963)

C. Hibbard, 'Charles I and the Popish Plot', Yale University PhD thesis (1975)

A.L. Hughes, 'Politics, Society and Civil War in Warwickshire 1620–1650', University of Liverpool PhD thesis (1980)

R. Hutton, 'The Royalist War Effort in Wales and the West Midlands 1642–1646', University of Oxford D. Phil. thesis (1980)

A.M. Johnson, 'Buckinghamshire 1640–1660', University of Wales MA thesis (1963)

M.V. Jones, 'The Political History of the Parliamentary Boroughs of Kent 1640–1662', University of London PhD thesis (1967)

D.F. Mosler, 'A Social and Religious History of the English Civil War in the County of Warwick', Stanford University PhD thesis (1975)

P.R. Newman, 'The Royalist Army in the North of England', University of York PhD thesis (1978)

C.B. Phillips, 'The Gentry of Cumberland and Westmorland 1600–1665', University of Lancaster PhD thesis (1974)

J.T. Pickles, 'Studies in Royalism in the English Civil War 1642–1646 with special reference to Staffordshire', University of Manchester MA thesis (1968)

B.W. Quintrell, 'The Government of the County of Essex 1603–1642' University of London PhD thesis (1965)

R.H. Silcock, 'County Government in Worcestershire 1603–1660', University of London PhD thesis (1974)

N.R.N. Tyacke, 'Arminianism in England in Religion and Politics 1604–1640', University of Oxford D. Phil. thesis (1968)

M.D.G. Wanklyn, 'Landed Society and Allegiance in Cheshire and Shropshire in the First Civil War', University of Manchester PhD thesis (1976)

The University of Sheffield granted me a term of study leave to work on this book in 1975 and another one in 1980. Colleagues both at Sheffield and elsewhere have been more than generous with their time in reading and commenting on draft chapters. In this respect I owe much to Dr Barry Coward, Dr Mark Greengrass, Professor Kenneth Haley and Professor

Conrad Russell, who have read sections of the book at various stages, and to Professor Austin Woolrych, whose advice on the final draft of the whole book has been of great benefit. Responsibility for the text as it appears is of course entirely my own. Miss Lynn Baker, Miss Suzanne Duce, Miss Suzanne Hill, Mrs Patricia Holland and Peta Jones have coped with my handwriting and shared the typing.

My greatest debt as always is to my family. Tresna's support has been unfailing; Crispin and Dickon have given valuable help with the index.

Sheffield, March 1981   A.J.F.

Preface to the Paperback Edition

I have taken the opportunity provided by the reprinting of the book for this paperback edition to correct a number of typographical errors. I am particularly grateful to Anne Young who brought many of these to my attention. Debate about the origins of the civil war has continued unabated since 1981. Newly published work, too extensive to be listed here, includes Caroline Hibbard's book *Charles I and the Popish Plot* (Chapel Hill, N.C., 1983) and two important articles by John Morrill, 'The Religious Context of the English Civil War' in *Transactions of the Royal Historical Society* XXIII (1983) and 'The Attack on the Church of England in the Long Parliament 1640–1642' in D. Beales and G. Best, editors, *History, Society and the Churches: Essays in Honour of Owen Chadwick* (London, 1984).

Sheffield, April 1985   A.J.F.

Abbreviations

Add. MS	Additional MS
Andriette	E.A. Andriette, *Devon and Exeter in the Civil War* (Newton Abbot, 1971).
Baillie	R. Baillie, *Letters and Journals*, (Edinburgh, 1841), I.
BIHR	*Bulletin of the Institute of Historical Research*
BL	British Library
Buller	R.N. Worth, editor, *The Buller Papers* (privately printed, 1895).
CJ	*Journals of the House of Commons*
Clarendon	W.D. Macray, editor, *Clarendon's History of the Rebellion and Civil Wars in England* (Oxford, 1888).
Cliffe	J.T. Cliffe, *The Yorkshire Gentry from the Reformation to the Civil War* (London, 1969).
Cope	E.S. Cope, editor, *Proceedings of the Short Parliament of 1640* (Camden Society fourth series XIX, 1977).
Crawford	P. Crawford, *Denzil Holles* (London, 1979).
Crummett	J.B. Crummett, The Lay Peers in Parliament 1640–1644, University of Manchester, PhD thesis, 1972.
CSPD	*Calendar of State Papers Domestic*
CSPV	*Calendar of State Papers Venetian*
Dering	*A Collection of Speeches made by Sir Edward Dering* (1642).
D'Ewes (C)	W.H. Coates, editor, *The Journal of Sir Simonds D'Ewes from the First Recess of the Long Parliament to the Withdrawal of King Charles from London* (Yale, 1942).
D'Ewes (N)	W. Notestein, editor, *The Journal of Sir Simonds D'Ewes from the Beginning of the Long Parliament to the Opening of the Trial of the Earl of Strafford* (Yale, 1923).

DO	*The Diurnal Occurrences or Daily Proceedings of Both Houses in this Great and Happy Parliament from the Third of November 1640 to the Third of November 1641* (London, 1641).
Durston	C.G. Durston, Berkshire and its County Gentry 1625–49, University of Reading, PhD thesis, 1977.
EHR	*English Historical Review*
Evelyn	W. Bray, *Diary of John Evelyn* (London, 1879), IV.
Everitt	A. Everitt, *The Community of Kent and the Great Rebellion* (Leicester, 1965).
Fairfax	G.W. Johnson, *The Fairfax Correspondence* (London, 1848), 2 vols.
Gardiner	S.R. Gardiner, *A History of England 1603–1642* (London 1883–4), 10 vols.
Gardiner, *Documents*	S.R. Gardiner, *Constitutional Documents of the Puritan Revolution* (Oxford, 1906)
Harley	T.T. Lewis, editor, *Letters of the Lady Brilliana Harley* (Camden Society, first series, LI, 1853).
Harl.MS	Harleian Manuscript
Hibbard	C. Hibbard, Charles I and the Popish Plot, Yale PhD thesis, 1975.
Hill	Transcript of the Journal of Roger Hill (Buckinghamshire Record Office) by Mrs Anne Young.
Hirst	D. Hirst, *The Representative of the People?* (Cambridge, 1975).
HLRO	*House of Lords Record Office*
HMC	Historical Manuscripts Commission
HMC Buccleuch	*Historical Manuscripts Commission, Buccleuch MSS at Montagu House*
HMC Coke	*Historical Manuscripts Commission, Cowper-Coke Manuscripts*, II.
HMC Egmont	*Historical Manuscripts Commission, Earl of Egmont's MSS*, I.
HMC Montagu	*Historical Manuscripts Commission, Montagu of Beaulieu Manuscripts.*
HMC Portland	*Historical Manuscripts Commission, Portland Manuscripts.*
HMC Various	*Historical Manuscripts Commission, Various Manuscripts.*
Holmes	C. Holmes, *The Eastern Association in the*

	English Civil War (Cambridge, 1974).
Hughes	A.L. Hughes, Politics, Society and Civil War in Warwickshire 1620–1650, University of Liverpool PhD thesis, 1980.
Hutchinson	J. Sutherland, editor, *Lucy Hutchinson's Memoirs of the Life of Colonel Hutchinson* (Oxford, 1973).
Hutton	R. Hutton, The Royalist War Effort in Wales and the West Midlands, University of Oxford, D. Phil. thesis, 1980.
JBS	*Journal of British Studies*
JEH	*Journal of Ecclesiastical History*
JMH	*Journal of Modern History*
Johnson	A.M. Johnson, Buckinghamshire 1640–1660: A Study in County Politics, University of Wales, MA thesis, 1963.
Keeler	M.F. Keeler, *The Long Parliament* (Philadelphia, 1954).
Kenyon, *Constitution*	J.P. Kenyon, *The Stuart Constitution* (Cambridge, 1966).
Ketton-Cremer	R.W. Ketton-Cremer, *Norfolk in the Civil War* (London, 1969).
Knyvett	B. Schofield, editor, *The Knyvett Letters* (London, 1949).
Larking	L.B. Larking, editor, *Proceedings in Kent* (Camden Society, LXXX, 1862).
LJ	*Lords Journals*
Manning	B. Manning, *The English People and the English Revolution* (London, 1976).
Morrill, *Revolt*	J.S. Morrill, *The Revolt of the Provinces* (London, 1976).
Nalson	J. Nalson, *An Important Collection of the Great Affairs of State* (1683), II.
Nicholas	G.F. Warner, editor, *Correspondence of Sir Edward Nicholas*, Vol I, 1641–1652, (Camden Society, new series, XL, 1886).
Ormerod	G. Ormerod, editor, *Tracts relating to Military Proceedings in Lancashire during the Great Civil War* (Chetham Society, II, 1844).
Oxinden	D. Gardiner, editor, *The Oxinden Letters 1607–1642* (London, 1933).
PCR	*Privy Council Registers in Facsimile* (London, 1967–8).

Pearl	V. Pearl, *London and the Outbreak of the Puritan Revolution: City Government and National Politics 1625–1643* (Oxford, 1961).
Pennington	D. Pennington, 'The Making of the War 1640–1642' in D. Pennington and K.V. Thomas, *Puritans and Revolutionaries: Essays in Seventeenth Century History presented to Christopher Hill* (Oxford, 1978).
PRO	Public Record Office
RO	Record Office
Rushworth	J. Rushworth, *Historical Collections* (1680–1722), 10 vols.
Russell, *Origins*	C.S.R. Russell, editor, *The Origins of the English Civil War* (London, 1973).
Russell, *Parliaments*	C.S.R. Russell, *Parliaments and English Politics 1621–1629* (Oxford, 1979).
Shaw	W.A. Shaw, *A History of the English Church 1640–1660* (London, 1900).
Slingsby	D. Parsons, editor, *The Diary of Sir Henry Slingsby of Scriven* (1836).
SR	*Statutes of the Realm*
Steele	R. Steele, *Tudor and Stuart Proclamations* (Oxford, 1960), I.
Sussex	A.J. Fletcher, *A County Community in Peace and War: Sussex 1600–1660* (London, 1976).
Townshend	J.W. Willis Bund, editor, *The Diary of Henry Townshend* (Worcestershire Historical Society, 1915).
TRHS	*Transactions of the Royal Historical Society*
Twysden	'Sir Roger Twysden's Journal', *Archaeologia Cantiana*, I, 1858.
Underdown	D. Underdown, *Somerset in the Civil War and Interregnum* (Newton Abbot, 1973).
VCH	*Victoria County History*
Verney	F.P. Verney, editor, *Memoirs of the Verney Family* (London, 1892), 2 vols.
Verney, *Notes*	J. Bruce, editor, *Notes of Proceedings in the Long Parliament by Sir Ralph Verney* (Camden Society, XXXI, 1845).
Wallington	N. Wallington, *Historical Notices of Events in the Reign of Charles I* (London, 1869).
Wedgwood	C.V. Wedgwood, *The King's Peace* (London, 1955).

Wormald   B.H.G. Wormald, *Clarendon* (Cambridge, 1964).
YPL   York Public Library
Zagorin   P. Zagorin, *The Court and the Country* (London, 1969).

List of Maps

Note on Sources and Quotations

In quoting from original sources I have modernized spelling and capitalization and occasionally supplied punctuation necessary to the sense of the passage. Dates are given in Old Style but with the year regarded as beginning on 1 January.

I have sought to keep the footnotes as concise as possible by making use of a long list of abbreviations. All books and articles not in this list have been given their full title, and place and date of publication the first time they are cited and a short title thereafter. Almost all the contemporary pamphlets that I have used are in the Thomason Collection in the British Library. Unless the text makes the title of the pamphlet cited obvious, I have normally supplied the British Library reference together with a sufficiently specific title for it to be possible to identify the item concerned without difficulty in other library catalogues. Full titles can be checked in G.K. Fortescue, *Catalogue of the Pamphlets collected by George Thomason*.

Introduction

The seventh of November 1640 was the fifth day of a new parliament, the second to be held that year, a parliament which, though no one would have believed it if they had been told, was to sit for more than 12 years. Arthur Capel, from Hertfordshire, gave others their cue when he stood up in the House of Commons with a petition in his hand. County agendas began to pile the table. Harbottle Grimston, with a powerful piece of rhetoric, called for a committee to consider them so that 'laws may be contrived and found for the preventing of the like mischiefs for the future'. The veteran Sir Benjamin Rudyerd harnessed the rising tide of emotion by harping on the 'destructive counsels' which rang 'a doleful deadly knell over the whole kingdom'.[1] Then John Pym rose. He was a man in a hurry, more passionate than in his deft summary of grievances to the Short Parliament on 17 April, less coherent in what he said. The speech was probably an inspired response to the day's debating. He began by sweeping aside Grimston's demand for new laws: 'we have good laws yet they want their execution; if they are executed it is in a wrong sense.' There was a design, Pym insisted, 'to alter law and religion', or, as another version of the speech has it, 'to alter the kingdom both in religion and government'. The papist conspiracy against the nation provided an overall perspective for a mass of discontents that Pym knew were seething in men's minds. Yet it was far from merely a propaganda device. Pym was utterly convinced that a conspiracy existed.[2]

With Pym's speech on 7 November 1640 provincial and national politics were fused. He concentrated men's minds: some of his listeners probably failed to grasp fully what he meant; many had not worked out the implications of his words. Nevertheless, for a rare and brief moment, the mood was one of complete unanimity. So menacing did the threat appear to be from above, that members did not stop to consider the process of events, involving riots, mutinies and a taxpayers' strike during the summer, which had brought them together. They did not ask each other about their priorities when religious zeal clashed with the preservation of social order or when the pursuit of evil counsellors involved making new laws. They

1 Rushworth III, Part I, 21, 24–6, 34–7; *D'Ewes (N)*, pp. 5–7.
2 *D'Ewes (N)*, pp. 7–11; Kenyon, pp. 190, 203–5.

were conservative men who did not appreciate the complexities of a potentially revolutionary situation. None of them would have believed that within two years the nation would be at war within itself.

It is proper to start an account of the outbreak of the civil war with Pym, since he was the acknowledged leader of the Long Parliament from its inception until his death just over three years later. Such was the authority he had achieved with his masterly speeches on 17 and 28 April, that everyone assumed he would be the outstanding figure in the new assembly.[3] Thus when Sir Richard Skeffington sent his advice to a newly elected friend, Sir Edward Dering, about the need for a long session, he added 'this is my earnest request to my dear friend Mr Pym'. Sir Simonds D'Ewes, unable to be up for the opening week, sent Sir Nathaniel Barnardiston a letter of apology for him to deliver to Pym.[4]

The threat posed by the contagious disease of popery had been the constant theme of Pym's parliamentary career ever since his maiden speech in 1621. He was convinced of the indefatigability of papists: 'for having gotten favour', he told the Commons in 1621, 'they will expect a toleration, after toleration they will look for equality, after equality for superiority, and after superiority they will seek the supression of that religion which is contrary to theirs.' He repeated the charge in the printed version of his speech of 7 November 1640, where he declared that the design against the kingdom was maintained by papists 'who are obliged by a maxim in their doctrine that they are not only to maintain their religion but extirpate others'.[5] Purity and unity of religion for Pym was the basis both of the rule of law and of the mutual obligation of King and people. He was one of those who believed, the historian of the 1620s parliaments has said, that 'the world was a perpetual struggle between the forces of good and evil, of Christ and Antichrist, a battle in which there was no resolution short of final victory'. His task was hunting the forces of evil. His maiden speech revealed his view of evil as something so universal that, unless checked, it was 'apt to multiply' until it pulled down church and state. On this occasion he attacked John Shepherd, a church papist MP, for seeking to 'divide us among ourselves, exasperating one party by the odious and factious name of Puritans.' Shepherd had opposed a bill for better observance of the sabbath on the ground that it was a 'Puritan' bill.[6]

The watershed in Pym's career was the rise of Arminianism. For him the Arminian assault on predestination was much more than simply an assault

---

3 Cope, pp. 7, 148–57, 299–302; Kenyon, pp. 197–203.

4 BL Sloane MS 184, fol. 192, Harl, MS 384, fol. 66r.

5 W. Notestein, F.H. Relf, H. Simpson, editors, *Commons Debates 1621* (New Haven, 1935) II, 463; Kenyon, p. 204.

6 C.S.R. Russell, 'The Parliamentary Career of John Pym 1621–9', in P. Clark, A.G.R. Smith, N. Tyacke, editors, *The English Commonwealth 1547–1640: Essays presented to Joel Hurstfield* (Leicester, 1979), pp. 151–2.

on Protestantism. He saw it as 'an attempt to subvert the state, both by depriving it of that religious unity without which it could not function, and by destroying that unity between king and people without which no government could be other than arbitrary.'[7] The Arminians, it has been shown, attempted a far-reaching redefinition of puritanism.[8] Pym found this utterly offensive. 'By dividing the kingdom under the name of Puritans, labouring to bring His Majesty in jealousy with his subjects and to stir up others in hatred against such', he believed, they were raising sedition. Richard Montagu, he alleged, had even laboured to bring some of the bishops 'into dislike with His Majesty as dangerous persons'. Hence Pym's sudden acquisition, between the parliaments of 1626 and 1628, of an intense concern with the rule of law and the ancient constitution. The rule of law guaranteed true religion, just as the common body of Protestant belief underpinned political consent.[8]

The case in the 1628 parliament of Roger Manwaring, a clergyman who Pym believed to be an Arminian, brings us to the final link in his chain of thought. Manwaring had preached that the Forced Loan was due by the law of God, which caused Pym to accuse him of 'a wicked intention to avert His Majesty's mind from calling of parliaments.' And

> if parliaments be taken away, mischiefs and disorders must needs abound without any possibility of good laws to reform them; grievances will daily increase without opportunity or means to redress them, and what readier way can there be to distractions betwixt the king and people, to tumults and distempers in the state than this?

The effect of Manwaring's remarks, Pym argued, was to turn the king's subjects against him and thus to dissolve the ancient constitution. Not long after this, Christopher Sherland spoke of Arminians running with papists to flatter great men and 'oppress the subject', while John Hampden commented that religion was likely to be altered by the duke of Buckingham's means. Thus, among a small circle of leading MPs, the notions of alteration of religion and government and of a popish and malignant party set upon the destruction of the Protestant state were born.[10] Our story starts here.

In an obituary tribute, Oliver St John revealed that around 1630 Pym, fearful about popery overwhelming the kingdom, thought seriously of making 'some plantation in foreign parts, where the profession of the gospel might have a free course'.[11] Instead he stayed in England and for the

7 Russell in Clark, Smith, Tyacke, editors, *The English Commonwealth*, p. 60.
8 N. Tyacke, 'Puritanism, Arminianism and Counter-Revolution' in Russell, *Origins*, pp. 119–43.
9 Russell in Clark, Smith, Tyacke, editors, *The English Commonwealth*, pp. 160–4.
10 *Ibid*, p. 163; Russell, *Parliaments*, pp. 375, 379–80.
11 Cited in Russell in Clark, Smith, Tyacke, editors, *The English Commonwealth*, p. 164.

next ten years he was forced to watch political developments from the sidelines. During this period the popish plot became the fixed principle of all his political thinking and its shape, finally unveiled on 7 November 1640, was clarified in his mind. Obviously in that speech Pym relied much on hearsay and the dramatizations of popular gossip; he accepted much for which he had no proof; details slipped easily into place in a mind becoming used to seeing everything in terms of a single conspiracy against Church and state. Yet there was far more to the plot than misunderstanding of the policies of Laud and misinterpretation of the inclinations of the king. A full account of its genesis is needed and an investigation of how far it was built on fact and how far on fantasy and irrational hysteria.[12] All that can be attempted here is a brief comment on what Pym knew of Catholic and Arminian activities and how he wove his story together.

As the king's affection for his wife blossomed during the 1630s Catholicism was more and more openly practised at court. By the end of the decade not only the queen, the Capuchins under her protection and the queen mother, but all the resident ambassadors of Catholic princes as well, kept chapels open to the public.[13] A mutual agency between the Stuart court and Rome was established with the encouragement of the queen's confessor Robert Philip, Lord Cottington and Sir Francis Windebank. George Con, papal agent from 1636 to 1639, drew courtier families like the Howards and Villiers into closer identification with Catholic interests and achieved a wave of conversions.[14] He also gathered around the queen a clique of seasoned Catholic proselytizers and intellectuals, such as Sir Kenelm Digby, Toby Mathew, Walter Montagu and Sir John Winter.[15] All this Pym must have known or suspected. In his 7 November speech he described the purpose of the mutual agency as the extirpation of Protestantism.[16]

Con urged the king to take up arms against the Scots and engaged in various schemes during 1638 and 1639 to aid the royal campaign by military and financial means. When the earl of Arundel, the head of a family stiff with Catholics, was appointed commander-in-chief of the English forces, he travelled to his frequent meetings with the king in Con's coach, emblazoned with the papal arms. Some of the most prominent Catholics in the kingdom, such as the earl of Worcester and the marquis of

12 Caroline Hibbard's very important Yale PhD thesis 'Charles I and the Popish Plot' (1975), shortly to be published, will fill this gap. Meanwhile see C.M. Hibbard, 'Early Stuart Catholicism: Revisions and Re-Revisions', *JMH* LII (1980), 1–34. I am deeply grateful to her for allowing me to make use of her work, on which the next three paragraphs are largely based.

13 Hibbard, pp. 50–5, 118–9; Wedgwood, pp. 121, 247–8.

14 Hibbard, pp. 65–117, 121–5; Gardiner VIII, 235–43; G. Albion, *Charles I and the Court of Rome* (London, 1935), pp. 145–248; L. Pastor, *History of the Popes* (London, 1938), 312–24.

15 Hibbard, pp. 144–51; Wedgwood, p. 210; R.W. Smuts, 'The Puritan Followers of Henrietta Maria in the 1630s', *EHR* XLIII (1978), 40–1.

16 Kenyon, *Constitution*, pp. 199, 204.

Winchester, responded enthusiastically to the Scottish war.[17] Most of this must have been common knowledge in Pym's circle. Gossip about a solid phalanx of Catholics in the army sent north fitted easily into a jigsaw of evidence and suspicion which almost pieced itself together. Pym believed the Scottish war was an expedient to weaken England and Scotland as a prelude to international Catholic designs: 'that when we had well wearied ourselves against one another we might be both brought to what scorn they pleased.' The popish plot, Pym told his colleagues on 7 November 1640, had been carried out 'first softly, now by strides'.[18] In the period 1638 to 1640, he pronounced in his later manifesto the Grand Remonstrance, 'this faction was grown to that height and entireness of power that now they began to think of finishing their work.'[19]

From early 1639 onwards the king's inclination to turn for foreign help against his domestic enemies became increasingly evident. An abortive plan for importing Spanish mercenaries that spring may have been kept secret.[20] But the earl of Strafford's negotiations with Spain in the summer of 1640, in order to obtain loans of money, were less well concealed. At the same time there was much talk of the papist army Strafford had raised in Ireland being thrown into the balance against the Scots.[21] Thus it was not so far-fetched for Pym to claim, as he did at the opening of the Long Parliament, that the Spanish fleet carrying an army intended for the Netherlands, which was badly mauled by Admiral Tromp in the Downs in October 1639, was part of a design for the destruction of English laws and religion. He connected this fleet with plans 'to bring soldiers from beyond sea' and the existence of an Irish army 'to bring us to a better order'.[22]

Pym's charge in April 1640 that there had been a 'universal suspension of all laws' against papists was unfounded, though recent research suggests that the composition system for recusancy fines imposed in the 1630s put few Catholic families under intolerable financial pressure.[23] But his accusation that the Caroline regime had introduced 'innovations in religion' was absolutely correct. Since the 1629 parliament the Arminian episcopate had mounted a campaign to change the face of the nation's religious life. Their emphasis on ritual and ceremonies, Pym contended, was 'to make us

17 Hibbard, pp. 190–273; Gardiner IX, 26; Wedgwood, pp. 232, 242, 250–1, 265–6; Baillie, p. 216; *CSPV 1636–9*, p. 273.
18 B. Whitelocke, *Memorials* I (London, 1682), 131; *HMC Portland* III, 57; Kenyon, pp. 204–5.
19 Gardiner, *Documents*, p. 215.
20 Hibbard, pp. 277–80.
21 *HMC Portland* I, 3–4; Gardiner IX, 57, 96, 131–2, 156, 175, 184; Wedgwood, pp. 299–301, 328, 350, 352–3.
22 Kenyon, *Constitution*, p. 205; *D'Ewes (N)*, p. 51.
23 Cliffe, pp. 218–21; T.S. Smith, 'The Persecution of Staffordshire Roman Catholic Recusants 1625–1660', *Journal of Ecclesiastical History* XXX (1979), 327–50. For the view that Catholics were treated severely see M.J. Havran, *The Catholics in Caroline England* (Stanford, 1962); K.J. Lindley, 'The Lay Catholics of England in the reign of Charles I', *JEH* XXII (1971), 199–219.

more capable of a translation': 'altars, bowing towards the east, pictures, crosses, crucifixes and the like, which of themselves considered are so many dry bones, being put together to make the man.'[24] So far as Pym was concerned Arminianism and Catholicism were virtually indistinguishable. In 1643 he accused the bishops of introducing 'Arminian or papistical cere-monies, whether you please to term them, there is not much difference.'[25] Protestants must be prepared for their conversion to popery; Puritans 'must be either rooted out of the kingdom with force or driven out with fear'. Pym saw these two policies as complementary aspects of the same design. Thus, he could accurately point out, the full weight of ecclesi-astical censure had been brought to bear on nonconformity, which had been redefined in the process. He had observed 'the daily discouraging of all godly men who truly profess the Protestant religion, as though men could be too religious'.[26]

This then was the scope and shape of the plot. But for how many others besides Pym did it provide a compelling framework for the priorities and plans of the new parliament? In the 1620s Pym, we should remember, had often been a one-man band. His fierce attack on Shepherd for seeking to divide the nation in 1621 did not catch the mood of the House; he was exceptionally quick off the mark in recognizing the significance of the Arminian issue in 1624; and even in 1628 the number of anti-Arminian speakers was comparatively small. It was only in the brief session of 1629 that general concern about the growth of Arminianism emerged and that the House as a whole began to grasp the notion of a conspiracy to alter religion. During the 1630s Pym had no opportunity to propagate his views. He did not establish wide contacts in gentry circles but preferred to live reclusively in the company of men of like mind such as John Hampden, Christopher Sherland and Sir Nathaniel Rich.[27]

Neither Sherland nor Rich lived until 1640. Of those elected to the Long Parliament 156 had sat in 1628–29: only ten of these men had spoken previously about Arminianism.[28] Moreover all had lived for more than 11 years away from the overheated atmosphere of Westminster. Many had no doubt lacked the compulsive interest which led Pym to follow political developments so carefully. Indeed one of the reasons for Pym's pre-eminence in November 1640 was simply that he was far better informed than anyone else.[29] Some MPs had probably read one of the political libels circulated in 1639 and 1640, which connected the activities of the papal

24 Kenyon, *Constitution*, pp. 199–200.
25 BL E 91 (34): *A Declaration and Vindication of John Pym*.
26 Kenyon, *Constituion*, pp. 200, 204; Gardiner, *Documents*, p. 216.
27 Russell, *Parliaments*, pp. 31, 164, 345, 404; Russell in Clark, Smith, Tyacke, editors, *The English Commonwealth*, pp. 148–9, 152.
28 Keeler, p. 15; Russell, *Parliaments*, p. 435.
29 Cope, pp. 138–40, 145–8; *HMC Portland* III, 25–66; Rushworth III, part I, 24–6.

agent, the queen and court Catholics such as Matthew and Winter.[30] Nevertheless there were undoubtedly many to whom the plot as a whole was a revelation and very few, besides his intimate friend Hampden, who heard no more from Pym than they believed already. Pym's task was formidable. If parliament was to follow his leadership, the majority of its members – in the Lords as well as the Commons – had to be convinced of his case that there was a more urgent task than condemning ship money, examining Star-Chamber procedure or reforming the lieutenancy system. The deepest irony of our story is that the further parliament plunged into investigating and combating popish conspiracy the more the plot seemed to become a self-fulfilling prophecy.

If it is proper to start this book with Pym, it is also appropriate to start it with the petitions that began to pile the clerk's table on 7 November 1640, since county petitioning exemplified the complex and sensitive relationship between parliaments and the gentry communities of the shires. Between the 1590s and 1640 relations between monarch and people were strained by inflation, disunity in religion and Stuart incompetence. Interest in parliaments, and expectations of them, grew as they came to be regarded as the salve for the nation's ills.[31] Yet at the same time the future of parliaments seemed to be in doubt. Much as the Stuarts valued parliaments as a point of contact between central and local government, the record of the 1620s shows that there was good reason for them to question their usefulness.[32] It has been suggested that the series of decisions to widen the franchise in particular boroughs made by the Commons between 1621 and 1641 arose from 'the sense of a desperate need to preserve parliaments'. These decisions reflected an unthinking defensive reaction, an assumption that the more voters there were the more difficult they would be to ignore, terrorize or bribe.[33]

Resistance to Stuart innovations prompted the growth of national political consciousness.[34] The provinces were becoming more fully informed, as the secrecy of parliamentary discussion came to be increasingly disregarded and reports circulated more readily. In 1626 the first manuscript newsletters aiming at a full narrative appeared; two years later both these 'True Relations' and speeches copied by hand were widely available.[35] Local communities increasingly pressed for accountability.

30 *CSPD 1639–40*, p. 246; *CSPD 1640–1*, p. 126.
31 C.S.R. Russell, *The Crisis of Parliaments* (Oxford, 1971), pp. 286–329; Russell, *Parliaments*, particularly pp. 1–84; *Sussex*, pp. 231–3; A. Hassell Smith, *County and Court* (Oxford, 1974), pp. 314–32.
32 C.S.R. Russell, 'Parliamentary History in Perspective', *History* LXI (1976), 1–27; Russell, *Parliaments*, p. 48.
33 Hirst, pp. 65–89.
34 R. Ashton, *The English Civil War* (London, 1978), pp. 67–8.
35 W. Notestein and F.H. Relph, editors, *Commons Debates for 1629* (Minneapolis, 1921), pp xx–xxiv. I am grateful to Conrad Russell for information on this point.

Edward Alford's plea in 1621 that members should 'have some care saving our reputations' lest it should be said 'that we should do nothing but give away their money and do nothing for them' was not just a tactical ploy. Many MPs shared his anxiety about going home with no justification at hand when they were asked about the granting of subsidies.[36] The emergence of the county petition, a collective statement of opinion carrying the authority of leading magnates, was only a small step from the practice, known in some counties at least before 1640, of briefing knights of the shire on the county's needs.[37] Petitioning complied with the traditions of legitimism and deferential protest which characterized English politics between 1603 and 1640.[38]

Members for Essex, Hertfordshire, Middlesex, Northamptonshire, and Suffolk presented petitions to the Commons in April 1640. These counties, by contrast with some others far from London, had suffered heavily from military taxation, ship money and purveyance.[39] Political awareness was correspondingly advanced. The gentry of remote counties such as Pembrokeshire and Carmarthenshire at this time showed 'a minimal grasp of significant political principles and a dogged introspectiveness'.[40] The fact that in October 1640 18 shires sent their knights with a formal agenda of grievances indicates that, over the summer, the urgency of the national crisis of confidence had penetrated many minds. This time not only southern and eastern shires but a wide arc of counties from Devon to Northumberland were involved.[41]

Long Parliament petitions mark an important stage in the evolution of a responsible relationship between members and their own neighbourhoods. There was an understanding that the county representatives would be engaged in a comprehensive investigation into the nation's ills, some of which were common to all regions while others affected particular shires. MPs were expected to regard the petitions as containing general guidance about the matters they should urge their colleagues to pursue most vigorously. Some knights without petitions in their hands were anxious to assure the House that they too had been entrusted with a specific programme. Sir John Culpepper, carrying his petition 'in his mouth', announced that he had the grievances of Kent 'in charge from them that sent me'. Lord Digby explained that at the Dorset election meeting a list of the county's complaints had been read to the freeholders present 'who all

---

36   Zagorin, pp. 86, 108; Hirst, pp. 157–81; R.E. Ruigh, *The Parliament of 1624* (Cambridge, Mass., 1971), p. 57 n.

37   D. Hirst, 'Court, Country and Politics before 1629' in K. Sharpe, editor, *Faction and Parliament* (Oxford, 1978), pp. 129–31.

39   *CJ* II, 5–6; Cope, pp. 273–8; M.D. Gordon, 'The Collection of Ship Money in the reign of Charles I', *TRHS* IV (1910), pp. 141–62.

40   H. Lloyd, *The Gentry of South West Wales* (Cardiff, 1968), pp. 120, 211.

41   *CJ* II, 22–5, 25–9; *D'Ewes (N)*, pp. 6, 16, 20, 22–3, 34–5, 542; Hirst, p. 183.

unanimously with one voice' approved it.[42]

The responsiveness of the provinces as a whole to national events increased enormously between November 1640 and the battle of Edgehill two years later. So stirring and so alarming were the political developments of this period, that anyone who was at the centre of things found himself pestered for news and information. Young men in London felt keenly their obligations to relatives: to deny him news, wrote John Turberville to his father-in-law, in one of four letters during the first ten weeks of the session, 'were to deny the love and service I owe you'.[43] William Eliot was full of gratitude for the bulletins his brother-in-law Sir Simonds D'Ewes sent down weekly by the Godalming carrier.[44] Sir John Holland's long account of the latest parliamentary business on 23 March 1642 was clearly written at the instruction of its recipient, his East Anglian compatriot Sir Robert Crane.[45] When news was lacking or diurnals were unobtainable, London correspondents knew that silence would not suffice. Excuses and expressions of confidence that the next week would see much accomplished were a regular feature of their letters. 'For news I cannot write anything of certain', declared Thomas Barrow to his brother-in-law Henry Oxinden on 24 June 1641, 'here is much business in hand but as yet here is nothing brought to perfection.'[46] It was surely better, Robert Appleton pleaded after scribbling a page of hearsay to a Suffolk cousin a few weeks later, to send rumours than nothing at all.[47]

There was much variation in the scope and quality of the information the localities received between 1640 and 1642. Captain Edward Rossingham's news service, subscribed to among others by the earls of Leicester, Northumberland and Salisbury, was factual and informative about parliamentary proceedings.[48] But for the spice of gossip, so essential for interpreting Whitehall and Westminster developments, there was nothing to beat the breathless summaries of obliging friends and relatives. It was the detail that mattered.[49] One newsletter of June 1641, for example, related that an angry exchange between the earl of Essex and Lord Saville over the Star Chamber bill had been 'passed over in the House although much talk of it in the town'.[50]

It quickly became clear that quill and ink alone could not satisfy the hunger for news. At first the stationers concentrated on official productions,

42 Rushworth III, part I, 30–4.
43 W.C. and C.E. Trevelyan, editors, *Trevelyan Papers*, part III (Camden Society, LV, 1872), 195–203.
44 BL Harl. MS 382, fols. 90–106; 383, fols. 191r, 197r.
45 Bodleian Tanner MS 66, fol. 299r.
46 BL Add. MS 28000, fol. 97.
47 Bodleian Tanner MS 66, fol. 110.
48 Cope, pp. 35–7; BL Add. MS 11045, fols. 132–47; *HMC DeL'Isle and Dudley MSS* VI, 338–66.
49 E.g. Northamptonshire RO Isham Letters 236.
50 Bedfordshire RO J 1386.

such as orders of the Houses and articles of impeachment, together with outstanding speeches and sermons. As early as 14 December 1640 Sir Simonds D'Ewes was sending down printed speeches and petitions to his wife in Suffolk, with the advice that she should 'lend them to whom you please'.[51] Diarists like John Rous in Suffolk and Henry Townshend in Worcestershire began to enter important items; the printed papers of 1641 and 1642 in numerous family collections testify to assiduous and widespread collection.[52] The issue of two vast compendiums, 963 pages in all, in November 1641, gave men a chance to catch up on items they had missed as 'separates'.[53] The first newsbooks appeared in the same month. They were normally published on Monday to catch the mails leaving London for the north on Tuesday morning. Many of the early ones were shortlived, but during 1642 confidence in a regular market led to continuous pagination from number to number within a series.[54]

The accuracy of certain items could not be relied upon: speeches, for instance, ranged from those based on a fair copy provided by the author, through those that bore marks of compilation from MPs' jottings, to complete fabrications. Newsbooks were often dull since editors moved cautiously in the new atmosphere of relaxed censorship, adopting an impersonal style and a neutral tone. The local news 'treads but the steps of corantoes', remarked a Norwich writer to a London correspondent who had obliged him with a more colourful version of events.[55] Controversial matters were avoided. He would 'not find above three lies but many truths left out', Lord Montagu's informant wrote, sending down a diurnal in February 1642.[56] For all these deficiencies, the efforts of the printers and stationers brought sighs of relief to overworked London correspondents. 'I desire you to send down the most material latest printed books by the Friday and Thursday posts constantly', Henry Oxinden of Barham in Kent wrote to a friend on 8 August 1642. His bills would be paid: 'if your leisure will not permit you to write what news is stirring yet pray enclose them in a paper and so send them.'[57] Printing made Sir Edward Littleton nonchalant about the whole business of reporting by June 1642. 'The king declares and we declare', he told his Staffordshire friend Sir Richard Leveson, 'were not all the news in print I should write more largely.'[58]

Once they reached the countryside letters were passed from hand to

51 J.O. Halliwell, editor, *The Autobiography of Sir Simonds D'Ewes* (London, 1845), I, 255–7.
52 J. Rous, *Diary* (Camden Society, LXVI, 1856), 98; *Townsend*, I, 9–22; *Buller*, pp. 28–53.
53 *Speeches and Passages November 1640 to June 1641* (1641); DO; *HMC Buccleuch*, p. 289.
54 J. Frank, *The Beginnings of the English Newspaper* (Cambridge, Mass., 1961), pp. 20–29; *D'Ewes (C)*, pp. xx–xxii.
55 Bodleian Tanner MS 66, fol. 181.
56 *HMC Montagu*, p. 147.
57 BL Add. MS 28000, fol. 218.
58 Staffordshire RO D 868/2/34.

hand. The rounds of county hospitality became a forum for argument and speculation; quarter sessions and assizes were used to exchange rumours and opinions. Yet in the end every family depended for a consecutive picture of political developments on its own informants and while some were wonderfully served others had cause to chafe. The elder Sir John Coke, a retired secretary of state living at Melbourne in Derbyshire, received at least 50 letters from his son, who was a knight of the shire, between November 1640 and March 1643. Lady Brilliana Harley, isolated at her castle of Brampton Bryan in Herefordshire, replied to about 100 letters from her son in the same period.[59] Others kept very closely in touch included the aged Lord Montagu at Boughton in Northamptonshire and Lady Sussex at Gorhambury in Hertfordshire. Some districts were undoubtedly much better supplied than others. 'I know you hear all the news before we do . . . for we see not the face of a soul', declared a north Yorkshire writer to Sir Ralph Verney in Buckinghamshire.[60] Thomas Knyvett assumed at the end of 1640 that if he told his Norfolk friends things a week old he would be 'tedious to the reader'. But Francis Cave complained from near Coventry in February 1642 that he received 'such straggling news printed' he knew not what to believe.[61]

Many in the localities were undoubtedly insatiable readers. But no one outside London could hope to achieve more than a partial and incomplete view of the political process that led to civil war. The pattern of relationships from which war emerged was highly complex. One important element in this pattern was the relationship between gentry communities and parliament, another was the relationship between Westminster and the City of London, and another again was the taut three-sided relationship between the king, parliament and the Scots. Between 1640 and 1642 more than 200 petitions in all were presented to the king or parliament. The activities of religious radicals, both in London and beyond, exercised a significant influence on the movement of opinion about reform of Church government and the liturgy. The London citizens showed themselves capable of making their own impact on parliament decision making. The relationship between the Long Parliament and local communities was thus a dynamic one from the moment that members assembled with petitions in their hands. Westminster was merely the focus for a debate which involved the whole political nation and the Scots as well.

It is right to look to the early years of Charles I's reign for the beginning of that 'mutual commerce of fear' which we have to understand if we are to explain why politcal deadlock ended in war. By 1628 Charles and Laud had destroyed the religious unity of England, which many gentry saw as

---

59   *HMC Coke* pp. 262–333; *Harley*, pp. 100–198.
60   *HMC Montagu*, pp. 129–60; *Verney* II, 85.
61   *HMC Various Collections*, II, 259; *HMC Egmont*, I, 163.

the foundation of monarchy, liberty and law. The eventual outcome of the division created by the promotion of Arminianism in the 1620s was the division Pym created in 1641 by his attempt to use parliament as an instrument to ward off popish conspiracy. In this sense religious issues provided the fundamental cause of the civil war. But any such assertion carries the danger of over-simplifying the events of 1641 and 1642. It is the many-sidedness of the political process of these years that needs to be stressed at the outset.

Moreover the political crisis which is the subject of this book has to be investigated at two levels, since misunderstanding is of its essence. Men's actual intentions must be distinguished from their assumed and alleged intentions. The political debate was conducted in emotional and often highly dramatized terms. Gossip and rumour fanned the flames of crisis. Normally sane and balanced men became the prisoners of their own fears and imaginings. When war came there were some who were able to articulate the principles and convictions for which they fought. Yet even they, let alone the many who found it impossible to attach themselves steadfastly to one side or the other, had not sought war. This was a war that nobody wanted, a war that left men bewildered and that they marvelled at as it broke out by fits and starts all over England in the summer of 1642.

1

Settlement

I hope that we shall not now lop the branches but stub up the roots of all our
mischiefs: which will be as the safer so the shorter work.

Sir Nathaniel Barnardiston to Sir Simonds D'Ewes,
30 October 1940[1]

I have often thought and said that it must be some great extremity that would
recover and rectify this state; and when that extremity did come, it would be a
great hazard whether it might prove a remedy or ruin. We are now, Mr
Speaker, upon that vertical turning point . . . .

Sir Benjamin Rudyerd,
7 November 1640[2]

Never had one parliament so many great affairs.

Sir Edward Dering,
21 June 1641[3]

It was easy to see the new parliament of November 1640 as a panacea. The
Yorkshire knight, Sir Henry Slingsby, expected 'a happy parliament
where the subject may have a total redress of all his grievances'. Francis
Read reported 'the strong expectation of much ensuing good'.[4] 'For ever
be this parliament renowned for so great achievements, for we dream now
of nothing more than of a golden age' wrote John Bampfield from
Somerset. 'But I stay you from better occasions', ended Sir John Trevor's
steward Samuel Wood on 18 December: he concluded his lengthy account
of the state of the peaches, quinces and crab-apples in the family's North
Wales orchards with an expression of concern 'for the happiness and
blessed end of the parliament'. 'Your praise sounds in all corners of the
land', declared Sir Richard Skeffington to Sir Edward Dering from
Warwickshire. He urged that the Commons should 'lay aside all your own
affairs' and that the parliament should 'not break up until businesses be
thoroughly settled'.[5]

1 BL Harl. MS 384, fol. 66r.
2 Rushworth III, part I, 25.
3 *Ibid*, 293.
4 *Slingsby*, p. 64; *CSPD 1640–1*, p. 139.
5 *HMC 15th Report*, appendix, VII, 164; Clwyd RO Glynde MS 3275; BL Sloane MS 184, fol. 19.

Religious radicals were on tenterhooks and the Londoners' petition for root and branch abolition of episcopacy soon encouraged their hopes. 'We cease not to pray for you and that great assembly', declared Stanley Gower to Sir Robert Harley: 'if the Lord turn away our captivity we shall be like them that dream.' Lady Brilliana Harley replied excitedly to her son's first bulletin. These widespread expectations explain the patience and passivity of the localities during the first months of the parliament's life. None of the Westminster news, D'Ewes's brother-in-law told him in February 1641, ruffled his confidence that 'a blessed communion between the king and his people' would emerge. 'I submit my weakness to the wisdom of our sages', wrote Sir Thomas Wodehouse to his Norfolk kinsman Sir John Potts on 23 April, 'and only will assume this honest part of interest in the commonwealth as to applaud and honour those who are sound and serviceable thereto of which noble number you are so eminent.' Parliaments were expected to produce settlement, unity and accord. Any other outcome of this assembly was too shameful for MPs and too surprising for observers to contemplate.[6]

Some of the early speakers dilated upon the providence of the second meeting of the year. 'Out of all question some great work is here to be done,' announced the garrulous Sir John Wray on 12 November, 'something extraordinary is here to be decreed or else God and the king beyond all our expectations, at the last breath, would never so soon have cemented us again to meet in this great council.'[7] First reports from London suggest a mood of euphoria. 'Great matters are expected', declared the Wigan burgess Alexander Rigby on 10 November. 'They go on very cheerfully and courageously', heard Henry Oxinden. 'Now reformation goes on again as hot as toast' Thomas Knyvett told a Norfolk friend. 'Here is a busy parliament and like to prove a very happy one', a correspondent wrote into Wales.[8]

On 17 December the Somerset lawyer John Pyne sent a full progress report to his friend Thomas Smyth, left chafing in the country after failing to find a seat. He mentioned the Londoners' Root and Branch petition, the committee set up to prepare a charge against Lord Keeper Finch and the judges and the vote declaring void the canons made in Convocation that summer. 'So now you may see we fly at all', he declared, ' 'tis thought tomorrow we shall desire the Lords to sequester the archbishop.' Only those who had been closely involved in the government of the previous decade had cause to be apprehensive. 'I pray God to bless us all in these

6 BL Loan MS 29/172, fol. 309r; Harl. MS 382, fol. 90r; Bodleian Tanner MS 66, fol. 65r; *Harley* p. 100; Russell, *Parliaments*, pp. 53–4; M.A. Judson, *The Crisis of the Constitution* (New Brunswick, N.J., 1949), pp. 1–107.
7 BL E 196 (10).
8 *HMC Kenyon MSS*, p. 59; *Oxinden*, p. 186; *HMC Various* II, 259; A.H. Dodd, 'The Civil War in East Denbighshire', *Denbigh Historical Transactions* III (1954), p. 47.

dangerous times', wrote Sir John Coke to his father, once Charles I's secretary of state, 'and to settle truth and peace amongst us'. Knyvett, home in Norfolk for Christmas, related to his wife how he met his friend John Buxton out hunting and compared notes about the Westminster news. Buxton, a ship-money sheriff who had made himself many enemies over his collection of the arrears on the 1638 writ, was dejected about his fate. The Commons had already set up a committee to receive petitions concerning rigorous levying of ship-money. 'Thus we make one another merry in this whipping time', observed Knyvett, 'if ever Astraea will appear in her glory in Westminster Hall again, sure 'twill be after this purgation.'[9]

Between 1558 and 1629 parliament had shown its inability to sustain a constitutional struggle with the Crown. The catchphrase was always 'grievances before supply', yet time and again subsidies had been voted and grievances left unredressed.[10] 1566, 1614 and 1626 were the only occasions when the Commons made a serious attempt to attach conditions to the supply of money.[11] When Charles I made it clear in 1628 that he would not accept a general bill for the liberties of the subject which was to be sent up with the subsidy bill, members put their trust in the Petition of Right. As an attempt to bind the Crown by law this proved wholly inadequate. In April 1640 there was a return to the grievances-before-supply formula, but this time there was a generous spirit among some backbenchers that might have enabled Charles to do business with parliament. Instead the outcome was deadlock and a rapid dissolution.[12] Pym and his closest colleagues probably had these lessons in mind when they decided, at a private meeting a few days after parliament assembled, to concentrate their attack on individuals rather than drive forward a programme of legislation.[13]

But Pym was also thinking of course about how best to root out the Catholic conspiracy. Statutes were useless for this purpose. In a speech on 7 November, following Pym's, Sir John Clotworthy gave MPs an account of the state of Ireland, stressing the power and corruption of the Catholic Church and the weakness of the parliament there. Members listened with respect to a man who could speak of Ireland's condition from long personal experience. There were two armies in existence there, Clotworthy explained: the new one consisting of 10,000 men, 8000 of them papists, 'as

9 Bristol RO 36074/139a; *HMC Coke*, p. 264; *Knyvett*, p. 96; Ketton-Cremer, pp. 92–9, 102–3.
10 C. Russell, 'Parliamentary History in Perspective, 1604–29', *History* LXI (1976), 1–27.
11 G.R. Elton, 'Taxation for War and Peace in Early Tudor England' in J.M. Winter, editor, *War and Economic Development* (Cambridge, 1975), pp. 45–8; Russell, *Parliaments*, p. 49.
12 E.R. Foster, 'Petitions and the Petition of Right', *Journal of British Studies* XIV (1974), 40–5; Russell, pp. 109–10. See the account of this parliament in the Grand Remonstrance, Gardiner, *Documents*, pp. 217–8.
13 Zagorin, p. 207.

well disciplined an army as any in the world that hath not seen enemy and as well paid' and the old Protestant one, which was a year in arrears with its pay. The impeachment of the earl of Strafford followed four days later. It was merely the centrepiece of a day's debating, in an atmosphere of frantic alarm, during which Pym began to educate his colleagues in the full horror of the papist design. Strafford was the arch conspirator. He was accused, above all, because, as the Commons declared at a conference with the Lords that day, he 'had a design to bring over the Irish army into England.' The seven articles of treason read on 24 November enlarged upon Pym's case against Strafford: popery had flourished during his rule in Ireland without restraint, he had stirred up enmity between England and Scotland and he had incensed the king against parliaments.[14] Strafford had to die because he was held responsible for the Catholic plot and he frightened the leaders of this parliament as no one else did.[15] He had 'laboured to set division, to alienate the hearts of people and destroy the kingdom'. The people might be instigated to rise against their monarch or they might passively submit. In either case it was on his shoulders that the imminent destruction of the kingdom would lie.

MPs heard a good deal more on 11 November about some of the other aspects of the conspiracy. Pym himself spoke of William O'Connor the Irish priest, a servant to the queen mother, who alleged 'many thousands were in pay . . . ready to cut all the Protestants throats' and also about information that the earl of Worcester was preparing a papist army in South Wales. Alexander Rigby sketched the links between the queen, the papal agent Rosetti and the Catholics of Lancashire, which involved a weekly fast for 'the design in hand'. Over the next weeks committees followed these and other leads. The pursuit of Sir Francis Windebank over his protection of recusants, for instance, arose directly from his 'carelessness' in the case of O'Connor and allegations that he had called those who opposed ship money traitors. His flight was naturally taken as proof of guilt.[16]

No doubt it took time for many MPs to piece together Pym's jigsaw in their own minds. Strafford's trial, rather than the popish conspiracy in its entirety, was seen by correspondents as the main business of the first weeks. Nevertheless a period of sustained attention to various threads in the plot at the end of January did much to alert the House. The king's reprieve of the Jesuit priest John Goodman on 22 January was the catalyst. Isaac Pennington, who had quickly established himself as the chief

14 *D'Ewes (N)*, pp. 13–14, 24–30, 60–2, 532; C.V. Wedgwood, *Thomas Wentworth, First Earl of Strafford* (London, 1964), pp. 310–21; Gardiner IX, 231–6, 240–1.

15 Hibbard, pp. 343–4, 372–3; G.E. Aylmer in W. Lamont, editor, *The Tudors and Stuarts* (London, 1976), pp. 125–6.

16 *D'Ewes (N)*, pp. 24–7, 47, 89–91, 103, 277–8; *CSPD 1640–1*, pp. 415, 426; Gardiner IX, 243.

intermediary between the Commons and the City's money bags, announced the next day that the £60,000 loan which the alderman had offered towards satisfying the Scots would not be paid. London was suddenly full of rumours: that the earl of Leicester, as the king's ambassador, had received Windebank at Paris, that Lord Keeper Finch, another delinquent in exile, was entertained by the queen of Bohemia at the Hague. Six weeks had now passed with no response to the radical citizens' Root and Branch petition.[17] Goodman's reprieve, noted one observer, gave 'a jealousy to the citizens that they were but deluded and made them doubt of the reformation that was promised'. Many took it as a deliberate pretext for saving the lives of Strafford and Archbishop Laud.[18]

The Commons took offence at the king's action in reprieving Goodman as stridently as the City. It was a signal for the start of the hunt for popery at court. During the next few days MPs learnt about the role of Rosetti in the queen's household and the masses that were open to all at Denmark House, St James's and the chapels of foreign ambassadors. They were told about the contribution from Catholics for the Scots war organized by the queen's secretary, Sir John Winter. They heard Walter Montagu and Sir Kenelm Digby being examined about the fragmentary evidence of a secret hierarchy of the popish Church in England. They began to understand the connections Pym was driving home, as Alexander Rigby reported 15,000 indictments for recusancy at the last sessions in Amounderness hundred of Lancashire, that arsenal of papist strength, and Clotworthy insisted that the Irish army 'were to have landed in some part of those counties where the earl of Worcester was to levy his forces'. It was in the midst of all this, conveniently enough for the Commons leaders, that the detailed charges against Strafford were read on 28 January. The centrepiece of the case remained the earl's introduction of the Irish army to overpower English resistance.[19]

By the end of February Robert Baillie could report that 'the combination of the papists with Strafford's Irish army, to have landed not in Scotland but Wales' was 'more and more spoken of.'[20] On the 13th the Commons had asked the Lords to get the king to disband the Irish army, disarm all recusants and remove the queen's chief papist favourites – Digby, Matthew, Montagu and Winter – from the court. After some dispute about whether disbandment of the Irish or Scottish army was the greater priority, the Lords accepted the Commons' first demand, stipulating that the Protestant army in Ireland should be reinforced. Yet it was not until 27 March that the king was formally requested to act in the matter. Digby,

17 *D'Ewes (N)*, pp. 277–8; Gardiner ix, 264–5; Hibbard, pp. 352–3; Pearl, pp. 198–206.
18 *HMC De L'Isle and Dudley MSS* vi, 371; Baillie, p. 295.
19 *D'Ewes (N)*, pp. 290–2, 295–8, 301–2; Gardiner ix, 269–70; Hibbard, pp. 354–71.
20 Baillie, p. 304.

Matthew and Montagu meanwhile had left England and MPs were pressed by the peers to drop their campaign against Winter on the grounds that the queen's sympathetic influence had secured the passing of the Triennial Act and that a Frenchman as queen's secretary would be more dangerous than a 'great papist'.[21] According to Sir John Coke, even Pym and his closest allies were divided over how Winter should be treated. In any case Strafford's trial at this stage became the absorbing drama of the moment and wider aspects of the papist conspiracy were temporarily neglected.[22]

Archbishop Laud, it was reported, wept when he entered his lodgings in the Tower on 1 March. His unpopularity in London was such that he was cursed as a traitor on his way there and the Lieutenant of the Tower had to draw out the yeomen to prevent a riot at his arrival. Some, wrote an observer of the scene, 'vowed to kill him in the coach'.[23] There was a certain irony in the fact that Laud, who had so firmly dissociated himself from Con's activities, should have been impeached on the charge of attempting to reconcile the English Church with Rome. Yet in a sense Laud was a better scapegoat than Strafford for the nation's troubles. Harbottle Grimston's powerful speech on 18 December, painting him as 'the root and ground of all our miseries' convinced the House. It was he who had advanced Strafford and Windebank, as well as Wren and the other 'wicked bishops'. 'He went about to subvert all the laws both of God and men' : this was Pym's summary of the impeachment articles. Laud was seen as having prepared England for the introduction of popery. His introduction of idolatry and superstition, his publication of 'popish and false tenets', his patronage of scandalous clergy, his suppression of preaching, his deprivation of godly ministers, and his inducement to the king to make war on the Scots were all contrived to damn him. In his speech justifying the impeachment on 26 February, Pym returned to the central theme of his parliamentary career, the evils of division between king and people. By all his policies, and above all by 'bereaving' the kingdom of parliaments, Laud had 'endeavoured to deprive the king of the love of his subjects'. In essence the case against both Strafford and Laud rested on the same grounds, but whereas it was necessary to pursue Strafford to his death Laud was regarded as so contemptible that he could be safely left to lie neglected in prison.[24]

Combating the papist design was the negative side of Pym's policy; fiscal

---

21 *D'Ewes (N)*, pp. 357, 359–60, 392–3, 484, 486–9, 492–4, 498; BL Harl. MS 6424, fols. 230–240; Hibbard, pp. 376–82; Gardiner IX, 289–90.

22 *HMC Coke*, p. 275.

23 Bedfordshire RO J 1378, p. 1: Hugh Floyde to Sir Roland St John, 4 March 1641; H.R. Trevor-Roper, *Archbishop Laud* (London, 1965), pp. 405–6.

24 *D'Ewes (N)*, pp. 169, 394–7, 413; Rushworth III, part I, 196–202; Gardiner IX, 248–9, 297–8; Trevor-Roper, *Laud*, p. 407.

reform and a plan for bridge appointments were its main positive elements. Overall Pym's strategy, formulated in conjunction with his patron the earl of Bedford and other confidants like Hampden, was a strategy for settlement. The sanctity of the king's revenue was an 'obsessive theme' which, it has been shown, ran through many of Pym's speeches in the 1620s. His was an accountant's mind: his detailed knowledge of royal revenue was evident on numerous occasions in the parliaments that met between 1621 and 1629. Pym believed that the sure foundation for a strong monarchical state was a regular and secure revenue.[25] He hated those who tried to defraud the king; he was enthusiastic about giving subsidies. In the autumn of 1640 he was working with Bedford on a constructive plan for settling the king's finances. The deal envisaged was the establishment of the royal revenue on a new basis in return for control of certain vital offices – the bridge appointments – which would provide Pym and his associates with a firm grip on the machinery of government. There was nothing new in men who had opposed royal policies being taken into government. Sir Thomas Wentworth was merely the most spectacular recent example. Thus the leadership's strategy made sense. It was based on a realistic and reasoned assessment of the government's situation. Why then did it fail? A close examination of the politics of the period from November 1640 to June 1641 is necessary to answer this question.

Nothing preoccupied men so much in the first months of this period as speculation about Strafford's fate. Many expected that the earl would 'not be concerned in his life', reported Sir Baynham Throckmorton on 21 November, 'but those of the select committee in the Lower House that have the managing of that business do not at all doubt to produce and prove abundant matter to make good the accusation of high treason against him'. 'His friends begin to forsake their hopes and mourn already', wrote William Davenant dejectedly on 19 January. In Somerset the rumour was that Strafford would be acquitted since 'favour and friends at court are powerful advocates'.[26] From London on the other hand Thomas Knyvett reported on 2 March that it was 'thought he will suffer for all his policy'. Coke agreed, telling his father a few days later that it was 'generally conceived that he shall suffer'. 'He hangeth equally in the balance of men's opinions, whether he shall live or die', ran another report of 5 March.[27]

Public interest grew as the trial developed. 'I find no man now at leisure', wrote Sir John Temple to the earl of Leicester on 25 March, 'everyone is engaged, and that passionately, either for my lord of Strafford's preservation or his ruin.' 'There hath been little done but what concerns his

25 Russell in Clark, Smith, Tyacke, editors, *The English Commonwealth*, pp. 152–5; Russell, *Origins*, pp. 110–16; Russell, *Crisis of Parliaments*, pp. 329–31.
26 Bristol RO 36074/136d; Staffordshire RO D 1778 Ii/12; *Camden Society*, LV (1872), 208.
27 *HMC Various* II, 260; *HMC Coke*, p. 275; *HMC Kenyon MSS*, p. 61.

lordship', Temple reported on 1 April. Thomas Smyth confessed in a letter he wrote the previous day that he was 'wearied out daily' with attending, but there was obviously no keeping him away. Westminster Hall became more and more overcrowded. On 6 April the Commons talked of preventing members from smuggling in their friends. Later a committee was set up to keep the doors and ensure that MPs found places. Knyvett's letter to Buxton, urging him to come up from Norfolk, illustrates the excitement the trial created: ' 'tis worth a hundred mile riding . . . bring your lady too, for she may be placed to see and hear as much as the men.'[28]

So convinced were MPs of Strafford's moral guilt that few had at first questioned the legal case against him. Sir Ralph Hopton's suggestion, when Pym presented the preliminary charge on 24 November, that it should be for high treason and 'other misdemeanours' hints at the doubts already present in his mind about the treasonable nature of some of the earl's more obnoxious activities. When the whole charge was read on 30 January, Sir Guy Palmes and Sir John Strangeways, two seasoned MPs apparently experiencing similar qualms, moved 'to know the witnesses' that would offer proof.[29] These were spiritied interventions but the points made were not taken up.

Strafford was charged with attacking three crucial elements in the constitution: parliament's sole power to legislate, its sole power to tax and the security of living under known rules of common law. Since he had so many enemies, it was easy to collect evidence against him. But it was hard to make it appear that he had committed treason. Essentially the prosecution case depended on a theory of accumulative treason which earlier cases had done no more than hint at. In an attempt to make a bridge between the doctrine of treason against the king's person and the doctrine of treason by alteration of government, Oliver St John pursued a tortuous argument about the constructive compassing of the king's death, by making him so odious that the people would rise against him.[30]

Strafford conducted his own defence with eloquence, passion and dexterity. On the second day he made a heartfelt appeal to the Commons for their 'gracious opinion' of him, offering to go 'in peace and quietness to my grave, leaving all public employments whatsoever'. His decrepit physical appearance made his tenacity all the more impressive. 'He looks bad, as if he could not live long', one observer had reported in November. Throughout the trial he was suffering grievously from the stone.[31]

---

28   Larking, p. 42; *HMC Various* II, 262; BL Harl. MS 163, fol. 9r; 477, fol. 470v; Add. MS 36828, fol. 58v; Bristol RO 36074/156a; *HMC De L'Isle and Dudley MSS* VI, 393, 396.

29   *D'Ewes (N)*, pp. 60–3, 303–4; Gardiner IX, 270–1.

30   C.S.R. Russell, 'The Theory of Treason in the Trial of Strafford', *EHR* LXXX (1965), 30–50.

31   J. Rushworth, *The Trial of Thomas Earl of Strafford* (1680), p. 116; *Camden Society* LV (1872), 196; BL Sloane MS 1467, fol. 26r.

Newsletters support Laud's judgement that the earl 'got all the time a great deal of reputation by his patient, yet stout and clear answers'. Coke, who thought 'his personal worth very hardly to be equalled', noted on 17 April that he had asked for no advice at all from his counsel on matters of fact or law.[32] Knyvett reported that he spoke with 'bravery and modest courtship of both Houses and in such language as begets admiration in all the beholders'. Temple's verdict was equally generous: 'Truly his lordship carries himself very gallantly, showing much courage and greatness of mind in this affliction, yet with so much modesty, meekness and humility as none can tax him of arrogancy, contempt of his accusation or any the least neglect to his accusers'. Even when irritated by an 'exceeding tedious' answer Strafford had made, D'Ewes had to admit its 'great subtlety and judgement'.[33]

From the start Strafford set out to deride the managers' theory of accumulative treason: 'when a thousand misdemeanors will not make one felony, shall twenty-eight misdemeanors heighten it to a treason?' 'Almost every article sets forth a new treason that I never heard of before', he mocked. As the trial became more openly a ruthless campaign to eliminate a political enemy his jibes went home. At the start John Hampden tried to ensure that Strafford was not allowed to speak in his defence until the Commons' managers had set out all the evidence. After two days an order was pushed through the House that members should not talk to the accused during the trial. Some had been seen to do so in a 'familiar manner'. Tension between the managers and the peers grew: there was suspicion of some lords who, 'upon every slight occasion', used the earl's interjections to call for an adjournment. D'Ewes, annoyed by Strafford's 'impertinences' such as 'telling us about his dinner with the mayor of Dublin', proposed a conference with the Lords on the fourth day of the trial to press them to shorten the earl's speeches. The failure of D'Ewes's motion is an indication of the rift that was opening inside the Commons, as the managers' tactics alienated backbench opinion.[34] They 'so banged and worried his lordship as it begets pity in many of the auditors', declared Knyvett. Temple spoke of the 'vehemency and sharpness' with which the managers sought to fasten their charge upon the accused.[35]

The Commons' leadership made its anxious wish for Strafford's death too obvious. There were tactical errors, such as the bullying of the earl's witness Sir William Pennyman on 24 March. Time and again the managers were outmanoeuvred; six articles were dropped for lack of proof. Too many of the charges turned out to be composed of malicious gossip

32 W. Laud, *Works* III, 440; *HMC Coke*, p. 279.
33 *HMC Various* III, 261; *HMC De L'Isle and Dudley MSS* VI, 393; BL Harl. MS 162, fol. 362r.
34 Rushworth, *Trial of Strafford*, p. 145; J.H. Timmis, *Thine is the Kingdom* (Alabama, 1974), pp. 72–3; BL Harl. MS 162, fols. 347r, 357r, 359r.
35 *HMC Various* II, 261; *HMC De L'Isle and Dudley MSS* VI, 393.

and hearsay. John Glyn's offer of new evidence on the two crucial articles, the 15th and the 23rd, on 10 April reflected the managers' panic. When the peers decided that Strafford should have the same concession, the Commons walked out. Sir Arthur Haselrig introduced his attainder bill that day because it had become clear that the case against Strafford could not be legally proved. Temple recorded that most of the peers had reached this conclusion by 8 April. Some MPs had certainly been discussing the use of attainder for several days. Haselrig believed there was no time to waste since it was essential to send the bill to the Lords before they came to judgement on the impeachment.[36]

Thus Haselrig's attainder bill was intended, as one newsletter put it, to 'supply the defect and make him more odious', or, as a recent commentator has put it, 'to piece out a want of evidence'.[37] Pym and Hampden at first resisted the new course of action. Indeed on 12 April Pym persuaded the Commons to climb down on the demand to present new evidence, which had produced the rupture in its relations with the Lords. His vigorous reiteration of the treason case on 13 April showed that his resolve to remove Strafford had not weakened, but he was concerned to avoid offending the Lords and hoped they would expedite their judgement.[38] The debates of 15 and 16 April about whether the Commons should continue to attend and participate in the trial were long and contentious. Pym had the support of Hampden, William Strode and Sir Walter Earle; influential men like Henry Marten and Sir John Culpepper and young fire-brands like John Hotham rallied to Haselrig and the lawyers in charge of the case, who had lost patience with the Lords. Reluctance to abandon the trial altogether was based on a perfectly intelligible viewpoint, as D'Ewes recognized: there was no reason to think that if the case that had been made did not persuade the peers to find Strafford guilty a bill of attainder would.

But Pym's tactical stand masked a much more important split in the House of Commons. His delay in throwing himself wholeheartedly behind the attainder encouraged an identifiable Straffordian faction to emerge. 'I was much amazed to see so many of the House speak on Strafford's side', noted D'Ewes on 14 April.[39] For the next week St John and a small group of associates struggled to combat a sustained backbench revolt against the attainder bill in committee. There were times when it might have

36 *HMC De L'Isle and Dudley MSS* VI, 398; Timmis, *Thine is the Kingdom*, pp. 64–130.
37 Bodleian Tanner MS 66, fol. 51r; J.H. Timmis, 'Evidence and 1 Eliz. I, Cap. 6: The Basis of the Lords' Decision in the Trial of Strafford', *Historical Journal* XXI (1978), 683.
38 P. Christianson, 'The Peers, the People and Parliamentary Management in the First Six Months of the Long Parliament', *JBS* XLIX (1971), 594–5; Gardiner XI, 328–34; Zagorin, pp. 220–1.
39 J. Forster, *The Debates on the Grand Remonstrance* (London, 1860), pp. 137–41; BL Harl. MS 163, fols. 45r, 47r, 52r, 53r; 164, fols. 966v, 967, 973; Timmis, *Thine is the Kingdom*, p. 145.

foundered on the deep concern of members for constitutional propriety and legality. The House was more divided than it had yet been since parliament met. The 14 April, when the trouble began, was the day after the earl's masterly summing up in his own defence. Members had listened to his strong and moving speech, three hours long according to one report, an appeal to the Lords based on equity and logic, ending with a biting attack on the managers' attempts to create new treasons: 'I speak in defence of the commonweal against their arbitrary treason.'[40] The speech, we are told, did 'abundantly satisfy many of those which were present'. 'He moved the hearts of all his auditors', declared Bulstrode Whitelocke, 'some few excepted, to remorse and pity.'[41] In the bitter and confused debate on the second reading of the attainder bill feeling ran so high that some tried to evade the orders of the House by speaking twice to the matter in question. The decision to sit as a committee on the afternoon of 14 April was intended to ensure that 'every man's conscience might be fully satisfied' that the offences charged against Strafford constituted high treason.[42]

For three days argument raged on the motion, eventually carried on 16 April, that Strafford had 'endeavoured to subvert the ancient fundamental laws of these realms of England and Ireland and to introduce an arbitrary and tyrannical government, against law'.[43] There were two questions which left many MPs uneasy. Had Strafford endeavoured the subversion of laws? Did such illegal acts as had been proved against him in fact tend to the subversion of the fundamental laws? Brave speeches were made in the earl's defence. Robert Holborne 'argued as strongly as his counsel could have done'.[44] Culpepper, seeing the impact of his defence of Strafford on 14 April, called for the motion to be put.[45] There were sharp passages between managers and backbenchers. When Edmund Waller asked what the fundamental laws were, John Maynard told him that anyone who did not know them 'is no fit man to sit here for he would do little good'.[46] In short there was a growing sense of dissatisfaction. According to Temple 'many of the ablest of the House and chiefest lawyers' disliked the attainder process. Sir John Coke's report on 17 April that it was 'agreed on all sides that the laws are not subverted' may have only slightly overstated the mood.[47]

More hard driving was needed before the next stage was achieved: the vote in the committee of the whole House on 19 April, after six hours'

40 Rushworth, *Trial of Strafford*, pp. 633–60; Bodleian Tanner MS 66, fol. 57.
41 BL Add. MS 11034, fol. 138r; Whitelocke, *Memorials*, p. 43.
42 BL Harl. MS 163, fols. 43r, 44r.
43 *CJ*, II, 122.
44 BL Harl. MS 163, fol. 45r; 164, fol. 974r.
45 BL Harl. MS 476, fol. 453r.
46 BL Harl. MS 476, fol. 180r.
47 *Verney*, pp. 48–9; *HMC Coke*, p. 278; *HMC De L'Isle and Dudley MSS*, VI, 401.

debate, that Strafford's attempt to subvert the fundamental laws was treason. D'Ewes thought it had 'treble affirmatives at least to the negatives', but a substantial group were wholly unconvinced.[48] The earl's motives were the great stumbling block. Coke was probably representative of the dissentient viewpoint:

How far a man may take upon his conscience to determine what the intentions of another man were in doing of such particular actions is a point worth some consideration with those that are to judge in a case of blood: and how agreeable it is that the punishment should precede the promulgation of the law . . . And it was never heard that intentions were reckoned for treason in any other case than where the conspirator intended or endeavoured the death of the king . . . an indifferent man may perchance satisfy himself upon the whole matter that certainly this earl never had any such intentions as to subvert the law.[49]

In the final stages it was the 23rd article which became the sticking point for many. The managers insisted that Strafford's alleged advice to Charles I to use his army in Ireland to reduce the kingdom of England was treason by statute. Yet this was their weakest ground, since under an Elizabethan statute conviction for treason required two witnesses. They only had one. Everyone remembered the dramatic session on 5 April when the elder Vane, garrulous with nerves, recalled Strafford's words about using the Irish army only at the third interrogation. Several of the peers had immediately shown their dissatisfaction with his evidence; other counsellors came forward to contradict him. Newsletters commented on the 'single testimony argued home to the point' that day.[50] The general unease is shown by the attempts on 14 and 20 April, thwarted by the managers, to have the earl of Northumberland's testimony read, which flatly opposed that of Vane. 'By God's law matter of fact is to be established in the mouth of two witnesses at least', thought Coke, reflecting that a man who sought 'to bring cold and impartial thoughts along with him' might question whether Strafford's crimes were 'of that exorbitant nature they are publicly declared'. A few dared shout no when the motion was put on 20 April that the earl's incriminating words at the Council board amounted to treason.[51]

Before the final vote on the attainder bill was taken on 21 April there were two dramatic interventions. Gervase Holles told his colleagues that 'being in a case of blood his conscience being not satisfied it would be murder in him which was but justice in the House.' Lord Digby went much further with his appeal against 'committing murder with the sword of justice'. The vulnerability of Vane's evidence was the centrepiece of his

48 *CJ* II, 123; BL Add. MS 11045, fol. 139v; Harl. MS 164, fol. 981r; *Verney*, pp. 56–7.
49 *HMC Coke*, p. 278. .
50 Timmis, *Thine is the Kingdom*, pp. 106–19, 221–2; BL Sloane MS 1467, fol. 27r.
51 BL Harl. MS 163, fols. 76, 78r; 476, fol. 179v; *HMC Coke*, p. 278.

argument: 'he who twice could not remember a thing might the third time forget something and this it is which doth utterly overthrow his testimony in law.' Digby reminded MPs that at times the most learned lawyers among them had been 'diametrically opposite', which was indeed true.[52] John Wilde and Robert Nicholas, for example, were assertively anti-Strafford; Orlando Bridgeman, John Selden and Robert Holborne had leapt to his defence.[53]

It would be wrong to assume that because only 59 men in the end had the courage to vote against the attainder the rest followed Pym and Haselrig with clear and confident hearts. Already by 21 April the citizens of London were organizing their petition for Strafford's death. Digby, aware of the mounting popular pressure, urged his colleagues to ignore it. There were also rumours of the Scots transporting their forces by sea to London. Lord Capel later maintained that he gave his vote for the attainder 'out of base fear of a prevailing party'. The matter greatly troubled him. Just before his execution in 1649 he attributed his 'unworthy cowardice not to resist so great a torrent as carried that business' to his frailty of nature.[54] There were probably a good many who found themselves caught between 'fear of Mr Pym', which an MP told one of Strafford's friends gave them no choice, and their consciences. It was easiest in this dilemma to rely on the Lords throwing out the bill. Some, as they watched the subsequent fortnight unfold, must have quickly regretted their acquiescence. Only five days after giving his vote for the attainder, Sir Edward Hyde was hinting to the earl of Essex that imprisonment for life might be the more just punishment.[55]

Little more than half the House, 263 MPs, voted on 21 April; less than a fortnight previously 295 had voted in another division. It is hard to say how many either left London in the midst of the final debates, like Sir John Strangeways and Framlingham Gawdy, or were absent at the momentous division. John Hampden, of all people, according to some notes made by Edward Nicholas, left the chamber while the vote was being taken. 'Some expounded it casual', he recorded, 'others that he would seem to wash his hands in that connection though he applauded the success.' It is hard to interpret the behaviour of those who made no good excuse. Can we believe Sir John Coke, who maintained in a letter to his father that he was 'casually away that evening, not expecting that vote', when abstention clearly had an appeal for thoughtful and worried men? Coke was at this time becoming

52 BL E 198(1); Harl. MS 476, fol. 612 includes a verbatim account of Digby's speech which was later rearranged for printing.
53 Harl. MS 163, fol. 64r; 164, fols. 966v, 972; 476, fols. 178v, 179r, 604–8; Add. MS 14828, fol. 38; Bodleian Tanner MS 66, fol. 69r; *Verney*, pp. 48–58.
54 *HMC Coke*, p. 278–9, 283; BL E 198 (1); *CSPD 1640–1*, pp. 524–5; A. Capel, *Excellent Contemplations, Divine and Moral* (1683), pp. 138–9, 197.
55 Wedgwood, *Strafford*, pp. 367–8; Clarendon I, 320.

disillusioned with the pressures and persuasions of Westminster politics. 'The experience I have had', he told his father, 'shall teach me whilst I live to beware of the public stage and to keep my thoughts at home, for I think I shall never go with any tide.'[56]

In the Lords, as in the Commons, it was concerted party manoeuvring which did most to secure Strafford's downfall.[57] The supporters of the bill among the peers focused the House's attention on the two articles of the charge, the 15th and the 23rd, which were reducible to the treason statue of 1352. Then they pushed through a crucial motion to break the normal rules of evidence: 'in the discussing the matter of fact in this whole cause, the rule shall only be the persuasion of every man's conscience'. On 6 May the matter of fact in article 23 was duly voted as proven, despite the lack of supporting testimony for Vane's. The portions of the Journal which were later obliterated show that there were ten divisions in all between 5 and 7 May. It was rumoured that of around 80 peers who had regularly attended the trial 30 might support the attainder, but 50 would oppose it. On 4 May 70 peers attended; only 45 did so on 7 May when the crucial vote was taken. In the interval there was much popular intimidation and, probably more significantly, the House decided that every peer should take the Protestation, a move that demoralized Strafford's friends and certainly kept the Catholics among them away. In the end the attainder only passed by 26 votes to 19.[58]

Some may have expected Strafford's death to ease political tension. On the contrary, it was bound to exacerbate it, since it had become clear that the king's attitude to the plan for bridge appointments rested on parliament's willingness to spare Strafford's life. At the end of April Bedford was working hard to convert influential men to a scheme for Strafford's removal from the political scene. Clarendon has given us a vignette of these negotiations with his acount of the conversation between himself, the marquis of Hertford and the earl of Essex in the course of which Essex made his celebrated pronouncement that 'stone dead hath no fellow'. On 7 May Secretary Vane was optimistic about settlement. He expected a resolution by the king very shortly 'to reconcile himself with his people and to rely upon their counsels, there being now no other left'. Two days later Bedford died. He was probably the only man that both Charles and Pym could be expected to trust as an intermediary.[59]

---

56   *CJ* II, 118–9, 125; BL Add. MS 14829, fol. 39r; 31954, fol 181r; *HMC Coke*, p. 283.
57   BL Harl. MS 6424, fols. 59v, 60r, 64v; C.S.R. Russell, 'The Authorship of the Bishop's Diary of the House of Lords in 1641', *BIHR* XLI (1968), 230; *EHR* LXXX (1965), 30.
58   Bodleian Tanner MS 66, fol. 77; Timmis, *Thine is the Kingdom*, pp. 166–9; P. Christianson, 'The Obliterated Portions of the House of Lords Journals dealing with the Attainder of Strafford 1641', *EHR* XLV (1980), 339–53; Manning, pp. 8–18; Pearl, pp. 216–7; Rushworth, *Trial of Strafford*, p. 751; Wedgwood, *Strafford*, p. 375; Christianson, *JBS* XLIX (1977), 597–8.
59   *CSPD 1640–1*, p. 571; Clarendon I, 318–21.

Strafford's death was preceded by a fortnight of political panic in London. Between 24 April, when the Commons received a petition against the earl from 20,000 Londoners, and 10 May, when Charles at last signed the death warrant, attitudes were struck which could not easily be unlearned.[60] The king saw the impact that massive crowds could make on Westminster decision making. Although the demonstrators were 'for the most part men of good fashion', they included 'mechanic people out of Southwark'.[61] MPs and citizens swallowed wild rumours: that the king intended to use the northern army against parliament, that Strafford would be rescued from the Tower, that the French were about to invade. One reporter spoke of 'the greatest treason discovered in England since the powder plot'.[62] An incident on 5 May illustrates the atmosphere in the City. When someone leaving the debate said there was 'hot work and a great fire within' he was taken literally. 'A sudden bruit ran through the City', related Baillie, 'that the papists had set the Lower House on fire and had beset it with arms; in a clap all the City is in alarm; shops closed, a world of people in arms runs down to Westminster.'[63] In the debating chambers emotions ran high. Men lived on their nerves. Temple told Leicester on 22 April that he thought the uncertainty over Strafford's fate and money for the armies presaged 'some great inconvenience to this state'. Not only was the City refusing to lend but he had heard that in some districts the countrymen would not pay their subsidies. 'God keep the parliament together, things are near to a crisis I fear', wrote Sir John Coke to his father on 28 April. 'As I said at Christmas and often since', reiterated Sir Edward Dering to his wife on 2 May, 'we shall be cured with a confusion.'[64]

The Protestation, drawn up behind closed doors on 3 May, was intended as a bond to hold MPs tightly together when dangers threatened. It could be seen as a purely internal affair. But for the Commons leadership it had from the first an avowedly public and propagandist purpose. An oath of association, declared Strode, would 'show loyalty'; it would 'clear us from all jealousies', added Holles, and 'manifest to the world our unity one with another'. The broad form the Protestation finally took – an oath in defence of 'the true reformed Protestant religion', the king, parliament and 'the lawful rights and liberties of the subject' – encouraged Pym to adopt it as a political weapon. An order for it to be printed was pushed through on 5 May so that it could be imposed on the whole adult nation. The leadership had found itself an ideological test, 'a shibboleth', as they put it in

60 Manning, pp. 8–18; Pearl, pp. 216–18.
61 Bodleian Tanner MS 66, fol. 83; *DO*, p. 90.
62 BL Harl. MS 477, fols. 470v, 497v; *HMC Montagu*, pp. 129–30; *CSPV 1640–2*, pp. 150–1; *HMC Egmont*, p. 134, Gardiner IX, 342–67; Russell, *Crisis of Parliaments*, p. 334.
63 Baillie, p. 352; *DO*, p. 93.
64 *HMC, De L'Isle and Dudley MSS* VI, 401; *HMC Coke*, p. 281; Larking, p. 46.

July, 'to discover a true Israelite'. There were objections from some, like Orlando Bridgeman, who doubted the legality of imposing an oath without the king's consent. But the answer to them was a bill. Meanwhile, all MPs were pressed to send copies into the localities, indicating the enthusiasm with which the Protestation had been taken at Westminster and recommending its nationwide adoption.[65]

Making Strafford 'the greatest example of these times' provoked bitter political controversy.[66] Since Digby had scriveners make copies of his speech and encouraged the printing of 500 copies, it was soon the talk of the nation.[67] Nine different pamphlets were on sale about Strafford before the end of May.[68] Newsletter accounts of his death emphasized his courage and 'generous carriage' at the end. The *Brief and Perfect Relation* of the trial was a sophisticated and powerful Straffordian tract.[69] There was little the Commons, or the Wardens of the Stationers Company whose help they sought, could do to check this spate of Straffordian publicity.[70] The much-read compendium *Speeches and Passages*, printed in the autumn of 1641, included Digby's speech, in defiance of the parliamentary ban on it, as well as the earl's speech from the scaffold.[71]

Once the identity of the Straffordians was well publicized they went in fear of their lives. Some MPs who were wrongly suspected of voting against the attainder were treated roughly: both Sir John Strangeways and Sir John Brooke complained in the Commons on 4 May that they had been nearly pulled to pieces. Strangeways reported on 1 June that some MPs were still suffering 'great abuses'.[72] One of the earl's supporters, William Taylor of Windsor, had the list of Straffordians waved in his face by an angry constituent and was forced to justify himself.[73] Taylor's bold answer, that in passing the attainder parliament had committed 'murder with the sword of justice', was too daring a slight for the Commons to pass by. When his words were reported on 27 May there was general support for his permanent expulsion, especially since it was recalled that at Strafford's arraignment he had smuggled in a friend and refused to remove him though an MP was thereby left standing. On the same day the House ordered investigation of the case of a Gloucestershire minister, who was said to have accused parliament of maliciously executing Strafford 'for fear

---

65 BL Harl. MS 477, fols. 484–6, 494; *CJ* II, 132–3, 135–6; *LJ* IV, 338; Verney, *Notes*, p. 67; Gardiner, *Documents*, pp. 155–6.
66 *HMC Coke* II, 266, 279.
67 BL Harl. MS 479, Fol. 797v; Bodleian Rawlinson D MS 1099: 13 July.
68 G.K. Fortescue, *Catalogue of the Thomason Collection* (Kraus, 1969), pp. 11–13.
69 BL Sloane MS 1467, fol. 37v; 3317, fols. 21–2.
70 *CJ* II, 146, 168; Bodleian Rawlinson D MS 1099, fols. 41v–42r.
71 *Speeches and Passages* (1641), pp. 213–32.
72 BL Harl. MS 477, fols. 488v, 509r; *DO*, p. 115.
73 *DO*, p. 111; BL Sloane MS 1467, fol. 72r; Bodleian Rawlinson D MS 1099, fol. 17v; Keeler, p. 358.

he should do some of them harm'.[74]

Thus the reverberations of Strafford's death were louder than anyone can have expected. The Commons leadership struggled to dampen controversy. They managed to resist the suggestion that a committee should investigate the breach of privilege involved in the divulging of the names of the Straffordians.[75] But they could not prevent a row over Digby's speech on 1 June. A motion that a committee should examine the printing of it produced 'a mixed cry of yeas and noes of difficult judgement'. When the Speaker ruled that the noes had it, Digby seized the chance to protest his innocence in the matter: his speech, reported one newsletter, 'a little blunted those sharpest gentlemen which were so high against him'.[76] The leadership had its revenge on Digby in July when, faced with the full story of his propaganda activities on Strafford's behalf, the backbenchers, with the exception of a few like Strangeways and Edward Kirton, turned firmly against him.[77]

A year after Strafford's death Margaret Eure, a bewildered Yorkshire gentlewoman, wrote that she was in 'a great rage with the parliament . . . for they promised us all should be well if my Lord Strafford's head were off and since then there is nothing better'.[78] The search for a scapegoat served Pym in 1641 no better than it had done Sir John Eliot in the 1620s. The trial merely showed the ruthlessness and singlemindedness of the harshest men in parliament, men who it was apparent were ready to override the law. St John's remark that 'it was not cruelty to knock foxes and wolves on the head', a blunt statement of political necessity, quickly became celebrated.[79] To a few especially perceptive provincial observers it seemed that Pym's whole strategy was wrong: 'I began to be much troubled', wrote Sir Roger Twysden, 'that they did not so much seek to redress things amiss as to spend time in setting out the miseries we lay under in quarrelling at offenders.'[80] The most important legacy of the trial was apprehension about the methods of the parliamentary leadership. On 1 June Sir John Strangeways, protesting that the Straffordians were 'posted and much traduced', threatened to leave parliament if the right of members to speak their conscience without intimidation was not secured.[81] Some men began to voice their fear of being muzzled inside the House or bullied outside it.

According to Hyde there was nothing which the leaders of the Commons more abhorred during the first months of the parliament than the prospect

74 BL Harl. MS 477, fols. 564, 565v; *CJ* II, 158–9.
75 BL Harl. MS 477, fol. 488v; Clarendon I, 307–8.
76 BL Sloane MS 1467, fols. 71v–72r.
77 *CJ* II, 209; Bodleian Rawlinson D MS 1099: 13 July.
78 *Verney*, pp. 90–1.
79 Wedgwood, *Strafford*, p. 270.
80 *Twysden*, p. 188.
81 BL Sloane MS 1467, fol. 72r.

of the English and Scottish armies being disbanded.[82] Pym and his closest associates certainly saw the Scots as deliverers. During November and December 1640 they feared another speedy dissolution. Thus they were bound to regard the presence of the Scots as an essential guarantee that the new parliament would survive. Some MPs spoke of the Scottish army, reported Robert Baillie on 12 December, as 'a most happy mean for all their desires . . . . the dissolving it were their utter ruin'.[83] Backbenchers tended to look at the matter differently, assuming that a quick treaty and disbandment of the armies would be a primary objective. There was a strong tradition of racial hostility, as James I had discovered when he sought union between the two nations.[84] Sir John Holland's proposal of two alternatives on 9 November indicates that he was one of those who lacked sympathy for the Scots from the start: he wanted 'a soft and mild reconciliation or else to expel them by force'. Alexander Rigby probably thought in weeks not months when he wrote to his brother on 23 December about parliament's efforts for 'a happy issue of the treaty'.[85]

Any attempt openly to delay the treaty would have been controversial. Pym's policy towards the Scots had to be equivocal. But there is no evidence that he or his associates put pressure to slow the pace of the treaty negotiations behind the scenes, either on peers who acted as English commissioners, such as Bedford, or on the Scottish commissioners. Such delays as occurred during February and March reflected the complexity of the business. The peers, anxious as the earl of Bristol put it on 6 March that the Scots might 'summer here', bickered among themselves about what could be done to expedite matters, but they were sensible enough to heed Viscount Saye's warning that 'spurring the Commons out of their own pace might offend them and beget an impediment.'[86] The lower House was not slack. They responded within a week to Lord Paget's request on 27 January that they should agree the sum to be given in the form of a 'brotherly assistance' for the Scottish charges, an essential preliminary at that stage to further discussion; in March it took only three days for the House to consider the important eighth article concerning the demolishing of the fortifications at Berwick and Carlisle and to report back to the Lords.[87]

Those most hostile to the Scots proved ready to challenge the leadership view that they should be treated as friends and brothers. Sir William Widdrington was censored for calling the Scots rebels; Gervase Holles was

82 Clarendon I, 284.
83 *HMC Various*, p. 259; Baillie, p. 280; Russell, *Crisis of Parliaments*, pp. 329–30; Pearl, p. 198.
84 See for instance T. Northcote, *Notebook* (London, 1877), p. 63; *Knyvett*, p. 97.
85 *D'Ewes (N)*, p. 16; *HMC Kenyon MSS*, p. 60.
86 BL Harl. MS 6424, fols. 23–24v, 46; D. Stevenson, *The Scottish Revolution 1637–1644* (Newton Abbot, 1973), pp. 214–23.
87 *D'Ewes (N)*, pp. 293, 317, 434, 451; Baillie, p. 312.

suspended from the House for declaring that some of the articles of the treaty were dishonourable.[88] Now and again the divergencies of attitude present in the Commons were sharply presented. Despite the Scottish commissioners soliciting of 'all their friends in both Houses', opposition emerged to Henry Marten's motion on 3 February that the Brotherly Assistance should be fixed at £300,000. Digby tried to have Marten called to the bar for his statement that the presence of the Scots on English soil was 'just if not necessary'.[89] Sir John Strangeways, who had earlier suggested that the English army should be ready to fight the Scots, was also openly antagonistic. He was joined by John Selden, who declared that no money should be promised until the Scots had departed: 'it was against divers statutes to aid or assist them coming with swords in their hands.'[90] Three weeks later Strangeways moved for action to rid the kingdom of the Scottish army: if they stayed after 16 March, he declared, they should bear their own charges out of the £300,000.[91]

At the end of February opinion in London was shifting against the Scots. The declaration issued by the Scottish commissioners that they wished to see episcopacy abolished in England produced 'one of the greatest distempers' in the Commons that D'Ewes had witnessed. Baillie commented that it 'put our enemies on their tiptoes' and 'made sundry of our seeming friends turn their countenance'. Men who previously 'thought the progress and success of their affairs had some dependence upon our army' were changing their tune, the Scottish commissioners told their commander Alexander Leslie on 13 March.[92] In the provinces also there was a growing revulsion from the prospect of the Scots dictating English affairs. In a letter from Cheshire on 21 March, Viscount Cholmondeley expressed the hope that they would soon go home 'and give us leave to make in England ourselves without their directions'.[93] Pym was so alarmed at the Scots' tactical error that he persuaded their commissioners not to insist on their demand being presented to parliament for a while. He feared that if the fragile unity of the House was broken on this issue at least a hundred of those 'set to oppose' Strafford might defect.[94]

Between November 1640 and April 1641 the arrears of pay of the two armies mounted and the impoverishment and distress of the counties faced with supporting them became lamentable. Northern MPs, badgered by friends at home who wrote of the burdens of billeting and supply, were in

88 *D'Ewes (N)*, p. 20; *CJ* II 128; Rushworth III, part I, 168–9.
89 BL Add. MS 31954, fol. 183r.
90 *D'Ewes (N)*, pp. 184; 317–8; Baillie, p. 297.
91 *D'Ewes (N)*, p. 398.
92 *D'Ewes (n)*, pp. 417–8: Baillie, pp. 305–6; *Calendar of Wynn Papers*, p. 270; Gardiner IX, 296–7.
93 BL Add. MS 36914, fol. 199.
94 Crawford, pp. 48–9; Gardiner IX, 299–300.

full cry as soon as parliament assembled.[95] 'The Scottish army begin to be in necessity', reported Sir Baynham Throckmorton as early as 21 November, 'the northern counties being not able to raise and pay the contribution any longer'. On 17 December the earl of Bristol warned that the Scots in their 'want and distress' might be forced to plunder the counties which were already under contribution. In January 1641 an officer reported that English soldiers, who were already notable sheep stealers, might mutiny before long. In March Thomas Knyvett retailed rumours of 'much disturbance in our army in the north . . . for soldiers will not starve.'[96]

Two papers about conditions in the north brought matters to a head. On 17 March parliament heard from the Scottish commissioners that their army was reduced to such extremity that, unless money was forthcoming at once, 'they must either starve or . . . break their limited bounds.' A few days later a letter from the officers of the English army to the earl of Northumberland was being circulated. They complained about the neglect of their pay, yet expressed their readiness, with the coming of spring, to engage the Scots, who had 'already moved in part, though under pretence of enlarging their quarter'.[97] The explosive situation in the north accounts for the extraordinary and impractical proposal, reported by Sir John Hotham from the committee on the king's army on 1 April, for disbandment of the English troops on 16 April rather than a renewal of the cessation of arms. It seems that Hotham and some of his northern friends, having recently secured a commission of oyer and terminer for the leading Yorkshire gentry to discipline the king's army, now adopted the hazardous view that the Scots might be made to accept virtually any conditions they were offered. Disbandment would follow the rapid completion of the treaty and the Scots' march home. But there was no chance of raising the £110,000 due to the Scots in a mere fortnight. The committee hoped to postpone payment of the whole of the Brotherly Assistance.[98]

Hotham's plan of action produced a long debate on 6 April. The over-riding concern of most MPs seems to have been to ensure that the English officers did not take matters into their own hands, as their letter hinted they might do. Hotham had already moved on 2 April that any in the army who offered violence to the Scots unprovoked or raised men without leave should be declared enemies of the state. A resolution followed on 6 April that the army should not 'march or advance' without specific directions from the king with the consent of parliament. This was generally

95 *D'Ewes (N)*, pp. 20, 38, 380, 432; BL Add. MS 11045, fol. 132v; *Fairfax* I, 103–4.
96 Bristol RO 36074/136d; *D'Ewes (N)*, p. 165; Gardiner IX, 308; *HMC Various* II, 262; *HMC 5th Report*, pp. 51, 435.
97 *LJ* IV, 187; *CJ* II, 106; *CSPD 1640–1*, pp. 507–8; see also *HMC De L'Isle and Dudley MSS* VI, 389–90, 392–3.
98 BL Harl. MS 162, fol. 391r; *CJ* II, 115; *HMC Egmont*, p. 132; Pennington, p. 170.

acceptable but Arthur Capel's attempt, leading an anti-Scots faction, to add to the resolution a 'declaration of the Scots to be enemies of the state if they did move in an hostile way' proved controversial.[99] Capel and his friends seem to have hoped either to rid the country of the Scots when the cessation ended or to drive them out. They were not able to carry the House, as a summary of the debate in one newsletter indicates: 'some would have the Scots declared enemies if they pass the Tyne and our soldiers rebels if they disband; some speak of sending a new general.' This reporter concluded that most MPs 'would fain keep the armies in their posts if it be possible'.[100]

Nevertheless, whereas from December to March the cessation of arms was renewed without much argument, when the vote on renewal came on 9 April it provided the occasion for the longest and most heated debate on the Scottish issue of the whole session.[101] Denzil Holles argued vigorously for the leadership viewpoint; the Newcastle member Sir Henry Anderson opposed renewal and moved the programme Hotham's committee had set out. At seven o'clock the anti-Scots faction forced a division, after the Speaker had ruled that the shout of those in favour of renewal of the cessation had carried the day.[102] Pym's majority in fact proved to be only 39. In a sense this debate was a charade, because those who were hostile to the Scots had little sense of the current political realities. Yet it demonstrated that the Scots, like Strafford, had divided the parliament to a degree no one expected in the first euphoric days.

By May the situation was grim: parliament had sat for six months, the news from the north was daily more alarming. In April a mutiny at Berwick, where the garrison was suffering 'extreme and urgent necessities', involved capture of the mayor and release of prisoners in the gaol. Sir Michael Ernley reported that he was mobbed by soldiers seeking their pay: 'we will have money, we are men come for the king's service, we will not be slaves to serve but will be maintained like men'.[104] Sir John Conyers was another officer who was frantic about supplies, the morale of his troops and the intentions of the Scottish army.[105] On 7 May he reported a riot in which 'some of both parties were slain'; the army was in no state, he warned the new lieutenant-general the earl of Holland, to resist a Scottish advance. Sir Jacob Astley stressed the difficulties faced by the officers in maintaining any kind of discipline.[106] Northumbrian and

99 BL Harl. MS 163, fol. 405r; 164, fols. 951v, 958r; *CJ* II, 116.
100 BL Sloane MS 1467, fol. 28r.
101 *D'Ewes (N)*, pp. 106, 215, 326–7, 460.
102 BL Harl. MS 163, fol. 963; Bodleian Tanner MS 66, fol. 50.
103 *CJ* II, 118.
104 BL Harl. MS 477, fols. 458v, 460v; 478, fol. 605v; 6424, fol. 56v; *HMC Egmont* p. 133.
105 *CSPD 1640–1*, pp. 531–2, 535.
106 Bodleian Tanner MS 66, fols. 55, 63, 69, 90, 91; *LJ* IV, 224; BL Harl. MS 477, fol. 532r; 6424, fol. 69r.

Durham gentlemen, meanwhile, told a tale of 'utter desolation': so much money had been drained from the county and so much corn and hay had been given to make up the payments to the Scottish army that seed corn was short and the people were likely to starve.[107] Sir Henry Anderson alleged that the Scots forced towns to bring in oats and beans and then resold them to the countrymen at dear rates. A letter read in the Commons on 1 May expressed northern fears that delays over the treaty would lead to 'a combustion and intestine war': 'in our country the laws are still silent and the courts of justice sit not, that except the fear of God and hope of a settled peace every man would do that which seems good in his own eyes.'[108]

With the survival of parliaments secured by the Triennial Act and the act against the dissolution of the current assembly, the case for urgent attention to the treaty and disbandment was unanswerable. D'Ewes sensed the mood among members, increasingly anxious about satisfying country expectations, when he reminded them on 6 April that nothing would render them more acceptable at home 'than the glad tidings of a firm and assured peace'. But money was the great obstacle. In general the House had been as sour and obstructionist over fiscal matters during the first six months of this sitting as they often were in the 1620s.[109] Members were reluctant to accept that subsidymen should bear the cost of paying off the armies. There was a search for scapegoats for the war. In November Sir Thomas Widdrington spoke hopefully of raising money from monopolists and delinquents; both he and Sir John Coke advocated penalizing the bishops for the new canons of 1640.[110] There was talk of exploiting dean and chapter lands, papists and the wealthiest clergy. Pym and Bedford had well thought out plans along these lines, but most members merely absorbed wild and ephemeral rumours about solutions to the financial problem. One newsletter in May 1641 reported that £900,000 might be raised from dean and chapter lands by turning all leases into fee farms. D'Ewes produced an idiosyncratic suggestion which exhibited his class consciousness: jumped up men who had bought 'titles bigger than they can support' should help maintain the armies as a 'first step to the punishment of their ambition'. But as he himself pointed out, it was all too easy just to go on discussing these 'far and remote remedies'.[111]

Subsidies meanwhile came slowly and grudgingly, despite relentless pressure from the more responsible of Pym's associates like the office holders Sir Benjamin Rudyerd and Sir Robert Pye:[112] It took from 12

---

107 Bodleian Tanner MS 66, fol. 85; BL Harl. MS 477, fol. 532r; 6424, fol. 69v.
108 BL Harl. MS 477, fols. 481–2, 504–5.
109 BL Harl. MS 163, fol. 405r, see e.g. 1625, Russell, *Parliaments*, pp. 256–9.
110 *D'Ewes (N)*, p. 34; BL Add. MS 11045, fols. 132v, 144r, 145r.
111 Russell, *Origins*, pp. 112–13; Bodleian Tanner MS 66, fol. 93v; BL Harl. MS 163, fol. 106r.
112 Northcote, *Notebook*, pp. 106–7.

November to 16 February to get the first bill through the Houses. Further subsidies were voted on 20 February, with 129 members opposing, but the new bill did not receive the king's assent until 13 May.[113] Members were capable of bursts of generosity when political exigencies dictated. In the midst of panic fears of a dissolution on 21 November, MPs had rushed to follow Arthur Capel's lead in giving bond for £1000 of the £100,000 loan raised in the City for the armies. Again in March, when it was vital to get money advanced on the subsidies, numerous members agreed to lend or give security. But few at this stage were really prepared to face the implications of the fiscal situation. 'Half a dozen more must follow before all things can be made even' noted one reporter, announcing progress on the second batch of subsidies in March.[114]

Tax collection was always slow, the more so when subsidies came rapidly on each others' heels. Since the first act was only passed on 16 February it was impossible to keep to the timetable of payment of the first two subsidies by 10 March. The Cheshire commissioners were reported to be having difficulty in finding collectors to undertake the work soon after that, because 'the pre-fixed day is past of payment and they dare not assign new ones so as nothing is done'. There was similar trouble in Devon and Sussex.[115]

Parliament's prolonged dependence on borrowing put Isaac Pennington in a strong position. The City's loans, he and his friends realized, could be made a bargaining counter against Strafford. 'Money was to be had' insisted Sir John Culpepper, reporting on the unsuccessful visit of a parliamentary deputation on 27 February, but delays in removing Strafford troubled the merchants. 'The delay of justice was a chief reason that retarded men from lending', admitted the Lord Mayor himself a month later.[116] The citizens' petition to parliament on 24 April made the Mayor's point explicit: only the disposal of Strafford, they believed, could secure their religion, lives, liberties and estates. It was useless to talk of raising money for disbandment, declared D'Ewes a few days later, since the door was shut and they all knew 'what key alone can open it'.[117]

Yet it was not simply Strafford's evident ability to keep his enemies at bay that worried the City merchants and populace. Hyde found the City 'melancholy to see two armies kept on foot at so vast a charge . . . when all the danger of a war was removed'. A pattern of insecurity and unrest was already present in London by February 1641. At the end of March Knyvett wrote of the 'new jealousies' in the capital. Strafford's trial was

---

113 *D'Ewes (N)*, pp. 382–4.
114 *Ibid*, pp. 51–3, 435–9; BL Sloane MS 1467, fol. 26r.
115 *SR* v, 59; BL Add. MS 36914, fol. 206; *D'Ewes (N)*, pp. 485–6; Pennington, p. 166n.
116 *D'Ewes (N)*, p. 417; BL Harl. MS 162, fol. 379r.
117 BL 669 f 4 (13); BL Harl. MS 163, fol. 105r.

'not half-way ended', bemoaned Thomas Smyth in a hasty report to his bailiff: 'if he be not more speedily despatched the kingdom will be undone and I fear we shall have somewhat to do to rid the Scots and bring this parliament to a successful conclusion.'[118] Men who were bewildered by a political crisis that was beginning to gather around them resorted to defensive mechanisms. The earl of Bristol at a conference of both Houses on 23 March, regretting that City merchants refused to lend despite offers of personal security as well as the subsidy bill, commented perceptively:

> The cause of this hindrance must be some apprehension of damage, which the kingdom hath and particularly the City of London in that they fear unquiet and dangerous times, and so loth to part with money; for we cannot but conceive there is money in the kingdom and in the City. This fear is that which maketh them all keep the wealth they have to serve their turns in extremity of danger.[119]

Thus in the eyes of the most politically conscious community in the nation the problems of November 1640 to May 1641 – Strafford, the armies and money – became inseparable.

Many expected political progress once Strafford was removed. 'God send us now a happy end of our troubles and a good peace', reflected the elder Vane. Coke hoped for 'those happy times that this city expects'. 'Now I suppose the other business of the kingdom will receive freer passage and quicker despatch', wrote a Yorkshire correspondent to Lord Fairfax.[120] The provincial clamour for reform and settlement demanded a response after so many months of expectation. On 13 May the Commons set in motion serious discussion of the knighthood fines and ship money; on the 15th committees sat on Star Chamber, Archbishop Laud, Bishop Wren and the delinquent judges; on the 21st the House decided that the treaty should be taken in hand every morning at 9.00 and every afternoon at 3.00.[121] 'There is hope His Majesty, after he hath yielded my Lord of Strafford, will not stand at anything', declared Viscount Falkland on 15 May, urging his colleagues to concentrate on the essentials for a firm peace.[122]

Thus in the short run there was a new sense of optimism and urgency. Sir Edward Dering's suggestion on 18 May that the Commons should decide 'what must be done before we part and to turn all that may stay till we meet again' was in tune with the general mood. A decision had already been taken to accept no new business for a month. Dering went further, moving that the committee which had been set up in January to purge the House's proliferating committees should be revived, 'by reason of eight

118 Clarendon I, 284; *HMC Various*, II, 262; Bristol RO 36074/156a.
119 *CJ* II, 111.
120 *CSPD 1640–1*, p. 571; *HMC Coke*, p. 282, *Fairfax* II, 107.
121 *DO*, pp. 102, 104; *CJ* II, 146, 153.
122 BL Sloane MS 1467, fol. 38r.

months' session almost, the sickness of the pox and plague increasing, the necessity of composing the state and Church in those things wherein this House had (upon just grounds) disjointed them'. The outcome was a drastic reduction of committees leaving only 20 in being: only the 'prime and most public causes' would receive debate in the parliament's first session, Francis Gamul told his father-in-law Sir Richard Grosvenor on 25 May.[123]

These moves answered the backbench mood. There had been signs for some months that many MPs were becoming fretful. Rents were high in London and only the most perceptive had expected a long stay. Lady Maynard took a lease on a house for six months in October 1640 because her husband believed parliament would sit until midsummer. Sir Thomas Barrington, conceding that he would be much in the capital for some while, moved from lodgings in Fleet Street to a house leased from a speculative builder in Great Queen Street in March 1641. But few were as comfortably placed as Barrington, whose new home in a fashionable district had a coach house, a stable and a large garden.[124] In many men the political stalemate of the period from February to May had induced a sense of frustration. 'The proceedings in parliament quicken not', observed Sir John Temple in a letter to Leicester on 11 February: 'till they discern what will become of my lord lieutenant they will not, I believe, do any thing considerable for the king's service, neither will the Scottish army depart.' 'Our businesses are great and many which makes our pace through them slow', Lord Fairfax told his brother on 16 February. The following month he confessed himself to be 'wearied with much toil and infirm in this evil air'. He was already pessimistic about what might be done in making 'examples of offenders' before a recess.[125] Sir John Wray reminded colleagues on 16 February that the parliament was already exceptional for its length: 'we have many irons in the fire . . . but we have not struck one stroke with the right hammer, nor riveted one nail to the head.' They had sat long, complained Denzil Holles when he delivered the Protestation to the peers on 4 May, yet they had 'all this while but beaten the air and striven against the stream'.[126] Lack of progress in reform 'after long and laborious endeavours' was one of the reasons for a public fast in April.[127]

Pym and his closest colleagues shared the backbench sense of frustration but their view of the political situation made them in less of a hurry to get home. They had become obsessed by conspiracy. For Pym himself the hunt for the army plot conspirators became the overwhelming priority:

123 Larking, p. 47; BL Harl. MS 477, fol. 537r; 2081, fol. 93; *CJ* II, 149, 153, 162.
124 BL Harl. MS 384, fol. 66r; A. Searle, 'Sir Thomas Barrington in London 1640–1644'. *Essex Journal* II (1967), 35–41.
125 *HMC De L'Isle and Dudley MSS* VI, 380; *Fairfax* II, 41, 81–2, 181.
126 BL E 196 (10); Rushworth III, part I, 243.
127 *CJ* II, 129.

everything else – money, the treaty, delinquents, legislation – was secondary. The army plot so unnerved him that by the beginning of May he had begun to abandon the mediatory political stance of November 1640 in favour of a harder line. He was taut and determined in the debate on 3 May which brought the Protestation into being:

> I am persuaded that there was some great design in hand by the papists to subvert and overthrow this kingdom . . . and though the king be of a tender conscience, yet we ought to be careful that he have good counsellors about him and to let him understand that he is bound to maintain the laws and that we take care for the maintaining of the word of God.[128]

Here was a new and more challenging note that belied the whole strategy of behind the scenes negotiation and settlement on the basis of bridge appointments.

The best defence against the papist threat, in Pym's view, was the propagation of constant awareness of it. In this sense Clarendon was right in saying that he exploited the army plot for his own ends and sought to manipulate public opinion. Pym's closest allies became practised in the papist smear, watching for every revelation they could turn to account. Thus the attack on a JP carrying a list of recusants through Westminster Hall in November 1640 led Denzil Holles to warn of the possibility of a 'general assassination'. Anyone who spoke up for the bishops, insisted Haselrig on 12 June 1641, was 'papist or popishly affected'.[129] In the critical period before the attainder of Strafford became law there was much deliberate rumour-mongering. For instance, fears of a French invasion had been current for several months: twice since January peers had moved for a fleet to set forth in the Channel 'because the French are making great preparations'. Pym found these fears easy to play on. It was very probable that French forces were 'now at the waterside and ready for this kingdom', he told the Commons on 7 May; at a conference with the Lords a few days later he made much of the landing of 3000 French foot soldiers at Granville. The presence of a French fleet in the Channel, actually bound for Portugal, gave some plausibility to the fears of French invasion.[130]

Pym's insistence that he himself should investigate the army plot with the help of a highly select committee, which would work in secret, undoubtedly magnified public awareness of the dangers that parliament had escaped. He filled the close committee, as it came to be called, with six of his most trusted lieutenants: Clotworthy, Fiennes, Hampden, Holles, Stapleton and Strode.[131] Although the committee made no announcements

128 BL Harl. MS 477, fol. 485r; Clarendon I, 329–30; Verney. *Notes*, p. 67
129 Clarendon I 348–54; Gardineer IX, 239–40; BL Harl. MS 478, fol. 654r.
130 BL Harl. MS 477, fol. 500; 6424, fols. 7v, 56r, 66r.
131 *CJ* II, 135–8; *LJ* IV, 235; L. Glow; 'The Manipulation of Committees in the Long Parliament' *JBS* XXXVII (1965), 46–7; Gardiner IX, 357–8 has Culpepper, a mistake for Stapleton.

during the five weeks when its enquiry was in progress, rumours about those who had fled ensured that the plot was kept in the news. On 6 May Henry Jermyn was said to be riding for Weymouth; on the 15th William Davenant's capture at Faversham was reported; the same day the Commons heard the picaresque story of Henry Percy's attempts to hire a boat on the Sussex coast with the tale that he had to flee because he had wounded a man.[132] There were also fresh rumours about the French. On 13 May a letter was read from Dover about 10,000 soldiers said to be massed at Calais and 100 barrels of powder alleged to be stored in strangers' houses in the town.[133] Newsletters regaled the provinces with much of this gossip but reminded readers that it was 'yet secret what the many crimes objected against' the plotters might be.[134]

In so far as political polarization existed in the House of Commons in May and June 1641 a man's attitude to the papist conspiracy was the acid test of where he stood. Belief in its potency was an article of faith among those most closely in touch with the counsels of the leadership. They found the kingdom 'surrounded with variety of pernicious and destructive designs, practices and plots against the well-being of it, nay the very being of it', Holles told the Lords on 4 May. Doubtless Sir Robert Harley was in deadly earnest when, sending down the Protestation to the Herefordshire JPs on 8 May, he spoke of parliament's care to preserve their 'fundamental laws and liberties from such pernicious counsels and conspiracies as threatened their subversion'.[135] The celebrated scare on 19 May shows the readiness of many to panic. When two fat MPs, standing to catch every word of a report by Sir Walter Earle on the army plot, broke a board in the gallery, members rushed from the House 'scared out of their wits'. Sir John Wray declared he smelt gunpowder. Some men fell on one another in the crush. In Westminster Hall Sir Robert Mansel tried to stop the head-long rush, drawing his sword and bidding them 'stand for shame, but no man stood with the good old knight'.[136]

On the other hand the reaction to another incident in the Commons about the same time hints that there was also a strong vein of scepticism about the papist conspiracy. When Thomas Earle cried 'treason, treason' at the fall of a piece of ceiling from the roof, some again drew their swords and ran out, but it was reported that 'they all returned well laughed at by the rest'. Sir Arthur Haselrig made a fool of himself by clinging in terror to an angel on the roof of the debating chamber, which produced the derisive

---

132 BL Harl. MS 477, fols. 499v, 530.
133 *Ibid*, fol. 524r; *CJ* II, 145.
134 BL Sloane MS 1467, fols. 38–9.
135 Rushworth III, part I, 242; BL Loan MS 29/173, fol. 101r.
136 BL Sloane MS 1467, fol. 39v, Harl. MS 477, fol. 457v; Nalson II, 191–2; Rushworth, *Trial of Strafford*, p. 744; the incident is misdated by Gardiner IX, 359 and others.

comment that he had flown 'to the horns of the altar'.[137] When Holles announced 'some imminent danger' being agitated against parliament by the papists on 17 May, he failed to persuade backbenchers to agree to an immediate debate, instead of another session on the treaty with the Scots, despite his being seconded by 'three more of the close committee and divers others'.[138] Two days later Pym tried the dramatic tactics of interrupting a debate on the treaty to tell the House that letters from abroad opened that week had revealed 'some things of great importance'. It was essential, he argued, that the close committee should continue to open all letters from overseas. But he had begun to adopt a defensive tone: 'Whereas it is conceived by some that this design is of no importance, the truth is we have reason to give God thanks for our great delivery.'[139] There was no question of the House treating Pym's or Holles's revelations with the scorn reserved for a melodramatic colleague like Sir John Wray, whose portentous announcement that he knew of three Catholic priests lodged in one place 'proved to be a mere flame' when the place turned out to be the Spanish ambassador's house.[140] But there were days in May when the leadership seemed to be on shaky ground.

The reason that Pym's hold slipped was probably simply that there was a temporary relaxation of political tension. The possibility of a French invasion no longer nagged after the news that the regiments at Granville were intended for Picardy rather than the Channel Islands.[141] The king's assent on 18 May to the bill to protect parliament against dissolution contributed to a renewal of confidence. The bill had been drawn up to secure the loans from City merchants for paying the armies in the north at the instigation of Isaac Pennington. It removed a persistent cause of stress: at least three times since parliament met there had been sudden panics about an imminent dissolution.[142] There was also considerable progress with the treaty, though it had its rough passages.[143] A proposal by the Scots that war should never again be declared between the two kingdoms without the consent of their respective parliaments caused some difficulties; so did the Scottish demands for freedom of trade.[144] The Scots looked for a close union, whereas some English MPs were not prepared to trust them any farther than was necessary for an ending of the present quarrel. Edward Montagu, for example, regretted yielding 'to some

---

137 East Devon RO Drake of Colyton MS 1700A/CP 19; BL Sloane MS 1467, fol. 74r.
138 BL Harl. MS 477, fol. 534r; *CJ* II, 148; Crawford, p. 48.
139 BL Harl. MS 477, fol. 539; *CJ* II, 143, 150.
140 BL Harl. MS 163, fol. 740v.
141 BL Sloane MS 3317, fol. 22r; *CJ* II, 143.
142 Pearl, p.205; Gardiner IX, 359–61, 367; Bristol RO 36074/137b; Russell, *Crisis of Parliaments*, p.334.
143 *CJ* II, 148–71; BL Harl. MS 163, fol. 696r; 477, fol. 467v; 478, fol. 656r; *DO*, pp. 105, 109.
144 Gardiner IX, 377–8.

things which I wish we had not'.[145]

The long-term financial outlook also improved. Between 12 May and 15 June Pym swept all before him in the debates on the new subsidy bill. Since the parliament opened he had relentlessly pursued the principle of applying a fixed yield to the subsidy which he saw as the only solution to the disastrous decline in its yield.[146] The breakthrough came on 12 May, when the Commons voted a grant for paying the nation's debts to the armies of £400,000, which was to be collected from the counties in the proportions by which they had contributed to the subsidies granted in 1593. Certificates, the device by which 'gentlemen escaped in London for a song and so got a discharge for the country', were abolished.[147] A long series of resolutions reflected Pym's success in persuading the House to take a harsh line towards many who had at one time or another enjoyed fiscal privileges. Bids to get the lands of peers, cities, boroughs, colleges and wards excluded from the bill were defeated; peers indeed were to enjoy no immunity from contributing their share in each place where they held land. The Cinque Ports lost their long-established exemption; a petition from Norwich against its rating, the highest for a provincial town, was frostily rejected.[148]

This serious attempt to reform the subsidy was long overdue. But it provided no quick solution to the problem of paying off the armies, since the money raised by the new bill would not start coming in until the summer of 1642. MPs spent May and early June wrestling with stop-gap expedients: a newsletter reported numerous days taken up with 'the ever-lasting money business'.[149] There were occasional chinks of light. Backed by the 'old Northern men', Pym persuaded the House to accept a deal he had done with the customers by which they would pay £150,000 and thereby escape any charge of delinquency.[150] He spoke hopefully of employing the same tactics with the soap monopolists, because 'he made no question but there might be raised great sums from them'.[151] The Northumbrian MPs Sir Henry Anderson and Sir Thomas Widdrington broached a plan to raise a loan of £50,000 from the Merchant Strangers; Strode proposed that £80,000 should be obtained by a subsidy on the clergy.[152] Negotiations were also in progress with the Merchant Adventurers.[153]

---

145 BL Harl. MS 6424, fol. 55r; *HMC Montagu*, p. 130.
146 *D'Ewes (N)*, pp. 43–4, 134–6; BL Add. MS 11045, fol. 134v; Russell, *Origins*, p. 112; *Sussex*, pp. 202–10.
147 *CJ* II, 145, 168; BL Sloane MS 1467, fol. 39v.
148 *CJ* II, 145–7, 161, 175–6; BL Harl. MS 163, fol. 264r.
149 BL Sloane MS 1467, fol. 76r.
150 *CJ* II, 157, 161; *DO*, p. 110; BL Harl. MS 163, fol. 228r; 177, fol. 555r; Gardiner IX, 379.
151 Bodleian Rawlinson D MS 1099, fol. 24r.
152 BL Harl. MS 163, fol. 672v; 478, fol. 628v; 5047, fol. 23v.
153 *CJ*, II, 149, 160.

Finally there was a new vigour in May and June about the House's efforts towards abolishing the instruments of prerogative government. By 4 May the Commons had reviewed the cases of Bastwick, Burton, Prynne, Leighton and Lilburne and pardoned them all. The bill for reforming the 'unlawful proceedings' of the Privy Council and Star Chamber, which had been given its second reading on 1 April, was then in committee.[154] Rumours were leaked during May that Star Chamber might be abolished rather than reformed, so the report recommending its abolition on 31 May may not have been as much of a surprise as some like John Coventry and John Vaughan who opposed it pretended. This was an exciting moment.[155] The amendments in committee vastly expanded the scope of the bill, turning it into a comprehensive measure against the royal prerogative tribunals: the Council of the North, the Council in the Marches of Wales, the court of the Duchy of Lancaster and the exchequer court of the County Palatine of Chester were all to lose their Star Chamber jurisdiction. Limitations would also be placed on the judicial role of the Council. 'Westminster Hall must now be the all-sufficient place to answer all plaintiffs', concluded a newsletter report.[156]

For all these glimpses of an easier future, the first days of June brought two hefty blows to the morale of MPs: Sir Henry Vane's announcement of the full magnitude of the nation's debts and Nathaniel Fiennes's unravelling of the army plot. Vane's grim conclusion on 2 June, after telling a story of protracted negotiations and promises unfulfilled, was that £245,000 was needed at once to pay off the armies. If there was no other way, he suggested, all the gold and silver plate within 40 miles of London turned into coin should make up this sum. The south-eastern delegations naturally resisted a proposal that would hit gentry pockets hardest. They were full of objections. Plate was the wealth of the kingdom, observed Culpepper, 'the reserve of many years'. Hyde thought the scheme foolish because £20,000 at the most could be coined each week. He preferred a bill 'to cause every man to bring in all his money', except such as should be necessary to his 'private occasions according to his quality', but Holles immediately denounced this idea with the scathing comment that the same bill should provide 'meat and drink for nothing'. Only the Yorkshire member Sir John Hotham seems to have been wholly in favour of the plan for coining plate, seeing it as a gesture that would restore business confidence and cause merchants to lend.[157] When the bill to enforce the plan appeared on 10 June the effect of vigorous lobbying was evident: it

154 *CJ* II, 115; H.E.I. Phillips, 'The Last Years of the Court of Star Chamber 1630–1641', *TRHS* XXI (1939), 103–31; Larking, p. 44.
155 *CJ* II, 149, 151, 162; *HMC Montagu*, p. 130.
156 BL Sloane MS 1467, fol. 71; *Verney*, p. 101; Zagorin, p. 243.
157 BL Harl. MS 477, fol. 583v; *CJ* II, 164–5.

applied nationwide but only to men with more than £20 worth of plate and they were merely to bring in half their silver plate, for which they would be repaid from the subsidies. The bill was read twice that day. Nevertheless the House again showed its dismay by a long debate. 'It discovers the nakedness of this state', reflected one newsletter, 'whereby we must do that to help the Scots necessity (as they pretend) which must needs bring us into a greater.'[158]

The close committee's unveiling of the army plot, in a sitting on 8 June that ended in confusion at 8.30 p.m., was a magnificent tactical performance. Fiennes's long account, which had D'Ewes and Moore scribbling furiously to keep up, gathered a mass of hearsay and assertion into a plausible picture of a conspiracy which had threatened the nation from three directions, the army in the north, the Tower and France. His speech was interspersed with examinations read by Holles, Stapleton, Clotworthy and Strode. The plot was of course far less coordinated and more flimsy than the committee purported, but they had unearthed enough evidence to make it credible. There was the talk among discontented army officers, aggrieved at parliament's more favourable financial treatment of the Scottish army, of bringing the English army up to London; there were the attempts by certain courtiers to secure Colonel Goring's support, as governor of Portsmouth, in a shadowy design that was presumed to involve French troops; there was the order the king had given to Captain Billingsly to occupy the Tower of London with 100 men.[159] When Henry Percy's evidence was introduced on 14 June, it was abundantly clear that the king had rejected plans put to him for the army to overcome parliament.[160] But backbenchers had by then heard enough to satisfy them that they had been in mortal danger. When three colleagues implicated in the plot, Henry Wilmot, William Ashburnham and Hugh Pollard, were committed that day on suspicion of high treason, some were sufficiently terrified by the whole story to argue that they should be sent to separate prisons so that there was no possibility of their meeting.[161] This demand was the measure of the close committee's triumph. The full story of the army plot, with its overtones of papist conspiracy, alerted the Commons and raised the political temperature in both London and the provinces. 'He gave no clear satisfaction unto the House', declared an MP to a friend after Goring's declaration on 16 June, 'for it is said Mr Percy discovers more bloody business.' By 17 June printed versions of Percy's evidence,

158 Bodleian Rawlinson D MS 1099, fol. 33; Tanner MS 66, fol. 100r; *DO*, pp. 116, 118.
159 BL Harl. MS 163, fols. 675–85, 691r; 478, fols. 630–9, 645r; Sloane MS 1461, fols. 95v, 97r; Bodleian Rawlinson D MS 1699: 8 June, 10 June; *Verney*, pp. 85–92; *CSPD 1641–3*, p. 7; *HMC Montagu*, p. 130; *CJ* II, 171, 173; *DO*, pp. 153–5; Gardiner IX, 309–18, 384–5; B. Manning, editor, *Politics, Religion and the English Civil War*, (London, 1973), pp. 57–64.
160 BL Harl. MS 163, fol. 700v; *DO*, pp. 138–43.
161 *CJ* II 175; BL Harl. MS 163, fol. 703v; *Verney*, pp. 94–7.

Goring's declaration and Fiennes's report were on sale. 'We hear of many plots', wrote Lady Brilliana Harley to her son from Herefordshire on 25 June, 'one that London should have been set on fire and many plots against the parliament, that there were porters appointed to take notice of every parliament man's lodging.' Pym found he no longer had to make the running: on 15 June and again on the 21st there were calls for 'a report from the secret committee'.[162]

The return of political tension in June can also be related to the bad news from the north. On 7 June the Commons heard about the brutal murder by the English soldiers of one of their own number, Captain Withers, at Hull. The soldiers responsible defied the officers from the security of the town's blockhouses and demanded pardon for their barbarous action. 'We long to see the armies disbanded', wrote Thomas Stockdale from Yorkshire on 18 June, 'to prevent mutinies and other ill consequences of an idle undisciplined and unpaid army.'[163] No one had expected that ridding the country of the Scots would prove so long drawn out and frustrating. 'The Scots gather strength daily', reported the Chester burgess Francis Gamul on 25 May, 'and our army grows into want and distress, so that being thus divided in ourselves we foresee much misery and destruction which all our consultations cannot prevent I fear. God of his mercy put a happy end to all our troubles in the state.'[164] 'All the shifts that can be invented will not bring money to pay the Scots and the army', declared Maurice Wynn to his brother in Wales on 8 June. It was 'a business of great difficulty not easily effected', commented Sir Henry Slingsby in his diary, 'like the tossing three balls in one hand, which required both the eye and the hand to be very steady: when we treated of the demands of the Scots, our own business which concerned ourselves and our country was neglected; and when we considered of the ways and means to get money, to disband our armies and pay the Scots, our engagement grew the more and no money to be found to discharge them.'[165] Most MPs were still unwilling to face financial or military realities, although the pressure for disbandment was so great that detailed plans for organizing it had been prepared at Westminster by 15 June.[166] The previous week many had again opposed renewal of the cessation of arms; they were only persuaded to accept it by the argument that fighting and plunder of the north was the inevitable alternative. Some then demanded a public declaration that the renewal for a fortnight from 8 June would be the final one but the majority had more sense than to accept any such commitment. D'Ewes, exasperated, pointed out that a statement of

162   BL E 160 (14) (17) (18); Harl. MS 163, fols. 705v, 723v; *Harley*, pp. 136–7; Bedfordshire RO J1384.
163   *Fairfax*, p. 112; BL Harl. MS 478, fol. 624r.
164   BL Harl. MS 2081, fol. 93.
165   *Calender of Wynn Papers*, p. 273; *Slingsby*, p. 65.
166   *CJ* II, 174–7; *LJ* IV, 254–5, 275–6, 280; *CSPD 1641–3*, pp. 14–18.

this kind would only produce despair and cause people not to lend the money that was so desperately needed.[167]

The meagre parliamentary achievement since Strafford's death and the new anxieties of June turned commentators sour. 'The parliament is long in giving birth to their great affairs', complained Robert Appleton to a country cousin on 4 June. 'We are here still in the labyrinth and cannot get out', sighed Secretary Vane on 18 June. 'You may see in what a dangerous age we live', reflected Thomas Wiseman the same day, 'and shall do till the Scots be sent away.'[168] 'A general confusion amongst us may with great reason be apprehended', declared another observer of the London political scene.[169] 'I pray God all end well', wrote Sidney Bere to Sir John Pennington, 'but the appearances of confusion are very great.'[170]

So parliament was in its eight month and there was no end in sight. Why had no settlement proved possible? We have seen how the army plot and the crisis surrounding Strafford's death deepened the mistrust between the king and the Commons leadership. But it was not simply the events of April and May which destroyed the settlement plan. In one sense the gulf between the king and the House of Commons was huge even at the start. He had little understanding of their fears and emotions, their anxiety about the future of parliaments and the strength of their anti-Catholicism.[171] 'The queen is very angry but the king eats and sleeps well still', wrote a court correspondent on 8 May in the midst of the crisis in London over Strafford and the army plot.[172] Moreover between November 1640 and June 1641 Charles's irresolution and prevarication became plain. On 4 February, for instance, the king assured parliament that Count Rosetti would leave 'within a convenient time' yet he was still in the country in June. His talk on the same occasion of proceeding against Jesuits according to the statutes in force came to nothing. He refused to disband the Irish army on 14 April and again on the 28th then agreed to do so on 7 May; he passed the Triennial Act soon after he had insisted that it was something 'I cannot yield unto'; he vowed to save Strafford's life and then abandoned him.[173]

Charles's haughtiness with them made MPs bewildered and apprehensive. As early as 25 January he blamed them for 'distractions . . . occasioned through the connivance of parliament'. 'For there are some men', he charged, 'that more maliciously than ignorantly will put no

167 *CJ* II 170; BL Harl. MS 163, fol. 671r.
168 Bodleian Tanner MS 66, fols. 98r, 100r; *CSPD 1641–3*, p. 17–18.
169 BL Sloane MS 1467, fol. 99r.
170 *CSPD 1641–3*, pp. 24–5.
171 Rushworth III, part I, 24–40; C. Russell and G.E. Aylmer in W. Lamont, editor, *Tudors and Stuarts*, pp. 151–2.
172 *HMC Egmont*, p. 134.
173 *LJ* IV, 151, 207, 216; Zagorin, p. 219; Rushworth III, part I, 155; Gardiner IX, 290–1; Wedgwood, *Strafford*, pp. 371–7.

difference between reformation and alteration of government.' In February he accused them of selfishness: 'hitherto you have gone on in that which concerns yourselves to amend and not in those things which nearly concerns the strength of this kingdom, neither for the state nor my own particular.'[174] Yet when the king showed tact it was at once evident that there was an enormous fund of loyalty upon which he could have drawn. Sir John Temple reported that his speech on 4 February declaring his intention to suppress popery 'gave great satisfaction'. He would 'repose himself wholly upon the affection of his subjects', Charles told the elder Vane, when, during the May panic about coastal defences, he agreed to hurry the appointment of the earl of Salisbury as lord lieutenant of Dorset. The news, we are told, produced 'much joy in the House and many put off their hats in sign of thankfulness'. Vane was instructed to return the gratitude of the Commons, with a message that they hoped to make him 'as great, as glorious and as potent a prince as any of his ancestors ever were'. A proper response to the king's passing of the Triennial Act, Holles suggested and colleagues agreed, would be a second reading of the bill for the queen's jointure.[175]

It is an open question whether the king ever showed much inclination to look seriously at the deal that Pym and his closest associates had in mind. On the one hand there is no reliable evidence that Charles actually discussed with Bedford or with Pym himself the question of giving office to men like Saye, Essex, Holles and Mandeville, whose appointments were at one time or another rumoured to be imminent. On the other hand rumours about bridge appointments were very strong in January 1641. 'I understand the king is brought into a dislike of those counsels that he hath formerly followed and therefore resolves to steer another course', wrote Sir John Temple to the earl of Leicester on 21 January. Temple was full of optimism that 'bringing in of these new men' should 'make up an entire union between the king and his people'. Oliver St John was indeed made solicitor-general on 29 January, apparently at Bedford's instigation.

Whether or not Charles originally saw St John's appointment as the first of a series there is good reason to think that he had hardened his heart against the leaders of the Commons by June. He would not employ men whom he regarded as Strafford's murderers. He was frightened by the demonstrations against Strafford and he was doubtless aware of the rumours that popular pressure on the Lords might be repeated in the case of the Root and Branch bill, which had its first reading on 27 May and was sent to committee on 11 June. Other evidence of the turbulence and radicalism of the London populace, such as the spread of mechanic

---

174 Rushworth III, part I, 154, 188B.
175 *HMC De L'Isle and Dudley MSS*, VI, 376; BL Harl. MS 164, fol. 1006r; 477, fol. 511v; *D'Ewes(N)*, p. 365.

preaching, must have reached his ears.[176] Charles may also have harkened to the inaccurate court gossip which appeared in the Venetian ambassador's despatches at this time: that the Commons were protracting the treaty so that 'all their machinations', and in particular Root and Branch, could be 'carried to perfection'.[177]

Whatever degree of willingness the king showed to taking leading MPs into office, Pym was unable to fulfil his side of the bargain. In a harmonious debate on 14 December 1640, initiated by St John, ideas were set out for replacing royal income from monopolies, ship money, wards and impositions with an adequate and regular revenue. Pym called on the younger Vane, as treasurer of the household, to request the king to provide information about his revenue and expenses. A few days later when Charles returned his thanks and gracious acceptance of parliament's plans, Sir Robert Pye, who was then working on the revenue balances, confessed there would be some delay in providing them.[178] 'We are about, with the king's allowance already had, to take into consideration the king's expenses and revenue and to settle him a meet supply', wrote Alexander Rigby on 23 December. We have already seen why these promising beginnings came to nothing. Pym was unable to get willing cooperation over emergency fiscal measures to meet the expenses of the armies during the winter and spring let alone long-term financial reform. There was no evidence between November 1640 and May 1641 that the appointment of Bedford as treasurer and Pym as chancellor of the exchequer would in practice put the royal revenue in safe hands.[179]

Pym's difficulties in commanding the Commons in this period can be largely explained in terms of the divisions that have been discussed over Strafford, the Scots and money for the armies. Underlying all these divisions was the simple fact that his settlement strategy ran counter to all the conservative notions of members imbued with the country tradition. By and large backbenchers were responsive to the grievances of their local communities, irresponsible when it came to national contingencies. They were both defensive and obstructive by nature; Pym was neither. They thought in terms of legislation, both on constituency matters and national ills, as well as measures to enforce existing laws. Pym was much less interested in either than in seeking out the authors of the nation's calamities. He cared passionately about the fiscal basis of the state; they did not. They clung to the assumptions of the 1620s, which Pym regarded as

176 *HMC De L'Isle and Dudley MSS* vi, 366–8; Manning, editor, *Politics, Religion and the English Civil War*, pp. 47–8, 55.
177 *CSPV 1640–2*, p. 164.
178 *D'Ewes (N)*, pp. 146, 164; Northcote, *Notebook*, pp. 59–60; BL Add. MS 11045, fol. 135v.
179 *HMC Kenyon MSS*, p. 60; Russell, *Origins*, pp. 113–16.

rendered useless by experience.[180] The myth that parliament normally dealt with grievances first and came to subsidies last was regularly reiterated. The enthusiasm for a remonstrance to the king, both in November 1640 and again in April and May 1641, reflected a persisting trust in the methods of 1628, methods which had proved hollow.[181]

Pym either never understood the country viewpoint or he grasped it only to reject it. He had no county community behind him: twice in his youth he had tried to establish himself as a country gentleman, first in Somerset, then in Hampshire, but both times he failed. In the late 1630s he was living in the mansion of his friend Richard Knightley at Fawsley in Northamptonshire. There even today the deserted village site, with its manor and church cluttered with family monuments, perfectly expresses the intense atmosphere of estate Puritanism. This was an ideological community, a 'kind of classis' Hyde called it; its life style afforded Pym little insight into the world of county government, hunting and hawking that most MPs inhabited. He was not interested in that world in any case. He was a man of business, apparently without pastimes and without any desire to enjoy country relaxations.[182]

Most MPs regarded their accountability to those who sent them as their prime responsibility. The tradition of instructing borough members was well established in many towns. Exeter, Great Yarmouth and York were among the towns which set up committees with this object late in 1640; the Exeter committee was to meet weekly.[183] It was also common for boroughs to appoint agents to maintain regular contact with their parliamentary representatives. The Ipswich agents, for example, were given a general direction on 16 November 1640 to 'petition for such matters and things as they shall think fit for the good and benefit of this town' with the advice of the borough members.[184] Regional pressure groups quickly became identifiable in the Long Parliament. William Strode and other western MPs kept the investigation of the stannary courts and the problem of piracy before the House's attention.[185] A northern clique, which included Ferdinando Lord Fairfax, Sir John Hotham, Sir Henry Anderson and Henry Bellassis, acted in concert. Both D'Ewes and Clarendon used the shorthand 'the northern men'.[186]

180   Russell and Aylmer in Lamont, editor, *Tudors and Stuarts*, pp. 141–3; *History* XLI (1976), pp. 1–27.
181   *D'Ewes (N)*, pp 33, 555; *CJ* II, 115, 122, 130, 136; BL Harl. MS 163, fol. 106r; *HMC Montagu*, p. 130.
182   Russell in Clark, Smith, Tyacke, editors, *The English Commonwealth*, pp. 148–9; Clarendon I, 183; N. Pevsner, *Northamptonshire* (London, 1973), pp. 213–5.
183   Great Yarmouth Town Hall, Great Yarmouth Assembly Book C19/6, fol. 470v; YPL House Books 36, fol. 49v; Hirst, pp. 158–66.
184   East Suffolk RO Ispwich Assembly Book, C6/1/5, fol. 159v.
185   *D'Ewes (N)*, pp. 183, 187, 352, 471, 481.
186   *Ibid*, pp. 380–1, 511–2; BL Harl. MS 163, fols. 105r–228r; Clarendon I, 309, 315.

A minute book of the committee of trade for the period 10 November 1640 to 16 March 1641 gives some indication of the range of constituency business handled by the parliament in its earliest stages. Petitions of the clothiers of Worcester, the clothworkers of Leeds, the citizens of Chester with regard to transport of leather and the townsmen of Cley in Norfolk 'touching a stop of the passage of ships' to the town were among the matters considered.[187] Bills mentioned in the *Journals* are only a sample of the local initiatives undertaken since far more was expected of MPs than they were able to perform. Among those read in April 1641 were bills for regulating the company of woodmongers, the making of the new draperies and the manufacture of bricks.[188] Other proposed bills are recorded in borough minute books and correspondence. The puritan corporation of Ipswich, for example, wanted to confirm 'the perpetual election of the ministers' of the town by statute because this had lately been questioned.[189]

Many MPs undoubtedly did their best to fulfil their constituents' expectations. Sir Peter Heyman, from Dover, told his colleagues that they would be putting his own reputation at risk if they did not listen to his case for the traditional exemption of the Cinque Ports from the subsidy bill. This plea won the day for him against speeches from St John and Pym.[190] When the ports eventually lost this particular battle in the debates on the bill for £400,000, Sir Thomas Peyton composed an apologetic letter to the borough of Sandwich. He tried to sweeten the pill by emphasizing that none would escape 'this last and great tax'; the port's exemption, he asserted, would certainly be restored when things returned to normal.[191]

Two lists of topics for consideration in 1640 contain 27 and 43 items respectively. But parliament's cumbersome procedures and its traditions of talk and procrastination, all designed to secure consensus, now told heavily against it. Within two months business was hopelessly clogged. As in the 1620s, the Commons had mainly themselves to blame for their failure to select priorities and to drive through legislation.[192] The diaries of the first eight months leave the impression of a restless impetuous body, lacking a clear sense of direction, haphazard in the way it approached the task of reform. Grievances came tumbling on to the floor of the House; committee after committee was formed. At the first purge of committees on 12 January the number was reduced to 21.[193] Not only the proliferating committees for private bills were eliminated. A committee as dear to this

187 *D'Ewes (N)*, pp. 521–8.
188 *CJ* II, 122, 128.
189 East Suffolk RO Ipswich Assembly Book, C6/1/5, fol. 160r.
190 Northcote, *Notebook*, pp. 108–9; *SR* IV, 77.
191 *Oxinden*, p. 199.
192 Russell, *Parliaments*, pp 39–42; K. Sharpe, editor, *Faction and Parliament* (Oxford, 1978), pp. 23–8; Cope, p. 47.
193 *D'Ewes (N)*, p. 206; *CJ* II, 66, 162–3; Zagorin, pp. 241–2.

Puritan assembly as that for scandalous ministers, flooded by petitions against Arminian clergy, was discontinued in January and again in June only to be subsequently revived.[194]

The Commons were often perplexed and divided in these first months about what should be given priority. There were relapses into helpless inertia. D'Ewes sometimes noted a 'pretty silence': when no one seemed to know where to begin after prayers on 15 April, he warned that 'our delay by silence would be as dangerous as by unnecessary disputes'.[195] Loquacious men were not checked; irrelevance and egocentricity were the bane of the debating chamber. The House suffered from such characters as the vain and pompous Sir Edward Dering, anxious to display his classical learning and the witless Sir John Wray, who was always ready to throw in a piece of elaborate and patriotic rhetoric. D'Ewes himself was fussy and verbose, obsessed by his latest discoveries in precedent hunting. In so wayward an assembly it is not surprising that debates often ran into the ground. On 2 March, for example, two lawyers put lengthy arguments, one that the clergy should be charged with *praemunire*, the other that they were guilty of treason, for constituting the new canons. 'There followed a long silence and the Speaker stood up once or twice to know what question he should put'. When Orlando Bridgeman added to the confusion with a third legal opinion, the matter was deferred.[196]

It was hard for anyone to lead such a body of men. Full of individuals who were passionate and excitable, easily swayed by sudden changes of mood and sometimes swept by outbursts of violent emotion, early seventeenth-century parliaments were ill fitted to play a constructive role in government.[197] There were many days in the first months when Pym abandoned any attempt to guide the debates. Yet in the long run his assets were considerable. He had a coherent programme of action and he enjoyed the respect of a close-knit group of able and experienced members. Some of them, like Hampden and St John, were his confidants, while others like Holles, Strode and Sir Robert Harley were at this stage more loosely attached to his leadership.[198]

Pym also had powerful allies in the Lords, some of whom like his patron the earl of Bedford and the earl of Warwick, who in 1642 made him a trustee for his advowsons, were intimate friends. In fact some of Pym's new reputation in the Commons arose from his being known to be the chief spokesman of a distinct group of peers who shared his hatred of popery and

---

194 C. Holmes, ed. *The Suffolk Committees for Scandalous Ministers* (Suffolk Records Society XIII, 1970), pp. 9–10.
195 *D'Ewes (N)*, p. 380; BL Harl. MS 163, fol. 47r.
196 *D'Ewes (N)*, pp. 425–8.
197 Kenyon, *Stuart England*, pp. 36–7, 45–7.
198 Clarendon I, 263n; Zagorin, p 202.

his determination to remove Strafford and Laud from power.[199] Clarendon named eight men as the 'great contrivers and designers' in the Lords: Bedford, Saye, Mandeville, Warwick, Brooke, Wharton, Paget and Andover.[200] Six of them can be glimpsed in action early in the parliament. Brooke, Mandeville, Paget and Saye prolonged debate for two hours but finally failed to throw out the motion of the committee of privileges on 3 February that Strafford should be given a fortnight to answer the charges against him and that he should deliver his answer in writing. The insistence of the same group of men led to the bishops withdrawing when Strafford read his answer on 24 February. Warwick called for Laud's imprisonment and sequestration from all his offices when the archbishop appeared on 26 February; Brooke, Howard and Paget argued that the House should 'show no compassion to him who showed none to others'.[201] This leadership group in the Lords did not win all its battles.[202] But its vigour is evident several months before its first major triumph with the passing of the attainder bill.

What Pym lacked in the first months was consistent and unquestioning support from his closest colleagues. Holles, Earle, Fiennes, Hampden and Strode all obstructed the reform of the subsidy; Haselrig, as we have seen, led an initiative that put him at odds with Pym over Strafford. This dissent at the heart of the Commons leadership sprang from sympathy with the backbenchers country viewpoint. According to a diurnal, Pym's motion on 27 November that parliament should grant the king tonnage and poundage in recompense for ship money and his declaration that they would thereby make him the richest king in Christendom 'took well in the House'. But he was silenced by those, led by Earle and St John, who 'stood upon it to have grievances first reformed'.[203] Speeches by Strode and Pym in the debate of 23 December on voting more subsidies epitomized their difference in outlook. Strode opposed the motion for four subsidies, arguing for three at once and another later 'that the country may see we do it upon necessity and by degrees'. Pym wanted 'the present necessity not satisfaction of the country' to be taken as the overriding consideration.[204]

The two most important bills of the first six months soon acquired Pym's support but it is worth noting that they were independent initiatives. It was his country stance which led Strode to introduce his bill for annual parliaments which later became the Triennial Act, on 24

199 Russell, *Origins*, pp. 110–11.
200 Clarendon I, 241–4.
201 BL Harl. MS 6424, fols. 39r, 42v, 43r, 113r; *LJ* IV, 150, 171–3; Christianson, *JBS* XLIX (1977), 591.
202 Below, p. 120.
203 Russell, *Origins*, pp. 112, 115; *D'Ewes (N)*, pp. 34, 44, 75–6, 331; Northcote, *Notebook* p. 107; BL Add. MS 36828, fol. 12r.
204 Northcote, *Notebook*, pp. 107–8.

December, the day after the initial two subsidies had been doubled. He wished to provide 'somewhat to comfort the people', he announced.[205] Alderman Pennington's bill to prevent the king from dissolving parliament without its own consent was, as we have seen, a hasty expedient to satisfy parliament's supporters in the City of London.[206] Pym at this stage had no legislative programme. Statutes nevertheless were what the provinces wanted. It was not enough for parliament to condemn ship money, Thomas Stockdale told Lord Fairfax on 10 April: a declaratory act 'would give great satisfaction' and 'encourage subsidymen in their payments'.[207]

In the localities the spring brought disappointment at the evasiveness of newsletters, bewilderment and wild rumour. In Herefordshire, Lady Harley told her son on 3 April, 'they had broken the parliament and beheaded my Lord Strafford, which would not well hang together.'[208] Remote from the cockpit of the nation, it was easy for men to see events there as reflecting no more than manoeuvrings in a political game. Sir Roger Twysden was suspicious that Pym and his colleagues merely sought advancement: 'What was it to me whether the earl of Strafford or Mr Pym sat at the helm of government if their commands carried equal pressure?' Sir Thomas Wodehouse was still patient but he was becoming disillusioned, 'the skill', as it seemed to him, 'being only now to comply with greatness and to be still on fortune's side'.[209] From Westminster Sir John Coke echoed his thoughts, when he wrote to his father about the campaign against Strafford: 'if his impeachment hath been trained into this length by private practice for private men to work out their own ends and preferments thereupon, their ambition may perchance in the end cost them as dear as it hath the kingdom.' These harsh words suggest the risk Pym was running that his strategy would be misinterpreted as a crude bid for power. In the meanwhile euphoria had dissolved; conflict and factionalism had emerged. 'How like we are', wrote Coke on 24 April, 'to let this great opportunity slip out of our hands without much advantage to the public.'[210]

The stork which was seen 'to sit upon the House of Commons' on the last day of May 1641 did not prove, as men hoped it might, to be an omen of 'much peace and quietness'. Hyde believed the settlement strategy might have worked: 'it is a great pity', he wrote, 'that it was not fully executed, that the king might have had some able men to have advised him

205 *Ibid*, p. 112; *D'Ewes (N)*, pp. 188–9; BL Add. MS 11045, fol. 147v; Zagorin, p. 142.
206 Russell, *Crisis of Parliaments*, p. 334; Gardiner IX, 359–60; Bodleian Tanner MS 66, fol. 93r; DO, p. 93.
207 *Fairfax* II, 104, 202.
208 *Harley*, p. 126.
209 *Archaeologia Cantiana* I (1858), 188; Bodleian Tanner MS 66, fol. 65r.
210 *HMC Coke*, p. 280.

or assisted, which probably these very men would have done, after they had been so thoroughly engaged.' The plan for bridge appointments lived on, at the level of gossip and rumour, into July but it is hard to believe that it had any life in it after May. It is hard to say whether it ever had much at the best of times. Hyde's account of why the settlement scheme collapsed is probably substantially correct. Pym and Bedford had two conditions: that the king's revenue should be 'in some degree settled' first and that none of their 'chief companions' should be left out, 'who would be neither well pleased with their so hasty advancement before them, nor so submissive in the future to follow their dictates'. Charles had his conditions too: 'the king's great end was, by these compliances, to save the life of the earl of Strafford and to preserve the Church from ruin.'[211] We have seen that fiscal reform never got off the ground. According to Hyde, providing offices for Hampden, Mandeville and Essex was another stumbling block. Once Pym had thrown in his lot with Haselrig in mid-April there was no stopping the campaign to be rid of Strafford. Finally there was the question of the Church, which will be fully examined in chapter 3. Pym had not yet thrown himself behind the popular movement for religious reform but his radical allies were urging him to do so and his reputation was already tainted by association with Root and Branch. The king, already fearful for the future of episcopacy and the liturgy, had staked out a conservative position. When all these issues between the king and the leading members of both Houses have been taken into account the under-lying fact remains that settlement depended on an atmosphere of political harmony and purposefulness which it proved impossible to achieve. Unless the Commons was firmly led resolution dissolved into bickering; yet when Pym sought to drive forward his programme debate all too often became angry and contentious. Meanwhile enough seeds of mistrust were sown for the opportunity for settlement to be lost.

211 Clarendon I, 280–2, 431; Bedfordshire RO J 1382.

2

Propositions

That we might clear ourselves that we have desired nothing but what is just from the king during this parliament and not taken any advantage upon any pretended straits or necessities, as hath been falsely bruited at home and in other parts of Christendom.

John Pym in the House of Commons,
23 June 1641[1]

The Houses are full of jealousies and apprehensions though I believe without any cause.

Edward Nicholas to the earl of Arundel,
21 August 1641[2]

They [the Scots] have carried away our money and left us a disjointed and distempered kingdom; and whether the remedy they have given it be not worse than the disease they found it in I am yet to be satisfied.

Thomas Wiseman to Sir John Pennington,
26 August 1641[3]

The most unnerving news of the early summer was the king's decision to visit Scotland. Rumours of his going were current from the middle of May; he was at first expected to leave about 5 July.[4] The army plot was fresh in men's minds and the king's journey seemed fraught with dangers. When in addition the close committee received a report through an intercepted letter of a new design by Montrose, in conjunction with his brother-in-law and the lairds of Keir and Blackhall, against the earl of Argyll, their alarm intensified.[5] Haselrig reported the plot to the Commons on 22 June: he drew the conclusion that the king's journey would be dangerous until matters were 'better settled'.[6] The next day Pym spoke at length. It was the

1 BL Harl. MS 163, fol. 730r.
2 *Nicholas*, p. 22.
3 *CSPD 1641–3*, p. 105.
4 Bodleian Tanner MS 66, fol. 95; BL Sloane MS 1467, fols. 40r, 71r; *CSPV 1640–2*, p. 145; Bedfordshire RO J 1383.
5 Rushworth III, part I, 290–1; Gardiner IX, 395–8; Wedgwood, pp. 440–2.
6 BL Harl. MS 163, fol. 725v.

most important speech he made in the first session, a theatrical account of the dangers facing the nation shot through with his preoccupation with popery. Disbandment was essential, Pym asserted, before the king travelled north: 'there are many evil spirits in the army that might make evil broils'. He set out a new programme for settlement, arguing that its completion was imperative before the king could safely leave the capital. Measures for the defence of the ports and counties in Charles's absence, the disarming of leading papists, the removal of 'all bad counsellors' and the royal assent to the 'good laws now prepared' were among the priorities he adumbrated.[7] The provocative assumption behind the speech was that the roots of political tension lay at court.

Pym's speech on 23 June proclaimed a new policy which was infinitely bolder than the original settlement plan. Yet his underlying aims had not changed: the king should be given an adequate revenue and evil counsellors should be replaced by trusted men whom parliament respected. Taken overall the speech was positive and optimistic. Pym was eloquent about the possibilities once the immediate problems were solved. The parliament that was sitting, he declared, could 'lay a foundation for such a greatness of the kingdom, both in power at home and in reputation abroad, as never any of His Majesty's ancestors enjoyed.'[8]

The Ten Propositions, formulated by the close committee and adopted by the Commons on 24 June, embodied Pym's proposals: evil counsellors, popery and defence were the most substantial items. That day he took them as the heads for a conference with the Lords.[9] This was perhaps Pym's most triumphant hour. He had sensed the mood of the House with complete assurance; once the programme was before them they were clamouring for action. Thomas Tomkins and Herbert Morley moved that the queen mother might be banished as well as the Capuchin priests. The interest and excitement was such that when Pym went up to the Lords backbenchers packed out the Painted Chamber, leaving the Commons without a quorum to carry on its business. He introduced the new policy with a short oration on the importance of unity in parliament's 'one great end, to serve God, the king and the commonwealth'. He explained the origins of the Propositions: 'because they had lately found out very malignant and pestiferous designs set on foot, or plotted, to trouble the peace of the kingdom, the which though they were prevented, yet were still pursued'. Then Pym read the full text, embellishing it with a few stories of his own like the tale, intended to drive home the evil effects of monopolies, of a gardener who, being asked why the weeds grew so fast and the flowers so thin in his plot, answered 'that the weeds were the true children but the

7 *Ibid*, fol. 730r; 478, fol. 706; 5047, fol. 34.
8 BL Harl. MS 163, fol. 730r; Bodleian Rawlinson D MS 1099: 23 June.
9 *CJ* II, 183–5; *LJ* IV, 285–90.

flowers were but so many slips and bastards'.[10]

With the establishment on 26 June of a joint committee of both Houses to oversee the enforcement of the Propositions the assertion of Pym's leadership was complete. The Propositions became the crux of the rest of the session. The new course was an attempt to break the political deadlock; yet paradoxically it was a course that brought the possibility of violent conflict between king and parliament much closer. Not that the Commons leadership wished at this stage to bring about a permanent alteration in the balance of the constitution by asserting parliamentary authority.[11] Far from it: the Ten Propositions were emergency proposals to deal with an emergency situation. There was a strongly defensive note in Pym's speech. He wanted to remove 'the scandal that we desire things may weaken the crown'; he suggested a 'declaration that we have done nothing derogatory' and a general pardon 'as hath been usual at all other parliaments'.[12] The new policy was not exactly a petitioning policy nor a policy of confrontation. It was rather something between the two. Deep as Pym's fears were he was still loyal to the king. He still earnestly sought to reach an understanding with him. Yet for all this there was a challenging air about the Ten Propositions which was bound to offend the king. Behind the concern for parliament's reputation lay the germ of the parliamentary quest for support from the people. Behind the determination to root out papist conspiracy lay the obduracy with which men can cling to a programme on which have they staked their political fortunes.

The resort to a new policy reflected the isolation of the king and his court. Nothing had happened since Bedford's death on 9 May to give Pym and his colleagues hope that Charles would seek new intermediaries. Indeed it was becoming increasingly evident that the king had decided to take his advice from his wife and from a narrow circle of intimate advisers like the marquis of Hamilton and the duke of Lennox.[13] The factional, many-sided court of the 1620s and 30s, with its rich opportunities for patronage, had finally disappeared.[14] In these circumstances the elevation of George Digby, when he was in disfavour over his Straffordian activities, might be seen as a grievous tactical error; the king presumably saw it simply as a chance to reward one of the few aristocratic families that had shown any real sympathy for his plight since the previous November. His Dorset neighbour Sir Anthony Ashley Cooper spoke of Digby's 'pedantic stiffness' and his 'great expectations of himself'.[15] The Commons was angry and not many of the peers were well pleased, an MP reported,

10   BL Harl. MS 163, fols. 733–4; 5047, fol. 34v; E 160 (20); *CJ* II, 186; *LJ* IV, 285, 290.
11   C. Russell in Lamont, editor, *Tudors and Stuarts*, p. 153.
12   BL Harl. MS 163, fol. 730r; 5047, fol. 34.
13   Manning, editor, *Politics, Religion and the English Civil War*, pp. 68–70.
14   Russell, *Parliaments*, pp. 5–34.
15   A.R. Bayley, *The Great Civil War in Dorset* (Taunton, 1910), p. 36.

when only a few minutes before he was due to answer for the printing of his speech in favour of Strafford on 10 June, he was seen putting on his robes. He had escaped their ire by the skin of his teeth. During the following few weeks there were persistent rumours that the king would follow Digby's elevation by creating other new peers. Arthur Capel was in fact promoted on 5 August; the wealthy squire of Longleat Sir James Thynne and the unscrupulous but spectacularly successful businessman Sir Arthur Ingram were among others being mentioned as likely purchasers of peerages. Perhaps the king did contemplate building a party in the Lords at this stage. It was already obvious that it was his best bulwark in the defence of episcopacy. If he had set about doing so the parliamentary plan for 'an act or order that no honours or dignities shall be sold' could hardly have stopped him.[16]

The promotions Charles made on 8 August confirmed the impression that he was not seeking to build bridges with parliament. Lennox, a young man according to Hyde of 'small experience in affairs', was made duke of Richmond. The earl of Bath, Lord Dunsmore and Lord Seymour became privy councillors. Bath was old but politically inexperienced. He had quarrelled with Lord Brooke in March over Brooke's placing the king after God and parliament in order of importance; he was also said to be 'a very good friend to the bishops'. Dunsmore was described by Hyde as 'a man of a rough and tempestuous nature, violent in pursuing what he wished, without judgement or temper to know the way of bringing it to pass'. Seymour had once been one of the most vigorous country MPs but had been undergoing a transition to court allegiance since his elevation to the peerage in February.[17]

Earlier in the year the king had made a much more promising set of privy council appointments. On 19 February seven peers – Bedford, Bristol, Essex, Hertford, Mandeville, Saville and Saye – were sworn councillors; a few weeks later Warwick also joined the board. Hyde said it was the marquis of Hamilton who persuaded Charles to appoint these men as a declaration of his intention to cooperate in the reformation of abuses, 'being all persons at that time very gracious to the people or to the Scots'. 'For two or three days', reported Baillie, the king's action 'did please all the world.'[18] But the experiment proved disastrous. The most influential men seldom sat. Saye was only at five meetings between March and July, Mandeville at four, Warwick at two. According to Hyde, when they did attend the new privy councillors refused to give the king advice 'in those matters of the highest importance which were then every day incumbent

16 BL Harl. MS 163, fol. 690v; Befordshire RO J 1384; Gardiner IX, 386, 416; *LJ* IV, 297; *CSPD 1641–3*, pp. 38, 41, 53; Cliffe, pp. 95, 103; Keeler, p. 361.
17 Crummett, pp. 90–1; *HMC Coke* pp. 273–4; Clarendon I, 160; II, 533–4.
18 Clarendon, I, 258–9; Baillie, p. 305.

on him' because parliament was debating them, 'by whose wisdom', they insisted, 'he was entirely to guide himself.'[19]

At first there had been signs that the council might work with parliament in its programme of reform. In January it agreed to prepare a bill defining the authority of lord lieutenants.[20] However, Bishop Warner noted on 13 February that a parliamentary petition on the fears aroused by popery in Wales was read there 'yet nothing answered'.[21] By the spring the council was dealing with nothing but private petitions and routine economic regulation. It paid no attention to political fears and tensions. It was not even meeting as regularly as previously: there were fifteen meetings between November and January, ten between February and June, three in July, four in August. When Edward Nicholas came up to London for his month's attendance upon the council in July he found 'nothing of business acted worth the tediousness of waiting'.[22]

Caught in the maelstrom of distrust between the king and parliament the council had withered. Hyde, writing five years later with didactic purpose, blamed the king for undervaluing its wisdom and for failing to maintain its authority and lustre. 'The truth is', he declared, 'the sinking and near desperate condition of monarchy in this kingdom can never be buoyed up but by a prudent and steady council attending upon the virtue and vivacity of the king.' In his view the choice of new councillors in February 1641 was merely one of a series of errors. More serious was the king's decision in December 1640 to allow privy councillors to be examined on oath about discussions at the council board. This not only opened the way to the use by the Commons managers of Sir Henry Vane's evidence against Strafford. It frightened every councillor with the thought that he might be questioned about any rash or impetuous speech he made and thus, in Hyde's argument, it 'banished for ever all future freedom from that board and those persons from whom His Majesty was to expect advice in his greatest straits'.[23]

The eclipse of the council was perceptively discussed in the correspondence between Sir Henry Vane the elder and Edward Nicholas during August 1641. Vane hoped that once the treaty was completed and the king could return south, enough political confidence might return for the council, deprived for months of a voice, to reassert itself. From Edinburgh he urged upon Nicholas the importance of the council's meeting:

if it were but to prepare business for His Majesty's return, so that king and

19 *PCR* xii, 107–39; Clarendon i, 261–2.
20 *PCR* xii, 77–8.
21 BL Harl. MS 6424, fol. 20r.
22 *CSPD 1641–3*, p. 52; D. Nicholas, *Mr Secretary Nicholas* (London, 1955), pp. 132–4.
23 Clarendon i, 256–61; C.H. Firth, 'Clarendon's "History of the Rebellion" ', *EHR* xix (1904), 42–4.

people may go close together, by which means the honour of our nation may be raised upon such principles as in the famous times of his predecessors and made them glorious: and certainly there is now no other choice and it is high time all jealousies were removed, for until that be done who can give counsel that shall avail?

Nicholas was equally pessimistic about the council's being able on its own to do anything towards restoring political harmony. 'It would be a great quiet and happiness to the king and kingdom', he wrote, 'if all jealousies might be so removed as that there might be a right understanding between the king and his parliament, for I am of your honour's mind, till that be, all men will be afraid to give counsel'.[24]

There is regrettably little material which gives any real insight into the king's mind in the summer of 1641. But his speeches to parliament hint at an increasingly unyielding stance behind a show of graciousness. On 22 June he was sure that he had nothing to blame himself for: 'I have omitted no occasion whereby I may show such affection to my people as I desire my people should show to me; and not only so, but likewise in eschewing all occasions of dispute and in seeking to remove jealousies.'[25] He believed that he had been generous in bestowing favours. 'I have given way to every-thing that hath been asked of me by the whole parliament', he declared on 5 July, 'and therefore methinks you should not wonder if in something I should now begin to refuse.' He reprimanded MPs on this occasion for their 'demonstrations of discontent' that he had required two days to consider the bills abolishing Star Chamber and High Commission before passing them. He also lectured them about giving priority to vital matters before his departure to Scotland and leaving 'trivial and less important matters to another meeting'. Charles, in short, was impatient with parlia-ment and quite ready to see it adjourned. He had bitter memories of 1629 when he believed 'the sincerer and better part of the House' had been 'overborn by the practices and clamours of the other'. In 1641, as in 1629, he saw himself as facing a group of men who intended 'to erect a universal over-swaying power to themselves, which belongs only to us and not to them'.[26]

Yet the king's actual political intentions in the summer remain obscure. The central problem of what he hoped to gain by his visit to Scotland may never be resolved. S.R. Gardiner's hypothesis is probably the most compelling: that he sought 'so to pacify Scotland as to bring its influence to bear on England, or at least to prevent its influence being used against himself'. There is no good reason though to think the king went so far as actively to seek Scottish allies for a coup against the English parliament, or

24 *Nicholas*, pp. 9, 12.
25 *LJ* IV, 283.
26 *CSPD 1641–3*, p. 44; Gardiner, *Documents*, pp. 95–7.

indeed that he was seriously contemplating an attempt on his return from Scotland to dissolve parliament against its will. All this is not to say that Charles was entirely averse to plotting. There seems to be no doubt that he played a principal role in the conspiracy around June 1641 to bring the army up to London once the neutrality of the Scots was assured. This became known as the second army plot. The king sent down a petition which he inteded should be presented by the army to himself. The petition reflected his view of the political situation in London: 'ill-affected persons . . . backed in their violence by the multitude' were aiming to diminish the king's 'just regalities' and were putting the king and his peers in 'some personal danger'.[27] The petition did not specify precisely what the army was offering to do about this beyond defending the crown, the parliament, 'our religion and the established laws of the kingdom'. However, a newsletter account of the new plot, when the story emerged, summarized the impression it gave; 'that all the army might be licensed to come up to attend the parliament for their defence and if this were yielded to them to give into the House a declaration to let them know that they had wronged the king's prerogative and they were come to restore it.'[28]

This new army plot did not become public until the autumn. Parliament's behaviour towards the king in the summer must be understood in terms of rumours and assumptions about his intentions not in terms of what he in fact intended. Many thought that Charles would seek to use the army or the Scots to avenge himself on the Commons. The correspondence of the Venetian ambassador, an optimist about the king's fortunes, was full of such gossip.[29] Even before this gossip began some MPs were panicky about reports of their proceedings reaching the king. For instance some who feared that 'many things were divulged at court' by certain peers called for greater secrecy on 19 May. By August anyone suspected of keeping the king up to date with Westminster news attracted intense odium, as Edward Nicholas discovered.[30]

Seen as the settlement strategy in a new guise, the Ten Propositions policy was probably doomed from the start. Neither the king nor Pym any longer dared trust the other far enough. Pym's pursuit of the Propositions is nevertheless the central thread of the summer's politics. They were never presented to the king as a whole and were probably never intended to be.[31] Instead they came to be regarded as a working document. The king was petitioned about specific points as it was thought appropriate.[32] The

---

27   *D'Ewes (C)*, pp. 155–7; Gardiner IX, 398–9; Clarendon I, 323–5; Stevenson, *Scottish Revolution*, pp. 223–33.
28   BL Sloane MS 3317, fol. 49r.
29   *CSPV 1640–2*, pp. 153, 171, 177, 193, 205–6.
30   BL Harl. MS 477, fol. 539; *Nicholas*, p. 32; *Evelyn*, pp. 84–5.
31   Some historians have assumed they were presented, e.g. Zagorin, p. 247.
32   *LJ* IV, 287–8, 291, 306, 321.

new joint committee of 48, set up to enforce the Propositions, replaced the close committee during July as the key instrument of the leadership's management. It met regularly and from 8 July, at Pym's suggestion, it was agreed that it should sit as it thought fit without informing the Houses.[33]

The essence of the new policy was a programme of priority measures before the king went to Scotland. After a good deal of negotiation between the two Houses, Charles and the Scottish commissioners, it was agreed on 29 June that the king's departure should be fixed for 10 August. The Commons leadership would undoubtedly have preferred a longer breathing space, but the peers were sympathetic to the king's argument that he had promised by proclamation to be present at the opening of the Scottish parliament in July and if he more than slightly modified his plans it might 'breed jealousies'.[34] The priority measures, listed under the first two headings of the Propositions, consisted of disbandment of both armies, which implied completion of the treaty, the passage of certain reform bills, some of which were still before the Commons, and the settling of the king's revenue. So far as the legislation was concerned, most MPs probably had in mind the bills which were subsequently passed in July and August together with some others, particularly the Root and Branch bill, which was currently absorbing the evangelical aspirations of a substantial section of the Commons.[35] For a mere six weeks the task was formidable. Predictably there were some who were sceptical about so much being done. But many appear to have assumed that Charles would not leave until he had satisfied the basic requirements that had been set out for the contentment of his people. Thus it was the gossip during July that he would not stick to his plans. There was talk and preparation about the king's departure, reported Robert Hobart to a Norfolk friend, 'but the wiser sort do not believe will be this year'. 'It is generally believed', ran a newsletter account, 'that they will persuade His Majesty to put off his journey till September or Christmas.'[36]

By mid July enough had been done to encourage hopes that at least disbandment and a limited legislative programme might be achieved by 10 August. Five regiments at Hull for which money was available had been sent home; the Scots had made a modest retreat from the Tees.[37] Star Chamber and High Commission had been abolished. Progress had been made with other bills. Most important of all there was at last a prospect of money. Sir John Hotham had finally brought MPs to their senses about the nation's accounts on 17 June. He showed that, even if payment of the

33 BL Harl. MS 163, fols. 765r, 770v; *CJ* II, 216–7.
34 BL Harl. MS 163, fols. 741v, 742r; 479, fol. 742v; *CJ* II, 189–93; *LJ* IV, 290–5.
35 *LJ* IV, 286; below, pp. 102–7.
36 Bodleian Tanner MS 66, fol. 109r; BL Sloane MS 1469, fol. 17v.
37 *CJ* II, 184; BL Harl. MS 6424, fols. 80v, 83v; *CSPD 1641–3*, p. 30.

billeting money to the northern counties and half the officers' pay was delayed, £242,000 was needed at once. For 24 hours his announcement produced wild thrashing about. Pym had nothing to offer beyond a crazy scheme for making Spanish money current in England and a proposal for sending to provincial cities for help.[38] He was still optimistic about the Merchant Adventurers producing the £150,000 they had promised, though negotiations with them had faltered for several weeks and some, like Oliver Cromwell, had advocated breaking them off.[39] It was another of Isaac Pennington's proposals which gained favour with Hotham's hastily summoned committee for advancing money and which the Commons accepted in a modified form on 18 June. When Pennington first suggested a poll tax as the quickest solution to the financial dilemma on 8 June he was not popular. The form he envisaged for it, with masters paying twelve-pence each for their servants and landlords the same for their tenants, was not likely to appeal to an assembly of country gentlemen. But it was hard to object to a poll tax carefully graduated by social rank and wealth. The bill for it was read twice on 22 June; the committee stage was completed between 23 and 26 June; the bill went to the Lords on 29 June and the king gave his assent on 3 July.[40]

Thus by mid July everything depended on a quick national response to the poll tax. The statute directed payments to be made by all adults throughout the land, from a basic rate of sixpence up to a hundred pounds for a duke, within ten days of its proclamation in each locality; those living within ten miles of London were only given four days to pay.[41] It was an impossible timetable and there was exaggerated confidence in the outcome. Some talked of the tax bringing in 'a million at least'; a few like Edward Nicholas were more sceptical.[42] The provincial gentry displayed their accustomed sloth in collecting the tax and their habitual talent for evasion. Some, like the Norfolk knights who would not act because the statute did not give them their full titles, were blatantly obstructionist. Others, like Sir William Courtenay who insisted that there were farmers with twice or even four times his means who escaped more lightly, were merely pained. Difficulties in interpreting the statute were widely used as an excuse for delay. Status-conscious gentry suddenly sought to humble themselves. Thus Thomas Moreton reported the laughable spectacle of Cheshire's 'apple esquires that gloried in the title' who 'shrink up their title to be called gentlemen and save five pounds'.[43]

38 BL Harl. MS 163, fol. 715v; 478, fol. 685r; *CJ* II, 177–8.
39 BL Harl. MS 477, fols. 536v, 572r; *CJ* II, 161, 179.
40 BL Harl. MS 478, fol. 624v; *CJ* II, 183–92.
41 *SR* v, 105–10.
42 *CSPD 1641–3*, pp. 30, 49, 53.
43 *CJ* II, 230; *CSPD 1641–3*, pp. 66, 76; *Buller*, pp. 43–4; *Pennington*, pp. 167–8; BL Sloane MS 1467, fol. 19v; Harl. MS 163, fol. 789r.

Anxiety at Westminster increased as the poll money no more than dribbled in. MPs did what they could to invigorate local officers: in a letter to the mayor of Sandwich, for instance, Sir Thomas Peyton emphasized the need for haste and care. Yet only a miserable £18,000 was brought in by 29 July. Whilst a flurry of orders was distributed clearing up ambiguities or misapprehensions and directing the Lord Mayor to provide a daily account of the takings in London, parliament once again turned to negotiating loans from City merchants against the eventual yield of a tax they could not quickly enforce.[44]

In this financial gloom the king's announcement on 28 July that he would leave for Scotland on 10 August as planned came as a bombshell.[45] The days had slipped by: disbandment was far from complete and several important bills, including Root and Branch, were nowhere near ready for the royal assent. The whole Ten Propositions policy was suddenly in jeopardy. There followed a fortnight of hectic political manoeuvring. The Commons' first thought was to persuade the Scottish commissioners to disband their army on the day Charles left London, whether the treaty was signed or not. They hoped to delay payment of the first £80,000 of the Brotherly Assistance until 1 September. But the Scots could not agree to this expedient because, as they explained, they needed the money due on the Brotherly Assistance, as well as their whole arrears, to pay the debts to their army which were due before it disbanded.[46]

Briefly the Commons leadership was swung off balance. The king's message to the Lords, announcing his departure, with its silence on the implications for parliament's sitting, was unnerving. His talk of a commission of privy councillors 'for the ordering of the affairs of state and issuing out of proclamations upon emergent occasions' sounded ominous. It was enough to start rumours of an adjournment.[47] For several weeks, MPs had turned their backs on a situation they did not wish to face. At the committee hurriedly constituted on 28 July to consider the parliament's future, even Pym was unprepared, asking whether it could 'proceed with any business or whether we did not stand as it were thereby suspended.' There were plenty of views. Selden said the crown was usually represented by a peer in cases of the monarch's absence; Glyn regarded the precedents as unimportant since the late Act against dissolving the parliament authorized them to continue their sitting; D'Ewes went off to check the records but returned to say that he could find nothing relevant.[48] Pym opted for a petition to Charles for a *custos regni* with power to pass bills in his absence,

44 BL Add. MS 44846, fol. 7v; *CJ* II, 210, 221, 226–8; *LJ* IV, 327.
45 *LJ* IV, 331.
46 *CSPD 1641–3*, p. 63; *CJ* II, 229, 232, 236.
47 *LJ* IV, 331; *DO*, p. 316.
48 BL Harl. MS 163, fol. 800v; *CJ* II, 227.

a scheme which the Commons readily adopted. It was a measure of the distrust of Charles felt by many at this stage that the House decided to petition him for an act to confirm that his commission to the *custos regni* would not be terminated until his return to London.[49]

It was unfortunate that at this moment relations between the two Houses were worse than they had been for many months. They had become involved in an acrimonious wrangle over the Commons' bill imposing the obligation of signing the Protestation on all Englishmen.[50] The Lords dragged their heels over the scheme for a *custos regni* from 29 July to 7 August, partly no doubt because they feared it might be used to force through the Root and Branch bill or other radical religious measures. They tried to deflect the Commons with the suggestion on 5 August that certain peers should be authorized to pass specified bills relating to money and defence.[51] MPs quickly saw the disadvantages of this proposal. Falkland pointed out that matters might arise needing urgent attention which the commission did not warrant.[52]

On 7 August a new tactic brought the Lords into line. They agreed to a request from the Commons to petition the king to delay his departure for a fortnight. But their support rested on a narrow majority of 28 to 25 in a vote taken after a very long debate.[53] Furthermore time was running out. The decision to sit the next day although it was a Sunday indicated the Commons' alarm. They had two basic worries. Firstly, by the following weekend the king would be in the north or in Scotland with every opportunity to plot against them. Secondly, the obstacles to the completion of their legislative programme appeared insurmountable. Yet 'distempers and jealousies of the kingdom', the Commons argued, 'cannot be composed unless bills be prepared.'[54] On 8 August MPs gathered at St Margaret's, Westminster at 6 o'clock for a sermon by Edmund Calamy. They sat all day and rose that evening, D'Ewes recorded, 'full of care and distraction'.[55]

The king remained unyielding, both over any further delay and over the request for a general commission for passing bills.[56] There was much bitterness on 9 August while the bills for confirming the treaty and securing the Brotherly Assistance were being rushed through so that the king could give his assent to them before he left London. Cromwell insisted that he was not satisfied with the reasons offered by Charles for his going and reiterated the dangers of his passing through the armies. Sir

49   BL Harl. MS 163, fol. 807r; *CJ* II, 230.
50   Gardiner IX, 414.
51   *CJ* II, 235, 240, 242; *LJ* IV, 339–42.
52   BL Harl. MS 5047, fols. 55r–56r.
53   *LJ* IV, 350; BL Harl. MS 6424, fol. 88v.
54   BL Harl. MS 5047, fol. 56r; *LJ* IV, 349.
56   *DO*, pp. 33–4; BL Harl. MS 163, fols. 812v, 816r.

Henry Anderson made 'a bold speech of the dangers and fears'. Pym dramatized the nation's insecurity: the presence of the armies in the north, the army plot 'being fully proved', the danger to the king of mutinies and disorders 'which may happen in the best governed armies', the ill-defence of the kingdom against invasion, the reports that papists were well armed. All these, he insisted, pointed to the need for time and legislative action before the king could safely travel. The journey was so inconvenient, he concluded on a more threatening note than he had struck hitherto, that he held 'the advisers of it enemies to the state and may hereafter question them'.[57] More than at any time since parliament assembled the previous November Pym felt the ground shaking beneath his feet. Something of the atmosphere of panic that had marked the passage of the attainder bill also returned to the City of London at the king's going. When Charles came down to Westminster on 10 August he found a large crowd of citizens who 'set up a loud shout begging him not to go'.[58] The presence of the king was coming to be seen as a reassuring element as a pattern of political tension developed which left ordinary men bewildered and bemused.

With Charles's departure from London on 10 August the centrepiece of the Ten Propositions policy collapsed. But the failure to prevent his going made attention to the rest of the programme all the more urgent. So long as soldiers were kept together, commented Nicholas on 26 August, 'it will raise jealousies and animate factious persons, whatsoever the pretence may be'.[59] The best news of the month was the orderly departure of the Scottish army. On 5 August the Commons were at last able to announce that all the money was ready to satisfy their arrears and to pay the first instalment of the Brotherly Assistance; by 20 August the Scots had reached Morpeth; on 25 August the last soldiers crossed the Tweed.[60] There was much relief at seeing the backs of them. They had 'discharged their debts in England very honestly', according to a newsletter of 31 August, 'even by the report of those which came out of the north and love them not.'[61] Many had a 'good opinion' of them for their 'quiet departing', reported Thomas Wiseman to Sir John Pennington, though his own view of their intervention in English affairs was thoroughly jaundiced.[62]

This was not in fact quite the end of the story. The treaty was concluded and the public thanksgiving was duly performed on 7 September: at Oxford, for instance, the mayor and his brethren celebrated with wine and cakes and arranged bread and a bonfire for the poor. Yet the Scots were not

57 *CJ* II, 247–8; BL Harl. MS 5047, fols. 59v, 60r.
58 Gardiner IX, 418; *CSPV 1640–2*, p. 210.
59 *Nicholas*, p. 81.
60 *CJ* II, 235; *LJ* IV, 343; Bodleian Tanner MS 66, fols. 139, 156; BL Harl. MS 164, fol. 870r.
61 BL Add. MS 11045, fol. 140v.
62 *CSPD 1641–3*, p. 105.

prepared to disband their last 5000 foot until the walls of Berwick and Carlisle were slighted.[63] Moreover it was 18 September before disbandment of the English army was complete: the final stage, disbandment of the Berwick and Carlisle garrisons and shipping away the ordnance, took until the end of October.[64] Difficulties in getting in the poll money explain these further delays. On 25 August the treasurer of the army, Sir William Uvedale, had only received £5000 from Yorkshire and very little from the nine other counties due to send their money direct to York.[65] MPs sent frantic letters to comissioners in the counties: the armies presented a burden the kingdom 'must needs sink under', Sir Gilbert Pickering warned Sir Roland St John in Northamptonshire, unless some spirit was put into the business. There was no question, St John was advised, of disbandment without full pay. Sheriffs were told that parliament intended a review of the assessments and that it would deal severely with comissioners who condoned partiality.[66]

There was intense frustration at Westminster about the long tale of obstacles and delays. Furthermore, reports of robberies and violence by soldiers on their way home made MPs uneasy.[67] There were also fears that postponements in the disbandment programme might anger the Scots. It was an article of the treaty that the English should disband when the Scots marched away, Pym reminded the House on 16 August after a letter from the earl of Holland had been read, which announced that £140,000 was still needed for the English troops. 'When they see we do not disband', he asked, 'will they be gone?'[68] The tension showed itself in tetchiness and distrust towards Holland. The Commons were 'ill satisfied' when they heard on 19 August that, instead of disbanding the horse, he had given priority to relieving the countrymen of three regiments of foot who had long been 'disorderly and grievous' to them.[69] Holland's conduct could not actually be faulted: he was sensitive to his responsibilites and not unnaturally upset by parliament's reproofs, protesting that he assumed the initiative was in his hands since he had not been given precise instructions.[70]

Some of the mid-August jumpiness can be attributed to the rumours that a new conspiracy was hatching. These were inadvertently begun by

63 *DO*, pp. 352–3; Oxford Public Library: Council Minute Book, 1629–63, fol. 115v; BL Harl. MS 164, fol. 885v; Bodleian Tanner MS 66, fol. 176.
64 BL Harl. MS 5047, fol. 80r; *DO*, pp. 365, 369; *D'Ewes (C)*, p. 11; *CSPD 1641–3*, pp. 122–4; *Evelyn*, pp. 82–3; *HMC 5th Report*, p. 102.
65 Bodleian Tanner MS 66, fols. 132, 135, 137, 139, 145–6, 156, 162; BL Harl. MS 164, fol. 877v.
66 BL Harl. MS 164, fols. 859v, 864v, 877v; East Devon RO 1700A/CP22; Bedfordshire RO J 1387.
67 Bodleian Tanner MS 66, fols. 139, 162; *Buller*, p. 48.
68 BL Harl. MS 5047, fol. 75r.
69 BL Harl. MS 164, fol. 854v; Sloane MS 3317, fol. 32.
70 Bodleian Tanner MS 66, fols. 141, 164.

Holland himself when he hinted darkly in a letter to the earl of Essex about reports he had received of a 'general assizes and judgement intended upon his kingdom'. If there was real danger, commented Nicholas, he should not have been 'so obscure and brief'; if it was imaginary he had 'said too much'. The letter, which was quickly printed, 'put both Houses into a distemper'. There were some who were ready to believe that Holland was deliberately retarding disbandment 'for some design'.[71]

MPs returning home in September 1641 could boast of certain achievements in the last weeks of the session: there were the statutes against prerogative government as well as the treaty and the disbandment of the army in the north. But the Ten Propositions was a much broader programme than this. Counsellors, popery and defence of the kingdom were the three outstanding topics and little real progress had been made over any of them by 9 September. The conviction that evil counsels lay at the bottom of the nation's troubles had been a guiding principle for the Commons' leadership since November 1640. By June 1641 Strafford was dead, Laud mouldered in the Tower, Windebank and Finch had fled and impeachment hung over Bishop Wren and six judges. But the army plot showed that these moves were not sufficient. 'The same ill counsels which first raised the storm which almost shipwrecked the commonwealth do still continue', declared Holles in an impassioned speech at his delivery of the Protestation to the Lords on 4 May, 'they blow strong like the east wind that brought the locusts over the land.'[72] At the same time bridge appointments were coming to seem less and less likely. So it had become essential to bring the whole question of counsel into the open. All the same it was a momentous decision to include a clause 'about His Majesty's counsels' in the Ten Propositions. The idea of counsel was at the heart of the constitutional dilemma of 1641: the supposed effects of it were the fundamental cause of 'fears and jealousies', the future managing of it was the sticking point in the fraught relationship between Charles I and his parliament.

The first indication of the divisiveness of the counsellors issue came with the debate on 15 June about the earl of Newcastle's alleged involvement in the army plot. When Sir Hugh Cholmley, backed by Sir John Culpepper, moved that Charles should be asked to dismiss Newcastle from his governorship of the prince of Wales and appoint the innocuous earl of Berkshire, Edward Kirton and others sprang to Newcastle's defence. They also seized upon the constitutional principle that was at stake. It was the king's not parliament's role to choose the prince's governor, insisted Sir Henry Mildmay.[73] This incident perhaps taught Pym to tread warily. In his speech on 23 June he went no further than he had ever done before,

71   BL E 166(13); *Nicholas*, p. 16; *CSPD 1641–3*, pp. 93, 97; Clarendon I, 360, 379–80.
72   Rushworth III, part I, 243; Pennington, p. 173.
73   BL Harl. MS 478, fols. 668v–669r; 5047, fol. 23v.

simply including the traditional cry for 'all bad counsellors' to be removed. This was not bold enough for some of his close associates.

Pym's associates had made the running on this issue. On 28 May Holles and Strode proposed that parliament should appoint commissioners for the collection of tonnage and poundage who would hold the money raised in trust for the king, a scheme that fell through because MPs could not agree on nominations. Haselrig had moved, more generally, on 4 May that the Lords should be requested to join in a petition to Charles 'for the putting away of evil counsellors and placing others in their place'. The motion was 'well allowed', noted D'Ewes, but nothing was done. Pym's speech on 23 June prompted Haselrig to renew his motion; this time he had the vocal support of Sir Walter Earle. What is not clear is whether he had in mind a parliamentary role in the choice of counsellors when he spoke on 4 May and 23 June. Perhaps he hoped it would be enough to urge upon the king his responsibility to appoint good men or perhaps he was already thinking more radically.[74] His main concern on the latter occasion seems to have been that the House should 'not skim over but deal plainly', by naming names in the Propositions document. He returned to this aspect of the question on 24 June. The 'chief cause' was omitted, he declared, if the wicked counsel of Jermyn and Percy was not specified. But this was no moment for division among the leadership: Pym saw the need to soothe Haselrig and any other hotheads who were tempted to follow him. 'If His Majesty find them not we shall name them', he promised.[75] He expanded this assurance when he spoke to the Lords later in the day. Though at present they spoke in general, he told them, the king's failure to discover his evil advisers himself would 'cause the House of Commons to reduce this petition to names of particulars'.

The final wording of the third proposition shows that Pym's approach, let alone Haselrig's audacity, was too much for backbenchers. The close committee suggested that parliament should make suit to the king to remove 'such as have been active for time past and in furthering those courses contrary to religion, liberty, good government of the kingdom and as have lately interested themselves in those counsels to stir up division between him and his people.' This provocative wording, harking back to arguments used in the treason case against Strafford, was reduced to a more straight-forward and guarded request when Pym read the Propositions to the peers: 'That His Majesty may be humbly petitioned to remove such evil counsellors against whom there shall be any just exceptions.' The Commons also requested that the king be asked to commit 'his own business and the affairs of the kingdom to such counsellors and officers as the parliament may have cause to confide in' and to take their advice in

74 BL Harl. MS 164, fol. 999r; 478, fol. 706; 5047, fols. 34v, 35r; Crawford, p. 42.
75 BL Harl. MS 5047, fol. 36v.

appointing 'some person of public trust and well affected in religion' to care for the education of the prince.[76]

Thus no general attempt to control appointment of ministers or even to exercise a negative voice in their appointment was yet envisaged.[77] The overall impression is of confusion and uncertainty about how far the Commons should assert itself. Everyone agreed that the king had to take counsel, but Haselrig and Earle seem to have been alone in claiming that he should take it from particular people named by parliament. A peculiarity of seventeenth-century parliamentarians, recently noted, was that 'they thought of themselves as the king's council to such an extent that if one only read their speeches, one might forget that there was ever such a body as the privy council at all.' When the council as an institution was moribund and the king was more isolated than he had ever been before, there was a strong temptation to adopt a view of mixed monarchy which allotted a larger role to parliament. Yet between their saying the king was obliged to hear and follow their counsel in general terms and claiming a share in the sovereign power by appointing or approving his councillors was a psychological razor-edge so fine that some members did not know on which side they stood.[78]

The problem of the governorship of the prince was quickly settled. Newcastle, heavily in debt and anxious to escape to his Midland estates, resigned the position. But the king chose the marquis of Hertford in his place instead of Berkshire, whom some MPs had wanted.[79] Charles also replied to parliament's petition that he should remove evil counsellors with a flat denial that he had any, which he accompanied with a firm reprimand: 'nor doth he expect that any should be so unadvised as, by slanders or any other ways, to deter any that he trusts in public affairs from giving him free counsel.'[80] Parliament had been kept waiting a fortnight for an answer to their petition and in the meanwhile members had been apprehensive about the advice the king was being given. Many blamed the king's decision to take time to consider the Star Chamber and High Commission bills on 3 July on his advisers. 'It did much discontent us', noted John Moore, 'to see such ill counsel given to His Majesty.'[81] The king's intransigence produced dismay but it brought no dramatic change of mood. Nothing came of the gossip reported by Nicholas on 15 July that parliament would shortly name certain privy councillors 'whom they hold to be unfaithful'.[82]

76 *LJ* IV, 286; *CJ* II, 185.
77 For a different view see Zagorin, p. 247 and Kenyon, *Constitution*, p. 193.
78 C.S.R. Russell in *EHR* LXXX (1965), 36.
79 *CSPD 1641–3*, pp. 18, 38, 63.
80 *CJ* II, 208; *LJ* IV, 310.
81 BL Harl. MS 479, fol. 767v.
82 *CSPD 1641–3*, p. 53; BL Harl. MS 5047, fol. 36v.

Debates on 13 July and 9 August show clearly that the Commons as a whole was not yet ready to confront the king on the question of his councillors. The debate about Lord Digby on 13 July arose from the revelations in a committee report of his Straffordian publicity seeking, but it was given zest by the current rumour that the king was about to send him as ambassador to France. Henry Marten and Herbert Morley moved that Charles should be petitioned not to give 'any honour or employment' to Digby, who had 'deserved so ill of the parliament'. Sir John Strangeways and Edward Kirton divided the House on an amendment to make the request temporary, which they lost by a narrow margin. It is hard to say how far MPs swung to Digby out of sympathy for an ex-colleague, rather than through a desire to preserve the royal prerogative intact, but the strength of feeling is evident from the fact that the noes were loud and there was almost a second division on the substantive motion.[83]

The discussion on 9 August concerned the new privy councillors, appointed on Bristol's advice. The Digby family had dealt the Commons a series of snubs. Bristol himself had become a gentleman of the bedchamber and Lord Digby had been named ambassador to France despite the Commons' objections.[84] Haselrig again took the lead. He spoke bitterly of how he was 'grieved at heart at the three councillors made yesterday now that we so much desire good councillors'. 'How can we hope', he asked, 'to have good of them, recommended in secret, who carried themselves so in public?' To balance Bristol's appointments the Commons sought to persuade the king to promote the earls of Pembroke and Salisbury.[85] Pembroke had just been deprived of the office of Lord Chamberlain of the Household, which he had held for 15 years. He was respected by the Commons leadership for precisely the same reasons that he was dismissed by the king: his vote against Strafford was well known and he was alleged to have gone further than this by countenancing the May tumults at Westminster.[86] The proposal to ask the earl of Arundel to step down as Lord Steward of the Household, making way for Pembroke, was in effect an attempt to restore to influence a senior peer who had served the court for 40 years but was not slavishly attached to it. Salisbury, who it was suggested might become Lord Treasurer, probably had less political wisdom, but he was another peer with wide electoral interests and long administrative experience, both on the council and in the lieutenancy, one whom men like Pym had no hesitation in trusting. These recommendations for high office did not raise constitutional hackles to the same extent as the bid to exclude Digby from office, though Orlando Bridgeman

83 *CJ* II, 208–9; *DO*, p. 284; BL Harl. MS 163, fol. 781v.
84 *PCR* XII, 176; Gardiner IX, 416.
85 *CJ* II, 248; BL Harl. MS 5047, fol. 61.
86 *CSPD 1641–3*, pp. 62–3; *HMC Coke*, 281.

thought them derogatory to the royal prerogative. But when Cromwell tried to go further and make Bedford and Saye nominees for the guardianship of the prince of Wales, in addition to Hertford, he could not find a seconder. Neither the nomination of Pembroke nor that of Salisbury made headway in the Lords, despite vigorous efforts by Mandeville and Lord Andover to rally support for them.[87] The counsellors question was left in confusion and deadlock at the end of the session.

The Commons' unquestioning adoption of the programme of anti-Catholic measures in the Ten Propositions indicates the effectiveness of the leadership's propaganda. No evidence had ever been produced of a specific papist element in the army plot yet the impression had been fostered that the Catholics were somehow at the heart of it. The stationers' merchandise reinforced the leadership's efforts. The June publications included the dastardly tale told by William O'Connor of the papist conquest that would begin shortly. The Commons' unanimity may also be attributed to public awareness of the failure of earlier measures. The proclamations of 11 November and 8 March ordering recusants from the capital and Jesuits and foreign priests from the country had not been enforced; the papal nuncio was still in England; masses were still held and attracted considerable congregations at Denmark House, St James's and the houses of certain ambassadors. When Francis Rous reported that nearly three hundred people were seen coming from mass at the Portuguese ambassador's on 10 May, D'Ewes reminded his colleagues that both the king and Henrietta Maria had promised that these confluences would be prevented.[88] Furthermore, Catholic peers had used the writ of *certiorari* to suspend the operation of the recusancy laws against peers and their dependents. This was a legal loophole the Commons intended to close through the bill for taking the Protestation.[89] Finally in so far as the recusancy statutes had been more strictly enforced since parliament met, the outcome was statistics which tended to increase rather than allay alarm.[90] The horrifying figures for Lancashire have already been noted; 1750 convicted recusants were reported in Middlesex, 265 in Herefordshire.[91]

If any MPs needed further convincing that a fierce anti-Catholic drive was in order the three intercepted letters which Pym had ready to justify the measures he proposed on 24 June were more than adequate for his

87 *LJ* iv, 355; BL Harl. MS 6424, fol. 89v.
88 BL E 158(4): *A Discovery of a Late Plot*; Steele, nos. 1832, 1839; *LJ* iv, 151; *DO*, p. 22; BL Harl. MS 163, fol. 544r; *D'Ewes (N)*, p. 324.
89 *CJ* ii, 161–2, 168; *LJ* iv, 110; *DO*, p. 9; BL Harl. MS 478, fol. 619v; *HMC, House of Lords MSS* xi, 279–80; Essex RO Q/SB a 2/43; *D'Ewes (C)*, p. 68.
90 *CJ* ii, 137; *D'Ewes (N)*, pp. 288, 292; *Sussex*, p. 104; *HMC Buccleuch* iii, 388–9; *Townshend*, p. 22.
91 *CJ* ii, 148; BL Harl. MS 477, fol. 532v; Loan MS 29/172, fols. 369–70; above, p. 5.

purpose. They contained a heady mixture of wild and offensive talk. Two were written to the courtier Walter Montagu, one of the most notorious of the queen's close advisers: in one of these MPs were branded as Puritans, the other was intended to incite Cardinal Richelieu 'to some design against England'. The third letter brought to the attention of MPs a man who was henceforth to be a leading *bête noire*. It was written by the queen's confessor Father Philip. A priest called John Browne, examined in April, had brought Philip to Pym's attention, naming him as a chief agent in the design to convert England to Catholicism. He was drawn into the spotlight because of his position at court and because the others, like Montagu and Matthew, whom Browne named, had already left England. Whether Pym had any inkling of just how deeply Philip had in fact been involved in nego- tiations with the papacy for financial aid in return for the king's conversion is uncertain. In any case this letter, including as it did the provocative assertion that the Protestation was 'like the Scottish covenant but worse', effectively damned him.[92]

Disarming of papists was already on the Commons agenda.[93] It was discussed on 12 May, for example, after Pym had read Lady Shelley's celebrated letter hinting at a Catholic conspiracy against the 'hellish brood'.[94] But wide-spread disarming had previously been controversial. John Maynard had received strong support for his insistence on 15 March that no one should be disarmed 'till a law were made for it'.[95] In response to this view a bill was drawn up in May to allow JPs to search the houses of suspected papists for arms and to arrest 'some of the most active and dangerous'. Since this bill was before the Lords on 24 June the close committee saw no need to make an explicit reference to disarming in the Ten Propositions.[96] It was the House, responding to a bold call from Sir John Culpepper for the principal popish nobility to be imprisoned, who added the clause 'that His Majesty be moved to give his assent that the persons of the most active papists be so restrained as shall be necessary for the safety of the kingdom.'[97]

By August it appeared that only independent action by the Commons would achieve the disarming of papists. The peers had balked the Commons' proposal for action in conjunction with the crown by a series of queries as to what they meant by 'active papists' and how far the 'restraint' would extend.[98] When the disarming bill reached them they let it sleep. In a

92 *LJ* IV, 286; BL Harl. MS 163, fols. 732r, 763v; 478, fol. 708v; Hibbard, pp. 392–400; Gardiner IX, 134–5, 175, 244, 251–2, 310.

93 BL Harl. MS 478, fol. 706.

94 Verney, *Notes*, p. 67; *D'Ewes (N)*, pp. 16–17, 357–60; *CJ* II,144; BL Harl. MS 477, fol. 521r; Sloane MS 1467, fol. 82r.

95 *D'Ewes (N)*, p. 488.

96 BL Harl. MS 477, fols. 494r, 546r; *CJ* II, 165, 171; *LJ* IV, 306.

97 BL Harl. MS 163, fol. 734; *LJ* IV, 287.

98 *LJ* IV, 290.

few places meanwhile local authorities had taken matters into their own hands. At York three aldermen were appointed as early as 2 June to disarm papists.[99] But reports that JPs in certain counties like Breconshire and Glamorganshire were failing even to enforce the recusancy statutes encouraged MPs to press for action. The Montgomeryshire bench had even managed to remove a JP who insisted on presenting recusants.[100] Those who felt the papist menace to be especially threatening in their own counties took the lead. On 18 August the Lords did agree that, because there was 'more than extraordinary cause of danger' and 'divers former directions have been frustrated', commissioners should be sent into six counties to ensure that all convicted recusants were disarmed as the royal proclamation of 11 November had directed. The six counties chosen were Cheshire, Hampshire, Lancashire, Staffordshire, Sussex and Yorkshire. Lincolnshire and Nottinghamshire were added three days later.[101]

But it was those who had escaped conviction that most concerned the Commons. At a conference with the Lords on 18 August they stated their view that no privilege of parliament should be allowed in cases of conviction for recusancy and that all *certiograris* out of the King's Bench should be superseded. When they agreed to the ordinance for disarming recusants on 30 August the Lords finally accepted these provisions. The ordinance, indeed, was a far more draconian measure than any of the recusancy statutes. It took its justification from the allegation 'that popish recusants have always had and still have, and do practice, most dangerous and pernicious designs against the Church and state'. It argued that some papists had avoided conviction by 'subtle practices and indirect means', or 'being outwardly conformable' had let their children, grandchildren or servants 'be bred up or maintained in the popish religion'. All who had not been to church once a month, received communion within the previous year or taken the oath of supremacy and allegiance were to be disarmed. It was even enough for a man's children or grandchildren or two of his servants to be known papists.[102] This comprehensive scheme to stamp out popish conspiracy in the provinces was certainly taken seriously by many of those appointed as commissioners. JPs visiting Catholic magnates did not always find the bulging Catholic armouries they expected, yet not every papist storehouse was a chimera. On 2 November, for instance, Richard Whitehead reported a haul of arms for 300 horse and 1200 foot from Basing House, the home of the marquis of Winchester.[103]

But the main brunt of the attack on Catholics in the Ten Propositions

99 YPL House Books 36, fol. 57v.
100 BL Harl. MS 163, fol. 740v; 5047, fol. 72r; *CJ* II, 189, 257.
101 *LJ* IV, 369–70; *CJ* II, 267.
102 *LJ* IV, 369–70; *CJ* II, 267.
103 *Sussex*, p. 103; *D'Ewes (C)*, p. 68.

was directed at those at court rather than in the countryside. Henrietta Maria had always wanted to make her household a focal point for English Catholicism and since 1637 she had succeeded in doing so.[104] Londoners, who had rioted outside her and her mother's apartments more than once, knew very well what was going on and the queen's refusal to dismiss Sir John Winter had rankled with MPs during the spring.[105] The Commons wished to deprive the queen of her priests and put 'some of the nobility and others of trust into her service'. They wanted the college of Capuchins at Denmark House abolished. They were fearful that her projected journey northwards with her husband as far as Holmby House or Pontefract would make her a prey to conspirators and planned she should have a 'competent guard'. Pym knew very well the delicate ground he was treading when he made these proposals to the Lords. He intended 'nothing of disrespect' he asserted: 'it was a blessed thing to be kept from temptation and to be rid of those flies would gain the queen the love of the people in His Majesty's absence.' The sixth and seventh Propositions consisted of further measures for removing Catholic influence at court. The king should be sparing over licensing papists to come to court, English Catholic ladies should not reside there and no pensions should be paid to recusants overseas. Finally the Commons desired a statute declaring it to be treason for any papal agent to visit England.[106]

The Lords responded cautiously to this programme. They at once rejected the proposal that Catholic ladies should leave the court with the comment that the only papist lady there was of 'quiet condition'. On 8 July they went on to reject any approach to the queen over her priests since the marriage articles were emphatic that she should have spiritual advisers of her own choosing. The Commons persisted: the Capuchins were 'busy men in giving intelligence to foreign states, the carriage of whose letters in and out of England cost three pounds, ten shillings a week'; some aspects of the marriage treaty with France were 'contrary to law'.[107] But it was becoming clear that no active cooperation from the peers would be forthcoming. The joint committee found it impossible to reach an agreed formula about Catholic influence at court to put to Charles before he left London. Nor was there any sign of the proposed bill against papal agents visiting England.

The only positive developments in July were the long-delayed departure of the nuncio Rosetti and the queen's decision to abandon her journey to

---

104 Russell, *Parliaments*, p. 264; Smuts, *EHR* XCIII (1978), 40–3; J.P. Kenyon, *The Stuarts* (London, 1966), p. 79.
105 Gardiner IX, 133; *CSPV 1640–2*, pp. 91–2; R. Clifton, 'The Popular Fear of Catholics during the English Revolution', *Past and Present* LII (1971), 28.
106 *LJ* IV, 286; *CJ* II, 185; Bedfordshire RO J 1383, 1386.
107 *LJ* IV, 290, 306, 309; BL Harl. MS 163, fol. 770v.

drink the waters of Spa.[108] MPs' anxiety about the queen's movements while her husband was away had its origin in the rumours of early June that she might go north to Holmby or Pontefract.[109] When the news of her trip abroad broke on 14 July, the close committee quickly produced a clever set of arguments to stop it. Papists were gathering abroad ready to take this opportunity to launch their design; they had been selling their lands and were collecting money; the state would be impoverished by the jewels, plate and money conveyed with Henrietta Maria; she should be properly furnished and attended yet this would be a heavy burden at a time of necessity; her absence, if out of 'some discontent of mind', would be dishonourable to the nation at so unseasonable a moment.[110] This was veiled confrontation, nicely calculated to produce a royal retreat. She would never do anything to prejudice the kingdom having so much interest in its good, the queen told a parliamentary delegation.[111]

August brought little further comfort except for another departure, that of the queen mother. Her name had only been omitted from the Ten Propositions because the elder Vane declared she was about to leave England even then.[112] So far as the queen's priests were concerned the Commons got no further than obtaining a list of them, so there could be no confusion when a priest was arrested about whether he was under her protection or not. There was a sense of frustration when the list was read on 28 August. Some cried 'to have them all sent away, the mass that they celebrate being idolatry'.[113] All the evidence MPs received suggested that Catholicism was as strong as ever in the capital. On 16 August they received a petition from a 'multitude of poor tradesmen and artificers' complaining that papists who were French, Walloon and Dutch aliens were snatching their livelihoods at a time of plague and economic dislocation. Yet they had to be content with minor victories. The head of the Capuchins was firmly instructed neither to let his friars go abroad in the streets nor to allow English Catholics to attend his masses.[114] A fierce priest hunt brought the first execution of a Jesuit for 13 years. There were others who only escaped the fate of the aged William Ward at Tyburn through the intervention of the French or Venetian ambassador.[115]

As we have seen, MPs had long been concerned about the way ambassadors of Catholic states nurtured their faith in the capital. But it was hard to prevent attendance at their masses. When the constables went to carry

108 *CJ* II, 199.
109 *Calendar of Wynn Papers*, p. 283; BL Harl. MS 163, fol. 785r; *CSPD 1641–3*, p. 38.
110 *CJ* II, 210–11, 213; BL Harl. MS 5047, fol. 42v; Bodleian Rawlinson D MS 1099: 14 July.
111 *CJ* II, 215, 218; BL Harl. MS 479, fol. 812v; Gardiner IX, 406–7.
112 BL Sloane MS 3317, fol. 25v; Harl. MS 163, fol. 733; Add. MS 28000, fol. 115; *Evelyn*, p. 80.
113 BL Harl. MS 5047, fol. 79r; Sloane MS 3317, fol. 29v.
114 BL Harl. MS 164, fol. 839v; 478, fol. 898v; *CJ* II, 258; *LJ* IV, 362, 364, 367.
115 Gardiner IX, 411; Wedgwood, pp. 446–7; *CJ* II, 216.

out arrests at the Portuguese ambassador's in August the bellman sent his servants into the crowd with drawn swords to rescue the worshippers.[116] The Catholic ambassadors had never been so unpopular as they were by the end of August. Some Londoners flung stones at the home of the French ambassador in Lincoln's Inn Fields and assaulted his doors.[117] Yet it was not simply domestic prejudice which moved parliament to pass an ordinance to stop soldiers from the disbanded Irish army being levied by the Spanish and French ambassadors for service abroad.[118] Enthusiasts for the cause of international Protestantism like Sir Simonds D'Ewes saw the question in both offensive and defensive terms. It would be dishonourable, they argued, to assist the king of Spain in this way and it might dishearten the Protestant party abroad. Pym spoke of the levies on 8 July as 'a great scandal to our nation' and warned that they might be 'a drawing-off of others from our religion'. Rudyerd supported him.[119] The news in the last days of the session that the king of Spain was hindering English shipping at Calais provoked an upsurge of ancient belligerence: 'this puts the House into a great rage', noted one newsletter, 'everyone being desirous to consent to a war with the Spaniards in the West Indies.'[120] Proposals for a West India company, an old chestnut in Pym's circle, were discussed. An aggressive campaign would be aimed at taking the silver fleet, Hispaniola and Cuba. It was no time to be sending 4000 Irish into Spain lest Spain 'may the better send 4000 Castilians into the West Indies', declared the supporters of this end-of-term charade.[121]

The attention given in the Ten Propositions to defence of the kingdom was a logical consequence of the leadership's obsession with papist conspiracy. It had been foreshadowed by the moves made in the hectic days of early May when defence was a daily preoccupation. Three aspects of national security were covered: the trained bands, the ports and the navy. Many MPs probably took a jaundiced view of the condition of the local militias. The demand that the militias should be 'furnished with arms, powder and bullets', exercised and 'made fit for service' certainly suggests that some of them were alert to the possibility that standards had fallen during the previous decade.[122] In fact recent research has shown that the exact militia programme brought about a marked improvement in many of the county militias, which was probably largely sustained, where musters were held regularly, from 1630 to 1640[123] Nevertheless there is no question

---

116 *CSPV 1640–2*, pp. 145, 154; *CJ* II, 141, 202; BL Harl. MS 478, fol. 888v.
117 *HMC House of Lords MSS* XI, no. 3541; *LJ* IV, 389.
118 *CJ* II, 202, 275, 283; *LJ* IV, 374, 381–2, 390, 394; Clarendon I, 369–70.
119 BL Harl. MS 479, fol. 787r; 5047, fols. 40, 78r, 81v; Rushworth III, part I, 381–2.
120 *LJ* IV, 394; BL Add. MS 11045, fol. 141r.
121 BL Sloane MS 3317, fols. 24–6; Russell, *Parliaments*, pp. 262, 293–4, 299–300.
122 *CJ* II, 135, 138, 185; Pennington, p. 171.
123 L. Boynton, *The Elizabethan Militia* (London, 1967), pp. 267–9; *Sussex*, p. 184; D.P. Carter,

that there were startling deficiencies, of arms and ammunition for instance and in the repair of some of the south coast forts.[124]. Sir John Culpepper had mentioned the Kentish loss of 1000 'of our best arms' for the Scottish war. Much was now made of the vulnerability this imposed.[125]

The Commons had become aware in May of the constraints they suffered under in these matters. For example they asked Sir Walter Earle to ride home to see to the defences of Dorset on 7 May, only to find three days later that he had not been able to leave because he lacked a commission to act as a deputy to the new lord-lieutenant the earl of Salisbury, whose own commission had been delayed. They also found it hard to obtain information quickly about the defences of Portsmouth, the Isle of Wight and the Channel Islands, still less to apply costly remedies.[126] But the response of the peers to this item of the Ten Propositions agenda was so positive that it looked in late June as if remedies might quickly be applied. The Lords showed none of the scruples in this area that they did over Catholicism at court. On 26 June three of their number were deputed to approach the Lord Admiral for information on the state of the navy; on 8 July the peers were able to announce that the earl of Newport had completed a survey of the main forts and castles and found them very defective.[127]

Progress was not fast enough, however, to satisfy all MPs. On 12 July several moved that 'some order be taken for furnishing magazines and commanding the trained bands if occasion should be to use them this summer'. The same day the Commons embarked on a scheme for members to collect detailed information from the localities about the state of magazines and the control of forts and castles. A week later a comprehensive militia bill – 'concerning trained soldiers and for the providing of gunpowder and other munition' – was given a first reading.[128] The new sense of urgency was evident at a meeting of the joint committee for the Propositions, when the Commons pressed for deputy-lieutenants to be supplied from the subsidies, for the king to be moved to let them have gunpowder from his store and for the arms taken from several counties for the Scottish war to be restored to them.[129]

Thus by July 1641 control of the local militias was already a central issue

'The Exact Militia in Lancashire 1625–40', *Northern History* XI (1975), 87–106; G.P. Higgins, 'The Government of Early Stuart Cheshire', *Northern History* XII (1976), 43–6; for a more pessimistic view see Barnes, *Somerset 1625–40*, pp. 258–71.

124 BL Harl. MS 164, fol. 1004r; 477, fol. 527; *Sussex*, p. 190; P. Clark, *English Provincial Society from the Reformation to the Revolution* (Hassocks, 1977), p. 375; *Buller*, p. 46; H.J. Moule, *Catalogue of the Charters and Minute Books of Weymouth and Melcombe Regis 1252–1800* (Weymouth, 1883), p. 29.
125 Rushworth III, part I, 33; *CJ* II, 257–8.
126 *CJ* II, 142, 148; *LJ* IV, 249, 251; *PCR* XII, 109, 127; BL Harl. MS 477, fols. 510v. 534v.
127 *LJ* IV, 290; BL Harl. MS 163, fol. 770v.
128 *CJ* II, 208, 216; BL Harl. MS 163, fol. 779v; 478, fol. 706.
129 *LJ* IV, 309.

in the relationship between the king and parliament. It was to remain so throughout the months when distrust and misunderstanding were driving them towards war. Pym, indeed, had put his hands firmly and confidently on the question in his speech on 23 June. For him national security was bound to be the immediate and overriding consideration when the monarch intended to abandon his country while papist enemies were massing against it. 'The king going we shall be naked', he declared.[130] The fullest account of what Pym said was as follows:

> that the forces of every county may be put into a posture of defence and that there may be provisions of arms and ammunition made in every county and lord lieutenants and deputy-lieutenants men of trust and such as shall be nominated in the parliament for the ordering and commanding of the forces of the several counties as occasion shall require.

John Moore's version of the speech confirms the crucial point: 'we take care to elect such as this House shall think fit'. In the 1620s Pym had persistently supported abortive bills to clarify the constitutional status of the militia. He may well have held radical views on this subject then. Certainly by June 1641 he felt no qualms about claiming parliamentary control of local forces. But even this was not enough: he wanted the parliamentary appointees to take an oath that they would 'endeavour themselves for the good of the commonwealth'.[131]

Pym's thinking about control of the militia was undoubtedly far ahead of that of most of his colleagues in the summer of 1641. Always the practical politician, he sought a wording for the Ten Propositions that would command general assent. He contented himself with the request 'that there may be good lieutenants and deputy-lieutenants and such as may be faithful and trusty and careful of the peace of the kingdom.' Before long he had brought the joint committee for the Propositions some way along with him. On 12 May Bristol reported to the peers that the committee desired lieutenants and their deputies 'may be such persons as both Houses approve of'.[132] The militia bill, read on 19 July, sought to go further: to enshrine the principle of parliamentary nomination in statute by listing the persons MPs had chosen to command the trained bands county by county. It may seem curious, in view of Pym's caution a month previously, that no one objected that the bill invaded the royal prerogative. Again the leadership's skill at instilling the idea of national emergency is evident. The bill was designedly a temporary measure, intended to give the parliamentary nominees extensive powers only until the following April. The nation's

130 BL Harl. MS 5047, fol. 34.
131 Bodleian Rawlinson D MS 1099: 23 June; BL Harl. MS 478, fol. 706; Russell, *Parliaments*, pp. 222, 385; R.C. Johnson, M.F. Keeler, M.J. Cole, W.B. Bidwell, *Commons Debates 1628* (New Haven, 1977) IV, 293, 297.
132 *LJ* IV, 287, 309.

defences were believed to be weak. Moreover there were cautionary tales to be heard, like the one about the earl of Bridgewater's telling the Herefordshire deputies to obey the commands of the papist earl of Worcester and another, not yet public but perhaps whispered, about a Montgomeryshire gentleman who kept possession of the county magazine in defiance of the Bench. In this atmosphere it was hard to oppose a bill that appeared to do no more than borrow certain prerogative powers for nine months.[133]

It was the subject's liberties, interestingly enough, rather than the royal prerogative that concerned some MPs when the militia bill was read on 19 July. The reputation of the lieutenancy had been badly tarnished by deputies' efforts to enforce the exact militia programme and by impressment for the Scots war. There were complaints when the Long Parliament met about deputies abusing their office in a number of counties including Leicestershire, Worcestershire and Yorkshire; a committee for investigating their oppressions was set up and directed to draw a bill for restraining their power.[134] Other priorities had prevented that bill from appearing, yet here was a bill that gave the lieutenancy even greater powers than its most stalwart advocates believed it possessed in the 1630s. These were the grounds on which 'divers spake against it to cast it out'. But the bill passed its first two readings and was sent to a committee under Sir Walter Earle: some had argued 'that it might be made a good bill and the power might be put into the sheriff or some others'. The committee's decision to put local military control on the same basis as collection of subsidies, by appointing large groups of commissioners in each county, eventually mollified those who had unhappy memories of abrasive caucus government by deputy lieutenants.[135]

There was undoubtedly much enthusiasm about purging the lieutenancies. MPs responded readily to Earle's request on 29 July for county delegations to report on whether their lieutenant and deputies were 'fitting to enjoy their places'. By 5 August he had collected 400 nominations for the bill; delegations behind with completing their lists were to consult the next day.[136] At that point the bill was stymied by the king's departure. It was prominent in the list of bills which the Commons wished the king to pass by commission in his absence but the commission was not forthcoming.[137]

During the last weeks of the session the leadership felt too vulnerable simply to let matters rest. The Tower and the south coast caused particular anxiety. The lieutenant of Dover Castle, the duke of Richmond, had gone

133 BL Harl. MS 163; fol. 791r; 164, fol. 1004r; 5047, fol. 72r; *D'Ewes (N)*, p. 348.
134 *D'Ewes (N)*, pp. 145, 243, 425, 445–6, 453.
135 BL Harl. MS 163, fols. 791r, 805v; *CJ* II, 222.
136 *CJ* II, 228, 238; BL Harl. MS 163, fol. 805v; 479, fol. 844v; Bodleian Tanner MS 66, fol. 118.
137 *CJ* II, 250; BL Harl. MS 5047, fol. 60v.

with the king; the Isle of Wight's governor, the earl of Portland, was said to have a papist wife and papist children and servants; Guernsey was rumoured to be under the control of Henry Jermyn. The Ten Propositions had suggested that parliament should receive a list of those who governed the ports and be ready to alter it 'upon reason'.[138] So a committee of defence was appointed on 14 August, at Pym's instigation, to prepare a plan for joint action with the Lords. Since the king had made the earl of Essex captain general of forces south of the Trent, military measures taken with his cooperation appeared both loyal and legal. Falkland and Culpepper sat on the new committee together with Sir Thomas Barrington, Earle, Strode and the younger Vane.[139] This was a united front: men who were divided about episcopacy and the liturgy could nevertheless still work whole-heartedly together over national security. By the time the recess came the committee had a few initiatives to its credit. The earl of Newport, as constable of the Tower, was told to reside there and arrangements were made for it to be guarded by the men of Tower Hamlets parish. Ten ships were sent forth until 1 December to patrol the English Channel. The earl of Holland was instructed to ensure that the large stores of ammunition at Hull were not moved without parliament's approval. This was a meagre outcome, however, in the light of the broad programme of defensive renewal set out on 24 June. Hopes of musters and training before harvest and a busy period of restoring fortifications were dashed. It was small comfort that one of the king's last actions before leaving was to pass the short bill removing all limitations on the making of gunpowder, which had been in short supply for some months.[140]

Taken as a whole the Ten Propositions agenda for restoring political confidence proved unattainable. Yet it is arguable that Pym's achievement between June and September was a remarkable one. In view of the difficulties he faced, simply to hold the Commons together and on course and to maintain some kind of working relationship with the Lords was a hard enough task. In the first place epidemics threatened the sitting. From May onwards smallpox and plague were spreading in the city. MPs were under pressure from relatives leaving London to travel with them and there was talk of moving parliament to Oxford.[141] The plague reached Chancery Lane and Holborn by mid July and Westminster by mid August: on 16 August the Lords closed the water-gate on the Thames and directed that members' coaches should wait nowhere but in New Palace Yard.[142] D'Ewes hurriedly looked for new lodgings which were 'sweet and in a good

138 *Nicholas*, p. 12; BL Harl. MS 163, fol. 806r; *LJ* IV, 287.
139 *CJ* II, 257; BL Harl. MS 478, fol. 897r; Pennington, p. 176.
140 *LJ* IV, 316, 356, 366, 369, 377–8; *SR* V, 131; Pennington, p. 175.
141 East Devon RO 1700A/CP19; BL Harl. MS 477, fol. 535v; *Calendar of Wynn Papers*, p. 273.
142 BL Tanner MS 66, fol. 110v; *Nicholas*, pp. 14, 37; *CSPV 1640–2*, p. 207; *LJ* IV, 365.

air'. On 26 August the Commons ordered a strict watch on infected houses in Westminster; by 6 September the district was so badly affected that the public thanksgiving for peace with Scotland had to be held at Lincoln's Inn.[143]

MPs were anxious about their personal survival. When Sir Guy Palmes announced he had been in a house infected by smallpox and desired leave 'till he might see himself past danger', the House assented with alacrity. When it was reported that Sir Richard Shuckburgh had lodged in a plague-ridden house in the Strand he was hastily bundled out with leave to go into the country.[144] The epidemics also disturbed men's sense of equilibrium. Pennington presented a petition for a public fast from the Londoners on 26 August, in view of the progress of plague and sickness and fears that the weather threatened a dearth.[145]

Sheer exhaustion with the political world of Westminster also took its toll. There was talk of a recess the next month during June.[146] It grew harder to resist the call of country pursuits; pressure from home was growing. He was afraid the session would drag on to a 'broken and imperfect conclusion', Sir Edward Dering told his wife on 20 May, 'and I shall have no patience to stay it out, especially if new afflictions be with thee.' If the sitting was going to be any further prolonged, Lady Harley told her son on 26 July, she hoped her husband would 'come down for a little time.'[147] Responsibilities called men home. His son loitered, failed to attend family prayers and spent as much time in play as 'following the book', reported Thomas Smyth's steward at the end of June. Furthermore his presence was required on the bench, since brewers serving unlicensed alehouses in the Bristol district were gaining licences by cozening less experienced JPs.[148] D'Ewes was reprimanded by his brother-in-law for neglecting his wife and his health: 'in almost three quarters of a year you have not enjoyed any freedom of air'. There were some though who deliberately waited in London to fight local battles. 'I wish myself heartily at Melbourne', sighed Sir John Coke on 14 July, irritated at being delayed over the impost on lead in the new book of rates, a vital matter for Derbyshire's economy.[149]

Tempers were shorter, political frustrations were keenly felt, during a long hot summer. Working conditions had deteriorated: on 24 June Edmund Waller moved that the House might be kept 'sweet and clean'. Foolish interventions received sharper reprimands: Sir John Clotworthy's proposal of a bill for the gelding of Jesuits on 19 July was greeted with

143 *CJ* II, 273, 281; BL Harl. MS 382, fol. 99r.
144 BL Harl. MS 163, fol. 805v; 164, fols. 827v, 871v; *CJ* II, 238, 250.
145 *CJ* II, 273, BL Harl. MS 163, fol. 897r.
146 Bodleian Tanner MS 66, fol. 100; BL Harl. MS 163, fol. 251r.
147 Larking, p. 47; *Harley*, p. 142.
148 Bristol RO 36074/140c.
149 BL Harl. MS 382, fol. 93r; *HMC Coke*, p. 289.

'much laughter'. D'Ewes thought such a diversion thoroughly inappropriate, 'when we had so many great businesses lying upon our hands and are so straitened for time'.[150] The tiredest man of all may have been Speaker Lenthall. He had never been able to arrive late or slip away early. His control of debate was still impeccable, his wit consistently sharp. It was not fit for members 'to sit as they were going to execution', he told Sir John Digby on 9 June when he perched himself on the ladder to the gallery instead of finding a proper seat.[151] On 30 June Lenthall decided that the time had come to declare a view about ending the session. He presumed, he announced after prayers, that the recess would begin at the king's departure on 10 August, so the House should apply itself to settling religion and abolishing all monopolies: this 'would be all we could do' and in doing this much 'we shall fully satisfy the country'.[152] But Lenthall was naive if he really thought he could satisfy the leadership with this limited programme. By mid August he was visibly tiring and on one occasion he refused an afternoon sitting on grounds of ill health. No one can have been more relieved than he when, after he had 'neither eaten nor drunk' all day, the Commons reluctantly accepted his ruling at seven o'clock on 9 September that there should be no new motions.[153]

Under these conditions it is not surprising that attendances were dropping. The high spring turnouts of more than 300 were not achieved after May; 13 July was the last occasion before the recess that as many as 200 members voted in a division.[154] By then the drift home was accelerating. In August, recorded Hyde, 'very many of both Houses . . . conceiving that there was no more to be done till the return of the king, save only the procuring money to finish the disbanding, went into the country.' The leadership had resisted backbench pressure in July for fixing the date of the recess. As D'Ewes shrewdly remarked, there was nothing so effectual for keeping men in London as 'the uncertainty of our rising'. But in August the problem went deeper than stopping the flight from London, as Hyde explained: those who stayed became 'less solicitous to attend the public service but betook themselves to those exercises and refreshments which were pleasanter to them'.[155] Pym may have found a thin House easier to manipulate than a full one, but in August he faced a real threat of having no House at all.

As early as 15 June lack of the quorum of 40 delayed the start of the

150   *CJ* II, 186; BL Harl. MS 163, fol. 791r; Bodleian Rawlinson D MS 1099; 19 July.
151   BL Harl. MS 478, fol. 644r; *CJ* II, 172.
152   BL Harl. MS 163, fol. 750r; 479, fol. 753r.
153   BL Harl. MS 164, fol. 859r.
154   V.F. Snow, 'Attendance Trends and Absenteeism in the Long Parliament', *Huntingdon Library Quarterly* (1955), 303; *CJ* II, 209.
155   Clarendon I, 281–2; *CJ* II, 220; BL Harl. MS 164, fol. 869r.

afternoon session.[156] The assumption among MPs that they should arrive early and see out the day seems to have gradually collapsed as the summer wore on. A month of many late sittings in July may have done much to discourage steady attendance.[157] The order of 26 July that public bills should only be read between nine and twelve o'clock marked an acceptance that numbers would remain low early in the morning and in the afternoon.[158] Thereafter the problem of keeping the Commons quorate became acute. MPs took to trooping out in bulk to hear the endless conferences with representatives of the Lords; delays in getting started after the midday break became frequent. Nor did a fresh start guarantee a solid afternoon's work. At one point on the afternoon of 13 August, after Lenthall had tried rather petulantly to cancel the afternoon sitting unless a penalty of £5 was imposed for absence, there were 'scarce 40 in the House'. Yet this sitting in fact continued from three until seven. On another occasion debate would have ground to a halt had not Lenthall ruled that the House was quorate because some members were employed in its service outside the chamber.[159]

The leaders of the Commons did what they could to combat absenteeism. The summons to all members on 7 August, 'in regard of the great and weighty affairs that import the safety of the kingdom', shows that they recognized the seriousness of the problem. The rollcall fixed that day for 18 August duly took place, but it is doubtful whether it brought more than a very few men back from the provinces.[160] Pym got by through expedients like opposing colleagues' requests for leave and calling out men known to be in London from their lodgings.[161] Once the day of adjournment was settled on 26 August interest waned even further. The final sittings in September were only achieved because a group of around 60 stalwarts made a personal commitment to be present.[162] The recess, in short, was forced on Pym and his closest colleagues.[163] The intensity of the plague and smallpox at Westminster made it inevitable, even if backbenchers had not voted with their feet. The epidemics were running their usual course, reaching a peak in September when they carried off about 300 people a week.[164] This was the pattern seasoned Londoners had come to expect: D'Ewes argued on 10 August that the grant of tonnage and poundage

---

156 BL Harl. MS 478, fol. 673r.
157 Clarendon I, 363; BL Harl. MS 163, fols. 757v, 764r.
158 *CJ* II, 224.
159 *CJ* II, 217, 233; BL Harl. MS 164, fols. 812v, 827r, 835r, 837v, 843r, 884v.
160 *CJ* II, 244, 263.
161 BL Harl. MS 164, fols. 843v, 850r, 851v.
162 BL Harl. MS 164, fol. 887v.
163 Clarendon I, 386.
164 *LJ* IV, 379; *CSPD 1641–3*, pp. 105, 120; *Calendar of Wynn Papers*, p. 274; *HMC Coke*, pp. 291–2, 294; J.F.D. Shrewsbury, *A History of Bubonic Plague* (Cambridge, 1970), p. 389.

should be extended to 1 December so there was no risk of MPs having to reassemble in September or October with plague at its height.[165]

From November 1640 to June 1641 Pym's leadership of the Commons was a prolonged wrestling match with a capricious assembly; from June onwards it became much more assured. His tactics were often brilliant, his sense of timing was acute, his exploitation of anti-Catholic propaganda was consistently adept. By keeping the army plot constantly on the agenda in July and August, for instance, he did much to revive flagging spirits and maintain awareness of the national peril.[166] By establishing a committee of six, two from the Lords and four from the Commons, to oversee the completion of the treaty in Scotland and preserve good relations between the two kingdoms, he did something to counter the nervousness about the king's activities there.[167] Pym knew when to hold the House in check and when to give it its head. Thus when a petition for a trading company with America and Africa was greeted with a burst of belligerent enthusiasm on 30 August, Pym brought weight and authority to a project close to his own heart: ''tis very hopeful if the Spanish party at court undermine it not.'[168]

There were still times when Pym was at odds even with his closest colleagues. When he tried to get the minimum payment for the poll tax doubled no one supported him.[169] He was almost on his own when he advised the House on 3 July to assent to the king's passing the poll tax bill without the reform bills that had been sent with it.[170] Nevertheless the inner circle, most of whom sat on both the close committee and the committee for the Propositions, were much more loyal and united in the summer than they had been previously. There was much greater identity of interest between them and they were probably meeting much more regularly in private.[171] There was commitment to a coherent programme of action and a shared conviction about the necessity of its implementation. This programme was largely spelt out in the Ten Propositions but it also included the Root and Branch bill which, as will be shown in the next chapter, made good progress in committee between 11 June and 3 August. The initiative for the bill had come from Haselrig, Cromwell and Vane but Pym came into line behind it immediately he saw the favourable response it received on 27 May.[172]

As the summer wore on and the country called many backbenchers

165   BL Harl. MS 164, fol. 826.
166   *CJ* II, 223–5, 255–6; BL Sloane MS 1467, fol. 17r; Bodleian Rawlinson D MS 1099: 23, 24, 26 July; Gardiner x, 2.
167   BL Harl. MS 164, fol. 825v; *CJ* II, 249; Rushworth III, part I, 376; Zagorin, p. 248.
168   BL Harl. MS 5047, fol. 79r; *CJ* II, 276; Keeler, p. 219.
169   BL Harl. MS 163, fol. 746r; *CJ II, 191.*
170   BL Harl. MS 163, fol. 759r; *CJ* II, 198; *DO*, pp. 180–1.
171   Clarendon, *Life* (1857) I, 74–5.
172   *Dering*, p. 62, below, p. 101.

home, matters rested increasingly with a core of activitists. Sir Baynham Throckmorton implicitly accepted their importance when he urged Thomas Smyth, in a letter of 14 June, to prepare Westminster opinion for the case he intended to present against Sir John Winter: 'make as many members of the House (especially that are active men) as you can in the business.'[173] The ability of men like Holles and St John to command the activist core is a striking feature of the summer debates. After a long debate on Henry Wilmot's petition for bail on 3 July, for example, the House set it aside when Holles and Strode opposed it, hinting that the close committee had new matters to prove against him.[174] Pym owed much in these months to his most trusted men. Holles was consistently energetic, so was Earle, a man with an impeccable oppositionist pedigree and one who shared Pym's fiery anti-Catholicism.[175] They had cooperated by insisting that some papists' lodings in Chancery Lane be searched for arms just before the parliament opened. Earle's services went far beyond his masterly chairmanship of the committee on the militia bill. Having sat in parliaments since 1614, he was deeply respected for his wisdom and experience. On 6 August, for example, the Commons turned to him for advice on a point of order.[176] Earle was also adept at inculcating tension. His advice on 12 July brought an order for a new report 'concerning the design' from the close committee. His ringing declaration, when there was talk of a recess on 22 July, that it was 'too dangerous a time to name it' closed the debate.[177]

A close working relationship between the two Houses was a prerequisite for the success of the Propositions policy. By July Pym had some cause for confidence over this. His formal contacts with leading peers have gone largely unrecorded but it seems plain that the numerous conferences between the two Houses noted in the *Journals* are only one side of the picture. The proximity of the debating chambers meant that peers mingled easily and frequently with leading members of the Commons. D'Ewes, for example, noted on 14 July how he had met Essex and Bristol leaving the Lords and gathered from them the latest news about the disbandment. Even the conference were becoming less stilted: on 25 June D'Ewes commented in his diary that the peers 'stood bare all the time as well as we'.[178]

It was no easier in the summer than it had been in the spring for Pym's allies in the Lords to command the House. During June they were engaged in a running battle with the earl of Manchester over the Star Chamber bill.

173 Bristol RO 36074/136e.
174 BL Harl. MS 163, fol. 759v.
175 Keeler, pp. 165–7; Crawford, pp. 39–56.
176 BL Add. MS 11045, fol. 131; Harl. MS 164, fol. 811r.
177 BL Harl. MS 163, fol. 779r; 479, fol. 821v.
178 BL Harl. MS 163, fols. 738r, 785v.

Manchester threw down the gauntlet by an assertion that the king possessed 'a regal and a legal prerogative', to which Saye replied that he did not expect to have heard such language again in parliament 'for he knew no power but legal which would make the king the most glorious prince in the world'. A few days later Manchester affirmed that the king's prerogative was 'so riveted and inherent in him that it could not be limited by any law, that he might take any cause out of any court of justice and judge it himself, that the Star Chamber was a court that regulated all other courts of judicature, that it curbed the nobility and awed the gentry'. Essex answered that these were precisely the reasons he would have it abolished, 'they having laboured all this parliament to make themselves freemen and not slaves'.

Another unpredictable element in the situation was the episcopal party, whose blocking of the bishops exclusion bill demonstrated the susceptibility of many peers to a conservative case. There was also a tradition of independent speaking at conferences which made it hard to hold the peers to a common line. After Lord Robartes had argued openly against Saye, who was putting 'the sense of the House', on 30 June the leadership moved to restrict this: 'when a preparation and ground is made and resolved on here . . . and the major sense of the House agrees upon that . . . no Lord is to speak contrary' was the decision of 1 July. Yet soon after the earl of Southampton produced a written paper of amendments at a conference about the bill for disarming recusants which Bristol and Saye said they had never seen before.[179]

Pym knew the Lords would not be bullied. There was nothing he and his friends there could do to further certain bills such as those for disarming recusants or against pluralities. But he found the peers could be cajoled. Negotiations over the Star Chamber, High Commission and poll tax bills were protracted and all these bills carried substantial Lords' amendments when they reached the statute book. But the important thing was that they got there.[180] In the case of the bill against the dissolution of the parliament the peers were persuaded to drop a severe amendment that would have limited its force to two years only.[181]

Towards the end of July falling attendances were having an even more dramatic effect in the Lords than in the Commons. After several weeks of constructive meetings, mutual effort to implement the Ten Propositions was grinding to a halt. Pym was sufficiently worried by 22 July to initiate an agreement that the Lords would not adjourn without 'two days warning

179　Bedfordshire RO J 1384, 1386; BL Harl. MS 163, fol. 792r; 6424, fols. 73r, 78v; *LJ* IV, 296.
180　*CJ* II, 191, 193–4, 196–7; *LJ* IV, 297, 299, 302–3, 305–6; BL Harl. MS 163, fols. 747r, 748v, 750v, 751v, 754–5; 479, fols. 743v, 753v; 6424, fol. 12; *DO*, pp. 165, 176–7; H.E.I. Phillips 'The Last Years of the Star Chamber', *TRHS* XXI (1939), 129–30.
181　*D'Ewes (C)*, p. 244.

to debate it' and information to the Commons beforehand.[182] Then came the serious breach between the Houses on 29 July over the peers' rejection of the bill imposing the taking of the Protestation on all adults, which was patently a device to root out Catholics. In their anger the Commons set about the impeachment of 13 bishops whom they held responsible for the canons of 1640 and whom they blamed for the fate of the Protestation bill. They also provoked the Upper House by printing their resolution that the Protestation should be generally taken.[183]

In early August all control of the Lords seemed to be slipping from the grasp of Pym's men there. After the king's departure peers were reported to be 'hourly leaving'; on 14 August a rumour that the Lords would adjourn, because so many were gone 'that the bishops will overrule by their votes', led the Commons to send up a stern reminder of the need to keep together.[184] But the fluid situation when attendances were dropping in fact played into the hands of Pym's friends, as an incident on 17 August shows. Essex, Mandeville, Paget, Saye and Wharton joined together to oppose the request of the impeached bishops to be given until Michaelmas to answer the Commons' charge. Finding a thin House sympathetic to the bishops, they used the ploy of adjourning it for lunch and returning in the afternoon with enough reinforcements to swing the assembly. The bishops were only given until 16 September to bring in their answer.[185] In the precarious last days of the session there were only around 20 peers who attended at all regularly.[186] The leadership enjoyed a major triumph with the ordinance for disarming recusants on 30 August but could not persuade a majority of colleagues to support the Commons order on worship and the prayer book. Thus the session ended with new recriminations between the Houses.[187]

Pym risked his political reputation on the Ten Propositions policy. It involved the acceleration of a process of invasion by parliament of the executive which had been going on since the previous November. The king's army had become more accountable to parliament. The navy was experiencing a similar change in the source from which decisions came. There were other spheres in which the role of parliament as an institution of government was expanding, such as trade and the punishment of Catholic recusants. This whole process was so gradual, the change was so subtle, that few can have been fully aware of it. What MPs were aware of was simply that they had never before sat for such long hours or worked so hard. Yet there was the danger that some might think that Pym had set his

182 BL Harl. MS 6424, fols. 70r, 82v; *LJ* IV, 324.
183 *DO*, p. 317; *CJ* II, 230; *LJ* IV, 333–9; Gardiner IX, 413–4.
184 *Oxinden*, p. 208; BL Harl. MS 5047, fol. 72r; Add. MS 28000, fol. 115r.
185 BL Harl. MS 6424, fol. 92; *LJ* IV, 367–8.
186 Clarendon I, 382.
187 *LJ* IV, 384–7; below, p. 117.

mind on a permanent change in the way the country was governed. The sharp debate in the Lords on 16 August over the Commons' request for a joint order forbidding the removal of the magazine at Hull illustrates the problems that could arise when a sense of constitutional proprieties was taxed. Several peers 'wished that they should write to keep it for the king's use and service'. It was only with difficulty that Saye, Mandeville and Wharton, who would 'by no means admit' this clause, had them overruled. In general, though, it is striking how little constitutional opposition Pym faced. No one in the Commons, for instance, appears to have objected to the executive measures proposed in May and again in August to defend the kingdom.[188]

The response of MPs to the first five parliamentary ordinances, passed in the last three weeks of the session, by and large bears out this impression of constitutional passivity. There was in fact confusion about the legal status of ordinances. D'Ewes was at his most misleading when he claimed on 28 July that there were precedents of parliament's passing ordinances in the king's absence, 'which are of the greatest authority next acts'. But hotheads like Strode were quick to make the most of his words.[189] The subject-matter of four of the ordinances made it easy for MPs to accept them without scruple. Two were innocuous: they established arangements for payment of the poll money at York and the thanksgiving for peace with the Scots. The ordinance forbidding Englishmen from taking military service with any foreign state may have seemed to many a very proper emergency measure. It was to remain in force for less than two months. The ordinance of 20 August legalizing the committee of MPs sent to Scotland was another emergency measure: nothing in their instructions actually broke new ground and although there was some confusion over their status their journey was generally agreed to be essential.[190]

Thus the ordinance for disarming recusants alone raised major constitutional issues. There is no doubt at all that it was a measure intended to broaden the definition of recusancy as well as enforce a neglected statute. The remark by one correspondent that its end was merely to quicken the execution of the law, 'which is only in the nature of a proclamation', illustrates the smokescreen which Pym put up. John Selden was not deluded: he told his colleagues in the Commons that the ordinance 'made new laws which it could not'. He particularly disliked the clauses which might 'bring men within the penalty of it for their children and servants' and the 'uncertain and general clause that persons suspected to be dangerous

188   BL Harl. MS 6424, fols. 84v, 92; *LJ* IV, 367–8; D.H. Pennington in R.H. Parry, editor, *The English Civil War and After* (London, 1920), pp. 28–30; Pennington, pp. 169–74.

189   BL Harl. MS 164, fol. 841v; 5047, fol. 62v; Gardiner X, 4.

190   *LJ* IV, 375, 379, 394; Gardiner X, 4–5, 9–10; Pennington, p. 174; E.R. Foster, 'The House of Lords and Ordinances 1641–9', *American Journal of Legal History* XXI (1977), 164.

should be disarmed'. An ordinance 'never was of any force', Selden added, 'to take away from the free subjects of England their goods against their will.'[191] This ordinance also upset Sir Roger Twysden, a Kentish antiquary with an exceptionally deep and perceptive understanding of the law. He was shocked that it reached to 'any that would be imagined popishly affected'. It may well have been he himself who challenged Sir Edward Dering at the Michaelmas quarter sessions with the awkward question that he records in his *Journal*: 'if a justice of peace should take away the goods of any man not prohibited by law the keeping of armour, whether he conceived that order of the Lords and Commons would save him harmless'.[192] Yet Selden and Twysden may have been virtually alone in sensing that the ordinances were incipient acts of parliamentary sovereignty.[193]

In view of his many difficulties and his deepening distrust of the king it is not surprising that Pym was becoming increasingly concerned with the public response to his policies during the summer of 1641. The initial version of the Ten Propositions, presented by the close committee to the House on 24 June, was soon in circulation as a printed pamphlet. The final version included the assertion that completion of a legislative programme 'concerning the reformation of Church and state', before Charles left for Scotland, would bring 'great advantage in His Majesty's own affairs and contentment of his people.[194] The implicit assumption was that parliament was accountable to the people. The Commons' campaign to win sympathy and support, which ran from the Protestation in May to the declarations of early September, arose from this sense of accountability. It also reflected a wounded sense of pride. This was plain in Pym's call on 3 May for 'some course to be taken to show that we stand for the defence of the king and the good of the kingdom' and in his anxiousness on 23 June to 'take away the scandal that we desire things that may weaken the crown'.[195] It was also plain in Holles's complaint to the peers on 4 May that 'our not effecting of the good things which we had undertaken for the good of the Church and commonwealth hath wounded our reputation and taken off from our credit.'[196]

The bill obliging all adult males to take the Protestation before Christmas was given its first reading on 6 May.[197] During the month copies of it

191 BL Add. MS 11045, fol. 140r; Harl. MS 164, fols. 858r, 876r; *LJ* IV, 384–7.
192 *Twysden*, pp. 187–97; J.M. Kemble, editor, *Certain Considerations on the Government of England* (Camden Society XLV, 1848), xlviii.
193 Zagorin, p. 249; Gardiner X, 2.
194 *CSPD 1641–3*, p. 38; BL E 160 (20); *LJ* IV, 286.
195 BL Harl. MS 477, fol. 484; 5047, fol. 34. For another version of Pym's words on 23 June see the first epigraph to this chapter.
196 Rushworth III, part I, 243; BL Harl. MS 5047, fol. 57r.
197 *CJ* II, 136.

were reaching many parts of England and its richly propagandist preamble about popish conspiracies, designs to introduce arbitrary government and 'jealousies raised and fomented between the king and people' was being read in council chambers and manor houses. Sir Robert Harley and Francis Coningsby urged the Herefordshire JPs to be forward in swearing the county; 'combination carries strength', wrote Oliver Cromwell and John Lowry requiring the subscription of the people of Cambridge.[198] There was undoubtedly some provincial enthusiasm. Thomas Stockdale, thanking Lord Fairfax for his copy, wanted lists of the refusers' names to be drawn up, 'so the strength of the adverse faction might appear'.[199] At Newcastle-under-Lyme 100 of the chief men of the town took the Protestation 'with much willingness and cheerfulness'. Lady Brilliana Harley reported on 21 May that it had been taken the previous Sunday in the Herefordshire villages of Brampton Bryan, Leintwardine and Wigmore. At Chester, Salisbury and probably a good many other towns the oath was taken by the mayor and aldermen at their assembly; at Rye 200 of the inhabitants were sworn as well. In Northamptonshire the JPs arranged for constables to summon 'as many as are willing' from the villages to take the Protestation at their divisional petty sessions.[200] Yet, despite these instances, only a small proportion of the whole populace can have subscribed voluntarily during the summer.

The Protestation arose from a yearning for unity yet paradoxically it was immediately divisive. Whereas the court of Common Council quibbled over the authorization of the oath many Londoners expressed their 'great joy and gladness' about it in a petition which was delivered on 4 May by the city MPs Matthew Cradock and Samuel Vassall.[201] The Commons' approval of Londoners taking the protestation was the signal for an energetic campaign by Edmund Calamy and other Puritan ministers to distribute copies and foist the business of general subscription on churchwardens. Radicals like Henry Burton meanwhile began to exploit the ambiguity of the religious clause of the oath in the cause of liturgical reform.[202] Some took fright at these proceedings. Sir John Strangeways, absent on 3 May, 'somewhat scrupled' the oath though he was persuaded to take it when he returned to parliament a few days later; the earl of Southampton, a critic of the campaign against Strafford, refused to take it. A rumour that Lord Digby did not subscribe was false but its circulation nevertheless attests

---

198 BL Loan MS 29/173, fol. 101r; Hirst, p. 186.
199 *Fairfax* II, 106–7.
200 Staffordshire RO D 868/2/30; *Harley*, p. 130; Chester RO DCC/47/26: Mayor of Chester to Sir Thomas Smith, 5 February 1642; Salisbury District Council Muniment Room, Ledger Book D, fol. 3v; *Sussex*, p. 252; Bedfordshire RO J 1385.
201 *CJ* II, 134; Pearl, pp. 115, 218.
202 Rushworth III, part I, 250; Bedfordshire RO J 1382, p. 2.

the significance that was attached to the Protestation.[203]

Holles did nothing to dispel the impression that the Protestation was intended as a symbol of factional loyalty when he told the peers on 4 May 'they thought it fit to give an account to those who had employed them . . . to give them a mark by which they might know who were good men, lovers of their country.'[204] Predictably, the Commons leadership was furious when the Lords finally rejected their bill to impose the oath on the whole nation.[205] They came as near as they could to defying the rejection by ordering their vote that anyone who did not take the Protestation was 'unfit to bear office in Church and commonwealth' to be printed and distributed.[206] There at the end of July the matter of general subscription rested. But when the Commons took steps for the guarding of the Tower on 28 August they directed that the men of the neighbourhood appointed to watch should first, with the inhabitants of the Tower itself, have the oath tendered to them.[207]

How justified was the leadership's alarm about the parliament's provincial reputation? Statutes were the best evidence of constructive effort as Pym knew very well. He remembered to urge on 23 June that public bills should be speeded 'for the satisfaction of the kingdom'. The legislative achievement of the subsequent six weeks was in fact impressive.[208] Statutes could be regarded as bargaining counters with local communities, though D'Ewes was being absurdly optimistic when he declared that if the bills removing the prerogative courts and establishing the poll tax were passed together '£100,000 might be paid in by that night.'[209] The bill preventing the king from dissolving the parliament was particularly important in this respect. 'It will give infinite content to the kingdom', reflected Lord Wharton, 'in point of assurance of justice upon delinquents and also in point of credit for the raising of such sums of money as must defray the great arrears.'[210] The abolition of Star Chamber and High Commission was 'a blessing which should encourage men to pay poll money cheerfully', John Bodville told his uncle in North Wales. No one could mourn the prerogative courts, Rye's MPs told the corporation, since they were 'a terror to all men'.[211] Reassurances of this kind probably did something to allay the frustration which had developed in the country over the spring and early summer.

203 BL Harl. MS 163, fol. 544r; Zagorin, p. 225; *A Brief and Perfect Relation* (1641), p. 88.
204 Rushworth III, part I, 242–4.
205 *CJ* II, 159, 176, 201, 208, 214, 216; *LJ* IV, 319, 328–9, 333; Gardiner IX, 413.
206 *CJ* II, 230; *DO*, p. 323.
207 BL Harl. MS 164, fol. 879v.
208 Bodleian Rawlinson D MS 1099: 23 June; Zagorin, pp. 243–4.
209 BL Harl. MS 163, fol. 759r.
210 Staffordshire RO D1778/1i/19.
211 *Sussex*, p. 251; *Calendar of Wynn Papers*, p. 273.

If statutes passed to secure the liberties of the subject gave country gentlemen good cause for gratitude there were other aspects of the political situation which they may quite properly have regarded with alarm. There were a number of outbreaks of popular activism, such as fenland enclosure riots, during the summer, besides the scattered incidents of religious unrest which will be discussed in the next chapter.[212] It seems clear that a false impression of the intentions of a reforming parliament underlay some of these disorders. Fenmen near Bourne jeered at an order of the peers of 6 April which gave possession to Sir William Killigrew, saying 'if it had been an order of the House of Commons they would have obeyed it'. The riots in Windsor Forest in August and September undoubtedly reflected frustrated expectations: the Commons were told that the people had 'risen by scores and hundreds and set upon the king's deer . . . and killed some under pretence of the late statute for limiting the bounds of forests'.[213]

The overall provincial mood between June and September 1641 remains hard to assess. News of the main political developments – the army plot, the king's journey, disbandment, Root and Branch – certainly reached the gentry even of the most far-flung countries. But it was difficult for them to understand political events that were only explicable within the whole pattern of Westminster and Whitehall politics. In November 1640 there had been identity of mind and interest between MPs and their country neighbours; by the following summer they had in one sense drifted apart. Those who sat at Westminster had undergone the most intense political experience of their lives. Those left behind had pursued the usual rounds of administration, sport and hospitality: their preoccupations remained essentially local as they waited passively for the 'good success of the parliament'. In the north the repayment of billeting charges had become the outstanding political issue. Radnorshire gentry nagged Sir Robert Harley about the burden 'their country suffered from maimed soldiers. The Cheshire JPs chased the deputy-lieutenants for their accounts for military costs in the previous years. The west country hoped for the reform of the stannary court and action against Turkish pirates. The corporation of Worcester sought exemption from the Council in the Marches of Wales. Reading aldermen pressed on their MPs a bill about artificers and handicraftsmen.[214]

Even the best-informed provincial observers were inadequately equipped to grasp the full significance of each parliamentary report they

212 Bodleian Tanner MS 66, fol. 178; *Nicholas*, p. 78; *CJ* II, 252, 263–4, 269, 274, 281–2; Manning, pp. 122–38; below, pp. 111–14.
213 *LJ* IV, 428; BL Harl. MS 164, fol. 900v; 5047, fol. 81r; Manning, pp. 188–90.
214 *Buller*, p. 47; *DO*, p. 327; *CJ* II, 178, 180, 190, 194, 237; BL E 168 (14): *The English Post*; Loan MS 29/173, fol. 140v; Cheshire RO QS Book 9a, fol. 46r; S. Bond, editor, *The Chamber Order Book of Worcester 1602–50* (Worcester Historical Society, new series, VIII, 1974), pp. 47, 345; J.M. Guilding, editor, *Reading Records*, IV, 17.

received. They were often puzzled. After all they had not actually heard the emotive speeches of Pym and his closest allies. 'I wonder, I confess, that the papists do not appear to be of the party and confederacy', wrote Sir Baynham Throckmorton to Thomas Smyth on 14 June after he had absorbed the news of the army plot. ' 'Tis wondrous strange that businesses of expectation are carried out with so miraculous a justice and secrecy', remarked a correspondent from Ely on 1 August.[215]

The tendency of gentry and countrymen still to see Catholic conspiracy on an essentially local scale illustrates the gulf that had opened between Westminster and the provinces. The grounds for scares were often fanciful, like the Rye boys' story of armed men drilling in the fields in September 1640 and the Herefordshire gossip in November that as much meat was dressed at Sir Basil Brooke's house daily 'as three cooks can make ready and it is not seen or known who eats it'. What really frightened Protestants was the prospect of a Catholic gentleman becoming so mighty locally that he could exercise the implacable malice with which papists were credited and which was expected of them in unsettled times. Thus Throckmorton explained to Smyth on 14 June that Sir John Winter's possession of the Forest of Dean gave him 'the disposing . . . of 20,000 acres of ground to make a plantation of papists upon it and to have so great a power to command thereby over all that country'.[216] A few days before Nathaniel Stephens had presented a petition from the forest community against Winter for transporting arms, which rested on precisely this fear. Reports current in the Basingstoke district in August 1641 that the Catholic marquis of Winchester had arms for 1500 men in Basing House raised the same kind of alarm.[217]

The sense of impending national crisis which Pym had sought to maintain in London was missing in the localities. This was the mental vacuum which the Commons leadership sought to fill when they revived the project for a remonstrance. If the nation could not be bound by oath, it was all the more essential for it to be wooed. Lord Digby had proposed a remonstrance to the king in November 1640; Pym had something very different in mind in July 1641: a declaration to the people. On 3 August the committee of 24, which had discussed the remonstrance at intervals during April and May, was supplanted by a new committee of eight. The membership of the new committee proclaimed the seriousness with which Pym was now pursuing the scheme: it consisted of Culpepper, Earle, Fiennes, Hampden, Pym himself, St John, Strode and Vane.[218] Sir Samuel

215 Bristol RO 36074/136e; E 168(14).
216 *Sussex*, pp. 102–3; *HMC Portland* III, 67, 69; Bristol RO 36074/136e; Clifton, *Past and Present* LII (1971), 23–53.
217 Bodleian Rawlinson D MS 1099, fol. 38v; *CJ* II, 263.
218 BL Harl. MS 163, fol. 826; 5047, fol. 62v; H.L. Schoolcraft, *The Genesis of the Grand Remon-*

Rolle, Alexander Rigby and the lawyers Glyn, Maynard and Selden were subsequently added, but it was undoubtedly Pym who wrote most of the remonstrance, probably with some help from Holles. Its content was summarized on 11 August as 'how we found affairs in Church and state, what we have done, how the king left affairs at his going'. The committee, it seems, was working in two halves. Fiennes and Vane took charge of the draft on the state of the Church, while the rest of the members concerned themselves with political issues. Why the separate drafts were not brought into the House on 14 August, as it was announced they would be, remains a mystery. Presumably other preoccupations intervened. What is clear is that when the project was renewed in October a complete draft was known to be at hand with little more work to be done on it, since a single meeting of the committee was regarded as sufficient to update it before it was presented.[219]

The autumn redrafting of the Grand Remonstrance probably accounts for the last 34 clauses of the final document: this section begins with references to the second army plot and the Irish rebellion. Eight other clauses were evidently added during the November debates, while a further six were substantially enlarged. With these reservations, the Grand Remonstrance can be treated as a statement by Pym's circle of the political situation facing England in August 1641. The preamble takes us directly into the inner recesses of Pym's mind. The decision to issue the Remonstrance, it explained, arose from the persistence of 'abounding malignity and opposition in those parties and factions' which had brought calamities and disorders upon the nation. The Commons had devoted itself to 'the public peace, safety and happiness' of the realm but had been continually hindered in its work by the malignant party, who fomented 'jealousies' between the king and parliament. Thus the time had come for the country to be given a full explanation of 'the root and growth of these mischievous designs'. The Remonstrance was intended as a progress report, an agenda for action and a statement of common political aims: the restoration of 'the ancient honour, greatness and security of this crown and nation.'[220]

'The root of all this mischief', the Commons leadership found, was 'a malignant and pernicious design of subverting the fundamental laws and principles of government, upon which the religion and justice of this kingdom are firmly established.' The common principles through which the design was promoted were already familiar through Pym's speeches. Firstly there was the campaign 'to maintain continual differences and

---

strance (Urbana, Ill., 1902), p. 23; W.H. Coates, 'Some Observations on the Grand Remonstrance', *Journal of Modern History* IV (1932), 1–5.

219 *CJ* II, 251, 253, 294, 298; BL Harl. MS 5047, fol. 62v; *D'Ewes (C)*, p. 51; *HMCC*, p. 295.

220 Gardiner, *Documents*, pp. 205–6, but this is not complete. See BL E 181(2): *A Remonstrance of the State of the Kingdom.*

discontents between the king and his people upon questions of prerogative and liberty', in order that the malignants could commend themselves to the king and obtain the highest offices in the land. Secondly the malignants allegedly sought 'to suppress the purity and power of religion'. We have seen how the notion that a strong Protestant church was the best bulwark of the English state had long been at the heart of Pym's defensive mentality. Thirdly they sought to encourage those parties who appeared propitious to their ends, the Arminians and 'libertines', and to split the common front presented by their enemies, by enlarging the differences 'between the common Protestants and those whom they call Puritans'. We have seen how Pym's anger at the use of 'puritan' as a term of abuse for all zealous Protestants dated back to the 1620s. 'They have brought it to pass that under the name of Puritans all our religion is branded', Sir Benjamin Rudyerd had complained in November 1640.[221] Finally the malignants had done their utmost to disaffect the king to parliaments by giving them a bad name and by encouraging him to seek extra-parliamentary sources of revenue.

The Remonstrance opened with a bitter partisan account of the misgovernment of England between 1625 and 1638. The king's fiscal, foreign and religious policies were blasted. Much emotional capital was sought from the government's treatment of individuals, especially Sir John Eliot: 'his blood still cries either for vengeance or repentance of those ministers of state who have at once obstructed the course both of His Majesty's justice and mercy.' The rigour of the episcopal courts was dramatized by the allegation that many thousands of the 'meaner sort of tradesmen and artificers' had been impoverished by their vexations. Perhaps the most striking aspect of this section of the Remonstrance is its sense of a group of people at the last ditch in their struggle to preserve parliament's role in the constitution and the subject's liberties. They dated the conspiracy against which they were engaged to the year 1625, when the Jesuits, who were the 'predominant element', had begun to 'revive and flourish'. The story thereafter revolved around the activities of three parties, the Jesuits, the bishops and 'such ministers as durst suppress the liberties of the kingdom'. The abrupt dissolutions of 1625, 1626 and 1629 were landmarks; the disregard of the Petition of Right was the best proof of the faithlessness of the Caroline regime.[222]

The second section of the Remonstrance dealt with the climax of the papist conspiracy between 1638 and 1640. The malignant faction had three principal aims: government must be freed from 'all restraint of laws concerning our persons and estates'; papists and Protestants must be

---

221 Gardiner, *Documents*, pp. 206–7; Rushworth III, part I, 224; see also Clark, *English Provincial Society*, p. 326.
222 Gardiner, *Documents*, pp. 206–15; Russell, *Parliaments*, particularly pp. 230–2.

combined in doctrine, discipline and ceremonies, 'only it must not yet be called popery'; and Puritans 'must be either rooted out of the kingdom with force or driven out with fear'. This was the period when the Catholics became 'another state moulded within this state'.

The Treaty of Ripon and the calling of a new parliament was the first serious setback the conspiracy had suffered. The king had the Scots not Strafford or Laud to thank for it. Their invasion could be excused since they were 'restrained in their trades, impoverished by the loss of many of their ships, and bereaved of all possibility of satisfying His Majesty by any naked supplication'. They had committed no spoil. Only duty, reverence to the king and 'brotherly love to the English nation' had stayed them from advancing beyond Newcastle.[223]

Thus the remonstrance committee reached the task of justifying their own sitting. They began by recalling the euphoria of November 1640: 'at our first meeting all oppositions seemed to vanish, the mischiefs were so evident which those evil counsellors produced that no man durst stand up to defend them.' They stressed the difficulties they faced: a backlog of 15 years of 'evils and corruptions', the chaotic state of the royal revenue, two armies to be paid and a nation sensitive to fiscal burdens after it had been exhausted by 'burdensome projects'. Then they set out a factual account of the achievements of nine months. Although parliament had been generous with subsidies, it had secured relief from the massive scale of Caroline fiscalism. Evil counsellors had been 'quelled'. The instruments of arbitrary government had been removed. Most crucial of all the survival of the current assembly and the summoning of future ones was assured as a 'perpetual spring of remedies'.[224]

On the face of it this looked an impressive performance. But, as the Grand Remonstrance confessed, the business of reform was by no means complete in August 1641. This was most obviously the case in the sphere of religion. Bills against superstition, pluralities and scandalous ministers were high on the list of 16 priorities drawn up on 9 August, when the Commons attempted to obtain a commission to complete the legislative programme in Charles's absence. Other bills lost at his departure included the controversial one for abolishing the Council in the Marches of Wales and a bill about piracy. Two major topics specified in the Remonstrance as outstanding were the establishment of the king's revenue, which implied investigation of abuses in expenditure, and reform of the law.[225] Awareness of this mass of unfinished business, which one commentator reckoned required the rest of the year, is evident in proposals for new bills during the

---

223 Gardiner, *Documents*, pp. 215–21.
224 *Ibid*, pp. 221–3.
225 BL Harl. MS 5047, fol. 60v; *CJ* II, 247–8; *HMC House of Lords MSS* XI, nos. 3514, 3530; Gardiner *Documents*, pp. 223–4,.

last weeks of the session. Fiennes for example, wanted a bill 'to assert our votes touching the canons'. Hampden prompted calls for another bill by his vehement criticisms of the 'indiscreet and vain' expenditure of sheriffs on feasting judges at assizes.[226]

If the legislative achievement was less than satisfactory, neither had much progress been made with the judicial campaign against evil counsellors. The committees met every now and then to work on the cases against Bishop Wren and Bishop Piers of Bath and Wells. John Pyne's judgement, in a letter to Thomas Smyth on 17 December 1640, that a 'speedy despatch of examinations' might deliver Somerset from Piers's tyranny within weeks appeared naive in retrospect. A move on 12 July to hasten the trials of Sir George Ratcliffe and Laud came to nothing.[227] The previous week the Commons had asked the Lords to set a date for the impeachment of Judge Berkeley, the most notorious of the six judges who had been bound over in December. They had also sent up the charges of crimes and misdemeanours against the other five men. This was an occasion for bitter speeches. Holles pictured the Commons delegation as having come 'to stand upon Mount Ebal, to curse these judges, to denounce a curse upon them who have removed our landmarks, have taken away the bound stones of the propriety of the subject, have left no *meum* and *teum*.' For all these brave words it had become plain that the difficulties of translating accusations into proof were insurmountable, even if full use was made of the theory of treason employed in Strafford's trial.[228]

The same difficulties in proving they had committed treason hindered vigorous prosecution of the army plotters, who appeared a more serious threat. The decision to charge Suckling, Percy and Jermyn with high treason on 12 August came after a long and contentious debate in which several influential lawyers like Bridgeman, Holborne and Selden had argued that there was no case to answer. Little further progress was made. The political necessity of charging the plotters was obvious to those who shared the leadership's preconceptions. 'If we do not punish this great offence we should draw on other rash adventurers', declared Robert Goodwin. George Peard thought the conspiracy had been 'a higher and more wicked plot' than the Gunpowder treason.[229] Just as in Strafford's case though, the political campaign was too blatant for a good many members. Pym found himself boxed in by the legal scruples of his colleagues. What was worse, John Selden dared to suggest on 25 August that the army plot was wholly 'pardoned and abolished' by the general

226 *CSPD 1641-3*, p. 38; BL Harl. MS 163, fols. 797r, 805v.
227 *CJ* II, 157, 159, 168, 172, 189, 191, 193, 199, 208; BL Harl. MS 163, fol. 779v; Bristol RO 36074/139a; Trevor-Roper, *Laud*, pp. 409-11.
228 *LJ* IV, 303; Jones, *Politics and the Bench*, pp. 142, 209-15.
229 BL Harl. MS 164, fols. 831v, 832r; 478, fol. 890r; *CJ* II, 253.

oblivion in the treaty with the Scots.[230]

Much had to be left unsaid in the Grand Remonstrance. The leadership could hardly tell the nation the true story of the promptings of conscience, genuine divisions and failures of nerve within parliament that had made the Ten Propositions a largely abortive policy. All the problems of the session had to be laid at the door of the malignant party. Evidence could be adduced for the assertion that the malignants had 'taken heart again' since their reverse the previous autumn. Some of their agents, it was alleged, had been given 'honours and offices'. Digby was almost certainly one of the recruits the committee had in mind. Difficulties in the prolonged negotiations with the Scots were attributed to the 'subtle practices' of the malignants to incense the Scots and parliament against each other. The army plot showed that the malignants had even laboured to corrupt MPs. Finally, and most obviously, the bishops and popish lords had consistently hindered the prosecution of delinquents and the passage of reforming legislation.[231]

Pym's alarm and fear for the future in August 1641 cannot be accounted for simply in terms of the failure of the Long Parliament to complete a huge programme of reform measures in nine months. For him statutes had been at best a sop to backbenchers and the country, at worst an irrelevance. The legislative achievement in fact gives a misleading impression of parliament's mood. No one was conscious of a constitutional revolution in the summer of 1641. As one historian has put it, legislative triumphs 'which a year earlier would have had men dancing in the streets were now largely meaningless'.[232] The two most vital bills, for disarming recusants and the militia, had failed. No remedy had been found to the machinations of evil counsellors and papists. The state was hopelessly vulnerable to the next manifestations of the conspiracy. All the leaderships' hopes had come to rest on the survival and credit of the parliament. This at least was an issue appropriate to a declaration to the people.

The most illuminating section of the Grand Remonstrance concerns the parliament's reputation with the king and his people. We know how apprehensive Pym and his allies were about this. 'He would have care taken that none should carry such tales unto Whitehall as was daily done in prejudice of the parliament', Essex told colleagues in the Lords on 14 June. Pym announced on 8 August that one of the reasons for sending commissioners into Scotland was to 'take off scandals that have been spread there and in both armies'. The Remonstrance defended parliament against two charges which the committee believed were central to the malignants' campaign of slander. The first was that parliament had acted in its own interest rather

230　*Evelyn*, pp. 75, 78; BL Harl. MS 164, fol. 869.
231　Gardiner, *Documents*, pp. 224, 227.
232　Kenyon, *Stuart England*, p. 129.

than the king's. The reply to this was that, on the contrary, parliament had indemnified Charles against a war wherein they were totally innocent to the tune of £1,100,000. Here the Remonstrance took on a shrill and neurotic tone. 'All that we have done is for His Majesty, his greatness, honour and support', insisted the committee, 'when we yield to give £25,000 a month for the relief of the northern counties this was given to the king, for he was bound to protect his subjects.'[233]

The second charge was that parliament had obtained from the king 'things very prejudicial to the crown both in respect of prerogative and profit'. This likewise was denied. Pym all along had declared that he was 'careful not to desire anything that should weaken the crown.' The case was argued with relation to four statutes. The Triennial Act, the Remonstrance shrewdly observed, need never be enforced if the king summoned parliaments at timely intervals. The act for the continuance of the present parliament, it was admitted, did seem to involve 'some restraint of the royal power in dissolving parliaments' but this was justified as an emergency measure without which MPs would have been forced to leave 'both the armies to disorder and confusion and the whole kingdom to blood and rapine'. Finally it was suggested that the profits accruing to the king from Star Chamber and High Commission were small and those from High Commission were in any case unjust.[234]

There were further aspersions which the Remonstrance sought to combat. It had a 'ready answer' for those who said the parliament had 'spent much time and done little, especially in those grievances which concern religion'. Observers should consider the 'long growth' of the national grievances that they had tackled, the determination of the delinquents they had pursued and the expenditure that faced them. A bright prospect was offered to those who grumbled about the burden of subsidies, heavier than that imposed by any former parliament, if they would but lift their eyes to the future. These charges would one day seem light in respect of the benefits that the nation would reap from a parliament that had devoted itself to constructive reform. Here was a note of unbounded confidence, a perception that the Long Parliament was bound to appear in retrospect as a turning point in England's history.[235]

Thus the Grand Remonstrance, as it stood in draft at the recess, was a skilful mixture of propaganda and sentiment, well calculated to evince sympathy and support. Its potential role in the country at large is obvious, but was such a declaration really necessary at Westminster and in London? Pym had certainly become vulnerable to the misunderstanding of those who did not accept the case for his policies and disliked the means he

233 BL Harl. MS 5047, fol. 57r; Bedfordshire RO J. 1384; Gardiner, *Documents*, pp. 224–5.
234 Gardiner, *Documents*, pp. 225–6.
235 *Ibid*, p. 226.

adopted. The myth of a small clique engaged in a conspiracy to overthrow monarchical authority was born during the spring and summer of 1641. A miasma of gossip and rumour already threatened the reputation of the parliamentary leaders. Their audacity provoked dislike. Many thought Strode wise because of his boldness of speech, Edward Nicholas noted in some jottings made about this time, which had 'drawn himself into the same conceit'.[236] Tales of their ambitions were exchanged. The most startling one, almost certainly without foundation, was that at a gathering at Mandeville's home in Kensington in August plans were made to seize the persons of the queen and her attendants. Essex, Saye, Wharton, Pym and Fiennes were among those said to have been at this meeting.[237]

Some were beginning to doubt and scorn Pym's alarmism. As early as 18 May there was a note of scepticism in Sir John Coke's account of the latest designs, which came to him 'from those that bear no good will to the Lord Strafford'. They had served well, he reflected, to keep the city 'in alarm against him'.[238] Men like Hyde, Falkland and Nicholas never became victims of the irrational fears of Pym's circle.[239] Sir Richard Cave, a newcomer to Westminster since he had only just been elected MP for Lichfield, informed Sir Thomas Roe on 20 August that he could find no grounds for the 'great jealousies and suspicions', though he expected attempts might be made to 'distrust such as will be frighted with pop-guns'.[240]

The best evidence that some wished to foster an interpretation of the session which reflected unfavourably on the Commons managers is the paper 'Queries to be decided by a Committee of the House of Commons', which was in circulation in August. It contained two principal accusations. First parliament was said to have kept the Scottish army in being to overawe the king. The implication, it was argued, might be that 'statutes enforced upon the king' were invalid. There was enough residual anti-Scots feeling in certain circles for this smear to damage Pym's reputation. The Norfolk recusant Sir Henry Bedingfield, for instance, discussing his fear of 'combustions in England and Ireland' in April, 'thereupon cursed the Scots as author of these troubles'.[241] The second charge was that the Protestation was an arbitrary act, which could not be imposed without the king's consent. It might, it was suggested, 'raise a sedition in pure zeal'. Here again, as we have seen, the anonymous paper was on promising ground. Other items in the list of queries included 'whether it be treason to be for or against the king?' and 'whether the subjects must rule the king or

236 BL Add. MS 31954, fol. 181r.
237 BL Harl. MS 6424, fol. 94r; *LJ* IV, 490; *D'Ewes (C)*, p. 353.
238 *HMC Coke*, pp. 282–3.
239 *Evelyn*, pp. 71–2; *Nicholas*, p. 72; *Wormald*, pp. 15–16.
240 *CSPD 1641–3*, p. 98.
241 *LJ* IV, 448.

the king the subjects?' The overall message behind the facetious format was that a particular faction, alleged to favour congregationalism rather than episcopacy, was determined to destroy the foundations of Church and state. Of course, the 'Queries' was a travesty of Pym's policies. But it was also an early indication of how effectively royalist propaganda could tug at men's sense of moderation and order.[242]

Above all it was the partisanship of Pym and his friends which was attracting unfavourable comment. They were regarded as a clique who expected unquestioning devotion and were merciless to their opponents. Thus Lord Cottington's withdrawal from public life was seen by one commentator as stripping himself to his skin to save his life: retirement from the mastership of the Court of Wards stopped the mouths of his 'greedy enemies'. The friendship of Pym's circle seemed to be becoming the prerequisite for a man's political safety.[243] Sir Ralph Hopton's petition against the earl of Manchester for bribery was opposed, Nicholas believed, because, though the offence was foul, he was protected on account of his son Mandeville's high reputation and 'his own industry in asserting the cause against Lord Strafford'. When Henry Burton was attacked for his pamphlet *The Protestation Protested*, Cromwell, Harley, Vane and others 'diligently attended the Committee to help this incendiary out of censure'.[244]

If little of this gossip made an immediate imprint on provincial opinion, an account by Sir Thomas Barrington of the mood of those he labelled 'malcontents' in Essex in September is nevertheless instructive. He found a 'strange tepidity' and 'needless scruples' about the execution of the ordinance for disarming recusants and recalcitrance among the poll money commissioners over the review of their accounts which the Commons had just ordered. He spoke of men's 'present spleen against some particulars'.[245] This evidence of resistance to Pym's policies in a county near London suggests that the reaction against his programme and methods was already finding local roots. Relief at the chance to get home may have distracted MPs from facing the political future, but the outlook was unquestionably bleak when parliament adjourned on 9 September. The recess came at last partly because of the plague, partly because with the news that the king had passed through the armies without incident a good many members relaxed their guard sufficiently to support a break.[246] The most important

242 *CSPD 1641–3*, p. 113; *D'Ewes (C)*, p. 327.
243 BL Add. MS 15567, fols. 30–1. This manuscript may have been written by Falkland, but it was certainly not the work of Mandeville as Zagorin suggests p. 207. See Crawford, p. 39n.
244 BL Add. MS 31954, fols. 182r, 185r.
245 Beineke Library, Yale University, Osborn Collection: Sir Thomas Barrington to Lord Howard of Escrick, 24 Sept. 1641. I am grateful to Professor Conrad Russell for drawing my attention to this document.
246 *CJ* II, 272; BL Harl. MS 164, fol. 870r; Gardiner x, 10.

outcome of the politics of November 1640 to September 1641 was that Charles closed his mind to negotiation and so did Pym. The defensiveness which lurks in every clause of the Grand Remonstrance had become a habit of mind among the parliamentary leadership, as the threat of popery and conspiracy became an ever more absorbing obsession. The less they trusted the king the more they wanted the future guaranteed. A strategy of pressure and persuasion had failed. Confrontation was established. It is at least arguable that an insoluble political crisis was bound to follow.

3

Episcopacy and the Liturgy

Never had any parliament any affair so great as this, which we call the bill of episcopacy . . . it is the great hope, or the exceeding fear of every man here and of all men abroad.

Sir Edward Dering in a speech to the House of Commons,
21 June 1641[1]

That which toucheth me to the quick at this time is the common prayer book.

Robert Abbott to Sir Edward Dering,
5 July 1641[2]

By your Majesty's timely moderation, you will put a bit in their mouths, who (upon a popular pretence of the relics of popery) cry down all that is of good order or decency in the Church.

Edward Nicholas to the king,
19 September 1641[3]

Controversy over the church was at the heart of the political debate before the civil war. With the relaxation of Arminian censorship, the institution of episcopacy was at once called in question and experimentation with forms of public worship became bolder and more widespread. Discussion of the future of the bishops and the liturgy focused men's minds on sensitive issues of authority and individual conscience. Between November 1640 and October 1641 the debate about religion became deeply divisive.

Alderman Pennington's presentation on 11 December of a petition against episcopacy 'with all its dependencies, roots and branches' was the most startling event of the first weeks of the parliament. Around 15,000 names were attached to it; about 1500 men accompanied it to Westminster, thronging 'the Hall and places thereabouts'. The petition had been formulated by the militant Puritans of the City. Pennington was its

---

1 *Dering*, p. 2.
2 BL Stowe MS 184, fol. 43v.
3 *Evelyn*, pp. 89–90.

organizing genius in the parishes around St Antholin's, where the Scottish Presbyterian Robert Baillie was lodging. 'The courage of this people grows daily, and the number not only of people but preachers who are rooting out of episcopacy', he reported excitedly on 2 December. The growing mood of anti-clericalism had been evident for some weeks. 'Our clergy', reported William Hawkins to the earl of Leicester on 5 November, 'begin to apprehend some danger seeing the people are so much bent against them'.[4]

The Root and Branch case was founded on the activities and attitudes of the Arminian episcopate. Twenty-eight articles dramatized the Arminians' iniquities in vitriolic language. Their imposition of a theological monopoly, their attacks on preaching, their encouragement of superstition and ritual which raised the expectations of the papists, their canons of 1640, the Book of Sports and their use of excommunication for trivialities were condemned; monopolies, impositions, ship money, the decay of trade and the war with Scotland, which threatened 'utter ruin', were all laid at their door. Episcopal government, the petition argued, was not *jure divino* but 'of human authority'; it was the cause of 'many foul evils, pressures and grievances to the people in their consciences, liberties and estates'; its abolition would make way for 'government according to God's word'.[5]

The provincial response to London's initiative was immediate. Kent and Essex led the way on 13 January and before the end of the month 11 other counties had joined them. Further petitions came in from Devon on 19 February, Lancashire and Nottinghamshire on 21 April, Lincolnshire on 27 May and Oxfordshire on 27 July. Somerset trailed the rest the following December.[6] Southern and eastern counties predominated, but as the map opposite shows the midlands, north and west also chimed in. At York the mayor and aldermen set up a committee on 24 January to consider whether the city should petition against episcopacy 'as Kent and other places have done'.[7] Since 19 counties issued specific demands for Root and Branch, it is appropriate to speak of a national petitioning campaign.

The atmosphere of expectation generated by the earliest fast sermons undoubtedly gave the campaign momentum. Stephen Marshall and Cornelius Burges began on 17 November with sermons that lasted seven

4   *D'Ewes (N)*, pp. 138–9; BL Add. MS 11045, fol. 135r; Manning, p. 5; Baillie, pp. 275, 288; Pearl, pp. 212, 230–2; *HMC De L'Isle and Dudley MSS* VI, 339.

5   Rushworth, III, part I, 93–6. For the extent of doctrinal Arminianism and sacramentalism among the parish clergy in the 1630s see N.R.N. Tyacke, 'Arminianism in England in Religion and Politics 1604–1640', Oxford D. Phil. thesis, 1968, pp. 251–9.

6   *D'Ewes (N)*, pp. 249, 282–3, 375; *CJ* II, 67, 89, 124, 226; BL Harl. MS 163, fols. 80r, 625r, 797r; Sloane MS 1467, fol. 146r; 669 f 4 (9).

7   YPL House Books 36, fol. 53r.

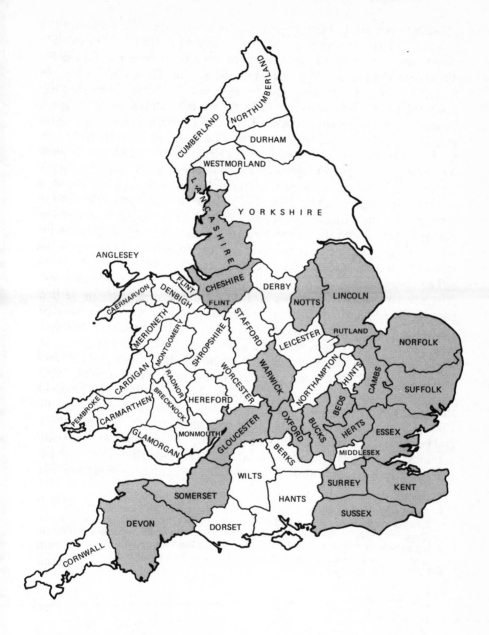

Map 1: Counties that petitioned parliament for the abolition of episcopacy during 1641.

hours between them. They argued that the Arminians were attempting to reverse the Reformation and bring back the yoke of Rome.[8] A newsletter noted how they pressed the Commons 'to go courageously forward'.[9] Thereafter the temper of participants varied, but all intended to rouse hatred of Archbishop Laud and his associates. Whereas John Gauden delivered an abstract and eirenic dissertation on 'truth and peace', Samuel Fairclough was more sanguinary.[10] Thomas Knyvett was one of those who enthusiastically reported these sermons. His comment is instructive: 'I go to church now to learn the old way to heaven'.[11] The message was anti-Arminian; there was a call for zeal. Yet Marshall, Burges and others were not yet openly calling for Root and Branch like the radicals of the London parishes who organized the December petition. It seems probable that the men who set the national campaign in motion came largely from outside parliamentary circles altogether: Kentish Puritans were circulating a copy of the London petition early in December and petitions were alleged to be in hand in several other counties before it was presented.[12]

The provincial campaign was essentially an anti-Arminian one. Arminianism had shattered the peace of the Church, dislocating the settled pattern of religious life. Bishop Bridgeman's drive for conformity in Lancashire and Cheshire had come as a shock to Puritan clergy and laity who had previously been leniently treated.[13] The dioceses of Bath and Wells and Ely had suffered severely at the hands of Bishops Piers and Wren. Ely was plagued with the fiercest visitation in living memory, based on a questionnaire comprising 147 articles. The city of York had endured the vigorous Arminianism of Archbishop Neile.[14] Gloucestershire's Bishop Goodman was accused in 1641 of being an enemy to all preaching and godliness.[15] In Hertfordshire Sir John Lambe had forbidden afternoon sermons; in Norfolk Clement Corbett had campaigned against conventicles and lectures; in Suffolk Thomas Eden had enforced Wren's orders

---

8 *DO*, p. 4; P. Christianson, 'From Expectation to Militance: Reformers and Babylon in the First Two Years of the Long Parliament', *JEH* XXIV (1973), 226–8; J.F. Wilson, *Pulpit in Parliament* (Princeton, 1969), pp. 36–46; E.W. Kirby, 'Sermons before the Commons', *American Historical Review* XLIV (1938–9), 531–3; H.R. Trevor-Roper, 'The Fast Sermons of the Long Parliament', in *Religion, the Reformation and Social Change* (London, 1967), pp. 297–303.

9 BL Add. MS 11045, fol. 144v.

10 *HMC Various* II, 259.

11 Larking, p. 25.

12 BL Add. MS 11045, fol. 135r; W.M. Lamont, *Richard Baxter and the Millenium* (London, 1979), p. 216.

13 Morrill, *Cheshire*, pp. 19–20; J.S. Morrill, 'Puritanism and the Church in the Diocese of Chester', *Northern History* VIII (1973), 150–4; R.C. Richardson, 'Puritanism and the Ecclesiastical Authorities: The Case of the Diocese of Chester' in Manning, editor, *Politics, Religion and the English Civil War*, pp. 3–33.

14 W.M. Parlmer, editor, *Episcopal Visitation Returns for Cambridgeshire* (Cambridge, 1930), pp. 72–6; *D'Ewes (N)*, p. 143.

15 *D'Ewes (N)*, p. 352.

for setting up altars; in Essex Robert Aylett had striven to eliminate Puritan sermonizing and congregational activities; in Nottinghamshire Edward Mottershed had achieved a remarkable degree of outward conformity by tightening up the presentment system.[16] By and large the counties which produced Root and Branch petitions were those which had received the firmest imprint of Arminianism.

Moreover the same counties mostly had some kind of Puritan tradition. The deep roots and abiding strength of Kentish and Suffolk Puritanism are well known. Laud showed his awareness of the Kentish tradition in his reports to the king between 1633 and 1639 and in 1634 he named Bedfordshire as the 'most tainted' part of the diocese of Lincoln.[17] In several cases there had been previous signs of opposition to the Arminians. The Hertfordshire grand jury had presented Laud's altar policy as an innovation.[18] Puritan JPs in Sussex had taken matters into their own hands, using quarter sessions to challenge Bishop Duppa; in Buckinghamshire Puritan magistrates had obstructed episcopal officers.[19]

Thus the involvement of Puritan gentry like Sir Philip Parker, Sir Oliver Luke, Sir William Masham, Sir Thomas Hutchinson, Sir Thomas Pelham and Ralph Assheton in the petitioning campaign was predictable.[20] But Sir William Brereton was probably the only leading figure whose commitment was based on much knowledge or heartsearching. He had visited churches of several denominations in the Netherlands and had also taken notes about the Presbyterian system in Scotland.[21] The rest may not have thought deeply about Church government or have had any constructive plans in mind for filling the void that would be left by the abolition of episcopacy. Besides the whole campaign, so radical in its declared aim, was in a sense very traditional. Arminianism was a particularly bitter grievance; the petition was the customary form of complaint. Therefore the appearance of men like Sir Arthur Capel and Thomas Chicheley in the ranks of the knights of the shire who rose to present Root and Branch petitions is less surprising than it might seem. These two men were both

16 BL Add. MS 11045, fol. 137v; Ketton-Cremer, pp. 62–88; Holmes, pp. 17–19; *D'Ewes (N)*, pp. 234–5; B. Levack, *The Civil Lawyers in England 1603–41* (Oxford, 1973), p. 178; R.A. Marchant, *The Church under the Law* (Cambridge, 1969), pp. 195–202.
17 Clark, *English Provincial Society* , pp. 149–84; P. Collinson, 'Magistracy and Ministry: A Suffolk Miniature', in R. Buick Knox, editor, *Reformation, Conformity and Dissent* (London, 1977), pp. 70–91. Laud, *Works* v, part 2, 318, 325, 331, 336, 346–7, 355–61.
18 BL Add. MS 11045, fol. 135v.
19 *Sussex*, pp. 92–3; Johnson, pp. 42–4; *Records of Bucks* VII (1892–6), 101–3; E.R.C. Brinkworth, 'The Laudian Church in Buckinghamshire', *University of Birmingham Historical Journal* v (1955–6), 31–59.
20 *D'Ewes (N)*, pp. 249, 282–3; Keeler, pp. 261–2, 268–9, 295; *Hutchinson*, pp. 16–17; R.C. Richardson, *Puritanism in North West England* (Manchester, 1972), p. 127.
21 Morrill, *Cheshire*, pp. 24–5.

Straffordians; both were of a conservative cast of mind. It is hard to see either of them as a convinced rooter.[22] But none regarded their role as curious when they presented their county petitions, since at that stage religious polarization had hardly begun. In the first months of the Long Parliament everyone agreed that reform of the Church was essential, while few had yet come to grips with the complexities of the Root and Branch issue.

Sir Edward Dering's adoption of a Kentish petition which was pressed on him by a group of wealden constituents shows how patronage could take place without total commitment. A man determined to make his mark at Westminster, Dering was impulsive by nature and thus susceptible to the persuasions of the radical cleric Thomas Wilson. Yet he thought the London petition too shrill and excessively long, so he wrote a new version that was shorter and milder. Its concluding request suggests that he was still open-minded early in 1641 about the bishops' fate. He may well have intended to be deliberately ambiguous: 'that this hierarchical power may be totally abrogated, if the wisdom of this honourable House shall find that it cannot be maintained by God's word and to his glory'. He could not approve of everything in the Londoners' petition, Dering told the Commons, but he found 'the greatest part so well grounded' that his heart went 'cheerfully along with it'. Later, defending himself against those who attacked him as a turncoat, he insisted that he had always been for 'most severe reformation' but had never professed himself for Root and Branch.[23] This was probably true.[24]

The potential divisiveness of the London petition was stressed by the elder Vane on the day it was presented. 'Take care that our divisions bring not worse evils than papists', he warned. Yet no one could gainsay its significance. D'Ewes believed that it was 'the weightiest matter that ever was yet handled in the House'.[25] In the interval before the petition was fully debated on 8 February 1641 contradictory rumours circulated. 'It is thought bishoprics to be brought to that pass as they shall consist merely *de spiritualibus* or otherwise no bishops at all', wrote one correspondent in January. Another thought the office would probably survive but the Arminians would be punished. Radicals watched the progress of the county petitioning movement with eager interest. More petitions earnestly praying that episcopacy may be utterly abolished were daily expected, Lord Andover told Thomas Smyth on 7 January. He was anxious to make local soundings: 'pray let me know what sense you have in the country

---

22 Keeler, pp. 126, 133.
23 Larking, pp. 19, 27, 38–42; Everitt, pp. 59, 62–3; *Dering*, pp. 1–2.
24 See below, pp. 255–6. D.M. Hirst, 'The Defection of Sir Edward Dering 1640–1', *Historical Journal* xv (1972), 196; W. Lamont, *Godly Rule* (London, 1969), pp. 83–8.
25 *D'Ewes (N)*, pp. 139–40; Northcote, *Notebook*, pp. 51–3; S. D'Ewes, *Autobiography* II, 254.

of these things', he asked in a postscript, 'and whether Somersetshire prepare any petition or no.'[26]

During December and January the controversy over Root and Branch took shape. The political implications of the issue began to emerge. 'Here will be the fountain of good or evil', declared Howard to Smyth, 'for I am credibly informed His Majesty can never consent to it and then it must necessarily put us all upon desperate courses.' There was consternation when the king confirmed his determination to defend the bishops in a speech to both Houses on 25 January. According to D'Ewes it 'filled most of us with sad apprehensions of future evils, in case His Majesty should be irremovably fixed to uphold the bishops in their wealth, pride and tyranny.'[27]

Two letters from John Pyne to Thomas Smyth, dated 17 December and 2 February, show how the Londoners' petition moved in six weeks from the edge to the very centre of one experienced country member's view of the parliament. Pyne was an impetuous man of strong convictions. On 17 December he was preoccupied with the Somerset campaign against William Piers, 'this notorious bishop'. He only mentioned Root and Branch in passing. By 2 February the bitter anti-Arminian had become a convinced rooter. 'The consideration of the opinion that episcopacy would come into debate', he informed Smyth, had given the Bridgewater by-election new importance. Pyne was anxious that 'an assured serviceable good member should be placed there', which meant Smyth, who was in fact elected, or his friend Robert Blake, rather than Sir Thomas Wroth, who Pyne thought 'would prove but disserviceable unto the public'.[28]

Interest in the outcome of the Root and Branch petitioning was undoubtedly intense and there were signs that tempers would rise. On 2 February, when the Commons investigated the attitude of some leading divines to the remonstrance subscribed by 750 clergy against Arminian theology and government, a conservative speech by Sir John Culpepper 'gave offence to many'. The remonstrance, which was not a specifically Root and Branch document, had been presented by Sir Robert Harley on 25 January. 'The heat in the lower House increases', noted Coke, reporting this debate. The 'high points' yet in debate and undetermined, Pyne told Smyth that day, 'will require great consideration and time, especially episcopacy which hath so many advocates and so strong a party in our House.'[29]

26 *Trevelyan Papers*, part III, 203; *Archaeologia Cambrensis* VI (1875), p. 202; Bristol RO 36074/137b.
27 Bristol RO 36074/137b; *D'Ewes (N)*, p. 281; *LJ* IV, 142.
28 Bristol RO 36074/139 a, b.
29 *HMC De L'Isle and Dudley MSS* VI, 365–6; *D'Ewes (N)*, pp. 277, 313–5; *HMC Coke*, p. 272; Bristol RO 36074/139b.

In the event the debate on 8 February was not as passionate as might have been expected. It was long, lasting at least eight hours and including contributions from some 60 members; it was also highly confusing, since positions taken up on the actual question at stake, whether the London petition should be referred to the committee on the ministers' remonstrance, tended to divert attention from the main issue. A large range of viewpoints on procedure concealed a much larger range still on the future of Church government. A few rallied to Digby's call for the House to reject the petition out of hand: George Fane, William Pleydell and John Selden for example. The largest group wanted it committed, either to the committee on the ministers' remonstrance or to the committee of the whole House; but this group included men like Sir Ralph Hopton and Harbottle Grimston who were firmly opposed to a Root and Branch solution. Others wanted to keep the petition before the House but had not decided where they stood. The determined and open rooters at this stage were a tiny minority, consisting of Nathaniel Fiennes, the younger Vane, Oliver Cromwell, John Pyne, Alderman Pennington and possibly a few leading figures in the county petitioning movement.[30]

The debate on 8 February was so incoherent that S.R. Gardiner's claim that 'two parties stood opposed . . . on a great principle of action' will not stand up.[31] Nor does Baillie's version of it as a premeditated attempt by an episcopal faction to rid the House of the London petition seem entirely convincing, though the case for episcopacy was certainly put much more strongly and repeatedly on 8 February than the case against it.[32] The general effect of the set speeches for the bishops by men like George Digby, Harbottle Grimston, Viscount Falkland and Sir Benjamin Rudyerd was undoubtedly sobering. They strengthened the mood Coke had detected a few days before, when he observed that supporters of the bishops were increasing: 'I doubt most are for their reformation only'.[33]

The resumed debate on 9 February was more bitter. The rooters tried to sway the House by having the Gloucestershire and Hertfordshire petitions read; the episcopalians, led by Sir John Strangeways, sought in reply to 'have the question of episcopacy put', confident that with a tide in their favour they could dispose of the matter once and for all. The emotional temperature was rising when Sir Francis Seymour proposed the compromise, gratefully accepted by MPs, of referring the London petition to a committee but reserving the actual question of episcopacy to the House. The function of the two days' debating had been to clarify an emerging

---

30 *D'Ewes (N)*, pp. 335–8; Shaw, pp. 23–6; D.M. Wolfe, editor, *Prose Works of Milton* (New Haven, 1953) I, 69; Clarendon I, 247–8, 309.
31 Gardiner IX, 281.
32 Baillie, p. 302.
33 Rushworth III, part I, 170–4, 183–7; *HMC Coke* II, 272.

factional situation. The division on whether new members, including Vane and Fiennes, should be added to the committee of 24 which was to consider the petition was seen by many as a vote for or against the small but assertive Root and Branch faction. The close result − 180 to 145 in favour of the rooters − indicated that, although many backbenchers were doubtless still bewildered and undecided, a polarizing process had begun.[34]

For some weeks after the February debate the rooters trimmed their sails to the wind, intending, as Baillie put it, 'to take down the roof first to come to the walls'. During a month of lengthy sessions, some of them attended by citizen petitioners and clerical remonstrants, the committee hammered out a programme of action based on common ground.[35] Although a few members showed 'great opposition', the House voted against the legislative and judicial powers of the bishops on 10 March; there was unanimous backing for the following day's resolution against clergy sitting on the county Benches or in Star Chamber. Thus, despite Sir Edward Hyde's obstruction, the bill to end the secular employments of bishops and clergy and exlude them from the Lords had an easy passage. It was sent to the Lords on 1 May.[36] But it may well be, as Hyde later alleged, that some reluctantly kept silent, seeing the bill as a minimum concession to the rooters and to the Scots.[37]

Anger with the Lords, rather than any desire to comply with the Scots who were pressing for conformity in Church government between the two nations, seems to have provided the main impetus behind the growing anti-episcopalianism of late May.[38] The rooters had failed to carry the House when they attempted to get the question of Church government taken first in the debates on the treaty with the Scots. But when it became clear that the peers refused to entertain the exclusion of the bishops many rallied to them. 'Now the Commons do all resolve to root them out root and branch and stick as close to it as ever they did to my lord of Strafford's business', related a newsletter on 25 May.[39] He hoped to hear soon of the 'turning out the bishops altogether', wrote Sir Baynham Throckmorton to Thomas Smyth on 14 June, 'since now there is no other remedy for cure of the disease'. According to another account, such friends as the bishops had in the Commons began 'more and more to fail them' at the end of May. The Chester MP Sir Francis Gamul expected that the growing animosity against the bishops at this time would destroy them.[40]

34 *D'Ewes (N)*, pp. 339–42; Shaw, pp. 29–42; Gardiner IX, 282.
35 Baillie, p. 307–8.
36 *D'Ewes (N)*, pp. 424, 452, 458–9, 464–73; BL Add. MS 36828, fol. 51v; Shaw, pp. 46–61; Zagorin, p. 237.
37 Clarendon I, 310.
38 *CJ* II, 148; Gardiner IX, 379–83; Crawford, pp. 48–9.
39 BL Sloane MS 1467, fol. 38r, 3317, fol. 21v; Devon RO 1700A/CP 19; *DO*, p. 109.
40 Bristol RO 36074/136e; BL Sloane MS 1467, fol. 81v; Morrill, *Revolt*, p. 41.

The rooters' choice of Dering to present their short and uncompromising Root and Branch bill on 27 May was a tactical move, intended to allay the suspicions of moderate backbenchers. Hyde noted his 'levity and vanity', which made him 'easily flattered by being commanded'. The presentation of Lincolnshire's Root and Branch petition provided an apposite moment. Necessity had driven them to it, Dering argued, emphasizing his reluctance to abandon all hope of reform by reviving 'the primitive, lawful and just episcopacy'. His was in no sense a committed Root and Branch speech.[41] But a second reading was achieved that day, after some fierce debating, by 139 votes to 108.

Then came the real battle on the question whether the bill should be sent to committee. William Pleydell demanded provocatively that the bill should be committed to the fire. Hampden, Strode, Holles, Pym and D'Ewes, who urged that the ensuing debate should be calm and rational, wanted the bill to go to committee. Falkland and Hyde, besides Pleydell, opposed them. The previous December D'Ewes had reverenced 'godly, zealous and preaching bishops'. Now he answered Pleydell's charge that the bill subverted religion and peace by insisting that both would 'continue the better though this bill pass'. Another member who announced his conversion was Sir John Wray, who had earlier prized a good Cranmer, Latimer or Ridley.[42] The bill was a last resort, he said, all other means of reforming episcopacy having failed. It would act 'as a vomit' to the bishops. The king was now bound to abolish a system of government upheld merely by ignorance and 'an unreasonable and evil custom'. The Ipswich burgess William Cage delivered a speech along the same lines, asserting that 'our bishops had well near ruined all religion amongst us'. His rhetorical appeal to MPs' sense of their responsibilities may have done much to sway the House. He feared God was angry with them 'for neglecting his service too long': if episcopacy remained intact at the end of the session 'certainly we do nothing, for as we should have a care of making of the peace and disbanding the army, so we must have a care of body and soul which so long have suffered under their government.'[43]

In the end the bill was referred to the committee of the whole House and debate was set for 3 June. The proposal came from Pym, the last speaker, and his words undoubtedly weighed most heavily. It was another instance of his assertion of strong leadership with an uncanny sense of timing. Pym had been stung by Falkland's accusation that the bill was 'like the killing of men, women and children'. He set out to show that Root and Branch was far from being a negative solution, indeed that it involved a constructive programme for the Church: 'I would have care taken that all godly

41 Clarendon I, 314; *Dering*, pp. 63–4.
42 *DO*, p. 112; *D'Ewes (N)*, p. 140; *Speeches and Passages*, pp. 401, 403–4, 438–40.
43 BL Harl. MS 163, fols. 625r, 626r; 477, fols. 566–7; Shaw, pp. 78–81.

ministers may be provided for . . . and many other things there are which we must take into consideration which may be inserted into the bill.'[44] He struck the keynote of the debates that were to follow. Many of those who voted for Root and Branch on 27 May may have at first seen the bill primarily as a challenge to the Lords, a tactic designed to secure the passing of the bishops exclusion bill. Yet a crucial step had been taken in leading the Commons, a more volatile and emotional body on this issue than any other, towards the radical objective.

The Lords had voted after a 'long and serious debate' on 24 May that the bishops should retain their places in the House. Whereas 25 peers were ready to exclude the bishops on that occasion, 30 to 40 voted on the other side together with 10 bishops who were present. Viscount Saye and Sele and Lord Brooke were probably the only two peers vehemently opposed to the institution of episcopacy at this stage. The argument that the exclusion bill was a presumption which boded ill for the future of the House as a whole certainly weighed heavily. On 8 June the peers reconsidered the bill and because the rooters among them insisted that its minor clauses could not be taken separately the House rejected it at the third reading by a solid majority. Powerful speeches on behalf of the bishops had been made by the earls of Arundel and Dorset. A newsletter of 2 June explained the bishops' dilemma. On the one hand, many argued that there was no way of preserving the office 'but by their voluntary yielding of their right in parliament'; on the other hand, to yield would be seen as 'a great step towards the abolishing of the whole order'. The king might regard it as an inducement to pass a Root and Branch bill, when he had 'an offer made him not of their revenues only but of the whole hierarchy'.[45]

Between 27 May and 11 June, when the committee stage of the Root and Branch bill was begun, it became certain that the episcopate provided a solid core of votes in the Lords which would block all measures of thorough-going ecclesiastical reform. The leadership's response was to stress the alleged implication of the bishops in the army plot. Fiennes insisted in his report from the close committee on 8 June that they and the clergy 'did maintain 1000 horse for this purpose'.[46] John Barry had linked the two issues in a letter written on 31 May expressing the view that there would be a decision about the fate of the bishops within a few days, since 'much of the business of the state depends upon that'. The decision taken by the Commons leadership, at a private meeting on 10 June, to press the bill in committee the next day was based on a sensitive appraisal of the mood at Westminster.[47] A newsletter recounted how three times, on 3, 7

44   BL Harl. MS 477, fol. 567v.
45   BL Sloane MS 1467, fols. 72v, 76v–78v; Harl. MS 6424, fols. 70r, 71v; Clarendon I, 309, 312–13; Bedfordshire RO J 1383, p. 2; Crawford, p. 50.
46   BL Sloane MS 1467, fol. 95v; *LJ* II, 165, 167; Bodleian Rawlinson D MS 1099, fols. 38r–40v.
47   *HMC Egmont*, p. 136; BL Harl. MS 163, fol. 306v; Zagorin, pp. 202, 239.

and 10 June, members had crowded the chamber expecting the committee stage, but the full House 'being for the vantage of episcopacy, the enemies thereof purposely avoided the question' and let those who cried for the treaty or money to take priority have their way.[48] Meanwhile more backbenchers showed their hands in the House or in correspondence. John Coventry and Edward Partridge, who wished the bill put off till Domesday, emerged as episcopalians. The Welsh MP John Bodville spoke passionately in favour of the bill on 3 June: 'we could not expect any fruit of our endeavours except we first cleanse the House of God'.[49] Sir Ralph Verney wrote approvingly of the idea of abolition, 'if it be desired', to the countess of Sussex on 7 June. An ugly scene that was just averted that day may have given Pym a hint that a tide was running in his favour. John Griffith's peroration in favour of the bishops was interrupted by members who called him to the point; when he replied offensively they began to cry him to the bar.[50] By Thursday 10 June Fiennes's revelations had sunk in and the Lords were known to be adamant. The time was ripe for a surprise move. It was so successful that even D'Ewes was caught unawares. Expecting no initiative until after the weekend, he was taking the Westminster air when he heard that the bill was being discussed. He went scurrying to his lodgings to collect his notes.[51]

The Root and Branch debates between 11 June and 3 August were long and sometimes wearisome. On 27 July a newsletter reported that the bill, already 20 sheets, had been the principal business of the previous week; by August it had grown to 40 pages.[52] No copy of it as it stood on 3 August has survived, but its main provisions can be reconstructed from the *Commons Journals*, parliamentary diaries, diurnals and newsletters. Episcopacy was to be replaced in two stages: a synod of divines was to devise the new form of Church government which the Commons intended should be established by 1 March 1642; in the meanwhile parliament was to take all ecclesiastical jurisdiction into lay hands and proceed with a massive redistribution of the Church's financial resources.[53] On paper it may all have looked deceptively simple. From 1 August all writs for ecclesiastical affairs were to be directed to nine commissioners in each shire, chosen by its parliamentary delegation. The county commissions were to have power to coopt in the case of the death of serving members. Clergy who attempted to retain their jurisdiction would incur a *praemunire*. The lay commissioners, who would be quorate with five attending, were given virtually 'the whole power which the bishops hold'. 'We shall have nine lay bishops for one

---

48 BL Sloane MS 1467, fols. 96r, 98r; *CJ* II, 159, 165–6.
49 BL Harl. MS 163, fol. 665r, 477, fol. 586r.
50 *HMC 7th Report*, p. 435; BL Harl. MS 478, fol. 624.
51 BL Harl MS 164, fol. 1014; Shaw II, 82.
52 *CJ* II, 173–234; *Dering*, pp. 3–4, 119.
53 *HMC Coke*, p. 288; BL Sloane MS 1467, fol. 17r.

consecrated', commented an opponent of the scheme.[54] The only limitations were that five clerical deputies were to ordain and act in certain
matters of heresy and schism; and neither they nor the lay commissioners
were to exercise powers of excommunication, which, together with the
death penalty for heresy, parliament reserved to itself.[55] The lands of deans
and chapters, together with all impropriations and advowsons belonging
to bishops, were to be managed by feoffees, whereas the rest of the bishops'
lands were to go to the king. Reasonable maintenance was to be reserved
for the episcopate and the cathedral clergy during their lives.[56]

In retrospect it is not so much the simplicity but the staggering boldness
of the bill which impresses. Yet the rooters carried the House with them
and, if other matters had been less pressing, the committee stage might
well have been completed before the recess and the bill presented to the
Lords. How can their triumph be explained? In the first place the timing
was exact. The bill went through its first stages on the tide of anger at the
peers' rejection of bishops exclusion and during the tedious committee
stage the exodus of MPs from London was accelerating. Secondly the
ground was well laid. In a series of sermons preached to them between 4
April and 20 June, MPs were subjected to a spate of radical propaganda.
Preachers like Henry Burton, whose sermon *England's Bondage and Hope
of Deliverance* set out the case for a Church based on 'that which Christ
hath set up in his word', certainly made a significant contribution to
preparing parliamentary opinion for Root and Branch.[57] John Moore took
extensive notes on Burton's sermon at the back of his diary of the
Commons's proceedings.[58]

Not that any of the sermons directed the Commons towards the interim
solution they subsequently formulated; indeed there was an enormous gulf
between their thinking and that of ministers like Nathaniel Holmes, who
urged MPs to build the new Jerusalem in a congregational way. Holmes
looked for the purity of the 'particular corporation' of gathered saints; they
sought a national Church and a system of social and moral control.[59] But
the preachers communicated a sense of apocalypticism and put Root and
Branch in the context of the popish conspiracy. The chiliastic note was
heard inside the Commons in June from the younger Vane:

> That which I assure you goes nearest to my heart is the check which we seem to
> give divine providence if we do not at this time pull down this government. For
> hath not this parliament been called, continued, preserved and secured by the

54 Bodleian Tanner MS 66, fol. 110r; BL Sloane MS 1467, fol. 19v; *DO*, pp. 288–9; Gardiner IX,
    408.
55 Verney, *Notes*, pp. 104–5; *DO*, p. 290; BL Harl. MS 5047, fols. 30r, 41r.
56 *CSPD 1641–3*, p. 49; Shaw I, 90–7.
57 Wilson, *Pulpit in Parliament*, pp. 43–52, 256, 275–80.
58 BL Harl. MS 478, fols. 728–35.
59 *JEH* XXIV (1973), 232–5.

immediate finger of God, as it were, for this work? Had we not else been swallowed up in many inevitable dangers by the practices of these men and their party?

With the army plot revelations heightening the House's sense of urgency, it is hard to overestimate the impact of these words. The day Vane spoke D'Ewes declared that God had not blessed the bishops exclusion bill 'because we did our work by halves'.[60] The same note is to be found in the correspondence of parliamentary families. Hearing a rumour that the Root and Branch bill was passed, Thomas Harley wrote excitedly to his brother on 21 June 'which I hope is true for the Lord hath a time when he will root them out and I believe this is the time'.[61]

The hallmark of the interim scheme embodied in the Root and Branch bill was its thoroughgoing Erastianism. As the bill evolved it became more and more blatantly a bid for power by country gentlemen. On 21 June Sir Edward Dering's plan for 'an old primitive constant presbytery' of around 12 clergy was swept aside in favour of Vane's proposal for commissioners chosen equally from among laity and clergy.[62] The subsequent removal of the clergy and reduction of their role to a minimum indicates the strength of support for lay initiative and control. According to one account, ministers would even be 'censurable before the lay commissioners' for their preaching.[63] The House was not impressed by William Pleydell's reiteration of the argument that laymen could not exercise spiritual functions. D'Ewes told him scornfully that 'every grown man' knew that anyway much of the scope of ecclesiastical jurisdiction was by ancient common law only triable in the lay courts. John Selden's firm insistence that laymen might act in the Church courts seems to have clinched the matter.[64]

The county delegations assumed that they and their friends would staff the commissions. Indeed the Lancashire MPs were so eager to go into action that by 14 July they had agreed upon the composition of the county's commission, which was to include six of their own number.[65] The procedure for appointing ordination committees enabled the lay commissioners to ensure that the task was given to men dependent on their patronage. It neatly fitted the provincial pattern of social relationships between Puritan gentry and divines and the tradition of local recruitment into livings.[66] The gentry wanted no check on their power. Thus the

60 BL Harl. MS 163, fol. 694r; Nalson II, 276–9; Shaw I, 85–7.
61 BL Loan MS 29/163, fol. 115r.
62 Rushworth III, part I, 293–6; *DO*, p. 157.
63 BL Sloane MS 1467, fol. 20r.
64 BL Harl. MS 163, fols. 776, 777v; 479, fol. 794r; Shaw I, 95.
65 BL Harl. MS 479, fol. 800v, misunderstood by Gardiner IX, 408.
66 *Sussex*, pp. 72–3; Richardson, *Puritanism in North-West England*, pp. 115–52.

Commons threw out Hyde's proposal from the chair that appeals should be allowed from county commissioners to the two commissions which were to be set up to execute the archiepiscopal jurisdiction of Canterbury and York.[67]

But there was much more than self-interest involved in the backbench support for the Root and Branch bill. It was after all highly constructive. Settlement and order, reform and renewal, were the prospects it offered. 'For piety', declared D'Ewes on 27 July, 'we know the way to maintain it is to abolish whoring, swearing and drinking and to increase preaching and praying.'[68] By taking over, rather than abolishing, the Church courts MPs looked for moral reform. By their control of ordination they hoped to improve the qualifications and standards of the clergy. The role of the commissioners, announced Vane on 21 June, would be to advance deserving men and turn out others.

The House's purposefulness is particularly evident in the decision about deans and chapters. Members recalled the arguments they had heard on 15 May between the representatives of the deans and the Puritan divines who debated before them. Burges had attacked the cathedral men for their failure to preach. What good books had they written, he asked? How much had they done for learning? 'There were other places', he declared, 'as well as they which send forth as good scholars, as at Eton and Merchant Taylors school'. The cathedrals had long been seen as 'dens of loitering lubbers'.[69] George Peard suggested that they should provide the solution to the problem of paying off the armies in the north, since, he calculated, £900,000 might be raised by letting the lands for 21 years and three lives.[70] Rumours that cathedral lands would be diverted to secular uses had been current for some months. But few Puritan members could in conscience support a proposal like Peard's, tempting though its acceptability to many of their constituents might be. By the decision on 15 June to reallocate the resources of cathedrals, they sought instead to achieve an adequate maintenance for all the clergy. There were plans for giving special attention to poorly maintained chapels of ease in the vast parishes of the Pennines and to other livings worth under £100.[71] No wonder moderates like Sir Benjamin Rudyerd, who called on 11 June for reform and purging rather than 'innovation, demolition or abolition', were brought into line. No wonder radicals like Stanley Gower in Herefordshire, labouring in a

---

67 BL Harl. MS 163, fol. 723.
68 Ibid, fol. 798r. See my article 'Concern for Renewal in the Root and Branch Debates of 1641', in D. Baker, editor, *Studies in Church History* XIV (1977), pp. 279–86.
69 BL Sloane MS 1467, fol. 39v; Harl. MS 477, fol. 520–2; *CJ* II, 144–5; Shaw, pp. 54–9; C. Cross, 'Dens of Loitering Lubbers' in D. Baker, editor, *Studies in Church History* IX (1972), 321–7.
70 BL Harl. MS 477, fol. 517r.
71 BL Stowe MS 184, fol. 29r; Harl. MS 5047, fols. 30r, 40v, 41r.

county almost bereft of preachers, responded enthusiastically. The scheme, he told Sir Robert Harley on 9 August, 'would get bishops down with ease and acclamation'.[72]

As the interim scheme for Church government was elaborated the ground was steadily cut from under the episcopalians' feet. Edmund Waller's call for a 'causeway of earth and stone' before the bishops were removed, lest sectarianism should 'overflow all the grounds', was answered; so was Sir John Culpepper's demand for an aristocratic rather than democratic form of government.[73] The committee stage was a masterpiece of parliamentary management. Admittedly invitations to dinner at Pym's lodgings and earnest discussion during a ride in the fields between Westminster and Chelsea with Nathaniel Fiennes failed to convert Hyde, but neutralized in the chair he was nothing like as successful in obstructing the bill as he later alleged.[74] Taking the bill piecemeal and voting it clause by clause at the end of each day's debating was brilliant tactics. The debates were very long and by each evening only the most committed were left, which occasioned Falkland's celebrated remark that 'they who hated the bishops hated them worse than the devil and they who loved them did not love them so well as their dinner.'[75] The episcopalians objected to the procedure but precedents for it were successfully maintained.[76]

The episcopalians retreated in face of a barrage of propaganda. Bishops had plotted treason since the days of St Augustine and had always opposed reform, insisted Oliver St John; they had ever been anti-monarchical, argued Holles; they were enemies to parliament, said Sir John Clotworthy; they had trampled on the laws of the kingdom and stopped the fountains of justice, declared Haselrig. Vane contributed the papist smear: their soil was Rome, 'the planters the spirit of Antichrist, the nature of the tree from the fruit'. Fiennes was bitterly anti-clerical, painting the episcopate as 'prejudicial to the honour of the nobility and gentry'.[77] By July Pleydell fought on almost alone. But as early as 11 June he had been laughed at, when Sir Neville Poole interrupted him to request translation of the lengthy Latin quotations he was reading from the bible in his hand. Sir John Culpepper relapsed into pleas for the unfortunate cathedral men thrown out of their livings. Sir Edward Dering later printed a speech against the bill which he said he had intended to make at the third reading, but meanwhile he was silent. A motion by Sir John Evelyn on 21 July that the House should be called before the bill was read, that it might 'pass in a full House', was rejected since he was foolish enough to propose it during

72 Nalson II, 300; *HMC Portland* III, 79.
73 BL Sloane MS 1467, fol. 101r; Bodleian Rawlinson D MS 1099: 11 June.
74 Clarendon I, 362–3.
75 BL Harl. MS 478, fol. 650v; Clarendon, *Life* I, 90–1.
76 BL Harl. MS 478, fol. 651r.
77 Bodleian Rawlinson D MS 1099: 11, 12 June; BL Harl. MS 478, fols. 646v, 650v, 653v, 655r.

the reading of another bill.[78]

The day before the recess D'Ewes, who was so encouraged by the progress of the Root and Branch bill on 28 June that he thought there was no need to specify a rating for bishops in the poll tax, reflected sorrowfully on the failure to complete it. Though much time and energy had been given to it, he observed, it 'had yet proved too great to pass out of these doors'. Administrative inertia was partly responsible for the failure to see the bill through. D'Ewes had seen the bill become bogged down in detail. The suggestion on 27 July that the disposal of cathedral lands should be fully set out in it, for instance, had irritated him since he realized that gathering information about revenues and inadequate livings would be a lengthy business.[79] The vigour was lacking among many county delegations, at this stage of the session, to nominate commissioners as they were told to do, let alone to initiate large-scale surveys.[80] But the principal reason the bill was not discussed after 3 August was probably that the month simply proved too hectic. The crisis of the king's departure for Scotland preoccupied the House. It forced immediate political considerations to the forefront of men's minds and kept them there, despite an abortive attempt, 'upon several motions', to revive the bill on 13 August.[81]

The rooters largely had things their own way in the provinces throughout the first session of the Long Parliament. The episcopalian response to the numerous Root and Branch petitions was meagre. The only petitions in favour of the bishops read in the Commons were the ones from Oxford and Cambridge universities on 11 May; by then tentative moves towards mounting similar petitions in London, Devon and Surrey had fizzled out.[82] The London petition, which had been 'much laboured' in the City in January when there were hopes of exceeding the 15,000 hands secured by the rooters, was apparently abandoned in February because its sponsors drew the optimistic conclusion from the two days of debating in the Commons that 'the function of bishops was like to stand'.[82] Only in Cheshire did the radical faction find itself faced at once with a vigorous and persistent antagonist. Sir Thomas Aston was an improving landlord, obsessively preoccupied with the preservation of social order, who had sat in the Short Parliament but lost his place in the autumn. He countered Sir William Brereton's petition to the Commons with an episcopalian one to the Lords, which was only read after long debate and stiff opposition from

78 BL Harl. MS 163, fols. 693v, 705v, 706r, 775v, 776r, 790r, 793v–794r; 478, fol. 649v, 673; *Dering*, pp. 119–61.
79 BL Harl. MS 163, fols. 745v, 797v; 164, fol. 913.
80 *DO*, p. 319.
81 *CJ* II, 255; BL Harl. MS 163, fol. 836r.
82 *CJ* II, 144; Baillie, p. 296; *D'Ewes (C)*, p. 291; *Buller*, p. 33; BL E 156 (22); *HMC, De L'Isle and Dudley MSS* VI, 371, 381.

Saye, Brooke, Paget and Mandeville.[83] Brereton was able to run rings round Aston at Westminster. He wrote a new county petition, simply doubling the totals of the various categories of Aston's supporters and he mobilized friends among the Cheshire clergy to mount their own petition discrediting him. Aston then overreached himself by sending parliament a new Cheshire petition without circulating it among the gentry at home. This provoked 48 of them to sign an 'Attestation' rebuking him for his temerity, which was presented to parliament by Peter Venables, Brereton's fellow knight of the shire, on 22 May. Thus though he had some supporters in Cheshire Aston was isolated in London; even the Lords ignored him.[84]

If it was not until the autumn of 1641 that a nationwide reaction to the dominance of the Root and Branch minority at Westminster made itself felt, an impression of their ruthlessness and determination nevertheless became established during the summer. A link between the Commons leadership and the London citizens was quickly assumed. 'The multitude will again press upon the Lords', wrote a commentator about the Root and Branch bill on 2 June, 'as they have done formerly in the case of mỹ Lord of Strafford and you know how ill a precedent to judge is club law.'[85] Another observer expected the City to prove 'as turbulent as on Strafford's cause'. He hoped 'they might not be frightened again here with a rabble of the base multitude', asserted Lord Saville in a heated exchange with Pym's men in the Lords on 14 June. 'They did not know any were feared by the multitude', he was told in reply. The author of the Straffordian tract *A Brief and Perfect Relation* suggested that the bishops who sought to persuade the king to pass the attainder by arguing that it would prevent the ruin of the kingdom were setting a dangerous precedent, since 'the next tumult will be against their liturgies, surplices and church ornaments'.[86]

Much more than episcopal government was at stake in 1641. This was why religious controversy became so intense. 'All the pulpits do now ring of the disorders of the clergy both in doctrine and discipline', reported one newsletter at the end of 1640.[87] From the reign of Elizabeth until the 1620s Puritan gentry and countrymen had been able to worship much as they pleased in their parish churches. Mangling and truncating of the prayer book service had largely escaped censure.[88] There were many in the House of Commons who had been stung by the Arminian attempt to enforce conscientious and exact observance of the prescribed liturgy. They

83 *CSPD 1640–1*, p. 528; BL Harl. MS 6424, fol. 43r.

84 BL Add. MS 36913, fol. 62; Harl. MS 477, fol. 546v; 2081, fol. 93; Morrill, *Cheshire*, pp. 44–53.

85 BL Sloane MS 1467, fol. 72v.

86 *CSPD 1641–3*, p. 16; Bedfordshire Ro J1384, P 3; BL E 417(19): *A Brief and Perfect Relation*, p. 93. I am grateful to Miss Sylvia Kingman for this reference.

87 BL Add. MS 11045, fol. 144v.

88 Collinson, *Elizabethan Puritan Movement*, pp. 356–71.

appreciated from their local experience the point of D'Ewes's story on 19 December about the aged Suffolk countryman who, comparing Bishop Wren's policy to Queen Mary's, declared that he had 'lived to see the old religion restored again'.[89] One did not have to be a rooter to do so and it was the anti-Arminianism of the Root and Branch petitioning movement, as we have seen, that gave it impetus. Thus there was general support for a campaign to reverse the liturgical innovations of Laud and his colleagues. In a symbolic gesture on 22 November MPs insisted that before they received communion at St Margaret's the rails should be pulled down and the table should be removed from its altarwise position.[90] Two months later a bill to remove altar rails and relics of idolatry was given two readings, but it was then lost in committee. The bill proposed an orderly scheme for abolishing the Laudian framework of worship: commissioners were to oversee the removal and sale of altar rails, giving the money raised to the poor; they were to ensure that all pictures and images in churches were taken down before Easter.[91]

The Commons did not pause to assess the probable reaction to these initiatives. There had been a number of incidents of the people violently destroying altar rails in Hertfordshire and Essex the previous summer. Some needed no urging to continue the process. John Tombes, for example, explained to Sir Robert Harley that he turned the communion table at Leominster as early as December 1640, 'hearing of the proceedings in the House of Commons concerning altars and the Laudian canons'.[92] By January 1641 rails were being removed parish by parish in London and several counties. 'Altars begin to go down apace and rails in many places', wrote Anna Temple from Warwickshire to her daughter in Sussex. Much of the stained glass in the Oxford college windows had been 'pulled down voluntarily', reported the earl of Leicester's solicitor on 14 January, 'and the altars turned into tables and stand east and west'.[93] The Staffordshire Bench heard on 23 March about 'malignant persons' who had destroyed the rails at Wolverhampton and moved the table from the chancel into the nave. The removal of rails at St Warburg's, Chester and the nearby village of Neston was reported the following month. A dramatic and symbolic burning of the Latton altar rails by a group of servants and apprentices occurred in Essex. William Skinner, one of those involved, told a JP that he had pulled the rails out of the church 'because they gave offence to his conscience and that the placing of them was against God's laws and the

---

89 *D'Ewes (N)*, p. 171.
90 BL Add. MS 36828, fol. 9v; *HMCV*, II, 259–60; Crawford, p. 46n.
91 *CJ* II, 79, 84; *D'Ewes (N)*, p. 356; BL Add. MS 36828, fol. 37v.
92 *CSPD 1640–1*, pp. 69–70, 140; Essex RO QSR 311/46 (I am grateful to Mr James Sharpe for this reference); J.S. Cockburn, editor, *Crime in England 1550–1800* (London, 1977), p. 105; *HMC Portland* III, 76; *Diary of John Rous*, p. 99; Gardiner IX, 176.
93 Baillie, p. 293; East Sussex RO Dunn MS 57/54; *HMC De L'Isle and Dudley MSS* VI, 364.

king's . . . and because the rails had been pulled down in other places without punishment'.[94]

The explosiveness of the liturgical issues quickly became evident. Much more was involved than the spontaneous destruction of altar rails. On 10 December the Lords heard about a disturbance in the Essex market town of Halstead, when the prayer book was kicked up and down the church and the curate's surplice was torn from him and rent in pieces. On 16 January they considered the case of some baptists of St Saviours, Southwark, who maintained that they only owed civil obedience to the king. The strength of the London separatist community had been evident four years previously when it contributed significantly to the great popular demonstration in favour of the Puritan martyrs Bastwick, Burton and Prynne. In the interval the government had failed to break the separatists' organization and will. As the weakness of the Laudian regime became plain during 1640 they grew bolder. On 22 October a meeting of the Court of High Commission, which had summoned certain leading separatists, was broken up. A few days later a mob ransacked St Paul's looking for the High Commission's records.[95]

By December 1640 the increasingly confident sectarian challenge to the established Church was producing anxiety. Edward Kirton opposed the commitment of the Root and Branch petition because he thought there might have been Baptists among the petitioners. William Pleydell commented bitterly, in the same debate, about pamphlets and sermons 'utterly subverting the foundations of truth'. Ferdinando Lord Fairfax wrote in March that he hoped the House would leave the liturgy alone 'which many shoot at'. 'I pray most humbly to God for the Church's safety from innovation', wrote Viscount Cholmondeley from Cheshire, where Samuel Eaton was expounding a full separatist condemnation of the Church of England.[96] From Kent, where separatist congregations had multiplied in the 1630s, Robert Abbott warned Dering on 15 March about the new expectations of sectaries who 'stick not only at our bishops, service and ceremony but at our Church'.[97]

During the spring and summer of 1641 there was a growing awareness of how religious radicals were threatening social and political order. It was not simply that the London citizens were seen as providing the motive

---

94　Staffordshire Ro Q/SR, E 1641, fols. 11, 12; BL Add. MS 36914, fols. 211, 224–5; Essex RO Q/SBa 2/41; Morrill, *Cheshire*, p. 36.

95　*LJ* IV, 107, 133–4; Gardiner IX, 215, 266; M. Tolmie, *The Triumph of the Saints* (Cambridge, 1977), pp. 46–8; *HMC De L'Isle and Dudley MSS* VI, 339.

96　*D'Ewes (N)*, p. 337; Rushworth III, part I, 186–7; *Fairfax* I, 180; BL Add. MS 36914, fol. 199; Morrill, *Cheshire*, pp. 35, 37; P. Christianson, *Reformers and Babylon: English Apocalyptic Visions from the Reformation to the eve of the Civil War* (Toronto, 1978), p. 199; Richardson, *Puritanism in North West England*, pp. 40, 137.

97　BL Stowe MS 184, fols. 27–8; Lamont, *Godly Rule*, p. 88; *Historical Journal* XV (1972), 202; Clark, *English Provincial Society*, pp. 370–1.

force behind the Root and Branch movement. From May to September the parliamentary pulpit was monopolized by divines like Nathaniel Holmes who expounded the possibility of the national Church being replaced altogether by gathered congregations. The millennial tone of this preaching undoubtedly alarmed some MPs. 'You have great works to do, the planting of a new heaven and a new earth amongst us', announced Stephen Marshall in his thanksgiving for the deliverance of God's people on 7 September. He was much less radical than Holmes but on this occasion he was ready to combine celebration with exhortations to MPs to continued tearing down Babylon and building up Zion. It was well known that both the preachers that day enjoyed the patronage of the earl of Warwick.[98] Another radical peer, Viscount Saye and Sele, had now been heard to argue that conscientious disapproval of the liturgy could provide a case for congregational separation. In a speech on 6 March that shocked many of his colleagues but was quickly printed, he suggested that the imposition of a set form of worship for all usurped 'the gifts and graces which Christ hath given unto men' and induced superstition: 'as if because some men had need to make use of crutches, all men should be prohibited the use of their legs'. Some began to blame parliament for encouraging radical citizens and countrymen to raise their hopes too high. Between December 1640 and the following spring the Commons committee for scandalous ministers received around 900 petitions.[99] 'The monstrous easy receipt of petitions makes authority decline', Sir John Danvers told its chairman Sir Edward Dering on 15 March, in a letter expressing his fears about 'orderly government' in Wiltshire. Robert Abbott wrote in similar terms from Kent.[100]

Parliament was kept constantly aware of the turbulence of sections of the London populace. In May a paper was set up at the entrance members normally used: 'The voice of God is the cry of the people; bishops the limbs of Antichrist and the plague of the kingdom; destroy them and take away Antichrist'. A few weeks later the Lords heard about the destruction of more altar rails in Southwark and about some Brownists who kicked the communion bread about St Olave's church, when the curate gave the sacrament to the parishioners kneeling.[101] Disorders reported from the localities were equally disturbing. At Sir John Culpepper's instigation, the Commons sent for a man who had delivered a paper to his minister telling him 'his function is Anti-christian, his church is no church'. At the end of July *The English Post* contained a despatch from Banbury about the town's

---

98 Christianson, *Reformers and Babylon*, pp. 204–21; Wilson, *Pulpit in Parliament*, pp. 43–53.
99 BL Harl. MS 165, fol. 1021r; 6424, fols. 44–5; E 198 (16); Larking, pp. 80–240; *CJ* II, 54.
100 BL Stowe MS 184, fol. 31r; Lamont, *Godly Rule*, pp. 87–91.
101 BL Harl. MS 6424, fols. 69v–70r, 72v, 73r; Sloane MS 1467, fol. 85r; Rushworth III, part I, 284; *LJ* IV, 270–1, 277–8, 295; *HMC 4th Report*, p. 74; Manning, pp. 33–4.

presumptuous sectarians who had 'an intolerable measure of the spirit amongst them'. A Dorchester correspondent complained in the same issue about the 'pestilent sects couched in London' and described the town's hopes for 'a pious reformation, not confusion in the Church or absolute abolition'. Even convinced rooters were unnerved. Stanley Gower wrote to Sir Robert Harley from Herefordshire on 9 August about Brownists there who 'discourage your reformation of our Zion'. He urged that the Commons should 'timely meet with this anarchy and confusion'.[102]

The most alarming development in London was the spread of mechanic preaching. This was publicized by John Taylor's *Swarm of Sectaries and Schismatics* which attacked the 'prating of cobblers, tinkers and chimney-sweepers'. The pamphlet's satirical woodcut of Samuel How, the most famous lay preacher of the Laudian decade, addressing his audience from a tub, made it instantly marketable. On 5 June Holles reported to the Commons that 'many shopkeepers and others took upon them to preach in the City'; two days later, when a horseman, a beavermaker and a customer were publicly admonished, it was revealed that one of their sermons, an hour and a half long, had attracted a crowd of 3000.[103] The horseman was John Spencer, once a coachman to Lord Brooke, who in October 1641 published a treatise defending himself against the evil aspersions cast upon him. The beavermaker was John Green. Such preaching, declared Holles, was against the honour of the House, 'as if instead of suppressing popery we intended to bring in atheism and confusion'. 'Divers spake and all disliked the practice of these men', noted D'Ewes.[104] Sir Henry Slingsby was disgusted that the men who appeared before the House 'thought so well of themselves, as they thought none so worthy as themselves'. Green boldly maintained that providence 'cast him upon the place' and that God had revealed to him 'the knowledge of his word in some measure'; Spencer insisted that he was 'able in Christ to preach'. D'Ewes suggested an act for 'severe punishing of tradesmen and other ignorant persons who shall presume to preach' but nothing was in fact done to check them.[105] In August the Venetian ambassador reported the spread of lay preaching and the appearance of women in the pulpits. One pamphlet claimed the discovery of women preachers in Cambridgeshire, Kent, Middlesex and Wiltshire. Another described the 'combustion' at St Anne's, Aldersgate on 8 August, when Marler the buttonmaker had to be dragged from the pulpit by the churchwardens. His sermon was ridiculed with the comment that he 'drew out his words like a Lancashire bagpipe and the people could

102 BL Harl. MS 478, fol. 689r; BL E 168 (14); *HMC Portland*, III, 79.
103 BL E 158 (I); Tolmie, *Triumph of the Saints*, p. 36; *CJ* II, 168, 170; Bodleian Rawlinson D MS 1099: 5 June.
104 Tolmie, *Triumph of the Saints*, pp. 26, 39; BL, E 172 (4): *A Short Treatise*; BL Harl. MS 163, fol. 662r.
105 *Slingsby*, p. 69; BL Harl. MS 165, fol. 1015; 478, fol. 627r.

scarce understand any word'.[106]

Whereas Spencer and Green had founded their own separatist congregations in 1639, many of the new lay preachers seem to have been individuals lacking congregational roots who harangued casually assembled groups of citizens. There was probably no massive increase in the number of fully organized separatist congregations in the capital during 1641. The meetings of the 17 lay preachers listed in *The Brownists Synagogue* varied from twice a week to fortnightly. These men attracted more or less regular congregations at published venues in the City. Their offence lay not so much in their separatism as in their social status and their determination to preach in public as 'chosen vessels of honour' inspired to show forth God's word.[107]

Confusion about the meaning of the religious clause in the Protestation added to the unrest of the summer. The clause had been a principal debating point on 3 May, when some MPs recognized that the declared intention of parliament to protect 'the true reformed Protestant religion, expressed in the doctrine of the Church of England against all popery and popish innovations' could be interpreted in various ways. Henry Marten wanted colleagues to unite themselves 'for the pure worship of God'. But some members 'who were more tender towards the Church', seeing 'some hint intended' against bishops and the liturgy, argued that 'the word discipline might be adjoined to the word doctrine'. They failed in this attempt to turn the Protestation into a bulwark against religious change and suffered a more significant defeat when the explanation of the religious clause of the oath was issued by the Commons on 12 May. The House had not meant to maintain 'any form of worship, discipline or government; nor any rites or ceremonies of the said Church of England'.[108]

Radicals were bound to take this explanation as an invitation to expound their own interpretation. Henry Burton did so anonymously in his *Protestation Protested*, the most notorious pamphlet of the summer. He argued that those who took the Protestation were bound by their oath to abolish the ceremonies and liturgy as well as the government and discipline of the established Church. We have seen how several MPs close to Pym, like Harley and Vane, sought to protect Burton's freedom to publish at the committee for printing. Indeed his pamphlet was saved from being burnt by their efforts. They had also managed to prevent it being read in the House as Pleydell wanted, knowing it would inflame anti-sectarian feeling. There was probably nothing that did the leadership more harm in July 1641 than its association with this radical propagandist whose brain, so the

---

106 *CSPV 1640–2*, p. 188; BL E 166 (I): *A Discovery of Six Women Preachers*; E 189 (6): *A True Relation of a Combustion.*

107 BL E 172 (32): *The Brownists Synagogue*; Tolmie, *Triumph of the Saints*, p. 35.

108 Verney, *Notes*, p. 67; BL E417 (19); *A Brief and Perfect Relation*, p. 89; *CJ* II, 145.

rumour went, was cracked. Burton's sermon at St Margarets was seen as an outright attack on 'organs, bishops and the liturgy'. He told MPs that England still lay under 'an Antichristian, Babylonian, Egyptian bondage'. More than one newsletter noted that many of the congregation were shocked and offended by his language.[109]

Burton had added fuel to the flames of controversy. John Geree the minister of Tewkesbury, was plain in his reply entitled *Vindiciae Voti* that the Protestation should not lead men to oppose the religion established by law. A correspondent into Norfolk commented favourably on Geree's tract, but it seems that many were left bewildered.[110] The minister of Sudbury was pleased when D'Ewes sent him a personal interpretation of the House's sense.[111] In Kent meanwhile the Protestation was used to justify attacks on the prayer book.[112] Some London youths used it to vindicate their burning of the altar rails of the church of St Thomas the Apostle. The lecturer at Newington in Surrey was so concerned at Burton's influence in his village that he proclaimed a protestation of his own to maintain ceremonies.[113]

Whereas by August solid progress had been made towards reforming Church government, the liturgical issues remained open and alarming. Worship and ceremonies seemed more pressing matters to MPs than episcopacy in the last weeks of the session. At the same time the claims of reform and of order were coming face to face. MPs were having to work out their priorities. Thus when Walter Cradock appeared before the House on 26 June to plead for the cause of preaching and godliness in Wales the response was divided. D'Ewes suggested that there should be a dispensation for people to travel to hear sermons outside their own parish in districts where there were few preachers. But the Welsh MPs Charles Price, a firm episcopalian, and William Herbert reported that Cradock had 'preached strange doctrines one of which was that Christ died like a slave'.[114] A curiously ambivalent order of the House of Commons on 8 August reflects the dilemma that was felt. Churchwardens throughout the nation were to remove rails and set communion tables in their traditional position. But the House 'doth likewise declare', the order went on, 'that they hold it fit that no man shall presume to oppress the discipline or government of the Church established by law'. This was the outcome of a long debate begun by Isaac Pennington, who called for a declaration

109 *CJ* II, 206; BL Harl. MS 163, fols. 775v, 776r; E 158 (14); Bodleian Tanner MS 66, fol. 109r; Bedfordshire RO J 1386, p. 2; Gardiner IX, 353; W. Haller, *Liberty and Reformation in the Puritan Revolution* (New York, 1955), p. 145; Christianson, *Reformers and Babylon*, pp. 200–1.
110 BL E 170 (9); Bodleian Tanner MS 66, fol. 95r.
111 BL Harl. MS 160, fol. 153.
112 BL Stowe MS 184, fol. 430; *Historical Journal*, XV (1972), 205.
113 BL Harl MS 163, fol. 707r; *CJ* II, 177; *HMC 4th Report*, p. 80; Manning, p. 34.
114 BL Harl. MS 163, fol. 740v; *CJ* II, 159.

against the Laudian altar policy. In the course of it Harbottle Grimston urged the Commons to deal severely with separatists like those at Colchester who brazenly insisted that 'our Church was not the true Church'. Three years previously Grimston's father had lectured the Essex grand jury, in his charge at the Chelmsford assizes, about ensuring the prosecution of those who failed to use the prayer book and about combating independency.[115]

As the end of the session came in sight the most important consideration to many Puritan MPs was achieving something. They dared not go home empty-handed. Their constituents had waited nearly ten months: D'Ewes stressed 'the hope and expectation with which we have all this time fed them'. Indeed he called for a declaration to the kingdom that, although the business of the armies had kept them from religious reform, it would be at the top of their new agenda in October.[116] Since bills in committee on pluralities, ceremonies and the sabbath could not be quickly completed, the solution adopted on 1 September was a general order intended to undo Laud's altar policy, eradicate innovations such as bowing at the name of Jesus, crucifixes, candles and images and enforce strict sabbatarianism. JPs and mayors were to report any who disobeyed to parliament when it reassembled. The order was an expedient. There had been hopes of achieving some of the same ends through legislation. Thus a bill had been read on 15 July for 'abolishing of the cross in baptism, the surplice, bowing at the name of Jesus, standing up at the gospel, *Gloria Patri* and etc.'[117]

But the matter did not prove so simple. The order frightened episcopalians like Sir John Culpepper and Lord Falkland; they had reached their sticking point. Unless it was accompanied by a declaration against 'such as did vilify and condemn the common prayer book established by act of parliament', Culpepper maintained, tumults might follow. Culpepper in other words saw the order as going beyond the anti-Arminian common ground. He had some cause for alarm. For the sabbatarian clause specified that ministers and preachers should be encouraged to give afternoon sermons on Sundays. Afternoon sermons, forbidden by Laud but so dear to Puritan hearts, were integral to the Puritan tradition of reform stretching back to the 1560s. Liturgical uniformity, a crux of debate since Elizabeth's reign, had become the central issue at stake. Between 1 and 9 September the Commons became more deeply divided over the wording of the general order than they had been at any stage of the session over episcopacy. Four votes taken in this period produced majorities ranging from six to eighteen; Edward Nicholas commented to the king on the

---

115 *CJ* II, 246; BL Harl. MS 164, fol. 816v; 478, fol. 872v; 5047, fol. 58r; Russell, *Parliaments*, p. 431.
116 BL Harl. MS 164, fol. 913.
117 Gardiner, *Documents*, pp. 197–8; Shaw, pp. 111–13; *DO*; p. 288.

'dissonance' in the House's proceedings.[118] On the one hand there were those who harkened to Culpepper's cry for order, on the other those who, as D'Ewes put it, desired 'a thorough reformation in matters of religion'.[119]

After two hours' debate on 1 September the conservatives carried the House with their view that the general order should contain a commitment to the integrity of the liturgy as it stood. They had touched a tender Puritan nerve. The freedom to adapt and abbreviate the liturgy was one which ministers had enjoyed largely unchecked until the rise of Arminianism. Was the nation now to be told simply patiently to tolerate the prayer book when, as D'Ewes reminded MPs, it included about 40 'material adulterations' inserted by Dr Cosin? William Prynne had listed a number of these alterations, including the omission of the clause in the collect for the royal family naming the king as 'the father of thine elect' and the rewriting of the Gunpowder plot prayer of deliverance so as to apply it to Puritans rather than papists.[120] A committee which had just investigated the matter reported that there was much in the prayer book never established by parliament but 'put in by the fancy of corrupted brains'. 'The preciser members', a newsletter noted, 'objected there were many things in the liturgy contrary to the word of God.'[121] One of these MPs was Oliver Cromwell, who spoke of passages which 'learned and wise divines could not submit to and practice'. The more radical Puritan MPs were horrified to discover that many of their colleagues were willing, in their dread of social disorder, to enforce an Arminian liturgy.

Thus the radical faction was forced on the defensive and given no option but to seek some escape for tender consciences through the wording of the addition. Pym, Harley and D'Ewes were balanced by Falkland and Culpepper on the committee responsible for formulating a new clause for the general order. The wording which emerged on 6 September was as follows: 'that none should condemn, abuse or deprave the book of common prayer to the actual disturbance of the divine service'. The key words in the furious debate on this clause were 'deprave' and 'actual'. If the radicals could get 'actual' retained, men would still be able, as Culpepper put it, 'to speak and preach what they would' against the prayer book, 'so as it came not to open force and blows'. If they could get 'deprave' removed, Puritans would be freed from the vexation of prelates who, according to D'Ewes, 'did make this word of so large an extent' that any criticism of the liturgy, however mild, was comprehended by it. They lost both votes.[122] Only a few weeks previously Pym and his associates had been able to bind the House

---

118 *CJ* II, 279–81; *Evelyn*, p. 86.
119 BL Harl. MS 164, fols. 888, 896r.
120 BL Harl. MS 164, fols. 888–90; 698gl: W. Prynne, *A Quench-Coale* (1637). I am grateful to Dr Nicholas Tyacke for drawing my attention to Prynne's pamphlet.
121 BL Sloane MS 3317, fol. 25v; Add. MS 11045, fols. 142r–143v.
122 *CJ* II, 278–81; BL Harl. MS 164, fol. 895r.

together, during the Root and Branch debates, and lead it in a radical direction. Now the tide was ominously turning.

Most seriously for Pym's leadership, the campaign to root out Arminianism and propagate Puritan reforms at the end of the session brought a major row between the two Houses. His allies in the Lords had never been as effective in the religious as in the political sphere, though they had probably done something to soften the harsh punishments dealt out by bishops and conservative colleagues to sectaries. Bishop Hall certainly accused Mandeville of condoning the Southwark disturbances in January 1641 and Bishop Warner of Rochester was angry that the sectaries escaped lightly.[123] When the Commons' general order was debated on 8 September the few radicals found it impossible to secure its acceptance. Their colleagues were cautious: they supported the removal of altar rails and also of images of the Virgin Mary, if they had been set up within the previous 20 years, but as for bowing at the name of Jesus they resolved that it should 'not be enjoined or prohibited to any man'.

Impatient with the way the peers were taking their text to pieces, the Commons went ahead with printing their general order.[124] This unilateral action was more than the conservative majority in the Lords could stomach. On 9 September they carried a motion, by eleven votes to nine, for publishing their order of 16 January that divine service should be performed 'as it is appointed by the acts of parliament of this realm'. In effect the House's stand was with Culpepper on the integrity and enforcement of the prayer book. Six peers – Bedford, Warwick, Clare, Newport, Wharton and Mandeville – entered their protestations in the Journal.[125] The Commons were desired to join in publishing the Lords' order, but they in turn were so incensed at this attempt by the peers to impose an opposite policy to their own that, so far from doing so, they published an explanation of their decision: they thought it 'unreasonable, at this time, to urge the severe execution of the said laws' and they expected the people 'quietly to attend the reformation intended'. Harley and the younger Vane would have gone further and made it plain that no order by the House of Lords could bind the nation without the Commons' consent. Whatever course he took Pym could not conceal the deadlock from the public. But before the session ended he at least managed to reverse his defeats over Culpepper's addition, since the general order was recommitted on 6 September on the grounds that the House customarily took a second look at matters which caused discord and dissatisfaction. When it reappeared

---

123 BL Harl. MS 6424, fols. 6v, 7r; C.S.R. Russell, 'The Authorship of the Bishop's Diary of the House of Lords in 1641', *BIHR* XLI (1968), 229–36.
124 *CJ* II, 283; *LJ* IV, 392; Steele, no. 1886.
125 *LJ* IV, 395.

two days later, Pym had mustered enough support to get the addition omitted.[126]

Copies of the Commons' general order were circulated nationally but enforcement depended on local initiatives. Men like Sir Robert Harley and John Hutchinson needed little prompting. Sir Robert Harley wrote peremptorily to the churchwardens of Leominster about the five crucifixes he noticed in the church and churchyard there.[127] John Hutchinson persuaded the minister of a church near his home, probably Colston Basset, to break the stained glass windows there showing Christ on the cross, the Virgin and St John and to blot out some 'superstitious paintings' on the walls.[128] Ralph Josselin recorded the removal of the stained glass at Earls Colne. The order gave lesser men the courage to demand reform: an Essex hundred jury presented churchwardens for failing to remove altar rails at the sessions on 5 October.[129] Certificates showing that communion tables had been returned to their traditional position came in from certain parishes, like Kingsland in Herefordshire.

But enforcement sometimes met a fierce response. The churchwardens' removal of a crucifix on the churchyard cross at Kidderminster provoked a minor riot; a Bromsgrove man later boasted that the stained glass there would have been removed had he not prevented it. There was a similar dispute in Gloucester. The struggle between Calvin Bruen and the subdean of Chester, who refused to take down the glass in the cathedral windows, was still not resolved the following March.[130] In at least four parishes of the city of London, as well as some country ones, there was determined resistance by ministers or churchwardens to the removal of altar rails.[131] At St Giles Cripplegate, certainly, and perhaps elsewhere, this resistance was not inspired by mere blind conservation or petty factionalism. Those who opposed the House's orders at St Giles maintained that the rails had been in position there for nearly 80 years and that they assisted 'more speedy administration of the sacrament'.[132] The Commons were in deep water once they sought to impose uniformity where custom was all important and diverging attitudes were long established. For example a good many who had no time for Arminianism sincerely believed that bowing at the name of Jesus was warranted by 'scripture and the practice of

---

126   BL Harl. MS 164, fol. 896; 5047, fols. 83v, 84r; *CJ* II, 281–7; Gardiner x, 14–17.

127   *Evelyn*, p. 83; *DO*, p. 368; *CJ* II, 289, *HMC Portland*, III, 80–1; Manning, p. 35.

128   Hutchinson, pp. 54, 303. I am grateful to Mr Michael White for advice on this point.

129   A. Macfarlane, editor, *The Diary of Ralph Josselin 1616–1683* (London, 1976), p. 12; Essex RO Q/SR 314/61.

130   *HMC Portland* III, 80; N. H. Keeble, editor, *Autobiography of Richard Baxter* (London, 1974), pp 38–9; *CJ* II, 461, 534; BL Harl. MS 480, fol. 180r; Cheshire RO DCC/14/68; *HMC 5th Report*, p. 350.

131   *D'Ewes (C)*, pp. 3, 5, 7, 17; *DO*, pp. 369–70, 374.

132   *DO*, p. 368.

the Church of England' and that it should therefore be left as a matter of personal choice.[133]

The recess committee of the Commons was vigorous in pursuing its reform campaign. According to Hyde any who failed to submit when summoned were made to attend 'from day to day to their great charge and vexation.'[134] This policy undoubtedly heightened tension in London, yet there was no chance of achieving complete obedience. They 'might have complaints enough from all parts', noted D'Ewes at the committee on 20 October, if they set out to deal with 'all those that had slighted our orders'. As early as 6 September there were signs of the trouble parliament was running into, when Alderman Pennington reported that a Moorfields alehousekeeper was taking out a case in Common Pleas against local officers who were seeking to enforce the clause on sabbath observance.[135]

The Commons' campaign was seen by many as an invitation to sectarianism and disorder. Edward Reed reported the distempered condition of London to Sir John Coke on 20 September: some of 'those that would have themselves thought to be most holy' had torn the prayerbook during a service at the Old Jewry and were threatening to pull out the altar rails, destroy the organs and deface the monuments in St Pauls. 'The Brownists and other sectaries make such havoc in our churches', wrote Thomas Wiseman on 7 October, 'by pulling down ancient monuments, glass windows and rails, that their madness is intolerable.' There was a report of women tearing the prayer books and surplices in Newcastle, while in Norfolk and Suffolk 'they say that if a bishop come into those counties they will hang him up in his lawn sleeves'.[136]

In a sermon at St Paul's Cross on 10 October, subsequently printed, Thomas Cheshire attacked the iconoclasm and irreverence of recent weeks. He was scathing about the Puritan insistence on extempore prayer and bitter about the vilification of the prayer book and the abuse of ministers. 'There goeth a Jesuit, a Baal's priest, an abbey lubber, one of Canterbury's whelps', he alleged, had become 'the ordinary language as we walk the streets'. Meanwhile the monuments of benefactors to the City were defaced and he had found a woman allowing her child to urinate on the communion table at St Sepulchre's. God was dishonoured by the preaching of cobblers, weavers, feltmongers, tailors, and butchers, who took it upon them to interpret his word. Pamphlets in defence of them containing all kinds of heresy were circulated and the *Protestation*

133 *CSPD 1641–3*, p. 134.
134 Clarendon I, 387.
135 *CSPV 1640–2*, p. 222; *D'Ewes (C)*, p. 17; BL Harl. MS 5047, fol. 80r.
136 *HMC Coke* II, 291; *CSPD 1641–3*, p. 134; BL Sloane MS 3317, fol. 27r; *HMC Portland* III, 80; F. J. Varley, *Cambridgeshire during the Civil War* (Cambridge, 1935), p. 32.

Protested, 'a most viperous prodigious piece of knavery', was still generally
available. Cheshire's sermon amounted to a comprehensive indictment of
the religious policy of the parliamentary leadership.[137] It exemplifies the
divisions opened by the attempt, in alliance with radicals outside parliament, to cleanse the Church of Arminianism. The events of September
and October greatly increased the apprehensions of those who already
doubted the leadership's priorities. In the long run, moreover, the open
dispute with the Lords proved especially damaging. 'The late cross
orders', reported Nicholas to the king on 27 September, 'are so distasteful
to the wiser sort, as it hath taken off the edge of their confidence in parliamentary proceedings.'[138]

The reaction against the policies of the radical Puritans and the division
between the two Houses of parliament gave the king a golden opportunity.
As early as 25 January 1641 he had made it clear that episcopacy was a rock
to which he would cling. In a speech to both Houses he was sharply critical
of those who 'more maliciously than ignorantly will put no difference
betwixt reformation and alteration of government'. He blamed them for
irreverent interruptions of divine service and tumultuous petitioning. But
he also stated on this occasion that he was keen to reform the Church and
bring it back to the model of 'purest times of Queen Elizabeth's days'. It
was at the king's prompting that the Lords had reprimanded the
Southwark sectaries a few days previously.[139] Charles probably also did
something to encourage Bishop Williams in his efforts during March and
April to stimulate a movement for moderate reform through a Lords
committee on religious innovations. There was certainly a solid group in
the Lords working during the summer to deflect the campaign for Root
and Branch. On 1 July they introduced a bill into the Upper House for
'regulating' Church government.[140] Secretary Vane seems to have hoped
that Bishops Williams and Usher might produce a working compromise.[141]
So presumably did the king, who expressed his continuing concern about
the Church in his interview with Sir Edward Hyde before he left for
Scotland. But he had shown no signs up to then of building a party on the
basis of the Church issue.[142]

It was Edward Nicholas, anguished at the way religious passions were
splitting the country, who galvanized the king into action.[143] On 19
September he spelt out a programme which he believed would unite the

137   BL E 177 (3): *A True Copy of the Sermon on 10th October;* Gardiner *X*, 29–31; M. Maclure, *The
      Paul's Cross Sermons* (Toronto, 1958), pp. 254–5.
138   *Evelyn*, p. 93.
139   *LJ*, IV, 142; *HMC Buccleuch* III, 408; Christianson in *JMH* XLIX (1977), 588.
140   BL Harl. MS 6424, fols. 45v, 54r; Shaw, pp. 65–75; Gardiner, *Documents*, pp. 167–79.
141   *CSPD 1641–3*, p. 40.
142   Clarendon, *Life*, p. 93; Gardiner IX, 387.
143   *CSPD 1640–1*, pp. 484–5.

nation. In the first place he emphasized the harm that was being done to the king's reputation by the imputation that he favoured popery. The time was ripe for 'some public assurance to the contrary', which could best be achieved by filling vacant bishoprics with men 'of whom there is not the least suspicion of favouring the popish party'. These recruits would bring Charles new votes in the Lords for the preservation of episcopacy, the fundamental bulwark of his monarchy. Secondly Nicholas recommended that the king should seek to conciliate those who chafed at the imperfections of the liturgy by declaring his readiness to see reform by the clergy and parliament, 'which will prevent those that (in a zeal without knowledge) seek to overthrow the good government and order wisely established in this Church'.[144]

The apostil to Nicholas's letter of 5 October shows that the king had grasped the constructive purpose of the episcopal elections. He had 'altered somewhat from my former thoughts to satisfy the times', he announced. For his promotions to York, Norwich and Carlisle, Charles chose three moderate defenders of the Church: John Williams, Joseph Hall and James Usher. He gave Salisbury to Brian Duppa, the tutor to the prince of Wales. The five new appointments, taken together with these promotions, could be seen as a declaration against Arminianism and in favour of sound Protestant churchmanship. Nicholas had mentioned two of the new men, Ralph Brownrigg and John Prideaux, as 'plausible persons' who would satisfy men's minds and 'settle their affections to Your Majesty'.[145] The king chose men he knew well and whose advice he valued. The previous January he had summoned Usher, Brownrigg and Richard Holdsworth for a discussion about episcopacy when the debate on the Root and Branch petition was imminent. Four of the men appointed were royal chaplains and Brownrigg had accompanied him to Scotland, after gaining favour at court by a sermon in June in which he spoke 'like a strict moderate son of the Church'.[146] Brownrigg, Prideaux and Holdsworth had all been members of Bishop Williams's reform committee in the spring. Brownrigg, who went to Exeter, was a strict Calvinist but a champion of the liturgy; Prideaux, the new bishop of Worcester, also a theological conservative, was a tactful and impartial opponent of both radical Puritans and Arminians. Thomas Winniffe and Henry King, appointed to Lincoln and Salisbury respectively, were reputed to be mild and amiable. Holdsworth, who eventually refused the king's offer of Bristol, had been celebrated in his younger days as a moderate Puritan who preached with learning and eloquence. But his recent speech, as vice-chancellor of Cambridge, in favour of the existing state of the Church had alienated him

144 *Evelyn*, pp. 88–90.
145 *Ibid*, pp. 96–100.
146 *HMC De L'Isle and Dudley MSS* VI, 368; BL Sloane MS 1467, fol. 94r.

from radicals in the Commons.[147]

In an apostil of 18 October, the gist of which Nicholas circulated among the peers, the king said he would live and die for the Church. He had established a defensive standpoint.[148] Thus by the recess both the divisiveness of the religious issues facing parliament and their potential for party conflict were apparent. 'The schism between the Puritans and the Protestants becomes more and more evident', wrote the Venetian ambassador on 4 October, reporting the divided response of the people to the Commons' orders on worship.[149] On a few occasions in the first session diarists and reporters had slipped into discussing debates in terms of religious factions or parties. A writer in April, for instance, spoke of the 'precise party' when he was referring to the radical coterie in the Commons; another identified those in the Lords who sought to censure Sir Thomas Aston for his role in Cheshire petitioning as the 'zealous party'.[150] Occasionally an atmosphere of factional conflict had prevailed: in angry exchanges over Root and Branch on 27 May, D'Ewes was interrupted by 'divers who were for bishops' and encouraged with cries of 'well moved' and 'go on' from rooters.[151] Yet factional conflict had so far largely been contained. Emotional polarization had occurred nonetheless. The result was that schemes to reform Church government which sought to exploit the middle ground, and which on paper looked highly promising, had never been given a serious hearing in the Commons. Bishop Usher's plan combined presbytery with episcopacy, through the introduction of synods at each level from the province to the parish. Williams's plan was intended to ensure that bishops and cathedral clergy preached regularly and it also provided for the reform of abuses in the procedures of ecclesiastical courts.[152]

By October 1641 stalemate had been reached. Arminianism was virtually dead, since its episcopal champions were silenced and its most committed protagonists among the country clergy dared not risk the parliament's wrath. The ecclesiastical courts were grinding to a halt, since the act abolishing High Commission denuded them of coercive sanctions.[153] Yet county Root and Branch petitioning had ceased and the bill was in abeyance. There had been time for second thoughts but conservative opinion in the provinces had not yet crystallized.

The bitterness and determination left in the minds of both radical and conservative participants at Westminster were plain to see. For some

147 BL Harl. MS 6424, fol. 49r; M.H. Curtis, *Oxford and Cambridge in Transition* (Oxford, 1959), pp. 174, 225.
148 *Evelyn*, pp. 104–5.
149 *CSPV 1640–42*, p. 222.
150 Bodleian Tanner MS 66, fol. 50; BL Sloane MS 1467, fol. 26.
151 BL Harl. MS 163, fol. 625.
152 Shaw I, 65–75; *HMC 5th Report*, p 81.
153 *SR* v, 113; Zagorin, p. 243.

far-reaching reform of the Church remained paramount. Belief in the imminence of the millennium inculcated a drastic and sharply depicted view of the parliament's destiny. There were others – a growing number – who feared for the foundations of the state and society. By November 1641 many MPs probably shared the viewpoint of Sir William Drake, a normally silent Buckinghamshire scholar whose single printed speech, dated to that month, expressed the yearning for a middle way. There could be no peace, he declared, until some rule and uniformity was brought to the religious life of the nation, caught as it was 'in an uncertain condition between illegal innovations and superstitions on the one side and I know not what lawless and irregular confusion on the other'. It was natural for men to fly to extremes: held back for years by fear, they had now run into irreverence and 'contempt of God's public worship and ordinances'.[154]

From the moment the London citizens came down to Westminster on 11 December 1640, there was a current of alarm running against the demand for zeal. The elder Vane said that day he was 'scandalized that such a great number came'. The decision to seal up the roll of hands to the Root and Branch petition, 'that no man's name be seen', indicates the stunned reaction of MPs to mass intervention in their affairs. Presenting the Kentish petition a month later, Sir Edward Dering showed awareness of members' susceptibilities. His petition offered 'no noise, no numbers at your door'.[155]

Then there was Lord Digby's waspish attack on the manner of the London petition on 8 February. He called it a comet with a 'terrible tail' and beseeched the House 'not to be led on by passion to popular and vulgar errors'. 'What can there be of greater presumption', he asked, 'than for . . . a multitude to teach a parliament what and what is not the government according to God's word?' Isaac Pennington answered Digby: the petition was 'warranted by the hands of men of worth and known integrity'; it was presented without tumult; nothing had been done to 'rake up hands'; if some of the petitioners were of mean status 'yet if they were honest men there was no reason but their hands should be received'.[156] The conflicting pressures on MPs were sharply etched in this exchange. For radicals like Pennington association with men below gentry status was necessary and acceptable; for anyone who lacked his commitment of heart and mind Digby's smear was temptingly persuasive. Edmund Waller made Digby's point more fully on 17 May: 'if by multiplying hands and petitions they prevail for an equality in things ecclesiastical, the next demand perhaps may be *lex agraria*, the like equality in things temporal'. Waller's speech

154 BL E 199 (26); *D'Ewes (N)*, p. 117.
155 *D'Ewes (N)*, pp. 140–1, *Dering*, p. 19.
156 Rushworth III, part I, 170–4; *D'Ewes (N)*, pp. 335, 339.

was a direct attack on the methods of the radicals. His saw episcopacy as a 'counterscarp or outwork' of the whole political system which it was in the interests of all gentlemen to preserve.[157]

In the highly charged atmosphere created by the religious controversies that have been discussed in this chapter the subtleties of men's standpoints and the complexity of their views came to be ignored. Some men only objected to altar rails and candles, others went further and disliked surplices and kneeling; there was a large spectrum of opinion between those who merely wanted to do away with the Arminian innovations and those who aimed to rid the country of the whole Elizabethan liturgy. Lord Brooke's eloquent plea *The Discourse opening the Nature of that Episcopacy*, for instance, was an extreme statement, with its call for men to follow 'the ways of God's spirit'; so was Burton's apocalyptic pamphlet *The Protestation Protested*.[158] The parliamentary leadership was tarred with the views of these radical allies. Distinctions of viewpoint were not perceived and understood among those of conservative temperament and those prompted by social qualms.

Thus the stereotypes were formed. Just as the rooters dramatized the views of those who defended the Church, seeing them as ready to let in popery and condone immorality, so the episcopalians, clinging to the Church as the rock of order, were terrified by their own supposition that all radicals were at least potential separatists. When Nathaniel Fiennes told Hyde in the summer of 1641 that there were 'a great number of good men who resolved to lose their lives before they would ever submit' to episcopal government he was exaggerating the strength of his party. But in the long run his prediction 'that if the king resolved to defend the bishops, it would cost the kingdom much blood' proved correct.[159] During the summer and autumn of 1641 a new crisis within the parliamentary ranks became superimposed on the crisis of distrust between the king and the parliamentary leaders. There were political and constitutional issues involved in this second crisis, as we shall see, as well as religious ones. Yet religion was at the heart of it. The national debate about the Church was crucial to the process by which the political nation was becoming divided, the process which brought the emergence of two parties at Westminster and made civil war a possibility. This debate mattered so deeply to so many people that there was no question of its being halted. Two distinct patterns of thought can be detected among its participants: the keynotes were zeal and social conservatism. But men could not compartmentalize the religious questions that have been discussed in this chapter. By the autumn of 1641 the religious and political aspects of the overall national crisis seemed wholly intertwined.

157   BL E 198 (30); Sloane MS 3317, fol. 22r.
158   BL E 177 (22); W. Haller, *The Rise of Puritanism* (New York, 1957), pp. 332–8.
159   Clarendon, *Life* I, 91.

4

Parliamentary Factionalism

> Then Mr Hotham proceeded and showed . . . that if this were permitted in the House that anyone might make himself the head of a faction here, there would soon be an end of the liberties and privileges of parliament and we might shut up the doors.
>
> The journal of Sir Simonds D'Ewes,
> 24 November 1641[1]

> The said Mr Chillingworth being brought in again . . . the Speaker laid open to him the greatness of his offences, in reporting we had sides and parts in the House which was but one body, so to set a division amongst us.
>
> The journal of Sir Simonds D'Ewes,
> 4 December 1641[2]

Eleven weeks elapsed between the beginning of the recess on 9 September and the king's return to London on 25 November. They were weeks of persistent expectation of his coming and puzzlement at his failure to appear.[3] In a letter to the Lord Keeper, read in the Lords on 26 October, Charles excused his long absence and promised to return with all possible speed.[4] There was much speculation during September and October about the impact the king would make on the confused political scene. Many put their hopes in his presence. The earl of Bristol, writing to Sir Thomas Roe, reflected that the achievement of peace and quietness in the northern kingdom might be a 'good inducement' to the ending of England's distractions. Thomas Wiseman thought that if the people's hearts could be bent to the king, 'as they ought to be and as he deserves', the great distempers 'imminent to Church and people' might yet be composed. 'The general wishes are that the king were in England again', Sir John Coke told his father. Few were as gloomy as Edward Nicholas, who saw 'no hope but that we shall before long fall into a very great confusion if God be not extraordinarily merciful to us'.[5]

There were probably very few MPs, besides Pym, who took no holiday

1 *D'Ewes (C)*, p. 192.
2 *Ibid*, p. 234.
3 *CSPD 1641–3*, pp. 115, 125, 128; *HMC Coke*, pp. 292, 294; *DO*, p. 365; BL Sloane MS 3317, fols. 25r, 27r.
4 BL Harl. MS 6424, fol. 97v.
5 *CSPD 1641–3*, pp. 126, 128, 130, 134; *HMC Coke*, p. 293.

at all. Forty-seven men were nominated to the Commons committee appointed to meet twice a week during the adjournment. Sir Thomas Barrington reported in a letter of 24 September that 30 of its members had been at the most recent meeting, but there were attendances as low as 19, on 18 September, 16, on 12 October, and 12 a week later.[6] The plague, after seeming to diminish during September, reached its height in the first week of October.[7] Moreover conscientious men, who had toiled for much of the previous ten months, were desperate for country relaxations. Melbourne's hawks and spaniels, together with the good company of Derbyshire friends in the evenings, would much refresh Sir John Coke, his friend Edward Reed told Coke's father on 20 September. MPs returning home were joyfully welcomed. The bells were rung at Hatfield Broadoak when Sir Thomas Barrington arrived on 10 September: a hundred of the Essex gentry had set out to meet him, he related to Lord Howard of Escrick, 'only upon hearsay of my coming and missing me yet divers came the next day and made such public signs of love as if I had been of far more use to them than my meaner abilities admit'.[8] The recess was an opportunity to take stock of the political situation, to report to colleagues on the Bench at Michaelmas quarter sessions and to discuss the issues of the moment with relatives and friends.[9]

Those who did remain at Westminister gave energetic attention to the problems of day-to-day government, though their grumbles were reported. 'I hear some say that between attendance of the committee and serious expectation what may become of business the next sitting of parliament', reported Reed, 'they have but little pleasure.'[10] The recess committee met 11 times in all, skipping only one of its appointed sessions. Among other things, it saw through the final stages of the disbandment of the army and of the garrisons at Berwick and Carlisle, it issued directions for securing the English Channel and it imprisoned the army plotters Sir John Berkeley and Captain O'Neale, when they appeared to submit themselves.[11] There was some relaxation of political tension, yet there were two kinds of men, disbanded soldiers and zealous enforcers of the general order on religious innovations, whose activities gave political commentators cause for concern. The soldiers had serious complaints about the way they had been treated at the disbanding but honest citizens found their thieving no less

---

6 Beineke Library, Yale University, Osborn Collection: Sir Thomas Barrington to Lord Howard of Escrick, 24 Sept. 1641; *CJ* II, 288; *D'Ewes (C)*, pp. 2, 8; BL E 172 (17): *The True Copy of a Letter*, p. 5.
7 *CSPD 1641–3*, pp. 126, 128, 134.
8 Clarendon I, 389–90; *HMC Coke*, p. 291; Essex RO D/DBa A2, fol. 62r; Beineke Library, Yale University, Osborn Collection: Barrington to Escrick, 24 Sept. 1641.
9 *Sussex*, pp. 252–3.
10 *HMC Coke*, p. 291.
11 *DO*, pp. 363–76.

intolerable for that. 'Troopers commit diverse outrages by the highway', wrote Barrington to Escrick on 24 September, telling the story of the robbery and murder of a wool merchant near Baldock. Tweny-six 'great robberies' had been committed in 24 hours between Tottenham High Cross and London, a correspondent informed Lord Montagu on 14 October. Reed predicted growing anarchy, in a letter to Sir John Coke a few days later, unless the soldiers and the 'over-busy men in the affairs of the Church' were brought to heel.[12] The committee did its best to disperse the soldiers but it had no authority to take speedy action on their petitions. It did nothing, on the other hand, to quell the religious disputes in various City parishes, which were prompted, as we have seen, by the Commons' own assertive policy. Pym's argument to the reassembled MPs on 20 October that the committee's initiatives to enforce the general order were necessary to prevent men coming to blows was disingenuous.[13]

Pym's chairmanship of the Commons's recess committee brought him to the apogee of his power. All official correspondence and petitions went through his hands; he determined the order of business; he signed executive orders like the letter to Sir John Pennington on the disposition of ships in the Channel. Yet he never stepped outside the instructions the House had prescribed: the keynote of his chairmanship was constitutional propriety.[14] Thus, when Berkeley and O'Neale came to him at his lodgings, he insisted that he had no power to advise them about their submission to parliament. When, sitting with one colleague, he was asked to give an opinion on the legality of the imprisonment of 100 poor men by King's Bench, he declared that it did not befit him to pronounce on a matter which 'only appertaineth to the two Houses of parliament, the judges and learned of the law'. Pym's style was to confide, reassure and admonish. He told the minister and parishioners of St Margaret's, New Fish Street 'to live lovingly together' after they had fallen out over a lectureship in the parish.[15] 'I would not willingly have you abide about the town for fear of scandal', he advised the troopers who came with petitions on 5 October, 'there are many and great misdemeanours lately committed here in this country and all is laid upon your back.' He urged them to return to their parents and kinsfolk, with the assurance that he accepted their case and would prefer their petitions to the Lord General: 'you are to be nourished by us being members of the same body politic.'[16]

For all this, when power was concentrated in so few hands Pym's

---

12 Beineke Library, Yale University, Osborn Collection: Barrington to Escrick, 24 Sept. 1641; *HMC Montagu*, p. 131; *HMC Coke*, p. 293.
13 BL E 172 (25): *A Discovery of Many Robberies; CSPD 1641–3*, p. 134; *CJ* II, 289, 291, 293.
14 *D'Ewes (C)*, pp. 1–11; BL Stowe MS 184, fol. 45; Pennington, p. 177.
15 *CJ* II, 290; *DO*, pp. 368, 371, 374.
16 BL E 172 (14): *Pym's Speech at the Committee.*

political supremacy was bound all at once to appear ostentatious and blatant. 'You know what letter was truly wanting – R', Sir Peter Wroth noted caustically about the printed version of the general order on the liturgy which concluded with the subscription John Pym.[17] The most dramatic manifestation of the personal hostility Pym was suffering at this time was the plague-sore incident on 25 October. This was a well planned attempt at assassination. The gentleman on horseback who gave a porter the letter to Pym, with 12 pence to deliver it, in Ludgate made it clear that he intended it to be opened in the presence of the House. The filthy and bloody rag, drawn through a plague sore, which fell from the letter when Pym unsealed it sent a shiver through the chamber. 'Do not think a guard of men can protect you if you persist in your traitorous courses and wicked designs', declared the anonymous assassin. 'If this do not touch your heart', it concluded viciously, 'a dagger shall.'[18]

Pym's unpopularity must be seen in the context of a strong wave of animosity against the parliamentary leadership as a whole. 'Pestilent libels spread abroad against the precise Lords and Commons' are first mentioned in a letter of Thomas Wiseman's on 7 October. The same week Giustinian, the Venetian ambassador, remarked on the bills attacking leading MPs which had been 'posted in public places'. According to Thomas Smith, numerous libels were still being 'thrown up and down in abuse of the best in parliament' soon after the Houses resumed on 20 October. The peers devoted much of their first day's debating to the question of how to proceed against the authors of a 'scurrilous and slanderous libel', which had 'much traduced' some of their number.[19]

The libel the peers discussed was almost certainly the 'Protestants Protestation', which was widely circulated at this time. It was directed against 14 peers and 13 of the Commons. 'Saye the Anabaptist' was alleged to be the leader of a 'pack of half-witted Lords', which included Bedford, Brooke, Essex, Mandeville, Warwick and Wharton; Pym, Hampden, Holles, Haselrig, Marten, Pennington, St John, the younger Vane, and Venn were among those attacked in the Commons. The continuity between this slanderous paper and the provocative 'Queries to be decided by a Committee' which had been circulated in the summer is plain, but the phrasing was now more bitter. The new libel described a conspiracy against 'the king, the crown and posterity'. Its crucial elements were the subjection of religion 'to be merely arbitrary', the prostitution of the honour of England by beggaring the nation to the Scots, and the destruction of all freedom of speech in parliament.[20]

17　*CSPD 1641–3*, p. 132.
18　BL E 173 (23); *A Damnable Treason; D'Ewes (C)*, p. 37; BL Sloane MS 1467, fol. 152r; Gardiner x, 38.
19　*CSPD 1641–3*, pp. 134, 147; *CSPV 1640–2*, p. 225; *D'Ewes (C)*, p. 10; *DO*, p. 371.
20　*HMC Salisbury MSS* xxiv, 277.

Dissatisfaction with Pym's leadership of the Commons was not confined to the political underworld of London. Some backbench MPs were beginning to talk openly of their dislike of the tactics employed by his clique. They complained, Giustinian reported in September, that everything had been 'guided by the sole arbitrament of a few individuals' who prevented others from giving their views.[21] Several MPs resisted a proposal on the day parliament reassembled that Berkeley and O'Neale should be examined by the close committee but they were overruled. They 'spake very vehemently against having any more of close committees' and insisted that it was an ancient privilege of the House to attend committees if they so wished.[22] Sir Peter Wroth was one of those who believed that the time had come for Pym's supremacy to be challenged. He told Secretary Vane, in a letter urging him to be back in London for the new session, that a 'well-grounded counsel' was needed, based on 'God's law and the present law of this kingdom', to choke off Pym's men, who he feared still expected advancement at the king's hands and the completion of their designs.[23] The bridge-appointments scheme may in fact have flickered into life at the end of September when a paper of Mandeville's was delivered to Henrietta Maria through the good offices of Lady Carlisle.[24]

The most damaging charge in the 'Protestants Protestation', if it could be sustained, was that the parliamentary leadership was hand in glove with London radicals. Thus, according to the libel, Pym and his clique had 'protected the ignorant and licentious sectaries and schismatics to stir up sedition, to bring in atheism and discountenanced all reverend ministers and have endeavoured to take away the common prayer book'.[25] Those who wished to slander the parliamentary leadership were on strong ground here since over the summer an identity of interest between it and the radical Puritans of the City had been commonly, though quite incorrectly, assumed. This is clear from the way that conservative observers like Sir Peter Wroth interpreted the outcome of the London mayoral election on 28 September: the defeat of the City radicals was read as a reverse for Pym. 'The Puritans if I may give that name to factious people whom you and I know', wrote Wroth to Secretary Vane, 'were overcome with hisses.' Wroth was undoubtedly right to ascribe the election of the rich silk merchant Sir Richard Gurney to the political and religious reaction that was gathering strength.[26] But the conclusion he drew that, with firm action, the reign of King Pym might quickly be brought to a close was

21 *CSPV 1640–2*, p. 222.
22 *D'Ewes (C)*, p. 16.
23 *CSPD 1641–3*, pp. 135–6.
24 *Evelyn*, p. 92.
25 *HMC Salisbury MSS* xxiv, 277.
26 Pearl, p. 124; *Evelyn*, p. 98; *HMC Coke*, p. 293; R. Ashton, *The City and the Court 1603–1643* (Cambridge, 1979), p. 204.

naive.[27] He oversimplified the complexities of the political situation. He did not understand how the obsessive anti-Catholicism of Pym and his friends would sustain them through bitterness and confrontation. Nor did he grasp either the appeal of their propaganda or the impetus which the Puritan yearning for religious reform gave to their cause.

Pym, Mandeville, the younger Vane and others certainly met regularly during the recess and discussed letters received from Hampden and Fiennes in Scotland, at Mandeville's home.[28] Nicholas described their mood as 'very jocund and cheerful' in September.[29] But there is good reason to think that it darkened as the new session approached. The libels in the streets were profoundly disturbing. Pym was probably already affected by that deep sense of persecution and injustice, which eventually led him in March 1643 to issue a declaration and vindication intended to clear his name. Moreover, according to Hyde, the ill humour of the parliamentary leaders was being fed at this time by the earl of Holland, a disgruntled cast-off favourite of Henrietta Maria, now newly returned from his northern command to his home in Kensington.[30] Pym and his friends were alert for new trouble. The Incident, as the shadowy plot in Edinburgh against Hamilton and Argyle was called, revived all their deepest fears. There was some kind of plan to seize the two noblemen and carry them on board a ship lying at Leith. On hearing of it, we are told, Pym 'rode post haste to tell Mandeville particulars'.[31] Whether or not Charles was implicated in the Incident does not really matter for the purposes of Westminster politics, since his involvement was immediately taken for granted by Pym. In fact he seems to have known that some sort of intrigue for helping him was afoot and to have stood idly by, without either stopping it or securing its success. When, in an atmosphere of wild rumour, he came to the Scottish parliament on 12 October to declare his innocence, he was accompanied by several hundred armed royalists. Expecting to be seized in their lodgings Hamilton, his brother the earl of Lanerick and Argyle left Edinburgh that day for the safety of Hamilton's castle.[32]

The very obscurity of the Incident made it doubly alarming to Pym. The facts reported by his colleagues in Edinburgh were few, but the impact the plot had made on the Scottish political scene was undeniable: parliament was investigating it, the single Scottish regiment not already disbanded had been called to defend the capital, guards were set and the ports shut up.

27   *CSPD 1641–3*, p. 132.
28   Clarendon I, 387–8; *CJ* II, 290; *Evelyn*, pp. 93, 95–6.
29   *Evelyn*, p. 95.
30   BL E 91(4): *A Declaration and Vindication of John Pym; EHR* XLIII (1978), 30–45.
31   BL Sloane MS 1467, fol. 153r.
32   Gardiner X, 23–7; D. Stevenson, *The Scottish Revolution 1637–1644* (Newton Abbot, 1973), p. 238.

Pym delayed revealing the new conspiracy till he had collected every bit of information on which he could lay his hands. His announcement of it to the recess committee on 19 October was portentous. He had received several accounts, he told his colleagues, of 'some great and dangerous design plotting again here at home wherein he did now believe there was a correspondence with those conspirators of Scotland'. Thus Pym sought to embroider and dramatize the Incident, jumping to the conclusion that its coincidence with the reassembly of the English parliament implied that a new gunpowder plot was hatching.[33] The committee swallowed Pym's story: the guards and watches of the City and suburbs were at once doubled. Through the cooperation of the earl of Essex, moreover, they were able to make further provision for parliament's safety. As Captain General south of the Trent, Essex called out the whole of the Westminster trained band to attend the Houses as they reassembled on 20 October and ordered the lord lieutenant of Surrey to have some trained horse in readiness to suppress 'disbanded soldiers and other disorderly persons' in London and Westminster.[34]

These were the trappings of the new emergency Pym created. Its purposes quickly became apparent. But first, after giving the House a lucid and concise summary of events since 9 September, including the tale of the Incident, Pym sat back and let others do his work for him. Rudyerd, D'Ewes and Earle were among those who pressed for a conference with the Lords to provide for the safety of the kingdom and of parliament. D'Ewes fanned the flames of anti-Catholicism with a fierce speech against papists and the clergy, 'the true root and spring whence all these conspiracies do arise'.[35] Pym could not have asked for a truer echo of his own thoughts and feelings. His programme became clear in the course of the day's debating. In the first place two new committees should be chosen, one for 'securing the kingdom', the other to examine traitors. Secondly, the Commons should unite with the Lords with four objectives: to 'root out papist lords and bishops', quash evil reports of the House, look to public business, and provide money for 'maintaining of our public faith'. There was nothing new in this plan of action. Pym still put his trust in a scheme for settlement, though circumstances now forced him to select priorities. Yet there was much that was predictable about his programme. He explained that the recess committee had got no further than asking the royal officers to provide a balance sheet of the king's finances and he obviously regretted its failure to come to grips with the problem of improving the revenue.[36] His renewed concern for parliament's reputation reflected his awareness of the

33 *D'Ewes (C)*, pp. 8–10; *Evelyn*, p. 107; Clarendon I, 389–90, 393–5; *CSPD 1641–3*, pp. 137–9.
34 Clarendon I, 391; *Evelyn*, p. 107; Pennington, pp. 176, 178.
35 *CJ* II, 289–91; *D'Ewes (C)*, pp. 11–14.
36 *CJ* II, 289; *D'Ewes (C)*, p. 15.

viciousness of the libels in the streets.

The Incident was perfectly timed to allow Pym to resurrect the spectre with which he had kept the Commons in thrall from May to September. Pamphlets describing its ramifications were quickly on the streets; newsletters were full of it.[37] Pym skilfully painted it as an extension of the long-standing Catholic conspiracy. There were Jesuits 'lurking about many places of the kingdom'; much was made of the suspected Catholicism of the earl of Crawford, one of the leading conspirators, which suggested a 'correspondency with the like party here'. Pym even alleged that the Scottish conspirators had been involved in the army plot. He also pointed to the disastrous consequences if, with peace only just established between the two nations, a rebel Scottish party should seize on the vulnerable garrisons of Berwick and Carlisle. In September Pym had written in his own hand, as chairman of the recess committee, to get the guns from Berwick and Lindisfarne into safe hands in the Tower.[38]

The magnitude of the Incident snowballed as the story was told and retold. The tale, complained Nicholas, was passed on 'according to the sense and affection of each several auditor and so become very uncertain'. The game Pym and his associates were playing, he reflected, had become familiar: 'the alarm of popish plots amuse and fright the people here more than anything and therefore that is the drum that is so frequently beaten upon all occasions.' The 'worst of businesses' were credited, he declared, and they silenced 'what they like not'.[39] But Nicholas could not deny the effectiveness of Pym's tactics. Many MPs and London observers still appear to have accepted his version of events uncritically. Thus Edward Reed, who confessed on 24 October that he was not yet clear how or from whence the danger used to justify a daily guard at Westminster threatened, nevertheless spoke approvingly of Pym's strategy: 'Mr Pym is a very careful man both for the keeping quiet of the House and people and to farther the reformation of that which is amiss in government.' Hyde observed, more bitingly, in retrospect that the Incident had 'a strange influence at Westminster and served to contribute to all the senseless fears they thought to put on'.[40]

Yet, for all the advantage the Incident gave him, Pym did not, even for a few hours, have things all his own way. Nicholas's warning to the king that if he was not home on 20 October there would be few 'that will dare to appear here to oppose the party that swayeth' was perceptive in the sense

---

37 BL E 173 (12, 19, 29), E 199 (19); Sloane MS 3317, fol. 45r.
38 *D'Ewes (C)*, pp. 15, 21, 29; *CJ* II, 290; *DO*, p. 380; Houghton Library, Harvard University, English History MSS, autograph file. I am grateful to Professor Conrad Russell for providing a copy of this document.
39 *Evelyn*, pp. 113, 118.
40 *HMC Coke*, p. 293; Clarendon I, 390.

that the contrary faction to Pym's was at first small.[41] But the determination displayed by the king's friends early in the session must have surprised his anxious counsellor. On the very first day, Falkland and Hyde stood against the tide, moving that the Incident should be left to the Scottish parliament to disentangle and urging colleagues 'not to take up fears and suspicions without very undoubted grounds'.[42] Much troubled, they had hurried that day to see Nicholas in case he could supply them with a full and accurate account of events in Scotland that would serve to confound Pym's sensationalism. Twice in the next few days, Nicholas emphasized to the king how disheartened his sympathizers were at being kept in the dark about the true dimensions of the plot.[43] Nevertheless their efforts to discount it did not go unheeded. One newsletter remarked that 'the courtiers make a slight matter of the conspiracy', although letters from Scotland spoke of it as 'a treachery of most dreadful consequence'.[44] If the simple test of a man's politics was still his attitude to the alleged papist conspiracy against the state, broader questions such as whom to trust – Pym or Charles – were being thrust into the forefront of men's minds.

'Perfecting businesses formerly begun' was the succinct description given by one commentator on the Commons' programme in the first weeks of the new session.[45] Exclusion of the bishops from the Lords was the first item on Pym's agenda. He knew that there remained very broad support for it on two grounds. Many regarded the bishops as a fifth column, accepting D'Ewes's charge that they 'correspond with the Romanists and discover the secrets of our state to foreign parts'.[46] Many also, whether or not they were rooters, recognized that it was essential for the progress of religious reform that the episcopate should be brought low.[47] The new bishops exclusion bill, introduced by Sir Gilbert Gerrard on 21 October, was read twice that day. The bill was to come into force on 10 November and Pym's intention was almost certainly to rush it through the House before members had found their feet again. Because of the plague many of those who had returned from the country were living out of town and their attendance was limited by the problems of commuting.[48] Although the bill's passage was rapid – the committee stage was completed on 22 October and it was passed on the 23rd – it was strongly opposed by a few individuals. Hyde fought it at every stage. He argued in turn that it was

41 *Evelyn*, p. 98.
42 *D'Ewes (C)*, p. 15; Clarendon 1, 395.
43 *Evelyn*, pp. 107, 110, 112.
44 BL Sloane MS 1467, fol. 153r.
45 *CSPD 1641–3*, p. 143.
46 *D'Ewes (C)*, p. 14.
47 See below, p. 218.
48 BL Harl. MS 6424, fol. 97; *HMC Coke*, p. 293.

against the privilege of the peerage to deprive them of any of their members, that the bill debarred men in orders from being masters of colleges, and that the House was still too thin for a bill of such importance to be given its final reading.[49]

The omens of the early autumn for the relationship between the Lords and Commons were not good. The first session had ended on a note of friction and a futile dispute in September, between the recess committees, about whether the commoners should be allowed to wear their hats at conferences, symbolized the malaise between the two Houses.[50] Predictably the bishops exclusion bill brought a major impasse. Now that it was abundantly plain that the Commons leadership intended exclusion as merely the first stage towards Root and Branch, Pym's allies were even less likely than in May to make any headway. Nor did Brooke, Essex and Mandeville manage to persuade their colleagues to take up the demand, delivered by Holles on 22 October, that the 13 bishops impeached for their part in making the 1640 canons should be 'brought to speedy answer'. The accused bishops were finally given until 10 November to bring in their answer, after the Commons' proposal had been fiercely resisted by the earls of Bath and Bristol, together with Lord Brudenell.[51] By 27 October when Pym argued at a conference between the Houses that, as an interim measure, the 13 impeached bishops should be excluded from voting, there was complete deadlock.[52]

In the Commons, meanwhile, it had never been more vital for Pym to retain a personal hold on the hour by hour course of debate.[53] His difficulty was that he could not be everywhere at once. He was so busy with the close committee examinations of Berkeley and O'Neale, and with preparing for conferences with the Lords, in the last fortnight of October that he was bound to be away from the Commons for considerable periods of time. Without him MPs were sometimes in a daze. When he went to fetch a letter from his lodgings on 22 October, for example, we are told that the House sat 'a good whiles silent'. On other occasions, lacking a firm lead, back-benchers readily turned to the mundane matters that they had been led to believe parliaments were normally about, such as the trade in currants and the low price of wool.[54]

Hyde and Falkland were probably in the House more of the time at this period than Pym himself. They were quickly joined, as emerging leaders of a powerful royalist faction, by Sir John Culpepper, Sir John Strangeways

49 *D'Ewes (C)*, pp. 21–2, 25–8, 30–2; Clarendon I, 401; Gardiner X, 37–8.
50 *D'Ewes (C)*, p. 4; *DO*, p. 367; *CSPD 1641–3*, p. 133.
51 *D'Ewes (C)*, p. 24, *CSPD 1641–3*, pp. 147, 163; BL Sloane MS 3317, fol. 53v; Harl. MS 6424, fol. 97r.
52 *LJ* IV, 407–8; *D'Ewes (C)*, p. 43.
53 See for instance *HMC Coke*, pp. 293–4.
54 *D'Ewes (C)*, pp. 24–26, 41–2, 52.

and Sir Edward Dering. On the important question of the validity and enforcement of the general order of 9 September about the liturgy, the backbenchers swung into line behind them.[55] Moreover a row on 26 October shows that, so far as tactics were concerned, Hyde could be a match for Pym. The point at issue was whether the Commons should name the offences of the 13 impeached bishops as treason. When the proposal that it should, made by Strode and backed by Holles and Haselrig, was opposed by Hyde, Pym successfully imposed a diversion. Yet Hyde won a small victory that day when he subsequently moved, in reply to Pym, that the question of naming the bishops' crime should not be taken up again before eleven o'clock in the morning. Since the House was normally meeting at ten, to allow commuting members time to arrive, the suggestion of an hour's moratorium seemed perfectly reasonable. Those who saw the chance of exploiting a thin early morning assembly disappearing cried 'no, no', but D'Ewes noted that their call for a division was shouted down.[56]

If Pym lost a little ground during the first ten days of the new session, there was no question of the sense of emergency, which was so vital to his control, becoming entirely dissipated. 'Bad news out of Scotland continues', a newsletter report of 28 October ran, 'but it is so dangerous men dare not write those particulars which they know.'[57] Uncertainty about the nature and extent of the Incident, together with the tumultuous behaviour of the troopers who were still badgering parliament for their pay, provided Pym with the excuses he needed to retain the guard at Westminster. 'We still live here as in a garrison town' commented one correspondent on 29 October.[58] Next day Pym brought before the House the close committee's discovery of the second army plot. This was another masterly performance. As in May and June it was the popish ramifications of the treasonable designs to use the army against parliament which Pym sought to impress. The queen's confessor, Father Philip, and the queen mother's confidant, Monsigot, he alleged, were daily contriving new plots; recusants in Hampshire were gathering forces and holding secret meetings; 'the conspiracy went round and there was a compliance in this new design both in Scotland and England.' Pym focused the attention of the Commons on the danger of allowing the prince of Wales frequent access to the queen's court at Oatlands. Indeed the prince's constant residence at Richmond, under the eye of his governor the marquis of Hertford, was essential 'to secure him from all plots'. The peers concurred in this view and Holland was sent to explain to the queen why they were so

55 See below p. 287–8.
56 *D'Ewes (C)*, pp. 39–40.
57 BL Sloane MS 1467, fol. 152v.
58 *DO*, p. 381; *D'Ewes (C)*, pp. xxvi, 37.

careful of the prince's safety.[59] For the first time in the new session a major initiative which was antagonistic to the court had been carried through without opposition from Hyde or his associates.

The second army plot had hardly taken root in men's minds when news of the Irish rebellion broke on 1 November. It was brought to the Commons by 17 privy councillors led by the earl of Leicester, the lord lieutenant, who had heard from Ireland the previous day. Hyde records the immediate reaction of the Commons: 'there was a deep silence . . . and a kind of consternation, most men's heads having been intoxicated, from their first meeting in parliament, with imaginations of plots and treasonable designs through the three kingdoms.' MPs were stunned, not because the rebellion was unexpected, but because the worst they had feared had happened. 'I often foretold what I feared', noted D'Ewes in cipher that evening.[60]

A quarter of the pamphlets collected by the bookseller George Thomason during November and December 1641 concerned the Irish rebellion. Their titles, *Bloody News from Ireland*, for example, and *Worse and Worse News from Ireland*, promised atrocity stories within; their contents amply fulfilled such expectations. According to these graphic accounts neither the aged, nor women, nor the very young were being spared barbarity and murder. Many of the pamphlet stories were wildly exaggerated, or even fabricated, yet, since the stereotype of the Irish papist as one capable of any barbarity had been so thoroughly inculcated, they were taken as the simple truth of what was happening across the Irish Sea.[61] Parliament received numerous shocking accounts.[62] Londoners absorbed the pamphlets with fascinated horror: 'all the news and speech is here of the rebellion', a correspondent wrote into Norfolk on 6 November.[63] The previous day's traditional bell-ringing and festivities throughout the nation to celebrate the gunpowder deliverance had suddenly taken on a new significance.[64]

All at once Pym's political advantage, briefly in the previous days less certain, was restored. His whole policy appeared justified. Many others beyond his circle shared the assumption that the rebellion was the first stage in a well planned and deeply laid design against Protestantism. This view was constantly reinforced over the next weeks. Owen O'Connolly,

---

59 *D'Ewes (C)*, pp. 58–9; BL Sloane MS 3317, fol. 54v; Harl. MS 6424, fol. 98v; *CSPD 1641–3*, p. 147.

60 *D'Ewes (C)*, pp. 61–3; Clarendon I, 398.

61 K.J. Lindley, 'The Impact of the 1641 Rebellion upon England and Wales 1641–5', *Irish Historical Studies* XVIII (1972), 145–6.

62 *D'Ewes (C)*, pp. 180, 283–5, 247–8, 350–1, 354–5.

63 Bodleian Tanner MS 66, fol. 199. See also BL Sloane MS 3317, fols. 36v, 39r; *Calendar of Wynn Papers*, p. 224.

64 Staffordshire RO D 113/A/PC/1; Essex RO D/DBa A2, fol. 64r; B.H. Cunnington, *Annals of Devizes* (Devizes, 1925) I, 102.

examined before the committee set up to suppress the rebellion, confessed he had heard the conspirators say 'they had good friends in England, the bishops and some privy councillors, and that nothing was done at the Council table in England but it was presently known in Ireland, in Rome and in Spain.' There was much reported gossip about the Romish religion shortly being established in England and the worst of the plot being yet undiscovered.[65] Then came Sir John Temple's report from Dublin on 30 November that the rebels had begun 'to grow so confident of their prevailing in Ireland as they did begin to advise of the invading of England'.[66] There were probably few informed Londoners who had any confidence during the last two months of 1641 that the rebellion could be contained across the Irish Sea. Many spoke of the intention to invade as a fact. D'Ewes was one of these, Nehemiah Wallington was another. 'All these plots in Ireland', he was convinced, 'are but one plot against England, for it is England that is that fine sweet bit which they so long for and their cruel teeth so much water at.'[67] 'The Irish profess they will root out the English and commit diverse barbarous cruelties upon them', Sir John Coke told his father on 24 November, reporting the common gossip. At Christmas one correspondent told a Devon friend that the rebels were publicly declaring their intention to 'come over into England where they have a great party and settle their religion here'. The general mood in London is well summarized by Henry Oxinden's letter to his cousin in Kent on 18 November.

> For news truly I was never so wise as that I could write any, pray pardon me therefore, that which is either too uncertain or too desperate and dangerous to write, nay some of it to think. If there be not a distemper and confusion in this kingdom far greater than hath yet been in the other two, verily God must work wonders and miracles again which I beseech him of infinite mercy to do.[68]

The rebels' claim that they had a commission from the king under the Great Seal was almost certainly false.[69] Yet Pym immediately assumed that the rebellion had been instigated at court. They had 'just cause of belief' that the commotions in Ireland were the effect of evil counsellors about the king, declared the Commons to the committee of both Houses at Edinburgh. The remarkable speech that Pym made to the Lords, when he delivered instructions to this committee on 8 November, gives more specific insight into his mind than any of his other speeches in 1641 which are fully documented. The subject of his discourse was evil counsels and

---

65 *Irish Historical Studies* XVIII (1972), 152–3; BL Sloane MS 3317, fols. 36r, 46r; *D'Ewes (C)*, p. 108.
66 *D'Ewes (C)*, p. 348.
67 *Ibid*, p. 121; Wallington, pp. 41–2.
68 *HMC Coke*, pp. 294–5; East Devon RO 1700 A/CP 20; BL Add. MS 28000, fol. 132.
69 R. Dunlop, 'The Forged Commission of 1641', *EHR* II (1897), 529–33.

Pym reached the heart of his argument in four steps. First he sought to show 'that the dangers which come to a state by ill counsels are the most pernicious of all others', because they were of the nature of 'diseases which proceed from the inward parts, as the liver, the heart or the brains' and therefore hard to cure. Secondly, the persistence of evil counsels at the English court was amply proved, he maintained, by the 'mischievous designs' of previous months. Thirdly, he suggested, in a revealing analysis of how he saw the political crisis, that the evil counsels of 1641 were more mischievous and dangerous than those of former times. Counsellors in the past had tried to please kings in their vices, 'from which our king is free'. They had promoted excessive reliance on the prerogative, which brought 'many miseries but not ruin and destruction'. What distinguished the ill counsels of this time was they they 'were destructive to religion and laws by altering them both'. Thus Pym came to the crux of his speech, which shows so clearly how the Catholic conspiracy, his haunting obsession, pervaded all his thinking that it deserves to be quoted at length:

> These ill counsels have proceeded from a spirit and inclination to popery and have a dependence in popery and all of them tend unto it. The religion of the papists is a religion incompatible with any other religion, destructive to all others, and doth not endure anything that opposes it: whosoever doth withstand their religion, if they have power, they bring them to ruin. There are other religions that are not right but not so destructive as popery is. For the principles of popery are destructive to all states and persons that oppose it, with the progress of these mischievous counsels. They provide counsellors, fit instruments and organs, that may execute their own designs and turn all counsel to their own ends. And you find that, now in Ireland, that those designs that have been upon all three kingdoms do end in a war for the maintenance of popery in Ireland and would do the like here if they were able, they are so nutritive as to turn all to their own advantage.[70]

This was the speech of a man whose sense of defencelessness had been brought to fever pitch, who really believed, as he explained, that there had been 'common counsel at Rome and in Spain to reduce us to popery', who lived in terror of the great fleets which he thought neighbour states were preparing against England. In November 1641 Pym still clung to the hope that the king could be persuaded to understand his viewpoint, when there was so much in his political programme for the king's benefit. Alteration of counsels, he urged the Lords, would bring great advantage to the king in his own designs: 'honour, profit . . . at home, peace and union and better respect from abroad'. Even now Pym's vision of what might lie beyond the political settlement he searched for had not entirely faded. On the other hand there is a perceptible hardening of Pym's attitude about this time. For all the talk of evil counsels he was thrusting home the conspiracy to the king himself, whose fidelity to protestantism was now in doubt. Though he dared not actually say it, Pym had probably concluded that the king had forfeited obedience. Treason not tyranny, as Baxter was later to emphasize, was the crucial issue.[71]

This fascinating testimony makes Pym's vigilant investigation of every whisper of conspiracy in the weeks following the outbreak of the Irish rebellion entirely comprehensible. Indeed it makes sense of the threats to use the rack on one priest, thought to be a 'great conspirator', unless he would confess all. Pym and those close to him did not fabricate the plots they laid before the Commons, as Thomas Wiseman scoffed at them for doing.[72] They were merely frightened men who gathered and circulated some of the combustible material of a bewildered nation. They did no more than treat every man's revelations, however far-fetched, with equal seriousness.

Plots came on each others' heels during November 1641. On the 11th Sir Walter Earle brought information that 40 Irish, meeting daily in Milford Lane under a colonel, 'were feared to consist of a body of 1000 men in several places and might occasion us much danger'. They were in fact being gathered by the French ambassador for service abroad, since the ordinance inhibiting him from recruiting had expired on 1 November. The same day, George Peard maintained that papists had set Guildford on fire once and would have done so again had not a good watch prevented them. Next day, Sir Harbottle Grimston directed the House's attention to a Colchester woman with arms in her house and correspondents in Ireland.[73] More elaborate and startling than all the rest was the plot related by the tailor Thomas Beale on 15 November. He had come hot-foot from Moorfields where, he alleged, he had heard two men discussing a design, instigated by some catholic priests, for 108 appointed men to kill 108 peers and MPs, 'all Puritans', either as they entered their coaches at Westminster or their lodgings. The assassinations, planned for 18 November, would be accompanied by a tumult in the City and papist risings in six counties, which included Buckinghamshire, Lancashire, Warwickshire and Worcestershire.[74]

Nicholas told the king on 18 November that 'many wise men' gave no credit at all to Beale's plot.[75] But for those in daily attendance at Westminster a succession of scraps of evidence made it hard to ignore his story. Earle had a letter from Portsmouth read on the 15th, which reported that a post went from there to Oatlands, where the queen was staying, several times weekly and 'that the papists and jovial clergymen thereabouts

71 Lamont, *Richard Baxter*, pp. 93–5.
72 *CSPD 1641–3*, p. 168; BL Sloane MS 3317, fol. 47r.
73 *D'Ewes (C)*, pp. 119–20, 135.
74 BL Sloane MS 3317, fol. 37v; *D'Ewes (C)*, pp. 144–5; *LJ* IV, 439–40; *CSPD 1641–3*, pp. 168–9.
75 *Evelyn*, p. 138.

were merrier than ever'. On the 17th Pym told of six papists 'this night come out of Lancashire armed with swords and pistols'; others the same day expressed fears, based on news from home, of recusants stirring in Herefordshire, Lancashire, Warwickshire and Wales.[76] D'Ewes, a sceptic at first, confessed that a letter which was read from Lord Strange about the sense of insecurity in Lancashire convinced him that Beale's story was true.[77] As the dreaded hour approached searches and watches in London were stepped up. On the night of the 17th the Lord Mayor rode up and down the streets till three o'clock 'apprehending a number of papists and other suspicious persons'.[78] Yet when the plot proved a chimera, public gullibility hardly declined. On the 27th MPs heard a new tale of a wandering papist, armed with pistols, who, when he was arrested in Buckinghamshire, tore the letters he carried into pieces. Hampden triumphantly announced he had all the pieces, collected for the attention of the close committee.[79]

The immediate outcome of the Irish rebellion was that, by heightening tension at Westminster, it made the old agenda both more urgent and more convincing. The leadership had little difficulty in carrying the Commons along with them in a vehement campaign against papist conspiracy in the localities. Thus, twice in November, members were to be found in the unseemly posture of compiling lists of innocuous country gentlemen, believed, because they were 'chief papists', to constitute an immediate danger to the kingdom and therefore to be fit to be imprisoned. When Pym invited the delegations from the six counties mentioned by Beale to name names on 15 November, other MPs from Dorset, Hampshire and Pembrokeshire rushed in with their own accusations. The rabble-rousing display of vindictiveness which followed probably served merely to magnify men's fears, though some who kept their heads later rose to defend men who they knew were being unjustly treated. After prolonged disputes about how many names should be on the list, nine counties, thought to be 'most stored with papists and in that respect most dangerous', were singled out.[80]

Much energy was devoted to persuading the Lords to cooperate in the imprisonment plan. Some had been secured in 1588, they were reminded, 'on suspicion of danger'. Four conferences were held on the subject between 6 and 19 November. Finally on 22 November the peers accepted a list of 65 men to be imprisoned but insisted that the confinements, for one

76   *D'Ewes (C)*, pp. 146, 163, *CSPD 1641–3*, p. 180. For provincial fears of popery at this time, see below pp. 200–7.
77   *D'Ewes (C)*, pp. 152–3.
78   *Ibid*, pp. 155, 163; BL Sloane MS 3317, fol. 47v; *Evelyn*, p. 139.
79   *D'Ewes (C)*, pp. 201–2.
80   *D'Ewes (C)*, pp. 146–75.

year, should be backed by statute. The requisite bill was greeted enthusiastically in the Commons, but by the end of the month it had foundered on the refusal of the Lords to leave the manner of restraint of the commoners on the list to the lower House.[81]

The vigour with which the imprisonment of leading Catholics was pursued owed something to the sense of frustration in the Commons at the failure of other anti-Catholic measures. The Lords ignored a proposal that all servants of the royal family should take the oaths of allegiance and supremacy or lose their places. The dissolution of the college of Capuchins was accepted in principle but not carried out. The Venetian ambassador denied that he harboured any English priests. An act for more speedy conviction of recusants stuck after its first reading on 4 November.[82] The Commons enjoyed only two small victories: the imprisonment at last of Father Philip and an exodus of papist peers from the capital after the Lords had agreed to confine Catholics to within five miles of their homes. This degree of cooperation was probably a sop to those who argued in a long and heated debate on 9 November that the House should exclude the papists in their midst. Lord Brudenell, one of the recusants the Commons wanted imprisoned, had challenged the motion with an insistence that, summoned by the king, he could not depart without his leave, yet he went quietly within a week or two. Whereas there were occasions early in 1641 when as many as six known Catholics were present in the Lords, none appear to have attended after the end of November except Earl Rivers who put in occasional appearances for another two months.[83]

MPs were inclined to blame the peers for the lack of progress in improving the nation's defences at this time. The vulnerability of Hurst Castle, Milford Haven and the magazine at Montgomery, said to be 'in the hands of a great recusant's servant', particularly bothered them.[84] In the case of Milford Haven, which the Lords insisted 'could not be well fortified' and was best defended from the sea, their inertia is plain. Nevertheless they had a fair point when they reminded the Commons that they had gathered information about the state of forts and castles in the summer and it was not up to them to raise the money for repairs. Moreover the Commons' victimization of the earl of Portland, the governor of the Isle of Wight, on the basis of mere hearsay was excessively highhanded. When Portland protested his 'real detestation of popery' and declared before his colleagues on 18 November that 'his father bred him a Protestant and he

81 *Ibid*, pp. xxviii, 160–2, 172–4, 191; *CJ* II, 318–9, 321, 324, 325–7; *LJ* IV, 441, 446, 450–1, 456; BL Sloane MS 3317, fols. 37v, 49v.

82 *LJ* IV, 426–7, 448; *CJ* II, 305, 315, 320, 365; *D'Ewes (C)*, pp. 98, 115; BL Sloane MS 3317, fols. 136r, 147v.

83 *LJ* IV, 429; *D'Ewes (C)*, pp. 71, 408–11; *Evelyn*, pp. 132, 139; *HMC Buccleuch* III, 411; BL Sloane MS 3317, fol. 36r.

84 *D'Ewes (C)*, pp. 69, 149, 153; BL Sloane MS 3317, fol. 47r; *CJ* II, 300.

would ever live and die one' the case against him collapsed.[85]

It was predictable that the November emergency would bring a new drive by the Commons leadership for full control of the county militias. Oliver Cromwell, then an increasingly vocal backbencher, took the lead in this matter at a conference with the Lords on 6 November and ten days later the Commons sent up a draft ordinance. It put all authority over the nation's military strength in the hands of the earls of Essex and Holland, two men with considerable military experience who were now wholly in the counsels of the leadership. The powers claimed for them, south and north of the Trent respectively, were made quite explicit: 'they may nominate particular men of trust in every county to take care of the militia'. Here was the summer's abortive militia bill in a new guise, in one sense a more radical guise since the ordinance did not set up a temporary system as the bill had done but was to remain in force as long as parliament required. Yet arguably the ordinance looked less radical than the bill had done because it was closely in line with the scheme that the king had established for national security when he left for Scotland. Furthermore the men nominated both supposedly still enjoyed royal favour. In any case the ordinance appeared much too innovatory for many of the Lords and within two days it had been returned to the Commons 'with some alterations'.[86]

Whereas some of the leadership's efforts to apply the remedies they thought necessary led to new clashes with the Lords, others widened the breach within their own chamber. By early November, as we have seen, Pym was more incensed than ever about evil counsellors. The question of ministerial appointments had never been far from his mind since the previous June, but it is hard to interpret his thinking on the matter just before the Irish rebellion broke. Did he, as Nicholas asserted, make plans during the recess to press nominations to the Lord Treasureship and other offices, after hearing about the act passed in Edinburgh giving the Scottish parliament a role in important appointments? The king's concession was certainly very well known and much discussed in London. Nevertheless, Pym's silence on the question early in the session suggests that he may have decided, in the interests of harmony, to bide his time on an issue that he knew was divisive. If so, Robert Goodwin's motion on 28 October was an independent initiative, which is very much how it looks. D'Ewes thought that Goodwin's and Strode's speeches that day were premeditated but this need not be taken to imply that they had sought Pym's advice.[87]

Unless parliament acted to remove such evil counsellors as remained

85   *LJ* IV, 427, 443, 446; *D'Ewes (C)*, pp. 63–4, 67, 154, 161–2.
86   *D'Ewes (C)*, pp. 97–8, 145, 147; *LJ* IV, 441–2; *CJ* II, 316, 320; Pennington, p. 176; W.C. Abbott, *The Writings and Speeches of Oliver Cromwell* (Harvard, 1937) I, 140–2.
87   *Evelyn*, pp. 91, 93, 97–8; *D'Ewes (C)*, pp. xxx–xxxi, 45; Stevenson, *Scottish Revolution*, pp. 235–6.

'and to prevent others from coming in hereafter', declared Goodwin, 'all we had done this parliament would come to nothing and we should never be free from danger.' Seconding him, Strode took up the implication of Haselrig's speech on 23 June: his speech contained the first specific claim that parliament should exercise a 'negative voice' in royal appointments. Bold as this was as an attempt to bring MPs off their psychological razor-edge, the motion on 28 October was undoubtedly badly timed. It came out of the blue and opened a new division within the ranks of Pym's supporters, making it impossible to disregard any longer the convenient ambiguities of the statement on counsellors in the Ten Propositions. Not only did predictable champions of the king's prerogative, like Falkland, Holborne, Hyde, Strangeways and Waller engage themselves. Others, like D'Ewes, found their moderate constitutional sensibilities jolted by Strode's audacity. Choice of counsellors, D'Ewes insisted, was 'an ancient and undoubted right of the crown, which rights I shall ever maintain whilst I sit in this House'.[88]

The controversy no doubt would have been renewed when the committee appointed on 28 October to draw a petition to the king 'touching privy councillors, officers and ambassadors' reported. But the Irish rebellion intervened and on 4 November the Commons heard that the Scottish parliament, approached by Charles, had offered their assistance towards its suppression. This information placed Pym in a dilemma. He could not contemplate allowing the king even partial control over forces to be sent to Ireland, while he was under the sway of mischievous counsellors who might turn armed men against the Commons leadership itself. Yet here was a brotherly gesture that could hardly be refused. Caught off balance, Pym made an unusually impetuous intervention. No one was more ready than he to engage everything to end the rebellion, he announced on 5 November, but he feared that as long as the king listened 'to those evil counsellors about him' all would be in vain. Thus the instructions to the committee at Edinburgh should contain an addition 'that howsoever we had engaged ourselves for the assistance of Ireland, yet unless the king would remove his evil counsellors and take such counsellors as might be approved by parliament we should account ourselves absolved from this engagement.[89]

If he had tried to justify the constitutional innovation he was now demanding on grounds of precedent, as he had apparently been thinking of doing, he would certainly not have prevailed. It made better sense to sweep past practice aside and take a stand on the grounds of political emergency. In this sense the tactics were right. All the same Pym had put himself in an

---

88 *D'Ewes (C)*, pp. 44–7; *Evelyn*, pp. 115–6. For a different view see Zagorin, pp. 247, 253–4.
89 *D'Ewes (C)*, pp. 47, 94; Clarendon I, 399.

absurd position. How could parliament possibly refuse to carry out its manifest duty of defending the realm from popery? Suddenly Pym confused his backbenches by appearing to contradict everything he had striven for. He also, of course, faced a barrage from the royalists. 'By such an addition we should as it were prevail upon the king', objected Hyde. Waller neatly compared Pym's motion to Strafford's alleged advice to the king that he was absolved from all rules of government if parliament failed to supply him with money. This daring bid to turn the tables indicates the growing confidence of the royalist faction.[90]

Pym extricated himself from this fracas with remarkable skill, though in doing so he had no choice but to make his proposal more open and drastic. On 8 November he brought in a new formulation. Unless Charles accepted the principle of parliamentary approval of royal officers, 'though we would continue in that obedience and loyalty to him which was due by the laws of God and His Kingdom, yet we should take such a course for the securing of Ireland as might likewise secure ourselves.' Again debate was furious. Orlando Bridgeman stood firm on the king's prerogative, which gave room for removing counsellors but not approving them. Culpepper was with him: 'that we could not desire this of right'. Waller thought that a system of parliamentary approbation would hinder the preferment of members of the House and counsellors' freedom of speech. Pym sought to satisfy all objectors. He emphasized the moderation of his proposal and the distinction between nomination and approbation. They were merely discussing a petition not an act. The public counsels of the king were a matter of public interest. A positive response from the king would 'discourage and dishearten the rebels that have bragged that they have in court the king's friends'. His arguments carried the day by a majority of 151 to 110.[91]

This recovery after he had slipped so badly may appear surprising. Obviously it is a tribute to Pym's personal standing and to his superb debating powers. But the vital distinction between the two formulations of the Additional Instruction was that the second was realistic while the first was not. Though there were difficulties in the offing over money and the cooperation of the Lords, the threat to act against the Irish rebels without Scottish help did not appear an idle boast. By 8 November the Commons had already obtained the peers' agreement to an ordinance for raising volunteers under the earl of Leicester and for supplying them from the royal magazines with arms and munitions. They had also issued directions for the arms and ammunition at Carlisle to be sent to Carrickfergus. Backbenchers took this parliamentary assertion of executive powers for granted. Involvement with the armies in the north had accustomed them to

90 *D'Ewes (C)*, pp. 94–5; D.H. Pennington in Parry, editor, *English Civil War*, pp. 32–3.
91 *D'Ewes (C)*, pp. 99–102, 105; Gardiner x, 56–7.

dealing with many aspects of warfare.[92]

The contentious Additional Instruction was never in fact sent to the committee in Edinburgh because the Lords, prompted by the king himself, threw it out after hearing well judged speeches against it by Bristol and Digby. Pym talked of sending it without the concurrence of the peers but never did so.[93] It should not be discounted though because it was abandoned. By causing Pym hastily to switch his tactics on the key issue of royal counsellors, the Irish rebellion had made a distinct mark on the growth of factional tension within the Commons.

The most illuminating political document of 1641, as we have seen, was the Grand Remonstrance. In the end it was also the most divisive. The remonstrance committee's final draft was brought into the Commons on 8 November. During the next fortnight it became a principal item of business and a good many additions and deletions were made as it was taken clause by clause. The intense emotions the document generated became progressively more apparent and the denouement was keenly anticipated.[94] Some well affected to him opposed the Remonstrance 'with unanswerable arguments', Nicholas told the king on 19 November, 'but it is verily thought that it will pass notwithstanding.'[95] The debate from noon on 22 November until two o'clock the next morning, which ended with the Remonstrance being carried by 11 votes, is one of the most celebrated incidents in the story of the origins of the civil war. Awe at what the House was contemplating mixed with anxiety and emotion during those exhausting hours. If the Remonstrance passed, observed Sir Edward Dering, much of Christendom would 'quickly borrow the glass to see our deformities therein'.[96]

Why did Pym revive the Remonstrance project and what did he hope to achieve by it? The final section, added in November, spelt out the implications of the second army plot and the Irish rebellion. No doubt in their defensiveness the final clauses, like the rest of the document, expressed the committee's collective mind but the pen was unmistakably Pym's. We find the familiar landmarks of his mind. His conviction, for instance, that 'the religion of the papists hath such principles as do certainly tend to the destruction and extirpation of all Protestants' was repeated. The Remonstrance ended with his long-established vision of religious unity at home as a preliminary to engagement in the ideological struggle abroad: both charity and 'wisdom for our own good' bound the English government to seek the liberty, safety and prosperity of the foreign Churches, 'for by this

92 *LJ* IV, 424–5, 430; *Evelyn*, p. 132; Pennington, pp. 162, 179–80.
93 *Evelyn*, pp. 129, 133; *D'Ewes (C)*, pp. 104–5, 125, 140–1.
94 *CJ* II, 294, 298, 308–9, 311, 316, 317, 320, 321; *D'Ewes (C)*, pp. 51, 106–7, 111, 143; *JMH* IV (1932), 6–7.
95 *Evelyn*, p. 141.
96 *Dering*, p. 108.

means our own strength shall be increased and by a mutual concurrence to the same common end we shall be enabled to procure the good of the whole body of the Protestant profession.'[97]

The autumn developments made an appeal to the people more imperative even than it had been in the summer. The 'people's good opinion', Nicholas had reflected on 27 September, was the parliamentary leadership's 'anchorhold and only interest'. 'To wash off the calumnies which are said to be cast on the parliament and to secure themselves in the good opinion of all men' was Sir John Coke's summary of the leadership's purposes. Pym hoped to bring the House into line behind a document that was designedly conciliatory towards conservative opinion in a number of important respects. For a few days after its introduction it looked as if a bid for consensus might succeed. On 10 November Sir Edward Dering clearly still expected the House to reach a point when it could distribute copies of the declaration without a division.[98]

The Remonstrance did after all contain little that was obviously radical. Root and Branch was dropped in favour of a proposal for a synod of 'grave, pious, learned and judicious divines', whose task it would be to present parliament with a blueprint for Church government. Slanders about parliament's intentions to 'abolish all Church government' and 'leave every man to his own fancy for the service and worship of God' were rebutted. A request for a standing commission which would use all due means for the execution of the recusancy laws was unexceptional. The militia issue was omitted altogether. The counsellors issue was stated in the moderate form of a plea that the House had 'great reason to be earnest' with the king not to appoint unsuitable men. Favourers of papists, those who spoke contemptuously of either House and agents of foreign princes of another religion were categories it was urged he should avoid. Such men, the Remonstrance explained, might be objectionable although no legal case for impeachment could be made out against them. This approach to the issue of appointments contrasted sharply both with Goodwin's motion and with Pym's words on the very day the Remonstrance came before the House.[99]

The bid for consensus was only a failure because the royalist faction, perhaps quite understandably, was not prepared to take what was on paper at face value. The arguments in the debates on the document primarily concerned the policies which were believed to lurk behind the leadership's manifesto. So when it came to the question of counsellors, for instance, the royalists assumed the Remonstrance was a declaration of intent to grasp a power of approbation. Orlando Bridgeman countered this with the usual

97 BL E 181 (2): *A Remonstrance of the State of the Kingdom*; Gardiner, *Documents*, pp. 205–6.
98 *Evelyn*, p. 93; *HMC Coke*, p. 295; *JMH* IV (1932), 6.
99 Gardiner, *Documents*, pp. 227–32.

royalist assertion that ministerial appointments were 'one of the choice jewels of the king's crown'. Pym and his friends, in their replies, were in disarray. Pym himself stood his new ground and maintained that to desire Charles 'to advise with us about it' was reasonable after the country had suffered so much by counsellors of the king's own choosing. Denzil Holles and John Maynard, on the other hand, trying to be conciliatory, pointed to the wording of the declaration before the House. 'We only beseech the king to choose good councillors', declared Holles.[100]

Nowhere is the gap between what the Remonstrance said and what it was taken to imply more obvious than in the debates on religion. In these debates those, like D'Ewes, who had returned from the country with a sense of spiritual urgency, intent on completing a programme of reform, stood face to face against those, like Hyde, who could honestly say they thought the important work in this sphere was done and 'all particulars were in a good condition if we could but preserve them'. In calmer times these differences of approach might have been reconcilable; with insecurity and emotion uppermost they were disastrous for unity. Although the Root and Branch bill had been laid aside it was assumed by conservative MPs, just as it was by most of the peers, that it would be forced through in the wake of bishops exclusion. Although even the most zealous Puritans in the House wished to do no more than reform the liturgy, Hyde was no doubt right when he said that 'many sober good men were afraid the common prayer book should be taken away'. 'Impudence and ignorance is now grown so frontless', declared Dering on 20 November, 'that it is loudly expected by many that you should utterly abrogate all forms of public worship and at least, if you have a short form, yet not to impose the use of it.'[101] In view of the fears about order in the Church that had been aroused almost anything the Remonstrance said on the subject was bound to be controversial. No matter that Pym's whole policy over religion had been negative since 20 October.

The tide had been running particularly strongly the royalists' way, so far as religion was concerned, ever since parliament reassembled. During the recess Sir Edward Dering had the unnerving experience of being challenged about the general order on the liturgy, when he sat on the Kentish bench at the Michaelmas sessions. He had been asked, probably at the instigation of Sir Roger Twysden, who was shocked by the illegality of the Commons' proceedings, whether the order was intended to suspend divine service as it was then by law established.[102] On 21 October he took the offensive with a bold speech against the validity of the order. He warned colleagues that it was being questioned by good friends of the House, men

100 *D'Ewes (C)*, pp. 184–5; Verney, *Notes*, pp. 123, 125.
101 *D'Ewes (C)*, pp. 46, 151; *Dering*, 102. See also *CSPD 1641–3*, pp. 165, 212; Larking, p. 74.
102 *Twysden*, pp. 190–1.

who had sent them as trustees: 'They know they did not send us hither', he avowed, 'to rule and govern them by arbitrary, revocable and disputable orders especially in religion.' Dering went on to argue that, in any case, the wording of the order implied that it would expire at the reassembly of the parliament. No one apparently dared challenge this reading.[103]

In another speech, which he never actually delivered, Dering planned to argue that it was 'a dangerous time to make any determinations in matter of religion': 'men are nowadays many of them more wise and some of them more wilful than in former times.'[104] He had accurately sensed the mood among many of his colleagues. Backbench opinion was plainly with Dering on 21 October, even if Nicholas's summary that the general order was 'conceived by most . . . not to be justifiable by law and therefore not binding' somewhat exaggerated the decisiveness of the mood. Henry Marten's brazen suggestion that Dering should withdraw, while members discussed his offence in presuming to arraign an order of the House, fell very flat.[105] In these circumstances the leadership had no option but to backtrack and they hastened to adjourn debate when the validity of the general order was subsequently raised.[106] There were other instances of the strength of the conservative reaction inside the Commons. Pym only won a narrow victory when he sought to petition Charles to delay his appointment of new bishops. A 'tedious' four-hour debate was necessary on 18 November to keep a petition from Nottinghamshire in favour of episcopacy out of the House. Edward Kirton had another petition of his own devising against Anabaptists and Brownists ready to present.[107]

The first two religious clauses of the Remonstrance to produce major clashes were ones that launched undiscriminating attacks on the episcopate. Men like Culpepper, Dering and Falkland found it intolerable that the whole clerical estate should be blamed for the canons of 1640 and that every single bishop had been held responsible for introducing 'idolatrous and popish ceremonies'.[108] They were sufficiently sympathetic to the Laudian Church to appreciate that it included men like John Davenant and Joseph Hall as well as Arminians like John Cosin and Matthew Wren.[109] Falkland, inspired by the Great Tew discussions, was open-minded towards all those who favoured moderate churchmanship.[110] Dering, for all his reforming zeal in 1640, had probably never been one of those who lumped together Laud and all his colleagues. This was part of

103　*Dering*, pp. 78–81.
104　*Ibid*, pp. 81–4.
105　*D'Ewes (C)*, pp. 20, 149–51; *Evelyn*, p. 110.
106　*D'Ewes (C)*, pp. 19–20, 79, 81.
107　*Ibid*, pp. 51–4, 165–6, 176.
108　*Ibid*, pp. 117, 151–2.
109　Gardiner, *Documents*, pp. 85, 230; *Dering*, pp. 111–12; Lamont, *Godly Rule*, p. 92.
110　Wormald, pp. 240–82.

his dilemma in 1641. He was in touch with men like Richard Holdsworth, who in a recent letter had blamed the sad condition of the Church on the 'indiscreet and offensive practices of some of our own order, by their intro- duction of superstitious rites and preaching of unsavoury doctrines'.[111]

The persuasiveness of the royalist faction is evident from the narrow majority of 25 by which Pym saved the clause on the bishops' introduction of 'idolatrous and popish ceremonies' on 16 November. The same day he twice gave way before the royalists on the more crucial issue of the liturgy: both a clause justifying disuse of the prayer book and another defending the House's stand against the peers in September were omitted without a division. Yet the royalists won an even more striking victory. Culpepper and Falkland joined the committee that had drafted the Remonstrance when it was sent back to them for reconsideration in the light of the House's discussions.[112] Two new clauses which were subsequently added bear the unmistakable mark of their thinking. One of them was a rejection of the malicious slanders levelled against parliament about its intention to 'destroy and discourage learning'. Horrified by mechanic preaching and sectarian excesses, the conservatives saw the whole discipline of theology as under attack. Dering spoke at length on this point in his final speech against the Remonstrance.[113] The other new clause was an extraordinary conjunction of different priorities. It seems to show Pym compromising with the conservatives. On the one hand it declared that it was far from the Commons's purpose 'to let loose the golden reins of discipline and govern- ment in the Church, to leave private persons or particular congregations to take up what form of divine service they please'; on the other hand it expressed the House's desire 'to unburden the consciences of men of needless and superstitious ceremonies, suppress innovations and take away the monuments of idolatry'.[114]

Uncertainties will remain about some of the dealing that went on over the religious clauses of the Remonstrance. The outcome was a set of state- ments that appear confusing, ambiguous and even contradictory. But there is little doubt who came off best. The royalist case was coherent and staunchly argued. Many were coming to see the prayer book and episcopacy as bulwarks of order. The royalists' plausibility on these issues surely goes far to explain the massive vote against the Remonstrance.

For all its importance, however, religion was probably not the main cause of the polarization of opinion that occurred over the Grand Remon- strance. The overriding issue, at this climacteric of the Long Parliament, was trust. The committee responsible for drafting the Remonstrance was

111 Larking, p. 53.
112 *CJ* II, 317.
113 *Dering*, pp. 112–18.
114 Gardiner, *Documents*, p. 229.

composed of men who, despite their genuine protestations about wanting to make him great and glorious, did vehemently distrust Charles I. They made their suspicion of him obvious at several places in the document. Thus they were attacked by D'Ewes for the suggestion that Charles had passed some of the reform statutes with a 'seeming unwillingness' and by others for implying that the king was personally responsible for the persecution of Sir John Eliot. Their sheer terror about Charles's intentions prompted the arrogant statement that the king 'had not bread to put in his head nor was able to subsist but by the bounty of his people'. This was omitted also following Falkland, Hyde and Bridgeman's objections.[115]

As a piece of calculated self-justification the Remonstrance was bound to alienate those who had been unhappy with the leadership's plans and methods for some while. But what really shocked many was its provocative tone and its popular purpose. Sir John Coke described it as 'a bitter story of the worst actions which have passed since His Majesty's reign until this present hour, with a comparative of the happy government under this parliament.' He went on to note that, whereas other remonstrances had been complaints of the people to the king, 'some say this is a complaint of the king to the people.'[116] The Remonstrance was without precedent; it was inflammatory; it might provoke a contra-remonstrance from the malignant party in the name of the king. These were the points put most forcefully in the final debate by Bridgeman, Culpepper, Dering and Hyde, men who desired to cajole the king rather than goad him, and to tempt him towards a settlement by concealing his errors and giving him the benefit of the doubt.[117] Hyde, no doubt with the September experience over the liturgy in mind, also stressed the dangers of the Lords, who were left unconsulted, issuing a contra-remonstrance.[118] Dering brilliantly summarized the royalist case in the celebrated histrionic outburst during which he assured his colleagues that none of his Kentish constituents looked 'for this at your hands'. Perception of an impending breakdown of social and political order underlay his avowal that he 'did not dream that we should remonstrate downward, tell stories to the people and talk of the king as of a third person'.[119]

Was it proper and necessary, at a moment of political emergency, for this story, in this shape, to be told to the nation? This was the insistent question which the leadership had to answer. Their performance was impressive. John Glyn, Hampden, Holles and Rudyerd all contributed trenchantly, emphasizing the positive aims of the Remonstrance, parliament's need to be proud of its achievements and its responsibility to satisfy those who had

115 *D'Ewes (C)*, pp. 143–4, 183–6, Verney, *Notes*, pp. 121, 124.
116 *HMC Coke*, p. 295.
117 *D'Ewes (C)*, pp. 183–4; Clarendon I, 417–8.
118 I owe this point to Miss Gillian Milne.
119 *Dering*, pp. 108–9.

given it their trust. 'The kingdom consists of three sorts of men, the bad, the good and the indifferent and these we hope to satisfy', declared Holles: 'they can turn the scales.' Pym's argument, in a well organized speech which took the main points made against him one by one, was the argument of necessity. 'He had thrust home all the plots and designs to the court', he claimed, 'and it is time to speak plain English, lest posterity shall say that England was lost and no man durst speak truth.' 'Nothing but a declaration can take away the accusations that lie upon us', he affirmed; the Remonstrance would 'bind the people's hearts to us, when they see how we have been used.' Yet again Pym held out his often repeated vision of national revival: 'if this king will join with us we shall set him upon as great grounds of honour and greatness in that all the world shall not be able to move him.'[120]

How MPs voted on the Grand Remonstrance is largely a mystery. When Hampden, Holles and Pym have been put on one side and Culpepper, Dering, Falkland and Hyde on the other, there are not many more whose decision is recorded. What is clear is that votes on this measure cannot be regarded as invariable pointers to civil-war allegiance. Three out of nine opponents mentioned by Sir John Coke to his father – John Crew, Sir Robert Pye and Alderman Soames – became parliamentarians.[121] A large diversity of motives certainly lay behind men's decision to give their voice one way or the other. Some seem to have been pulled in two directions by their response to different parts of the declaration. Hyde confessed he disliked the narrative but accepted the case for a progress report. Rudyerd went along with the 'historical part', but was concerned that the 'prophetical part' would lead the world to expect things that parliament might not be able to perform.[122] D'Ewes found the conflict between his attachment to constitutional precedent and his desire for religious reform so uncomfortable that he left the debate soon after four o'clock with a remarkably convenient but probably quite genuine cold. There were some particulars, he confessed in his journal, he 'could not in my conscience assent unto', although his 'heart and vote went with it in the main'. But perhaps the oddest reaction to our eyes was that of Sir Thomas Peyton who thought the whole debate on 22 November tedious 'beyond all example and precedent'.[123]

What then was the pattern of parliai. ntary business in the first five weeks of the new session? Men trickling back from their vacation in the last days of October found themselves plunged into a period of hectic day-to-day politics punctuated by a series of emergencies.[124] The atmosphere of

120 *D'Ewes (C)*, pp. 184–5; Verney, *Notes*, pp. 122–5.
121 *HMC Coke*, p. 295.
122 J.A. Manning, editor, *Rudyerd's Memoirs* (1841), pp. 222–3.
123 *D'Ewes (C)*, pp. xli, 183, 185.
124 *D'Ewes (C)*, pp. 22, 25, 31; *CJ* II, 294; *HMC Coke*, p. 293–4.

the new session was manifested in the procedures adopted. On 16 November all committees except five crucial ones were suspended. Midday breaks were abandoned and the House often sat late. The Speaker's exhaustion is a measure of the pace the Commons set itself: on 30 October he had to excuse himself for a while; on 19 November he complained that he could not go on sitting 'daily seven or eight hours'; on 3 December he wrote to Secretary Nicholas begging him to obtain the king's assent to his retirement. Yet, for all the striving of these weeks, there was little achievement and a deepening sense of paralysis. 'Notwithstanding all the discourses in parliament, I see nothing put into action', wrote Nicholas on 12 November.[125]

The House of Commons was numbed because the consensual system of parliamentary politics on which members had been nurtured was breaking down. In a recent discussion of this system its two guiding principles have been defined as 'the primacy of debate and the unanimity of resolution'. The first of these principles had been gradually eroded between November 1640 and September 1641. The campaign against Strafford swept men along to a predetermined conclusion. The House was rushed into the Protestation, without being given time to assess the implications of Pym's plan to turn it into a national political test. The Ten Propositions were hastily formulated but forcefully imposed on the House. Pym had always been impatient of long debate, seeing it as an obstacle to action.[126] At the critical moments of 1641 the essence of his leadership was thus the tactical denial of debate: matters were always alleged, at such moments, to be too desperate to allow for pondering and thoughtful consideration. Yet debate was taken seriously by all those who had any experience or knowledge of parliament's accepted role in the constitution. Men came to Westminster expecting to listen, weigh arguments and be convinced, not to be manipulated or conquered. In debate all were traditionally equal: this was why the rule that no member could speak twice to an issue was normally enforced. Each contribution to debate was treated on its merits. Empty rhetoric was derided; pedantry and self-importance, as D'Ewes discovered but would never have admitted, were disdained. The qualities that were valued most highly in an MP were clarity of argument and altruism. Thus Pym's reputation stood so high at the start because he was, in Sir Thomas Peyton's words, 'an ancient and stout man of the parliament that ever zealously affected the good of his country'.[127]

Parliament's established procedures were designed for an institution which met to get business done: this primarily meant the creation of

---

125   *D'Ewes (C)*, pp. 58, 317; *CJ* II, 317; *CSPD 1641–3*, p. 190; *Evelyn*, p. 134.
126   I am grateful to Professor Conrad Russell for this point.
127   M. Kishlansky, 'The Emergence of Adversary Politics in the Long Parliament', *JHM* XLIX, (1977), 619; *D'Ewes (C)*, p. xl.

legislation. The committee system served to shape bills in the light of arguments put on the floor of the House, to allow compromises and to deflect opposition. The presumption was that once a bill was reported it would usually pass the House. Divisions on bills were rarely necessary.[128] The Long Parliament had respected these norms. The reason that the Commons so nearly reached unanimity on the Root and Branch bill was that debate was given full rein and waverers were given time to come round. But the problem was that the exigencies of warfare and the year's unending plots and emergencies were imperceptibly turning the Commons from a legislative body into something quite different.

The royalist faction whose emergence has been a principal theme of this chapter disliked the leadership's sensationalizing of popish plots, its bullying tactics to secure assent to its policies, its attempts to push through radical constitutional measures and its piecemeal encroachment on the executive powers of the king and the privy council. Unanimity of resolution, the second fundamental principle of the consensual system, broke down in the autumn of 1641 because the royalists, though not numerous, were strongly committed, very energetic and increasingly confident that they commanded significant support. Pym was fighting for his political life against an assertive alternative leadership. The vote on the Grand Remonstrance showed how evenly matched the factions were, much more so than some had cared to admit a few days before. How wrong Cromwell was when he said the Remonstrance would pass with very little debate.[129]

The hallmarks of the royalist programme were defence of the Church and the king's prerogative and resistance to the rumour and innuendo with which Pym and his associates worked to magnify the sense of emergency at Westminster.[130] Differences of emphasis between the leaders of the royalist faction, such as between Falkland and Hyde over religious issues, were less important than the sense of acting in concert which now held them together with those like Bridgeman and Waller, who earlier in the year must have felt they were voices crying in the wilderness. Confidence in the persuasiveness of the conservative case grew with each little victory. Moreover it was constantly fed by Edward Nicholas, a tireless worker in the royal cause. He was the king's mouthpiece, corresponding avidly with Edinburgh, absorbing and fulfilling the king's instructions.[131]

In the Lords, as well as the Commons, there was bitter conflict during the first weeks of the new session. Although the debates themselves are poorly documented, the establishment of a royalist phalanx by the queen, acting on her husband's instructions, is fully recorded. The shrewdly

128 *JMH* XLIX, (1977), 620–3; Russell, *Parliaments*, pp. 5, 35–40.
129 Clarendon I, 419.
130 *Evelyn*, p. 116; *D'Ewes (C)*, pp. 15, 26, 30, 45, 63–4; Wormald, pp. 17–27.
131 *Clarendon* I, 311–312; Wormald, pp. 282–9; *Evelyn*, pp. 92–3, 97, 100, 113.

concocted list of 11 peers 'fit to be sent for', which she sent to Nicholas on 5 October, showed Henrietta Maria's political instincts. Some, like Bristol, were obvious nominees. He told Nicholas that, although there were rumours he and his son would be questioned in parliament, nothing would deter him from performance of his duty. Others chosen were more than likely to be reliable. Lord Poulett was an unusual figure in that he was a firmly Calvinist royalist, who had already acted the part of a stout advocate of the Caroline regime on the local stage.[132] The earl of Nottingham's loyalty was unquestionable. Although he scarcely had a political career behind him, he was alleged on 13 July to have ordered a personal copy of Digby's speech on Strafford's attainder from a scrivener.[133] The earl of Bath, as we have seen, was deeply conservative. The earl of Cumberland was an amiable scholar more at home in his library or in the saddle than at Westminster but there was every reason for the crown to trust him. Lord Seymour had been pulled into the royal orbit by his recent promotion.[134]

The rest, though less easily assessable, might reasonably have been expected to rally to the king's cause. The young earl of Devonshire, an energetic lord lieutenant in Derbyshire, had attended the House consistently earlier in the year. So had Lord Coventry, the son of a devoted servant of the king. In fact all those summoned in the first instance did attend regularly between November and the following January, except Lord Cottington, the earl of Newcastle and Poulett, who was somewhat erratic.[135] Newcastle was certainly disenchanted with political life at this time and there may be some truth in the story that he resigned his office of governor to the prince in May 1641 in fear for his life and estates.[136] Cottington, confined to his chamber at Fonthill with the stone and gout, had a perfect excuse for his failure to appear.[137] During November the queen thought it wise to add reinforcements to these initial recruits. She also instructed Cottington to send two proxies that he held besides his own. The earls of Caernarvon and Southampton and Lord Dunsmore quickly answered the royal summons and became assiduous attenders.[138]

Once in place the peers chosen for their sense of duty were regularly encouraged by royal messages conveyed through Nicholas. To divert parliament from other mischiefs, Bristol should renew the dispute between the Houses over the Protestation. 'Command the Lord Keeper in

---

132 *Evelyn*, p. 110; Clarendon II, 531–2; Barnes, *Somerset*, pp. 281–98; I am grateful to Professor Conrad Russell for drawing my attention to Poulett's will: PRO, Prob. 11/207/45.

133 BL Harl. MS 479, fol. 797v.

134 Wedgwood, *The King's War* (London, 1958), pp. 110, 118.

135 L. Beats, 'Politics and Government in Derbyshire' (Sheffield University PhD thesis, 1979), pp. 54–69; Crummett, pp. 42–3, 145–7.

136 *CSPD 1641–3*, p. 38.

137 M.J. Havran, *Caroline Courtier* (London, 1973), p. 153.

138 *Evelyn*, pp. 128–9, 137.

my name that he warn all my servants to oppose it' ran the king's apostil when he heard about the motion in the Lords to exclude papist peers.[139] The results of all this management were impressive: bishops exclusion, the Commons' anti-Catholic measures, the draft militia ordinance and the Additional Instruction were each in turn blocked by the royalist faction.

Despite what was happening men found it impossible most of the time to think of the Houses of Parliament as assemblies divided into factions. 'If you set Pym, Holles and Hampden aside, the best of the House voted against it': Sir John Coke's account of the outcome of the Remonstrance debate was free of personal allegiance and of factional assumptions.[140] Members expected the internal workings of parliament to conform to the notions of unity and harmony that held their political world together. They clung to the concept of a myriad of correspondences linking the various members of the body politic. Court and country, they believed, depended on each other for their mutual well-being. This was equally true whether they were engaged in the nation's business in their own neighbourhoods or at Westminster.[141] Thus there were times even now when ingrained attachment to old ways prevented division. The compromise clause that emerged when Culpepper and Falkland joined the Remonstrance committee is the classic example.

Besides, old tensions cut across the factional conflict. The leadership still faced opposition from members imbued with the country viewpoint. When Vane urged on 11 November that raising money to equip an army for Ireland should be the first priority, he was resisted both by Henry Marten and by Strode, who insisted that there should be no discussion of subsidies 'till the Remonstrance were passed this House and gone into the country to satisfy them'. A few days previously Edmund Waller and Pym, strange bedfellows, had stood together in defence of a bill for impressment of soldiers for Ireland which was attacked by Marten and Sir John Hotham. Marten denounced it as 'against the liberty of the subject'.[142]

Such debates, though, were exceptional; most of the time the new factional pattern applied. Its real implications came home to many in the early hours of 23 November when George Peard moved that the Remonstrance should be printed. This was the final provocation for many and Geoffrey Palmer asked that all those who wished should have their protestations entered in the Journal: 'some waved their hats over their heads', according to D'Ewes, 'and others took their swords in their scabbards out of their belts and held them by the pummels in their hands setting the lower part on the ground, so as if God had not prevented it there

139 *Evelyn*, pp. 110, 132.
140 *HMC Coke*, p. 295.
141 Hirst in Sharpe, editor, *Faction and Parliament*, pp. 123–4.
142 *D'Ewes (C)*, pp. 83, 120–1; Gardiner x, 69.

was very great danger that mischief might have been done.' The clerk had started to enter a list of names before the House came to its senses. When it did so it recoiled in horror. So disturbing was the memory of that scene, MPs had to find a scapegoat. Palmer went to the Tower for speaking in a manner that tended 'to draw on a mutiny'. A few days later William Chillingworth joined him, when he was censured for his talk, in a private conversation at Sir John Strangeways' lodging, of 'parties or sides in the House'.[143]

The word party had not yet become a description of political organiza-tion and structure; it had no ideological connotations. There was no accepted terminology for adversary politics since there was no regular experience of them. Thus factions and parties were synonymous to con-temporary minds with 'cabals' and 'juntos'. The very use of such terms implied a corruption of the traditional political system in which the public good came before private or sectional interests. In so far as Pym on one side or Hyde and Falkland on the other acted as managers of a group who pursued common aims, they did so in the sincere belief that they were in search of the common good. Yet it was impossible, in this primitive stage of party politics, for ordinary MPs to look rationally on their programmes and choose between them.[144]

Confrontation between the parliamentary leadership and the crown became endemic after the recess. There had been a good deal of confronta-tion during the summer. But the difference between the summer and the autumn of 1641 was that, whereas in June Pym had been able to hold parliament together when he declared a programme for settlement on his terms, in November he was challenged at every vulnerable moment by a royalist faction that set out to offer the Commons an alternative leadership and he was balked all along the line by the solid phalanx of conservative peers who had taken control of the Lords. Pym was discovering that it was only by stoking the fires of anti-Catholicism that he could keep his cause alive, yet the more he did so the deeper grew the gulf of understanding between his circle and royalist observers of the Westminster debates such as Secretary Nicholas. It had become very difficult, one historian has perceptively remarked, 'for anyone in the court circle to make sense of the behaviour of Pym and his allies'.[145] It had become equally difficult, of course, for them to make sense of the attitude of those who still trusted the king and his advisers.

Two insistent problems underlay the sense of political emergency at the end of November 1641. One was the emergence of a new pattern of

143   *D'Ewes (C)*, pp. 186–7, 192–6, 216, 232–3, 320–3.
144   *JMH* XLIX (1977), 624–7.
145   Pennington in Parry, editor, *English Civil War and After*, p. 31.

parliamentary politics which men had hardly begun to grasp or accept. The other was uncertainty about where power lay. The elder Vane's hope that the privy council might be revived, that it might 'prepare business' indeed for Charles's return 'so that king and people may go close together', had not been fulfilled. The council met several times during and after the recess but the attendance lists explain why it discussed nothing but uncontentious routine matters: Saye and Mandeville, Pym's men, sat beside Bristol, the king's protagonist in the Lords.[146] Although doubtless some of those who attended the council at this time still regarded it as a potential instrument of political settlement, views about the necessary preconditions for that settlement so divided the council's membership that it remained in limbo.[147] The council was caught between a king whose most treasured prerogatives had been openly questioned and a parliament whose piecemeal involvement with armies had provided a taste of executive power.[148]

Once the king was back in London these matters would have to be resolved. The stage was set for a reassertion of royal power but the chances of anything Charles might attempt breaking the political deadlock were minimal. Pym's faction was too frightened to give way, too powerful to conquer. The king was not going to see himself permanently deprived of his authority to appoint his own councillors or control the militia once he was fully aware how much sympathy and support he had gained at Westminster. Civil war requires two sides, each controlling forces comparable in size and resources. The reality of it was still some way off. Nevertheless a resort to violence of some kind had begun to look very likely.

146 *PCR* xii, 183–94.
147 E.g. M.L. Schwarz, 'The Making of a Roundhead Peer: The Opposition of Viscount Saye and Sele in Pre-Civil War England', *Duquesne Review* xviii (1973), 22–8.
148 Pennington, pp. 162–81.

5

Political Crisis

Now all things hastened apace to confusion and calamity from which I scarce saw any possibility in human reason for this poor Church and kingdom to be delivered.

> The journal of Sir Simonds D'Ewes,
> 24 December 1641[1]

There is now nothing sought for so much as guns and trimming up of old ones.

> John Dillingham to Lord Montagu,
> 30 December 1641[2]

I was never comfortless though somewhat perplexed at these times, which have caused many here to die through fear.

> John Berners to John Hobart,
> 24 January 1642[3]

When would the king return to his capital? The news from Ireland made this question daily more insistent during November 1641. 'If there be not a hearty and perfect union between the king and his people here', wrote Nicholas to Sir John Pennington on 11 November, 'we shall be presently confounded, having in His Majesty's dominions so many great distractions.' Many still believed the king's presence might be a salve for the nation's sores. 'I pray God bless our good king and send him safe hither again', reflected Thomas Wiseman. Surely Charles's presence was 'never more necessary', declared the earl of Northumberland. The Lords decided on 1 November to urge the king to hurry home; Nicholas begged him to do so in every letter to Edinburgh.[4] Only in Pym's circle was the king's arrival at Whitehall awaited with dread. Some of his allies, probably led by Saye and Mandeville, opposed a motion at the privy council on 29 October that parliament should be moved to hasten the king's journey. 'I observe,' noted Nicholas, 'that every one of Your Majesty's privy councillors is not

---

1 *D'Ewes (C)*, p. 347.
2 *HMC Montagu*, p. 139.
3 Bodleian Tanner MS 66, fol. 246r.
4 *CSPD 1641–3*, pp. 162–3, 165, 168; *Evelyn*, p. 130; BL Harl. MS 6424, fol. 198v.

fond of your speedy return hither.'[5]

The king's confidence had been enormously boosted by his reception at Edinburgh. 'Methinks', he told the citizens there after the bonfires and feastings, 'I see already how the sun of our happiness begins to show his face through the thick clouds of distraction.'[6] The conviction that he had secured a personal triumph in Scotland sustained him through the following weeks, stormy though they were to be.[7] Meanwhile, the king's implacable distrust towards the men he saw as his determined enemies in the English parliament hardened. Charles was already deeply suspicious of all Pym's actions. 'I pray God it be to good purpose and there be no knavery in it', he wrote when he heard that the recess committee was about to tackle the question of the royal revenue. He was delighted that the Houses had ended the session at odds over the liturgy. He was adamant that he would not grant his English subjects the concession of a say in ministerial appointments that he had made in Edinburgh. The king's caustic comments embroidered each paragraph of Nicholas's reports. 'I hope some day they may repent their severity', was his apostil to the news of the recess committee's refusal of bail to Berkeley and O'Neale.[8]

Whereas all the summer it is hard to say that the king had a clear policy at all, by the early autumn there is no doubt that he was in a mood to assert himself. His episcopal appointments we have seen showed sense and moderation. We have also seen that he now exhibited a clear understanding of how a well managed House of Lords could serve his purposes. A further element in his strategy was an alliance with the City of London. There had been no close alignment between the City government and the court in the previous months. Indeed the causes of friction between the king and the leading merchants in the previous decade had been manifold. With the exception of a few concessionaires, the City aldermen had been alienated by Charles's policies. Thus Sir Henry Garway, Lord Mayor in 1641, had given evidence against Strafford at his trial.[9] There was much ground to be made up and the first sign that the king realized this was his direction to Lord Keeper Littleton on 7 September to inform the citizens that he would put right certain omissions in the tonnage and poundage bill detrimental to their interests. 'Tell the City in my name', he wrote, 'that though their own burgesses forgot them in parliament, yet I mean to supply that defect out of my affection to them, so that they may see that they need no mediators to me, but my own good thoughts.' This initiative, Nicholas reported later, 'wrought much upon the affections, not only of the

5 *PCR* xII, 193; *Evelyn*, p. 117.
6 BL E 166(5): *A Relation of the King's Entertainment into Scotland*.
7 *Evelyn*, p. 80; Gardiner x, 18–27.
8 *Evelyn*, pp. 85, 91–2, 95, 97, 104.
9 Ashton, *City and the Court*, pp. 157–208; *English Civil War*, pp. 92–6.

merchants, but of divers others in this City'.[10]

It is hard to tell exactly how Charles saw the future of the parliament. In October he thought of adjourning it outside London, where the mob he believed was simply Pym's creature: he toyed with Cambridge as a new venue. He presumably envisaged dissolving the parliament before too long with its own consent. Although there was now an act limiting his rights in this matter, he had every reason from precedent to expect he would succeed. But with the Irish Rebellion dissolution was no longer a practical option, because it was necessary to raise another army. A new strategy was needed leading not to a dissolution but to the achievement of a royal majority at Westminster.[11]

The king's resolve was strengthened by his experiences on his journey south. Wherever he halted, his people received him joyfully. York's reception was particularly magnificent: constables with flaming torches lined the street, cleaned of dirt and manure for the occasion, as the royal party came down past Marygate Tower. The mayor and aldermen welcomed the king in full regalia and the waits played on Bootham Bar. That night he was feasted and presented with £100 in a purse; next day, after lodging as Sir Arthur Ingram's guest, a cavalcade accompanied him to Tadcaster. In gratitude the king knighted five of the leading citizens and promised to look favourably on their petition for a new court to bring back trade to the city, which was alleged to be languishing without the business that had been drawn to it by the Council of the North.[12]

As Charles approached London the speeches he heard were everywhere highflown and bursting with deference. 'Our wives conceive with joy, our children's tongues are untied with alacrity and each one doth strive to cry welcome home to so indulgent a sovereign', York's recorder had declared, in an emotional account of the city's 'sea of joyful tears'. At Stamford the mayor, describing himself as the king's 'abject lieutenant', boasted the loyalty of the town; at Huntingdon the mayor harped on the dangers posed by 'sects and schisms' and besought Charles to restore the religious unity of Elizabethan and Jacobean times. A delegation of Cambridge academics came to meet him there, primed with eulogistic Latin.[13]

For weeks before he came, Nicholas had been assuring the king of the welcome in store for him 'by the better sort of Londoners'. The royal approach to Whitehall was carefully planned, with Nicholas playing the

10 *Evelyn*, pp. 81–2, 95; *Pearl*, pp. 122–3.
11 *Evelyn*, p. 104. The argument of this paragraph is based on a valuable discussion with Professor Conrad Russell.
12 YPL House Books 36, fols. 61v, 62r; *HMC Various MSS* VIII, 55–6; *Fairfax*, p. 269; D.M. Palliser, 'A Crisis in English Towns? The Case of York 1460–1640', *Northern History* XIV (1978), 114, 121.
13 A. Kingston, *Hertfordshire during the Civil War* (London, 1894), p. 29; BL E 199 (32): *Five Most Noble Speeches*.

role of master of ceremonies. Charles, he insisted, should not miss the opportunity to show graciousness to his people on the last stage of his journey, 'and to speak a few words to them, which will gain the affections (especially of the vulgar) more than anything that hath been done for them this parliament.' On 24 November the Hertfordshire gentry and free-holders waited on the king from a mile outside Ware and rode with him to Theobalds. The Lords did not sit that day, since most of them were waiting with the queen and prince to receive their sovereign.[14]

25 November was a day of festivity and entertainment. The royal family, attended by a number of peers, travelled by coach from Theobalds to Stamford Hill, where they were joined by the sheriffs of London and Middlesex, trumpeters and 72 men arrayed in the scarlet cloaks trimmed with silver lace which were the colours of the City. The main procession awaited the king in the fields outside Moorgate. A tent had been pitched for the chief dignitaries since the morning was 'gloomy and cloudy'. In an elaborate speech of welcome, Sir Thomas Gardiner, the recorder of London, offered the citizens 'hearts and affections, hearts of true subjects, full of loyalty to you our king and sovereign'. At this point the king mounted a steed, whose saddle was embroidered with gold and silver, and the rest of his party transferred to a sumptuous coach. The officers of the City and the chiefs of the livery companies, 'habited in plush, satin, velvet and chains of gold', led the procession down Cornhill. There timber platforms for the liverymen were covered with blue cloth and adorned with the companies' ensigns and pendants; even the housefronts were 'beau-tified with rich tapestry'. The same care and attention had been given to the interior of the Guildhall, where the banquet consisted of four courses and 'plenty of all delicates'. The afternoon procession to Whitehall was if anything even more impressive, since, by four on a wintry day, it was necessary for the footmen to replace the truncheons they had carried in the morning with lighted torches. The conduits in Cheapside and Fleet Street ran with wine, trumpets, church bells and 'city music' saw the king on his way: 'in their passage by the south door of St Paul's church, the choir (with sackbuts and cornets joining with them) sang an anthem of praise to God and prayers for Their Majesties long lives which pleased His Majesty so well that he gave them an extraordinary respect.'[15]

This celebration was the climax of the rapprochement between the crown and the City. The king and queen were 'resolved to have been much taken' with their welcome 'though the entertainment had been worse', explained William Montagu to his father, 'and they have, they say, a policy in it to see if they can gain the City'.[16] In his speech Charles granted some

---

14 *Evelyn*, pp. 102, 128, 139, 143–4; BL Sloane MS 3317, fol. 150r.
15 *Ovatio Carolina*, in *Somers Tracts* IV, 137–51; BL E 177 (13), *King Charles his Entertainment*; E 177(17): *Great Britain's Time of Triumph*; Rushworth III, part I, 429–32.
16 *HMC* Buccleuch I, 286.

'few reasonable demands' made unto him, mentioning particularly the restoration of the City's confiscated estates in Ulster.[17] Other points that had been raised included abolition of the corporation of the suburbs, an innovation of the 1630s that was much disliked, and alterations to the City's charter to concentrate power in aldermanic hands.[18] Yet for all this the king was foolish to take the magnificence of his welcome at face value. How wrong he was in the conclusion he drew, replying to Sir Thomas Gardiner, 'that all these tumults and disorders have only risen from the meaner sort of people' and that the 'main part of the City' was wholly loyal.[19]

What the king experienced on 25 November was an official and organized demonstration, not a spontaneous one. It had gone ahead despite the efforts of the City's MP, John Venn, to dissuade the Common Council from it 'as a thing displeasing to parliament'. A strong undercurrent of dissatisfaction remained. There was much gossip about parliament being offended at the City's generosity and so many libels against the entertainment had been dispersed in the streets that two companies of the trained bands stood ready on the day. There was also a man at every door 'sufficiently appointed to be ready upon all occasions to appease any disorders'. The author of the royalist account *Ovatio Carolina* was evidently relieved that the arrangements for lining the streets with representatives of the City companies ensured that the spectators were kept in good order.[20]

The king's speech on 25 November was a premeditated gambit. The next few days made it clear that wooing the City had become the cornerstone of royal policy.[21] On 3 December when, apparently at Henrietta Maria's suggestion, the king returned hospitality to the City fathers at Hampton Court, he accepted assurances that the demonstrations at Westminster since his return were due to 'the meaner sort of people' from the suburbs, who were beyond the Lord Mayor's jurisdiction. Furthermore he agreed to spend Christmas at Whitehall, instead of Hampton Court as he had planned, so as to promote the political confidence and trade of the capital. Five aldermen and two sheriffs were knighted that day and the delegation was 'bountifully feasted'.[22] The king and the City magistracy had knowingly entered a relationship of mutual flattery for political ends. The magistracy saw in the crown a bulwark against the growing disrespect and turbulence of the London populace; the crown saw

17 Rushworth III part I, 430.
18 *CSPD 1641–3*, pp. 177–8; Ashton, *City and the Court*, pp. 158–61, 165–7, 209.
19 *Somers Tracts* IV, 142.
20 *Ibid*, 140, 145; *D'Ewes (C)*, p. 202; *Evelyn*, p. 144, *HMC Coke*, p. 295; Pearl, pp. 126–7.
21 Gardiner X, 83–4.
22 *Somers Tracts* IV, 148–50; BL E 199 (28); Rushworth III, part I, 432–4; Pearl, p. 129; *CSPD 1641–3*, p. 192.

in the aldermen political allies against the House of Commons. The potential importance of the new partnership was obvious to all and was viewed according to men's political assumptions: William Montagu saw cause for alarm, declaring that if the City did not hold firm 'we are all undone', whereas Thomas Wiseman's hopes of settlement and an end to sectarian activity correspondingly rose.[23]

The 3 December knightings were only a part of the bonanza of honours and office-giving on the king's return from Scotland. The Lord Mayor and recorder of London received knighthoods; so did Edward Nicholas, who was also rewarded for his labours with a secretaryship of state. The duke of Richmond became steward of the king's household and his brother, Lord Aubigny, master of the queen's horse.[24] These appointments, together with the elder Vane's dismissal from the secretaryship, induced a spate of rumours about a wholesale reshuffle, which would dispose of Essex, already dismissed from his generalship south of the Trent, Hertford, Holland, Newport and Saye. 'They talk much that the king is often very private with Digby and Bristol and that he looks but overly upon the good lords', reported William Montagu to his father on 27 November. A fortnight later, relating a list of likely appointments, Montagu was even more convinced that 'the good party' was tottering.[25]

In fact the expected dismissals did not occur and it became apparent that, despite rumours to the contrary, the king meant to bring into government a broad spectrum of moderate opinion from the highest social ranks. This was the policy announced in Charles's answer to the Grand Remonstrance, written by Hyde, whom the king had recently taken into his confidence.[26] Earnestness of the royal intentions was signified by the revival of the council. The king himself took the chair at well attended meetings on 11 and 26 December, 1 January and 3 January; other meetings were also held during December. Moreover not all the business transacted was merely routine administration: Pym would have approved of the decision on 15 December, for instance, to send a commission to North Wales to investigate a plot to seize Conway Castle.[27]

But the king's strongest asset was a distinctive and plausible set of policies. The proclamation of 10 December which directed that, while parliament was considering how 'all just scruples may be removed', the prayer book should be followed throughout the land was bound to appeal to many who were unhappy about the religious disorders of the summer and autumn. A petition from Cheshire defending bishops and the liturgy

---

23 *HMC Buccleuch*, p. 286; *CSPD 1641–3*, p. 168.
24 Rushworth III, part I, 429–30; *Evelyn*, p. 145.
25 *HMC Buccleuch*, pp. 286, 288; Gardiner x, 97–8.
26 Gardiner, *Documents*, p. 235.
27 *PCR* XII, 199–207.

was read in the Lords on 20 December by the king's express command.[28] Thus the restoration of order in the Church, which was predicted in the congratulatory pamphlet *King Charles his Entertainment*, appeared to be in prospect:

> Demy powers of parliament shall find a royal guerdon
> Religion that in blankets late was tossed
> Banded, abused, in seeking almost lost
> Shall now be married and her spouse adore.[29]

The king also made plain his genuine concern to crush the Irish rebellion, urging parliament to give it foremost priority.[30] Less ostentatiously, but equally sensibly, he took steps to reform his expenditure. He was not prepared 'to live longer from hand to mouth', he told the council on 11 December, and it would be dishonourable for him to accept any more temporary grants of tonnage and poundage. He would not infringe his subjects' liberties, nor let himself be starved, nor be 'bought out of any more flowers of the crown'. So a commission to examine the royal accounts was established with a view to retrenchment. He would subsist, Charles announced, 'though below his kingly dignity, upon his own revenue without burdening his subjects'.[31] A newsletter account of his speech in parliament on 2 December summarized the king's overall mood: 'he had settled Scotland in peace and quiet and left it a flourishing kingdom and it should be now his endeavour to make this so too.' Because we know that within a few weeks Charles had turned to violence, it is easy to miss the fact that he was well set at the beginning of December 1641 to prevail by constitutional means. His proclamation for all MPs to come up from the country by 12 January indicates that, although implacable against a few, he had set his mind on working with parliament.[32]

Balked by a powerful royalist faction within their own House, Pym and his closest allies knew very well that they could be destroyed by a firm alliance between the king and the Lords. Pym was now helpless and frustrated. The anti-Catholic programme was at a standstill. The entreaties of the queen that Father Philip should be released, so that she could make her confession, were resisted, but this was merely holding ground already won.[33] No progress was made towards ending the stalemate with the Lords over the bill for imprisoning recusants: some MPs were so

---

28 *LJ* IV, 482; Gardiner, *Documents*, pp. 232–3.
29 BL E 177 (13).
30 Gardiner X, 89, 99; *EHR* II (1887), 527–33.
31 *PCR* XII, 200–1.
32 BL Sloane MS 3317, fol. 44r; Steele, no. 1905; Kenyon, *Stuart England*, p. 137.
33 *D'Ewes (C)*, pp. 178, 190, 317; BL Sloane MS 3317, fol. 52v.

disappointed about this that they brought in a new bill for disarming them.[34]

The appointment of counsellors remained a hazardous topic on the floor of the Commons. Pym tacitly recognized this when, in the petition to accompany the Grand Remonstrance, he abandoned his recent demands and returned to a simple request that Charles should remove evil counsellors and 'employ such persons . . . as your parliament may have cause to confide in'.[35] In so far as the counsellors issue was kept alive at this stage it was done so by the most traditional of means. Despite what had actually happened in the 1620s, there was still a deep sense that political demands were given both respectability and persuasiveness when they accompanied supply.[36] Thus, when they sent up the tonnage and poundage bill on 29 November, the Commons renewed their request of 9 August that the Lords should join with them in petitioning for the earl of Salisbury to become Lord Treasurer and the earl of Pembroke Lord Steward. Despite the unheeding response of the peers to these suggestions, and the king's appointment of Richmond instead of Salisbury, at least one backbencher, Walter Yonge, was all for pegging away along these lines. He called on 18 December for Sir Henry Vane to be 'put into the next bill of tonnage and poundage to be continued treasurer of the navy'.[37]

Finally, there was the question of the militia. With the king's return to London, Essex's commission to command the trained bands had expired. Strode, seizing upon the uncertainty as to where military authority lay on 27 November, called for a bill for 'putting the kingdom in a posture of defence', but Sir Walter Earle reminded him that there was already a bill in existence to that end, the bill he had chaired in committee during July.[38] Here again Pym seems to have lain low. The militia bill introduced by Haselrig on 7 December probably owed nothing to him. Rather it was St John who took the initiative, impatient with the failure of Earle's committee to tie up the summer's bill and anxious to put control of the military strength of the kingdom on an unambiguous footing. St John apparently felt that the House's votes against the arbitrary proceedings of lord lieutenants and their deputies had permanently blasted the old system. His new bill was a sincere attempt to clarify the issue.

Seldom in parliamentary history have good intentions been so misunderstood and misinterpreted. The bill settled the militia under a Lord General and the navy under a Lord Admiral, rigorously defining their powers. Blank spaces were deliberately left for the names of the men to be

34 *CJ* II, 330–1, 333, 349, 355, 357; *D'Ewes (C)*, pp. 237, 340.
35 Gardiner, *Documents*, p. 205.
36 *History* LXI (1976), pp. 5–12.
37 *D'Ewes (C)*, pp. 207–8, 312.
38 *D'Ewes (C)*, p. 202; *CJ* II, 325.

appointed and the bill's time span. The response was anguished. In vain did St John explain 'that the House might . . . put the power into such hands as they thought proper, which, for ought he knew, might be the king's and he hoped it would be so'.[39] Not only royalists like Culpepper and Waller were on their feet. Even the stalwart Essex oppositionist Sir Thomas Barrington disapproved of the bill as too 'unlimited and arbitrary'. The tide of dismay was plainly much too strong for it to be turned by Haselrig, St John and Strode. The first reading was not taken but the House decided by a majority of 33 that the bill should not actually be rejected. In view of this hostile reaction the bill's supporters bided their time: a first reading was achieved on 21 December and a second one three days later but there was no pressure to send it to committee.[40]

The short shrift St John was given is only comprehensible when his bill is compared with the one that had been chaired by Earle. Whereas this bill gave full military authority over the whole country to a single person, the earlier one had merely placed control of each county's forces in the hands of resident gentry. This bill named no names, while the intention in the summer had been to list the militia commissioners county by county, just as subsidy commissioners were listed in the subsidy acts. There was also the element of uncertainty about how long the bill would apply, which prompted fears that it would be irreversible, while the summer's bill had been specifically limited to a period of nine months.[41]

Pym's apparent neglect of his main political objectives in these weeks may not have been entirely tactical. He was preoccupied with the problems of raising an army for Ireland. It was he who usually reported from the committee for Irish affairs, who handled such details as the equipment of volunteers raised in Cheshire with stockings, shoes and caps and who set in motion the public collections for refugee Protestants.[42] The impediments to effective action were numerous and raising troops at all involved a nagging dilemma. There was no cause to doubt the loyalty of the new lord lieutenant of Ireland, the earl of Leicester, but Pym was intensely suspicious that disaffected officers who had fought in the Scottish war would grasp the chance to take commands in an army that could easily be turned against parliament. There was talk of the Commons approving all officers before they were employed.[43]

Money as usual was at the core of Pym's difficulties. At first the Commons rested its hopes of crushing the rebellion on a meagre loan of £50,000 from the City, only £15,000 of which had been raised by 18

39 Clarendon I, 365–6, 444–6; *D'Ewes (C)*, p. 245.
40 *D'Ewes (C)*, pp. 244–6; Verney, *Notes*, p. 132; Gardiner X, 95–6.
41 *D'Ewes (C)*, pp. 326–7, 346; *CJ* II, 351.
42 *D'Ewes (C)*, pp. 210, 250, 254, 277; K.S. Bottigheimer, *English Money and Irish Land* (Oxford, 1971), pp. 32–6.
43 *D'Ewes (C)*, p. 165; *CSPD 1641–3*, p. 164.

November. The return to the nightmare world of military finance brought out all the customary obscurantism of MPs imbued with the country viewpoint. D'Ewes raised hopes of scapegoats among delinquent bishops and judges; others talked of raising money from recusants and the monopolizers of salt, soap and wine. Not until 14 December did the House face realities and decide to give immediate attention to the previous summer's bill for a subsidy of £400,000. But even then the fiscal expedient which was soon to be embodied in the act for adventurers in Ireland was already in some men's minds. In the petition which accompanied the Grand Remonstrance the Commons had asked the king not to alienate any lands which might become forfeit as a result of the rebellion, since out of them satisfaction could be offered to those who would bear the cost of the war.[44]

There were other obstacles besides lack of funds. The impressment bill was held up, first by the earl of Manchester and Lord Littleton, who opposed the clause denying the king's right to compel men to military service outside their own county, then by Charles himself, who told the Lords he would only pass it so worded that it did not diminish his prerogative.[45] Meanwhile, protracted negotiations with the Scots over their sending 10,000 men into Ulster were complicated by the reluctance of some peers to see English soldiers in Ireland outnumbered by Scots and the Scots arriving there first.[46]

We are left with a general impression of long and exhausting parliamentary sessions to remarkably little effect. Settlement came no nearer in December 1641. Private bills, Sir Thomas Peyton told his Sandwich constituents on 23 December, had been 'remitted to a time which God must appoint'. When the current emergencies were in hand, he had explained a fortnight before, the next priority would be 'the business of public concernment', the remainder of the reform programme, in other words, on which MPs had set out so hopefully just over a year before.[47] Yet reforming energy had not quite petered out even in this difficult period. During December the bills concerning piracy and the relief of captives at Algiers completed their passage; the committee investigating the destruction of timber in the Forest of Dean put in some useful work; a bill for the confirmation of the subject's liberties was given a first reading.[48] There were also occasional stabs at the Puritan agenda for spiritual and moral renewal. The committee appointed in June to bring in a bill against scandalous ministers was revived on 21 December. Three days later John Wilde, the increasingly energetic recorder of Worcester, presented an

44 *D'Ewes (C)*, pp. 121, 133, 164, 284–5; *CJ* II, 355, 357; Gardiner, *Documents*, p. 205.
45 *LJ* IV, 462–3, 473–4, 481; *CJ* II, 335, 337–8, 341; BL Sloane MS 3317, fol. 51r; Clarendon I, 440; Gardiner X, 95, 99.
46 Clarendon I, 438; *CJ* II, 331; *D'Ewes (C)*, pp. 333–4.
47 BL Add. MS 44846, fols. 8v, 11r.
48 *CJ* II, 329–32, 350, 354, 356; *D'Ewes (C)*, pp. 236, 325, 335, 346.

ordinance to quicken the enforcement of the laws against swearing, drunkenness and profanation of the sabbath.[49]

The clearest indication of the political bankruptcy of the parliamentary leadership in December 1641, and of its desperation, was the attention given to scapegoats. The pursuit of 'delinquents', which was the label now given to all those believed to have parliament's ruin at heart, became the motif of the leadership's policy. But the only concrete result was the expulsion from the Commons on 9 December of four MPs implicated in the first army plot. There was no prospect of bringing other delinquents low while they were protected by the peers and the crown. 'The proofs are so broken', noted Nicholas with regard to the case against O'Neale, 'as they will not make a full and clear evidence.' Yet the impeachment went ahead.[50] Hunting and exposing delinquents had become essential simply as a means of rallying support during a prolonged and exasperating political deadlock.

The earl of Bristol and his son Lord Digby were obvious new targets. Bristol came under attack when his involvement in plans for a truce between Holland and Spain, to be mediated by Charles, was revealed to some MPs by the French ambassador. A letter of 1625, alleged against him, made it appear that he had tried to persuade the king to turn papist and Cromwell smeared him with implication in the first army plot.[51] Digby, meanwhile, provoked the Commons by a speech on 23 December, in which he accused MPs of invading the privileges of the Lords and the liberties of the subject. It was widely discussed: as one newsletter put it, he had 'bespattered the House of Commons as much as one would do his cloak in riding from Ware to London'.[52] The campaign against both men reached a climax on 29 December, when there was a concerted move by John Glyn, Holles, Pym and Strode, among others, to press the Lords for Bristol's removal from court and for justice against Digby.[53]

Even more obnoxious than the Digbys, to Pym's mind, were the 13 bishops, impeached in August but still not in his clutches.[54] At a conference with the Lords on 13 December, he read an inflammatory and partisan account of the episcopate's political stance, which he wanted published, with the concurrence of the Lords and the king, as the preamble to a declaration concerning the Irish rebellion:

> Before the Scots were declared rebels or one drop of blood shed the bishops were so zealous against them (they being Protestants) they made prayers, enjoining those prayers to be read in all churches, wherein they do declare them

49 *CJ* II, 348, 353, 356; *D'Ewes (C)*, pp. 308, 333, 343–4.
50 *D'Ewes (C)*, pp. 234, 258–60, 303–5, 336; *CJ* II, 332, 337; *Evelyn*, p. 141.
51 *D'Ewes (C)*, pp. 352–3, 357–8.
52 *HMC Montagu*, p. 137.
53 *D'Ewes (C)*, p. 361; Crawford, p. 59.
54 *D'Ewes (C)*, pp. 130, 133–6, 221, 240, 280.

rebels, pray for confusion upon all their designs. But now in this business against the Irish rebels, wherein religion is so much more concerned and so much of our brethren's blood hath been shed, neither they nor any of their episcopal function have so much as prayed or implored God's assistance against such barbarous cursed rebels.[55]

The same day Holles launched a forthright attack on the bishops as religious innovators, calling them 'instruments of the devil striving to increase and build his kingdom to the decay of the propagation of the gospel'. He blamed them for fomenting divisions in the kingdom, for favouring the Irish rebellion and for oppressing parliament's proceedings.[56]

This note of hysteria was bound to exacerbate the vicious factionalism within both Houses. The royalists resisted every piece of leadership provocation and implacability. Thus a plan put forward on 8 December for a declaration that neither the king nor parliament would ever consent to the toleration of Catholicism in Ireland met the objection from Culpepper that it would drive loyal papists into the arms of the rebels.[57] Three days later, Haselrig overplayed his hand when he attempted to hasten the execution of all the seven priests whose reprieve was being sought by the French ambassador. It emerged that two of them had been prisoners ever since the proclamation of 11 November 1640 ordering recusants to their homes and both were then spared in close divisions.[58] Religious controversy also smouldered. Some passages were amended in Pym's petition to the king to accompany the Grand Remonstrance, after they had been criticized by Strangeways and others. They were said to scandalize the discipline of the Church established by law.[59]

The most heated debate came on 15 December over whether the Remonstrance should be printed. William Purefoy moved that there would be no readier means of raising money for the Irish war than by sending it into the kingdom. Many took his cue to cry 'order it, order it'; by candlelight in the gathering winter dusk the matter was 'argued with great vehemency'. So bitter was the discussion that when the order for printing went through by a majority of 52, giving Pym his only major triumph of the month, the defeated royalists revived the issue of entering protestations.[60] The Commons returned to the question a week later. Hyde then suggested that any MP should be allowed to protest before a vote that, if a particular decision was taken, his name should be entered as a dissentient. In other words, he wanted the House to recognize the existence of factionalism,

55 *Ibid*, p. 281–2; BL Sloane MS 3317, fol. 42v.
56 BL E 199 (48): *Denzil Holles Esq. His Worthy and Learned Speech.*
57 *CJ* II, 335–6; *D'Ewes (C)*, pp. 254–5; BL Sloane MS 3317, fol. 42v.
58 *D'Ewes (C)*, pp. 270, 273–4, 288; *CJ* II, 339.
59 *D'Ewes (C)*, pp. 204–6, 254, 298–300.
60 *Ibid*, pp. 294–5.

which was just what most members were not willing to do. The failure to establish a right to protest on 20 December left the royalists in an unhappy dilemma: 'we must submit to a law when it is passed', declared Robert Holborne, 'but if we may not ask leave to protest we shall be involved and perhaps lose our heads in the crowd, when there is nothing to show who is innocent'.[61]

In the Lords there was a long-established tradition of entering protestations, though it had never been used for factional purposes. So far the deadlock there remained unacknowledged. Pym's attempt on 3 December to attach those peers 'more careful for the safety of the kingdom' in a joint approach to the king over the House's obstruction of bills vital to the nation's security came to nothing.[62] Not until 24 December, when he sent up a declaration about the king's appointment of the desperado Colonel Lunsford as lieutenant of the Tower, did an open break occur.[63] The appointment was offered as proof that the papist conspiracy was 'very near to maturity'. Pym wanted a joint plea to Charles to protect parliament from 'the cruelty and rage of the papists', but, after a long argument, the royalists won a deferment of debate for three days. The protestation entered against this decision by 22 peers was both factional and frankly political. The list of protestors, which included Brooke, Essex, Holland, Mandeville, Saye, Warwick and Wharton, read like a rollcall of Pym's staunchest allies.[64]

The divisions within both Houses were the common gossip of the capital. 'I begin to be of your Lordship's mind that we are running to ruin', wrote William Montagu to his father on 2 December: 'sects in the body and factions in the head are dangerous diseases and do desperately threaten the dissolution of a well governed estate.' 'Now I think is the vertical point of the times', he reflected a week later, perhaps in a deliberate reference to Sir Benjamin Rudyerd's printed speech.[65] On 16 December he had a nice tale to illustrate his reading of the month's politics. Bishop Williams and the earl of Warwick had exchanged 'some hot words', when Williams refused to withdraw from a discussion about the fate of the condemned priests: 'the bishop saying "Sir" was mistaken to have said "Sirra" and called to the bar.' 'It is dangerous to suppose parties in either House', Montagu concluded, 'but the bloods of men severally affected are up, you may see by their catching'. Others were equally alarmed. Sidney Bere predicted that divisions 'on points of so high nature' would bring 'confusion and combustion'; 'the differences between both the Houses are

---

61 *Ibid*, pp. 320–3; Verney, *Notes*, p. 136.
62 *D'Ewes (C)*, p. 228; Verney, *Notes*, p. 131; *HMC Buccleuch* I, 288; *CJ* II, 330.
63 *Sussex*, pp. 54–5; Rushworth III part I, 459–60; *D'Ewes (C)*, pp. 339–40.
64 *LJ* IV, 489–90; *D'Ewes (C)*, pp. 346–7; Zagorin, pp. 274–5.
65 BL E 196 (2); see page 1.

now very great', wrote a correspondent into Devon, 'which cannot last long.'[66] D'Ewes was plunged in gloom by the news that 22 peers had protested against a decision of their House. 'My only hope', he recorded, 'was in the goodness of that God who had several times during this parliament already been seen in the Mount and delivered us beyond the expectation of ourselves and of our enemies from the jaws of destruction.'[67]

Awareness of what was happening inside the Houses of parliament was one element in the growing sense of crisis during December 1641. Observation of the occurrences outside it was another. The king's decision to attempt a coup cannot be properly assessed until we have taken account of the political impact, during the five weeks following his return to Whitehall, of the London populace. The new-found alliance between the king and the leading aldermen of the City quickly proved a broken reed. 'Since the king's coming all things have not happened so much to his contentment as by his magnificent entertainment was expected', reflected Robert Slingsby on 2 December.[68] By then the control of London by men like Sir Thomas Gardiner, Sir Richard Gurney and Thomas Wiseman was under threat. A massive demonstration at Westminster on 29 and 30 November was the first shot in the citizenry's campaign to proclaim their alliance with the parliamentary leadership. The appearance of the London crowds at Westminster can also be seen as a defiant reply to the organized junketings of 25 November. Much worse from the City governors' point of view was to come. They failed to halt the mobilization of a petition which carried the signatures of 15,000 citizens by the time it was presented by the experienced oppositionist alderman John Fowke on 11 December.[69] More important still, in the Common Council elections on 21 December, the old leadership was displaced by men of active parliamentary sympathies, many of them radical Puritans. These elections forestalled the incipient aldermanic counter-revolution and 'transformed the political scene in London'.[70]

The king's promotion of Lunsford on 22 December could not have been worse timed.[71] He had been convicted for the attempted murder of his Sussex neighbour Sir Thomas Pelham and was reputed a man of 'desperate fortune'. Within hours a petition was being formulated to express men's fears that the Tower in his hands might prove prejudicial to the City.[72] Next day it was reported that merchants were withdrawing their bullion from the mint within the Tower, 'because they will not trust their treasure

66 *HMC Buccleuch* I, 287–9; *CSPD 1641–3*, p. 192; E Devon RO 1700A/CP 20.
67 *D'Ewes (C)*, p. 347.
68 *CSPD 1641–3*, p. 188.
69 Manning, pp. 52–4, 61–4.
70 Pearl, pp. 132–8; Ashton, *City and the Court*, pp. 205–6, 212–13.
71 *CSPD 1641–3*, p. 210; *D'Ewes (C)*, pp. 330, 336.
72 *LJ* IV, 487; *CJ* II, 354; *D'Ewes (C)*, p. 340.

under the command of the new lieutenant'. The panic over Lunsford triggered a new wave of demonstrations which continued for three days, despite the fact that on the Lord Mayor's advice Charles had dismissed Lunsford before they began. From 27 to 29 December, Westminster was in uproar. The bishops became the scapegoats for all the ills of the commonwealth: the coaches entering and leaving New Palace Yard were relentlessly searched; some of those arriving by boat were prevented from landing. When Williams grabbed a youth who was shouting 'no bishop, no bishop', to carry him into the Lords, 'the rest of his fellows came jostling in upon the archbishop in such a rude manner that the archbishop escaped very hardly with his life.'[73]

The new feature of the post-Christmas demonstrations was the emergence of a party of royalist officers ready to combat the citizens. They were disgruntled professional soldiers, many of them snobbish and swaggering men, who were waiting for their arrears of pay and lobbying for new commands in Ireland. Nehemiah Wallington, an eyewitness, was not exaggerating when he said that their 'fierce countenances and deadly weapons' alarmed the Londoners with the thought that no good was meant towards them.[74] The first encounter took place inside Westminster Hall on 27 December. Lunsford himself was there; so was one Captain Hyde who threatened to 'cut the throats of those roundheaded dogs that bawled against bishops'. The citizens were eventually driven from the Hall, although, according to one observer, they 'fought like enraged lions'. The fray continued outside with the people tearing bricks and tiles from the walls of the Court of Requests to defend themselves. Lunsford was eventually forced to escape by wading out to a boat on the Thames. Next day the focus of trouble was Westminster Abbey: when the crowd forced one of the doors, in an attempt to rescue some apprentices detained by Williams for questioning, they were driven back by stones from the abbey roof and the swords of the archbishop's gentlemen. The fiercest clash of all occurred on the third day in Whitehall. The crowds pressed about the gates abusing the officers, led by Lunsford, who had offered the king their services and a running battle developed in the street. Although no one was killed on the spot in these skirmishes, a celebrated casualty was Sir Richard Wiseman, who died later of wounds received outside the Abbey and was given a martyr's burial. According to information given to the Commons in January, three or four others died from wounds received in Whitehall; many were certainly injured in the battle there.[75]

The political campaign which ended in this bloody affair had been

73 E Devon RO 1700 A/CP 20; *LJ* IV, 598; *CSPD 1641–3*, p. 216; Manning, pp. 76, 90–4.
74 Wallington, p. 279; Manning, pp. 72–3.
75 BL Sloane MS 3317, fol. 35, Add. MS 14827, fol. 10r; E 181(9): *A Bloody Massacre; CSPD 1641–3*, p. 216–7; Manning, pp. 76–85.

initiated by merchants, shopkeepers and craftsmen. Gravity and modesty were the keynotes of the presentation of the new petition from the Common Councilmen to parliament on 11 December. MPs had heard rumours of a crowd of 10,000 Londoners, but 'divers of the richest citizens in coaches' came instead. If notice had been given of the petition's delivery, Fowke explained, 'there would have come down a tumultuous number of people'.[76] Evidently there were a good many substantial men in London, some of them probably old hands with experience of the petitioning campaigns of December 1640 and April 1641, who read the political crisis in much the same terms as Pym. The 11 December petition shows that they shared his wildly exaggerated assessment of the popish danger and regarded bishops exclusion as the best means of calming the capital. The committee which visited the Guildhall about a loan for the Irish war had been told, the petition reminded the Commons, that the abolition of the political voice of bishops and popish lords was a necessary preliminary to progress in reformation and accommodation with the crown.[77]

Thus popular demonstrations at Westminster began as an orderly extension of the petitioning movement. Some of those who were in the crowds on 29 and 30 November explained in a petition a few days later that they wanted to know what had become of their former petitions.[78] But Alderman Fowke and his friends appreciated just how much popular pressure was building up. They could not in fact contain it. A new petition from the London apprentices on 23 December, discreetly presented, nonetheless indicated the rising tide of radical opinion. If it echoed much of the case made on 11 December, the language was sharper and this time the demand for Root and Branch was spelt out.[79] Men of lesser social rank were taking charge. 'The prentices dare give out', reported one newsletter, 'that they will be able if need be to over-match a royal coup.'[80]

Yet it is hard to say how much leadership was involved in the demonstrations of 27 to 29 December. In a sense lack of leadership seems their most obvious characteristic. Clearly there were religious radicals who urged their friends to join them down the road to Westminster. There may have been something more formal, such as notices in shops and alehouses, but the only specific evidence we have of drumming up support is the paper thrust into the hands of the minister of Christ Church for him to read to the congregation on 19 December:

Sir be pleased to direct your prayers to God and move the congregation of saints

---

76 *D'Ewes (C)*, pp. 270–1; BL Sloane MS 3317, fol. 41r; Pearl, p. 222.
77 BL 669 f 4 (33); *CJ* II, 314; *D'Ewes (C)*, pp. 319–20; Pearl, pp. 210–35.
78 *D'Ewes (C)*, p. 222.
79 Society of Antiquaries: *The Humble Petition of the Apprentices* (1641); *D'Ewes (C)*, p. 337; *HMC Montagu*, p. 137.
80 BL Sloane MS 1467, fol. 146r.

here met to join with you that he would be pleased to assist the apprentices and others with strength and power and to bless their undertakings, which are speedily to root out superstition out of this and all other Churches and to extirpate all innovations of the bishops and clergy.[81]

It is not in fact fanciful to see a good deal of spontaneity about the demonstrations. A pattern of political uncertainty and related economic dislocation had become familiar to Londoners over the previous two years. The money market became tight, dealings fell off, people were put out of work. In September 1640 business was virtually halted by fears about the war with Scotland; much the same happened in the two months before Strafford's execution. This time the depression was more serious and far reaching. Trading in the capital, the 11 December petition asserted, was 'much more of late decayed than it hath been for divers years past, no man following his trade cheerfully while the lives of himself and family and the public safety of the kingdom are in danger.'[82] Many of those who clamoured at Westminster against bishops were probably not clear in their own minds what precisely they intended. They were motivated by a general sense of panic; they were struggling to articulate some kind of understanding of a political and economic crisis that was largely beyond their comprehension. Thus a tallowchandler of Coleman Street, caught up in a crowd coming down the Strand, said he was 'afraid in regard of papists and others ill affected'. John Broome of Bread Street 'came to hear news'. When 200 men, 'sworded and staved', gathered round Sir John Strangeways to demand 'his vote for the putting down of the bishops', most of them had no idea who he was, until someone identified him as 'one of the greatest enemies we have'.[83]

Hostile observers alleged that the Westminster crowds were composed of separatists, but there are good reasons for regarding this charge as simply a predictable slander.[84] Many of the mechanic preachers who had been so active in the summer were certainly still attracting regular congregations in December. Nevertheless the total membership of the separatist congregations was probably only about a thousand and there is much evidence that their leaders were intensely unpopular.[85] Prophet Hunt had recently been 'almost pulled in pieces' at the Exchange and forcibly removed from the gallery of St Sepulchre's church because he attempted to interrupt the service with a text from *Revelation*. In Fleet Street apprentices and others had attacked the home of the leatherseller Praise-God

81 BL E 181 (1): *An Order from Parliament read in Every Church.*
82 Rushworth II, 1264; BL 669 f 4 (33); B. Supple, *Commercial Crisis and Change in England 1600–1642* (Cambridge, 1959), pp. 125–31.
83 *D'Ewes (C)*, pp. 211, 213; Manning, p. 53.
84 *CSPD 1641–3*, p. 192; Manning, p. 53.
85 Tolmie, *Triumph of the Saints*, p. 37.

Barebone, when he preached for five hours to a congregation of 150.[86] In his tract *New Preachers New*, published about 20 December, John Taylor blamed the mechanic preachers for enticing men 'to neglect their callings and trades two or three days a week' and encouraging them to censure their neighbours. The revival of pamphlet controversy about lay preaching at this time suggests that the separatists were cast in the role of scapegoats rather than popular heroes.[87] There were obviously some radical Puritans like John Lilburne present among the Westminster crowds but sustained separatist leadership can be discounted.[88]

The anger of the crowds was directed against the Lords and on the face of it the leaders of the Commons had good reason to welcome them. Yet their presence brought an unexpected dimension to Westminister politics which, at the very least, MPs were bound to find disconcerting. The incident on 29 November, when the crowds invaded the Court of Requests and pressed against the door of the Lords, was a warning of the difficulties in retaining order once large numbers were assembled. The guard under the earl of Dorset could not get the citizens to stir an inch: 'I saw and heard my Lord of Dorset entreat them with his hat in his hand', reported William Montagu, 'and yet the scoundrels would not move'. It was only when Dorset ordered the guards to fire that they adopted firm measures, fending the people off with their cuirasses and threatening them with their pikes until they dispersed.[89]

Dorset's rash order, fortunately disobeyed, inevitably became a factional issue. The leadership of the Commons was already incensed that the king, on his return to London, had replaced their guard, under Essex, with a body of militiamen under a peer whom they distrusted. The royalists, taking the opposite view, argued that the citizens were tumultuous, defended Dorset's action and pursued information they obtained that the City MP, John Venn, had deliberately called down citizens in arms. Strangeways even tried to implicate Venn in a 'conspiracy for the destruction of some members of this House.'[90] Nothing was proved but MPs were left with a deep sense of unease about popular intervention in their affairs, thoughtfully summarized by the sober Norfolk Puritan Sir John Holland:

> It hath ever been observed in every well governed state as a thing of dangerous consequence to suffer the people to assemble and arm at their own wills and pleasures and though I am as confident as any man can of the fair and clear intentions of the citizens that have resorted in such numbers, in such manner,

86 BL E 180 (25): *The Discovery of a Swarm of Separatists*; E 181 (1): *An Order from Parliament read in Every Church*.
87 BL E 180 (26): *New Preachers New*.
88 Tolmie, *Triumph of the Saints*, pp. 48–9.
89 *D'Ewes (C)*, pp. 211, 213, 222; *HMC* Buccleuch I, 287.
90 *D'Ewes (C)*, pp. 213–4, 225–6, 229–31; BL Sloane MS 3317, fol. 38r.

to our doors, that it is rather for the preservation of our peace and safety than of disturbance, yet truly I conceive it cannot stand with the wisdom of this House to permit it, in respect of the danger in the possible consequence thereof . . . though the intentions of these citizens be peace, yet God only knows what the issue may be, possibly such as may endanger the reputation of all the proceedings in this parliament.[91]

Pym's attitude to the tumults is hard to determine. He certainly wished to protect the right of petitioning: 'God forbid that the House of Commons should proceed in any way to dishearten people to obtain their just desires in such a way', he declared.[92] He may well have been instrumental in several moves to keep the channels of communication open between the Commons and the City. When the JP George Long acted on a warrant from the Lord Keeper and sent down a guard to Westminster he was put in the Tower. An inquisition by some Surrey JPs into alleged 'riots and routs' at a petitioning meeting in Southwark was quashed. Moreover, according to Hyde, the witnesses about Venn's part in bringing down citizens at the end of November were kept from the House by leadership manoeuvres.[93] But when it came to massive demonstrations and bloodshed in the streets Pym's stance was bound to be equivocal. A calculated appeal for popular support appeared far too dangerous, yet Pym was much too terrified of papist conspiracy and of the king's personal antagonism to condemn the demonstrations once they had begun. Social disorder threatened Pym's standing because it seemed to confirm the worst fears of his enemies about an alliance between the Commons leadership and the City radicals. By 29 December it had become urgent to bring the crowds under control, though whether John Venn was simply acting on his own initiative when he appealed to 2000 apprentices that day for peace and quietness is uncertain.[94]

Between Christmas and the news of the king's intention to impeach five members of the Commons nine days later, fear and distrust pervaded London politics. On the evening of 29 December Charles feasted the cavaliers who had shed citizen blood in the Whitehall skirmish that day.[95] Next morning many of the Commons heard the Lord Keeper read the protestation of 12 bishops who, prevented from sitting by the affronts of the people, insisted that all the orders of the House since 27 December were null. They had appealed to the king to secure their rights. By doing so they handed Pym back the political initiative. He moved that the doors be shut and that no one should leave, then portentously announced that there

91   *D'Ewes (C)*, pp. 218–9.
92   Gardiner x, 118.
93   *D'Ewes (C)*, pp. 268–71, 283; Clarendon, i, 453–5.
94   BL E 181 (21): *A True Relation of the Most Wise Speech by Captain Venn*; Manning, pp. 86–7.
95   BL E 201 (5): *Diurnal Occurrences*, 27 Dec — 3 Jan.

was a design to be executed upon the House of Commons that very day.[96]

Such dramatic tactics were well timed. In a House thinned by Christmas absences, there was much 'alacrity of spirit' against the bishops for their unadvised and indiscreet action. They were immediately impeached for their 'insolent and traitorous' protestation, which the Commons were sure they would never have dared make 'without some back in their design'. Only a single member questioned the accusation and he did so because he thought the bishops were stark mad rather than guilty of treason and that they should be sent to Bedlam.[97] Hyde included a long and bitter passage in the *History of the Rebellion* about the ambition and imperiousness of Bishop Williams, the instigator of the protestation, the decoy duck as one satire painted him, who had so foolishly led his brethren into the Tower.[98]

Lunsford's appointment, the riots and the bishops' rash action had transformed the political situation within the Commons. It is not really surprising that Pym's reading of the latest events was generally accepted, since unnerving rumours that 'the king would be king again' had been current for several weeks. As early as 30 November there was talk of some MPs being accused of treason 'within two or three days'.[99] Papist scares had also continued unabated.[100] The only disagreement on 30 December was over the best means for the Commons to secure themselves. Pym wanted the London trained bands to be mustered: others, who thought this too provocative, preferred an adjournment to Guildhall. Finally the House decided to renew pressure on the Lords for a guard under the earl of Essex. Although the removal of 12 bishops had strengthened the hands of Pym's allies in the Lords, they were not able to swing their colleagues behind this plan, so the day ended with an agreement that MPs' servants should bring pistols with them in the morning and that three MPs who were Westminster justices should set a strong watch of halberdiers.[101]

Public opinion in London had never been so aroused. Horror and alarm at the experiences of the previous few days was the common coin of street meetings, tavern talk and newsletters. Thomas Coke spoke of 'the saddest and most tumultuous Christmas that in all my life I ever yet knew'; Robert Slingsby of the 'maddest Christmas' he ever saw. Bulstrode Whitelocke later described the street battles as a 'dismal thing to all men'.[102] A backlash had begun which could rapidly have undermined parliament's reputation. John Dillingham told Lord Montagu that there was a 'general crying down

96 *D'Ewes (C)*, pp. 364–6; Gardiner x, 120–3.
97 *D'Ewes (C)*, pp. 365–8, 374; *CJ* II, 343, *LJ* IV, 496, 498.
98 Clarendon I, 464–76.
99 *D'Ewes (C)*, pp. 165, 175–6, 212, 215, 261; BL Sloane MS 3317, fol. 150r.
100 *D'Ewes (C)*, p. 300; BL E 181 (9): *A Bloody Massacre*; E 181(17): *The Attachment . . . of a Frenchman.*
101 *D'Ewes (C)*, pp. 365–8; *LJ* IV, 496, 498.
102 *HMC Coke*, p. 302; *CSPD 1641–3*, p. 217; Manning, p. 82.

the Brownists' and a growing belief 'that all that go to Westminster in this tumultuous way are such'. 'In case we fall out', he predicted, 'I see clearly that not the religious in general but even parliament men will be voted such.'

By 30 December many citizens had resolved to shut up their shops and desist from trade 'in case things take not issue'. If three or four hundred did this, avowed Dillingham, all would 'grow to confusion suddenly'. New invasion rumours spread like wildfire: one was started in Cheapside by a Frenchman who announced that, 'if there should fall out any hurlyburlies here', 15,000 of his countrymen would soon be on Englishmen's backs. The capital longed for catharsis during these last December days. Meanwhile, for the first time since the emergencies of the year began, there was sober talk of civil war. Thomas Smith heard 'of nothing but drawing of swords and a war between the Protestants and papists which God forbid'. 'If there be a hundred to one of our side and yet the papists and that party shall have more armed men than we, as I believe they will, how you think things will go?': this was the question that Dillingham put in all serious-ness to Lord Montagu.[103] Insofar as people contemplated civil war at this stage, they did not envisage a war between king and parliament but a war between parliament and its papist enemies.

31 December began with a new flutter of alarm in the Commons when Haselrig reported that a papist gentleman was publicizing his hope before long to 'see half a dozen parliament men hanged'. In an atmosphere of heightened emotion the House produced a comprehensive set of emer-gency measures. A committee of lawyers was established for bringing the bishops to speedy trial. Another committee was given the task of furnish-ing the kingdom with gunpowder and arms. Enquiries were made about the beating of drums in London to raise the volunteer army that Charles had promised to send to Ireland. Holles, meanwhile, led a delegation to the king to request a guard under Essex. There was 'a malignant party bitterly envenomed against them daily gathering strength and confidence', he told Charles, accusing the cavaliers of steeping their hands in blood at the king's gates and menacing parliament with insolent speeches. Pym and his henchmen were now more firmly in charge than they had been for many weeks. Over the weekend, sitting as a committee at Guildhall, Pym, Holles, Strode and a few others prepared a new manifesto. They were still at work on it on Monday morning, 3 January, when they heard that there were '500 commanders about the court ready to be employed upon any desperate design'. Back at Westminster in the afternoon, Pym had scarcely finished his report when the blow so long expected and so much rumoured at last fell.[104]

103　*HMC Montagu*, p. 139; *D'Ewes (C)*, p. 360; *CSPD 1641–3*, p. 215.
104　*D'Ewes (C)*, pp. 371–7; *CJ* II, 364–6; Rushworth III, part I, 471–3; BL E 201 (6): *Diurnal*

Charles I had long been convinced that a small group of MPs were deliberately conspiring against him. In the parliament of 1628–29, he had claimed, 'the sincerer and better part of the House' were overborne by 'the practices and clamours' of a few malevolent men who did their utmost to sow and disperse jealousies. Their intent, he believed, was power: 'to break through all respects and ligaments of government and to erect a universal over-swaying power to themselves, which belongs only to us, and not to them'. Seven articles of high treason were preferred against the five members. The first one repeated the charge the king had made in the declaration at the dissolution of parliament in 1629. For the rest, the charges show that the king shared the views of those who had mounted the propaganda campaign against Pym and his clique in the summer and early autumn. The five members, it was alleged, invited the Scots to invade and endeavoured 'to subvert the rights and the very being of parliaments'. They were also charged with raising and countenancing tumults against the king and parliament.[105] If Charles suspected that Pym had a hand in summoning the crowds that clamoured for Strafford's death, he was bound to deduce that by December appealing to the populace had become a matter of policy.

The general grounds of the king's coup are thus plain. But the decision to act was very likely a sudden one. It seems unlikely, as some have suggested, that Charles was implicated in the bishops' protestation and that the accusation of the five members was merely an extension of the same design.[106] He responded impetuously to the protestation, hurriedly sending it to the Lords because he was afraid, according to Hyde, that the peers might take the opportunity provided by episcopal absences to pass the exclusion bill.[107] It was probably after he had done this that he first heard the rumour, suddenly current on 30 December, that the leaders of the Commons intended to impeach the queen.[108] Whether there was any substance in this story is uncertain.[109] For Charles, in any case, it was the last straw. Decisive action always came easiest to him when those he loved were apparently in mortal danger: in May, over Strafford, he retreated, in January, over Henrietta Maria, he attacked.

Lord Digby was almost certainly the man who brought Charles to the sticking point. Digby's fatal infirmity, noted Hyde, was 'that he too often thinks difficult things very easy'. Although he had good cause to reflect bitterly on a decision which amounted to repudiation of the counsels of moderation that he had been offering, Hyde's account rings true: 'the king

Occurrences, 2–10 January.

105 Gardiner, *Documents*, pp. 83–99, 236–7.
106 Gardiner x, 123–4; Wormald, pp. 43–5.
107 Clarendon I, 473–4.
108 *HMC Montagu*, p. 139; Gardiner x, 128; Clarendon I, 555; Wormald, p. 50.
109 BL Sloane MS 3317, fol. 35r.

was the unfittest person alive to be served by such a counsellor, being too easily inclined to sudden enterprises and as easily amazed when they were entered upon.'[110]

The story that the king was contemplating making Pym chancellor of the Exchequer on 1 January is ridiculous and its survival in modern accounts is entirely due to a single gossipy letter from Sir Edward Dering to his wife.[111] But the promotions that were made on the eve of the king's coup make sense. Falkland, who became a secretary of state, and Culpepper, who became chancellor, were among those accounted by Sir John Coke 'the best of the House', parliament men whose qualities were recognized by every backbencher. Falkland, recalled Hyde later, 'was wonderfully beloved by all who knew him as a man of excellent parts'; Culpepper was 'generally esteemed as a good speaker' and much respected for his clear summaries of the points at issue in debates.[112] In the king's mind the appointment of these two men, who had shown him such loyalty in the previous weeks by their promotion of a royalist viewpoint, and the treason charge against five members who planned his ruin were two sides of the same coin.

The king's choice of victims was perhaps predictable. There were others more radical than several of the five members certainly, like Henry Marten, Nathaniel Fiennes or the younger Vane, but all those charged had some special claim on the king's wrath. Pym picked himself of course and so really did Hampden, the taciturn Buckinghamshire patriot, who had sat with Pym in every parliament since 1621. Holles had earned his place as a personal enemy by his behaviour at the end of the 1629 session. He had been consistently active in the Long Parliament and Charles had very recently been reminded face to face that he had few subjects who were more uncompromising. Strode was another experienced oppositionist, celebrated for his boldness and vehemence, whose prominent role in attacks on the royal prerogative over the previous weeks was no doubt well known to the king. Finally there was Haselrig, a younger man with no parliamentary experience before 1640.[113] He was a friend of Pym's and had taken his children into his house during an outbreak of the plague in 1638.[114] He had an outstanding record for assertiveness in 1641 on the critical issues of Strafford's attainder, Root and Branch and the militia.

Everything went wrong for the king from the moment the attorney-general read the treason charges before the Lords on 3 January. Digby, who had apparently promised to maintain the charge against Mandeville,

---

110   Clarendon I, 457–63.
111   Larking, p. 66; Gardiner X, 127; Wedgwood, *King's War* p. 50.
112   *HMC Coke*, p. 295; Clarendon I, 457.
113   Gardiner VII, 74–6; Crawford, p. 67; Keeler, pp. 201–2, 213, 220, 318–9, 355.
114   I owe this information to Professor Conrad Russell.

instead whispered to him that Charles was mischievously advised and walked out of the chamber. He probably panicked as he watched the peers' faces.[115] The House's response to the charge was cautious: they appointed a committee to investigate whether the king was acting within his legal rights. Later in the day they agreed to join with the Commons in a petition for a guard that both the king and parliament could trust. The Commons concentrated on the breach of privilege by royal officers who had sealed Pym's trunks, study and chamber. There was no question of their meekly delivering those of their number who were accused to the sergeant-at-arms who came to arrest them.[116]

The king's decision to visit the Commons himself, taken it seems on the evening of 3 January, probably reflected the promptings of Digby and the queen. His delay of some 18 hours in carrying it out, while the news of his intentions leaked out, made it certain he would fail in his purpose. Pym teased Charles into the action which lost him more face than any other in his entire life: he and the others attended as usual on the morning of the 4th and even returned after the lunch break. The king set out, so the story went, 'upon notice that the five persons were in the House'. The intended victims ran things so fine that, according to Haselrig's later account, they were not yet on the water when the king entered the chamber. Yet there was surely some advance planning about making an escape.[117]

The significance of the king's abortive coup for our story lies in the impression it left and the interpretation MPs and others put upon it. It was generally assumed that a bloody outcome had only been avoided by the extraordinary providence by which the House received warning of the king's coming. About 400 men, many of them armed, came with the king: 'desperate soldiers, captains and commanders', Roger Hill called them in his diary, 'papists, ill-affected persons, being men of no rank or quality, divers of them being traitors in France, Frenchmen fled hither, panders and rogues'. Eighty or so of them, with swords or pistols, waited in the lobby while Charles was inside the chamber, 'so thirsty after innocent blood', according to D'Ewes, 'as they would scarce have stayed the watchword if those members had been there but would have begun their violence as soon as they understood of our denial.' They had a resolution, recorded Hill, if the accused men sat still 'to fall upon the House of Commons and to cut all their throats'. This was the story that sunk in over the next few days. Meanwhile, the stunned reaction to Charles's unprecedented appearance and his halting speech was an adjournment until the following afternoon. D'Ewes went home and made his will.[118]

115 Clarendon I, 484.
116 *LJ* IV, 500–2; *D'Ewes (C)*, pp. 377–8.
117 Bodleian Tanner MS 66, fol. 234; Clarendon I, 484; Gardiner X, 133–41; Wedgwood, *King's War*, pp. 52–5; Crawford, pp. 64–6.
118 Hill: 4 Jan; *D'Ewes (C)*, pp. 381–4; BL Harl. MS 163, fol. 121v.

In a desperate attempt to redeem his abortive coup, Charles went down to the City on 5 January. The hostility of many of the citizens was unmistakable. His meeting with the Common Council at Guildhall turned rowdy, despite his promises to suppress both popery and sectarianism and to protect parliament's privileges. 'The king had the worst day in London yesterday that ever he had', reported John Dillingham to Lord Montagu, 'the people crying "Privilege of Parliament" by thousands and prayed God to turn the heart of the king, shutting up all their shops and standing at their doors with swords and halberds.'[119] With the five members and Mandeville snugly hidden away, in Coleman Street according to one account and in Red Lion Court according to another, the City was now in mortal fear of the king and his cavaliers. A rumour the next evening that Charles intended to fetch out his victims by force brought huge crowds into the streets, with whatever arms they could lay hands on: women provided hot water to throw on the invaders, stools, forms and empty tubs were hurled into the streets 'to intercept the horse'. Panic and hysteria accounted for at least one death and several miscarriages that night.[120]

'I pray God we find not that we have flattered ourselves with an imaginary strength and party in the City and elsewhere which will fall away if need should be'. Thus did Sidney Bere, a secretary at court, ponder the king's reception in London.[121] The truth was dawning in Whitehall, between 4 and 10 January, that, for all the swashbuckling of the cavaliers and the protestations of young loyalists at the Inns of Court, the king had lost control of his capital.[122] From 6 to 10 January the Commons met daily as a committee, either at Guildhall or Grocers Hall. In the absence of its leaders, others had quickly stepped forward, perhaps under instruction from the City hideout. The speed with which the committee appointed on 5 January produced a declaration 'ready penned' suggests prearrangement. John Glyn, Nathaniel Fiennes, Sir Philip Stapleton, the younger Vane and John Wilde were the most prominent men in Pym's absence. At the meetings in the City the Commons investigated what had happened on 4 January, vindicated the House's privileges and denounced the king's 'false, scandalous and illegal' proclamation for apprehending the accused men.[123]

The control of the Common Council of London by parliament's most vigorous supporters, established in the 21 December elections, was strikingly demonstrated by its appointment on 4 January of a committee of

119 *HMC Montagu*, p. 141; *CSPD 1641–3*, pp. 241–2; *Somers Tracts* IV, 348; Wallington I, 282; Gardiner X, 142.
120 *CSPD 1641–3*, p. 245; *D'Ewes (C)*, p. 392; 'A Letter from Mercurius Civicus to Mercurius Rusticus' (1643) in *Somers Tracts* IV, 587–8; Manning, pp. 97–8; Crawford, p. 65.
121 *CSPD 1641–3*, p. 248.
122 *D'Ewes (C)*, p. 376 n.
123 *D'Ewes (C)*, pp. 387–402; Clarendon I, 486; Crawford, p. 66.

safety. The very next day the Common Council adopted a petition, drafted by this committee, which strongly condemned the king's proceedings.[124] During parliament's stay in the City the bonds between it and the new rulers of the Common Council were drawn tighter. Prompted by the committee of both Houses for Irish affairs, which was working hard at the urgent business of crushing the rebellion under the chairmanship of Sir Robert Harley, the committee of the Commons resolved that a strong guard from the City was essential when sessions were resumed at Westminster. The next step was the appointment of a subcommittee of MPs to meet regularly with the City's committee of safety over the necessary arrangements.[125] Sir Richard Gurney was helpless in the face of these moves. The king tried to revive the alliance between the royalist aldermen and the crown in a message on 3 January but it was in fact in pieces. Gurney dared not veto the committee of safety's petition, which was presented to the king in his name; he feared to issue the royal proclamation impeaching the five members; on his way home from conducting Charles to Temple Bar on 5 January, he was even pulled from his horse and had his mayoral chain torn from his neck by an angry crowd.[126]

The royalist faction in parliament was utterly discredited by the king's decisive action on 4 January. In their 'grief and anger' that the violent party at court had seized the initiative, Hyde, Falkland and Culpepper were stunned into meekly accepting the decision to adjourn to the City.[127] Only a few brave spirits spoke up for Charles, like Sir Ralph Hopton who excused his bringing armed men on the ground that some of the servants of MPs, attending in the lobby, had carbines and pistols. Hopton thought the king's speech 'full of grace and goodness'.[128] There were undoubtedly others, both inside and outside parliament, who shared his view of the matter. 'Our good king is much abused', wrote Captain Carteret to Sir John Pennington on 6 January. 'My heart pities a king so fleeting and so friendless, yet without one noted vice', Sir Edward Dering told his wife a few days later.[129]

The king had sympathizers but where it mattered, in these desperate days for him, he lacked support. The precautionary decision by the most faithful royalist MPs to stay away from the committee in London, because when the five members appeared and their colleagues refused to deliver them they would appear accessories, was no help to Charles.[130] Well

124 *CSPD 1641–3*, pp. 238–9; Pearl, pp. 141–4; Zagorin, pp. 289–90.
125 *D'Ewes (C)*, pp. 393, 396–7 n, 399; *CSPD 1641–3*, p. 248.
126 BL 669 f. 4 (42); Pearl, p. 144; Bodleian Dep C MS 164, no. 6; *Somers Tracts* IV, 590; BL E 201 (7): *Diurnal Occurrences*, 3–10 January.
127 Clarendon I, 487, 493; Wormald, pp. 48–9.
128 *D'Ewes (C)*, p. 386.
129 *CSPD 1641–3*, p. 241; Larking, p. 67.
130 *CSPD 1641–3*, p. 243.

attended meetings of the Privy Council were held on 6 and 8 January, but nothing was done at them to tackle the roots of the crisis. A request to the chief justice of King's Bench to examine a scandalous pamphlet containing a pirated version of Charles's speech in the Commons and a letter to Gurney directing him to seek out the authors of the panic on 6 January were attempts to deal with symptoms not causes.[131] Meanwhile in private, as so often, the king received conflicting advice. Whereas Digby and other hotheads pressed for force, it was reported that some 'well-affected nobles to both sides' were labouring to pacify him.[132] Two minor pieces of conciliation were insufficient to make any real impact on the mood of the City. A ship from Berwick, loaded with arms and ammunition and moored near the Tower, was given orders to fall down the river to Gravesend 'to take away all occasions of fright and jealousies'. And in a declaration of 8 January the king denied any intention of questioning any more MPs, as was rumoured, and insisted that he would proceed against those already accused by 'the exact rule of law and justice'.[133]

Charles's decision to leave Whitehall on 10 January was another impetuous move, taken against the advice of Essex, Holland and Lord Keeper Littleton.[134] So sudden was it that the royal family spent several nights at Hampton Court and then Windsor in straitened circumstances. One story was that the princes slept the first night in the same bed as their parents, another that they made do with 'three beds and one chamber'.[135] It was only with hours left that the king had taken stock of the preparations being made for the reassembly of parliament the next day and decided he could not face the humiliation of watching the triumphant five members pass his own doors. Dering regarded the last-minute appointment of Philip Skippon as sergeant major-general of the trained bands to attend parliament as a deliberate move 'to the king's terror'.[136] The tale later became current that the king abandoned his capital because he was 'like to have been torn in pieces by the citizens'. This was a gross exaggeration, yet it is undeniable that the plans of the committee of the Commons contained an element of intimidation and that when the king slipped away from Whitehall that January afternoon, he was in fear of his wife's, if not his own, life.[137]

So embarrassing were the multiple offers of support received by the committee of the Commons for the return to Westminster, that the apprentices were persuaded to stay at home to guard the City and the Southwark militia agreed to provide an ancillary demonstration of strength

131 *PCR* XII, 208–10.
132 Clarendon I, 485; *CSPD 1641–3*, p. 245.
133 *D'Ewes (C)*, p. 402; *CSPD 1641–3*, p. 244, 246–7.
134 *CSPD 1641–3*, pp. 252–3.
135 *CSPV 1640–2*, p. 281; Bodleian Tanner MS 66, fol. 242r; *CSPD 1641–3*, p. 256.
136 Larking, pp. 67–8.
137 Bodleian Tanner MS 63, fol. 81r; *D'Ewes (C)*, pp. 400–1; Clarendon I, 507; Gardiner X, 148–9.

in the fields at Lambeth.[138] The actual procession down the Strand was led by the eight City companies under Skippon, followed by an enthusiastic crowd of citizens. The five members and the rest who had attended the City sessions, together with Viscount Mandeville, embarked at the Three Cranes. Eye witnesses commented on the 'brave show on the water': there was a fleet of boats, armed with muskets and ordnance 'which gave volleys all the way they went' and 'gallantly adorned with flags and streamers'. Trumpets, drums and martial music accompanied the MPs all the way to Westminster. This was how Pym and his associates celebrated, with noise and colour to bring the tidings of victory, with a sombre message for the future that few dared contemplate on that exciting day. It was as much like a triumph as setting a guard, one observer noted.[139] More than 2000 men in arms and citizens thronged Westminster Hall and its environs that evening, many of them proudly displaying the Protestation: some carried it on the top of their pikes, some as a 'little square banner' on sticks or poles, some had it affixed to their muskets, 'one had it fastened upon his breast and it was also wrapped upon one of the ensigns'. D'Ewes, deeply impressed by this massive display of loyalty, was coming to see the Protestation as a talisman. 'It appeareth', he wrote in his journal, 'that we did not only at first prevent that dangerous design of the earl of Strafford's escaping justice by it, but that now and at several times since it was a very special means under God to preserve us in safety.'[140]

During the rest of January the collision course between the king and parliament, now increasingly evident to all, was given concrete expression by measures and counter-measures. Everyone grasped the military importance of Hull, whose magazine contained 20,000 arms, 7000 barrels of gunpowder and 120 field pieces.[141] The king's attempt to seize this invaluable arsenal and vital port by appointing the earl of Newcastle as governor was thwarted by young John Hotham's rapid journey up the Great North Road, though it was a while before the mayor, unwilling to become embroiled, was persuaded to admit his men.[142] The celebrated hurlyburly at Kingston on 12 January was a shadowy affair, though Digby does seem to have carried some kind of directive from the king to Lunsford and the cavaliers who were assembled there. Dramatized accounts of the fracas caused the Commons to issue a strongly worded order for sheriffs to check on unlawful assemblies.[143] Suspicious that the king had some kind of

138 *D'Ewes (C)*, pp. 400–1.
139 *CSPD 1641–3*, p. 252; *CSPV 1640–2*, p. 281; J. Vicars, *Jehovah-Jireh* (1644), p. 69; Bodleian Tanner MS 66, fol. 242r; Rushworth III, part I, 484; Clarendon I, 510. Mandeville did not, as Gardiner states (X, 151), travel in a carriage.
140 BL Harl. MS 163. fol. 318r.
141 BL Add. MS 14827, fol. 1v.
142 BL Harl. MS 162, fols. 336v–337v; *CSPD 1641–3*, pp. 253–4, 256; *CJ* II, 371–2, 387; Gardiner X, 152–3.
143 *CJ* II, 372–3, 379; BL Harl. MS 480, fol. 18r, E 131 (15): *A True Relation of the Late Hurlyburly*

design on Portsmouth, the House directed the governor of the town to deliver it to no one without parliament's express command and it also hastily discussed measures for paying the garrison's arrears. A bill was rushed through and presented to the king for the adjournment of parliament from Westminster to the City. Before the end of the month the trained bands of four southern counties had been called out to deal with Lunsford's cavaliers, Skippon's power had been enlarged to give him effective command of the Southwark and Middlesex militias as well as the London one, and the mayor of York had been ordered not to dispose of the 'king's arms and munitions' there without parliament's directions.[144] Parliament, in other words, was moving swiftly in the wake of political crisis towards asserting comprehensive executive authority.

The unanimity of both Houses in making these moves was the unanimity of shock and bewilderment. The events of the previous few weeks appeared to have shifted the secure foundations of social and political order. The even tenor of the gentry's material life went on undisturbed. Sir Thomas Barrington and his family, for example, living comfortably in their new Queen Street home, were enjoying a normal supply of delicacies from the London markets: oysters, sprats, larks, pheasants, woodcocks, sweet lemons and violet comfits.[145] Yet the month's correspondence testifies to the pervasive sense of political crisis. Henry Oxinden's letter to his Kentish cousin on 27 January is the classic statement of the mood in London's gentry circles:

> I find all here full of fears and void of hopes. Parents and children, brothers, kindred, I and dear friends have the seed of difference and division abundantly sowed in them. Sometimes I meet with a cluster of gentlemen equally divided in opinion and resolution, sometimes three to two, sometimes more odds, but never unanimous, nay more I have heard foul language and desperate quarrelings even between old and entire friends and how we can thus stand and not fall, certainly God must needs work a miracle parallel to some of his great ones in the old time.[146]

Oxinden's account cannot be dismissed as overdramatization since others wrote in similar terms. 'I fear I shall scarce ever write you good news again', began John Berners in a letter of 10 January to a Norfolk cousin. 'My lines are like my thoughts, disturbed', he scrawled as his hectic account of the latest events straggled down the second page, 'but I trust God will turn all to the best.' 'The times are dangerous to discourse what I might', Thomas Wiseman told Sir John Pennington on the 14th, 'only if

---

at Kingston; Gardiner x, 154.
144   *CJ* II, 370–1, 373, 376, 384, 390; *LJ* IV, 515.
145   Essex RO D/DBa A 14, fol. 23v.
146   *Oxinden*, p. 272.

God do not speedily look upon us we are like to perish'.[147]

Men expected a drop in the political temperature with the king's departure from Whitehall. Factions were less hot, noted Robert Slingsby on 14 January, 'since with the malignant party' out of town 'the language of the parliament' predominated. But the language of parliament was so harsh that the sense of relief at Charles's going was short-lived and it was quickly replaced by despondency about the future and by feelings of desolation. The monarch's absence from his capital came to be seen as a factor prolonging the crisis and making a return to political harmony impossible.[148] With invasion fears rampant, stories circulating of the Irish being resolved for Lancashire and new pamphlets resurrecting the papist conspiracy pouring from the presses, the search for scapegoats became a general preoccupation.[149] Many were disposed to blame the cavaliers, who were seen to have displaced traditional royal advisers such as the peerage. 'The myrmidons are become absolute courtiers', wrote John Berners, retailing the common tittle-tattle, 'and frequently go into the privy chamber and talk with both Their Majesties.' If distractions followed, Thomas Smith told Sir John Pennington on 17 January, 'it will be from some factious firebrands that trouble the court, abuse His Majesty and seek to fish in troubled waters.'[150] There was another view, which was succinctly summarized by Wiseman in his letter to Pennington on the 14th: 'the liberty of the press, the liberty of factious preaching of ill-affected ministers . . . and the liberty that tumultuous persons have taken to themselves by their unlawful meetings in the City, has poisoned the obedience of too many of His Majesty's subjects.' It was implicit in this interpretation that Pym's clique was responsible for the crisis. Sir Edward Dering was undoubtedly of the same mind as Wiseman, though, writing to his wife on 13 January, he contented himself with the bemused remark that at Westminster 'every day we have a sufficient guard against no enemy.'[151]

There was as much confusion about what would happen next as about whom to blame for what had happened already. Wild speculation flourished. Parliament was said to be going to crown the prince of Wales.[152] The king was variously supposed to be moving to Woodstock, York, Plymouth and Portsmouth.[153] He was credited with considerable military forces at Windsor, where wagons laden with arms and saddles were allegedly being

147 Bodleian Tanner MS 66, fol. 234; *CSPD 1641–3*, p. 255.
148 *CSPD 1641–3*, pp. 254, 257.
149 *HMC Montagu*, p. 140; *Oxinden*, p. 273; BL E 131 (14): *A Great Conspiracy of the Papists*; E 131 (16): *Matters of Note to all True Protestants*; E 181 (33): *The Papists Design against the Parliament and City of London.*
150 Bodleian Tanner MS 66, fol. 246r; *CSPD 1641–3*, p. 257.
151 *CSPD 1641–3*, p. 255, Larking, p. 68–9.
152 BL Harl. MS 162, fol. 325v.
153 BL Harl. MS 383, fol. 197r; E 201 (8): *Diurnal Occurrences*, 10–17 Jan.; E 201 (10), *Diurnal Occurrences*, 17–24 Jan.; *CSPD 1641–3*, p. 254; *HMC Montagu*, p. 144.

brought in.[154] There was talk of charges against further MPs – Earle, Fiennes and St John – and against more of the peers, including Brooke, Essex, Paget, Saye and Warwick. Orlando Bridgeman received a mysterious letter warning him to withdraw from the Commons lest he suffer 'among the Puritans'.[155] Among those who dared look ahead there was a predictable diversity of views. Whereas Sidney Bere thought the onus was on parliament to prevent confusion by producing constructive proposals for the king's return 'with his contentment', John Dillingham reckoned that 'unless there be some yielding to the House of Commons all will suddenly be on fire', Thomas Smith likewise trusted those who ruled in parliament as 'honest and able men', who might yet secure peace and tranquillity.[156]

If well informed observers had such difficulty in making sense of the political crisis, it is not surprising that at the lower social levels it was viewed in crude and simplistic terms. 'The king was no king because he did not take up arms against the Scots', avowed one Londoner, 'Pym was King Pym and that rogue would set all the kingdom by the ears, and the parliament were fools and made none but fishmongers and fools of the committees.'[157] Another bold spirit said 'he would go 20 miles to see Mr Pym hanged and would then cut off a piece of Mr Pym's flesh to wear about him in remembrance of him.'[158] Petty factionalism aggravated local tensions. In Stepney two parties were at daggers drawn. Richard Cray used his authority as constable to disarm the watch set up by some of the Puritans in the parish during the panic of 6 January and hindered the radical preachers Jeremiah Burroughs and William Greenhill. He and his friends declared they would rise with the papists, if the chance came, against 'Puritans and Brownists'. They derided the five members as men that 'did carry two faces under one hood' and called for the cutting of the throats of 'damned Puritan whores'.[159]

For the poor the central reality was the economic depression, which deepened during the first weeks of the New Year. A spate of petitions echoed the fears and repeated the recipes in the Common Council petition of 11 December. The mariners and seamen of London and the Thames estuary were the first in the field on 8 January. On the 26th the young men, apprentices and seamen portrayed the City's trading as 'extraordinarily decayed'.[160] A delegation met in Moorfields and walked from there to Westminster, with printed copies of another petition representing the

154   *CJ* II, 379–80; BL Harl. MS 480. fol. 18r.
155   *CJ* II, 369.
156   *CSPD 1641–3*, pp. 253, 257; *HMC Montagu*, p. 145.
157   BL Harl. MS 162, fol.323v, 480, fol. 12v.
158   *D'Ewes (C)*, p. 397.
159   BL 559 f 4 (43): *The Petition of the Inhabitants of Stepney*.
160   Bodleian Ashmole 1026 (11): *Petition of the Mariners and Seamen*; Steele, no. 1961.

misery of the poor in their hands.[161] On 31 January a petition alleging the support of 15,000 poor labouring men explained that they had already sold or pawned part of their goods for food and they could not pay their rents. A few days later the 'distressed tradesmen's wives and widows' told the same story.[162] The master and company of silk throwers complained on 12 February that, because of the interruption of trade, 200,000 poor people living in and around the City were likely to be in extremity.[163] By then however the immediate economic crisis may have been almost over, since merchants had begun to bring their bullion into the mint again by the end of January and with the resignation of Sir John Biron as lieutenant of the Tower trade seems to have picked up. The security of the Tower was the foundation of London's economic and political confidence; so greatly was Biron distrusted that it had been blockaded by land and sea.[164] One of the reasons for the consternation of the Stepney Puritans about their contentious neighbour Richard Cray was that he had just been made a warder in the Tower.[165]

In what sense then was the period from November 1641 to January 1642 one of political crisis? Charles had charged the five members because he believed that a settled conspiracy by a small clique to bend him to parliament's will had reached fruition. Parliament responded assertively to the abortive coup because most members took the king's initiative as the final proof they needed of the long-established design of which Pym had spoken so often. The distrust that in the end made civil war unavoidable was founded on these two competing myths. The king left London with a fixed conviction that his capital was in rebellion against him. He set his mind against returning until he had brought the parliamentary leaders and the City populace to heel. Whereas for a time it had looked doubtful whether Pym's supremacy in parliament could survive, he now came back to the helm with everything in his favour.[166]

Distrust festered in the body politic over the next months as the king and parliament tried the loyalty of the nation and sought to raise armies. Meanwhile the terms 'roundhead' and 'cavalier' had gained currency. They were used as terms of abuse in the street battles of December 1641, applied to the rabble and to provocative activists among the king's supporters.[167] But already they enshrined the stereotypes that were to be constantly

---

161 BL 669 f 4 (54): *A Petition of Many Thousand Poor People*; Steele, no. 1972.
162 BL 669 f 4 (55): *The Petition of 15,000 Poor Labouring Men*; 669 f 4 (57): *The Petition of many hundreds of Distressed Women*.
163 BL 669 f 4 (60): *The Petition of the Silk Throwers*; Manning in Parry, *English Civil War and After*, pp. 10–12.
164 *LJ* IV, 521; *CSPD 1641–3*, pp. 253–4, 265, 269, 277–8, 281; Gardiner x, 162–5; BL Harl. MS 480, fols. 26r, 27r.
165 BL 669 f 4 (43).
166 Clarendon I, 505.
167 Gardiner x, 121.

reinforced in the propaganda war that lay ahead. Already the distortions of fear and hatred overlay much of the positive idealism that would eventually carry men into one camp or the other. Already, as we have seen in this chapter, there was a willingness to characterize the conflict in the harsh terms of a struggle between papists and Puritans. This absurdly simplified it, yet it pointed accurately to the dramatization and rhetoric, the delusions and misunderstanding, that make the origins of the civil war so complex a story.

6

Petitions

The Remonstrance is printed and certainly will give abundant satisfaction to all that yet know little of what hath passed.

John King to Martin Calthorpe,
24 December 1641[1]

We need not entreat you to ease our great pressures, which in our souls, bodies and estates we have long groaned under, for we are most sensible of your cares, wisdoms, unwearied labours and faithful endeavours to do what our hearts can desire.

Petition of Leicestershire,
15 February 1642[2]

Peace and religion are the works of absolute perfection which being united make a state unconquerable.

Petition of Hampshire,
11 March 1642[3]

When John Hampden's friends and neighbours rode in to Westminster with their Buckinghamshire manifesto on 11 January 1642 a new campaign of county petitioning was off the mark.[4] In scale and energy this movement, a remarkable manifestation of the support for Pym's policies in the localities, soon dwarfed the Root and Branch campaign of the previous year. Petitioning had become the most potent weapon in the provincial armoury. The parliamentary diarists quickly gave up summarizing the new petitions: the Lincolnshire, Northamptonshire and Oxfordshire ones, noted Framlingham Gawdy on 10 February, were 'much like the rest'; Sussex on 17 February and then Dorset on 19 February spoke 'much to the effect of former petitions', D'Ewes recorded.[5] The basic similarity of the petitions has misled some historians into assuming that they were organized or managed from the centre.[6] On the contrary, they deserve

1 Bodleian Tanner MS 66, fol. 218.
2 BL E 135 (13).
3 BL 669 f 4(77).
4 Bodleian Tanner MS 66, fol. 242r.
5 BL Add. MS 14827, fol. 36v; Harl, MS 162, fols. 389v, 393v.
6 Wedgwood, *King's War*, p. 62; Ashton, *English Civil War*, pp. 148–9.

recognition as an authentic expression of deeply felt local opinion. They were not in fact as uniform as they appear at first sight and, in so far as they do present a unanimous view, this merely reflects a common reaction to the political crisis. The petitions will be used in this chapter, together with other evidence, to illuminate the mood of the provinces in the first months of 1642.

Of the 40 English counties, 38 sent up petitions for presentation to parliament between December 1641 and August 1642 and Wales also added its voice.[7] All of them except Westmorland's were in fact in by May. Complementary petitions to both Houses were sent by 22 counties.[8] In a few cases, moreover, the counties produced more than one petition: thus the Hertfordshire and Surrey gentry mounted petitions in December and revised versions in the new year; Suffolk provided a long statement on 31 January and a further petition a week later; gentry from all over Yorkshire joined in petitions which were presented on 15 February and 11 April, but they had been preceded by those of the Cleveland district who presented their own petition on 9 February. By and large local communities acted one after another as they heard what friends and neighbours were doing. Petitioning snowballed from the shires near London, like Buckinghamshire, Essex, Middlesex and Suffolk. The stragglers were counties towards the periphery of the nation, like Monmouthshire, Herefordshire and Northumberland. The two counties left out were Cumberland and Gloucestershire, which chose to address views that were certainly not palatable to him to the king and ignored parliament.[9]

A number of towns joined in the petitioning movement: in January representations were received from several Devon towns; in February Dover, Ipswich, Norwich and Salisbury followed suit; in March the Commons heard from the Cinque Ports and King's Lynn, in May from Tewkesbury.[10] Other towns probably discussed petitions but lacked the energy or unanimity to see them through. Dorchester for instance sent up a petition which it seems was not presented. A Bristol petition was first mooted on 15 March, when a committee of the Common Council to devise it was established. On 26 May, when it had still not been sent, the Council recognized that it would have to be amended in the light of new developments; on 11 July, finally overtaken by events, it was abandoned.[11]

One of the Yorkshire petitions provides a useful case study of procedure and organization. In a letter of 28 January, Thomas Stockdale reported to

---

7 *CJ* II, 346–595, 710; Derbyshire RO Chandos-Pole-Gell MSS, Nottinghamshire Petition; BL E 201(31): *A True Diurnal*, 14–21 March, p. 13.

8 *LJ* IV, 506–711; V, 10, 66, 92.

9 BL E 133(7): Petition of Gloucestershire.

10 *CJ* II, 428, 440, 449, 464, 452, 466, 537–8, 593; *LJ* IV, 611; Andriette, p. 46; BL E 135(35): Petition of Ipswich.

11 Dorset RO B2/16/4: Dorchester Corporation Minute Book 1637–56, under 28 Jan. 1642; Bristol RO Common Council Proceedings III, fols. 118v, 119, 120r, 122r.

the county MP Ferdinando Lord Fairfax that a number of gentry had met and 'resolved upon petitions to the king and parliament'. The leading gentry of the shire were subsequently summoned to York to frame and sign petitions prepared in draft by the sheriff and several JPs beforehand. Some wanted a full-scale campaign for signatures at this point, but Stockdale persuaded the sheriff, Sir Thomas Gower, to send up the petition addressed to parliament straight away. The gentleman appointed to present it carried copies and covering letters for the knights of the shire. Meanwhile further copies were circulated throughout Yorkshire for 'the general subscriptions of the multitude', which, Stockdale promised Fairfax on 18 February, would shortly reach him in London.[12] The Yorkshire petition was only unusual in that it was presented as a single sheet, before the concurrence of the whole county had been obtained. Its prestige did not in fact suffer because in an accompanying letter, which Speaker Lenthall read to MPs, the sheriff declared that it came with the 'hearts' affections' of 'most of the gentlemen in that country'. A mere three weeks elapsed between the initial meeting and the presentation of the petition on 15 February.[13] The crucial ingredients of the petitioning movement were all present in this case: the more or less formal meetings of the gentry, the close cooperation between the organizers and the shire knights in preparing the ground for the moment of delivery, and the drive for signatures.[14]

The hardest question to answer about the county petitions is how much of the spectrum of gentry opinion each one represents. Organizers saw them as rallying points, intended to bring a sense of unity as signs of division were beginning to emerge. 'I have done my endeavour so to couch our desires in moderate terms as none may check at the matter', Stockdale reported to Fairfax with respect to the draft he had framed. The close link between an MP and an energetic friend in the shire was often crucial to getting a petition off the ground. In Derbyshire for example the initiative lay with Sir John Curzon and Sir John Gell. In the case of Northamptonshire Sir Gilbert Pickering's prompting was important. Some petitions never represented the views of more than a clique among the gentry. Herefordshire's is the classic example: there the mounting of the petition opened up a quarrel that, as we shall see, fatally split the county. Sir Robert Harley, the ringleader, probably did not attempt to circulate his draft, spoken of lovingly by his wife as 'our Herefordshire petition', among the leading families. Westmorland's petition, straggling the rest in August, was reported to be a reply by one group of gentry to another group that had petitioned the king 'in a private way'.[15]

12 *Fairfax*, pp. 344–5, 362, 364–5.
13 *CJ* II, 433; BL Harl MS 480, fol. 149r; HLRO, Main Papers, 15 Feb.: Yorkshire Petition.
14 For another case study see my article 'Petitioning and the Outbreak of the Civil War in Derbyshire', *Derbyshire Archaeological Journal* XCIII (1973), 34–8.
15 Fairfax, p. 349; *Derbyshire Archaeological Journal* XCIII (1973), 34; Bedfordshire RO J 401;

Most of the petitions though do seem to have been genuine attempts at representing a consensus. Discussion of the contents was the rule rather than the exception. In some cases one of the best known hostelries of the county town was the venue for an initial debate, the White Hart at Derby, for example, or the Swan at Northampton.[16] The Oxfordshire gentry formulated their petition at a meeting to take the Protestation.[17] In other cases more authoritative backing was sought from the start by discussion of the petition at quarter sessions or assizes, and involvement of the grand jury, the traditional instrument for expressing the voice of the county. Hampshire's petition was based on a grand jury presentment received by the judge at the Lent assizes. Devon's petition to the Lords was drawn up at the Epiphany sessions.[18] The role of signatures attached to Staffordshire's petition was headed by the 12 JPs and 17 grand jurymen who had supported it at the assizes.[19] Sir Thomas Gower told Lord Fairfax when he sent him a new Yorkshire petition on 8 April that he had been enjoined 'by the county now assembled' at the assizes to desire him to present it.[20]

The actual debates over the wording of petitions are almost undocumented, but a letter from Sir Gilbert Pickering to Sir Roland St John illustrates the misunderstandings that could arise. St John had expressed the disquiet of some Northamptonshire gentry that the county's clause about employing men ill-affected to religion in places of power and trust was intended as an attack on the earl of Peterborough, the current lord lieutenant who was under suspicion for mixing with papists. Pickering sought to reassure him by explaining that a clear distinction was intended between national grievances, of which this was one, and 'particular grievances of the county'. 'His lordship was never once thought of in the petition by me', he declared, 'and I dare say I can procure the like protestation from every man that was at the penning.[21]

There was always an element of charade about county petitioning. Organizers eagerly sought both the respectability of institutional backing and the impact of numbers. The Root and Branch campaign of 1641 had seen some startling affirmations of numerical support: petitions from Lancashire, Suffolk, Hertfordshire and Norfolk claimed 4488, 4400, 2800 and 2000 hands respectively.[22] But understanding observers had learnt

Harley, pp. 121, 148; BL E 202(30): *A Perfect Diurnal*, p. 8; for Lord Brooke's probable role in the Warwickshire petition see Hughes, pp. 229–30.

16   *CSPD 1641–3*, p. 279.
17   Bodleian Z, 1, 17(19): Oxfordshire Petition.
18   *CJ* II, 474; *LJ* IV, 536, 640; BL 669 4 (77); East Devon RO Quarter Sessions Order Book 1640–1651; J.S. Morrill, *The Cheshire Grand Jury* (Leicester, 1976), pp. 6, 36–7.
19   HLRO, Main Papers, 16 May 1642: Staffordshire Petition.
20   Bodleian Dep C MS 153, no 14.
21   Bedfordshire RO J 1402; BL Harl. MS 162, fol. 380r; 480, 131v.
22   *D'Ewes (N)*, pp. 282–3; BL Harl. MS 163, fol. 80r.

that the number of signatures and marks attached to a petition testified more to the vigour with which it had been organized than the degree of enthusiasm for its contents in a particular locality. Everything depended on the time and trouble that was taken, as Thomas Stockdale explained in a letter about his efforts in Claro wapentake, after he had amassed 530 subscriptions, 'all men of good substance', in only a few days.[23] The massive rolls of paper and parchment, made up of parochial returns stitched together, that now rest in the House of Lords are a monument to the industry displayed by many of those who were in charge of the petitions at the county level. D'Ewes became so used to seeing these huge rolls dumped on the table in the Commons that he noted how unusual it was that Staffordshire's petition, presented on 14 May, consisted of a top sheet 'and then the names of those that had subscribed filed together like a chancery bill'.[24] Petitioning had reached a new scale in 1642, as the numbers game demonstrated. Essex demanded attention with 30,000 hands, Suffolk with 14,000, Surrey and Shropshire with 10,000, Norfolk with 8000. Other counties were more modest in their aspirations: Hertfordshire and Middlesex declared 4000 supporters, Berkshire 3000. But even Rutland's 560 hands was an impressive turnout for so tiny a county.[25]

The collection of returns from scattered rural parishes could be a lengthy business. Derbyshire's petition, presented on 14 March, had been signed at Baslow and Ashford a month previously; Cleveland's petition, which reached Westminster on 9 February, was subscribed at Ingleby Greenhow on 26 December and Marton on 2 January. Responsibility for parochial subscriptions rested in the last resort either on constables or ministers. Sir John Gell used his authority as a JP to compel active support from constables in Derbyshire, but it seems to have been much more common to circulate petitions through the clergy.[26] Ministers clearly approached their task in various ways. In Essex many apparently thought it was sufficient to read the petition from the pulpit, obtain some kind of verbal assent from the congregation and send in a list of those present. Some took the petition to be directed to the literate only and secured the signatures of those substantial householders who could write, ignoring the rest of the populace. But, in Cleveland, Derbyshire and Middlesex at least, the majority were more conscientious. The ministers' returns from these districts mostly consisted of an amalgam of signatures and marks. Some of them were hopelessly disorganized, a few were impeccably planned. Few

---

23 *Fairfax*, pp. 375–6.
24 BL. Harl. MS 163, fol. 118v.
25 *CJ*, II, 404; Society of Antiquaries: Shropshire Petition; HLRO, Main Papers, 29 March 1642: Rutland Petition; BL E 131 (24); E 134 (21); E 201 (12); Harl. MS 162, fol. 360v; 480, fols. 41r, 81r; Add. MS 14827, fol. 58r.
26 *Derbyshire Archaeological Journal* XCIII (1973), 36.

sought to compete with the minister of Ashford, who provided splendidly ruled lines and little boxes for men to make their marks.[27]

The sense of parochial leadership felt by ministers is evident from these documents. Their names head the lists, often pushed spaciously across the page as if to emphasize their importance beside villagers who could only manage a crabbed hand, a scrawl or an ungainly mark. Sometimes they appeared side by side with a resident gentleman. A few of the men who turned the petitioning movement into such a massive display of loyalty to parliament had already made a name for themselves outside their parish or have done so since. We find Stephen Marshall in charge at Finchingfield in Essex, Ralph Josselin's neat signature beside that of his patron Richard Harlackenden at Earls Colne, Immanuel Bourne's at the top of a good showing of names for Ashover in Derbyshire.[28] By and large though the parish organizers were men unknown in the wider world, expressing the trust of their own little community in parliament at a time of political bewilderment. All his parishioners, noted the minister of Beeley in Derbyshire, did 'willingly consent' to join the leaders of the shire in their humble supplication to 'the honourable assembly of parliament'. 'The names of the inhabitants in Winshull that freely and heartily pray for the good of the parliament and the furtherance of the petition', the minister there inscribed his page.[29] What it all meant to those whose mental horizons were bounded by the nearest market town, to illiterate countrymen preoccupied with the harsh realities of a farming life, is hard to say. For many no doubt detailed prescriptions were transmuted into a general haze of anti-Catholicism. Neither among the gentry nor among the countrymen was there as yet any sense of course that loyalty to the representative body of the nation might come into conflict with or even preclude loyalty to the king.

If the county petition was designedly a political act, what could be more appropriate than a handsome cavalcade to accompany it? This was the thinking in Buckinghamshire, whose gentry's ride to Westminster on 11 January, though it shocked some like Sir Edward Hyde, was hailed by many as a magnificent gesture on a day already decked with parliament's triumph.[30] Nothing quite like it had been seen before: 3000 of the participants were on horseback, 'riding three and three' with swords at their side and the Protestation in their hats and hands. At one point the

---

27   HLRO, Main Papers, 20 Jan. 1642: Essex Petition; 24 Jan. 1642: Middlesex Petition; 10 Feb. 1642: Cleveland Petition; 26 Feb. 1642: Derbyshire Petition, fols. 15–16, 19; Holmes, pp. 26, 28.

28   Clarendon I, 401; Wilson, *Pulpit in Parliament*, passim; A. Macfarlane, *The Family Life of Ralph Josselin* (Cambridge, 1970), p. 347; R. O'Day, 'Immanuel Bourne: A Defence of the Ministerial Order', *JEH* XXVIII (1976), 101–14.

29   HLRO, Main Papers, 26 Feb. 1642: Derbyshire Petition, fols. 23, 102.

30   Clarendon I, 510–12.

procession reached all the way from the Royal Exchange to Newgate. Their 'fair and orderly manner' dazed the Londoners. When the petition had been presented, they waited more than two hours for parliament's answer, standing and pressing towards the door.[31] Predictably other counties sought to emulate Buckinghamshire. The crowd accompanying the Kentish petition on 8 February was variously estimated at between 7000 and 10,000; at least 3000 came from Essex and 1000 or more from Bedfordshire and Suffolk. Not all these demonstrations were as well organized, it seems, as the Buckinghamshire one. Indeed they were probably largely spontaneous expressions of enthusiasm which rather alarmed some MPs. In Essex the official delegation consisted merely of 20 chief knights and gentlemen, attended by about 200 horsemen. Oxfordshire's delegation surpassed Northamptonshire's on 10 February in terms of sheer numbers, but what mattered, William Montagu told his father, was that Northamptonshire's petition was 'the best attended by gentlemen of quality' of any yet delivered.[33]

Some counties chose an MP to act on their behalf and present their petition. Thus Derbyshire called upon Sir John Curzon, one of their knights of the shire, Cleveland on Sir John Hotham, Staffordshire on the earl of Essex, their lord lieutenant, for their petition to the peers.[34] More commonly a leading gentlemen from the shire, almost invariably a baronet or knight, carried the petition into the Commons: Sir John Burgoyne acted for Bedfordshire, Sir George Chudleigh for Devon, Sir William Waller for Hampshire, Sir Robert Carr for Lincolnshire.[35] When a knight of the shire rose to announce the arrival of his countrymen at the door his whole experience of representing his friends and neighbours suddenly came into focus. This was a moment to glory in, a moment when the distance between Westminster and home fields and lanes all at once seemed shortened. 'Men of great quality', were come from Middlesex, declared Sir Gilbert Gerrard on 24 January; some 40 'of the best of that country' had brought Northamptonshire's offering, Sir Christopher Yelverton told his colleagues on 10 February; 'there is not above three or four gentlemen of quality but have their hands to it', avowed Sir Edmund Moundeford, ushering in Norfolk's petition on 4 March.[36] Whatever the words they chose, those who moved the acceptance of the county petitions did so

31 Bodleian Tanner MS 66, fol. 242r; BL Harl. MS 162, fols. 314v, 315v; E 201(8): *Diurnal Occurences*, 10–17 Jan.; E 181(36): *The Parliament's Answer to the Two Petitions of Buckinghamshire*; Vicars, *Jehovah-Jirah*, p. 70.

32 BL Harl. MS 480, fol. 125r; Add. MS 33936 fol. 258r; Sloane MS 3317, fols. 31v, 35v; E201 (11): *Diurnal Occurences*, 17–24 Jan; E 201(27), *A Perfect Diurnal*, 14–21 March; *Trevelyan Papers* III, 217.

33 *HMC* Buccleuch I, 291; BL Harl. MS 480, fol. 127v.

34 *Derbyshire Archaeological Journal* XCIII (1973), 34; BL E 148(27); Harl. MS 162, fol. 370r.

35 Steele, no. 2042; BL Harl MS 163, fols. 28r, 343v; 480, fol. 127r.

36 BL Add. MS 14827, fol. 58r; Harl. MS 480, fols. 50v, 130r.

secure in the knowledge that this was one time when they could be sure of grasping the attention of their colleagues.

In several cases the orchestration of the final stage of the petitioning process was very much a family affair. James Fiennes, the eldest son of Viscount Saye, who sat for Oxfordshire, announced his county's delegation and his brother John presented the petition. When it had been read James Fiennes moved the customary thanks: 'there were many of very great quality', he insisted, 'and though the malignant party went about to poison the fountains, yet God hath opened their eyes.'[37] Sir Nathaniel Barnardiston moved the reception of the Suffolk petitioners, who were led by his heir Sir Thomas.[38] Somerset's petition was introduced on the motion of Sir Peter Wroth and then spoken to by his brother Sir Thomas.[39]

The speeches made by those who presented them must have warmed the hearts of MPs as much as the petitions themselves. Sir Thomas Wroth, noted a diarist, 'at our bar compared this House to the day of judgement'. He hoped that Somerset would be harkened unto like the rest, although he brought 'no numerous or multitudinous troop' but merely '1000 hands to attest their approbation and assent'.[40] The Buckinghamshire freeholders, explained one of their representatives, had come out of a sense of loyalty and protectiveness, 'not counselled thereto by any but hurried along with apprehensions of the dangers this honourable House was in which they had set forth at large'.[41] Mr Bacon from Essex had two things to insist upon: 'the settling of religion and the relief of our brethren of Ireland'. He concluded, recorded the diarist, 'that they would desire us to believe that they have their mooring by us and that their lives and fortunes shall be laid at our feet'. Bacon was in fact so verbose that, when he left the chamber, Sir Thomas Barrington hastened to excuse his countryman, if he 'had committed any error', but the apology was brushed aside.[42]

The petitions were public utterances intended for general consumption. Most of them were printed, either as broadsides or in pamphlet form, within a few days of their acceptance at Westminster. The capital avidly absorbed them and they were often commented upon in letters to friends in the country.[43] What then did they have to say? Most of them opened with a paean of praise for the Long Parliament's achievements to date. Rutland, for example, could never sufficiently express its gratitude 'for the great works that have been done for the good both of Church and commonwealth'; Shropshire deemed the parliament's efforts worthy of 'perpetual

---

37   BL Harl. MS 162, fol. 377v; 480, fol. 127v.
38   BL Harl. MS 162, fol. 360v; 480, fol. 81r.
39   BL Harl. MS 164, fol. 226v; 480, fol. 172r.
40   BL E 200(33): *A Speech spoken by Sir Thomas Wroth.*
41   BL Harl. MS 162, fol. 314v.
42   *CJ* II, 387; BL Harl. MS 480, fol. 41r.
43   E.g. Staffordshire RO D 868/3/14 f 4 (15).

and grateful memory'. Berkshire praised MPs' 'piety, courage and constancy', Derbyshire their 'patience' and 'unwearied diligence', Essex and Hertfordshire their 'indefatigable labours'.[44] Some counties put their thanks in general terms, others particularized. Cheshire and Lancashire provided two of the fullest statements. The treaty with Scotland, the suppression of Star Chamber and High Commission and the abolition of ship money were mentioned by Cheshire, together with action against monopolists and 'the unlimited power of the prelates'. Lancashire's catalogue included the purging of the 'fountains of government', 'the blessed union of two kingdoms to the terror of our enemies', the expunging of innovations from the Church and the restoration to the people of 'courage, industry and vivacity of spirit, by the freedom of their persons and estates'.[45] Each county found its own emphases: Hampshire made much of the Triennial Act, Hertfordshire welcomed the bloodshed saved by the peace with the Scots, Surrey commended the action taken against 'oppressive courts' and illegal impositions, Sussex the 'opening of the mouths of faithful ministers long since silenced' and the release of 'those who were in prison and exile'.[46]

A sense of the parliament's destiny, of its appointed role in bringing to an end a period of arbitrary government by a 'full and complete reformation', was common to all the petitions.[47] England, they avowed, would eventually emerge from the shadow of disaster as surely as it had emerged from the crises of 1588 or 1605. The Cambridgeshire petition made specific reference to 'former deliverances whose memories we yearly celebrate'.[48] Providence, declared the Staffordshire gentry, was carrying the parliament through its most difficult straits. In several cases the petitioners recalled the euphoria of the first months.[49]

Plainly then, those who wrote the petitions were closely in touch with the parliament's progress. But they took the story very much at face value and they did not appreciate all the complexities of the factional situation that had developed at Westminster. In the 1620s men had become used to accepting parliament's failure to complete its business because there was so often the excuse of a premature dissolution.[50] This time, so it appeared to provincial minds, there was no reason why they should not get on and finish the job. Northamptonshire, for instance, spoke of 'good beginnings' which encouraged the expectation of a complete and happy settlement, Staffordshire of past services which they took as 'fair pledges of the healing

---

44 BL 669 f 4 (15), f 6 (1); E 133 (15); E 134 (13); Society of Antiquaries: Shropshire Petition.
45 Ormerod, pp. 2–3; BL E 148 (12).
46 BL E 134 (21), (35); E 133 (15); 669 f 4 (77).
47 *LJ* IV, 648.
48 BL 669 f 4 (83).
49 BL 669 f 6 (14).
50 Russell, *Parliaments*, pp. 36–7.

of the unsupportable grievances both ecclesiastical and civil which the Church and state groan under'. Only two petitions opened on a sour note. Somerset omitted thanks and painted the first 15 months of the parliament as a period of marking time while 'distractions and dangers daily multiplied'. The Wiltshire gentry complained that so far they had merely 'paid taxes impoverishing their estates to promote the common good' while awaiting remedies for their grievances.[51]

A sense of political crisis, the petitions suggest, only enveloped the provinces in the last months of 1641. The essence of it was fear and alarm about a malignant party, which was thwarting parliament's work and had brought reformation to a halt. None of those who took the lead in their county petitioning campaigns believed that enough had been done already to secure the nation against a recurrence of arbitrary government. Moreover Puritan gentry felt utterly frustrated at the failure of the religious reform movement to get off the ground. After a period of joyful hopes, the Leicestershire petitioners explained to the Lords, they were once more 'thrown into a sea of dangers and distractions'. Unless those who hindered reform were removed, insisted the inhabitants of Buckinghamshire, they had 'not the least hope of Israel's peace or to reap those glorious advantages, which the 14 months seedtime of your unparalleled endeavours hath given'.[52]

Papists were seen as the core of the malignant party and fear of popery was the most prominent theme running through the petitions. The Irish rebellion was accounted the prelude to the papists' wider designs. It brought to the surface the deep loathing for Catholicism felt by a generation educated in the Foxeian tradition and imbued with a sense of popery as a debasement of Christianity, a system of idolatry and error.[53] 'The insurrection of the papists', declared Staffordshire, 'may be reckoned of not only as a rebellion but a horrid persecution of Christ in his truth and members.'[54] The provincial terror about the implications of the rebellion had three main sources. There was the atrocity propaganda, which was undoubtedly widely circulated outside London. By the first weeks of 1642 there were also numerous Protestant refugees tramping the English roads, seeking aid and spreading panic reports. 'The distressed Protestants do animate the people here against the popish party', Thomas Stockdale told Lord Fairfax from Yorkshire on 14 January, 'and make them distaste them exceedingly.'[55] Finally in coastal districts there was sometimes the

51   BL E 135 (36), (46); E200 (33); 669 f(14).
52   *LJ* IV, 589; BL E 181 (29).
53   C.Z. Weiner 'The Beleagured Isle: A Study of Elizabethan and Early Jacobean Anti-Catholicism', *Past and Present* LI (1971), 27–62; R. Clifton, 'Fear of Popery' in Russell, *Origins*, pp. 144–67.
54   BL 669 f 6 (14).
55   *Fairfax*, p. 299; *Irish Historical Studies* XVIII (1972-73), 143–50. Local records contain many

confirmation which searches of ships driven into port could bring to anti-Catholic prejudices. A Bilbao ship, for instance, taken in St Ives in February, was found to contain not only priests, friars, wheat and wine but also crucifixes, beads and some teeth alleged to have belonged to St Peter. The large stores of beeswax found in a ship bound from Dunkirk to Ireland, inspected in the Isle of Wight, were assumed to be intended for making 'tapers for the mass priests'.[56]

Popular fears of popery found a range of different expressions and varied in intensity according to particular circumstances.[57] Joseph Lister of Bradford later recalled in his autobiography the atmosphere of heightened emotion that pervaded the Puritan communities of the West Riding in the months following the Irish Rebellion. A young boy of 12, he grew 'weary of so much fasting and praying'. It was a chance incident, he explained, that turned tension into panic. The congregation at a fast in Pudsey broke up in confusion when some refugee Protestants, reported to be approaching Halifax, were taken for the rebels themselves intent on re-enacting the Irish massacre: 'some ran out, others wept, others fell to talking to friends and . . . the people's hearts failed them with fear.'[58]

Fear of a full-scale papist invasion, common in London, was otherwise largely confined to the west coasts. Besides the boatloads of refugees arriving at the ports, there were landings by Irish papists in Somerset and Cornwall.[59] Some of them who reached Minehead in January 1642 roamed the town with swords and pistols, others in Cornwall that month were expected to fire towns, villages or houses.[60] It is not surprising, in this context, that a man examined in Plymouth in March found a ready audience for his tale that the pope's legate was sitting in counsel with the rebels, who boasted of invading England shortly.[61]

Wales was equally on edge. A paper about Monmouthshire, written in May, explained that the houses of the chief papists were placed near fair landings and that the daily confluence of strangers to them brought terror to the county. The papists, it was alleged, could bring 100 horse into the field at short notice against the Protestants' 20. The gentry were mostly

references to the refugees, e.g. Nottinghamshire RO PR 1760: Upton constables' accounts, p. 10; Dorset RO B2/16/4, under 3 Feb; B3/M2: Bridport bailiffs' accounts 1641–2; P9/CWI, Charlton Marshall churchwardens' accounts 1641–2; LL631, a transcript of Milton Abbas churchwardens' accounts p. 29; Gloucestershire RO D 2071/A3, Chipping Sodbury bailiffs' accounts, fol. 35r.

56 BL E 135 (2): *Exceeding Good News from the Isle of Wight*; E 135 (5): *A True Relation of Certain Passages which Captain Basset brought from Cornwall*; see also *CJ* II, 448, 466.

57 Staffordshire RO D113/A/DC/1; William Salt Library, Stafford, SMS 402; *Irish Historical Studies* XVIII (1972-3), 148–50.

58 T. Wright, editor, *The Autobiography of Joseph Lister* (London, 1842), pp. 6–8.

59 J. Latimer, editor, *Annals of Bristol* (Bristol, 1900), p. 155; *CJ* II, 467, 491, 578; Bodleian Tanner MS 63, fol. 43v; Wedgwood, *King's War*, p. 72. rl.

60 BL Harl. MS 162, fol. 353r; 164, fol. 235v; *CJ* II, 392.

61 BL Harl. MS 163, fol. 21v.

dependent on the earl of Worcester by reason of 'leases tithes, bargains, favours and flatteries'; the commonalty did not realize the danger that threatened them 'having lived in blindness without preaching'. All in all the county had never been 'more naked and less provided for war'. The leading citizens of Pembroke saw the Milford river as an obvious invasion point. Some of those arrested locally had refused the oaths of supremacy and allegiance, the mayor told the Speaker of the Commons on 12 February. And 500 or 1000 armed men, he believed, could easily 'possess themselves of the whole country and fortify Pembroke town with the castle and other strong places', which would not 'lightly be regained'. In June Sir Hugh Owen complained to colleagues at Westminster that his Pembrokeshire countrymen were 'so little regarded in respect of their safety as if they were no part of the kingdom'.[62] Caernarvonshire experienced a heady mixture of internal and external anxiety when news spread of a plot to surprise Conway. The local JPs attributed it to fears arising from the presence of known papists in the area, the weakness of the town and castle defences and the proximity of Ireland, 'being within eight hours' sail'. The conspiracy was only accepted as groundless after a thorough search of recusants' houses.[63]

No other district felt the impact of Protestant refugees so severely as Cheshire and Lancashire. As early as 6 November 1641, Sir John Trevor's steward reported many women and children arriving daily at Chester. In January 1642 a correspondent from there spoke of Irish gentlewomen offering themselves in service, 'having been left to their very skin in the wide world'.[64] Yet it is Lancashire, rather than Cheshire, which provides us with much of the outstanding material relating to anti-Catholic hysteria. Nowhere else in England was Catholicism so deeply rooted as in the hundreds of Amounderness, Leyland and West Derby, and nowhere else was the ideological conflict between Protestant and Catholic already felt as keenly.[65] Even the horrific tale that MPs heard on 21 February about a gentleman who had discussed plans with a Catholic priest to make 'fireballs and grenados', so that when the Irish landed 'all the towns of Lancashire should upon one day be burned and then the papists to rise', may well have been true.[66] In their petition of 12 March, the Protestant gentry stated their candid opinion that the 'massacre' in Ireland might be

---

62 Bodleian Tanner MS 66, fol. 265r, Dep C MS 168, no. 175; *HMCP* I, 31; BL Harl. MS 163, fol. 146v; 480, fol. 73r; see also *D'Ewes (C)*, p. 153.

63 *CSPD 1641–3*, pp. 170, 270; *Calendar of Wynn Papers*, p. 275; *Irish Historical Studies* XVIII (1972–3), 154–5.

64 Clwyd RO Glynde MS 3275; *HMC Montagu*, p. 146; *CJ* II, 417; *Irish Historical Studies* XVIII (1972–3), 148.

65 C. Haigh, *Reformation and Resistance in Tudor Lancashire* (Cambridge, 1975), pp. 247–95; Richardson, *Puritanism in North-West England* pp. 151–70; J. Bossy, *The English Catholic Community* (London, 1977), pp. 91–5.

66 *LJ* IV, 606–7; BL Harl. MS 480, fol. 160r.

'transported hither from the opposite shore where the number of popish recusants and the opportunity of landing may invite an invasion.'[67] The most convincing testimony of all to the heightened emotional atmosphere of the shire is the extraordinary letter written by Lord Strange to his son-in-law Lord Wharton on 13 November 1641. He was undoubtedly at that time in great perplexity, torn between duty to his neighbourhood and the desire to escape the seat of imminent conflict. The struggle in Strange's mind is symbolized by the sorrowful statement that he now felt bound to 'shut and watch those doors that you have sometime known all night open':

> It is so far in winter that there is no possibility of remove, else we might leave the safety of this country to the keeping of them that take on greater power than your father . . . some do me the honour to say they cannot think to be so secure when I am gone . . . if ever need was to look to Lancashire in our sin it is now . . . I have too much interest to forget how deeply I am concerned.[68]

Petitioners living away from the west coasts pursued a more subtle line of argument about the significance of the rebellion for the nation's troubles. For them the crux of the matter was the effect of rebel successes on native papist morale. The expectation that English papists would seek to emulate their Irish coreligionists was widespread. Hampshire believed they were confederate with the rebels and 'would do the like execution here'; Dorset noted their own papists' 'contemptuous and insolent carriage'; Wiltshire expected the Catholic 'rage and insolency' in their midst; Essex found their papists 'very insolent and ready to act the parts of those savage bloodsuckers in Ireland'.[69] Attitudes among native papists, needless to say, were grossly overdramatized; numbers were considerably exaggerated. Warwickshire was said to be swarming with recusants. The Ipswich petition stressed the 'numbers, liberty, power and boldness of the papists and their party'. Suddenly every move that local Catholics made was noted with suspicion or even openly misinterpreted. The petitions testify to a new obsession with the pattern of Catholic sociability. Dorset reported night meetings and 'more than usual flocking together and posting up and down', Berkshire 'frequent assemblies and consultations' of priests and Jesuits. The tale in Monmouthshire was that native Catholics were taking up most of the great houses near them for popish strangers and 'retaining men of great rank' in their homes.[70]

The tense and nervous attitudes revealed by the petitions make the numerous Catholic panics that occurred between November 1641 and the following April wholly comprehensible. Ralph Josselin characterized this

67 Ormerod, p. 4.
68 Bodleian Tanner MS 66, fol. 203; *D'Ewes (C)*, pp. 152–3.
69 BL 669 f 4 (77); 190 g 12 (56); E 135 (46); E 134 (13).
70 BL E 135 (27), (35); 190 g 12 (56); 669 f 4 (75); f 6 (20).

period as a time of 'hopes and yet sometimes fears'.[71] Men looking for trouble found it where it did not exist. The panics fall into several categories. Key points of the kingdom, highly sensitive to the possibility of surprisal, like Berwick, Carlisle, Hull and Portsmouth, were particularly vulnerable to false rumour.[72] Estates and homes of leading Catholics aroused watchful interest. Thus, in a typical case, the countrymen around the home of Lady Rivers of Hengrave in Suffolk were much troubled by the 'great resort' of papists there and by a story that she owned more than 100 arms.[73] A scare in Oxford was begun by a labourer who saw a loaded wagon at the house of Charles Green, a convicted recusant living in St Giles.[74] Then there were the running scares, which show that general rumours of a Catholic rising could spread with amazing speed: the West Riding panic recalled by Joseph Lister is one example and the Brampton Bryan panic of 19 November, which reached Bridgnorth, more than 50 miles away, in a single night is another.[75] Finally there were localized alarms caused simply by wild and irresponsible talk. 'Ere long blood should be sold as cheap as milk', declared a man at Eltham in Kent in January 1642, exacerbating fears surrounding a recusant neighbour. Sheffield apprentices were in uproar the next month after the earl of Arundel's armourer, alleged to be a Catholic, had announced that before Mayday there would be such a peal rung by the papists of the town 'as had not been heard these hundred years'.[76]

The map opposite gives some impression of the distribution of Catholic panics in this period, but much evidence has of necessity been omitted from it because it is too unspecific. The Commons, for instance, took action to disarm suspected persons in Bedfordshire during December, Gloucestershire, Lincolnshire, Northamptonshire and the East Riding during January and Cheshire and Staffordshire during March.[77] It was predictable that Lancashire, Hampshire, Sussex and Monmouthshire were among the counties which had been drawn to the attention of the House for special vigilance.[78] MPs received numerous stories of papists foregathering: a Staffordshire man was alleged to be buying up the provisions in all the local markets, Cumberland papists had never before 'kept

---

71 Macfarlane, editor, *Josselin's Diary*, p. 12.
72 *CJ* II, 346, 378; *HMC 5th Report*, p. 7; *D'Ewes (C)*, p 302; *HMC Portland*, I, 28–9; *CSPD 1641–3*, p. 258; R. Clifton, 'The Popular Fear of Catholics during the English Revolution', *Past and Present* LII (1971), 29–31.
73 *CJ* II. 378, 387, 396, 431; BL Harl. MS 162, fol. 324v; 480, fols. 122r, 144r.
74 M.G. Hobson and H.E. Salter, editors, *Oxford Council Acts 1626–65*, pp. 104, 363–4.
75 B. Manning in Parry, editor, *English Civil War and After*, p. 6.
76 *CJ* II, 373; HLRO, Main Paper series, 11 Feb. 1642: Sir Edward Rhodes to Ferdinando Lord Fairfax; BL Harl. MS 480, fols. 77r, 144r.
77 *D'Ewes (C)*, p. 335; *CJ* II. 354, 371, 387, 455, 490; BL Harl. MS 480, fol. 39r.
78 *D'Ewes (C)*, p. 122.

Map 2: Towns and villages which experienced Catholic panics, November 1641–April 1642.

greater families', Yorkshire ones arranged 'hunting matches to the terror of the people'.[79]

Catholics had become the scapegoats of a nation plunged into a political crisis that left it bewildered and uncomprehending. Very likely recusants did draw together at a time when they felt themselves hated and threatened in their own neighbourhoods. But where they did so their intentions were certainly largely pacific and defensive. Staffordshire recusants who held an open-air mass at Mow Cop in May confessed to a JP that they foregathered there in fear of laws such as the statute which made them traitors for entertaining Jesuits. The story told in the January 1642 pamphlet *A Bloody Plot* about a Derbyshire gentleman who was storing gunpowder in a vault beneath the church and collecting arms in his house may not have been fabricated, even if the suggestion that he was conspiring with three others to blow up the church and congregation is improbable. Nor does the account of an innkeeper's servant who conducted a well dressed stranger to Raglan Castle in November 1641, where he was shown scores of horses in the stable and an enormous armoury, sound entirely fanciful, though his reasons for suspecting the man were trivial to say the least.[80]

Several generations of Protestant gentry had treated their Catholic neighbours with intermittent respect, tolerance and even lenience. Some of the alarms of 1641 and 1642 centred, it is true, on strangers or newcomers to a district. Yet the conclusion is inescapable that men became inconsistent in their attitude to the Catholics in their midst under political stress. In many cases latent hostility took hold of men's minds, though some felt the dilemma that stories of local plots and designs imposed. 'The men named are of good ability, of seeming civil behaviour and quiet neighbours', declared the three Lancashire JPs who investigated the fireball plot in February 1642, 'but earnest, forward and hearty recusants.' They were evidently reluctant to believe the worst of neighbours against whom they bore no grudge, but they were moved by the possibility that some part of the dangers so much spoken of throughout the kingdom might hang over their own district.[81] The circulation of letters and pamphlets, together with the insistent tattle of marketplace and alehouse, forced gentry in authority to be wary and energetic in pursuing every piece of hearsay. As the sense of national peril became increasingly pervasive, local panics were bound to be treated seriously, even by the more sceptical.

At the popular level anti-Catholicism provided a political language that everyone could handle. When Walter Hill, a townsman of Stafford, met

79 *HMC 5th Report*, p. 13; BL Sloane MS 3317, fols. 30r, 37v; *LJ* IV. 579.
80 BL E 149 (25): *Strange News from Staffordshire*; E 134 (8): *A Bloody Plot practised by some Papists in Derbyshire*; E 176 (13): *A Great Discovery of a Damnable Plot at Raglan Castle*; HMC Coke p. 305.
81 *LJ* IV, 606–7; Russell, *Parliaments*, pp. 69, 154–5.

some troopers who were bound for Ireland, he wished them God speed, since they were 'going to fight against our enemies the papists'. He could not resist the chance of trying to divert them into a punitive raid on local Catholics, including Lady Stafford, 'an alone woman' with no armour at her disposal but allegedly a 'great store of money'.[82] There were many no doubt who saw things in these black and white terms. Nevertheless it would be wrong to make too much of fear of popery plain and simple. In the last resort it is the emotional standpoint of individuals that we know most about. When the Cheshire gentleman Henry Delves explained that his purchase of arms for 182 cavalry was for himself and his friends 'to defend themselves against the popish faction and league', his motivation rings true.[83] Nor can Lady Brilliana Harley's absorbing fear of papists be questioned, despite her protestations in November 1641 that she was contemplating taking a house in Shrewsbury for the children's sake rather than her own: 'if the papists should rise or there should be any commotion', she believed, a town would be safest. But her son Edward, she confessed in the same letter to her husband, was doubtful whether the papists had any strength and disliked her plan for abandoning the family home.[84] Edward Harley was not alone in his scepticism. Sir Thomas Holland, a 'very old and unwieldy' deputy-lieutenant, was criticized for carelessly slighting the plot against Conway and Beaumaris; and Bishop Prideaux of Worcester rapidly dismissed the panic in Oxford as a mere excuse for 'jealousies' without cause.[85] William Dobbins, writing to Sir Philip Percival on 15 February 1642, was more prepared to contemplate the possibility of external invasion than internal conspiracies: 'as for our homebred enemies the papists', he confided, 'I doubt not now of quieting them.'[86]

There were also those who were declared enemies of the papists but cannot be said to have feared them. Thomas Stockdale's comments on the Catholic problem in the West Riding were calm and rational. As a Puritan, a JP and a subsidy commissioner he did not underrate it: he possessed a list of some 532 recusants in Claro wapentake and in February 1642 ordered a general search throughout it for priests and arms. 'The forces they are able to make out are not much considerable,' he concluded, 'yet their consultations may conduce to the prejudice both of Church and commonwealth.' The Irish rebellion simply provided an 'apt occasion' for a pet scheme of his, by which two-thirds of the revenues of recusants' estates could be

82 D.A. Johnson and D.G. Vaisey, editors, *Staffordshire and the Great Rebellion* (Stafford, 1964), p. 21.
83 BL Harl. MS 480, fol. 150r.
84 *HMC Portland*, III, 81–2.
85 *CSPD 1641–3*, pp. 170, 258.
86 *HMC Egmont*, p. 165.

perpetually employed to uses of the government.[87]

The petitions were not so naive as to attribute the whole political crisis to the papists alone. Many of them seized upon the supposed links between the Arminian episcopate and Catholics, placing stress on the efforts of popish lords and prelates to retard reform measures at Westminster. Some implied that the conspiracy went wider still within the Church, drawing in the clergy as tools of the bishops. There was also a general disposition to regard evil counsellors, monopolists and projectors as Catholic allies.[88] Thus the papists were merely the most dangerous of the nation's enemies because they stirred others into action. As Thomas Stockdale put it, 'there are other humours in the body politic of this state, that are made fluid, and will move with them when there shall be opportunity.' Although he was dubious about the power of Yorkshire Catholics, Stockdale was always ready to blame the Jesuits for anything. He saw the attempt on the five members, for example, as a Jesuit plot 'to set a jealousy between the king and parliament'.[89]

The county petitions were the response to a call for partnership signalled by the Protestation and the Grand Remonstrance. Whereas in the summer of 1641 there was a gulf in understanding between the parliamentary leadership and the leaders of county communities, by early 1642 that gulf had closed. Both now saw the causes of the political crisis in much the same terms. Sheer frustration and even the wounded sense of pride which Pym and his circle felt so sharply had communicated itself to provincial observers. Thus the Hertfordshire gentry regretted the attempts by the malignant party to render the Commons 'not only contemptible but also burdensome to the people' and the Northamptonshire gentry hoped that the Remonstrance would remove aspersions cast by 'malignant spirits' upon parliament's proceedings.[90] Eleven of the county petitions and several urban ones included specific references to the Remonstrance. The narrative section had brought home to them the full tally of grievances and pressures suffered by the nation during the 1630s, declared the Shropshire petition.[91] Warwickshire was grateful for so comprehensive a statement 'of their sad condition and cure thereof'.[92]

So the Grand Remonstrance had abundantly satisfied many in the country. Men relived the seesaw of despondency, hope and new despair between 1639 and 1641 as they read the printed copies. Gratitude swelled in them as they assimilated the tale of achievements; grief, as the Dorset

87 *Fairfax*, pp. 229–30. 286, 377.
88 E.g. BL E 133 (15): Hertfordshire Petition; E 134 (21): Middlesex Petition; E 135 (36): Northamptonshire Petition.
89 *Fairfax*, pp. 286, 297.
90 BL E 133 (15), p. 5; E 135 (36).
91 Society of Antiquaries: Shropshire Petition.
92 BL E 135 (27); (35), p. 4.

petition explained, replaced it as they observed how MPs' godly endeavours had been hindered by malignants.[93] Surrey appreciated the
manifesto's 'full and satisfying account' of the 'great and hitherto
invincible obstructions of reformation'.[94] Cheshire regarded it as a 'looking
glass for this age and full justification . . . in all suceeding generations'.[95]

The obstructionism of the Lords and the pressure of other business had
brought the campaign to impose the Protestation on a nationwide basis to a
temporary halt in the summer of 1641, but the five-members crisis, as we
have seen, swept the anti-Catholic oath back into prominence. Throughout January 1642 the Protestation was constantly before Londoners' eyes:
'the roundheaded apprentices flock in troops to the parliament house with
the Protestation on the top of their swords', wrote John Turberville to
John Willoughby on 29 January, 'and their long ears cannot endure to hear
the name of a bishop'.[96] The speaker's letter to sheriffs on 20 January,
ordering that the oath should be taken by all adult males, stressed that this
had always been the Commons' intention. Printed copies reached the
localities, often with exhortatory letters from MPs, during late January
and early February and during the next weeks the nation was sworn village
by village.[97]

For those who oversaw it the business was time consuming: ministers,
churchwardens and constables had to be instructed in the process of taking
the oaths, certificates had to be collected in, the inefficient had to be
chivied. The pattern in Sussex was probably fairly typical. A meeting was
held at Lewes early in February at which most of the JPs took the oath,
further meetings in the market towns followed a few days later and the
parochial subscriptions were virtually complete by the end of the month.
The most common practice seems to have been for villagers to take the
Protestation at the bidding of the minister after one of the Sunday services.
Many of the returns indicate the care with which parliament's orders were
obeyed. Some who failed to appear at public meetings were visited in their
homes. When excuses were made for the old and sick, those at sea and those
away from home, there was often a note that they were good Protestants.[98]
In some counties, such as Lancashire and Yorkshire, it proved impossible
to complete the task by 12 March, the deadline laid down by parliament,

93 BL 190 g 12 (56).
94 BL E 134(21).
95 BL E 148 (12).
96 *Trevelyan Papers*, part III, 217.
97 *CJ* II, 389; R. Garraway Rice, editor, *West Sussex Protestation Returns* (Sussex Record Society,
    V, 1906), 1–4; Gloucestershire RO D2510/15.
98 HLRO, Protestation Returns, particularly Haytor hundred, Devon; Dufton, Kirkby Thore and
    Milburn, Westmorland; Derbyshire RO 803m (Gresley letter book), fols. 39–40; YPL House
    Books 36, fol. 67r; Townshend, pp. 46–8; *Fairfax* pp. 362–3, 365, 375, 377–8; Garraway Rice,
    editor, *West Sussex Protestation Returns*. I am grateful to Ms Lynn Beats for drawing my
    attention to the Derbyshire reference.

but there is no evidence of heeldragging among JPs or constables.[99] Some parish officers may have doubted the point of the exercise but at least their costs were recoverable. At Thorpe in Nottinghamshire the constables paid out four shillings and fourpence in all for their copy of the Protestation – for which they paid sixpence – and their expenses at meetings.[100]

Predictably, since it was just then in the front of their minds, many counties made a specific reference to their engagement to aid and succour parliament. Derbyshire wrote of that 'happy Protestation so providently commended unto us'; Staffordshire accounted it 'wise and religious' and told the Commons they conceived 'their own lives and liberties to be shipped in one bottom with yours'. In Sussex there were rumours that some of the peers 'discountenanced' the Protestation, so the petitioners urged the Lords to support the Commons' initiative for nationwide subscriptions.[101]

The petitions were propaganda documents designed to prompt effective action. What solutions did they have to offer? Their programme, in essentials, was simply Pym's programme of June 1641, brought up to date to account for new circumstances. The four central elements remained Catholics, evil counsellors, defence and reform of the Church. The critical preliminary to success with this programme, as many counties stressed, was the cooperation of Lords and Commons. The February and March petitions expressed a new optimism in this respect. Bedfordshire, on 16 March for instance, spoke of its joy at the concurrence of the Houses 'upon which the prosperity and welfare of our Church and state depends'; Cambridgeshire the same day was 'much cheered with the good hopes conceived of your lordships further care and zeal for a perfect cure for the future.'[102]

There could be no eradication of the Catholic danger without the relief of Ireland, 'the crying object of our pity', in Sussex's words, 'and subject of our enemies' cruelty'.[103] The call for speedy succour to the Protestants there was the common coin of all the petitions. Some counties were bold enough to put the blame for delays fairly and squarely on the Lords: when the blood of their brethren cried aloud to heaven for justice and vengeance, the Yorkshire petitioners told the peers on 15 February, 'hindering supplies to support the small remainder of those which yet remain unslaughtered hath rendered the former untainted honour of this nation an object of scorn and obloquy.' Hertfordshire's verdict on 25 January and Surrey's on 4 February were equally harsh. Hertfordshire attributed the

99   Bodleian Tanner MS 66, fols. 284, 293r; Bedfordshire RO J 1389.
100   Nottinghamshire RO PR 5767.
101   BL 669 f 4 (14), (80); *LJ* IV, 591.
102   *LJ* IV, 647–8.
103   BL E 134 (35).

persistence of the rebellion to the peers' failure to grant commissions to those who were ready to take up arms, to pass the impressment act and to accept 'the worthy offer of the Scotch nation to send 10,000 soldiers thither'. Surrey identified a party within the Lords who, they alleged, had resisted the efforts of their colleagues and of the Commons to hasten relief.[104]

Nineteen counties made a specific request for the disarming either of recusants or of all papists. Neither the royal proclamation of 11 November 1640 for disarming convicted recusants, nor the controversial and much more draconian disarming ordinance of August 1641, had been generally enforced. Cheshire, Lancashire, Nottinghamshire, Staffordshire, Sussex and Yorkshire, all given special attention the previous summer, were among the counties that issued new calls for total disarming. Even where something had been done there was a conviction that it was not enough. Several counties felt that such inspections as had been carried out were unlikely to have been adequate. 'Papists are so superficially disarmed, to the great animating of them in their pernicious practices', complained Rutland.[105] Oxfordshire wanted JPs to be given powers to administer oaths to servants and tenants, as well as their masters, when they visited papist manor houses, since searching alone had been 'commonly frustrated'. The petitions suggest that many shared the fears of the three Lancashire JPs who complained that in recusant homes 'made anciently of purpose for private conveyances, many things may be unfound of us'. The Monmouthshire gentry felt so incapable of the task of laying bare the papist armouries that they wanted the county's Catholics to be disarmed 'by some stronger force than our own'.[106]

For all this pessimism it should be noted that in some areas disarming was still regarded as a practical policy and had been vigorously pursued. In Devon, for instance, the Bench had established a comprehensive scheme for constables to sequester the arms of recusants and certify two justices of their proceedings, basing their action on the statute 3 James I, c.5.[107] But the widespread sense of helplessness is evident in the numerous requests for all papists to be confined to the neighbourhood of their homes and in the measures in this direction already taken in some localities. York city council was following a general direction from the county magistrates when it ordered on 31 January 1642 that all recusants should be visited by the constables and charged 'to keep themselves within their confines according to the law at their perils'.[108] Confinement was a temporary

104 *LJ* IV, 540, 563, 587.
105 Ormerod, p. 4; Derbyshire RO Chandos-Pole-Gell MS: Nottinghamshire Petition; BL 669 f 6(14); E 134 (35); E 135 (31); E 148 (12).
106 *LJ* IV, 606; BL 669 f 4 (65), (80); f 6 (1), (20); E 134 (21).
107 East Devon RO QS Order Book 1640–51 (Michaelmas sessions 1641).
108 YPL House Books 36, fol. 65r; *Fairfax*, p. 344.

panacea. As the Oxfordshire petitioners pointed out, it could prevent 'meetings for plots in London and elsewhere'.[109] The harsher alternative of imprisonment, proposed by Culpepper in June 1641 and enthusiastically discussed by the Commons in November, also received some support. Four counties – Bedfordshire, Berkshire, Northamptonshire and Rutland – made an unambiguous demand for the imprisonment of the most dangerous and active papists.[110]

So, despite the serious efforts in some districts to execute the available anti-Catholic legislation since the Long Parliament met, there remained a good deal of unease about its effectiveness.[111] Twelve shires, together with Ipswich and King's Lynn, made general requests for firmer enforcement of the statutes. Derbyshire, Kent and Surrey urged that special attention should be given to discovering and rooting out Church papists. Cambridgeshire and Sussex drew attention to papists' 'subtle conveyances of their estates', by which forfeitures were avoided.[112] Two counties proposed new powers for JPs: Berkshire wanted them to be allowed to examine papists on oath about 'bringing in arms to strengthen themselves'. Devon's prescriptions included an 'edict giving power to some of us to suppress meetings of recusants and Church papists' and warrants for searching foreigners at the ports who might be 'Jesuits disguised as merchants'. Devon also required the banishment of all papists who were not native, on pain of death, and the speedy execution of the Jesuits who had been condemned in December 1641.[113] Essex and Rutland supported them in the latter request.[114]

Another issue that was still alive was the influence of Catholics in local government. Their exclusion from the county Benches and other commissions is known to have been a slow process, but it is somewhat surprising to find four counties still worried in 1642 about their political influence at the local level.[115] Cheshire asked that papists should be 'put out of commission', Devon that they should be removed from colonelcies, captaincies and offices at the county's ports, and Lancashire that they should be deprived of any ports 'or other strengths' still in their keeping.[116] In Sussex, which requested that 'none popishly affected may have any place or trust in the kingdom', we know that there was a growing animus at

109 BL 669 f 4 (65), (77), (80), (83); E 134 (35); E 135 (36); Z 1 17 (59); *LJ* IV, 573, 579; Derbyshire RO Chandos-Pole-Gell MS: Nottinghamshire Petition.
110 BL 669 f 4 (75), (82); 669 f 6 (1); E 135 (36).
111 J.S. Cockburn, editor, *Western Circuit Assize Orders* (Camden Society fourth series XVII, 1976), p. 224 and above p. 59.
112 BL 669 f 4 (80), (83); E 134 (35); E 135 (36); *LJ* IV, 563.
113 BL 669 f 4 (75); E 181 (27).
114 BL E 134 (13); 669 f 6 (1).
115 R.B. Manning, *Religion and Society in Elizabeth Sussex* (Leicester, 1969), pp. 241–53; *Sussex*, p. 101.
116 BL E 148 (12); E 181 (27); Ormerod, p. 4.

this time against Sir Henry Compton, who throughout the 1630s had performed a remarkable political balancing act. The head of a wholly Catholic household, he had not only avoided conviction for recusancy, but had also, both socially and administratively, held his place within the charmed circle of county affairs.[117]

In conclusion the petitions provide massive evidence of a new determination to combat and root out popery. Nowhere is this more strikingly demonstrated than in the demand by six counties for the 'utter abolition of the mass'. Previously on this issue class solidarity had come before anti-Catholic sentiment, whatever distaste men felt for the forms of worship practised behind some park fences. But in the political tension of 1642 a good many people found the very thought of the mass unbearable. Moreover the mass at court, that open wound in the body politic, provoked the same horror in some parts of the countryside as it did in parliament. Bedfordshire and Kent specifically desired that the mass should be suppressed both at court and in the countryside.[118]

Eighteen county petitions took up the issue of evil counsellors, Rutland claiming pride of place in this respect by its forcefulness and its sense of the threat they posed to parliament's standing: 'that the hearing and censuring may be speeded . . . of all those who have been in eminent degree delinquents, especially in the ministry . . . by the delay of whose trials, the malignant party is (as we humbly conceive) much encouraged, the orders of this honourable House disobeyed and publicly slighted, thereby contemning the indubitable and ancient authority of parliaments.'[119] By early 1642, as most counties realized, it was the punishment rather than the discovery of delinquents which was glaringly urgent. The most dangerous delinquents of all, many believed, were the bishops: 'the great remoras', the Surrey petitioners called them, 'at which all our pious endeavours for the nation's welfare stop'.[120] Thus bishops exclusion was a vital ingredient in the petitioning programme and its achievement in February 1642 became a matter for tributes in the later petitions of the series. The Warwickshire delegation wrote a special preamble, explaining to the peers that they had met the news of their agreement to exclusion on the road to London and they found new hope in the countryside at this pledge that the Lords would join with the Commons 'for the public good'.[121] No Catholics actually sat in the Lords in 1642 but the point remained that bishops exclusion made the political rights of Catholic peers, surely potential evil counsellors if anyone, appear all the more blatant. The Rutland gentry

117 *LJ* IV, 591; *Sussex*, pp 97–8.
118 BL 669 f 4 (82); 669 f 6 (1); E 134 (35); E 148 (12); E 135 (36); *LJ* IV, 579; *D'Ewes (C)*, p. 375.
119 BL 669 f 6 (1).
120 BL E 134 (21).
121 BL E 135 (27) (36); 669 f 4 (65), (77), (80); *LJ* IV, 591; Society of Antiquaries: Shropshire Petition.

thought it 'against reason that papists should vote in points of that religion whereunto they are professed adversaries, or in matters of state to which they can be no fast friends, especially now that so great a party of papists are in open rebellion.'[122]

No one expected that the malignants responsible for the political crisis would be brought to heel within a few days or weeks, so securing the nation while parliament worked for settlement was necessarily a major objective. Invasion rumours did not only focus on the Irish rebels. Many believed that foreign aggressors would choose a moment of internal weakness to strike. Thus Surrey's petition spoke of the 'malice of enemies abroad sharpened by enraged fugitives driven forth by parliament's justice'.[123] According to one tale spread by a Dover resident, the French were so oppressed with taxes 'as they had scarce bread left and would be willing to partake of their plenty of England'.[124] Sir John Culpepper, rejecting the notion of sending English arms to Scotland to replace those sent from there into Ireland, was expressing a Kentishman's traditional caution: 'we should expose ourselves to the danger of our neighbour nations who were potent in arms.'[125]

What really frightened men was the sheer vulnerability of the English coasts. All the way from Northumberland round to Lancashire the same sorry story was told. The mayor of Berwick expounded the inadequacy of the town's defences. Both Colchester's blockhouse and Landguard Fort at Harwich were seriously decayed; guns there were without carriages and ammunition was lacking. Essex and Kent were still pleading for the restoration of their arms, which had been borrowed by the crown for the Scottish war.[126] The corporation of Dover reported that the castle was in 'great decay', the carriages and platforms for the ordnance were 'broken' and the supplies of gunpowder were almost exhausted.[127] Other Cinque Port fortifications were in no better condition and Dungeness Roads, as the ports pointed out, had a low shore ideal for landings. The Sussex petitioners called for speedy measures to protect its coastline, 'more than 70 miles naked to the sea'.[128] The complaints of the Hampshire gentry about the state of the county's castles and forts were given substance by independent accounts of the defences at Carisbrooke, Hurst Castle and Portsmouth.[129] The Dorset gentry insisted that they were in special

122 BL 669 f 6 (1).
123 BL E 134 (21); see also BL Harl. MS 383, fol. 201r.
124 Bodleian Tanner MS 66, fols. 88, 252r; BL, Harl. MS 162, fol. 373v.
125 *D'Ewes (C)*, p. 293.
126 *HMC 3rd Report*, p. 84; BL E 134 (13), pp. 2, 4; E 135 (36); *LJ* v, 126; Rushworth III, part I, 33; Essex RO Q/SR 313/34: Grand jury presentment 13 July 1641.
127 Kent RO, *Colonel Lunsford his Petition also the Petition of Dover.*
128 BL 669 f 4 (86); E 134 (35).
129 BL 669 f 4 (77); *CSPD 1641–3*, p. 271; *HMC 3rd Report*, p. 84.

danger, since persistent invasion rumours infested the shire and their situation invited it, 'being champion and bordering on the sea'. Foreign designs were so much feared in Devon that the gentry wanted to put Plymouth under daily guard by the trained bands.[130] Cornwall drew attention to its lack of gunpowder and the seriously decayed state of the castles at Pendennis and St Mawes; the harbours of Fowey and Helford were also 'fit to be fortified and put into trusty hands'. The shrill note struck by some of these southern communities reflected bitter experience of the failure by central government in the 1620s and 30s to maintain or strengthen their scattered bastions and blockhouses.[131]

The coastal inhabitants of Wales and the north west felt equally unprotected. Monmouthshire declared itself 'wholly unprovided for.'[132] The mayor of Pembroke complained that the deputy-lieutenants neglected his town, refusing to deliver arms from the county magazine for a posse of musketeers to defend it, to exercise the trained bands or to set any watches. 'We have not in this brave river of Milford,' he wrote on 17 February, 'one piece of ordnance mounted'. Anglesey petitioned their lord lieutenant on 22 March about the island's defences.[133] Cheshire asked the Commons for a new magazine and blockhouse to command the passages of the Dee and Mersey. Lancashire, 'seated in the mouth of danger', requested a fleet of small ships to guard its coast.[134] Even inland counties recognized that the coasts were a priority. Northamptonshire, for example, specifically mentioned the Tower and the Isle of Wight.[135]

Many of the petitions called for the passing and enforcement of the militia ordinance. Local initiatives indicate the urgency with which this was regarded. The Cambridgeshire gentry and freeholders, staging a mass appearance at quarter sessions in February, put pressure on the lord lieutenant for musters, regular drilling and replacement of defective arms. Some Shropshire gentry petitioned parliament for speedy provision of money to pay officers and soldiers of the trained bands and of arms and ammunition to train them.[136] The Commons' declaration in January 1642 about securing the counties and dispersing unlawful assemblies encouraged sheriffs and JPs to take specific measures. Friends of Hampden's in the Chilterns mustered the trained bands. The Leicestershire JPs attended a special meeting with the constables of the hundreds to discuss the state of the county militia.[137] The Worcestershire Bench ordered militiamen to be

130 BL 190 g 12 (56); E 181 (27).
131 BL E 143 (19); *Sussex*, pp. 188–924.
132 BL 669 f 6 (20).
133 *HMC Portland* I, 31–2; *CJ* II, 492.
134 BL E 148 (12); Ormerod, pp. 3–4.
135 BL E 135 (36).
136 *LJ* IV, 531, 612; *CJ* II, 455; BL. Harl. MS 480, fols. 173v–174r.
137 *CSPD 1641–3*, p. 259; PRO SP 16/488/90.

ready at an hour's warning furnished with powder, bullets and match. Night watches were doubled in Warwickshire.[138] The Monmouthshire magazine was guarded by selected men who were 'soundly settled' in the established religion. The Commons, not satisfied by this measure, ordered the removal of the magazine from Monmouth to Newport, a direction the JPs found it impossible to enforce, such was the power of the earl of Worcester in the shire town. The Yorkshire sheriff and JPs, meeting on 28 January, decided to erect an elaborate scheme for county defence: a foot company was set to guard the magazine, kept at the King's Manor at York, the lord lieutenant was to be moved to commission colonels and captains to exercise their men weekly and the arms of the trained bands were to be checked and improved. This bold programme, which ran far ahead of Westminster directions, was shortlived because it encountered resistance from the gentry of the shire, who doubted its legality and disliked the cost it involved.[139]

So there was a good deal of defensive activity in the first weeks of 1642, but those responsible for it were in no sense looking to civil war or acting on behalf of parliament against the king. Their prime concerns were the papist threat and local order. The Chiltern muster was a pro-Hampden demonstration but it was also prompted by news of the Kingston hurly-burly, which the Buckinghamshire men offered to suppress 'in array of war'. The Shropshire petition was due to the 'insolences and robberies' of troops on their way to Chester, 'whither it is said many popishly affected do go in the quality of volunteers'.[140] The Yorkshire scheme like the Monmouthshire one was based on fear of Catholics. Thomas Stockdale, its chief protagonist, hoped to pin the charge of maintaining a guard for the magazine on local recusants. 'Where sudden insurrections are to be prevented there I conceived that *salus populi suprema lex*', he told Lord Fairfax on 4 February, excusing his failure to act 'strictly within the compass of the letter of the law'. The main point of the petition of Cleveland, presented in the Commons the following day, was that its inhabitants had lost most of their arms in the Scottish war, whereas the papists in Yorkshire had still not been disarmed.[141] Besides these specific anxieties, there was probably a widespread sense that the condition of the local militias had deteriorated. There is no firm evidence that the annual muster, so beloved by the government in the 1620s, had taken place in a single county since the Long Parliament assembled. The Dorset petition

138   S.C. Ratcliff and H.C. Johnson, editors, *Warwick Country Records* II, XXIV, 116; Birmingham Reference Library Hanley Court MSS, Box 5, 398265–7.
139   BL Harl MS 163, fol. 54r; Bodleian Dep. C MS 165, no. 36; Tanner MS 66, fol. 254; *CJ* II, 415, 503–4, 549; *LJ* V, 57; *HMC Coke* p. 312; Webb, *Herefordshire in the Civil War*, pp. 30–2, 103–4; YPL House Books 36, fol. 87r; Fairfax, pp. 343–4, 348, 362, 365, 378, 381.
140   *LJ* IV, 531; BL Harl. MS 162, fol. 331v.
141   *Fairfax*, pp. 347–8; BL Harl. MS 162, fol. 370r.

was sharply critical of its new lord lieutenant, the earl of Salisbury, for his failure to appoint captains 'to muster or discipline' the trained bands.[142]

If the political agendas of the counties hold no great surprises, neither do their desiderata with regard to the Church. Many of the petitions employed a common argument, echoing Pym, that the Arminian changes had undermined the Protestant foundations of Church and state and that they threatened true religion. The points against the Arminians made endlessly at Westminster by the more zealous MPs were repeated time and again.[143] There was an implicit assumption in many cases that king and parliament stood together against the Arminian innovators: Nottinghamshire, spelling this assumption out, asked that 'idolatry and superstition may be totally extirpated by a thorough reformation, as well court as country, unto which particular we doubt not but the King's Majesty (having made so many full declarations and protestations against the same) will be graciously pleased so far to condescend as not to suffer that in any which good King Asa would not suffer in his own mother.'[144] Other counties which stressed the need to root out superstition and idolatry included Leicestershire, Warwickshire and Wiltshire.[145] There were numerous forceful condemnations of the Arminians. Derbyshire and Hampshire, for instance, referred to the corruptions in the Church, Bedfordshire to 'burdensome ceremonies'.[146] The Devonshire gentry objected to the views they had heard propounded 'that we may without danger receive into our Church ceremonies of the Church of Rome and that the Church of Rome in fundamental points does not err.'[147] Only a few of the petitioners specifically mentioned the Commons' orders of 8 September 1641, but those that did so, like the Oxfordshire and Sussex ones, were convinced that they had been widely flouted by cathedral and parish clergy. Oxfordshire pressed the Lords to question heads of colleges about whether their altars, images and crucifixes had been demolished as the Commons insisted.[148]

Several petitions stressed how much the universities had to answer for. 'The nurseries of our public ministry', lamented Ipswich, had been almost overwhelmed by 'popery, Arminianism and superstition'.[149] The Cambridgeshire gentry demanded 'orthodox and prudent governors' in the university, 'to provide that purer authors may be read to students'.[150]

142 BL 190 g 12 (56).
143 Rushworth III, part I, 21–40, 170–87; BL Add. MS 34485, fol. 77.
144 Derbyshire RO Chandos-Pole-Gell MS: Nottinghamshire Petition.
145 BL E 135 (13), (27), (46).
146 BL 669 f 4 (77), (80), (82).
147 BL E 181 (27).
148 BL E 134 (35); 669 f 4 (65).
149 BL E 135 (35).
150 BL 669 f 4 (83).

Distant counties like Staffordshire and Sussex, as well as neighbouring ones like Bedfordshire, Northamptonshire and Warwickshire, included a demand for the universities to be purged and reformed.[151] Nor was it only doctrine that was at stake. Northamptonshire blamed the universities for corruption of manners, a complaint enlarged upon by Rutland: 'by their looseness in government', it was alleged, 'youth being there first corrupted in conversation and doctrine become afterwards infectious and of evil example to the country.'[152]

There was much frustration at the delays in bringing the leading Arminians to justice. Nowhere was the hatred of a single individual stronger than in East Anglia, where Wren's activities had been well publicized by William Prynne's scurrilous pamphlet *News from Ipswich*, which went through four editions between 1636 and 1641. Yet early in 1642 the impeachment of Wren still lagged and the bishop continued to perform episcopal acts, such as the institution of clergy, from the Tower. Pleas for speedy justice against him came from Cambridgeshire, Ipswich and King's Lynn.[153] Provincial communities, it seems, found it hard to accept that Arminianism was dead and they had little confidence that it was safely buried. The 'utter quelling the pride, insolency and tyranny of the prelates' was prominent, for example, in Rutland's agenda.[154]

Since it was at the level of the parish that most men had experienced the impact of Arminianism, the call for the removal of scandalous ministers was almost universal in the petitions. That it should have come from 22 counties is some measure of the atmosphere of bitterness, the vendettas and the factionalism that Arminianism had brought to the countryside. The flood of petitions to the Commons' committee for scandalous ministers is further proof of Arminianism's divisiveness.[155] But this committee had achieved virtually nothing in 1641; such was the pressure of business that it was several times discontinued and subsequently revived. Inertia at the centre had given Arminians in the provinces the utmost encouragement.[156] The 'base ministers' of the county had 'raged more' since they knew of intentions to petition against them, Sir Anthony Weldon told the Kentish knights of the shire in May 1641, and were 'as insolent as ever in this part'.[157] Arminian assertiveness on behalf of Strafford has already been mentioned and the prominent role of Arminian

---

151 *LJ* IV, 575; BL 669 f 4 (14), (82); E 134 (35); E 135 (27).
152 BL 669 f 6 (1).
153 BL 669 f 4 (83); Z 1 17 (59); E 135 (35); E 137 (21).
154 BL 669 f 6 (1).
155 See my article 'Factionalism in Town and Countryside: the Significance of Puritanism and Arminianism' in D. Baker, editor, *The Church in Town and Countryside* (Studies in Church History XVI, 1979), pp. 291–300.
156 Holmes, editor, *Suffolk Committees for Scandalous Ministers* pp. 9–11; Shaw II, 176–9.
157 Larking, pp. 48–9.

clergy in local factionalism during 1642 will be discussed in chapter 9.[158] The pattern of parochial conflict is nicely summarized by the case of Mr Andrews, vicar of Busbridge in Surrey. A petition against him, 'very foul yet strongly proved', had been organized in his village and obtained substantial support at the opening of the Long Parliament. The following July it was reported that Andrews still carried himself with 'proud and insolent demeanour' and that, together with another of like mind, he slighted 'all passages against them in the House of Commons'. Villagers who protested at their vicar's prayers for Bishop Wren were told that he would pray for him 'till the Upper House and the king hath declared it'. Andrews never preached; he continued his commemoration of the dead; and he still refused communion to one whose 'conscience would not suffer him to kneel'.[159]

There is good reason to think that the Andrews case was by no means an isolated one. The magnitude of the problem in Surrey is suggested by its inclusion in the county's petition to the Lords in February 1642: no composure of the nation's distractions could be expected 'so long as our churches do abound with superstitious clergymen, many of whom, lying under the censure of parliament, for their own security breed and foment divisions and factions, thereby to thwart and overthrow the proceedings of this parliament.'[160] 'The superstitious innovating ministers are not punished', declared Rutland, 'who to escape just censure foment factions against the parliament.' 'We still suffer under the malign influence of some of the parties, who either are not cast out from us or boast of their hopes to return and do as formerly', affirmed Ipswich.[161] The conviction that Arminianism was still a potent force becomes understandable in view of this evidence of the vigour of Laud's allies among the parish clergy. Their determination to maintain their local footholds shows they believed they had friends in high places whose battles were not all lost.

So much for the petitioners' attempts to clear the ground. When we turn to the positive side of the religious programme, we find it was no other than the authentic Elizabethan programme of reform, resting on the twin foundations of sabbatarianism and preaching. Thus Cheshire demanded 'the due sanctification of the sabbath' and Rutland a check on all profanation of it, 'by wakes, travelling far and nigh and other actions not warranted by God's word'.[162] Able, fit, learned, godly, conscionable, painful, zealous: these are the adjectives that recurred as the petitioners set out their ideal of a preaching ministry. They attacked the persistence of pluralists and

158 Above pp. 16–17; below pp. 291–2.
159 BL Harl. MS 382, fol. 106r; 383, fol. 201r; D'Ewes, *Autobiography*, II, 272–3.
160 *LJ* IV, 563.
161 BL 669 f 6 (1); E 135 (35).
162 BL E 148 (12); 669 f 6 (1); C. Hill, *Society of Puritanism in Pre-Revolutionary England* (London, 1946), pp. 30–123. 124–744.

non-residents; they stressed the urgency of improving the maintenance of the clergy.[163] The deficiencies of the parochial clergy were constantly reiterated. Herefordshire found the people sunk in 'ignorance, super-stition and profaneness', through the insufficiency and idleness of ministers. Hampshire feared that under 50 of its 250 parishes, Oxfordshire less than 30 of its 280, enjoyed the services of a constant preacher. The bane of the county, the Oxfordshire petition explained, were those who luxuriated in 'a rich lordship . . . a deanery, a prebend and two fat parson-ages and seldom preach at either'.[164] Bedfordshire wanted special attention to be given to the ministry in market towns and 'populous places', Suffolk to the oversight of patrons to ensure they did present able men.[165] Lancashire drew attention to the unusual problems, long glaringly evident, of remote chapelries, where a rough and ignorant populace had never received the benefit of an adequately paid and competent ministry.[166]

All this emphasis on preaching was of course music to the ears of those evangelical MPs, like Sir Simonds D'Ewes, who had backed the previous summer's abortive Root and Branch scheme. Plainly such men were merely the representatives of a broad section of gentry opinion that ran right across the country. The keenest Puritans had been working as indi-viduals for reforms along these lines ever since the parliament opened. Oliver Cromwell's presentation of a petition on 7 February 1642 from some Monmouthshire men, who had been presented at assizes for abandoning 'their parish church where there is no preaching' to hear sermons elsewhere, was typical of the constant Puritan initiatives.[167] Meanwhile those who were stuck at home had harried their knights and burgesses by post. Augustine Skinner's letter to Sir Edward Dering on 28 January is a classic example of constituency pressure. Hailing him as the man who had given the first assault against the 'Goliath of hierarchical episcopacy', Skinner made his expectations clear:

> I doubt not had not many calamitous and unthought of disasters happened in our state to stop the current of your desires, the Church of God had by this time tasted more sweetness from your endeavours than yet to our grief we can be sensible of. Our eyes and hopes are still upon you and our pressures, through the scandalous lives, neglective and cold abilities, or total disabilities to discharge their functions as they ought, of our clergy cry aloud for a speedy redress.[168]

163   BL 669 f 4 (82); E 135 (27), (36).
164   BL 669 f 4 (65) (77); 669 f 6 (19).
165   BL 669 f 4 (82); *LJ* IV, 573.
166   Ormerod, p 4; Haigh, *Reformation and Resistance in Tudor Lancashire*, pp. 20–30; C. Haigh, 'Puritan Evangelism in the Reign of Elizabeth I'; *EHR*, XCII (1977), 30–58.
167   BL Harl. MS 480, fol. 114r.
168   BL Stowe MS 744, fol. 13r.

We are reminded that, as one commentator has insisted, Puritanism cannot be equated with rejection of a status quo: 'it is possible and by the early decades of the seventeenth century preferable to consider Puritanism as embodying the mainstream of English Protestantism.' 'The impressively homogeneous religious world' of early seventeenth-century Puritanism has been revealed by recent research, a world built around the sabbath, around preaching, repetition, conference, prayer and psalms, around lectures-by-combination, public exercises, funeral panegyrics, days of solemn humiliation and fasting. The word of God – preached, repeated, discussed – was always at the heart of these well established patterns of religious experience, which had taken root in so many corners of the land.[169] The inroads made by Puritan religion, not only in the south and east but in parts of Yorkshire, Lancashire and other more remote counties, have been amply demonstrated.[170] The petitions merely confirm the strength and forcefulness Puritanism had attained as a lay movement.

Many men still believed themselves in 1642 to be in the first flush of the Reformation. The Long Parliament's mission included the completion of a basic programme of education and conversion. Both the debates of July 1641 on Root and Branch and the petitions of early 1642 show an outpouring of evangelical aspirations, together with a very practical and hard-headed concern to secure the Protestant basis of the English state. But what distinguishes the 1642 petitions from the Root and Branch petitioning movement of the year before is their moderate tone. This is a direct reflection of the way the country had taken fright at sectarianism and religious controversy. There is no doubt that the gentry who formulated the new petitions were deliberately playing down the vexed question of Church government. Just as Pym looked for consensus at Westminster by omitting Root and Branch from the Grand Remonstrance, so they put the unity and harmony of their county communities above private opinions about the future of episcopacy. In any case there were many zealous Puritans for whom Root and Branch was no longer or never had been an article of faith. Augustine Skinner, for instance, in his letter to Sir Edward Dering, wrote as follows:

> Sir, I praise God I am no separatist nor have I any spawn of schism in me. Make bishops Timothies by lopping off their temporal honours and employments

---

169 P. Collinson, 'Towards a Broader Understanding of the Early Dissenting Tradition' in C.R. Cole and M.E. Moody, editors, *The Dissenting Tradition* (Athens, Ohio, 1975), pp. 10–15; P. Collinson, 'Lectures by Combination: Structures and Characteristics of Church Life in Seventeenth-century England', *BIHR* XLVIII (1975), 182–213; P. Collinson, ' "A Magazine of Religious Patterns": An Erasmian Topic transposed in English Protestantism', in Baker, editor, *Renaissance and Renewal in Christian History,*, pp. 223–49.

170 J.A. Newton, 'The Yorkshire Puritan Movement 1603–40', *Transactions of the Congregational History Society* XIX (1960–4), 3–17; Richardson, *Puritanism in North West England;* J. Marchant, *Puritans and the Church Courts in the Diocese of York* (London, 1960).

and paring away their superfluities. Then will they be more apt to teach and watchful and able to rule the ministry. So let them be bishops still.[171]

Only five of the 19 counties which had called for Root and Branch in 1641 repeated the demand and of these only Hertfordshire, which attributed the national crisis to the 'continuance of prelacy', did so unambiguously. Cambridgeshire requested the removal of 'unwarranted orders and dignities', Bedfordshire, Kent and Sussex the establishment of a form of Church government agreeable to God's word.[172] Three counties which had not spoken on the matter the previous year – Herefordshire, Northamptonshire and Staffordshire – chimed in with similar formulations.[173] Colchester made no bones about its fears of future enthralment by bishops, chancellors and their officials, nor did Ipswich and the Cinque Ports.[174] This was as far, in public, as Puritan gentry were now prepared to go. The Cheshire gentry merely asked the Commons to diminish the vast revenues and power of the bishops, 'who else may in time again become as mischievous to the Church as they have formerly been to the state'. By this stance, aimed at consensus, they clearly hoped to hush the factional strife of the county and maintain the isolation of their conservative controversialist Sir Thomas Aston.[175]

The petitions that have been discussed represented a broad and considered response to the nation's problems. National ills were seen in national terms and parliament was seen as the institution best fitted to restore normality at a time of crisis. The petitions present incontrovertible evidence of the hold parliament had obtained on the nation's mind. In this sense it was in 1642 that the representative body of the nation finally came into its own. The 14 petitions which made an explicit mention of Charles's abortive coup are marked by concern that parliament's privileges should be secured and vindicated. Dorset regarded them as 'our dear and undoubted right', Essex as 'the strength and safety of your body and the inheritance of the subject', Hampshire as 'the chiefest and most real inheritance, purchased and left us by the great care and powers of our ancestors'.[176] Leicestershire wanted the 'actors of that most horrid, high and wicked attempt' made 'public examples to all posterity': 'the greatest hazard of our lives would not more affect us, which makes us restlessly to desire the bottom of this bloody design may be sounded.'[177] These reactions were perhaps predictable. After all the whole country tradition of

171 BL Stowe MS 744, fol. 13v.
172 BL 669 f 4 (82), (83).
173 BL 669 f 6 (14), (19); E 135 (36).
174 BL E 134 (13); E 135 (35); 669 f 4 (86).
175 BL E 148 (12).
176 BL 190g 12 (56); E 134 (13); 669 f 4 (77); Hirst, particularly pp. 132–88.
177 BL E 135 (13).

opposition to prerogative government during the 1620s and 30s was founded on the belief that ancient rights and privileges were in danger. It had been a defensive operation mounted by deeply conservative men.[178]

The petitions show that, however introverted county communities could become in normal times, they were not blind and unheeding about the significance of national perils.[179] They show, moreover, that the hunger for news so evident at this time represented a real involvement in political affairs and a sensitivity to national issues, even though petitioners often achieved effect by putting these issues in a local context. Yet, when all this is said, the particular and individual complaints which make these petitions local as well as national ones must not be ignored. Many of these were economic. The cloth trade, which had been sluggish for 18 months, ground to a halt in early 1642, bringing hunger and misery to such districts as East Anglia and the West Riding of Yorkshire, together with parts of Berkshire, Devon, Hampshire and Kent. (See Map 3, p. 224) Towns which petitioned about their difficulties included Colchester, Exeter, Gloucester and Marlborough. Essex, where sudden pressure on the land brought a massive rise in rents, and Suffolk were probably the counties worst affected.[180] A Commons committee investigated the trade in the new draperies and concluded that the remedy was in the Suffolk clothiers own hands. They had confessed that, of 16,000 cloths dyed azure blue made each year, only about 3000 were properly finished, 'which had brought a great discredit upon those cloths at Constantinople'.[181] But the committee, if they had been rather more sympathetic, might have given weight to political insecurity as a cause of trading disruption.

The counties have been portrayed in this chapter as presenting Pym with a mirror image of his own policies. Yet there was one important respect in which the mood of the localities early in 1642 differed from that of the parliamentary leadership. At Westminster there was a sense of outright confrontation with the crown from which there could be no drawing back. We find this entirely absent in the petitions. During the weeks they were being written and circulated many town councils looked to their defensive arrangements. But they were preparing not for civil war but for a national state of emergency based on the papist conspiracy. Thus in the anxious weeks following the Irish rebellion Stafford gave attention to the town butts, Exeter moved its ammunition stocks to a safer storage

178 Ashton, *English Civil War*, pp. 17–21; Hirst, pp. 157–81.
179 A. Everitt, 'The County Community' in E.W. Ives, editor *The English Revolution* (London, 1968), pp. 48–63; A. Everitt, *Change in the Provinces: the Seventeenth Century* (Leicester, 1969), pp. 8–12; *Sussex*, pp. 22–54; Everitt, pp. 20–83; Morrill, *Revolt*, pp. 13–31.
180 HLRO, Main Papers, 25 Jan: 1642: Petition of the Commons of Exeter to the Mayor; BL Harl. MS 480, fol. 125; E 200 (14); *Mr Grimston his speech in Parliament*: Steele, no. 1982; Manning in Parry, editor, *English Civil War and After*, pp. 9–10.
181 BL Harl. MS 163, fol. 76v; *CJ*, II, 532.

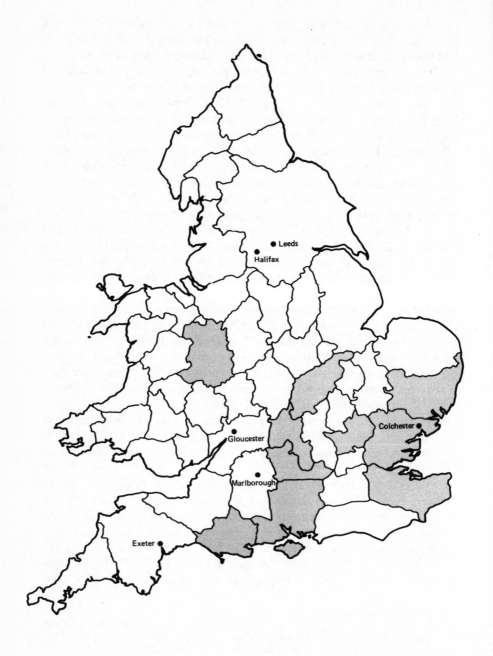

Map 3: Counties and towns that petitioned parliament about decay of trade, January–March 1642.

place, Coventry purchased 500 muskets. Exeter's changing attitude to the night watch charts the ups and downs of local alarm: originally set on 14 December, it was reduced in size on 20 December and then returned to its initial complement, after the news of the attempt to arrest the five members reached the city, on 11 January.[182]

The abortive coup brought the emergency home to many corporations. Braintree's Company of the Four and Twenty decided to buy six muskets for the defence of the town; the Gloucester corporation ordered 60 muskets and four new pieces of ordnance; at Norwich and York the militia captains were directed to check the citizens' arms. Coventry, Great Yarmouth, Northampton and Salisbury were among the towns which established a nightly watch managed by leading citizens at this time. Such towns also took precautions for the defence of gates and bridges by posts and chains. At Dorchester a special watch was set on the magazine during divine prayer and sermon on Sundays and fast days. Where church attendance was strictly enforced, this was obviously a time of particular vulnerability to surprise attack. The 'present troubles and dangers' caused the corporation of Great Yarmouth to appoint a committee to improve the town's fortifications; at Shrewsbury the corporation ordered that the cannon should be tested and stocked.[183] There were other towns which took matters in hand during March. Plymouth and Reading set a strong nightly watch; Newark bought powder and shot; Wigan mustered its soldiers, arranged for the erection of town butts and admitted two men as freemen so they might make 'warlike weapons for the safeguard of the town in any time of danger'.[184] The chronology of these initiatives was largely haphazard and it cannot be made to fit any coherent geographical pattern. There is nothing about them to suggest commitment to one side or the other in the growing conflict, or even any recognition that such commitment might very soon be required.

Neither townsmen nor country gentlemen were ready to face the possibility of civil war. In so far as petitioners glimpsed it at all, their object

182 William Salt Library SMS 402, fols. 110–11; East Devon RO Exeter Chamber Act Book 1634–47, pp. 250, 253, 257–8; Coventry RO A 14 (b), fol. 23a.
183 Essex RO D/P 264/8/3; Norfolk RO Norwich Court Book 1634–46, fols. 335v, 336v; YPL House Books 36, fol. 65r; Northamptonshire RO Northampton Borough Book 1628–1744, pp. 66–7; Great Yarmouth Town Hall, Yarmouth Assembly Book C19/6, fols. 498v, 499v; H. Beaumont, 'Events in Shropshire at the Commencement of the Great Civil War', *Transactions of the Shropshire Archaeological and Natural History Society* LI (1941–3), p. 14: Coventry RO Council Minute Book 1636–96, fols. 24v, 25r, 26v; Salisbury District Council Muniment Room Ledger Book D, fol. 6v; Gloucestershire RO GBR B3/2: Borough Minute Book 1632–56, pp. 205, 207; Dorset RO B2/16/4: Dorchester Corporation Minute Book, 1637–56, under 28 Jan, March, 1642; Town Clerk's Department, Newark: Borough Council Minute Books, under 20 March. I am grateful to Mr Michael White for the last reference.
184 *CJ* II, 494; J.M. Guilding, editor, *Reading Records* IV, 41; A.J. Hawkes, *Wigan's Part in the Civil War* (Manchester, 1932), pp. 100–1.

was to stave it off. Thus Derbyshire's petition gave comfort by holding out a vision of the future:

> England may still continue one of Christ's golden candlesticks; the ministers stars in his right hand, the whole kingdom and people in covenant with God and the blessed peace of the gospel, we may sit every man under his own vine and figtree and enjoy a happy peace to us and prosperity to the world's end.

Devon had decided to petition the king as well as parliament, the JPs and gentry told the peers on 25 January, 'being thence confident of these happy effects: instead of distractions unity; for remoras, celerity; for misunderstanding, correspondency'.[185] Here was an inkling, unusual in the January and February petitions, of the fact that the restoration of some kind of trust between the king and the leading men at Westminster had become the overwhelming political priority. Only Hertfordshire specified the 'misunderstanding between His Majesty and the parliament' as one of the causes of their fears.[186] Not until March, when Bedfordshire and Hampshire made something of it, was there much sign that the significance of the physical separation of the antagonists was grasped outside London.[187]

Because the petitioners did not feel strong personal distrust of Charles themselves, they could not be expected to understand how the whole political crisis had come to hinge on the breakdown of trust between a few men and their monarch. The petitions were manifestos of loyalty to parliament, but they were not declarations of loyalty to parliament against the king. On the contrary, they were suffused with loyalty to Charles as well as parliament. This loyalty still came naturally to almost everyone, even, for instance, to so zealous a supporter of the parliament as the Yorkshire gentleman Thomas Stockdale. There is no need to suppose he meant anything but what he said when he commented on the crisis in London to Lord Fairfax in January 1642. 'The king's goodness', he wrote, 'will, I hope, hearken to the advice of his Commons, which is the major and more infallible part of his great councils.' Grief not anger was the note commonly struck in reflections on the king's behaviour. The latest rumours about Charles's movements had made 'us somewhat fearful of the issue', D'Ewes's brother-in-law told him on 17 January, 'I pray God direct him for the best.'[188] 'I am sorry the king is pleased yet not to conceive any better thoughts of this parliament', wrote Lady Harley, when she thanked her son for Charles's latest declaration on 19 March.[189] We have seen how the king was welcomed on his journey down the Great North Road in

185 BL 669 f 4 (80); *LJ* iv, 536.
186 BL E 133 (15).
187 BL 669 f 4 (77), (82), (86).
188 Fairfax, p. 294; BL Harl MS 383, fol. 197r.
189 *Harley*, p. 152.

November 1641. When the news of his return to London reached towns on the other side of the country they rejoiced: bonfires blazed at the High Cross and outside the mayor's home in Bristol and the church bells rang at Bridgnorth.[190] This, like the speeches of recorders and mayors, was part of the ritual of deference. There is no reason to regard such expressions as empty gestures, yet what is hidden from us at this stage of the story is the extent to which the prestige of the monarchy had declined because of the policies Charles I had pursued. This is something that would only become apparent when men had to face the conflicting claims of king and parliament for allegiance in a civil war. At that point the persuasiveness of Pym's account of the papist conspiracy, on the one hand, and the strength of the king's hold on men's loyalty, on the other, would be of crucial importance.

Unfortunately the ideals of mixed monarchy and a balanced constitution, so aptly summarized in many of the concluding statements of the petitions discussed in this chapter, were of little use to men about to face these claims. The petitions show no signs of constructive wrestling with the constitutional dilemmas of the moment. In requesting the disposal of the militia 'as may consist with native liberties of the subject', Oxfordshire harked back to old controversies about the statutory basis of military obligations and ignored the urgent problem of how parliament and the crown might reach a working relationship over the question. Northamptonshire added to its agenda of eight measures for restoring political harmony the ambiguous advice that the Commons should use 'such lawful ways and means as the present necessity and desperate condition of the kingdom suggest'.[191] The petitioners were essentially escapist. They were horrified at the wounds in the body politic and yearned for them to be healed. Though none of them could yet see it, they were asking the impossible.

190 Latimer, editor, *Annals of Bristol*, p. 154; *HMC Various MSS*, IV, 434.
191 BL E 135 (36).

7

Confrontation

We should send to His Majesty for a present answer and if evil counsellors be not removed, the great council of the kingdom must.

> Sir Arthur Haselrig in the House of Commons,
> 4 February 1642[1]

So many false reports are spread abroad that a man knows not what to believe.

> Sir John Coke to his father,
> 27 March 1642[2]

Our choice is of the prime gentry and of one regiment of our trained bands . . . and that you may fully assure yourselves of our sole dependency upon the love and service of our own people, to live and die with them, we have armed these our subjects.

> The king's declaration to the Yorkshire freeholders,
> 3 June 1642[3]

The king stayed at Windsor for almost a month after he had abandoned his capital. Then he accompanied his wife to Dover. There was a tender farewell when she set sail on 23 February: Charles, we are told, galloped along the cliffs to keep her ship in sight as long as possible.[4] This vignette is important since Henrietta Maria had sworn her husband to be resolute in the policy of confrontation with Pym which was confirmed by the charges against the five members. 'The king's affection to the queen', wrote Hyde later, 'was of a very extraordinary alloy; a composition of conscience and love and generosity and gratitude . . . insomuch as he saw with her eyes and determined by her judgement.'[5] Henrietta Maria knew about civil strife; the thought of civil war did not appal the daughter of Henri IV. She went abroad to pawn the crown jewels and seek aid against the leaders of the English parliament. Charles in her absence would look for support in the north, making his base at York, and attempt to regain control of

---

1 BL Add. MS 14827, fol. 28v.
2 *HMC Coke*, P. 310.
3 BL E 149 (27): *His Majesty's Declaration at Heworth Moor*.
4 *CSPD 1641–3*, p 283; Gardiner x, 168.
5 Firth, *EHR* xix (1904), 250.

Hull.[6] When the Venetian ambassador had an audience with the queen at Greenwich on 10 February, she told him that 'to settle affairs it was necessary to unsettle them first as she considered it impossible to re-establish her husband's authority in any other way.'[7]

The king's dependence on his wife at this time reflected his sense of humiliation and betrayal. Hardly any of his counsellors except Falkland and Culpepper had rallied to him. There was 'no force with the king at the court', reported Culpepper after a visit to Windsor on 12 January; two days later Orlando Bridgeman returning avowed he had never seen so small a court.[8] Sir John Holland on 29 January spoke of 'a desolate court' with no noblemen and 'scarce three gentlemen'.[9] The Berkshire countrymen refused to assist with the royal carriages or cooperate with the purveyors. An attempt to raise the *posse comitatus* on the news of 1000 citizens coming with a petition fell flat. The crown's 'small attendance and pomp' on the road to Dover was also noted.[10] It was perhaps some comfort that so many Kentish gentry turned out to greet the royal couple when they rode across Barham Downs on the final stage of their journey.[11] The lesson was obvious: loyal subjects were to be found well away from the capital.

If this interpretation of the king's mind is correct then the whole of the conciliatory phase in royal policy between late January and mid February 1642 was no more than a tactic.[12] The exclusion of the bishops from the Lords, the most important sop of these weeks, seems to have been pressed on Charles by both Culpepper and the queen for rather different reasons. For Culpepper it was central to a bid for appeasement; for the queen it was merely a ploy that would help her husband to stand firm thereafter. The gossip for once may have been right: 'they say the king passes the bill quickly,' wrote William Montagu to his father, 'lest the queen should be thought to be a hindrance of it and now she is gone he is diffident of his own resolution and fearful he should have been wrought to have broken it if now he should have given them a denial.'[13] Henrietta Maria, in other words, knew the king's irresolution and sought to cure it by prompting a major concession together with a period of conciliation. The friendly message on 20 January, the declaration on 6 February that the king would drop his charges against the five members, the agreement on 11 February

6 M.A.E. Green, editor, *Letters of Queen Henrietta Maria* (1857), pp. 52–4, 112; Zagorin, pp. 297, 302.
7 *CSPV 1640–2*, p. 295.
8 *HMC Coke*, p. 304; BL Harl. MS 162, fol. 320v; Harl. MS 480, fol. 18r.
9 BL Harl. MS 162, fol. 358v.
10 Bodleian Tanner MS 66, fol. 242r; *CSPD 1641–3*, pp. 273, 281.
11 Everitt, p. 94.
12 For a different view see Wormald, pp. 53–67.
13 *HMC Buccleuch*, p, 290; Wormald, pp. 60–1.

to remove Biron from the Tower and the passing of the impressment bill on the 14th can all be seen in this context.[14] The king and queen may have hoped to produce some defections at Westminster by this course, but they had no expectation of ending the rebellion led by Pym without a resort to force.

The reunion with his eldest son at Greenwich on 26 February undoubtedly brought the king some solace. The Commons had made frenzied efforts to prevent the marquis of Hertford from taking him there. But their fears that Charles would send him overseas were without foundation.[15] The king wanted his heir by his side. It is interesting that he should have mentioned the boy when he discussed the form of the reply Hyde was drafting about the militia on 28 February. The phrasing did not bother him, he declared, 'for now I have gotten Charles I care not what answer I send them.' In his speeches to the MPs who brought parliament's latest messages at Theobalds on 2 March and at Newmarket on the 9th, Charles showed his increasing exasperation with those who believed he was seated at the centre of a web of conspiracy. 'What would you have?', he demanded. 'Have I violated your laws? Have I denied to pass any bill for the ease and security of my subjects? I do not ask you what you have done for me.'[16]

The journey to York was a leisurely and sometimes heartwarming affair. At Cambridge Charles heard an oration from the vice-chancellor and the scholars shouted *Vivat Rex* in welcome, but the failure of the sheriff and county gentry to appear was disconcerting. At Little Gidding he shot a hare in the fields. Yet the king's mood, as the prince reported to his sister Mary on 10 March, remained 'disconsolate and troubled'. They were 'now for York', wrote this anxious boy who was not yet twelve, 'to see the event or sequel of these bad unpropitious beginnings'.[17] Henrietta Maria continued to chide, and even to threaten retirement to a nunnery, if Charles's constancy failed, but her anxiety at every false rumour of his return to London was misplaced.[18] The king finally knew his own mind. There was hope beneath his apparent depression. 'He had heard the king say', an anonymous informant told Pym, 'that he had the nobility, the gentry and divers honest men of his side.' By alienating the cavaliers, Charles believed, Pym's men had 'prepared swords for their own throats'. He talked of an army of 16,000 men, commanded by the officers who had

14 *CJ* II, 416, 426, 429–30; *LJ* IV, 580–1; Gardiner X, 159–67.
15 *CJ* II, 379, 450–1, 457, 459; *LJ* IV, 608, 610, 617; *HMC Coke*, p. 308; BL Add. MS 14827, fol. 53.
16 Rushworth III part I, 524, 532; Gardiner X, 171–2.
17 BL E 201 (29): *A True Diurnal*, 14–21 March, pp. 4–5; Kingston, *Hertfordshire in the Civil War*, pp. 11, 37–8; Wedgwood, *King's War*, p. 76.
18 Green, editor, *Letters of Henrietta Maria*, pp. 52–8.

supported him at Whitehall, who would 'keep him in safety'.[19] At Doncaster on 17 March the king discussed with Sir Thomas Glemham a strategy for besieging Hull by cutting off its fresh water supply.[20] Every day, as he rode further from London, he kept the key to the cipher in which he and the queen exchanged letters in his pocket: it was a talisman in his time of trial.

Although he told the queen he found the county well affected, the first weeks at York were in truth a grievous disappointment to the king.[21] Observers noted his displeasure and his failure to reply when the recorder's oration on 18 March stressed his duty to 'hearken unto and condescend unto' parliament.[22] The county did not throng the court. At the end of March, according to one report, Charles had the company of only 39 gentlemen and 17 personal guards. Thomas Stockdale noted that the presence of the cavaliers, who spoke loud 'in their sense' of the nation's troubles, disturbed the local community.[23] Nor was the response of the peerage to the summonses to attend the St George's Day Feast at all encouraging.[24] Projecting the image of royalty in exile was no easy task. Ever since January Falkland had been assiduously circulating multiple copies of the king's declarations to sheriffs but this propaganda campaign was not yet showing results.[25] Petitioners from midland counties such as Derbyshire and Lincolnshire urged accommodation not war.[26] Gestures such as the proclamation at Stamford for enforcement of the recusancy laws and offers to the Yorkshire gentry to reduce the size of their trained bands, pay their billet money and restore the Council of the North on a just foundation provoked no enthusiasm for the royal cause.[27]

The key to understanding royal policy in April 1642 remains Charles's sense of desolation. He announced on 8 April that he had set his mind on going to Ireland in person. Since Yorkshire was unsympathetic, he would raise a guard of 2000 foot and 200 horse in Cheshire and arm them from the magazine at Hull.[28] No doubt the king did hope to bring the rebellion to an end, but in the main he was probably looking further ahead. He needed an army to crush the traitors at Westminster and the queen's projects of raising financial support for such a force from the Netherlands and

19 BL Harl. MS 163, fol. 32v.
20 J. Shaw, *Yorkshire Diaries*, p. 134.
21 Green, editor, *Letters of Henrietta Maria*, p. 59.
22 BL 669 f 3(61): *A Letter written by Master Simon Rhodes*; 669 f 3(63): *The King's Entertainment at York*; E 141(8): *The King's Noble Entertainment at York*.
23 Fairfax, pp. 390–1; BL E 143(8): *A True Relation concerning Nottinghamshire's Petition*, p. 4.
24 *LJ* IV, 675–8, 712–3, 715; *CSPD 1641–3*, p. 307; *HMC Buccleuch* I, 297.
25 BL Add. MS 14827, fol. 34v; *CJ* II, 402, 421, 496, 499, 510; *HMC Buccleuch* I, 296; *HMC 5th Report*, p. 15; Durston, pp. 133–4.
26 *Derbyshire Archaeological Journal* XCIII (1973), 36–7.
27 BL 669 f 3(57).
28 Bodleian *Petition of Yorkshire, 5 April 1642*, pp. 3–5.

Denmark at this stage still looked promising.[29] The king clung to the strategy he had worked out with his wife in the dark winter days at Windsor, even though it involved tactical concessions to parliament. Thus the militia bill that he offered to the Lords on 19 April made provision for the parliamentary nominees to hold office but for one year only; while the king was overseas the armed forces would be under the direction of parliament alone.[30]

There was no chance that parliament would agree to a militia bill on these lines or cooperate in raising the guard the king needed to go to Ireland. By the end of April his broad strategy was in ruins, above all because of Sir John Hotham's defiance on the walls of Hull.[31] Ever since he reached York, the county's gentry, fearing civil strife, had dissuaded him from attempting to take the town. Only a few hotheads and the queen's nagging pushed him into the humiliating journey and retreat on 23 April.[32] The events of that day must have deeply affected the king. Hotham's refusal to admit Charles to his most important port in the north was bound to harden still further the heart of a man of rigid temperament, whose office was the essence of his self-respect. It was an insult to his kingly dignity that he could never forget and that he was bound to revenge at the earliest opportunity.

So it is not surprising that the king showed a new waspishness in his dealings with parliamentary emissaries during the following weeks. Reading the instructions of the committee of MPs sent to York in May, he observed that he had 'heard of the great trust that is put in the king' but never of the 'great trust reposed in the parliament without the king'. If they tried to make a party in his temporary capital he would 'clap them up'. If the militia ordinance was executed parliament would receive just punishment. It was ironic that on the very day of this warning MPs carried out their first military review, of the London trained bands in Finsbury Fields. Charles dismissed the new petition for peace brought by the earl of Holland on 16 July as 'like a pill well gilded'. 'He had been robbed', he declared peevishly, and 'he sought his own.'[33]

May was spent, as Sir John Coke put it, 'labouring with the gentlemen of Yorkshire to engage them in the business of Hull'.[34] The case Charles put was that he needed a personal guard to defend him against 'sudden violence and affront'. Assemblies of gentry on 30 April and 12 May were given soft words about the king's pacific intentions and warned against the insinuations of the parliamentary committee, vipers in their midst who

29　*LJ* IV, 709–10; Gardiner X, 186–8.
30　Gardiner X, 186, 191; Zagorin, pp. 316–7.
31　*CJ* II, 534, 541; *LJ* V, 12–13; Gardiner X, 192–3.
32　Green, editor, *Letters of Henrietta Maria*, p. 59; below, p. 316.
33　BL Harl. MS 163, fol. 115r; Add. MS 14827, fols. 102r, 168r.
34　*HMC Coke*, p. 314.

alleged Yorkshire was becoming a seat of war.[35] Despite local dismay at the plan, Sir Robert Strickland's regiment of the North Riding trained bands was put on duty at York. By 20 May around 600 foot soldiers were billeted there; they were joined by a troop of horses under Sir Francis Wortley, selected in the first place at a review of the county's cavalry, which grew to about 140 by the end of the month.[36] The cost of all this was general political alarm, which the king tried to allay by a meeting of freeholders at Heworth Moor on 3 June.[37] Estimates of the numbers who attended vary from 40,000 to 100,000, but only a few of them can have heard the king's speech reiterating his concern for Yorkshire's welfare which was read in several parts of the milling crowd.[38] According to Lord Howard's report to parliament, many left 'saying they could give no account of the cause of their being called together'.[39] The meeting did little to further the king's cause.

'If I could be Pym with honesty', wrote Sir Edward Dering tartly to his wife on 13 January, 'I had rather be Pym than King Charles.'[40] Many London observers probably shared Dering's assumption that it was Pym who held the political advantage in the aftermath of the abortive coup. This was not how Pym or his closest allies saw things themselves. They had escaped with their lives but they now had incontrovertible proof that the conspiracy they had so long feared was hatching. When the Westminster sittings resumed on 11 January, Mandeville and the five members only dared return there by day. They were fed and lodged each night by friends in the City.[41] Moreover every sitting of parliament was attended by two companies of militiamen until 5 March, when the guard was at last reduced to a single company.[42]

The leadership's fearful state of mind in early 1642 is fully explicable in terms of the 4 January incident, the king's subsequent movements, the unsettled state of London and the persistent rumours of foreign invasion. The impudence of artisans, porters and even women who petitioned in such massive numbers was much remarked upon.[43] The invasion fears began with stories of great preparations in France during January. In

---

35 *CSPD 1641–3*, p. 324; *HMC Portland* I, 38–9; Steele, no 2138; BL 669 f 5(20): *His Majesty's Speech to the Gentry of the County of York.*
36 BL Add. MS 14827, fols. 105v, 112v; *LJ* v, 74, 79–80; *CSPD 1641–3*, pp. 322–3; *HMC Coke*, p. 316; *HMC Buccleuch* I, 301; *HMC 5th Report*, p. 148; Cliffe, pp. 332–3.
37 Rushworth, III, part I, 620; BL 669 f 6(15): *The Petition of Many Thousands of the County of York.*
38 BL 669 f 5(34): *His Majesty's Declaration to the Freeholders of the County of York*, p. 6; Northamptonshire RO Isham correspondence, 243; *CSPD 1641–3*, p. 336.
39 *LJ* v, 107; J.L. Malcolm, 'A King in Search of Soldiers: Charles I in 1642', *Historical Journal* XXI (1978), 257.
40 Larking, p. 68.
41 *HMC Buccleuch*, p. 290.
42 *CJ* II, 468, 577, 621; *LJ* IV, 596, 268.
43 E.g. *CSPD 1641–3*, p. 274.

March 60 French men-of-war were reported to be hovering between Brittany and Devon and there was news of men and horses ready for transportation in Normandy.[44] Then Pym's circle became more concerned about Danish activity. Digby, now in Denmark, was suspected to be deep in negotiation with the king there, who was 'much incensed against the parliament'. New rumours about Danish plans cropped up week by week during April and May. Finally, on 9 June, Pym announced that 20 Spanish ships were feared to be sailing for Hull.[45] What terrified him was the prospect of a joint invasion from Denmark and France or Spain at a moment of gross internal weakness. He had no reliable means for sifting false rumour from fact.

Within the Commons Pym faced a delicate factional situation. The incipient peace party contained various elements. There were some, like Sir Simonds D'Ewes, who still believed Pym's account of the political situation but simply recoiled at the prospect of war. There were others who now openly questioned Pym's story. On 4 March Sir Ralph Hopton objected to 'the design to change the true religion and settle popery' being named as the first cause of the political crisis in a new declaration: 'there had been such a design but it was now so far quashed as it could for the present be no cause of our fears and jealousies.'[46]

It is well known that for a while Culpepper, Falkland and Hyde played a double game. They participated in debates and then sent the king advance warning of parliament's moves, even 'heads ready framed for his answers and notes in the margin what was against law and what records made for him'. Gradually though the most seasoned advocates of the king's cause defected. Dering, who told a colleague that Pym and his men had set up 'the omnipotent power of legislation in this House' as a new idol for themselves, was expelled in February.[47] Hyde attended infrequently after the beginning of March, Culpepper and Falkland were present intermittently until June.[48] Their discomfort is tellingly illustrated by the fact that Culpepper had to reassure colleagues he was not for the popish party and by a letter from Falkland to Hyde on 23 March explaining that he must attend to take the chair in the committee on the charges against Judge Berkeley, since Falkland's bid to excuse him because he was ill had been jeered at by George Peard and Herbert Morley. They had insisted, because

44 *Oxinden*, p. 274; *CSPD 1641–3*, p. 275; *HMC Coke*, p. 304; BL Harl. MS 163, fol. 336r; 164, fol. 249r; 480, fols. 29v, 40r, 74v; Add. MS 14827, fol. 19v; Hill, p. 21.
45 *CJ* II, 484, 539–40; *LJ* IV, 655; *HMC Coke*, pp. 309, 313; Bodleian Tanner MS 66, fol. 298r; BL Add. MS 14827, fols. 74, 79v, 133, 195v; Harl. MS 163, fols. 37v, 84, 86v, 108v, 141r; E 201 (27): *A Perfect Diurnal*, 14–21 March, p. 8; E 201 (31): *A True Diurnal*, 14–21 March, p. 15; E 201 (32): *A True Diurnal*, 21–28 March, p. 7.
46 BL Harl. MS 163, fol. 14v.
47 BL Harl. MS 163, fols. 17v, 32v, 36v, 105v; Larking, p. 75.
48 *CJ* II, 512, 565, 567; BL Harl. MS 163, fols. 50v, 57v, 65r, 79r., 85v, 132v, 143v, 146r; 164, fol. 252v.

it was Hyde's attendance that was in question, that the House should not take notice of any man's being out of town without leave.[49]

Pym's task was further complicated by the increasing vehemence of some of the king's harshest opponents, such as Fiennes and Strode, and the provocative speeches made by two uncompromising advocates of parliamentary supremacy, Sir Henry Ludlow and Henry Marten. In a debate on the militia ordinance on 1 February Ludlow declared that 'the king is derivative from the parliament and not the parliament from the king and if he govern not by parliament then he govern by force and abuseth the law.' In May he dismissed a message from the king with the caustic remark that its author 'was not fit to govern nor wear a crown'.[50] Marten was equally audacious: in February he claimed that the king was bound to pass bills assented to by both Houses; in April he called for rejection of the king's militia bill for by accepting it 'we should condemn our own act and vilify the ordinance'; in May he demanded that MPs who remained at York on the king's orders should be expelled and replaced.[51]

These attitudes were extreme. Nevertheless there was no escaping the fact that a new kind of division was appearing between January and June 1642. Some, like Sir Robert Harley the recipient of letters bringing hopes of 'courage and comfort from the Lord', found it easy to go forward with Pym, but many were querulous and uncertain.[52] Pym had to take account of the majority who loathed the prospect of war. His strategy was not to form a middle group but simply to be a middle man, who sometimes worked alone, sometimes in conjunction with a few close allies like Hampden and St John. His heart was always with those who advocated meeting confrontation by confrontation, but his policy was a brilliant exercise in pursuing contradictory ends at the same time. It was a policy which represented the duality of his mind towards Charles I and gave scope to the political constructiveness which was a constant feature of Pym's parliamentary career. As he prepared for war Pym was always ready for accommodation, so long as it was based on complete security against those who sought to destroy the protestant state. For a time he probably believed a military bluff might work: he kept assuring his supporters that the king was too ill-beloved to raise an army.[53] Those who were with him at Windsor, Pym noted on 14 January, were not members of the ancient nobility or privy councillors but 'giddy-headed young men'.[54]

From 12 January onwards, when he called for Charles to be urged to dismiss the cavaliers and come back to Whitehall, D'Ewes's journal

49 BL Harl. MS 162, fol. 314v; Bodleian Clarendon MS 20, fol. 200; *CJ* II, 493, 508.
50 BL Add. MS 14827, fol. 25r; *HMC 5th Report*, p. 178; Clarendon II, 149.
51 BL Harl. MS 162, fols. 375v; 163, fols. 83r, 108v–109r; Zagorin, p. 316.
52 BL Loan MS 29/173, fol. 210r: Stanley Gower to Sir Robert Harley, 10 February 1642.
53 Rudyerd, *Memoirs*, pp. 232–3.
54 BL Harl. MS 480, fol. 18v.

becomes an intimate record of the mood and fortunes of the incipient peace party. D'Ewes himself was henceforth the weathervane of moderate opinion. That day hardliners managed to distract attention from Culpepper's offer to act as an intermediary towards a true understanding with the king. Next day Holles diverted the House from Sir Hugh Cholmley's motion for a message to Charles about parliament's grief at his absence.[55] At the third attempt, on the 14th, the moderates got a proper hearing. The leadership tactic this time was to capitalize on the rumours of the moment that there was an intention to send the prince of Wales out of England: the marquis of Hertford, as his governor, should take the boy into his custody. This motion produced a set-piece debate which exhibited two quite distinct viewpoints. The moderates argued that the initiative suggested would only increase distrust between king and parliament and that the king had a right to keep his son at his side. In any case, D'Ewes added, unless Hertford took sufficient strength with him to seize the boy Charles was unlikely to give him up. The decision that Hertford should merely attend the prince was a victory for the accommodation lobby. Pym saw the way the wind was blowing. The grand committee that followed on the causes of the political crisis sprang from his initiative; he began with the proposal that the House 'should first declare our love and loyalty to His Majesty'.[56]

In his speech on 14 January, D'Ewes reflected on the miasma of delusion and misunderstanding that lay upon the nation's affairs: 'we hear of several false reports that are raised touching our intentions to lessen the king's lawful authority, to prefer articles against the queen and to crown the prince and it is possible we may have false reports brought to us also of the king's intention towards us which may breed unnecessary fears in us.'[57] The moderate case was based on conciliation, trust and a search for objectivity. The king's friendly messages of 20 January and 6 and 13 February naturally raised men's hopes. For the next four weeks or so the tide appeared to be running in favour of peace.[58] D'Ewes saw the king's own goodness outweighing 'the dust and vanity of the evil counsels' and looked hopefully to a time when the guard at Westminster could safely be discharged.[59] London commentators were noticeably less despondent than they had been, remarking on the royal efforts to satisfy parliament, the dismissal of the cavaliers at Windsor and new rumours that Charles might return to London. 'God be thanked and continue this harmony', wrote

55   BL Harl. MS 162, fol. 322; *CJ* II, 375, 377.
56   BL Harl. MS 162, fols. 325v–327v; *CJ* II, 379.
57   BL Harl. MS 162, fol. 325v.
58   BL Harl. MS 480, fols. 424–430, 108, 109v–110r, 141; Gardiner x, 159–67; Wormald, pp. 53–9.
59   BL Harl. MS 162, fol. 337r.

William Dobbins to Sir Philip Percival on 15 February; 'this week hath produced so happy effects as gives us hopes of better times', Sir John Wray told Lord Montagu two days later.[60]

At no point in these weeks though did the peace party win control of debate. The discussion of the king's message of 6 February about the militia shows how things worked. Rudyerd moved for thanks and a plea for the king's return; Marten said 'he could not conceive it deserved thanks for that he conceived it to be a denial'; Pym soothed the House by agreeing that the message was gracious but he then ensured that the process of confrontation on the issue went forward as before.[61] By March the mood was darkening, as it became plain that MPs had fixed their minds on the militia ordinance as the bedrock of parliamentary policy. Everyone desired that the king should return to Whitehall, the countess of Lindsey told Lord Montagu, but few any longer had confidence he would do so.[62] MPs were much agitated at this time by passages in John Booker's latest almanac that promised 'cruel and bloody counsels'.[63] Perhaps there was truth in the story that Charles only went to York to keep his promise to the queen not to return to London until she could accompany him, wrote William Montagu to his father, and he did not therefore intend to set up his standard. But it was becoming impossible for men to know what to believe: 'the lies spread abroad are without number', Sir John Coke told his father.[64]

Individual moderates kept up a vigorous rearguard action as the drift towards war accelerated between March and June. When the votes against the king's attempt on Hull were about to pass, for instance, Sidney Godolphin and Sir Edward Alford insisted that the orders made in January authorizing Hotham to garrison the town should be read. No one of course had expected then that Charles would appear in person before the walls but the leadership had seen nevertheless that the wording of Hotham's instructions was quite unambiguous.[65] Most of the clashes between moderates and the men D'Ewes called the 'fiery spirits' occurred over the messages and declarations sent to the king. Many besides D'Ewes were undoubtedly shocked by the escalation of the paper war, though he was one of those who resisted the tide of bitterness most consistently.[66] On 8 March, following a lead given by Sir John Northcote, he objected to a request for the king to

60 *HMC Buccleuch*, I, 290–1; *HMC Coke* p. 306; *HMC Egmont*, p. 164; *CSPD 1641–3*, pp. 261–2, 278, 282.
61 BL Harl. MS 480, fol. 108.
62 *HMC Montagu*, p. 151; *HMC Buccleuch* I, 296.
63 K.V. Thomas, *Religion and the Decline of Magic* (London, 1971), p. 298.
64 *HMC Buccleuch*, I, 293; *HMC Coke*, p. 312.
65 BL Harl. MS 163, fol. 92v. For Godolphin see I. Coltman, *Private Men and Public Causes* (London, 1962), p. 136.
66 E.g. Edmund Waller, BL Harl. MS 163, fol. 125v.

'retract such things done by himself as, if they had taken effect, would have destroyed kingdom, parliament and justice'. On 15 April he advocated a Lords' amendment to the latest message by which a clause about the king 'deserting the government and protection of his people' would be omitted.[67] D'Ewes's watchfulness for allegations that could not be proved and offensive wordings quickly won him the hostility of the hardliners. He became a target for sniping and derision. But he was delighted on 14 April when the Speaker reproved some 'indiscreet and violent spirits' who interrupted his pedantic peroration about parliament's reply to the king's announcement of his plan to go to Ireland. He took the chance to lecture them about the need to weigh every expression, 'lest we precipitate things into a speedy confusion'.[68]

The factional divisions of this period were not reflected in frequent divisions but some of those that did occur are interesting. Twice the hardliners went too far on the basic question of trust: a motion to reject the king's request that the *Prince Royal* should go to sea rather than two other ships designated by parliament was lost on 7 March and an attempt to get the first clause of the king's latest message, which stated his right to veto legislation, voted scandalous failed on 2 April. On the first occasion the tellers were Hampden and Marten; on the second they were Marten and Glyn.[69] The second vote was in effect reversed six weeks later, when the House declared that the king was bound by his coronation oath to pass bills presented to him. The result of this motion, with Holles and Fiennes as tellers against Culpepper and Strangeways, is a striking indication of the way that opinion swung against the king in the aftermath of the attempt to take Hull.[70] Factional alignments are plain in a number of other divisions, particularly those that concerned the treatment to be accorded men charged as delinquents. The arguments for harshness or lenience in these cases reveal a common pattern, with future royalists like Bridgeman, Hopton, Killigrew and Waller rallying to accused men.[71] But how far the House as a whole voted consistently or recognized allegiance to a particular group of members is hard to say. The only MP who has left us a systematic record of his voting behaviour, Framlingham Gawdy, settled down into a steady peace-party supporter. Yet it would be dangerous to assume that his consistency was typical.[72]

Pym's overall aim was to hold the assembly together on the defensive course that he had mapped out so many times in 1641. His first problem was keeping the Commons quorate. Though the king's proclamation for

---

67 BL Harl. MS 163, fols. 24r, 75v.
68 BL Harl. MS 163, fols. 57v, 78v, 87.
69 *CJ* II, 469, 512; BL Harl. MS 163, fol. 60r: Rushworth III, part I, 539–40.
70 *CJ* II, 584.
71 *CJ* II, 450, 511, 543, 624; BL Harl. MS 162, fols. 355, 366r; 163, fols. 58v, 59v, 89r.
72 BL Add. MS 14827, fols. 11–134.

MPs to attend brought them flocking in during January, many did not stay long in London.[73] The intractability of the political crisis probably encouraged absenteeism as did simple exhaustion with political business. After all the length of the parliament was already unprecedented. They had 'been so continuously kept at work as we have very little time for any other employment', lamented Sir John Wray to Lord Montagu on 17 February. Thomas Smyth's energy for parliamentary affairs was rapidly dissipating that month: his mind was on tenants at home whom he suspected of cheating him and the preparedness of his horses for the journey by coach to Bristol.[74] By mid February the old danger of business grinding to a halt was ever-present again. When Pym and a few others went out to prepare an urgent paper on 22 February, there were not 40 left, so 'the Speaker came out of his chair and we discussed severally one with another for a pretty while.' On 3 June the afternoon session was delayed while the House 'stayed for company'; a few days later it was once abandoned altogether.[75]

The leadership never solved this problem and obtained solid and regular attendances, but by a series of expedients they did manage to alleviate it. They were certainly aware that gossip about absenteeism at this critical juncture could harm parliament's reputation.[76] Much tighter control over leave was imposed in 1642 than in 1641: some were refused it, others were questioned about their motives before it was granted.[77] From June it became common to specify the period of a man's leave. MPs were reprimanded for taking excessive holidays and even expected to give an account of themselves for such frivolities as going riding on a fast day. Mocking laughter greeted Richard King, who tried to excuse himself for three months' absence with a long and, according to D'Ewes, impertinent speech.[78]

Rollcalls were a familiar device but to make them effective the fines had to be collected, which they were not either in August 1641 or after a new one was taken on 16 April 1642.[79] It was only the news that many of the absent members were gathering at York that drove the Commons into severity. 'It is conceived it will be very strictly pursued', wrote Sir Edward Littleton to Sir Richard Leveson on 6 June, reporting the rollcall fixed for the 16th of the month backed by a penalty of £100.[80] The effect was startling but temporary: nearly 300 MPs attended on the day appointed, another 150 at least saw that they were properly excused and only about 45

73 *CJ* II, 400; *HMC Coke*, p. 306; *CSPV 1640–2*, p. 294; *CSPD 1641–3*, p. 282; Snow, *Huntingdon Library Quarterly* (1955), 303–4.

74 *HMC Buccleuch* I, 291; Bristol RO 36074/156b.

75 BL Harl. MS 162, fol. 401r; 163, fols. 144v, 152v; Add. MS 14827, fol. 130r.

76 Sharpe, editor, *Faction and Parliament*, pp. 11–12.

77 BL Harl. MS 163, fols. 19v–20r; *CJ* II, 439, 468, 632, 645.

78 BL Harl. MS 163, fol. 95v; *CJ* II, 549, 552; Keeler, pp. 240–1.

79 BL Harl. MS 162, fol. 398v; 163, fol. 34r; *CJ* II, 449, 479, 534.

80 Staffordshire RO D 868/2/34.

were unaccounted for. The House's displeasure, in the shape of a committee to receive their fine before they entered the chamber, was ready for men in the last category, but virtually none of them ever returned.[81]

Some persisted in their faith in rollcalls and wanted a surprise one every week, but the truth was that an adequate House could be secured simply by getting those resident in London to put their Westminster duties first.[82] Much juggling with the hours of sitting was undertaken with a view to encouraging a full day's work. In March it was decided that, instead of meeting at ten and as often as not rising very late, the House would begin at eight and sit till three without a break. Then there was a switch back to the late start; then the early start was tried again on 20 April, with a shilling fine on all those late for prayers. This at once proved generally unaccept-able.[83] Long dinner hours leaving the few to soldier on were the crux of the problem, as D'Ewes repeatedly emphasized.[84]

The secret of Pym's continued mastery of the Commons was his amazing omnicompetence. It was he who directed the acid paper dialogue with the king: he brought in the draft reply to Charles's message from Newmarket on 19 March; he proposed a committee should be sent to York on 29 March 'to beget a right understanding between His Majesty and the parliament' and nominated Fiennes and Stapleton; he insisted at the end of April that MPs should give priority to formulating an immediate reply to the king's declaration concerning his abortive visit to Hull.[85] Fiscal matters also received his constant attention. It was on his motion that a voluntary collection was made at the first sermon on 30 March for the distressed Irish Protestants, that payment was ordered on 2 April of the guard placed in the Tower the previous August, that the captains in the Scottish war were given their arrears of pay later that month.[86] Pym's searching eye for the detail of the conspiracy still kept members on their toes: on 15 January he moved for the arrest of a colonel 'beating a drum for soldiers under a pretence of going for France'; on 10 February he drew attention to dangerous books in Latin and Irish, which would 'discover some to have been here instruments of the troubles in Ireland'; on 11 June he reported a letter found in Oxfordshire declaring that the king would shortly 'come with horse and foot to the parliament'.[87] Time and again his sense of the right mixture of challenge, loyalty and concern for legitimacy enabled him

81   *CJ* II, 598, 602, 605, 630; BL Add. MS 14827, fols. 118v, 137v; Harl. MS 163, fol. 163v, E 202(8): *A Perfect Diurnal*, 13–20 June 1642.

82   BL Harl. MS 163, fol. 198v.

83   *CJ* II, 515, 522–3, 538; BL Add. MS 14827, fol. 72r; Harl. MS 163, fols. 48v, 50v, 81v, 83r; E 202(1): *A Perfect Diurnal*, 28 March-4 April 1642; *HMC Buccleuch*, I 296.

84   BL Harl. MS 163, fol. 76v.

85   BL Harl. MS 163, fols. 37v, 55v, 80v, 86v; *CJ* II, 486–7, 509, 535, 537; Rushworth III, part I, 570–1; *HCM Buccleuch* I 295.

86   BL Harl. MS 163, fols. 27v, 58v; 164, fol. 252v.

87   BL Harl. MS 480, fol. 25r: Add. MS 14827, fols. 37r, 135; *CJ* II, 382, 425, 456.

to bring the House round to his viewpoint. The diarist's summary of his speech on 1 February, for example, in the debate on the king's answer to the petition about the militia, hints at the power of his words: 'we have often complained of attempts against us, our guards taken from us. In times of danger by fire we must provide. We seek nothing but by consent and advice of parliament.'[88]

On numerous occasions Pym exercised his debating skills to hold the middle ground. Once, coming to D'Ewes's support, he himself amended the House's declaration about the king's proposed visit to Ireland at the clerk's table along the lines the diarist proposed.[89] On another occasion, when the fiery spirits wanted to declare that the king intended to make war against parliament, Pym inserted a saving clause that the king was 'seduced by evil counsel'.[90] There were other times when the leadership got their way by swift coordinated action. D'Ewes was surprised on 26 January when Pym and Holles suddenly pressed 'with great violence' for an immediate second reading of the new tonnage and poundage bill, which St John had just introduced. Several of St John's intimate friends then spoke against the bill and its commitment was rejected. 'I learned afterwards', D'Ewes noted in cipher, 'that he was commanded by His Majesty to bring in this bill.'[91] When the leadership unexpectedly called for a rereading of the king's latest message, laid aside in the morning, on 31 March D'Ewes took the charitable view that 'their hearts were so full of it as they could not refrain', but the signs of planning are unmistakable. A conference with the Lords followed on Pym's initiative, managed by Vane and Holles.[92]

Committee tactics changed in 1642. The close committee had provoked too much criticism and alarm, so Pym chose to use the much larger joint committee of both Houses for Irish affairs as a 'tacitly recognized parliamentary executive' and to work with other ad hoc groups as the exigencies of debate required. Thus committees of five and ten respectively prepared the agendas for the conferences with the Lords on 25 January and 29 March.[93] Pym had become flexible in the arrangements for committee sittings as well as over the kinds of committees he used. One tactic, tried on 3 February, was adjournment to the City for a day of committee work. The need to give the trained bands a day's rest was a good excuse. Pym and his henchmen sat at Merchant Taylors' Hall and other committees at Grocers' Hall.[94] Committees more usually sat before the House met for the day or

88 Hill, p. 21.
89 BL Harl. MS 163, fols. 24r, 74v; Zagorin, p. 316.
90 Crawford, p. 70.
91 Hill, p. 9; BL Harl. MS 162, fols. 351v–353v; *CJ* II, 396–7.
92 BL Harl. MS 163, fol. 56r; *CJ* II, 509–10.
93 *CJ* II, 393, 503; L. Glow, 'The Manipulation of Committees in the Long Parliament 1641–2', *JBS* (1965), 47–8.
94 *CJ* II, 410-11; BL Harl. MS 480, fols. 93v, 94v; *HMC Buccleuch* I, 290.

after it adjourned; occasionally they sat concurrently with the Commons. We have few accounts of committee debates, but D'Ewes's record of one he attended on 4 April to formulate a new declaration to the king suggests that Pym and his allies were sometimes more forthright in the committee chamber than they dared to be in the House itself. D'Ewes was shocked to hear Fiennes insist that the king was bound to assent to laws passed by both Houses and Pym declare that he had 'utterly denied' to pass the bill for indemnity of the five members.[95] This kind of talk may often have gone unchecked in a committee meeting, but any attempt to preclude discussion of policy by the House was likely to run into trouble. When John Wilde brought the names of Pym, Holles and eight others as commissioners for Irish affairs from a committee attended by only about 14 men on 4 February, the House divided and the nominations were thrown out in favour of a larger body.[96]

Careful preparation and seizing the opportunities of the moment remained the twin foundations of Pym's command of day-to-day debate. In the latter respect his response to the county petitions discussed in the last chapter was acute. There were many times between January and March when Pym and others harnessed the mood of excitement that their reception engendered to vigorous pursuit of the business of confrontation. 31 January is a good example. Early in the day two petitions were brought in, one from the poor tradesmen and artificers of London, the other, containing veiled threats of popular unrest, from Suffolk. At the bar the Suffolk delegation demanded that they should not be 'delayed with hopes'. Pym was quickly on his feet: 'there must be a speedy remedy. We must go up to the Lords. Thence help must come. If they will not all join, we must get such as we can and go to the king to take away the obstacles and that we may put the kingdom in a posture.' Progress was made that day over the militia ordinance, a new declaration, control of the Tower and the supply of gunpowder for county magazines.[97]

Unanimity with the Lords was the prerequisite for Pym's achievement of that domination of the whole parliamentary process which had never quite been his in early 1641 and had slipped decisively from his grasp in the autumn. The struggle by his allies there to wrest control of the Upper House from the royalist faction reached its climax between 17 January and 5 February. In the division on 24 January, over the Commons' petition for the forts and militia to be put in the hands of parliamentary nominees, the royalists held on by only eight votes. On 26 January and again on 1 February a core of 22 protesters stood together against the royalist

95 BL Harl. MS 163, fol. 61v.
96 BL Harl. MS 162, fol. 367v, 369v; *CJ* II, 414; Pennington, p.184.
97 Hill, pp. 19–20; *CJ* II, 404–6.

majority.[98] The break came on 5 February, when bishops exclusion passed the House. Accounts differ as to whether Pym's majority that day was 11 or 13, but the psychological effect is what matters: the royalist peers never regained the initiative and during that month, despite appeals from the king to them to stay at their post, a steady stream of them left, discontented and disillusioned, for their country estates.[99]

Whereas there were 60 to 70 regular attenders in the Lords during January, the average in February dropped to less than 40.[100] Were the royalists then simply driven out or intimidated into leaving by nasty incidents such as the mobbing of Richmond, Lord Keeper Littleton and others by porters and women petitioners on 1 February?[101] The story is not quite so simple. In all, 59 peers voted on the question of bishops' exclusion: 27 votes against bishops can be accounted for if we suppose that all those present who had protested in one of the divisions of the previous three weeks stood by the Commons again. All of them, except the earl of Clare, had in actual fact entered at least two protestations. John Moore's list of men 'against bishops' in his diary suggests the names of two more of their enemies at the final count. One was Lord Strange, who had not been present at the January divisions, the other was the earl of Manchester, who had probably chosen this moment to change sides.[102] The outcome shows that there must have been six or seven more royalist defectors and there can be no certainty as to who they were or why they chose this occasion to abandon the king's cause. We know that certain MPs, one of whom was Sir John Clotworthy, had recently taken to inspecting the Lords journal and there was undoubtedly much talk about the identity of the 'good and bad lords'.[103] Both Moore and Hill entered collated lists of the January protesters in their diaries.[104] Intimidation may have caused some men to change sides, but it is as likely that hard-hitting speeches by Pym and Holles, based on the latest petitions, had persuaded some of the peers that concessions to the Commons and to the people were necessary to preserve peace. Pym's speech at the 25 January conference, marked by sweeping language and unusual vehemence, was particularly widely reported and praised.[105]

Once Pym's majority was assured in the Lords, the relations between the

---

98 *LJ* IV, 521, 533, 543, 556; *HMC Coke*, pp. 304; Bodleian Tanner MS 66, fol. 248.
99 Hill, p. 30; *HMC Buccleuch* I 290; *LJ* IV, 612–3, 618–9; Bristol RO 36074/156b; Zagorin, p. 299.
100 HLRO, House of Lords minute book, no.5.
101 *CSPD 1641–3*, pp. 274, 278.
102 BL Harl. MS 480, fol. lv.
103 *CJ* II, 400; BL Add. MS 14827, fol. 17v; *HMC Coke*, p. 304; Clarendon I, 543.
104 Hill, p. 30*; BL Harl. MS 480, fol. 2v.
105 *LJ* IV, 559; BL Harl. MS 162, fol. 362v; E 200 (21): *A Speech delivered at a Conference*; E 200 (25):*Mr Holles his Speech*; E 201 (12): *A Perfect Diurnal*, 24–31 Jan., p. 4; *CJ* II, *395*; *HMC Montagu*, p. 145; C.H. Firth, *The House of Lords during the Civil War* (London, 1974), p. 111; Crawford, p. 69.

two Houses became relaxed, even bantering. The 23 February fast sermon was moved from Lincoln's Inn to St Margarets so there would be space for those peers who had said they intended to come. Sir John Holland explained to a Norfolk friend that when the Commons received a reminder on 23 March about the proceedings against Laud, 'by way of retribution' they pressed the peers to speed the trial of the delinquent judges.[106] The leading men in the Upper House were now Brooke, Essex, Holland, Mandeville, Pembroke, Robartes, Saye and Wharton. They had little difficulty in keeping at bay a disintegrating royalist faction, who entered their protestations in varying numbers on such issues as the militia, the declarations sent to Charles, the Kentish petition, Hotham's command of Hull and Warwick's command of the fleet. At the divisions on 2 and 5 March over the militia ordinance Pym's majorities were 22 and 17.[107] Attendances then were still running at just under 50, but the rate of abstention soon became more worrying and in May attempts were made to summon peers known to be at York.[108]

So far as policy was concerned Pym's priorities were the old priorities of 1641. The January fright was bound to put control of the local militias to the top of the agenda. The intention to enforce this was implicit in the declaration to the counties issued by the Commons on 12 January. A new committee to see the kingdom put in a posture of defence was established, on Oliver Cromwell's motion, two days later. The germ of the militia ordinance came on 18 January, with the decision of the committee of the whole House to appoint new lord lieutenants 'by ordinance of parliament'. They would exercise 'a standing power for the commanding of the military forces in every county'.[109] There was never any question in the new year of proceeding by bill.[110]

During the following weeks the Commons was led along step by step. Many of the more determined MPs played a part: Sir John Hotham and Strode opened the chorus of dismay at the king's first reply on 29 January; Fiennes insisted that the petition for control of forts, castles and the militia had been reasonable and 'nothing was granted'. When the king's final denial was read, Holles at once declared that parliament should enforce the ordinance on its own, Herbert Morley supported him and Marten wanted the ordinance printed and published.[111] The ordinance also brought William Pierrepoint into the limelight. This previously reticent Nottinghamshire gentleman chaired the committee responsible for the business with firmness and tact. He collected each MP's nomination for the

---

106 BL Harl. MS 162, fol. 398v; Bodleian Tanner MS 66, fol. 248; *CJ* II, 493.
107 *LJ* IV, 622, 627, 631, 643, 646, 656, 628, 697, 700; v, 4, 80.
108 BL Harl. MS 163, fol. 68v; *LJ* IV, 685, 708, v, 59.
109 *CJ* II, 372, 379–80; BL Harl. MS 162, fol. 328v; Add. MS 14827, fol. 7v.
110 Gardiner x, 155 was incorrect on this point.
111 BL Add. MS 14827, fols. 20v, 55v.

lieutenancy of his own shire and he managed the delicate matter of distributing the peerage whose loyalty could be counted upon across the English and Welsh counties with scrupulous care.[112] The debates on this aspect of the ordinance brought home the problem of local security and so gave backbenchers confidence in what they were doing.

Technically the militia ordinance did not pass both Houses until 5 March, but by a series of ten resolutions on 2 March the Commons cut through the tortuous process of negotiation with Charles that had dragged on so long and established their position. There was now no room for retreat. Only one man, William Pleydell, opposed these resolutions in the Commons and only twelve peers entered their protestations. Yet D'Ewes believed that everyone was alert to what was happening.[113] Two main reasons may be suggested for the near unanimity of parliament on 2 March. First many MPs were probably reassured by the leadership that the ordinance was precautionary and persuaded that a show of force had become necessary. Bulstrode Whitelocke's later account, which emphasizes the perplexity the ordinance caused in legal circles, includes a clear statement of Pym's case:

> That which wrought most upon me was the solemn protestations of the most powerful and active members that they had not the least purpose or intention of any war with the king, but to arm themselves for their necessary defence without which the king would so grow upon them and his evil counsellors so prevail, that they would undoubtedly bring their designs to pass of a speedy introducing of popery and tyranny. Whereas if they saw the parliament in a good posture of defence and the people generally would adhere to them as no doubt but they would, that then the king would be brought to a good accommodation and agreement with his parliament without a blow to be struck between them.[114]

Secondly there was the adoption, following the previous summer's precedents, of the instrument of an ordinance. The outward garb of the militia ordinance, a recent commentator has noted, was 'reassuringly respectable'. Ordinances, according to learned opinion at the time, required less ceremony than statutes and were usually temporary in effect. It is important to recall that, though the clause was eventually omitted, the militia committee first planned that their scheme would last for two years only. Above all ordinances did not require the king's assent as statutes did. Yet neither did they imply action taken against his will. Thus the leadership got the best of both worlds by using a constitutional device that was familiar in one sense, in that the procedure in each House was basically the

---

112 *CJ* II, 381, 405–6, 424, 426–8; BL Harl. MS 162, fols. 378–80
113 *CJ* II, 463–5, 467; *LJ* IV, 622, 627; BL Harl. MS 163, fol. 13v.
114 BL Add. MS 37343, fol. 249; see also *HMC Montagu*, p. 151; Pennington, p. 184.

same as the procedure for a bill, but potentially revolutionary in another.[115] Of course Pym's formidable debating powers did not still all doubts. Hence the resolution on 15 March, introduced by a committee hurriedly appointed the previous night, that the ordinance obliged the people 'and ought to be obeyed by the fundamental laws of this kingdom'. This we are told 'cost a long dispute', with some maintaining that 'nothing but a law could bind the subject' while others insisted that the ordinance 'was warranted by the law of God, by the law of nature and of necessity'.[116]

What mattered to Pym was that he had seen through a policy which had been the crux of his programme since the previous June.[117] He intended that the ordinance should be enforced but he bided his time for almost a month before the next move. Meanwhile many of the old lieutenancy commissions were brought in and surrendered to the clerk of the Lords and numerous deputy lieutenants were appointed on the nomination of the peers appointed to office or of MPs.[118] It was on 2 April that a message went to the Lords requesting that the ordinance should speedily be executed.[119]

In practical terms parliament's defensive arrangements during the first half of 1642 consisted of command of Portsmouth and Hull, whose garrisons were paid from various funds, and tentative moves towards a more general refurbishing and control of the forts of the kingdom. The regiment at Hull was increased from 700 to 1000 when the king reached York. At Portsmouth George Goring was involved in ambitious plans for improving the fortifications.[120] A contract for making nearly £5000 worth of gunpowder was negotiated in March by the committee responsible for seeing that supplies were available for county magazines.[121] But a bid by this committee to give saltpetre men leave to dig at will in men's dovecots was balked after D'Ewes complained that they often chose to dig when pigeons had young and that they might take bribes from those who wanted their dovecots left alone.[122] Gentry self-interest was already at odds with the incipient war effort. But local initiatives, as we have seen in relation to Monmouthshire and other places, were always encouraged. The townsmen of Lewes, for instance, were allowed to use some spare coat and conduct money for arms, ammunition and gun carriages. The

---

115 BL Add. MS 14827, fol. 32v; Foster, *American Journal of Legal History* XXI (1977), 158–61
116 *CJ* II, 478–9; BL Harl. MS 163, fol. 33r.
117 For a fuller account see L.G. Schwoerer, 'The Fittest Subject for a King's Quarrel',*JBS* XI (1971), 45–76.
118 *LJ* IV, 628–9, 637, 645, 649, 653, 659–60, 664, 671;*CJ* II, 483–5, 489, 492, 495, 497–8; *HMC Coke*, p. 310; Hampshire RO Herriard MS Box F9.
119 *CJ* II, 694.
120 *CJ* II, 427, 440, 457, 468, 495; BL Harl. MS 162, fol. 391v; 163, fol. 46r; Harl. MS 480, fol. 98r; Add. MS 14827, fols. 33r, 46r, E 201 (30): *A Continuation of a True Diurnal*, 14–21 March, p. 75, E 201 (37): *A Continuation of a True Diurnal*, 21–28 March; *LJ* IV 637–9;*CSPD 1641–3*, p. 271.
121 *CJ* II, 406, 457, 474, 476, 510, 571; BL Harl. MS 163, fol. 29v.
122 BL Harl. MS 163, fol. 71v–72r; *CJ* II, 527.

Caernarvonshire gentry procured parliamentary assistance for the release of a consignment of gunpowder for their magazine stayed by the officers at the port of Chester.[123]

The decisive moves towards setting forth a summer fleet contrast strikingly with these rather fumbling efforts to increase coastal preparedness. It consisted of 15 of the king's ships, manned by 2970 men and supported by 23 merchant ships.[124] An act for impressment of mariners, to remain in force until November, was rushed through both Houses and signed by the king by commission, with Marten alone opposing it on the grounds of the subject's liberties.[125] The captains of the fleet were considered and approved one at a time in the Commons and the leadership made plain its determination that the command would rest with the earl of Warwick, not Sir John Pennington as Charles insisted.[126]

Combating popery remained as intractable a business as ever. When Herbert Morley, a specialist in harrying the Capuchins, managed to arrest six of them in February, MPs had to content themselves with their being kept prisoners at Somerset House while the French ambassador negotiated their return home.[127] The execution at last of seven Jesuits was small comfort when papists still flocked to the masses at the ambassadors' houses. There was a new complaint on 9 May that the Portuguese ambassador had appeared on his balcony in Lincoln's Inn Fields to urge on his servants who sought to rescue some Catholics arrested for attending his mass.[128] A committee spent two sessions a week examining the obstructions to proceedings against recusants but no report was forthcoming.[129] A new bill for disarming recusants took from December to April to complete its passage through the Commons.[130] Many probably put more trust in imprisonment. A scheme was discussed for disposing of recusants thought to be a dangerous influence in their own shires to distant towns: Lancashire recusants, for example, would be sent to Coventry and Northampton, Hampshire ones to Abingdon, Monmouthshire ones to Nottingham and Cheshire ones across the country to Lincoln.[131] A new bill containing these provisions was quickly given two readings in March, but it stuck in committee. There was nothing for it but to press local authorities to make what use they could of the statute confining convicted

123 *CJ* II, 409, 470. For other examples see *CJ* II, 517, 524, 533.
124 *CJ* II, 378, 413–4, 420, 435, 466.
125 *CJ* II, 402–3, 407; *LJ* IV, 556; BL Harl. MS 162, fol. 363v; *SR* v, 137.
126 *CJ* II, 460, 474–5, 478, 513–4.
127 BL Add. MS 14827, fol. 53v; Harl. MS 163, fol. 13r; *CJ* II, 456, 458, 464, 610.
128 BL E 201 (33): *A Perfect Diurnal*, 21–28 March, p. 4; Harl. MS 163, fol. 112v; *CJ* II, 552; *LJ* v, 58.
129 *CJ* II, 414.
130 *CJ* II 387, 403, 415, 527, 542.
131 *CJ* II, 384, 402, 415, 422; BL Add. MS 14827, fol. 35v.

recusants to within five miles of their homes.[132]

Abroad all eyes remained fixed on Ireland, now so evidently the mainspring of the whole Catholic plot. There was no relief from the tale of anarchy and destitution until news reached London in March of the earl of Ormonde's relief of Drogheda. This was followed by his victory over Lord Mountgarret at Kilrush in mid April. The enemy's strength was much broken, reported Sir John Temple, in a letter read in the Commons a few weeks later.[133] Yet the English parliament could take little of the credit. Its response to the rebellion between November 1641 and the following summer has rightly been condemned as 'disjointed, halting and thoroughly Lilliputian'.[134] The initial force under Sir Simon Harcourt, consisting of 1800 men several hundred of them unarmed, did not even reach Dublin until 30 December. No reinforcements arrived until February. No order was made for levying the army of 10,000 men envisaged in parliament's original resolutions until April 1642.[135] 'I am sick to see so slow a proceeding above for the relieving of that sad country', wrote Francis Cave to Sir Philip Percival on 15 February, 'I pray God the blood of many cry not out against those that have been the causes of this slack sending.'[136]

There were several reasons for parliament's inept performance. In the first place there was a strong undercurrent of doubt about making a winter war. This explains the reluctance of the commander-in-chief the earl of Leicester and men like Sir John Clotworthy to cross the Irish Sea. The prospect of spending the winter in a country that was seen as barbarous at the best of times and was now plunged in violence was bound to be unappetizing. Clotworthy and others said they stayed for 'want of arms'; Leicester maintained that he was still owed arrears of pay for his diplomatic service in France and that he had no assurance facilities suitable to his station were ready in Dublin. D'Ewes found such excuses unacceptable. He was very sorry to see Clotworthy still in the House, he told him on 5 March, 'who I well hoped had by this time been victorious in Ireland'.[137] There were also difficulties over the negotiations for help from the Scots and administrative complications that defied even Pym's patient unravelling. In May for example 2000 soldiers were retarded at Minehead through lack of supplies.[138] It was a problem, moreover, to find officers whom parliament

132   *CJ* II, 470, 490, 527; BL Harl. MS 163, fol. 23v.
133   *D'Ewes (C)*, p. 227; *HMC Coke*, p. 314; *HMC Egmont*, pp. 145–75; BL Harl. MS 163, fol. 162v; Add. MS 14827, fols. 47v, 104r; E Devon RO 1700A/CP 20; *CJ* II, 556, 576; Gardiner x, 174–5; Wedgwood, *King's War*, p. 70–75, 85–8.
134   Bottigheimer, *English Money and Irish Land, p. 35.*
135   *HMC Egmont*, pp. 158–9; *CJ* II, 540; *D'Ewes (C)*, p. 124; Gardiner x, 173.
136   *HMC Egmont*, p. 163.
137   BL Harl. MS 162, fol. 370r; 163, fol. 20v; *LJ* IV, 679.
138   *CJ* II, 453, 456, 559, 582, 601; *HMC Montagu*, p. 145; Gardiner x, 166; Stevenson, *Scottish Revolution*, pp. 244–5.

was sure it could trust: several men were rejected because they had been in the king's party that came down to Westminster on 4 January.[139]

As always, predictably, the main impediment was lack of money. Pym, Earle and others constantly warned colleagues that the bill for £400,000 should be given the utmost priority.[140] The Commons did in fact work hard at it during February, sweeping aside every plea for exemptions and abatements.[141] Still it was not ready for the royal assent until 26 March and the earliest any money could be expected was the end of May.[142] When the Commons went back to their City friends they found themselves in the old vicious circle they had experienced in 1641. The City expected action on the basis of the loan of £50,000 already voted for crushing the rebellion and saw only inertia. Disappointment naturally brought recalcitrance.[143]

This financial deadlock explains the enthusiasm of the committee for Irish affairs for the proposals they heard on 11 February from a group of London citizens for putting the Irish war into the hands of undertakers. The act for adventurers in Ireland was passed on 19 March. The final blueprint apparently owed much to Sir John Clotworthy: he was publicly thanked both by Cromwell and Earle, chairman of the subcommittee responsible for the scheme.[144] The purpose of the act was to raise an expeditionary force supported by £1,000,000, given on the promise of 2,500,000 acres of Irish land which would become liable to confiscation. In short it established a lottery. The fundamental assumptions were that the rebels would be defeated and that there was enough self-interested colonialism among the wealthy English gentry for the plan to succeed.[145]

The second of these assumptions was quickly shown to be false. Indeed some were revolted by the propaganda which held out the possibility of extermination or mass expulsion of the Irish. A number of prominent MPs on the other hand set an example: Barrington, Hampden, Haselrig, Holles and Marten were among those who promised £1,000 or more. Others, like Sir John Coke who told his father he did not like the adventure, held back. By 10 April contributions from the Commons amounted to £55,000.[146] But the talk of 2000 London citizens laying down £500 apiece came to very little and the provincial response was miserable, despite a campaign to

139 *CJ* II, 398; Add. MS 14827, fol. 17r; Harl. MS 480, fols. 62v–63r; *HMC Egmont*, p. 164.
140 BL Harl. MS 162, fols. 365r, 385r.
141 *CJ* II, 408, 432, 440, 446–7, 449, 452, 454, 458, 464, 473; *LJ* IV, 643, 647, 674; *HMC Buccleuch* I, p. 290; BL Harl. MS 162, fol. 367v; 163, fols. 28v–29r; Add. MS 14827, fol. 27v.
142 *SR*, v, 145–67.
143 BL Harl. MS 162, fol. 348v; 163, fols. 341v–342v; 480, fols. 56v–57r; E 134(7): *A True Copy of the Masterpiece of all Petitions*, pp. 5–6; *CJ* II, 396; *LJ* IV, 534; Bottigheimer, *English Money and Irish Land*, pp. 39–40; Pearl, p. 207.
144 BL Harl. MS 162, fols. 388v–389r; Add. MS 14827, fols. 42v–43r.
145 *CJ* II, 467–8; *LJ* IV, 593–5, 598; *SR* v, 170–2; Bottigheimer, *English Money and Irish Land*, pp. 40–7.
146 BL 669 f 5(3): List of MP subscribers; J.R. MacCormack, 'The Irish Adventurers and the English Civil War', *Irish Historical Studies* x (1956), 30–58; *HMC Coke*, p. 315.

publicize the plan at the Lent assizes. 'Here none would adventure purchase of land in Ireland', the sheriff of Herefordshire, where less than £100 had been collected, reported to Sir Robert Harley on 11 July.[147] The only counties which subscribed at all liberally were Devon and Somerset. The decision to open the scheme to new categories of investors and extend the time limit for subscriptions exposed the basic miscalculation on which it had been based.[148]

People were much more prepared to contribute to the benevolence for relief of Protestants who had fled from Ireland than to the adventurers scheme. They could do this with little harm to their pockets and the plight of the refugees anyway came much nearer home. The benevolence was given statutory backing on 31 January and collections were made in most places between March and May.[149] Berkshire, Buckinghamshire, Kent, Leicestershire and Sussex were among the most generous counties. The total yield of £45,000 was an impressive testimony to the way that squires and ministers had drummed the Irish catastrophe into the mind of the nation. Many thousands yielded a few pence each when the plate went round under their sharp eye at a fast-day service.[150]

Not until 20 May did the Commons come to terms with the disastrous fiscal situation. The whole of the £400,000 tax, which was coming in more slowly than it should have done, was mortgaged to accumulated debts and the next instalment of the Brotherly Assistance. £40,000 was still owing to the northern counties for billeting, for instance, and there were huge debts on the navy account.[151] As usual MPs were more voluble than constructive. It was predictable that there would be no positive response to Pym's proposal of a bill taxing the kingdom with £50,000 a year for seven years 'for present security'. Plenty of alternatives were mentioned. John Crew wanted to stumble on with a piecemeal system, proposing a bill for £200,000 for 1643. Haselrig, supported by John Glyn, would have put the adventurers project on a compulsory basis for all with incomes over £100 a year. William Wheeler was for 'taxing the better sort of people'; Sir John Culpepper suggested the wealthy should pay a tenth of their rents 'at a just value'.[152] The ingrained determination of MPs to shift financial responsibilities was evident in the outcome, a bill to foist the cost of the Irish war on the papists of the kingdom. The House had landed itself with another

---

147   BL 669 f 4(76): letter to sheriffs; Guilding, editor, *Reading Records* IV, 42; BL Loan MS 29/174/274r.

148   *LJ* IV, 615; V, 154; *CJ* II, 463; Bottigheimer, *English Money and Irish Land*, pp. 45, 51–2; H. Hazlett, 'The Financing of the British Armies in Ireland', *Irish Historical Studies* I, (1938), 30–1.

149   *CJ* II, 349, 350, 352, 381; *LJ* IV, 529, 554; *SR* V, 141–3.

150   *CJ* II, 588; PRO SP 28/191–3; *Sussex*, p. 256; *Irish Historical Studies* I (1938), 26–8; Bottigheimer, *English Money and Irish Land*, p. 47.

151   Hill, p. 49; BL Harl. MS 163, fol. 109v; Add. MS 14827, fol. 125r; *HMC Coke*, pp. 314–5.

152   BL Add. MS 14827, fol. 110v; *CJ* II, 584; Keeler, p. 387.

elaborate and impractical project and little immediate progress was made with its implementation.[153]

Parliament's efforts to bring in arrears of the poll money and the 1641 subsidies and hasten the new subsidy payments were obviously not enough.[154] Loans once again were the only answer. £20,000 provided by the Merchant Adventurers was immediately swallowed up by transport and equipment charges of men ready to leave for Ireland.[155] On 3 June the City livery companies at last bowed to the exhortations of Pennington and the earl of Warwick, but the £100,000 they promised came in slowly.[156] In view of this bleak situation Pym's battles over the fixed-yield subsidy in the summer of 1641 may appear to have done him little good, but it is worth remembering that if it had not been for those victories parliament would by this stage have been in a far worse financial plight.

With the approach of war our interest naturally focuses on parliament as an executive institution but those who sat out the winter of 1642 still regarded the normal business of parliaments as legislation. Reading bills brought a comforting feeling that conflict might not after all be inevitable. Among those introduced in February were a bill to penalize monopolists in wine, intended as D'Ewes put it 'to invite all these delinquents to a composition', a bill against the transport of native wool, and a bill vindicating the five members.[157] In March progress was made with the bill for enfranchisement of the palatinate of Durham.[158] In April bills were read for relief of captives taken by Turkish pirates, for improving the postal service, for satisfaction of the damages sustained by certain MPs imprisoned in 1629 and for restitution from the soap boilers of Westminster.[159] New bills in May were concerned with the increase of new buildings, the relief of maimed and shipwrecked seamen, the import of currants, draining the Fens and the incorporation of the Merchant Adventurers.[160] The last was a quid pro quo for the loans the company had provided. None of this legislation, apart from the bills about the five members and export of wool, made any progress in the Lords; most of it was still in committee during the summer.[161] Nevertheless it provides ample evidence that county petitioners did not cry in vain and that the reforming impulse of November 1640 was not dead.

Much more time than was spent on these miscellaneous matters was

153 BL Add. MS 14827, fol. 123r; *CJ* II, 604; Bodleian, Tanner MS 63, fol. 32.
154 *CJ* II, 538, 547–8, 556, 561, 565–6, 570, 584, 588–9, 620.
155 *CJ* II, 546, 556.
156 *CJ* II, 605, 609, 614; Pearl, pp. 207–9.
157 BL Harl. MS 162, fol. 370r; *CJ* II, 414–5, 436, 447–8, 451, 454, 456, 458, 462, 523–4; Pearl, pp. 290–1.
158 *CJ* II, 491, 519; Hirst, p. 176.
159 *CJ* II 516, 519, 522, 524, 527, 537, 544, 549; *HMC Coke*, p. 314.
160 *CJ* II, 557–8, 587, 592, 600, 607; BL Harl. MS 163, fol. 133v.
161 *LJ* IV, 649, 658.

given between January and May to bills about the church. Religious reform, we have seen, ground to a halt in the autumn of 1641 because the issues involved became so divisive. Yet Pym still believed that the Protestant foundations of the state could only be secured by thorough-going renewal and reformation. The synod of divines to determine the new form of Church government had been established policy for many months: nominations for it were considered one at a time between 20 and 25 April and a bill for the assembly to meet on 1 July was quickly passed by both Houses. The assembly was not convened because the king refused his assent.[162] A comprehensive bill about worship, introduced on 16 February, was intended to give statutory form to the general order of 9 September 1641 about innovations and to advance preaching and sabbatarianism. Its scope was very much wider than the abortive bill of the previous January to remove altar rails. One of its most important clauses was a directive that there should be a sermon or exposition of scripture each Sunday morning in every parish, besides weekday lectures where the parishioners desired them. This bill passed the Commons, after some lengthy debates in committee, but stuck in committee in the Lords.[163]

Other bills which answered petitioners' demands and Puritan members' aspirations were revived or introduced. The bill for punishing scandalous ministers, committed on 24 June 1641 and repeatedly called for since the recess, was eventually reported on 22 March.[164] It had become a draconian measure: men found guilty of favouring innovations during the previous three years, scandal in their lives or neglect of preaching for a period of six weeks could be deprived of their cures and replaced under a presentation made by the Lord Keeper. Commissioners were given power to empanel juries to try suspects. The bill was given a fair wind and it reached the Lords at the end of April.[165] Some work was put in at conferences between the Houses on the pluralities bill, introduced in February 1641 and since much amended by the peers.[166] A bill to give lecturers entry to pulpits they were barred from by beneficed clergy was planned but not introduced.[167] But a bill for the better maintenance of a preaching ministry, which had received its first reading on 30 October 1641 and was given attention in committee during April and May, was perhaps the most radical of all these

162 *CJ* II, 427, 528, 539–45, 568, 575–6, 579, 583, 599, 605, 609; *LJ* v, 76, 78, 84; *HMC Coke*, p. 315; Shaw I, 124–5.
163 *CJ* II, 436–8, 476, 489, 493–4, 510, 527, 531; *LJ* IV, 669, 679; Hill, p. 34; BL Add. MS 14827, fols. 44r, 65r; Harl. MS 163, fol. 30r; 480, fols. 134v, 154; E 201 (28): *A Continuation of a True Diurnal*, 14–21 March, p. 74; E 201 (35): *A Continuation of a True Diurnal*, 21–28 March; *CSPD 1641–3*, p. 286; Shaw I, 108.
164 *CJ* II, 183–4, 311, 353, 441, 491; Shaw, II, 179.
165 *CJ* II, 516, 520; *LJ* v, 19, 35; BL E 201 (32): *A Perfect Diurnal*, 21–28 March, p. 3; *HMC Montagu* pp. 148–9.
166 *CJ* II, 431, 438, 493, 539; *LJ* IV, 577, 582, 661, 701; v, 40, 43; Shaw, I, 111.
167 BL Harl. MS 164, fol. 238v.

measures.[168] It was an attempt to put the feoffees for impropriations scheme of the 1630s on a national basis. There was a long committee stage while MPs puzzled about how they could provide more adequately for the clergy without losing their many privately acquired rights to tithes.[169]

By all this work on ecclesiastical reform the leadership asserted the continuity of the Puritan evangelical campaign with the first session of the Long Parliament and beyond that with the final session of the 1628 parliament, when Pym had worked with men like Sir Walter Earle, Sir Nathaniel Rich and Francis Rous to give religion priority in the business of the Commons.[170] The cost was a renewal of acrimony. Some MPs called the need for an anti-Arminian campaign in question on 22 January, since 'all innovations were now well laid down'. But D'Ewes declared he had evidence some Arminian clergy had 'taken new heart', setting tables altarwise and replacing rails others had removed.[171] The motion on 17 February that omissions of the ceremonies in the liturgy should not be punishable while the intended reformation was in progress was only won by 117 votes to 113.[172] When the Colchester petitioners complained that the prayer book was a burden to their consciences, Orlando Bridgeman, Richard King and some others 'would not have them to have thanks for that part'.[173] When Cornelius Burges affirmed in his fast sermon on 30 March that only immediate reformation could bring security against the malignant party, some were so offended that it was a fortnight before the air cleared sufficiently for Haselrig to make an acceptable motion for thanks.[174]

Pym must have known very well that there was no chance of the religious bills reaching the statute book in the near future. Discussion of them though gave MPs their head, sustained a sense of purpose, helped to prevent that dissolution into recrimination in face of political deadlock which might have destroyed the parliamentary cause at this stage. Petitioners constantly referred to reform in the Church and this was an area where solid work could be done in response. Thus again the county petitions feature as a springboard to action. They were also important in themselves. They nourished the House's pride, its sense of accountability and confidence in its public trust. MPs busied themselves on committees appointed to consider the grievances of their particular districts and with

168 *CJ* II, 300, 496, 525, 534, 539, 549, 561, 578. I am grateful to Mrs Anne Young for the reference to the first reading.
169 BL Harl. MS 163, fols. 46r, 98r; C. Hill, *Economic Problems of the Church* (Oxford, 1956), pp. 245–74.
170 C. Thompson, 'The Divided Leadership of the House of Commons in 1629', in Sharpe, editor, *Faction and Parliament*, pp. 253–63; Russell, *Parliaments*, pp. 396–416.
171 BL Harl. MS 162, fol. 342v.
172 BL Add. MS 14827, fol. 10v; Harl. MS 480, fol. 155v; Hill p. 5; *CJ* II, 438; *HMC Montagu*, p. 144.
173 BL Harl. MS 480, fol. 41v; E 134(13): *Three Petitions*.
174 BL Harl. MS 163, fol. 71v; Wilson, *Pulpit in* Parliament, p. 64; Christianson, *Reformers and Babylon*, p.228.

executive orders that flowed from the information received from the localities.[175] The petitions fed their self-importance and helped them to endure sittings that wearied them as political business had never done before in their lives.

The popish conspiracy and county petitions were the starting points of this book. D'Ewes tellingly illustrated the significance of the relationship between them in 1642 when he told colleagues which point he thought most worthy of thanks in Staffordshire's petition delivered on 14 May:

> they conceive themselves to be safe only in the safety of this parliament as being embarked in the same ship with us, which if it were as generally believed as it is undoubtedly true, we should neither fear factions nor parties, but there is now a generation of wicked men risen up who think the safety of the kingdom doth no way depend upon the safety of the parliament.[176]

The concomitant of the House's self-consciousness and pride was an assumption that those who were not for them were indubitably against them. The leadership did everything possible to promote this view. A new committee was set up on 13 January, including Haselrig and Strode in its membership, to investigate information against those suspected of opposing parliament's proceedings.[177] Hunting delinquents rallied the Commons and helped Pym to hold the middle ground.

Lord Digby became the grand apostate. The rumour that he had contrived the articles against the five members was discussed on 29 January and a fortnight later the damning letter he had written to the queen from Middleburg was read.[178] The committee that presented his impeachment painted him as one who had made 'a strange progress of inveterate malice' against parliament. He had 'at first pretended service . . . that he might be the better able to do a disservice', tortuously labouring 'to raise a jealousy . . . between the king and his people and to possess His Majesty that he could not live with safety of his person amongst them'. Modern eyes may see courage and idealism in Digby's story as well as vanity and impetuousness, but MPs saw only blind ambition. This was the man, Sir John Evelyn reminded the peers on 26 February, who had stood behind the swaggering officers and assured them that 'the king went out of town but to save them from being trampled in the dirt.' He had 'fallen from us', reflected George Peard, 'and turned a Judas'.[179]

175   E.g. *CJ* II, 403–4, 411, 438, 491, 595.
176   BL Harl. MS 163, fol. 118v.
177   *CJ* II, 375, 377.
178   BL Add. MS 14827, fols. 10r, 21v, 40v, 41r; Harl. MS 480, fol. 148r; *CJ* II, 396; *CSPD 1641–3*, p. 286; Gardiner X, 167.
179   BL Add. MS 14827, fol. 47r; Harl. MS 480, fols. 18v–19r; *CJ* II, 442–3; *LJ* IV, 616; H.G. Tibbutt, editor, *The Life and Letters of Sir Lewis Dives* (Bedfordshire Record Society XXVII, 1948), pp. 14–16.

Some MPs took Sir Edward Dering's defection to heart quite as much as Digby's. In the first place the manner of the man riled his colleagues. The *Collection of Speeches* was so obviously a tendentious and rhetorical piece of self-advertisement that a lively debate followed Cromwell's motion on 2 February for it to be voted scandalous. Cromwell condemned the book as 'full of impertinences'; Marten said Dering had fouled the House 'with impiety, scandal and folly'. D'Ewes called him vainglorious: 'he doth so overvalue himself as if he had been able of himself to weigh down the balance of this House on either side when he pleased.' Dering had broken the Commons' rule of secrecy with 'premeditation and consideration' and his offence therefore put William Taylor's impulsive outburst at Windsor the previous year in the shade.[180]

The content of Dering's book explains the vehemence of the Commons' reaction. Here was the man who had promoted Kent's radical petition of January 1641 and presented the Root and Branch bill itself setting himself up as the champion of episcopacy and the prayer book. He was both offensive and derisive in the process, arguing, at least by implication, that the rooters were engaged in a design against the king and the kingdom. MPs were accused, Whitelocke noted, of making the king no monarch and of intending 'a funeral peal to religion'. To charge colleagues with 'impiety and disloyalty' was an offence, according to D'Ewes, of 'the highest, greatest and most transcendent nature that ever was committed by a member of this House'. To his enemies' fury Dering had even dared to name names: the device of initials in the margin was as transparent in 1642 as it is today. At least nine of those he lectured in his bitter postscript for having publicly taunted him with defection are easily identifiable: they are Sir William Brereton, William Cage, Oliver Cromwell, Nathaniel Fiennes, John Hampden, Sir Arthur Haselrig, Herbert Morley, William Purefoy and Nathaniel Stephens.[181] Robert Abbott reported to Dering on 26 February the story in Kent that the 'marginal characters of names without allegation of the reasons urged' accounted for the harshness with which he had been treated.[182]

In February 1642 most of Dering's colleagues believed that he was guilty of apostasy and historians have argued the same view recently.[183] But D'Ewes's dissent from that judgement deserves notice: 'I never thought

180 BL Add. MS 14827, fol.26r; Harl. MS 162, fol. 366r; 480, fols. 95v–96v.
181 BL Harl. MS 162, fol. 366r; 480, fols. 95v–96v; E 197(1): *A Collection of Speeches in matter of Religion*, pp. 162–3, 166. For Brereton see Morrill, *Cheshire*, pp. 23–5; for Cage, D'Ewes, *Autobiography* II, 247; for Cromwell, Abbott, *Writing and Speeches* I, 155–6; for Morley, *Sussex*, pp. 66, 133, 264–6; for Purefoy, D. F. Mosler, 'A Social and Religious History of the English Civil War in Warwickshire' Stanford University PhD thesis, 1975, pp. 22, 45, for Stephens, *CSPD 1639–40*, p.581.
182 BL Stowe MS 744, fol. 15.
183 Lamont, *Godly Rule*, pp. 83–93; Hirst in *Historical Journal* XV (1972), 196.

him a convert which made me when I first heard him speak in this House at a grand committee . . . earnestly in the matter of religion to stand up and say that I was very glad to hear that gentlemen speak as he did, for it was the first time that ever I heard him speak in the maintenance of a good cause.'[184] It seems probable that Dering was misunderstood, since, naive as it is, his testimony does hang together. Many, it has been suggested, were sobered by the developments of 1641. If he emphasized the conservative side of his thinking in 1642, whereas the previous year he had adopted the language of a radical, this perhaps merely testifies to Dering's innocence about the impact the debate about the Church would have when the parliament opened. It also points to the conceit which had made him take up a cause on behalf of constituents whose outlook was very different from his own. Dering's previous record shows his concern about Kentish separation: in 1635 he had acted as an informant to Laud about the activities of the trugger John Fenner of Egerton.[185]

Dering's conceit may also be the clue to the course and outcome of the 2 February debate. Two friends from his own shire, Sir Edward Partridge and Henry Heyman, urged a lenient sentence. Sir Ralph Hopton supported them, arguing that Dering should not be expelled because of his great abilities. D'Ewes spoke next, reacting caustically to Hopton's points. When he sat down, the Speaker whispered to some near the chair 'you may now see what Sir Edward Dering's friends have procured him by endeavouring to have a small censure put upon him'. In other words, the House was at its most passionate and it disliked special pleading. Earle, Hampden, Pym and others were able to capitalize on the tide of anger against a colleague whose arrogance diminished the usual sympathy shown towards men accounted among 'the best of the House'. The *Collection of Speeches* was voted scandalous, its author was disabled and after a close vote sent to the Tower, where he stayed until his fellow knight of the shire Sir John Culpepper procured his release nine days later.[186]

James Stuart, the young duke of Richmond, was rather a different kind of scapegoat. He was feared as a leading courtier who had accompanied the king to Scotland in the summer of 1641.[187] So many naturally assumed the worst of him when, in a rash and foolish outburst on 26 January, he moved that the Lords should adjourn for six months.[188] But Pym's call for his banishment as an agent of the malignant party so divided the Commons that a six-hour debate followed. It was so repetitious that D'Ewes, who was

184 BL Harl. MS 162, fol. 366r.
185 Kent RO U 350 C2/54. I am grateful to Miss Gillian Ignjatijevic for this reference. See also Clark, *English Provincial Society*, pp. 326–7, 370.
186 *CJ* II, 411, 426; BL Add. MS 14827, fol. 27r; Harl. MS 162, fol. 366; 480, fols. 95v–97r; *HMC Coke*, p. 295; *CSPD 1641–3*, p. 273.
187 Bodleian Tanner MS 66, fol. 242r; Crummett, pp. 21, 145–7.
188 *LJ* IV, 543; *HMC Coke*, p. 304; *CSPD 1641–3*, p. 274; Gardiner x, 160.

supping during the first two hours, believed he missed no points of substance. This was a classic case of the House whipping itself into a fury against a man whom it was easy to hate. A string of revelations shocked MPs. George Peard had an incriminating story to tell about Richmond's interference in the case against Percy and Jermyn. Henry Heyman alleged that as Lord Warden of the Cinque Ports Richmond had sent threatening letters to towns which refused to accept his nominations – who were monopolists and projectors – in the Long Parliament elections. John Lisle charged him with receiving a pension from the king of Spain and contriving the dissolution of the Short Parliament. Swallowing these accusations, even usually reticent backbenchers jumped on the bandwagon: Walter Long 'conceived that this lord was the engine by which the bishops turned and subsisted'; such dangerous words as Richmond's, avowed Sir John Northcote, 'ever were spoken and hatched by the Jesuits'; ' 'tis no less than to lose Ireland and to hazard this kingdom', declared Sir John Hotham. The hallmark of this debate was surging fear and emotion; the outcome was a handsome majority, in a very full House, for the leadership's motion that Richmond was fit to be accused as one of the malignant party, and an ill counsellor to the king. Dissent from the motion can be accounted for more in terms of doubts about the House's proper role in a case that had already been judged by the Lords than doubts about his guilt.[189]

The Commons handed out many summonses for delinquency and impeachments during these months. All sorts of men were brought into their net: the small fry included the hostile Kentish petitioners in April and men who had loosened their tongues against Pym or the parliament.[190] But all this activity was to little purpose since parliament lacked the means to bring its enemies low. Those who mattered most stayed free. Digby had fled; Dering was impeached for his role in the Kentish petition in March but escaped from the custody of a serjeant-at-arms; Richmond defended himself so well against the charges of the Commons that the case fizzled out.[191] Those who were imprisoned, like the attorney-general Sir Edward Herbert and Sir George Benion, were hardly exciting catches.[192]

The lesson of Strafford's case was that the treason law was inadequate as it stood to deal with parliament's political enemies. An attempt to revive the cases against the delinquent judges petered out because the lawyers were suffering a debilitating loss of confidence. Many of them had excused themselves, wrote Sir John Coke to his father reporting on the plans for Berkeley's trial, 'declaring themselves altogether unsatisfied of any treason

---

189 *CJ* II, 400; BL Add. MS 14827, fol. 17v–18; Harl. MS 162, fol. 355; 480, fols. 67v–69v, 70v–71v; Hill, pp. 11–16
190 E.g. *CJ* II, 432–3, 456–520, 552, 571.
191 *CJ* II, 401–3, 537, 552; *LJ* IV, 549–53, 703; V, 17–19; *HMC Buccleuch* I, 296.
192 *CJ* II, 394, 398, 407, 427–9; *LJ* IV, 683–5, 703, 717; Gardiner X, 167, 185, 194.

in his case'.[193] The trial of the 12 bishops impeached on 30 December had opened on 19 February only to be abandoned two days later.[194] A bill was brought in for the forfeit of the bishops' estates but MPs were so moved by the submissions which some of them made that, when the bill was reported on 21 March, they were given salaries for life and their families were allowed the inheritance of their forfeited lands.[195] Time and again the unpredictability of members when dealing with individuals, particularly those of their own number, was made plain. An incident like the expulsion of Robert Trelawney on 9 March could rack men's hearts. His statement, heard by a linen-draper at the Exchange, that it was treason for parliament to set a guard upon themselves without the king's consent could not be overlooked. Yet his abundant tears when the Speaker pronounced his sentence at the bar 'moved myself and divers others', D'Ewes recorded, 'to great pity and compassion, though I knew him to be a man opposite almost to all goodness.'[196] After 16 months of intense activity, MPs' feelings of shared endeavour were bound to be strong, but they had also built up a rancorous defensiveness which needed outlets of this kind.

MPs also needed continual reassurance about social order. The December riots had jolted everyone and the popular presence maintained at Westminster during January and February by women and poor tradesmen reminded members of how close London was to unrest.[197] Moreover the massive demonstrations that accompanied some of the provincial petitions were disturbing. There are signs of leadership co-ordination behind the moves made on 3 February to couch a letter restraining the East Anglian clothiers from stirring from their homes.[198] Neither pamphlet controversy nor sectarian audacities had been stilled. A militia company had to watch Cheapside Cross every night lest the apprentices should pull it down, when, ironically, it was Puritan MPs who had directed attention to it as a monument of idolatry in the 1620s.[199] In these circumstances Sir Benjamin Rudyerd's proposal of an urgent discussion on settling the distractions of the Church was bound to get a fair hearing. A declaration was issued on 8 April to allay public uncertainty about parliament's religious policies: nothing 'but what shall be evil and justly offensive or at least burdensome and unnecessary' would be taken away in the

193 *CJ* II, 499, 560, 566; *LJ* v, 81–2; *HMC Buccleuch* I, 294, *HMC Coke*, p. 315.
194 *CJ* II, 447–8; *LJ* IV, 609.
195 BL Harl. MS 162, fol. 398r; 163, fol. 14v; Add. MS 14827, fol. 71r; *CJ* II, 467, 517–18, 525, 560; *LJ* v, 42–3; *HMC Coke*, p. 314.
196 BL Harl. MS 163, fol. 26v; E 201(23): *A Perfect Diurnal*, 7–14 March, p. 14; *CJ* II, 473.
197 *CJ* II, 387, 407, 410, 413, 415, 439; BL Harl. MS 162, fol. 364v; Add. MS 14827, fols. 26v, 29v, 30v; E 201(13): *The True Diurnal Occurences*, 31 Jan.–3 Feb.; Manning, pp. 107–10.
198 *CJ* II, 412; BL Harl. MS 163, fol. 367v.
199 BL Harl. MS 163, fol. 66r; Sloane MS 3317, fol. 30r; *CJ* II, 519; *HMC Coke*, p. 304; Russell, *Parliaments*, p. 277.

reformation of government and the liturgy.[200] Moderates like Sir John Coke, who approvingly noted the intention 'to prevent the intolerable abuses daily committed', were duly appreciative. But some were merely further bemused. John Berners confessed to a Norfolk correspondent that he did not 'clearly understand' the new declaration and that he was convinced any major changes in the Church would beget 'great disturbance'.[201]

Censorship was another aspect of the maintenance of order which the leadership was bound to take seriously. Nothing systematic was attempted but a bill to regulate printing was talked of in March and an ordinance against scandalous pamphlets was passed in June.[202] The committee for printing investigated particular items brought to its attention and efforts were made in a few cases, such as the Kentish petition of 25 March, to see that all copies were burnt.[203] A variety of items understandably attracted MPs' displeasure. Thomas Kilcop's *Treatise of Baptism* was disliked because it declared that infant baptism had 'no footing in the word of God'. Some scurrilous pictures of Sir John Hotham on horseback on the walls of Hull showed the king in an abject posture beneath them. Sheer fabrications, like the false Hertfordshire petition drawn by a young Cambridge scholar at an inn to make a couple of shillings, were seen to reflect on the publishing trade as a whole.[204] But the sudden attack on many of the leading printers and stationers in March is harder to explain. It was certainly not an initiative of Pym's. He knew the propagandist value of the weekly diurnals and also appreciated how journalism contributed to the economy of the capital when trading was dislocated. He had made the point with regard to the players when Edward Partridge moved for all plays to be suppressed on 26 January.[205] The printers appear to have suffered from a surge of emotion among MPs about their privileges, which found expression in a strict order against publication of parliamentary news in any form. But within two months the order was quietly allowed to lapse and the presses were busy once more.[206]

So far this account of parliamentary politics in early 1642 has been concerned with the internal management of both Houses. Some aspects of the leadership's public stance emerged in the discussion of petitioning: the petitioners themselves, we have seen, were given thanks and encourage-

200 *CJ* II, 498, 514–5, 519, 522; BL Harl. MS 163, fol. 49r; Gardiner, *Documents*, p. 247.
201 *HMC Coke*, p. 312; Bodleian Tanner MS 66, fol. 10v.
202 *LJ* IV, 652; *CJ* II, 494, 516, 615, 628, 651, 743.
203 *CJ* II, 520, 553, 615; *LJ* IV, 651–2, 702; V, 78.
204 *CJ* II, 396, 550–1, 617, 621; BL Harl. MS 162, fols. 350v, 351v; E 1113(1): *A Short Treatise of Baptism*.
205 BL Harl. MS 480, fol. 63r; see also E 158 (13): *Sion's Charity towards her Foes in Misery*, p. 5.
206 BL Harl. MS 163, fol. 52v; *CJ* II, 500–1; *HMC Montagu*, p. 148; *HMC Buccleuch* I, 294–5; Fortescue, *Catalogue of the Thomason Collection* II, 371.

ment, the Protestation was imposed on the localities, measures for local defence were readily authorized. Something must now be added about the leadership's developing relationship with two vital allies, the Scots and the City of London. Attitudes to the Scots remained as ambivalent in 1642 as they had been in 1641. Fears that they had their own ambitions in Ireland hindered the negotiations for the Scots army to sail under English pay to Ulster. The first 2500 men actually landed in April but the terms of their intervention against the Irish rebels were not finally agreed until July.[207] Meanwhile Pym sought to ensure that the friendship between parliament and the covenanters was kept in good shape. The meeting of the Great Council of Scotland on 13 April was a useful occasion for reassurance: a powerful committee, chaired by Fiennes, formulated a declaration about preserving the brotherly affection between the two nations. The Scots were also kept up to date with the messages and declarations that formed the parliamentary side of the paper war.[208]

It has been shown that Sir Richard Gurney was brought low in January 1642, but the Lord Mayor did not abandon the struggle for control of the City government. For some months he successfully resisted the order of parliament that he should call a common council whenever the committee of safety required it, but on 10 August he was finally removed from office and sent to the Tower.[209] Both Gurney and the recorder Sir Thomas Gardiner gave full support to the challenge to the militia ordinance mounted by one of the common councilmen displaced in the December 1641 elections, Sir George Benion. He obtained more than 200 signatures to a petition protesting that the command of the City militia should rest in the Lord Mayor's hands, rather than in the hands of the men of mean estate named in the ordinance.[210] Taking his cue from Puritan petitioners, Benion used shops for collecting subscriptions, but one of the merchants who brought the petition down to Westminster on 24 February confessed that at the time he signed he knew nothing of the ordinance passed by both Houses.[211] Benion was quickly answered by Pym's supporters, who put forth a petition in the name of the Lord Mayor, aldermen and common council on 18 March vindicating the honour of the City against his 'false, scandalous and seditious petition'.[212] This was so 'singularly well penned',

207 Stevenson, *Scottish Revolution*, pp. 244–5.
208 *CJ* II, 517, 521–2; *LJ* IV, 707; BL Harl. MS 163, fol. 67v.
209 *CJ* II, 373, 376; *LJ* V, 192, 241, 280; *HMC 5th Report*, p. 36; Ashton, *City and the Court*, pp. 206–7, 216; Pearl, pp. 147–59.
210 *LJ* IV, 681–2; V, 230; BL E 201(32): *A Perfect Diurnal*, 21–28 March, p. 4, E 140(12): *The Petition of the Citizens of London*; HLRO, 24 February: Petition of London; *HMC Coke*, pp. 307–8; Gardiner x, 168.
211 *CJ* II, 452, 464; *LJ* IV, 701; BL Harl. MS 162, fol. 403r.
212 *CJ* II, 485; *LJ*, IV, 651–2; BL E 140 (18): *A True Copy of the Petition of the Common Council of London*.

Sir John Holland assured Sir Robert Crane on 23 March, that 'it travels the kingdom over in print'.[213] However that may be, Pym and his closest allies needed to cosset their City friends while Gurney and Gardiner were still there to stir up trouble and there was a current of dissatisfaction about the feeble use that had been made of money loaned for crushing the Irish rebellion.

Pym's achievement between January and June 1642, with the help of a few others who worked as hard as he did, was that he held parliament together and maintained his links with the City and the Scots. These were the months when he built the foundations of a parliamentary party ready, if the absolute necessity arose, to raise an army and fight the king. The mood at Westminster was often sad, often apprehensive, often hesitant. The sterility of many of the policies that were being pursued is evident. It was evident to MPs and this very sterility made men begin to face the fact that there was no answer to Pym's argument that assertive moves taken in a defensive spirit were the only course left open. The story is not simply one of confrontation but of mounting confrontation. The king's attempt on Hull and the news during May that he was raising forces to defend himself pushed the process forward. On 20 May parliament passed three votes charging the king with making war; on 1 June it agreed upon the Nineteen Propositions, an ultimatum so far as the leadership was concerned rather than a serious agenda for negotiation. With both these moves Pym exhibited his command of both Houses, using the Lords as a stalking horse. 'Some guess the Lords rather nurses than parents them', wrote Sir Edmund Moundeford to Sir John Potts in an account of the three votes.[214] They were presented to the peers by a new committee, chaired by Mandeville and including in its membership Brooke, Essex, Holland, Northumberland and Saye. The first draft of the Nineteen Propositions was the work of a committee of 16 peers, with Northumberland as chairman, established on 23 May. When this draft reached the Commons on 31 May a small committee was appointed to consider it. Fiennes, Hampden, Holles, Pym and St John were all nominated. Within a few hours Pym was back in the House with some amendments, five additional articles, a preface and a conclusion. As had so often happened before in this parliament, most MPs were too stunned by Pym's tactics to react.[215] Perhaps some members did grasp that the new document was an ultimatum but did not yet believe Charles was capable of resistance.[216]

The Nineteen Propositions repeated Pym's old blueprint for settlement, but it had now taken on so harsh a guise that had the king given way to

213 Bodleian Tanner MS 66, fol. 298v.
214 Bodleian Tanner MS 63, fol. 32.
215 *LJ* v, 76–7, 80, 89; *CJ* II, 600–1.
216 I owe this suggestion to Professor Austin Woolrych.

these dictated terms the balance of executive power would have swung violently in parliament's direction. The document amounted to a claim for parliamentary sovereignty just one month before Henry Parker published the first exploration of this concept in his *Observations upon some of His Majesty's late Answers and Expresses*.[217] Yet the leadership had not reached this point by cool deliberation. They were merely seeking new guarantees against a man they now totally distrusted. The framework of the Propositions is familiar. The preamble stated once more that the distractions of the nation 'have proceeded from the subtle insinuations, mischievous practices and evil counsels of men disaffected to God's true religion, your Majesty's honour and safety and the public peace and prosperity of your people.' The conclusion once again promised an increased royal revenue and loyal obedience so the king might reign in 'honour and plenty'.[218]

The substance of the Nineteen Propositions can be briefly summarized. Charles was asked to accept the militia ordinance, consent to the synod and the full programme of religious reform embodied in the bills before parliament, pass an act clearing the five members, restore men dismissed since November 1640, dismiss all his own forces and give up delinquents to such censures as parliament should determine. The main anti-Catholic measures were the exclusion of popish peers from the Lords, strict enforcement of the laws against Jesuits and recusants, parliamentary control of the education and marriage of the royal children and a bill for the education of the children of papists as Protestants. Parliament required alliances with the United Provinces and other neighbouring Protestant states, with a view to intervention on the continent on behalf of the Elector Palatine. The king was expected to surrender his rights of appointment to all the major offices of state and to the privy council and even his rights to issue patents of nobility. The depth of the leadership's distrust was plain in the statement that public policy should be 'debated, resolved and transacted only in parliament and not elsewhere' and in the provision for councillors and judges to take an oath that they would maintain the Petition of Right and the other reform statutes passed since 1640. The judges of assize and JPs would be set as watchdogs on those at the head of the executive and judiciary by a direction that they should enquire into breaches of these laws securing the subject's liberties at assizes and quarter sessions.[219]

The content of Pym's ultimatum emphasizes the inevitability of some kind of appeal to arms by June 1642. But what is really interesting about this constitutional document is that it was not formulated under the final provocation of the king's journey to York and his activities there in April

---

217 Zagorin, p. 348–9; J.W. Allen, *English Political Thought 1603–1644* (London, 1938), pp. 426–35; W.K. Jordan, *Men of Substance* (Chicago, 1944), pp. 426–35.
218 Gardiner, *Documents*, pp. 250, 254.
219 *Ibid*, pp. 250–4; Kenyon, pp. 196, 244–7.

and May. Between 15 and 24 January the Commons had spent much of their time discussing a new Declaration of Fears and Jealousies, which we know was drawn up by Pym himself.[220] This has been little noticed by historians, since, although it reappeared on the Commons agenda in March and May, it stuck in the Lords and was never published.[221] It was in effect a draft of the Nineteen Propositions and it included every single demand made on 1 June. Indeed several clauses, such as the one about resolution of public policy, were taken over verbatim.[222] As with the Grand Remonstrance in 1641, Pym staked out his ground and held to it, once the parliamentary circumstances permitted, with incontrovertible logic and determination. There were very few others who saw the political crisis as clearly as he did. It is time to turn to those at Westminster, at York and in the localities who did not share his or the king's mentality and who sought to resist the nation's drift into a struggle based at least in part on competing delusions.

220 *CJ* II, 382, 384, 386–7, 392; BL Harl. MS 162, fols. 330v, 335v, 341r; 480, fols. 44v–46v; Sloane MS 3317, fols. 34v, 35v; *HMC Montagu*, p. 144. For Pym's authorship see BL E 201(19): *A Continuation of the True Diurnal*, 21–28 Feb.
221 *CJ* II, 467, 470, 498, 526, 568–70, 575; *LJ* IV, 700, 712; V, 21; BL Harl. MS 163, fols. 17v, 19r, 118v; Add. MS 14827, fol. 61.
222 *CJ* II, 443–6; *HMC 5th Report*, p. 148.

8

Accommodation

God forbid that either king or parliament should by power and force go about to cure the present distempers for that course can produce nothing but misery, if not ruin, both to king and people.

> The earl of Northumberland to Sir John Bankes,
> 19 May 1642[1]

I did conceive the present differences between us and His Majesty do rather proceed from fancy and misunderstanding than from any real difference that is between us, whereby things appear in a prospect and at a distance otherwise than indeed they are.

> Sir Simonds D'Ewes in the House of Commons,
> 31 May 1642[2]

There are now some overtures of accommodation . . . and most men think they smell the air of peace. Yet provide for war.

> Sir Gilbert Pickering to Sir Roland St John,
> 13 July 1642[3]

Most Englishmen recoiled with dread at the prospect of civil war. The desire for accommodation was the insistent theme of gentry correspondence between March and November 1642, binding together men and women of widely different political views. We find it in many letters from the capital. 'God make us thankful for such a blessing there and pray for his mercies towards us here', wrote Sir John Holland to Sir Robert Crane reporting good news from Ireland on 23 March.[4] 'I hope notwithstanding all that hath passed we shall not go together by the ears', Sir John Coke told his father on 24 May. 'All do wish and pray for peace', Coke reported on 5 July, 'yet the going of affairs does not promise it.'[5]

There were still provincial correspondents in early March who ended their letters with a conventional encomium. Richard Harlackenden showed no awareness of how close the nation was to the brink on 7 March: he was praying, he told Sir Thomas Barrington, 'for your happy progress

---

1 G. Bankes, *The Story of Corfe Castle* (London, 1853), p. 123.
2 BL Harl. MS 163, fol. 140.
3 Bedfordshire RO J 1383.
4 Bodleian Tanner MS 63, fol. 32; 66, fol. 298v.
5 *HMC Coke*, pp. 317–9.

and success in yours and the rest indefatigable pains in this happy parliament'.[6] But the realities of the situation were sinking in and a conclusion in these terms was soon replaced by anxious enquiries for encouraging news. 'I have no news to write of that is good and you I presume as little', was the comment D'Ewes received from his brother-in-law on 25 March. 'Pray God', he added, 'send all for the best.'[7] Anxiety became the keynote of political comment. Each step towards war was greeted with surprise and speculation. John Dillingham, for instance, informed Lord Montagu in April that there were two views current about the news of the king's intention to go to Ireland, that it was 'a colour to raise men' and that he would 'fetch hither the Irish power'. He rejected both of them but he leaves the impression that he was reassuring himself as much as Montagu with his conclusion that the design was 'no more but to deliver the rebels from intended extirpation by some kind of accord'.[8]

The whole nation was now so alert that distance from London no longer implied any political isolation. Margaret Eure's letters to Verney from north Yorkshire show increasing despondency. 'All things grow on by degrees here, what will become of all I know not', she opined on 21 May, 'I doubt no good.'[9] Samuel Wood in north Wales, who had virtually ignored politics in his bulletins since December 1640, was seriously worried about what the future held. 'The Lord show his mercy to us all of his kingdom and continue our peace if it be his will', he wrote on 16 May, 'our fears do daily increase here whether upon just grounds or not God knows.' In his letter to Sir John Trevor of 6 August he showed more fortitude: 'I see the whole nation is almost every man furiously bent for war and bloodshed and do express themselves very boldly but I will not God willing shrink till I see more apparent fears. I hope God will guide us and provide means either by an accord in peace or a means to avoid the hazard.'[10] The postscript to Thomas Radcliffe's letter of 29 April to the steward at Thornhill in Yorkshire is equally evocative: 'I pray God we be not forced ere long to use other weapons.'[11]

One of the fullest and most interesting sets of correspondence is that of the aged Lord Montagu of Boughton, a quintessential moderate who had watched the parliament's progress with eager interest from his Northamptonshire home but was now becoming more and more disillusioned by its actions. 'It troubles my thoughts and grieves my heart to see how things are carried which are no way warrantable', he declared on

6 BL Egerton MS 2646, fol. 171; for Harlackenden see A. Macfarlane, *The Family Life of Ralph Josselin* (Cambridge, 1970), pp. 17, 63, 78, 191.
7 BL Harl. MS 382, fol. 160r.
8 *HMC Montagu*, p. 149.
9 *Verney*, pp. 85–7.
10 Clwyd RO Glynde MS 3275/3.
11 Nottinghamshire RO DDSR 221/95/2.

16 May. Montagu thought much harder than most observers about how parliament's achievements might be preserved in a context of renewed amity with Charles. He told his son in April that the only solution he could envisage was a speedy adjournment of the parliament to a place where the king could meet it without fear for his life. This was an intelligent paper plan even if it did not take enough account of the rooted distrust of the principal men on each side. May and June's developments greatly troubled Montagu; the letters he received from his brother the earl of Manchester, who was better placed than he to assess the political future, brought little comfort.[12]

The perception that internal military conflict threatened all the standards of civilized society as men knew it gave the accommodation movement its impetus. Edward Reed was one of the first to spell this out. If the king and parliament were not able to concur, he wrote on 4 April, 'the danger that poverty and want can bring will come on too fast.' 'I hope under colour of preserving the king's prerogative we shall not destroy one another', William Davy told John Willoughby on 28 May.[13] Six months later, in the midst of the first campaign, measured comments of this kind were replaced by shrill lamentations. The countess of Sussex, grieving at the loss of her kinsman Sir Edmund Verney at Edgehill where he was 'buried amongst the multitude', sent a series of distracted letters to his son Sir Ralph. 'If there be so little hopes of peace', she declared on 9 November, 'we are like all to be in a most miserable condition.'[14] Francis Newport's report from London to his uncle Sir Richard Leveson on 29 November is full of his longing for accommodation:

> As the face of public affairs now looks, there is nothing to be seen in it but ruin and desolation unless we speedily incline all hearts to some good accommodation . . . God grant that which is sour destroy not that which is sweet and that a happy agreement betwixt king and parliament may speedily prevent our ruin and destruction.[15]

Time and again in these letters God's name was invoked, in prayer by men who saw no other course, in praise by those whose localities for a time remained quiet.[16] The fatalistic and moralistic attitudes that were exhibited show that this was a society that found it hard to contemplate political change or upheaval, let alone regicide or revolution.[17] A sense of helplessness, of waiting upon God's judgement, pervaded England as it slipped

---

12 *HMC Buccleuch* I, 297, 300, 303.
13 *HMC Coke*, p. 313; *Trevelyan Papers*, part III, 210.
14 *Verney*, p. 123; *HMC 7th Report*, p. 442.
15 Staffordshire RO D 868/3/13a.
16 E.g. BL Add. MS 28000, fol. 217; Harl. MS 384, fol. 94; 669 f 6 (44): *News from York*; J. Adair, *Roundhead General* (London, 1969), p. 36.
17 P. Burke, *Popular Culture in Early Modern Europe* (London, 1978), pp. 174–5.

into civil war. A pamphlet relating the fall of a meteorite near Aldeburgh suggested that it was an omen of God's intention towards 'this sinful land and nation'.[18] Young William Sancroft, immersed in university politics at Cambridge, found time to comment in a letter to his family on 4 April about how things went 'very ill above'. 'I cannot but say', he predicted rather precociously, 'in the words of His Majesty in one of his messages there is a judgement of heaven upon this land if these things continue.' 'We upon the cold wolds are yet quiet I thank God', reflected a Lincolnshire gentleman on 16 April. 'I am persuaded things are now come to their ripeness', declared Lady Brilliana Harley the same month, 'and if God be not very merciful to us we shall be in a distressed condition.' 'God forbid that we should war here one with another', asserted Lord Strange to her husband a few weeks later.[19]

In a letter to Montagu on 11 May the countess of Lindsey expounded the view that the immediate future was 'not in the power of man's wisdom but from God, who governs all things for the good of his children'. Thomas Knyvett confided to his wife a fortnight later that he could foresee 'nothing but a public phlebotomy if God in his mercy doth not in time cast out these evil spirits from amongst us'.[20] 'It is his infinite mercy that we are not together by the ears already', one of Leveson's correspondents thought the following month. Henry Manners, another of Montagu's confidants, was sanguine by comparison. He refused to believe, he explained on 22 June, that either parliament or the king would actually start a war, but neither did he expect salvation by man's hand: 'there is hope in Israel and truly I am in the same opinion I was from the beginning, in God I trust we shall lose no blood.'[21] Isaac Seward's missive to Sir Robert Harley on 11 July was full of trepidation: 'the Lord . . . continue peace if it be his blessed will.' 'The Lord grant us faith and constancy to undergo all troubles that lie upon us', declared a Shrewsbury correspondent to a London friend on 30 September.[22] 'It hath pleased God to lay a heavy punishment upon this land by civil war', was Sir Edmund Sidenham's reading of the situation soon after Edgehill.[23]

What could men do to stop the war? For those in the localities petitioning was the only means, not a very effectual one at that, of influencing the national situation. Isolation of the home town, district or county was another matter which will be considered later. A new set of petitions emerged from anxious meetings in manor houses up and down the country

18 BL E 111(2): *A Sign from Heaven*.
19 Bodleian Tanner MS 63, fols. 2, 16r; *HMC Portland* III, 87; *Harley*, p. 153.
20 *HMC Buccleuch* I, 299; *Knyvett*, p. 105.
21 Staffordshire RO D 868/4/4; *HMC Montagu*, p. 154.
22 BL Loan MS 29/174/274r; J.R. Phillips, *Memoirs of the Civil War in Wales and the Marches* (London, 1874) II, 18.
23 *HMC 7th Report*, p. 442.

and from discussions on the Bench and among grand juries at assizes and sessions. 'The coming of His Majesty into the northern parts we observe troubles the minds of many of his loving subjects', began a group of gentry who sent a letter to Derbyshire friends and colleagues on 21 March summoning them to meet about a petition. They had gathered at Barlborough House on the Nottinghamshire side of the county and exchanged news about the petitions for accommodation that had been presented to Charles by other counties during the previous few days, as he passed through the north midlands.[24]

Petitions for accommodation were formulated and circulated in at least 17 counties between March and November 1642. Counties such as Cornwall, Kent, Lancashire, Lincolnshire, Nottinghamshire and Yorkshire presented more than one. Most of them were to the king but a few went to parliament. Some counties looked to intermediaries to mediate or forward their requests: thus in August the Somerset grand jury petitioned Sir Robert Foster, the visiting assize judge, and the Devon one presented three petitions, along the same lines as the county's pleas to the king and parliament, to Foster, the earl of Bath and the MPs for the county.[25] Certain towns also joined in the movement. The citizens of Westminster presented Charles with a request for reconciliation on 25 May; Chester asked the shire's commissioners of array to seek peace when they were in the city during August; the corporation of Salisbury sent their mayor and three aldermen to the Lords with an appeal for peace in October.[26]

The petitions simply put the apprehensions and unhappiness expressed in private correspondence in more formal terms. The gentry and free-holders of Rutland explained in their petition presented between Stamford and Grantham on the Great North Road how they believed that 'the joy of the whole land' was darkened by Charles's withdrawal from London 'in these times of imminent danger . . . to the raising of unspeakable fears in the hearts of your loyal subjects'. Nottinghamshire, in a petition signed by 4540 presented on 1 April, spoke 'from deep and bleeding sense of miseries of all sorts'.[27] Lancashire expressed its 'heartbreaking sense and sorrow', on 2 May, 'for the unhappy rents and distractions in Your Majesty's dominions, especially in session of so grave and religious an assembly'. When the king invited counties to declare their grievances by a letter read at assizes in July and August, the Buckinghamshire grand jury announced that their greatest grievance was 'the fear of civil war', occasioned by the

24 *Derbyshire Archaeological Journal* XCIII (1973), 34–5.
25 *CSPD 1641–3*, p. 371; BL E 112(14): *Three Petitions of Devon*.
26 BL 669 f 6(23): *Petition of Westminister*; Phillips, *Civil War in Wales* II, 9; Salisbury District Council Muniment Room, Ledger Book D, fol. 10r.
27 BL 669 f 6(1), (6).

Map 4: Counties where petitions for accommodation were circulated March – November 1642.

king's having raised an army which was 'a sight terrible to your people and not conducive to that amicable accommodation so much desired'.[28]

The Devon petitions are particularly full of pathos. The grand jury looked to the earl of Bath as a person of 'eminency and known interest' in the king's favour, they told him, to procure peace, 'that war, the greatest and worst of evils be not conceived and chosen for a means to heal our distempers rather than a parliament, the cheapest and best of remedies.' The 'war actually begun', Sir Robert Foster was informed, was 'a grievance tending to the dissolution of the ancient government of this kingdom'. 'Bind up our wounds', the grand jury pleaded with their MPs, 'heal our divisions, ere our disease become incurable.'[29] The Devonshire gentry also expounded their views in complementary petitions to the king and parliament. From parliament they sought mildness: 'two acts we chiefly pray for, one of forgiveness, another of forgetfulness.' 'Great hearts', they advised, 'are best wrought upon by submissive intercessions'; 'a few examples made upon delinquents are as prevalent warnings as a multitude.' Lamentable distractions and convulsions, they informed the king, made them fly to him 'as a physician to cure us and . . . as a compassionate father to relieve us'. How could they possibly choose between obedience to the militia ordinance and to the king's commissioners of array, they asked, when they felt gratitude, love and duty to him but also 'natural affection' to parliament and deep concern for its privileges? The naivety and bewilderment of the Devonshire phraseology indicates the tragedy of a war that men hated but could see no way to prevent. The petitions confessed as much: 'we are not presumptuous to petition for the way', was their message to the king, 'but humbly beg the end.'[30]

Another county which produced heartfelt propaganda against the war was Cheshire. Sir Thomas Aston had been outplayed and the sharp divisions of 1641 were temporarily overlaid. The June remonstrance was not directed to either side in the quarrel but was intended to influence all men of good will both inside the shire and beyond. In this sense it was unique. The remonstrance stressed the county's double loyalty and the inhabitants' intention to defend the Protestant religion both against 'sects and schisms' and against 'papists, Donatists and Arminians'. The conclusion was as follows:

> We cannot but look upon all such as unworthy of future happiness who do admit for current that dangerous and disloyal distinction (which rings too loud in our ears) viz. for the king or for the parliament. Our loyal affections and judgements will not permit us to style them true patriots and lovers of their country that are not cordially affected to our gracious sovereign, nor them good

28 Ormerod, p. 6; Johnson, p. 70.
29 BL E 112 (14).
30 *LJ* v, 295–6; Andriette, p. 54.

subjects that disaffect parliaments. The king and parliament, being like Hippocrates' twins, they must laugh and cry, live and die together; and both are so rooted in our loyal hearts that we cannot disjoin them.

These words were assented to in villages all over the county.[31] The organizers plainly hoped to give a lead that others might follow. There would be no civil war if all the country gentry refused to fight one.

The outstanding theme of the accommodation petitions to the king between March and August was the need for him to return to London. Unable to interpret the political crisis satisfactorily, the localities became gripped by the fact of the parties' physical separation, which was seen as having an almost mystical significance. Northamptonshire's petition brought out both the practical and psychological aspects of the matter. With Charles resident close by, parliament

may enjoy the influence of your royal presence amongst them and have a more easy and speedy access upon any emergent occasions unto your sacred person, which your petitioners believe will not only blast the designs of the popish discontented party, but will also make you absolute in the affection of your people and, removing the fears of your distracted subjects, will give life and vigour to the languishing body of your distempered kingdom.[32]

Petitions calling for the physical reunion of the parties at odds ranged from those, like Northamptonshire's, based firmly on Pym's account of the crisis, to those that combined sympathy for Charles's plight with a sense that this minimal concession was a necessary first step to settlement. The sternest lecture the king received was from Leicestershire when he appeared there on 18 June. Not content with reprimanding him for selling the crown jewels, the gentry made it abundantly clear what initiatives he should take. He should go south and listen to parliament, which could end the nation's differences 'by God's blessing and your assenting unto them'. The petition ended on an explicit note of warning. If it became necessary for parliament to declare 'the procurers of your and our fears, jealousies and amazements out of their known experience, we shall take upon us to remove from Your Majesty such prosecutors as are enemies to the state and hinderers to the tranquility of the same.'[33] The Nottinghamshire gentry were not mincing their words either when they told Charles to show his good opinion to parliament and trust the men at Westminster as 'the best supporters' of his wealth, honour and sovereignty. Nor indeed was Sir Thomas Barrington, in his counter-petition to a royalist one at the Essex assizes in July, when he informed the king that 'the influence of those virtues shining in you do best express themselves' in parliament.[34] But a

31 Morrill, *Revolt*, p. 159; Morrill, *Cheshire*, pp. 58–9.
32 Bedfordshire RO J 1405.
33 BL 669 f 6 (34).
34 BL 669 f 6 (6); BL Egerton MS 2651, fol. 119; Holmes, pp. 41, 248.

good many of these petitions adopted a deferential tone. Lincolnshire dressed up a demand for the king to reside near and 'listen to' his parliament in adulatory language. So did Hampshire, imploring Charles to revive their 'withered and dying hopes' by his 'gracious favour, presence and happy concurrence' with parliament.[35] Rutland stressed 'the foundation of everlasting comfort' which his presence at Whitehall would bring. The Derbyshire gentry debated the Nottinghamshire formulation only to reject it in favour of a straightforward and humbly worded request for the king to return south.[36]

These pleas of course were hopelessly unrealistic. There was no such panacea though people naturally looked for one. Some were beginning to grasp this as the summer wore on. In their second accommodation petition at the end of May, the Lancashire gentry recognized that certain 'differences and impediments' had to be removed before the king could return to the capital.[37] The Cumberland and Westmorland gentry, in a petition presented on 5 July, took up the idea Lord Montagu had been pondering of a new venue for parliament. Once some place of meeting was found 'free from exception both of danger and distrust', they believed, all the country's differences might be reconciled.[38] There was a growing awareness in the provinces of the role of hotheads, cavaliers at York and Puritan radicals in London, who fanned the flames of war. Leicestershire had asked the king to cashier the cavaliers; a Somerset petition, received in the Lords on 15 June, urged parliament to provide for Charles's security by declaring against tumults and suppressing seditious sermons and pamphlets.[39]

Whereas petitioners were outsiders with no more than a simplified version of the events which had produced political deadlock at their command, the peace party at Westminster was sustained by the experiences of 18 months' debating and the determination this had engendered to finish the task undertaken. We can only grasp the persistence of the moderate MPs if we forget the events of the next months and appreciate that the overwhelming certainty in the Commons during the spring and early summer was that Ireland was still the main priority. Peace at home was a prerequisite for crushing the rebellion. Many doubtless shared something of the sense of the parliament's destiny that still kept D'Ewes in the chamber with his notebook in his hand. 'God had been already seen in the mount', he reminded colleagues on 20 May, 'and let us still trust him to disappoint the designs of our enemies that they may not

35   BL 669 f 4 (87); E 112 (9), p. 4.
36   BL 669 f 6 (1); *Derbyshire Archaeological Journal* XCIII (1973), 37; see also Ormerod, p. 6.
37   Ormerod, pp. 10–11.
38   BL E 154 (46), p. 3.
39   BL 669 f 6 (34), (37).

come to force and violence . . . as long as it is possible we are bound to perform the trust of those that sent us hither by preserving the peace of the kingdom.'[40]

Persistence though, we have seen already, was not enough: Pym's command of the Commons never faltered in the weeks before the passing of the Nineteen Propositions on 1 June. It was so sure that he could afford to be magnanimous and to allow the moderates their little victories. Despite Strode's anger at the suggestion, he had the wisdom to let through Edmund Waller's addition to the brief of the new committee for the defence of the kingdom on 27 May 'so as to consider of all means for continuing and preserving the peace of the kingdom and the preventing of civil war'.[41] What committees recommended mattered rather than what they were told to discuss.

When moderate MPs heard the Lords' proposals for the new peace initiative at a conference on 30 May, they at once realized that the factional struggle had reached a turning point. Next morning Harbottle Grimston moved that instead of the Propositions a single petition should be sent to the king, 'not cloyed with any expostulation', begging him to return to his parliament. This move, he argued, would make it possible to raise loans for relieving Ireland immediately. D'Ewes was behind him, harping on the 'asperities' of former petitions and predicting that if the report from the Lords was heard the debate would be long and controversial.[42] It was of course, but Pym, as has been shown, swept the arguments for trust aside and parliament established its harshest terms.[43] The king's reply to the Nineteen Propositions has come to be seen as a masterly statement of the moderate royalist position.[44] When it was read in the Commons on 21 June many were shocked at its 'high language' and disappointed about what it said. Nevertheless when the debate on it opened two days later the peace party at once proclaimed themselves undismayed. The House must go on with accommodation, they insisted, treating the Nineteen Propositions as a working document. Charles had actually given some cause for optimism by his conciliatory tone on the proposals for educating papist children as Protestants and for allying with the United Provinces.[45] Concessions in return, it was possible to believe, might hasten settlement.

For a month or so from 21 June the Commons seemed to be pursuing contradictory policies at the same time. The truth was that Pym was playing a clever double game by letting the peace party have its head. At

40 BL Harl. MS 163, fol. 128v.
41 BL Harl. MS 163, fols. 128, 135; *CJ* II, 585, 593.
42 BL Harl. MS 163, fols. 139r–140.
43 *LJ* v, 90–2; *CJ* II, 599–600.
44 C.C. Weston, 'The Theory of Mixed Monarchy under Charles I and After', *EHR* LXXV (1966), 426–33; Ashton, *English Civil War*, pp. 164–6.
45 BL Harl. MS 163, fols. 207v, 210v; E 202 (11): *Diurnal Occurrences*, 20–28 June, p. 5.

the same time, as we shall see, he was preparing most thoroughly for war. When necessary he could employ the old trick of mastering the House with a sudden announcement, like the news of plans to besiege the earl of Stamford in Leicestershire which diverted attention from the Nineteen Propositions on 1 July.[46] He was also ready to stoop to conquer men's doubts. Thus he used a subtle line to hang on to the vital first proposition about appointment of counsellors on 23 June: 'we should propound it by way of approbation, whereby we give the king great advantage of honour . . . we do it not by way of compulsion, he abhors all such thoughts, but to lay it home to the king and let it lie upon his conscience.' His reply was adept when Thomas Tomkins tried to hold up the commission appointing the earl of Essex as Lord General on 15 July and it summarizes his tactics: 'if we receive a gracious message from the king, as I hope we shall, then we shall easily and quickly undo that which we have done. If not then we are in a forwardness.'[47] However there were times in these weeks when the course of debate angered the leadership and even Pym was temporarily put off his stroke. When a committee was appointed to find precedents for some of the parliamentary demands on 25 June 'but altogether to decline their former way of demanding them', Elias Ashmore related to a friend, Hampden, Holles, Pym and Strode with 'divers others of that side went out of the House in a discontent'.[48]

The crucial moment in the debates on the Nineteen Propositions came on 2 July when the Commons reached the article on the militia. Fiennes, Goodwin, Pym and Strode all reiterated the arguments about the legality of the ordinance. On the other side, Selden reminded colleagues of his objection to disposing of men's goods and persons by this means. But none of those who desired peace dared answer the leadership's insistent question: what assurance would subjects have of their safety if the execution of the ordinance was abandoned?[49] In their heart of hearts the majority still believed what Pym had told them all along. They were still possessed by the delusion of a Catholic and malignant conspiracy against the state. Besides there was now no question that the king was raising an army.

Thereafter the fortunes of the peace party began to fade, though there were two further initiatives in July. On the 6th that kindly Norfolk gentleman Sir John Holland, always an exponent of moderation, sponsored a new militia bill which left the lieutenancies in the hands of those appointed, mentioned the king's approbation of them, but glossed

46 BL Add. MS 14827, fols. 147v, 148r; *CJ* II, 650.
47 Hill, p. 103; BL Add. MS 14827, fol. 160v.
48 Morrill, *Cheshire*, pp. 41–2.
49 BL Harl. MS 163, fol. 254v; E 202 (12): *Some Special Passages*, 29 June–5 July; E 202 (13): *A Perfect Diurnal*, 27 June–4 July, p. 7; *CJ* II, 653.

over the problem of ultimate authority. The bill was to remain law until Lady Day 1644.[50] It was frostily received at first but read twice on 9 July and sent to committee. No further progress was made when it reappeared on 12 July.[51] Two days later a final petition for peace, which was actually no more than another demand for surrender, was sent to the king at Beverley.[52] For a few more days it gave the fainthearted something positive on which they could fasten their minds.[53]

Although the peace party failed to stop the war, its achievements in amending the Nineteen Propositions between 23 and 28 June are of considerable interest. Not a single article was retained as it stood, but the most drastic changes were made to Pym's programme for control of the executive. The claim to appoint privy councillors was discarded and the bid to make policy was much watered down. The limitation on the size of the council to between 15 and 25 was abandoned and the support of six councillors rather than the majority was established as sufficient validity for the council's acts. Control of appointment was whittled down from 15 major offices to eight. The king was also given *carte blanche* over the education of his children when parliament was not in session and the ban on royal marriage treaties was softened by leaving the king free to negotiate with protestants abroad without consent from Westminster.[54] In short the constitutional ambitions of the mass of backbench MPs remained almost as tentative in June 1642 as they had been a year before.

The leadership's radicalism of course was merely the measure of their distrust and the question of trust remained the fundamental issue at stake between the parliamentary factions. In an impassioned speech on 9 July, Sir Benjamin Rudyerd reviewed the history of the previous three years, declaring that if anyone had predicted the achievements of the Long Parliament they would have been thought 'a dream of happiness'. Yet now we are in the real possession of it, he went on,

> we do not enjoy it. . . . We stand chiefly upon further security, whereas the very having of these things is a convenient fair security, mutually securing one another. . . . Let us beware we do not contend for such a hazardous unsafe security as may endanger the loss of what we have already. Let us not think we have nothing, because we have not all we desire, and though we had, yet we cannot make a mathematical security. All human caution is susceptible of corruption and failing; God's providence will not be bound; success must be his; he that observes the wind and rain shall neither sow nor reap; if he do

50 Hill, pp. 122–3; BL E 202 (15): *A Perfect Diurnal*, 4–11 July, p 9; Ketton-Cremer, pp. 47–8, 117, 144.
51 *CJ* II, 659, 667, 671; BL Harl. MS 163, fol. 262v.
52 *CJ* II, 672, 694; *LJ* v, 206–7; BL E 202(16): *A Perfect Diurnal*, 11–18 July.
53 See the third epigraph to this chapter.
54 *CJ* II, 641–3, 646–7.

nothing till he can secure the weather, he will have but an ill harvest.[55]

This speech was probably the most perceptive account of how parliament had blundered into war that MPs heard in the summer of 1642. It must have struck a chord in D'Ewes's mind, since he had said much the same thing a good many times. Only three days before he had questioned the decision to send more troops to Hull with the same argument as Rudyerd used. 'We may kill one another to the world's end', he had told colleagues, by action of this kind,

> for if it shall be objected that we have no certainty of all that is promised us but that it is like a spider's web easily blown away, then to what end should we desire more? Nay if a monarchy continue amongst us, there must of necessity remain a confidence from the subjects towards the prince.

Unfortunately for D'Ewes, but not surprisingly considering his state of mind, he one day overstepped the mark, accusing the committee of safety on 23 July of copying passages from Henry Parker's *Observations* into their latest declaration to the king. His enemies jumped at the chance to challenge him and his humiliation that day, which to his dismay some treated as a joke, left a permanent mark on the diarist, who vowed he would no longer take notes and speak in debates.[56]

We know much less about the factional struggle in the Lords than that in the Commons. Quite clearly it was less fierce. Many of the most persistent royalist peers – Capel, Dover, Andover and Monmouth for instance – lost heart and departed for York during May.[57] Bristol was another who did so after making a final plea for accommodation. Hindsight enables us to appreciate the sensitivity of his appraisal:

> the greatest difficulty may seem to be how that which may be settled and agreed upon may be secured. This is commonly the last point in treaties betwixt parties and of the greatest niceness, but much more betwixt a king and his subjects where that confidence and belief which should be betwixt them is once lost.[58]

But if the analysis was acute it was hardly encouraging. By June and July there were less than 20 regular attenders in the Lords and the ostensible peace party, entering their protestations, consisted merely of the earls of Leicester and Rutland together with Lord Spencer.[59]

There is good reason to think, however, that a solid group of peers

55 Rushworth, III, part I, 753–4.
56 BL Harl. MS 163, fols. 259r, 291v, 292v; *CJ* II, 659, 691–2.
57 *LJ* v, 64, 73, 80, 92; *HMC Buccleuch* I, 302.
58 *HMC 5th Report*, p. 178; *CSPD 1641–3*, p. 342; Rushworth III, part I, 714–7; Zagorin, p. 320; *Knyvett*, p. 106.
59 *LJ* v, 59, 186, 190, 211, 250; *CSPD 1641–3*, p. 340; *HMC Coke*, p. 319; BL Add. MS 14827, fol. 125r; Harl. MS 163, fol. 281v; Bodleian Tanner MS 63, fol. 43r.

harboured serious doubts about Pym's course of action despite their showing loyalty. It is instructive to compare the standpoints of Essex and Northumberland as revealed in letters to Sir John Bankes at York. Essex in his letter of 31 May was concerned to defend his reputation against accusations he had heard or suspected that he was motivated by ambition. He knew 'none but must abhor' the deadlock between king and parliament, but he said nothing about accommodation, putting all blame for the crisis onto 'delinquents, papists and men that desire to make their fortunes by the troubles of the land'. Northumberland by contrast regretted the harshness of the paper war and expressed his earnest desire for accommodation. He understood the fears and misapprehensions that are the essence of our story. 'The alteration of government is apprehended on both sides', he wrote on 19 May: 'we believe that those persons who are most powerful with the king do endeavour to bring parliaments to such a condition that they shall only be made instruments to execute the commands of the king, who were established for his greatest and most supreme council.' His next letter shows just how far at odds Northumberland was with Pym's men in the House. Preparations being made for war were entirely defensive, he assured Bankes, and no constitutional revolution was at hand. 'Let us but have our laws, liberties and privileges secured unto us and let him perish that seeks to deprive the king of any part of his prerogative or that authority which is due unto him.' This statement was in direct contradiction of his at least tacit support for the Nineteen Propositions. But then Northumberland had always seen these as an agenda for negotiation, as the Commons moderates did, rather than as an ultimatum. All the things desired in them were not absolutely necessary for securing 'our laws, liberties and privileges', he told Bankes on 29 June giving his own interpretation of parliamentary policy, 'nor was it intended that those propositions should be insisted upon, they being petitions of grace not of right'.[60]

Others of Northumberland's mind were the earls of Holland and Pembroke who spoke strongly in favour of accommodation at a joint committee of both Houses on 9 July.[61] Holland subsequently carried the new peace petition to Beverley. Pembroke at this time was in the midst of a crisis of conscience prompted by two letters from Charles pressing him to go north. In a reply on 25 June he had offered protestations of obedience: 'wheresoever I am there is a heart full of loyalty and a tongue that speaks nothing but duty.' In a letter to Hyde on 30 June he explained his desire to be restored to the king's favour.[62] Another waverer from the leadership's

60 Bankes, *Corfe Castle*, pp. 122–3, 129–30, 138–9.
61 BL E 202 (14): *A Perfect Diurnal*, 4–11 July, sub 9 July.
62 *LJ* v, 208; G.A. Harrison, 'Royalist Organisation in Wiltshire' (London PhD thesis, 1963), pp. 73–6.

policy was the earl of Manchester. Though aged, ill and bewildered by events, he still attended the Lords. He thought the royal answer to the Nineteen Propositions would 'give great satisfaction to all the world', and bring reconciliation closer.[63]

The peerage were traditionally seen as the monarchy's closest counsellors. Many of them undoubtedly felt a special responsibility to the nation at this time. How was it that every day things appeared more desperate, Lord Wharton asked Bankes, when there were many prominent men at Westminster and at York 'that have public interests in the peace of this kingdom'? In neither case, he was convinced, were they turbulent or disloyal men, so surely they were prudent enough to 'prevent the ruin coming upon us'.[64] The difficulty was to find anyone who was trusted by both Pym and Charles. There was no question once Hyde, Falkland and Culpepper had become identified with the bitter tirades of the paper war of their being acceptable to the parliamentary leadership as mediators.[65]

Sir John Bankes came into the news in May and June because he told friends like Holles, Northumberland, Saye and Wharton before he left London that he intended to speak his mind and make the king struggle with his conscience. He was a man respected for his wisdom and good sense; his nomination in the militia ordinance as lieutenant of the Isle of Purbeck was a mark of the esteem in which he was held.[66] His friends took his cautious refusal to deliver an opinion either way on the legality of the ordinance in good part. Predictably, though, Charles wanted his Chief Justice of Common Pleas at his side and so on 4 May he summoned him to York.[67] In the next weeks his reports were much discussed at Westminster. Not that they brought any immediate joy: 'nothing of certainty' appeared in them Sir John Coke told his father on 24 May.[68]

Bankes's peace initiative did not start well because the king was already offended with him for his failure to protest against the militia ordinance. But many peers were gathering at York during May and Bankes certainly found sympathetic spirits to commune with. More than 30 members of the peerage were there at the beginning of June. Bankes's first move, in conjunction with Hertford and Saville, was an expression of disapproval to the king of the order for all Yorkshiremen charged with horse to attend him on 20 May. He also tried unsuccessfully to get him to countermand the royal order adjourning the Trinity term. The price of disaffection, he quickly realized, was high. 'I am here in a very hard condition where I may be

63 *HMC Buccleuch* I, 299, 307; BL Harl. MS 163, fol. 124r.
64 Bankes, *Corfe Castle*, pp. 132, 147.
65 Wormald, pp. 75–113.
66 Bankes, *Corfe Castle*, pp. 124, 129, 132, 139; *LJ* IV, 623.
67 *HMC 8th Report*, p. 209; *HMC Buccleuch* I, 300.
68 *HMC Coke*, p. 316.

ruined both ways', he wrote on 21 May.[69]

The king's announcement to the assembled peers of his intention to raise his standard at the beginning of June provoked alarm at court. Three men left York, having tried to dissuade him from this course, a few days later.[70] They were Clare, who in August threw in his lot with parliament, Dorset, whose advice was reported to have been very much against the king's expectation, and Salisbury, who told Northumberland in a letter that he valued his conscience above his office of Captain of the Gentleman Pensioners. Salisbury's departure for Hatfield was said to have been 'without any willingness of the king and with very little leave-taking'.[71] How long Bankes still struggled to change the king's mind is not certain but an accommodation campaign of sorts undoubtedly limped on at court until late August. The earls of Cumberland and Lindsey, for instance, petitioned the king to assent to the Nineteen Propositions and return to parliament. Cumberland at one stage was reported to be so disillusioned he was considering abandoning the court.[72]

Lord Saville, who went to York in fulfilment of his oath of office as Treasurer of the Household, was one of the most consistent advocates of peace. He later maintained that he did in fact succeed for a short time in securing the dismissal of the armed guards at York who presented a 'semblance of war' and that he was acting in this case at the prompting of the parliamentary committee led by Howard and Stapleton. He again cooperated with parliamentary emissaries when Holland's peace mission reached Beverley, using 'all his power' to dissuade the king from besieging Hull. He also opposed various recruiting expeditions such as the July visit to Coventry. Saville only abandoned his peace efforts when Charles marched westwards. He regarded this act as ending his obligation to attend the king since he had broken up his household.[73]

The earl of Rutland may also have attempted to influence the king. He was keeping in with both sides. On the one hand he had accepted the lord lieutenancy of Derbyshire in the militia ordinance; on the other he had lent the king his coach for the journey north from Belvoir in March, which brought him gracious thanks. He was at York in early July and there was speculation about his taking a mediatory line.[74] Another peer who would without doubt have liked to bring Charles back from the brink was Lord

69 Bankes, *Corfe Castle*, p. 135; *LJ* v, 74; BL 669 f 6 (26); Clarendon II, 186; Gardiner x, 205.
70 BL E 151 (10): *His Majesty's Resolution concerning the Setting up of his Standard*; Bodleian Tanner MS 63, fol. 43v.
71 *LJ* v, 284; Crummett, p. 348; *HMC Buccleuch* I, 305; *HMC Montagu*, p. 155.
72 BL E 150 (10); *HMC Coke*, p. 316; Crummett, pp. 341–2.
73 J.J. Cartwright, editor, 'Papers relating to the Delinquency of Lord Saville', *Camden Miscellany* VIII (1883), pp. 2–3, 25–6.
74 *HMC Buccleuch* I, 293, 303; *HMC Coke*, p. 319; *HMC Hastings MSS* II, 85; *Derbyshire Archaeological Journal* XCIII (1973), 38–9.

Montagu, but he was too infirm to stir from Boughton. He was in touch with Charles by correspondence and his brother told him of rumours that the king 'takes notice of your affection and some of your expressions'.[75]

The arrival of Holland's delegation at Beverley on 16 July led to a last frenzied effort to change Charles's mind. Hyde's later account is illuminating: the parliamentary messengers persuaded several nobles 'that the king's answer was too sharp and would provoke the Houses, who were naturally passionate, to proceed in the high ways they were in, whereas if the king would abate that severity of language . . . they were confident satisfaction should be given to all that His Majesty proposed.' Holland himself, playing the peacemaker, privately offered to undertake that conciliation would produce a friendly response. The king though would not accept the arguments put to him for withdrawing the preamble to his answer and softening its language.[76]

Yet there were a few who still persevered. On 25 August Charles was persuaded to send a message to parliament which suggested that a committee of an equal number of men chosen by each side should meet at a neutral venue to treat about peace. A few months later Lord Saville claimed that he was responsible for this initiative. The earl of Southampton supported it on the grounds that parliament would reject it, casting themselves in a bad light, and that it was a way of gaining time to strengthen the royalist army. The emissaries were Southampton, Culpepper and the earl of Dorset.[77] Despite the tactical considerations that were certainly involved, this last plea was an authentic expression of that dread of war which many of the nobility at court shared with the peace party at Westminster. 'Heaven prevent these storms', Dorset had written to his close friend the earl of Salisbury on 27 June, 'I am one of those that believe that an easy and safe way may be found to lead us all forth this dark and inextricable labyrinth.'[78]

'All men give not the same advice and when former counsels are rooted other counsels come too late'. With these words in a letter of 21 May, Sir John Bankes summarized the reason for the failure of the accommodation campaign at the court-in-exile.[79] The dominance of the cavaliers was evident almost as soon as the king settled at York. Some 20 Lincolnshire gentlemen lodged in the city on the night of 27 March. They had come peaceably enough with the county's petition pleading for Charles's return to London. But it was coronation day and in the disorder following the

75 *HMC Buccleuch* I, 306.
76 Clarendon II, 231–40; E 202 (21): *A Diurnal and Particular of the last week's Daily Occurrences.*
77 *LJ* V, 327–8; Clarendon II, 299–304; 'Delinquency of Lord Saville' in *Camden Miscellany* VIII (1883), p. 2.
78 Crummett, pp. 350–1.
79 Bankes, *Corfe Castle*, p. 134.

bonfires these roundheads, as they were unjustly called, were forced to defend themselves against a citizen mob set on by the cavaliers.[80] Such behaviour fits with the belligerence shown by individual cavaliers in reported conversations. He hoped the king would set up his standard and maintain his prerogative by force of arms, Colonel Francis Edwards had pronounced in a Covent Garden tavern on 5 March. The king would not 'stand to anything he says', complained Thomas Elliott on 5 May, otherwise 'we should have made an end of the business long since'.[81]

There was much confidence among the cavaliers at York in the summer. They jeered against parliament and talked optimistically about dividing the estates of MPs among themselves. They had the king's ear: 'it is certainly informed the king adhereth to the advice of the cavaliers and totally deserts the counsel of his peers' was the account in one July newsbook.[82] An unusual glimpse of royal decision making is provided by a report from York on 19 July. Colonel Lunsford was 'standing by' when Charles related to Lord Mowbray news which had just arrived of the clashes over the militia in Leicestershire. Mowbray advised he should go there himself and Charles spent much of the night making preparations. Next morning he set out, 'the cavaliers going along with him'.[83]

The attitudes of the combatants were so deeply entrenched that the defeat of the moderates on both sides should cause no surprise. When Sir John Culpepper came with the king's final message on 27 August, the war party divided the Commons on the motion that he should be expelled rather than admitted. They lost this vote but there was no opposition to the leadership view that there could be no treaty until Charles took down his standard. He would very likely yield to this demand, declared Strode at his most scoffing, 'because he can keep up no longer'.[84] Yet hope fed by rumour sustained men against the odds through the spring and summer months. The king would be at Whitehall again that day was the latest gossip, Henry King told a Norfolk correspondent on 12 March. A general intelligence ran through the City on 1 September that Charles had actually come to his parliament, 'the joy of which was unspeakable to the hearts of all and bonfires were made everywhere thereupon'.[85] People were living through a political experience they had never expected and for which they were totally unprepared. When Essex himself took horse at Temple Bar on

80 BL E 143(8): *A True Relation of some Remarkable Passages concerning Nottinghamshire Petition*, p. 4; E 143 (11): *Terrible News from York*; *HMC Coke*, p. 313; *HMC Montagu*, p. 148.
81 BL Harl. MS 163, fol. 124v; *CJ* II, 471; *LJ* v, 180. See also BL E 201 (22): *A Perfect Diurnal*, 28 Feb.–7 March, p. 3.
82 BL E 202 (15): *A Perfect Diurnal*, 4–11 July, p. 4; E 202 (19): *Some Special Passages*, 12–19 July, sub 18 July. See also Add. MS 14827, fol. 163v.
83 BL E 202 (21): *A Diurnal and Particular of the last week's Daily Occurences*.
84 BL Harl. MS 163, fols. 303v–307v; S.R. Gardiner, *History of the Great Civil War* (London, 1897) I, 14.
85 Bodleian Tanner MS 66, fol. 291r; BL E 202 (41): *A Perfect Diurnal*, 29 Aug.–25 Sept., p. 6.

9 September to join the parliamentary army, men's emotions were stirred to awe and wonder. 'God grant his excellency a happy journey', wrote one journalist, 'and give him favour in the eyes of our gracious sovereign that he may return with the olive branch of peace in his mouth.'[86] It was hard to understand or face the nation's slide into war. No one would have believed that once it was begun four years were to pass before it could be ended.

86 BL E 202 (44): *Remarkable Passages or a Perfect Diurnal*, 5–12 Sept., sub 9 Sept.

9

Royalism and Faction

Sir William Croft is much against the parliament and utters his mind freely
. . . . he told Mr Gower he was a mover of sedition . . . . they say the parliament
does their own business and not the country's.

Lady Brilliana Harley to her son Edward,
25 March·1642[1]

Mr Pym: that there be letters come out of Somerset that there is a faction there
to take part with the king against the parliament.

Journal of Framlingham Gawdy,
29 March 1642[2]

The strength of loyalty to parliament demonstrated by the county petitions, taken together with the massive support for peace discussed in the
last chapter, prompts an obvious question. How was it that Charles I
managed to wage war? The origins of royalism have so far only received
brief attention here at the level of parliamentary politics. This chapter is
intended to redress the balance. First it must be stressed that in a real sense
everyone was a royalist in 1641. The deep emotions of loyalty to the king
and the concepts of duty and obedience which rested in the last resort on
the Tudor theory of the godly prince were taken for granted while the king
himself did not appear to be in danger. All the publicity about the year's
politics concentrated on the danger facing parliament. Hence the themes
we have encountered in the petitions. The king's cause against parliament
first roused a response in some provincial minds when his championship of
the Church came to be understood and appreciated. Royalism emerged in
many counties through conservative petitioning campaigns about the
issues of episcopacy and the liturgy. Clergy were active from the start
alongside the gentry. Royalism as a coherent viewpoint, based consciously
on dislike of and opposition to the parliament's political policies and
methods, took longer to crystallize. But an attempt will be made by a series
of case studies to show how it did so. There was a stage in the polarization
of gentry communities, towns and villages which it would be inappropriate
to discuss in terms of royalist and parliamentarian parties since the very

1 *Harley*, p. 121.
2 BL Add. MS 14827, fol. 77v.

idea of such parties was still abhorred. The terms cavalier and roundhead, we have seen, were also still being used loosely and merely abusively. The origins of royalism can best be detected by a study of the factionalism of English society between late 1641 and August 1642.

Map 5 (opposite) shows that petitions in defence of the Church were produced and circulated in at least 22 English counties. There was also a single petition representing the views of the six shires of North Wales. Seven or more of these petitions were on foot before the end of 1641.[3] In a couple of cases counties provided petitions that were evidently based on a common model, but in general these petitions were no more stereotyped than those expressing loyalty to parliament.[4] The organization of them was along familiar lines. Ten Gloucestershire gentlemen gathered at Cirencester on 15 December 1641, for instance, circulated their draft to friends, urged the collection of signatures and notified them about their next meeting.[5] Most of the petitions were sent to the king, who ordered that a number of them should be printed as a collection on 20 May. Their authenticity did not make those that reached Westminster acceptable to the Commons, although sympathetic promoters did manage to get three of them read in the Lords.[6] 'All art is used to keep petitions for episcopacy from being presented to the House', Sir John Coke informed his father.[7]

The essence of the new petitions was the demand for confirmation of those fundamentals – episcopacy and the prayer book – which, in the county of Dorset's words, had served the Church well 'in the purest times of Queen Elizabeth and King James of blessed memory'.[8] The petitioners showed no interest in disputes about whether episcopacy was of human or divine origin; their arguments were based on tradition and achievement. In the first place, the sheer longevity of episcopacy was urged in much the same terms as it had been by MPs in the February 1641 debates.[9] Staffordshire confessed its fears 'that the sudden mutation of a government so long settled, so well known and approved, cannot recompense with any proportionable utility the disturbances and disorders which it may work by novelty'. North Wales found the bishops' antiquity 'a strong argument of

---

3　BL Add. MS 11055, fol. 130v; 29975, fol. 130; E 150 (28): *A Collection of Sundry Petitions*; E 201 (26): *A Continuation of the True Diurnal*, 7–14 March; Bodleian Tanner MS 66, fol. 181; Gloucestershire RO D 2510/14; *HMC Coke*, p. 295; *CSPD 1641–3*, p. 203; *CSPV 1640–2*, p. 242; Larking, pp. 60–2; J.W.F. Hill, editor, 'The Royalist Clergy in Lincolnshire', *Lincolnshire Architectural and Archaeological Society Reports* II (1940), 45, 49, 53–4, 78–9, 81, 85, 106, 108, 109. I am grateful to Professor Clive Holmes for drawing my attention to the last reference.

4　M.J. Mendle in Russell, *Origins*, p. 240.

5　Gloucestershire RO D 2510/13.

6　*LJ* IV, 467, 469, 482; *CJ* II 627; *D'Ewes* (C), p. 290; BL Harl. MS 164, fol. 226v; E 201 (14): *Diurnal Occurrences*, 7–14 Feb., sub 10 Feb.

7　*HMC Coke*, p. 295.

8　BL Add. MS 29975, fol. 130.

9　Rushworth III, part I, 183, 186–7; Nalson II, 298.

Map 5: Counties where petitions in defence of episcopacy and the liturgy were circulated, September 1641–May 1642.

God's special protection'. How could Protestants look papists in the face, asked Surrey, if they cast off a hierarchy held in veneration by ecumenical councils, learned fathers and constant martyrs for 1500 years?[10] The Gloucestershire gentry believed that government of the Church by bishops was the best form 'that any kingdom hath been blest with since the apostles' days'. Rutland was confident that 'Christ did clearly institute a disparity in the clergy.'[11] In short there was much sympathy for the view expressed by Sir Henry Slingsby in his diary that, considering the apostolic origins of episcopacy, 'it were not safe to make alteration from so ancient a beginning.'[12]

Secondly the institution of episcopacy was seen as appropriate for the state and society which it upheld. Several petitions echoed an argument Sir Edward Dering intended to use in the speech he wrote against the Root and Branch bill: 'reason and necessity' justified the bishops, just as a college needed a master, a ship a pilot, an army a general.[13] Herefordshire found episcopacy 'eminently serviceable to this commonwealth, most compatible with the civil government (into the fabric and body of which it is riveted and incorporate) and most apt and easy at all times by the state to be reduced into order'. Rutland was doubtful whether 'any innovated government can or will' subsist with monarchy; they dismissed Presbyterianism, which they took to be the only plausible alternative, out of hand, since it derived its authority 'from divine institution with more confidence, and more immediate derivation than episcopacy, though indeed most vainly as we conceive'. The Bedfordshire and Cheshire petitioners found the prospect of Presbyterianism equally alarming.[14]

Thirdly the petitioners sought to distinguish the faults of particular bishops from the question of the fate of the institution. It was a 'dangerous inference', declared the Bedfordshire petition, 'from personal abuses to conclude the eradication of the function'. There were many accounts of the bishops' positive achievements before and since the Reformation: Bedfordshire stressed 'the benefits to our religion from their piety, fortitude, examples, labours, martyrdoms'; Rutland mentioned their 'campaigns against heresy, their conversion of nations, their performance of miracles, their building of churches and colleges and their example by public acts of piety'. Herefordshire, Huntingdonshire and Staffordshire were among the counties that gave them particular credit for their leadership against popery. Rutland defended the bishops as men who advanced learning, which would be 'discountenanced' by their abolition; some other counties

---

10 BL E 150 (28), pp. 25, 29; E 151(11).
11 BL Add. MS 11055, fol. 130v; E 150 (28), p. 16.
12 *Slingsby*, p. 67.
13 *Dering*, pp. 129, 144.
14 BL E 150 (28), pp. 2, 17, 20, 40; *CSPD 1640–1*, p. 446.

were specially concerned about the preservation of cathedrals, whose revenues provided 'powerful encouragements of industry, learning and piety'.[15]

Horror at the confidence and audacity of sectarians was a main motive for the petitions. Oxfordshire requested the enforcement of the laws against sectaries 'of late dangerously increased among us'. The Kentish assizes petition included a reference to laymen who dared 'to arrogate to themselves and to execute the holy function of the ministry' and demanded action against 'the odious and abominable scandal of schismatical and seditious sermons and pamphlets'. Cornwall spoke of ill-affected pamphlets, 'which fly abroad in such swarms as are able to cloud the pure air of truth and present a dark ignorance to those who have not the two wings of justice and knowledge to fly above them'.[16]

The clearest statements of the anarchic implications of independency came from Huntingdonshire and Surrey. Through the claim by congregations to 'execute ecclesiastical censures within themselves', Huntingdonshire insisted, 'several and contrary opinions will soon grow and arise, whereby great divisions and horrible factions will soon ensue thereupon, to the breach of that union, which is the sacred bond and preservation of the common peace of Church and state.'[17] The Surrey petitioners, appalled by the uncontrolled experimentation of the capital and its environs, were fearful that Root and Branch would fuel the intemperance of the schismatics and embolden them to turn their zeal against the secular and civil power. If there was no power to restrain general discussion of the 'dark and intricate disputes about God's eternal decrees and purposes', there would be an 'open field ready to be sown with hatred and discord':

> The more vehement and popular part overswaying the more temperate and soberly learned, the matter may arise unto that height that either the truth may be deserted and the consciences of men left upon the rack or the contention and tumult wax so great as may cause the whole Church and kingdom not only to sigh and groan but to be put into great hazard of sinking under so great a burden.[18]

But it should be noted that only a minority of the petitions adopted these dramatized terms. Moreover Sir Thomas Aston was alone in echoing the specific point made by men like Strangeways and Waller in the Commons that social hierarchy was at stake.[19]

The argument over the liturgy, like that over episcopacy, reflected deep respect for custom. Ever since the Reformation, declared the Worcester-

---

15 BL E 150 (28), pp. 10, 19, 25, 34, 40; *CSPD 1640–1*, p. 446.
16 BL E 150 (28), pp. 22, 34, 39; *CSPD 1640–1*, p. 446.
17 BL E 150 (28), pp. 11–12.
18 BL E 151 (11).
19 *D'Ewes (N)*, p. 339; BL E 150 (28), p. 3; E 198 (30): *A Speech made by Master Waller*; Morrill, *Cheshire*, pp. 37, 50–1.

shire gentry, they had been 'blessed with a uniform liturgy ratified by law and with general consent received and continued amongst us'. Huntingdonshire recalled the 'great care, piety and sincerity' with which the prayer book had been 'revised and reduced from all former corruptions and Romish superstitions'.[20]

Cheshire, Cornwall, Gloucestershire, Somerset and Worcestershire were among the counties which complained that liturgy had been interrupted, neglected or depraved by those who disliked it. A petition circulated in Southwark included a full account of the way the prayer book was treated in the South Bank suburbs. Some ministers simply mocked it; some of the laity refused baptism, churching or burial according to the rubric and abused ministers who used the prescribed forms so fiercely that they dared no longer do so. The Cornish gentry asked parliament to clarify its policy over the liturgy, 'lest while you hold your peace, some rejecting it in part, other altogether, they vainly conceive you countenance them'. Kent provided a catalogue of the ways in which the fabric of religious life was being destroyed:

> The houses of God are profaned and in part defaced; the ministers of Christ are condemned and despised; the ornaments and many utensils of the church are abused; the liturgy and book of common prayer depraved and neglected; that absolute model of prayer, the Lord's Prayer, vilified; the sacraments of the gospel in some places unduly administered, in other places omitted; solemn days of fasting observed and appointed by private persons; marriages illegally solemnized; burials uncharitably performed.[21]

What is so interesting about these petitions is that, although they show no sympathy for Arminianism, they indicate that an alternative view of the Church from the Puritan one was firmly held by substantial numbers of people in the country. A strong sense of the corporate nature of the Church, something entirely missing in the Puritan agendas, underlies them. Archbishop Laud's concept of worship as solemn, dignified, uncontentious and evocative plays a part here, even if the ritualistic excesses of some of his episcopate had angered conservatives as much as radicals. Many, it has been suggested, were 'bored and repelled by the argumentative austerity of sermon-dominated Puritan services'.[22] The breakdown of order in the Church since November 1640, sketched earlier in this book, brought a reaction into the open in the localities more slowly, but in the end just as forcefully, as it did at Westminster. Under the stress of religious controversy the attachment of many to the forms and institutions of the Elizabethan Church settlement became evident. In late 1641 and 1642

20   *Townshend*, p. 45; BL E 150 (28), p. 10.
21   BL Add. MS 11055, fol. 131r; E 150 (28), p. 14, 21–2, 26, 38; E 151 (11).
22   Kenyon, *Stuart England*, pp. 113–4.

petitioners made it plain that the notion of an Ecclesia Anglicana, which embodied a middle way and was equally resistant to Romish superstition and Genevan innovation, had struck deep roots. Foxeian and Laudian propaganda, in a sense, had fused.[23]

Petitioning clashes over religion occurred in at least 16 counties. Thomas Holt, the minister of All Saints, Stamford in Lincolnshire, persuaded one of the aldermen to summon those who subscribed the county's Root and Branch petition in the town so that he could publicly reprove them and argue the unlawfulness of their action. When he later sent his clerk round the town with a counter-petition in the name of the shire those who refused it were again brought before the alderman. Huntingdonshire episcopalians alleged that the rooters' petition there was 'framed and penned in a close and subtle manner to import more than is first discernable to an ordinary eye'. Bedfordshire conservatives thought that countrymen were 'incapable of apprehending the subtleties and dangerous insinuations' of the Root and Branch petitions.[24] Nottinghamshire episcopalians were charged with gaining hands on the pretext that their petition was simply to abolish altar rails and that parliament desired countrymen to subscribe it.[25] 'Much pains hath been taken to get hands, no matter how foul or mean', reported an observer of the progress of the episcopal petition in Herefordshire to Sir Robert Harley. Villagers were certainly infinitely gullible. Robert Dore, the vicar of Ilsington in Devon, solicited hedgers, ploughmen and threshers to support a petition to uphold episcopacy: 'and some of them being asked what they had done said that now they should have peace for ever more, for these notes were to conclude peace.'[26]

The struggle in Cheshire to speak in the name of the county produced recriminations that lasted at least until the end of 1641. Calvin Bruen maintained that Sir Thomas Aston got signatures in the first place by pretending that he wanted to amend Church government rather than preserve the status quo. Some of the names he obtained, according to Bruen, were of people dead or at sea; others were madmen, children or papists.[27] In November 1641, Robert Hawkshawe deposed at Chester that he had signed a petition for the liturgy a second time and added two additional names.[28] Two other counties where feelings ran particularly high were Gloucestershire and Oxfordshire. John Smyth of Nibley in Gloucestershire, an enthusiastic organizer of the conservative petition in his district,

23 Lamont, *Godly Rule*, pp. 1–77.
24 BL E 150 (28), p. 9; *CSPD 1640–1*, p. 445; *Lincolnshire Architectural and Archaeological Society Reports* II (1940), 79, 84–5.
25 *D'Ewes (C)*, pp. 290–1.
26 BL Loan MS 29/173, fol. 106v; *Buller*, pp. 33–4.
27 BL Harl. 163, fol. 69r; 164, fol. 1012r; 478, fol. 604r; Add. MS 33936, fol. 232; 36914, fols. 210–11; *CJ* II, 123, 126.
28 Bodleian Dep C MS 165, no. 28.

wrote of the 'pulpit discourses' against the petitioners 'by the name of papists, common drunkards, base and lewd livers'. Some Puritan clerics there, it seems, were keeping the names of those who signed in the hope of calling them to account.[29] Across the other side of the county at Tewkesbury, the bailiffs bound to good behaviour a man who complained to them about being approached by those who sought to vilify parliament.[30] Oxfordshire became rent with discord when Sir William Walter, who had stood unsuccessfully for a knightship of the shire, challenged the hegemony of the Fiennes family with a conservative petition which he had had printed at Oxford. John Fiennes took offence at Walter's 'great labouring to raise a faction'.[31] When Walter appeared before the Commons on 17 March, MPs were not satisfied with his excuses that what he did was 'for the good of the whole county' and that only the hands of those 'ready and willing' were taken.[32] In this instance differences of view over the Church exacerbated a long-standing personal feud.

Many of the conservative petitions claimed huge totals of signatures: the six shires of North Wales led with 30,000 followed by Somerset with 14,350, Cheshire, Devon and Nottinghamshire with more than 6,000 apiece.[33] The explanation for these dramatic affirmations of support probably lies in the role of the clergy, who wooed the people from the pulpit and in the streets. D'Ewes's brother-in-law related from Surrey how his minister had pressed him so hard for his reasons for refusing to support an episcopal petition that 'some coarse language passed between us'.[34] There were two parties in enmity with the Church, William Clarke, a minor canon of Chester, told the cathedral audience there in November 1641: on the one hand the papists, on the other hand the Puritans, like Samson's foxes with firebrands in their tails.[35] The vicar of Ellaston in Staffordshire cried out against a parishioner who subscribed a petition sympathetic to parliament as a 'Puritan, roundhead and fool'.[36]

Catholic refusals of the Protestation in such areas as Lancashire and Sussex were predictable, but the extent of opposition among the conformist clergy is more surprising.[37] It shows the mark left by the controversy

---

29 G.A. Harrison, 'Royalist Organisation in Gloucestershire and Bristol' (Manchester University MA thesis, 1961), p. 31.
30 BL Harl. MS 162, fol. 394r; *HMC 5th Report*, p. 345.
31 BL Harl. MS 163, fols. 24r, 50r; E 150 (28), p. 36; E 201 (23): *A Perfect Diurnal* 7–14 March 1642; *CJ* II, 471, 499; Keeler, pp. 59–60.
32 BL E 201 (30): *A Continuation of a True Diurnal*, 14–21 March, p. 78.
33 BL E 150 (28), pp. 3, 9, 14, 24, 27.
34 BL Harl. MS 383, fol. 197.
35 Bodleian Dep C MS 165, nos. 28–31.
36 Johnson and Vaisey, editors, *Staffordshire and the Great Rebellion*, p. 42.
37 BL Harl. MS 163, fol. 21r; *Sussex*, p. 99; *HMC 5th Report*, pp. 127, 134; HLRO, Main Papers, Yorkshire protestation returns, Agbrigg wapentake; Bodleian Tanner MS 66, fol. 239r;

over Burton's *Protestation Protested*. In Lincolnshire two clerics refused to take the oath.[38] In Northamptonshire a curate pronounced that there was much in it 'contrary to a good conscience'. At Hardingham in Norfolk, Nathaniel Flick preached against it 'terming it the covenant' and condemned those who took it for acting 'against the king's prerogative'.[39] At St Paul's a Cambridge cleric argued that, though intended to a good purpose, the Protestation was 'converted to treasonable ends'.[40] At Muggleswick in Durham the minister affirmed before the congregation that it was false.[41] There was even one minister in Warwickshire who presented the JPs with his personal rewording of parliament's manifesto, which included his resolution to maintain parliament's privileges 'so far as I am, or shall be, rightly informed what they are'.[42]

By their activities in furthering petitions and resisting the Protestation clergy were preparing the ground for their main role in 1642 as the storm-troopers of the king's cause in the localities. So much attention has been given to two minorities among the clergy, the Arminians and the Puritans, that it tends to be forgotten that the clergy as a whole were a conformable body of men trained in a conservative academic mode and preoccupied by day-to-day pastoral work. They felt threatened by everything they heard about the proceedings of the Long Parliament and had no hesitation in looking to the leadership the king offered.[43] Between March and October numerous clergy read royal declarations from the pulpits and incited the people to resist parliament. The vicar of Cople in Bedfordshire, for instance, reminded his parishioners in July, after reading a missive from York, that scripture bade men obey the king but there was no scripture commanding them to obey parliament.[44] The minister of Boxted in Suffolk, Frederick Gibb, held meetings at shops and on village greens to expound the monarchical viewpoint and was instrumental in publishing the proclamation against levies without the king's consent in four villages.[45] The attempt by the minister of Coversey in Cambridgeshire to

---

Holmes, editor, *Suffolk Committees for Scandalous Ministers*, p. 37.

38 I am grateful to Professor Clive Holmes for this information.

39 BL Add. MS 14827, fol. 52r; E 201 (30): *A Continuation of a True Diurnal*, 14–21 March, p. 76; *CJ* II, 455.

40 BL Add. MS 14827, fol. 105r.

41 BL 669 f 4 (69): *A Most Lamentable Information*; M.E. James, *Family, Lineage and Civil Society* (Oxford, 1974), pp. 129–32.

42 HLRO, Main Papers, 29 March 1642: Petition of Christopher Harvey.

43 I am most grateful to Dr Ian Green for letting me see his forthcoming article in *Past and Present*, 'Career Prospects and Clerical Conformity in the Early Stuart Church', in which he makes this case.

44 E.g. *CJ* II 455, 581, 608, 654, 665, 673, 677, 683, 686, 659–6, 702, *LJ* IV, 715; *HMC 5th Report*, p. 33; *HMC Various Collections* I 320–1; Bodleian Tanner MS 63, fol. 21; Holmes, p. 35; *Sussex*, pp. 256–7; BL E 202 (25): *Some Special Passages*, 18–26 July.

45 Bodleian Dep C MS 165, no. 72; BL Harl. MS 163, fol. 285v; *CJ* II, 684; A.G. Matthews, *Walker Revised* (Oxford, 1948), p. 335.

have the earl of Essex proclaimed a traitor in Ely market place succeeded after an appeal to the Bench, despite the efforts of the mayor to prevent him.[46]

The pulpit propaganda of royalist clergymen ranged from instruction in the duties of a subject to crude abuse of the men at Westminster. Christopher Smith insisted in a sermon at Deeping St James in Lincolnshire that it was treason to obey any order of parliament which did not carry Charles's hand and seal.[47] At the Launceston assizes in August, Nicholas Hatch prayed publicly for his royalist patron Lord Mohun and then declared that 'the militia was in the king'. He tried to prove his point, the committee of MPs present related, 'with some rotten stories that are too troublesome to write'. Edward Jeffery preceded his sermon at Southminster in Essex on 14 August with a prayer for the bishops, 'the foundation and pillars of truth'. He preached a high doctrine of royal authority: 'the king hath not only power to command all your persons, but also power to take away your goods at his pleasure.'[48] About the same time Paul Gosnall, at Bradfield St Clare in Suffolk, offered prayers for the success of the royal forces 'and that those which took up arms against them, their arms might rot from their shoulders'.[49] Many urged parishioners to contribute generously to the royal cause, some of them with promises of the favour they would receive later if they did so.[50]

In certain counties activists made systematic use of the talents of the clergy who were sympathetic to the the king's cause. Sheriffs burdened godly ministers with a declaration against the militia ordinance, it was alleged in the Commons on 6 July, 'and forced them to read it in their churches, that it grew to be almost as great a snare as the Book of Sports had been.' It was much remarked upon during June that 23 ministers accompanied Henry Hastings on his recruiting campaign in Leicestershire.[51] The clergy were very active in Herefordshire and also in Cheshire, where the commissioners of array directed them in July to publish the royal commands and warrants on threat of expulsion from their benefices.[52]

Besides being based on dislike of its religious radicalism, the case against the parliamentary leadership in 1641 rested on the charges of ambition, factionalism and manipulation of business and on scepticism about the

---

46 A. Kingston, *East Anglia and the Great Civil War* (1897), pp. 53–4.
47 *CJ* II, 581, 608; Hill, p. 85; Matthews, editor, *Walker Revised*, p. 257.
48 *LJ* v, 275; Bodleian Dep C MS 165, no. 90.
49 Holmes, editor, *Suffolk Committees for Scandalous Ministers*, p. 28.
50 BL Loan MS 29/174, fol. 293v; E 112 (36): *A True Relation of Certain Passages*; E 202 (25): *Some Special Passages*, 18–26 July.
51 BL Harl. MS 163, fol. 152r; Hill, p. 107.
52 *HMC Portland* I, 43–5; see also BL E 151 (18): *A Relation of the Last Week's Passage in York and Hull;* J. Webb, *Memorials of the Civil War in Herefordshire* (1879) I, 93; Hutton pp. 16–17.

truth of the popish plot. To some extent the king, his sympathizers in the Commons like Hyde and Culpepper and those sections of the populace who engaged in street libels and abusive talk came to share a common view of their new parliamentary masters. Yet in 1641 the various strands in the royalist view of the incipient rebellion still ran apart. In 1642, allowing for the greater sophistication with which. educated men expressed it, the coherence of this view and its hold on supporters of the king at all levels of society became plain. Charles himself never doubted that the conspiracy against the crown which he had first detected in 1628 had reached fruition. After a serious attempt in March to plead for accommodation from the king's standpoint, Hyde seems to have adopted his view.[53] In the royal reply to parliament's declaration of 26 May about Hull, the moderate royalists spoke in the king's language of a 'faction of malignant, schismatical and ambitious persons whose design is and always hath been to alter the whole frame of government, both of Church and state, and to subject both king and people to their own lawless arbitrary power and government'.[54] As gossip proliferated certain themes which cropped up consistently became the starting points of popular royalism. The parliament had never been universally popular. Even before it opened it was slandered as 'a company of Puritan rascals, base fellows and base scabs'.[55] A Northamptonshire minister had expressed the opinion in January 1641 that 'parliaments in England never did good nor never would but that his hogs were fit to make parliament men of.'[56] By 1642 accusations that the country was being cozened by 'Puritanly rogues and roundheads' had become the common coin of town and village recriminations.[57] Many, predictably, continued to fasten their attention on Pym. Some were saying in February 1642 that the king's charge of treason made it lawful for any man to kill him. One man the following month told his tavern audience he 'could find it in his heart to cut King Pym in pieces'.[58] The story that he was penniless when the parliament assembled circulated widely. Since then he was alleged to have received sugarloaves as bribes to the value of around £700.[59]

The notion spread that all the parliamentary leaders were lacking substance and good sense. Boys, giddy-headed people, dogs and asses were among the terms applied to them.[60] The 20 most prominent MPs, one

53 Wormald, pp. 77–119.
54 Rushworth III, part I, 588.
55 *HMC Portland* III, 70.
56 *D'Ewes (N)*, p. 270.
57 Bodleian Dep C MS 165, no. 182; *CJ* II, 427; BL Harl. MS 163, fol. 99r; Essex RO Transcript 387: Information of Robert Meanes.
58 *CJ* II, 409, 450, 478, 651; see also BL Harl. MS 162, fol. 381v.
59 *LJ* v, 181; Bodleian Tanner MS 63, fol. 81r.
60 *LJ* v, 156; *CJ* II, 478, 534; BL Harl. MS 163, fol. 65r.

minister observed, were not worth 20 pence apiece; Pym himself, maintained another, was 'neither a scholar or a gentleman'.[61] Several peers attracted caustic abuse. A Londoner derided Warwick and Essex in August, vowing he would kill the latter wherever he met him. In September a Suffolk man called the earl of Pembroke a 'base lousy rogue and a pedlar'.[62]

> One cuckold, two bastards and a pack of knaves
> Strive to make subjects princes and princes slaves.

This couplet was going the rounds in East Anglia, with Essex reputed the cuckold and Holland and Warwick the bastards 'for their mother was a whore'.[63] An altercation between a Dorset man and a party of Somerset gentlemen he met on the road in August shows that, though the gentry were less ready to be scurrilous about men from their own class, they too saw the nation's troubles in personal terms. Lord Poulett, Sir John Stawell and Sir Ralph Hopton were among those present on this occasion. Asked which side he would take, the Dorset man said both, which they accepted, but when he confessed to knowing Sir Walter Earle he received a sharp reproof: 'then quoth the gentlemen thou knowest a rogue and a round-headed rogue and one that hath been the chief raiser of these combustions amongst us.'[64]

The supposed ambitions of Pym's clique became connected in men's minds with the idea of their self-interest. There was a story current in Colchester that Harbottle Grimston, the town's MP, could not buy the house he lived in without his father's help in 1640, but since then he had made £700 a year. One of the town's weavers spread the view that the members sat merely 'for their own ends to enrich themselves'.[65] A Canterbury cleric warned that Pym and his friends sought to defraud the people of their money.[66] An Ipswich man declared in August that they intended to run away with what money they could get 'when they have done'.[67] Richard Pauling, the rector of Wallingford, told his congregation about the same time that the parliamentary leaders were men of broken fortunes 'who have spent their means lewdly and cannot subsist but by this way of rebellion'.[68]

61 BL Add. MS 14827, fol. 77r; Harl. MS 162, fol. 381v.
62 BL E 202 (40): *A Perfect Diurnal*, 22–29 Aug., sub 22 Aug.; HLRO, Main Papers, 12 September 1642: Information of Samuel Crossman.
63 BL Harl. MS 163, fol. 88r; Bodleian Dep C MS 165, no. 82.
64 BL E 202 (41): *A Perfect Diurnal*, 29 Aug.–5 Sept., p. 2.
65 Essex RO Transcript 387.
66 HLRO Main Papers, 6 Aug. 1642: Petition of John Marston.
67 BL E 202 (37): *A Perfect Diurnal*, 8–15 Aug., p. 7.
68 Bodleian Dep C MS 165, no. 99.

Bullying and intimidation were widely seen as the characteristics of Pym's management. A Sidmouth man spoke of the leadership's 'new tricks and laws', a Huntingdon JP of how he had been convinced by the way parliament had set about its task that things would be no better.[69] There was a growing unanimity, in fact, between a section of the gentry and people that the methods and aims of Pym's faction threatened both order and fair government. The Colchester weaver cited above summarized the state of affairs in the Church: 'the king stands to maintain but one religion', whereas parliament 'stood to maintain all religions, Arminians, Brownists, Anabaptists and freewillers'.[70] Sir George Benion accused parliament of setting up an arbitrary power, which because it was exercised by 400 men would be worse than any arbitrary action Charles had attempted.[71] Sir Roger Twysden made the same political indictment: the people chose knights and burgesses 'with an intent to redress their grievances by laws and not to be absolutely the lords and masters of their judgements, as well in what is amiss, as obedience to the laws they shall establish.'[72]

Popular affirmations tended to be more colourful and dramatic than Benion's or Twysden's sober conclusions, but the notion that Pym's men sought permanently to alter the balance of the constitution was the common theme at both levels. 'If the king should go to the parliament', declared a Norwich man in a drinking circle at the Turkey Cock on 24 August, 'they would take away his prerogative and commit him to prison and take off his head.' The company had just drunk a health to the king and confusion to 'factious Pym'.[73] There were stories passed round in the summer of 1642 of Charles being fetched to London dead or alive, of his being kept in the Tower as a titular king, of the coronation of the duke of York in his place, of intentions to depose him and establish a form of government on the Dutch model.[74]

No single item better captures the spirit of all this criticism and popular ribaldry than the verses circulating in Staffordshire which came to the attention of the JPs there:

Change places Charles, put thou on Pym's grave gown
Whilst he in the Upper House doth wear thy crown
Let him be king awhile and be thou Pym
Then we'll adore thee as we now do him
And hang up bishops who so proudly strive

---

69 Andriette, pp. 53. 197; *CJ* II, 386, 409.
70 Essex RO Transcript 387.
71 BL Add. MS 14827, fol. 76v.
72 *Twysden*, p. 205.
73 Bodleian Dep C MS 153, no. 45.
74 *HMC 5th Report*, p. 439; BL Add. MS 14827, fol. 145v; *LJ* v, 226; Bodleian Tanner MS 63, fol. 81r.

To advance their own and their prerogative
And be content since roundheads call them Romans
To have some traitors in the House of Commons
Let us do what we list and thou shalt see
We'll all be kings as well as Pym and thee.

Framlingham Gawdy, no doubt accurately, dismissed these couplets as another libel against Pym.[75] But their equation of authority and might and the menace of the final line tells us much about why there was such a groundswell of opinion moving in the king's favour which he could exploit by publicity and propaganda.

The king's official printer, Robert Barker, was active in producing broadside versions of the various messages to parliament before he went north.[76] There was then a constant flow of items from his press at York – 73 original ones have been identified – and he was equally busy when he moved to Shrewsbury at the end of September.[77] Systematic circulation of royal propaganda by sheriffs was begun in some counties such as Herefordshire and Northamptonshire during February. But it was not until June that the campaign was in full swing. 'I pray you send us nothing that is printed at York for we have enough of them', wrote a correspondent from there that month.[78] Seven proclamations, all of them available in broadside form, became the basis of the king's effort to woo his gentry and countrymen. The first four, issued on 27 May, 18 and 20 June and 4 July respectively, all dealt with aspects of the militia issue. On 8 July Charles announced his intention of waging war on Sir John Hotham in Hull, while disclaiming any plans to fight parliament; on 9 August he declared Essex a traitor; on 12 August he proclaimed the raising of his standard at Nottingham ten days later. Throughout these proclamations as well as the longer argumentative pieces of the summer, Pym and his followers were painted as a clique inspired to mischievous designs against the peace of the kingdom and identified with such celebrated rebels as Wat Tyler, Jack Cade and Robert Kett.[79]

The propaganda campaign was efficiently organized. The Lord Mayor of London received 18 copies of the proclamation against seizing or removing magazines and 38 copies of the one about Hull. A man was arrested in Ware on 14 August for nailing up the proclamation against Essex during 'sermon time'. He was found to be carrying a cloak bag full of

75   Bodleian Dep C MS 164, nos. 11–12; BL Add. MS 14827, fol. 86r; *CJ* II, 548–9.
76   Steele, nos. 1946, 1977, 1988, 2017, 2029, 2039.
77   *Fairfax* II, 390; L. Hanson, 'The King's Printer at York and Shrewsbury 1642–3', *The Library* XXIII (1943), 129–31.
78   *HMC Portland* III, 84; *CJ* II, 480; BL E 151 (18): *A Relation of the Last Week's Passage in York and Hull.*
79   Steele, nos. 2150, 2186, 2194, 2208, 2216, 2242, 2244; *LJ* V, 112.

proclamations, letters and commissions of array and he confessed that he had already delivered proclamations at Lincoln, Boston and Cambridge.[80] Copies of the proclamations or notes of their having been received crop up in many county and borough archives.[81] Many local officers must have unhesitatingly obeyed the directions they received to promulgate the royal orders.[82] No one else seems to have had the courage of the sheriff of Essex, who simply presented the whole bundle he had received to the Commons.[83] Some though did hesitate: the under-sheriff of Middlesex kept the proclamation against the militia ordinance by him four days before he was 'at last so terrified that he read it'.[84] Others, like the mayor of Exeter and the sheriff of Hampshire, bought time by requesting parliament's views about their duty. A Berkshire high constable, ingeniously, hedged his bets by distributing copies of the deputy lieutenants' warrants under the militia ordinance together with the royal proclamations about the commissions of array.[85]

Wherever royal policy was openly pursued tensions simmering beneath the surface of local life were liable to come into the open.[86] During March a number of sheriffs tried to enforce the reading in parish churches of the very lengthy book of petitions and messages between the king and parliament over the militia. But at least two had difficulties in doing so. The constable of Southampton flatly refused to obey the sheriff. The constable of Wilby in Northamptonshire, incredulous about what was expected of him, sought an interview with Sir William Wilmore and told him he dared not publish the book without the consent of parliament. 'The king must be obeyed for all the parliament', Wilmore told him, threatening to send him to gaol for his disobedience.[87] One of Sir Richard Gurney's last acts of defiance was to have the commission of array proclaimed in the City on 10 June. When the sheriffs acting on his orders attempted to follow this up by reading the king's proclamation against raising forces a few days later, they were knocked off their horses by angry citizens.[88] A party of Reading townsmen thrust parliament's declaration against the commission of array into the hands of the deputy mayor as he was about to read the royal proclamations, but he told them stoutly 'he would take no notice of it nor of

80 *HMC 5th Report*, pp. 35, 37; E 239 (9): *A Perfect Diurnal*, 15–22 Aug.; Kingston, *Hertfordshire in the Civil War*, p. 18.
81 E.g. Gloucestershire RO GBR 1396/1501, fol. 178r; Derbyshire RO Chandos-Pole-Gell MSS 60/72; *HMC Kenyon MSS*, p. 61.
82 *HMC Portland* I, 47; III, 94; *CJ* II, 622, 681, 700, 787; Kingston, *Hertfordshire in the Civil War*, p. 14.
83 *CJ* II, 626.
84 BL Harl. MS 163, fol. 277v; *CJ* II, 683.
85 *LJ* v, 154; *HMC Buccleuch* I 296; *CJ* II, 670.
86 E.g. *CJ* II, 576; *Sussex*, p. 258.
87 BL E 201 (27): *A Perfect Diurnal*, 14–21 March, p. 5; *LJ* IV, 704; *CJ* II, 480.
88 *CJ* II, 657; Fortescue, *Catalogue of the Thomason Collection*, p. 122; Pearl, p. 155.

anything else that came from the House.'[89]

The king's systematic remodelling of the commissions of the peace was an important aspect of his propaganda offensive. Details of the changes he made in the composition of 14 Benches between 10 June and 7 August are recorded in the Crown Office docket book: 177 men were purged, 154 were added.[90] But the totals were much higher because appointments and dismissals on at least eight other Benches were never entered. Among these Kent lost 15 JPs, Yorkshire 20 and Northamptonshire all the deputy lieutenants named in the militia ordinance, while the Monmouthshire Bench was filled with dependents, men of 'mean condition', of the earl of Worcester.[91] The king's intelligence was good. 'I pray ask the opinion of your noble father concerning the list I showed you as well for putting out as in', wrote Sir Christopher Hatton, his agent in Northamptonshire, to a sympathetic neighbour, Sir Justinian Isham, on 5 June.[92] Besides well known antagonists like Earle, Holles, Ludlow, Marten and Vane, many others went out who had begun to or were about to show their hand on behalf of parliament: Sir William Masham and Sir Martin Lumley in Essex, for instance, Sir Richard Onslow in Surrey, Sir Edward Hungerford and Sir John Evelyn in Wiltshire. The 18 peers who suffered exclusion in one or more counties were all predictable victims, men who had stayed away from York and in many cases run with the leadership at Westminster.

Control of the commissions of the peace was an asset that parliament could ill do without. Since November 1640 members had been able to procure the removal of certain objectionable men in their counties and the appointment of some who were enthusiastic supporters of the reforms in progress.[93] The seriousness with which the leadership viewed the king's initiative is indicated by the appointment of a committee on 23 August to investigate it which included all the lawyers of the House.[94] But, with the Lord Keeper at the king's side, there was nothing parliament could do. Both in practical and in psychological terms, Charles had struck a shrewd blow to gentry communities that were striving to maintain unity and sound government in face of creeping disorder. In Sussex, for example, five of the most stalwart JPs in the east of the shire were replaced by men

---

89 *CJ* II, 670.
90 PRO C 231/5, fols. 527–36.
91 BL Harl. MS 164, fol. 260r; E 112 (9): *Petition of Suffolk to the King*; E 202 (12): *Some Special Passages*, 3–10 July; E 202 (15): *A Perfect Diurnal*, 4–11 July, p. 3; E 202 (23): *A Perfect Diurnal*, 18–25 July; E 239 (5): *A Perfect Diurnal*, 8–15 Aug.; *HMC Buccleuch* I, 306; *HMC Portland* III, 89; Webb, *Herefordshire in the Civil War* I, 104; Harrison, 'Royalist Organisation in Wiltshire', p. 439.
92 Northamptonshire RO Isham correspondence 243.
93 E.g. Hutchinson, pp. 53–4; *CJ* II, 409, 573.
94 *CJ* II, 738.

Map 6: Counties whose commissions of the peace were remodelled by the king, June–August 1642.

who were inexperienced in local administration.[95] The outcry was immediate. Factionalism was undoubtedly exacerbated. The grand jury of Hampshire told the king that their fears were increased by the displacement of many of the most 'worthy, faithful and able' gentlemen to whom they looked for support of 'our religion and laws' and 'maintenance of our peace'. The chief constables of Suffolk complained to those JPs who were still able to sit on 30 July about the dismissal of 'so many gentlemen of known abilities and integrity, without any fault of theirs that we know of or can imagine'.[96] Many in Yorkshire who sympathized with parliament were bitter about the expulsion of men 'well affected to religion and the commonwealth' like Sir Thomas Fairfax, George Marwood and Thomas Stockdale.[97] The restoration of all JPs removed from their places since April 1642 became an article of the abortive treaty of Oxford negotiations in 1643.[98]

The king knew very well that his best chance of influencing large numbers of people would come with the summer assizes, when gentry and freeholders flocked to county capitals for business and gossip, political discussion and social intercourse. So on 4 July he issued an open letter to the judges going on circuit which set out the royal stance and invited petitions in reply from grand juries, as long as they were penned 'in a humble and fitting way'. Charles had four main points. First, he reiterated his resolve to maintain Protestantism 'in its purity, without declining either to the right hand or to the left'. The judges should give special attention to the suppression of popery and the 'overhasty growth of Anabaptism and other schisms'. Secondly he stressed his determination to govern according to the law rather than in an arbitrary way: he would uphold parliament's privileges 'as far as may stand with the justice which we owe to our crown and the honour thereof'. Thirdly he directed the judges to suppress all riots and unlawful assemblies. Finally he told them to maintain order by seeing that rogues were apprehended and watch and ward was strictly kept, since the conditions of the times encouraged the unruly 'under hope of immunity, as far as they dare, to make a prey of our good subjects'.[99] There has perhaps been a tendency to ascribe the emergence of royalist sentiment too generally to an actual rather than hypothetical collapse of order in the summer of 1642, but the force of the king's final point could not possibly be lost on gentry in counties such as Berkshire, Essex and Lincolnshire

95 *Sussex*, pp. 257–8, 352–4.
96 BL E 112 (9): *Two Petitions*, pp. 4, 7.
97 BL E 107 (12): *An Extract of all passages from Hull, York and Lincolnshire*, E 112 (27): *Militia Old and New*, 669 f 6 (44): *News from York*.
98 Rushworth III, part II, 167.
99 *CSPD 1641–3*, pp. 349–50; J.S. Cockburn, *A History of English Assizes 1558–1714* (Cambridge, 1972), p. 239.

where forest and enclosure troubles were still rampant.[100]

Parliament's retaliation was to order the assize judges to read the Commons resolution that the commissions of array were illegal.[101] But the king certainly got the better of this battle. Sir Robert Foster on the western circuit did announce the parliamentary vote but he forbore to deliver an opinion of his own in the matter. Sir Thomas Malet refused to obey parliament's instructions at Maidstone and was subsequently arrested while sitting at Kingston. He had opened his circuit in Essex with a strong speech against the militia ordinance. Sir Edward Henden ignored the Westminster directions on the Oxford circuit and was impeached.[102] Sir Robert Heath made a speech arguing the legality of the commissions of array at York. There is some evidence that judges attempted to influence the composition of the grand juries so they would look favourably on the king's missive. Heath 'viewed and corrected' the panel presented by the sheriff at York the night before the assizes opened.[103] Brilliana Harley was told that Henden removed a man from the grand jury at Hereford, after whisperings in his ear by Walter Brabazon and Sir William Croft.[104] Parliament also failed to get Henden to ask the JPs and grand jury to disavow a royalist petition from Herefordshire which was circulating in London.[105]

'I found a very plausible acceptance and expression of much joy and contentment.' Foster's report to Secretary Nicholas on the reception of the king's letter in the west suggests that the point was generally taken that he desired a return to order. The Somerset grand jury's demand for the confinement of popish recusants also chimed in well with Charles's declared religious policy.[106] But it was in Kent and East Anglia rather than the west that the letter had its most heartwarming impact. In both Essex and Suffolk a hesitant group of royalist gentry were emboldened in July 1642 to declare their loyalty. The extent of support on the Bench for the Suffolk petition is uncertain but the Essex petition was signed by 25 JPs and six of the grand jury.[107] In both cases the petitioners promised to assist the king with their 'lives and fortunes'.[108] Here, in unpromising country, was a sign of the positive, even belligerent, royalism that the king needed to sustain his cause. But a newsbook, noting Sir Thomas Barrington's cross-petition to parliament in Essex, reported that the immediate outcome was

100 Manning, pp. 46–70; Morrill, *Revolt*, pp. 34–6.
101 *CJ* II, 685–6.
102 *CJ* II, 778; *CSPD 1641–3*, pp. 358–76; Cockburn, *English Assizes*, p. 239; BL E 202 (23): *A Perfect Diurnal*, 18–25 July; E 202 (37): *A Perfect Diurnal*, 8–15 Aug.; Harl. MS 164, fol. 260r; *LJ* v, 275.
103 BL E 107 (12); E 114 (36): *Special Passages*, 23–30 Aug.; *LJ* v, 303.
104 *HMC Portland*, III, 95.
105 *CJ* II, 694.
106 *CSPD 1641–3*, p. 375; Cockburn, *English Assizes*, p, 240.
107 BL Egerton MS 2651, fol. 118; Bodleian Tanner MS 66, fol. 110.
108 Holmes, pp. 41, 48 was mistaken on this point.

'much disturbance in the county'.[109]

A series of case studies will provide a broader perspective on the royalist standpoint and emphasize its coherence. The seven counties that have been chosen all reveal some kind of factional pattern in gentry circles. Cornwall, Herefordshire, Kent, Lincolnshire, Nottinghamshire, Somerset and Yorkshire were not necessarily the most royalist counties in the period from March to September 1642, but they are the counties in which the process through which royalism emerged is easiest to trace. The university towns and certain cathedral cities can be discussed in the same context, because their long-established patterns of urban factionalism make their politics peculiarly interesting.

In two counties – Herefordshire and Nottinghamshire – an incipient ideological split between the parliamentary delegation and a group of gentry at home gave impetus to factional division. In March and April 1642 nine leading Herefordshire JPs engaged in lengthy and acrimonious correspondence with Sir Robert Harley. His fellow knight of the shire was Humphrey Coningsby, a mere youth who had been elected against Harley's candidate to replace his father in November 1641.[110] Coningsby's role in the affair was negligible. Harley on the other hand was a formidable antagonist.[111] The JPs involved included Walter Brabazon, an enemy of the Puritan minister of Leominster John Tombes, Sir William Croft and that paragon of High Anglicanism Viscount Scudamore.[112]

The first hint that all was not well in the relationship between Harley and this gentry caucus came in February 1642, when the sheriff reported that the JPs were 'very cold' in assisting him to carry out the House's orders for securing the county and its magazine.[113] Meeting at Hereford on 5 March, the JPs penned a full account of their views which, they claimed, leaving aside 'an inconsiderable party of recusants of both kinds', were representative of the shire as a whole. Their main point was that the Protestation was not apparently intended to be a voluntary act, yet they did not know by what authority it was to be taken. They considered it needful that each individual should have the liberty to interpret the Protestation for himself, 'especially in the point of power and privilege of parliaments, whereof we may without shame confess our ignorance, since it hath of late raised questions between His Majesty and both Houses and between the Houses themselves'. This veiled attack on the arbitrary proceedings of parliament was joined with a reference to the conciliatory messages which

109 BL E 202 (23): *A Perfect Diurnal*, 18–25 July.
110 Keeler, p. 140.
111 For Harley's career see G.E. Aylmer, *The King's Servants* (London, 1961), pp. 372–9.
112 For Scudamore see G.E. Aylmer, 'Who was Ruling in Herefordshire from 1645 to 1661?' *Transactions of the Woolhope Naturalists Field Club* XL (1972), 375; for Brabazon and Tombes see *HMC Portland*, III, 76; Baker, editor, *The Church in Town and Countryside*, pp. 296–7.
113 *HMC Portland*, III, 84.

sprang from the king's 'great goodness' and a confident, but probably deliberately naive, statement that the nation's differences 'we conceive to our great comfort, are happily composed'. Finally the JPs defended the status quo in the Church, attacking both papists and sectaries. The distrust they felt for their representatives at Westminster is indicated by the most startling item in the letter, a request for a bill to reform parliamentary elections and provide means for knights and burgesses 'more diligently hereafter to attend that service in discharge of the great trust reposed in them'.[114] Never had the demand for accountability been so stridently expressed.

Harley's reply on 18 March was icily polite but wholly unyielding. Disavowing any desire to enter dispute, 'which would heighten the discourse but it may be lessen the satisfaction', he nevertheless treated his correspondents to a lecture on the care which parliament was devoting to its responsibilities. The constitution, Harley told them, 'is resolved into the prudential power of parliament, composed upon the three estates' and if any one of them

> either neglect his office or withold his influence, symptoms of ruin will quickly appear and the crisis of this great body will extremely be endangered. If any such prognostics now show themselves, it will be all our wisdoms to study the means of cure and humbly beseech the God of heaven to add virtual application to our endeavours, wherein we should not take up discontent but on very good grounds.

The Herefordshire justices, in other words, should remember their place. The Commons, Harley warned them, both haughtily and knowingly, might regard their letter 'as a character of disaffection to parliament's proceedings, especially if there should come a petition out of that county freely to avow the Protestation, which your letter seems so warily to decline'.[115]

A petition of loyalty to parliament had in fact been drawn up at John Tombes's home in Leominster on 4 March.[116] The circulation of this petition during the following weeks by Harley allies like Stanley Gower and the sheriff Isaac Seward brought a spirit of bitterness to the county. Sir William Croft, the assertive leader of the royalist faction, called Gower a 'mover of sedition' and engaged in hot dispute with a cousin of the Harleys.[117] To Lady Brilliana's dismay, his long-established friendship with the Harleys withered in the storm of political controversy: 'he never asked how your father did, spoke slightly and stayed but little', she

114 BL Loan MS 29/173, fols. 227v–229r; Hirst, p. 185.
115 Shropshire RO 212/Box 364.
116 BL Loan MS 29/173, fol. 226r.
117 *Harley*, p. 121; see the epigraph to this chapter.

reported to her son after Croft had paid her a call in June.[118]

On 28 April the JPs met to formulate another letter to Harley. Its angry tone reflected the tensions that had come into the open since 5 March. They pointed out that the petition to which Harley had referred did not actually mention the Protestation. In any case, so far from speaking for the gentry community, this petition represented only a few factious spirits: it 'would not have credit enough for you to tender it to the House'.[119] Other counties, the JPs declared, 'might swallow down their throats' arbitrary parliamentary directions: such was their care for the liberty of the subject that neither for 'fear of being sent for as delinquents nor being put out of commission' would they 'yield obedience to any authority that is not derived from His Majesty'. The justices offered Harley their own reading of the constitution:

> You tell us truly that the constitution of this kingdom is comprised of three estates . . . . it is a triple cord and it would be dangerous to untwist it: if you leave out either it will not be so strong. We do not yield any active obedience to His Majesty's commands, but such as are warranted by laws made by his authority and consent of both Houses . . . . Every one of the three hath a negative voice and if any should have power of binding it would be rather thought the king than the Commons. For we find in the statute books that those charters and other acts (which story telleth us cost our ancestors much blood) are yet there entered as proceeding from the free grace of the prince. All the land we hold is either mediately or immediately from him. He summons you to parliament and had always the power to dismiss you. By virtue of his writ we send you, not with authority to govern us or others, but with our consent for making or altering laws as to His Majesty, the Lords and Commons shall seem good. This is our stronghold, let us stick to that and not with grasping more lose the hold we have.

The JPs followed this with a trenchant attack on the crux of Pym's policy, the defence of the nation against the popish conspiracy. They scorned the talk of invasions from France and Denmark, which had not materialized; they dismissed the leadership's rabble-rousing anti-Catholicism. The papists were 'still underground as formerly and with us they are so quiet we have found no cause hitherto to apprehend any danger from them'. The overall message was clear: the onus rested on parliament to reach agreement with the king. They should start by settling his revenue and granting him tonnage and poundage for life 'as to his predecessors'. Above all the JPs looked for trust:

> His Majesty may find a confidence and love in his subjects some ways answerable to those great expressions this parliament hath obtained for us of his

---

118　*Harley*, p. 173; *HMC Portland*, II, 81.
119　*Harley*, p. 159.

unmatchable goodness and grace. That most pious, generous and princely confession of errors in government past we cannot sufficiently extol, and his resolution of governing by law for the future so gracious as what father to a son, or what ingenious man to another, would not so be reconciled and grow confident. Much more readily should the people run to meet such a father of the country.[120]

Harley ensured that, whereas the petition organized by his friends was duly presented on 4 May, the one in favour of episcopacy and the liturgy, planned by Walter Brabazon and signed by 68 gentry, 150 ministers and 3600 others, never reached its destination.[121] In Herefordshire though it was Brabazon, Croft and their party who held sway. So the Protestation was not taken village by village in March as it was in most other counties and as the summer went on Lady Brilliana was made to feel increasingly threatened.[122] When the royalists produced a resolution in the name of the county in June, Gower sent a copy to Harley explaining that the parliamentarian faction 'dare not appear (such is their malice and power) to oppose for fear of exasperating and further disturbing the peace of the county'. Gower alleged that the resolution had never been seen 'by above 50 in all the county'. What mattered of course was that it had the backing of most of the major gentry families besides the Harleys. When it was read to the trained bands no one objected and 'all cried God save the king'.[123]

The Herefordshire resolution was sent to the king at York bearing the support of the grand jury.[124] It exhibited a lofty strain of royalist sentiment that had not at that stage been heard from any other county. It is an important document in several senses. In the first place, its authors were remarkably well informed about the national political debate: the Kentish petition, the king's recruiting in Yorkshire and Sir Henry Ludlow's bold attack on the monarchy, for example, were all mentioned. Secondly, they had a clear understanding of the way the parliamentary leadership had maintained their following. 'Private combinations or chamber conventicles', hindrance of freedom of speech and denial of unsympathetic petitions were among the matters catalogued against them. Thirdly, the boldness of the resolution and the persuasiveness of its argument to all who had begun to doubt Pym's strategy is undeniable. Parliaments were the 'only good old way of physic' to cleanse distempers in the body politic. But this one, 'instead of restoring it to its primitive vigour and health', was driving it to 'a fatal period'. The Herefordshire gentry declared themselves for the Protestant religion, the king's just power, the laws of the land and

---

120 BL Loan MS 29/173, fols. 238v–239v. There are copies of this letter in Shrosphire RO 212/Box 364 and Staffordshire RO D 868/2/32.
121 BL Loan MS 29/173, fol. 206v; E 150 (28), pp. 39–40; 669 f 6 (19); *CJ* II. 560.
122 *Harley*, pp. 157–85.
123 *HMC Portland* III, 91, 93; BL Loan MS 29 174, fol. 287.
124 *HMC Portland* III, 92; *Harley*, p. 170.

the liberty of the subject. All these, they believed, had been violated by Pym's men: the Church had been assaulted in the 'inworks and skirts of it'; the king's person had been in danger from the rabble; men had been imprisoned contrary to the Petition of Right; an assembly of divines had been chosen without election by the clergy 'as if they were neither the king's subjects nor God's servants'. They would not suffer themselves to be swayed by any arbitrary government, nor cast off the yoke of one tyranny to endure a worse; they bound themselves, like the petitioners of Essex and Suffolk a few weeks later, to maintain the king with their 'lives and fortunes'.[125]

The ideological commitment of a section of the Nottinghamshire gentry had brought tensions into the open in 1641. The county's Root and Branch petition was almost certainly organized by the young Puritans like John Hutchinson, Henry Ireton and Francis Thornhaugh.[126] Hutchinson's father, Sir Thomas, a man with a high reputation for his hospitality and generosity, was knight of the shire and in this capacity he presented the petition in May.[127] It must have rankled with some because a counter-petition was organized and Robert Sutton, Hutchinson's fellow knight, tried unsuccessfully to get this received on 15 December.[128] There was then a clash at the epiphany quarter sessions in 1642 when Hutchinson's group failed to win full JP backing for a petition of gratitude and loyalty to parliament. One of the justices, Gilbert Boone, derided their manifesto as an assault on the king's prerogative.[129] At the assizes two months later though the incipient parliamentarian faction obtained the approbation of Judge Reeve for their outspoken accommodation petition to the king.[130] Sir John Biron and Sir John Digby meanwhile were emerging as the leaders of the county's royalist gentry. The kinship links between the Birons and Hutchinsons were strained by their diverging political views. Angry words passed between the two families over John Hutchinson's presence in the cavalcade that rode into York with the assizes petition.[131]

Distrust simmered until July when Biron and Digby, supported by the disaffected member for Grimsby, Gervase Holles, organized a meeting of the gentry to call Hutchinson to account. They seem to have possessed a copy of the Herefordshire JP's letter of 28 April, since some of the same phraseology appears in their letter to Hutchinson, which carried the signatures of 81 leading men in the shire. Indeed they might never have

---

125 Webb, *Civil War in Herefordshire*, pp 343–4; *CJ* II, 665–6, 683.
126 A.C. Wood, *Nottinghamshire in the Civil War* (Oxford, 1937), pp. 35–6.
127 *Hutchinson*, p. 15; Keeler, p. 227.
128 *D'Ewes (C)*, p. 290; Keeler, p. 356.
129 BL Add. MS 14827, fol. 54v; *CJ* II, 459; Derbyshire RO Chandos-Pole-Gell MSS: Nottinghamshire Petition.
130 *CJ* II, 522; *HMC Coke*, p. 309; BL 669 f 6(6); above, p. 271.
131 *Hutchinson*, pp. 53–4, 61–2, 72–3.

acted in this way without the Herefordshire example. Both in tone and content they followed it closely. Sweeping aside the papist conspiracy and invasion fears as mere pretences, the Nottinghamshire gentry emphatically rejected the independence of the knights of the shire and the actions parliament had taken on its own authority:

> We shall not conceive ourselves bound to obey one or both Houses without the king, but in such things as are according to the common laws of the land. . . . We never conceived your only votes should be our law nor conceived that we had such a power to confer upon you. And we require you not to lay any such command upon us, nor to engage us in any civil war for the maintenance of such votes, under colour of privilege, against our lawful king . . . we hope it will not be displeasing unto you, that we give you our sense freely, for you are us, and we hope you will not be unwilling to follow our sense, so far as you conceive it to be the sense of your county whose you are and for whom you serve.

Unlike the Herefordshire correspondence, the Nottinghamshire letter was quickly printed.[132] Some, like Sir John Coke, saw it simply as another attempt to bring national reconciliation, but within the county there can be little doubt that it exacerbated the enmities that had begun to flare.[133]

The Kentish assizes' petition of 25 March is the most celebrated of the county manifestos of loyalty to the king, partly because it was the first, partly because its attack on parliament was so forthright.[134] By their thorough investigation of its origins and persecution of its instigators, the parliamentary leadership gave the petition all the publicity its adherents could have wished. Yet they were not fools in seeing it, in Coke's words, as 'a practice to make a party'.[135] Essentially the petition was Dering's revenge. He would stop at nothing to discredit the House which had expelled him: 'the burning of my book cannot confute me, nor silence me in the way I go.' If his partner Sir John Culpepper was expelled too, he avowed, he would 'ride from east to west and visit all Kent but we would petition him in again'. Dering had come home, after his release from the Tower, to galvanize the county and his personal stand quickly crystallized factional loyalties. He boasted at the Maidstone assizes, with surpassing vanity, that 'he could get 40,000 hands to the petition and that they would all come up and deliver it'[136] He was either the hero or the villain of the hour. Sir Michael Livesey and his friends told Londoners, when they were there with the shire's petition of loyalty to parliament on 8 February, that they thought he deserved his censure. A royalist cleric deposed a few

132 BL E 154(45): *His Majesty's Declaration made June 13th 1642.*
133 *HMC Coke,* p. 319.
134 Gardiner x, 179–80. T.P.S. Woods, *Prelude to Civil War 1642: Mr Justice Malet and the Kentish Petitions* (Wilton, 1980), pp. 30–85, is an excellent account of the whole affair.
135 *HMC Coke,* p. 311.
136 Larking, pp. 74–6; BL Add. MS 14827, fol. 75v.

months later that he 'would see his heart's blood that should speak against Sir Edward Dering's petition although it should be his own father'.[137]

The unusual degree of formality in the procedure at the assizes for west Kent on 23 to 25 March is worth noting. Dering himself was appointed chairman of the grand jury. A committee of grand jurymen and the Bench met three times to discuss and amend Dering's draft. He had intended that one clause should question his own expulsion and request that in future no MP should lose his seat 'without just cause shown', but others thought this personal element inappropriate.[138] The petition was presented publicly in court in the presence of about 2000 people. This was no hole and corner affair, but a direct challenge to the Puritan and parliamentarian faction led by Livesey and Sir Anthony Weldon. Friends of Livesey's like Thomas Blount naturally resisted it: 'myself and others spoke against it', he later told MPs, 'because we should contradict the petition already delivered'. Such men thought Dering's petition showed insufficient gratitude for the work parliament had accomplished. In the end nine of the grand jury disowned the petition.[139]

So successfully had Dering and his friends stirred the county that their opponents felt bound to issue a new petition reiterating their zeal for parliament and vindicating the gentry community from the disloyal assizes manifesto. This provoked an angry scene at the Maidstone sessions on 20 April, when the cavalier squire Richard Lovelace, recently returned from service against the Scots, flourished the new document over his head and tore it in pieces. Young hotheads like Lovelace had taken over the circulation of the assizes petition and it was they who eventually presented it at Westminster on 30 April.[140] Only five days later the arrival of the reply organized by Blount and others was announced to the Commons by Augustine Skinner, who had acted with Blount at Maidstone and replaced Dering as knight of the shire. Six thousand signatures had been collected to this petition in a mere fortnight.[141]

No compromise was possible between the outright resistance to the militia ordinance and the religious conservatism of the assizes petition and the Puritan activism of men like Blount, Livesey and Weldon. The factions among the Kentish gentry were probably about evenly balanced in the summer of 1642, with a certain unease apparent in the alliance of cavalier hotheads and more moderate royalist gentry such as Sir Roger Twysden. A new round of petitioning in July and August confirms the impression of

---

137 *Trevelyan Papers* III, 217; HLRO, Main Papers, 6 Aug. 1642: Petition of John Marston.
138 BL Add MS 14827, fol. 77r.
139 *Twysden*, pp. 200–12; Everitt, pp. 94–6.
140 Everitt, pp. 100–104.
141 *CJ* II, 562; BL Harl MS 163, fols. 65r, 107v; Add. MS 14827, fol. 76r. For Skinner see Everitt, p. 77; Clark, *English Provincial Society*. pp. 350, 357, 360, 387 but Clark's characterization of him as a radical is confusing.

political stalemate.[142] It was a tactical blunder by the Commons to send 17 MPs for the county down in force as a committee to sit on the Bench, when news came of further trouble at the summer assizes. The pride of those legally appointed to sit was touched by this intervention and when they arrived on Saturday 23 July, after the assizes had opened, the justices were unwilling to make room for them. Only 9 of the 17 were in fact members of the commission of the peace. Neither then, nor after the weekend, would Judge Malet cooperate by allowing the committee to read the orders and instructions they had brought with them. The 25 and 26 July were spent in a desultory exchange of formal statements between the JPs and the committee. The former declared that the county enjoyed a 'secure peace' and that they had no power 'to place any on the Bench not sent thither by the like authority we sit there', the latter peremptorily required their colleagues and countrymen to do parliament's bidding. On 26 July Sir Henry Vane the younger asked that the grand jury might be sent to hear what the committee had to say. One part of the company hummed when Malet spoke, he later told the Commons, and the other hummed when he replied. The MPs were so totally balked that they eventually withdrew.[143] At this point the boldest of the Kentish royalists, perhaps prompted by Malet, adopted the tactic of Herefordshire and Nottinghamshire and formulated a set of instructions for the knight of the shire, Augustine Skinner, who was present in Vane's party. Parliament should deliver Hull to the king, restore to him the navy, lay aside the militia ordinance and adjourn to an 'indifferent place' where negotiations could be carried on with the king in safety. At the same time the royalists sent Charles a new declaration of loyalty.[144]

Once again the parliamentarian faction was not slow to reply. On 30 August Sir John Sedley, one of those who had informed upon Dering and his friends in March, presented a new petition to parliament. He assured the Commons that the July petition to the king had been 'contrived by a few malevolent and ambitious spirits only'. By contrast this petition, he declared, came 'guided hither with as many hearts as hands': it was 'all of a piece, speaking plain language, yet full of loyalty' and it had been 'embraced with such a unanimous consent of the entire body of the commonalty as that each man contested for the first subscription to it'.[145] No doubt Sedley's protestations were somewhat overdramatized, but the fact that he should have felt the necessity to speak in such terms is an indication of the rifts that had opened in a shire where the gentry were exceptionally united and close knit. It was ironical that Sedley had been

---

142 Clark, *English Provincial Society*, p. 388, Everitt, pp. 95–107 takes a rather different view.
143 *CJ* II, 690, 704; BL Harl MS 164, fol. 258; Woods, *Prelude to Civil War*, pp. 99–105.
144 BL E 112 (26): *Petition of Kent to the King*; Woods, *Prelude to Civil War*, p. 108.
145 BL E 113 (1): *Petition of Kent to Parliament*.

Dering's right-hand man in the 1640 elections.[146]

In Somerset, as in Nottinghamshire and Kent, rival factions had petitioned for Root and Branch and the preservation of episcopacy. The conservative party was almost certainly the stronger among the gentry and clergy: 200 knights and gentry together with 211 divines supported the petition sent to parliament in December 1641.[147] By March 1642 the parliamentary delegation was decisively split. The defectors included Sir John Stawell, John Coventry, a Straffordian who had opposed the Grand Remonstrance, Sir Ralph Hopton, whose stormy career had led to a spell in the Tower, and Edward Kirton, a constant antagonist of the leadership.[148] Stawell and Coventry appear to have been the initiators of a royalist campaign in Somerset. They began to talk of 'the king's side and the parliament's' and asked some leading families like the Luttrells of Dunster 'which side they would be on'.[149] Then, in May, Hopton and Thomas Smyth, another defecting MP, were reported to be 'planning a petition like that of Sir Edward Dering'. It was also rumoured that one of them had a commission from the king to oppose the militia ordinance if it was executed. Smyth brought his friend Sir Francis Doddington, his wife's kin the Pouletts and his stepfather Sir Ferdinando Gorges into the scheme.[150] A number of ministers were employed to read the petition in their churches. Old friendships, that between Thomas Smyth and John Pyne for instance, began to shatter as the county divided.[151]

Somerset's royalist petition, received with much disfavour at Westminster in June, combined an appeal to localist sentiment with a demand that parliament should fulfil the conditions laid down by Charles for his return to London. There were references to the Petition of Right and the impoverishment of the shire brought about by taxes levied since 1640. But in its main emphasis the argument was closely modelled on the Kentish petition at the Lent assizes: parliament must abandon the militia ordinance, put the peace and safety of the kingdom before disputes about prerogative and lay aside groundless fears and jealousies.[152]

Cornwall was apparently the only county where the standard petition of thanks and loyalty to parliament met with outright rejection at a public assembly of gentry. The grand jury at the March assizes laid it aside. It reached the Commons nevertheless, having, according to its opponents, been 'indirectly intruded upon divers persons, without reading or perusal,

146 Everitt, pp. 20–55, 72–4, 80–2.
147 *LJ* IV, 469; BL 669 f 4(44); Underdown, pp. 26–7.
148 *CJ* II, 159; *D'Ewes (N)*, pp. 337, 467; BL Harl. MS 163, fol. 42r; Keeler, pp. 144, 242, 349–50; Bristol RO 36074 (156); F.T.R. Edgar, *Sir Ralph Hopton* (Oxford, 1968), pp. 19–24.
149 BL Add. MS 14827, fol. 77v; *HMC Coke*, p. 311; *HMC Buccleuch* p. 295.
150 Bristol RO 36074; BL Add. MS 14827, fol. 95r.
151 *LJ* v, 133–4; Underdown, pp. 28–9.
152 BL 669 f 6(37).

many of them since retracting their opinions and wishing back their hands'. The section of the petition which called for abolition of all aspects of the liturgy 'not warrantable by God's word' and a form of Church government agreeable to his word probably accounts for the furore it caused. The foundations of Cornish royalism were spontaneous political conservatism and deep attachment to traditional ways in the Church. These sentiments were expressed in the petition of obedience presented to Charles on 26 June. The parish clergy were seen as the guardians of social and moral order: they should be orthodox and competent to preach; obstruction to the recovery of their tithes should be removed 'so those that minister at the altar may live by the altar'; statutes should be passed against adultery and to compel the refractory to pay their rates for the repair of parish churches.[153] The clergy played a principal role in organizing this petition. One of them John Smith, the rector of St Ewe, boasted that he had collected a thousand hands. He derided the Protestation and disparaged villagers who did not share his views as roundheads.[154]

The divisions in the large parliamentary delegation from Cornwall had gradually become apparent during 1641. There were eight Straffordians. There was also a solid phalanx of Puritan gentry, led by the experienced Francis Rous and including Sir Alexander Carew, Sir Richard Buller, John Bampfield and Anthony Nicoll.[155] Some of the same tensions between gentry at home and the knights of the shire such as we have seen existed in other counties were present in this case. In an abortive petition to parliament the Cornish gentry expressed their despair that those who should have been their 'hands and mouths' had failed to bring attention to local problems, the decay and poverty of the ports, for example, and harsh Exchequer amerciaments on Duchy tenants.[156] The complaint may have reflected general dissatisfaction with Carew, whose strong loyalty to parliament put him out of sympathy with many in the shire. Sir Bevil Grenville, the other knight, was in Hyde's words 'the generally most loved man in the county', but, probably through distress and perplexity at the course of events, he failed to give a positive lead when he came into the west in March 1642.[157]

The leadership of the royalist movement in Cornwall in the spring and summer of 1642 thus fell to the young Lord Mohun, the sheriff John Grills, the energetic Courtney family and John Arundel, the heir to that most perfect of Cornish manor houses Trerice. The petition formulated at a gathering at Lostwithiel and subsequently carried to York by Mohun

153 BL E 143 (19): *Petition of Cornwall*; E 150 (28): *A Collection of Petitions*, p. 40; M. Coate, *Cornwall in the Great Civil War and Interregum* (Oxford, 1933), pp. 28–29.
154 Bodleian Tanner MS 63, fols. 21–6.
155 Coate, *Cornwall in the Civil War*, pp. 26–8.
156 BL E 150 (28), p. 40.
157 *CJ* II, 463; Clarendon II, 452.

expressed the views of these men. Charles was urged to resist arbitrary government and alteration in religion. The petitioners were 'most feelingly grieved' for his discontents. They wished 'a confluence of all comforts, honour and happiness' towards him and offered to defend him 'against all persons whatsoever according to the oaths of supremacy and allegiance'.[158]

Finally in this series of case studies consideration will be given to Lincolnshire and Yorkshire, the former so close to Hull that it could not avoid political involvement in the summer of 1642, the latter inevitably a seat of factional war once the king's court was established there. Lincolnshire follows the familiar pattern of counties that became polarized early. Episcopacy and the prayer book had determined friends and enemies who expressed themselves in rival petitions.[159] A more unusual element was the trouble from April 1641 onwards in the fens. A small group of gentry actively involved in fen drainage gradually emerged as the core of the royalist faction in the county: the Bertie family, including the earl of Lindsey himself, Sir Edward Heron and Sir John Monson. The Commons committee which reviewed the legality of the undertakers' operations was dilatory in its proceedings. Meanwhile the commoners, taking matters into their own hands, dammed ditches, breached banks, drove cattle into arable enclosures and reaped the landlords' corn.[160] Robert Sanderson surely had the riots of the summer in mind when he preached a visitation sermon against the 'connivance and licentiousness' of the times in October 1641: 'we find, by late experience, what wildness in some of the lay people, what petulancy in some of the inferior clergy, what insolency in some both of the laity and the clergy, our land is grown into, since the reins of ecclesiastical government have lain a little slack.'[161]

When the king settled at York a number of the leading gentry attended the court. Sir William Pelham told his sister-in-law Brilliana Harley that he had refused a deputy lieutenantship under the militia ordinance and acted in this way 'being his servant and so bound by his oath'.[162] The earl of Lindsey's loyalty ran deep. His energetic efforts on the king's behalf caused parliament to vote him an incendiary on 6 June. A few days later he was reported to be planning a royalist muster in Lincolnshire. His son Lord Willoughby of Eresby had been with Charles at Hull on 23 April.[163]

158 BL E 150 (28), pp. 32, 40 E 151 (18): *A Relation of last week's passages in York and Hull*; Coate, *Cornwall in the Civil War*, p. 31.
159 I am most grateful to Professor Clive Holmes for making available his account, now published in *Seventeenth-Century Lincolnshire* (Lincoln, 1980), pp. 141–57, on which the following paragraphs are partly based.
160 *D'Ewes (N)*, p 19; *LJ* IV, 204, 208, 220, 269; Manning, pp. 128–31.
161 W. Jacobson, editor, *Works of Sanderson* (1854), II, 155, 161, 167.
162 *Harley*, p 161.
163 *CJ* II, 611, 619; *LJ* V, 30; *HMC Buccleuch* I, 297, 299; BL Add. MS 14827, fol. 90r.

In late May the Lincolnshire gentry were said to be 'most of them ill affected to the parliament'.[164] Nonetheless, as we shall see, Lord Willoughby of Parham executed the militia ordinance in June without undue difficulty.

The catalyst that brought the county's divisions into the open was the king's visit to Lincoln on 13 July. Next day the recorder Charles Dallison, who had welcomed the king enthusiastically, Sir Peregrine Bertie and Sir Edward Heron drew a petition to parliament demanding that the king should have Hull, the militia should be laid aside, tumults and licentious pamphlets should be suppressed and parliament should be adjourned to a place of the king's choosing. In short this was another agenda for reconciliation on the king's terms. It is hard to tell how widely support was canvassed. The petition apparently secured many baronets', knights' and gentlemen's hands but, brought by 'a simple fellow in a livery cloak' on behalf of Heron, it had a derisive reception. Sir Edward Ayscough and Sir Anthony Irby perused the signatures and concluded that 'the greater part of them were men of very mean condition and esteem.'[165] Later that same day, 18 July, Mandeville read the protestation of loyalty to parliament of the gentry and freeholders to Lord Willoughby, which he had been asked to send to Westminster. This was claimed to carry the support of 10,000 men.[166]

There were seeming contradictions in Lincolnshire's behaviour, to which we shall return, but the existence at this stage of the nucleus of two parties is not in doubt. In a 'humble gratulation and petition' pleading for isolation from the emerging conflict, presented on 1 August, the royalists did not disguise their standpoint. 'We will not contribute to the keeping of seas or towns against you', they declared, attacking parliament's diversion of the people's money to their own ends. Once again we find provincial observers of the Long Parliament's performance speaking of a new form of arbitrary government.[167]

By 1640 factional conflict was almost endemic in Yorkshire. During the previous two decades the assertive rule of Sir Thomas Wentworth had been the pivot of the county's politics.[168] But the outstanding issue of 1641 was the billeting money.[169] Many murmured against parliament for its failure to satisfy them and by December Thomas Stockdale was talking of

---

164 BL Harl. MS 163, fol. 130r.
165 BL Harl. MS 163, fol. 275r; Add. MS 14827, fol. 162r; E 108 (29): *Petition of Lincolnshire*; E 202 (19): *Some Special Passages*, 12–19 July, sub 18 July; J.W.F. Hill, *Tudor and Stuart Lincoln* (Cambridge, 1956), pp. 150–2.
166 *CJ* II, 683; BL Harl. MS 163, fol. 276v; Add. MS 14827, fol. 163v.
167 BL E 109 (27): *Petition of Lincolnshire*.
168 Cliffe, pp. 282–304; J.P. Cooper, editor, *Wentworth Papers 1597–1628* (Camden Society, fourth series, XII, 1973), 4–8, 79–318.
169 *D'Ewes (C)*, pp. 108–9, 114, 206, 256–7; *Fairfax* II, 215–20, 269–70, 376, 391.

an 'anti-parliamentarian faction', who used the issue to mobilize opinion on a wider range of subjects. The Knaresborough by-election the previous month had shown that religious issues provided combustible material for those willing to exploit them. Rumours that he had spoken against the prayer book were used to tar the candidacy of Sir William Constable.[170]

The national significance of the struggle for control of Hull was fully grasped. But in the locality it was also seen in terms of the personal rivalry of Sir Thomas Metham and Sir John Hotham, contestants for the hegemony of the East Riding. Metham had been one of Wentworth's deputy lieutenants and was suspected of Catholicism. One of young Hotham's anxieties in his first days at Hull was that the papists on Humberside were said to be arming themselves.[171] The 28 January scheme for guarding the magazine and exercising the militia, we have seen, was based on fears of a papist insurrection. Sir Edward Rodes reported that the county was in 'even greater perplexity' in February 1642 than it had been the previous year, when two armies menaced its livelihood.[172]

In the petitioning drive of that month Stockdale tried hard to achieve consensus. But his parliamentarian stance was actually blatant and, as he confessed in his letters, the petitions brought the county's divisions into the open. The organizers deliberately ignored some leading gentry, who they suspected would make difficulties about the congratulatory tone of the petitions to the Lords and Commons and the request to Charles that he should 'be advised by his parliament and remit those that he accused'.[173] Strafford's close friend Sir Edward Osborne was one of those so treated. The petitioners also found some obstruction in the villages: five ministers in Claro wapentake encouraged parishioners to refuse support.[174] Undoubtedly many were dismayed. There was talk of an anti-petition from the contrary faction but this did not materialize. Instead the king's sympathizers used both the Puritan and the billet-money sticks to beat their enemies. A false rumour that Puritan exercises such as fasts and days of humiliation were not acceptable to parliament was sedulously fostered. More ingenious still was the story that, since the county had offered to raise 3000 foot and 300 horse for its defence, parliament had decided that it could not really be in desperate straits for the payment of its billeting arrears. All hopes of these being paid could therefore be abandoned. These slurs so damaged parliament's reputation in Yorkshire that Stockdale, the sheriff Sir Thomas Gower and others called for reassurance from

---

170 *Fairfax* II, 266, 289.
171 Hill, pp. 2, 18; BL E 140 (4): *Master Speaker's letter to the Sheriff of Yorkshire*, p. 4; Cliffe, pp. 243, 290, 311.
172 *HMC 5th Report*, p. 7.
173 BL Add. MS 14827, fol. 41r.
174 *Fairfax* II 345, 372–3, 376; Cliffe, pp 303, 312, 319–320.

Westminster that the petitions had been well received.[175]

The king's failure to win wholehearted support in Yorkshire is one of the most important themes of the months that lead into civil war. In the first place then he came to a county that was already divided. Secondly it is crucial to note the economic circumstances of the region. The cloth trade was the lifeblood of the West Riding. By April 1642 the disruption of exports produced by Hotham's control of Hull was severely affecting towns like Leeds and Halifax. Many thousands of spinners and carders of wool were being put out of work.[176] By July the livelihood of 40,000 people was alleged to be threatened.[177] The sullen response of the Yorkshire gentry to the king's arrival has already been described. Charles brought the political crisis with him. The first reaction was to shy away from this unpalatable political fact and take refuge in unjustified hopes. The first week of April saw Stockdale treasuring gossip that the king had told the mayor of York he would 'shortly leave them' and recounting news of successes in Ireland, which should discourage 'the malevolent party' from raising insurrections.[178]

After the recorder's firm lecture on 18 March, the reaction of the corporation of York to the king's coming was supine. On 7 April they repudiated a petition put out in their name begging Charles to return to Whitehall.[179] They simply did what they could to keep order. There were already sharp divisions in the city between Puritans and religious conservatives. There had been a riot in February for instance, between 200 'blue ribands' and some citizens engaged in breaking stained-glass windows.[180] The cavaliers soon had a crowd at their bidding, who were persuaded that any pressure on the king to leave his northern capital was disloyal. The mobbing of the Lincolnshire petitioners on 27 March attracted much comment.[181] Stockdale, in York two days before, had already remarked upon the attempt by the court 'to have the roundheads cast into balance with the recusants' and made to appear no less obnoxious. But he recognized that the cavaliers' relationship with the citizens posed the same dangers to the king's reputation as the Westminster crowds had done to parliament's. 'I am confident such riots are most displeasing to the king', he wrote to Lord Fairfax, 'though I am persuaded the people are emboldened by his presence to act them supposing them acceptable to His Majesty.'[182]

175 BL E 140 (4); E 201 (28): *A Continuation of a True Diurnal*, 14–21 March, p. 78; *CJ* II, 479; *Fairfax* II, 377.
176 BL E 144 (6): *Petition of the Clothiers of Leads, Halifax and other parts*.
177 HLRO, Main Papers, 18 July 1642: Petition of the West Riding clothiers.
178 *Fairfax* II, 363–4, 366–7, 378, 380, 393–4.
179 BL E 143 (2): *A Message from Parliament*; YPL House Books, 36, fols. 70–1.
180 *Fairfax* II, 375.
181 *HMC Coke*, p. 313; *HMC Montagu*, p. 148.
182 *Fairfax* II, 390–1, 393.

A new round of petitioning was initiated by Sir Thomas Gower's call for a meeting at York on 25 March. Prompted by friends, Stockdale had framed the draft of a petition to Charles a few days before. But as soon as he started collecting signatures he found hesitation about its demand that the king should go back to parliament. At the York meeting many of the leading men of the shire refused to follow his lead and Stockdale was persuaded to withdraw his draft. After all the king had not sent to demand the surrender of Hull; instead he had made clear his gracious care for 'the peace and welfare of the land'. Stockdale saw the need to humour both sides. 'I hope we shall petition the king in such a style', he told Fairfax on 1 April, 'as shall please both him and parliament.'[183]

Sobered by the presence of the king in their midst, the Yorkshire gentry sought to contain their disagreements by a moderate line. They would be neither 'guided by the Kentish petition', nor slavishly follow the harsh terms of the Nottinghamshire petition, telling Charles to trust parliament. His confidence in the county's affections, they told the king, was a comfort, but 'fellow feeling of the passionate sorrows and heartbreaking apprehensions' of other districts drove them to speak. Yorkshire accepted all his assurances and would serve and protect him in any capacity they could 'according to law'. Yet it was said 'a kingdom divided cannot stand', so the search for 'fit means and expedients' to remove 'all distance and mis-understandings' between him and parliament was an urgent necessity. In a new petition to parliament the Yorkshire gentry adopted the same mediatory stance, emphasizing that neither the king's prerogative nor their liberties should suffer in the solution they proposed. These petitions, formally approved at the assizes on 5 April, were well calculated to secure a truce in the fraught politics of the shire.[184]

The truce was ended on 22 April when about 20 gentry petitioned the king to arm himself by seizing the Hull magazine, which it was known parliament intended to ship to London. This was the first step towards the emergence of a distinctive royalist party in Yorkshire. The continuity with previous factional struggles is notable: four men who had been dependents of Wentworth's in the 1630s – his brother Sir William Wentworth, Sir John Gibson, Sir Thomas Metham and Sir Francis Wortley – were chief figures behind this petition.[185] When it was reported in the Commons, Sir Hugh Cholmley noted that most of its signatories had Supported Strafford in his campaign during September 1640 to balk demands to the King for a parliament.[186] The response of the parliamentarian faction was immediate. A new petition formulated by Gower, Stockdale, Sir Thomas Fairfax and

183   *Fairfax* II, 389–95.
184   *LJ* IV, 710, 11; BL, E 143 (8): *A True Relation concerning Nottinghamshire Petition*, p. 4.
185   *LJ* V, 15; Rushworth III, part I 566.
186   Hill, p 50; *CJ* II, 544; Cliffe, pp. 321–2.

their allies took a hard assertive line. It disclaimed the advice given by a 'very small part of the gentry': the disposal of the Hull magazine was a matter for the king's 'great council', who could best judge the interests of the state. The king's task was to apply himself 'to all good means of union, that those duties which by the laws of God and men we owe . . . may not become a divided proposition'.[187]

The gentry came in to York from all three ridings on 30 April because Charles had summoned them to attend the court. Before he would receive another petition, which he doubtless guessed would be unpalatable, he insisted they should hear what he expected for his defence 'against all violence'. This was the first of his series of appeals to the Yorkshire gentry for help and vindication. The request for advice as to what action he should take in reply to Hotham's affront was an invitation to open factionalism. There was a short fracas, during which Wortley drew his sword and cried 'For the king, For the king'. Then two parties went off to prepare their separate statements, which summarized the opposing viewpoints. The parliamentarians would defend their monarch 'by all such ways as the law and our duty binds us', but offered nothing with regard to Hull. The royalists would defend the king's 'sacred person against all foreign and domestic enemies' and cautiously offered service against Hull however they were legally commanded. Both groups claimed they commanded majority support in the gentry community.[188] It is hard to judge where most men in fact stood and whether they themselves even knew.

There was nothing the parliamentarian gentry could do to stop the king's recruiting efforts during May, but the meeting called for 3 June on Heworth Moor seemed to provide an opportunity for propagandist campaigning. Sir Matthew Boynton and Sir Thomas Fairfax prepared a petition in readiness, which attempted to exploit neutralist sentiment. Yorkshire was still exhausted by the Scottish war, they declared, yet it found itself engulfed in the national political crisis, its settled life rent by 'factions and divisions'. They emphasized the imminent miseries threatening the whole nation and once more implored the king to assent to parliament's propositions for peace.[189] But when the day came it was obvious that the royalists were equally prepared and to prevent an open clash Sir John Bourchier acted as mediator. Both parties agreed to desist from collecting signatures on the Moor.[190] But this truce, like the previous one, could only be temporary, because in the intensely political atmosphere generated by the king's presence, the Yorkshire gentry were now well on

---

187 BL 669 f 6(9): *Petition of Yorkshire.*
188 *CJ* II, 556; BL Harl. MS 163, fols. 101v–102r; Add MS 14827, fols. 90v–91r; 669 f 5(22): *His Majesty's Demands to the Gentry of Yorkshire; Fairfax* II, 391.
189 *LJ* v, 109.
190 J.J. Cartwright, editor, 'Papers relating to the Deliquency of Lord Saville', *Camden Miscellany* VIII (Camden Society, new series, XXXI, 1883), p. 4; *LJ* v, 111; Gardiner x, 200.

the way towards dividing themselves into two camps.

The two ancient universities of Oxford and Cambridge, bastions of Arminianism, coexisted uneasily at this time with their townsmen and neighbouring gentry communities.[191] The academics were quick to answer the Root and Branch petitions of the counties with formulations of the conservative case.[192] The tensions between Puritan gentry of the county and the Cambridge academics had come into the open at the summer assizes in 1641, when there was an angry altercation about the exclusion of clergy from the commissions of the peace by the act abolishing Star Chamber.[193] The heads of eight Oxford colleges were only prepared to take the Protestation with certain reservations.[194] Town and gown relations were at a low point in both places early in 1642. The corporation's appointment of a lecturer to strengthen Protestant orthodoxy and a violent tavern outburst by Dr Shoulbridge about cutting Pym's throat are indications of the charged atmosphere in Cambridge.[195] Oxford's corporation chose this moment to abandon as an outworn superstition the traditional St Scholasticus day procession by 63 citizens to St Mary's to make a mass oblation for the students killed in a medieval riot. This degrading affair involved the mayor in wearing a halter about his neck and enduring the ritualistic jeers of the scholars.[196]

A common pattern of factional conflict is strikingly apparent in many cathedral cities during the 1630s. Canterbury, Chichester, Gloucester, Norwich, Worcester and York are among the cities where the same key issues disrupted peaceful relations between the leading Puritan aldermen and the clergy of the close. These included the immunities employed by inhabitants of the close, availability of sermons in the cathedral and seating arrangements for the mayor and aldermen.[197] The prolonged sitting of the Long Parliament naturally encouraged aldermen to assert themselves: in March 1641, for example, the corporation of Salisbury decided to petition parliament about the refusal of the close to contribute to certain payments.[198]

Cathedral clergy were more likely than those in the parishes to be

---

191 Curtis, *Oxford and Cambridge in Transition*, pp. 211–26.

192 *D'Ewes(N)*, p. 283; BL E 131 (8): *Petition of the University of Cambridge*; E 156 (22): *Petition of the University of Oxford*, E! 150 (28): *A Collection of Petitions*, pp. 4–8, 23.

193 BL 669 f 4(83): *Petition of Cambridgeshire.*

194 *HMC 5th Report*, pp. 130–1.

195 BL E 201 (28): *A Continuation of a True Diurnal*, 14–21 March, p. 77; E 201 (29): *A True Diurnal*, 14–21 March, p. 2.

196 Oxford Central Library, Council Minute Book 1629–63, fols. 113r, 118r, 121r, 128r.

197 Baker, editor, *The Church in Town and Countryside*, pp. 297–300; *Sussex*, pp. 234–7; J.T. Evans, *Seventeenth-Century Norwich* (Oxford, 1979), pp. 84–96; P. Clark, ' "The Ramoth-Gilead of the Good": Urban Change and Political Radicalism at Gloucester, 1540–1640', in Clark, Smith, Tyacke, editors, *The English Commonwealth*, p. 186.

198 Salisbury District Council Muniment Room, Ledger Book D, fols. 1v, 2v.

Arminians and they were particularly ready to give a royalist lead. In a sermon at Canterbury on 22 January, Thomas Paske told his congregation 'that the people were departed from the king, that they must come as Benhadad's servants did with halters about their necks'.[199] 'The pulpit is made a stage wherein to act their parts against the parliament', reported Stanley Gower to Sir Robert Harley on 8 May, in a letter describing how the royalist clergy at Hereford opposed those who sought to introduce an 'edifying lecture' with a stream of propaganda. 'I know not whether they have taught some of our gentry or these them', he observed, 'but they strive who shall outvie the other in their railing rhetoric.' In April Henry Rogers had preached a sermon comparing King Charles with David; in July he declared that 'as the limb of a man is not a man . . . no more is the parliament a parliament without the king.' He compared the seizure of the Hull magazine to a man robbing by the highway pretending he did it to give to the poor. The clergy in Hereford were clearly building up a considerable following: when a minister omitted to pray for the king there before his sermon on 20 June, two men heckled him and rang the bells to collect a crowd which jeered him as a roundhead.[200]

The mounting tensions in cathedral cities showed themselves in frights and arguments. The dean and prebendaries closed the gates and mounted a guard at Norwich following rumours that the apprentices intended to spend Shrove Tuesday pillaging the altar rails and organs in the cathedral. One man had told the dean that their having sworn the Protestation bound them to drastic action, but the clergy may have reacted over-sensitively to what was in fact a false alarm.[201] At Canterbury, where the minister of St Mary Magdalen, John Marston, was a principal royal protagonist, the bitterness between the two factions during the summer was reported to be such 'that we can hardly look upon one another in charity'.[202]

In Salisbury disputes between Puritan townsmen and the dean and chapter had found expression in the 1640 elections. In both cases Robert Hyde, the recorder of the city, was elected much against the will of some who identified him with the local ecclesiastical establishment and saw in his activites a threat to religion and the people's liberties.[203] The mayor in 1642 was Thomas Lawes, one of Hyde's allies two years before, but a man who wanted to hush the factional strife of the city as far as he was able. He committed one who said the members of parliament were all rebels to prison and hoped to have him sent to Westminster, but Hyde was uncooperative, saying 'he could find no fit time to move the House in it'.

199 BL Add. MS 14827, fol. 20v; Matthews, editor, *Walker Revised*, p. 202.
200 *Harley*, pp. 167, 170–1; *HMC Portland* III, 86–9; Matthews, editor, *Walker Revised*, p. 195.
201 BL E 140 (17): *True News from Norwich*; Ketton-Cremer, pp. 142–3.
202 HLRO, Main Papers, 27 June 1642: Letter from William Bridge and others.
203 P. Slack, 'An Election to the Short Parliament', *BIHR*, XLVI (1973), 108–14.

The receipt of the king's proclamations, though, was a test Lawes could not avoid. John Dove, a leading Puritan alderman, was quick to show him parliament's order against their publication. But Lawes knew his own mind: 'if the king's writ will not bear me out', he declared, 'I will suffer.' The basic emotions of the city are well illustrated by the assertion of John Joy, who also sought to dissuade Lawes, that he knew the papists were busy preparing horses and strength and therefore it was no time to hinder our preparation.'[204]

The emergence of royalism is thus a complex phenomenon. The patterns of thought which fostered and sustained it are plain enough, but the case studies that have been pursued here show the lack of homogeneity in the local conditions which gave it birth. Personal conflicts often became a striking element in the factional struggles of towns or counties but the struggles themselves were based firmly on the issues of the national crisis. There were other counties of course where royalism was at least as strong before August 1642 as in those discussed in this chapter, but where, because there was less division in the gentry community, the documentation is incomplete. These must surely include Cumberland, Lancashire, Monmouthshire, Northumberland, Shropshire, Westmorland and Worcestershire.[205]

In the period covered by this chapter fears, puzzlement and the search for understanding of the nation's differences became for many an almost daily preoccupation. On the road and the river, in the market place, manor house and tavern, 'what news' became the insistent enquiry of all men. It is appropriate to end with a vignette of village life, which tells us much about how the politics of the civil war were percolating the countryside. In August 1642 a London gentleman called Abraham Haynes took overnight lodging at the village inn of Sherston in Wiltshire. He was returning home from a journey on business to Gloucestershire, Worcestershire and Shropshire, so he was naturally supplied with the latest intelligence. Not that the men of Sherston were ignorant. The innkeeper Thomas Palmer could give a fair account of the Long Parliament's achievements, including its raising of large sums to pay the Scottish army. But by and large Sherston had absorbed one side of the story: Pym's side. That very day their company of volunteers was exercising in the street and it was Haynes's hearing the sound of a drum that brought conversation round to politics. 'Were there any roundheads there?' The innkeeper was genuinely puzzled at his question. He may have had no knowledge of the term. The

---

204 Bodleian Dep C MS 165, no. 79.
205 For Cumberland and Westmorland see BL E 154(46): *Petition to the King*; for Lancashire; Ormerod, pp. 8–35; for Monmouthshire, Bodleian Dep C MS 168, no. 175; for Northumberland, BL, Add. MS 14827, fol. 78v; *CJ* II, 504, 515, 548, 559; *HMC Coke*, p. 311; R. Howell, *Newcastle-on-Tyne and the Puritan Revolution* (Oxford, 1967), p. 144; for Shropshire and Worcestershire, Bodleian Dep C MS 165, no. 94.

volunteers, he explained, were 'a company of honest men that exercised themselves to do their king and country service'. Haynes began to tell him the other side of the story, wondering that the villagers could be 'carried away by pamphlets set forth . . . against the Lord's annointed'. What did he think then, enquired Palmer, 'might be the cause of the difference between the king and his parliament'? Haynes had all the answers: the prayer book was the outstanding issue at stake; the Scots, Wales and the marches would stick close to the king; parliament would shortly be overthrown 'and then he would warrant there should never be a parliament again whilst England was England'. All this was undoubtedly a revelation to the Sherston innkeeper, but for the moment at least he clung to the side of story that he had learnt and accepted.[206] All the time the historian has to amass and quantify experience. It is salutary to be reminded how particular were the conditions of the individual's perplexities.

206 Bodleian, Dep C MS 165, no. 94.

10

War Offensives

Here are arms raised daily and a great strength is raising for the defence of this city.

> Edward Reed in London to Sir John Coke,
> 14 August 1642[1]

There cannot be too often mention of the wonderful providence of God, that, from that low despised condition the king was in at Nottingham after the setting up of his standard, he should be able to get men, money or arms and yet within 20 days after his coming to Shrewsbury he resolved to march in despite of the enemy even towards London.

> The earl of Clarendon, *History of the Rebellion*[2]

There was no final certainty that there would be a civil war until the king and parliament had proved that they could raise rival armies. This chapter is concerned with the nature and effectiveness of the royalist and parliamentarian war offensives. Neither side could hope to collect a genuine national army; both were bound to concentrate on the recruiting grounds that circumstances offered. But both sides did attempt to wage a propagandist campaign for the hearts and minds of the people at large. The crucial instruments of these campaigns were the commissions of array and the militia ordinance, which will be discussed in general terms here and then more fully in the next chapter in terms of their local enforcement.

The commissions of array were the centrepiece of a broad royalist strategy that included paper propaganda, changes in commissions of the peace and special instructions to the assize judges. These other aspects of the strategy have already been considered. Such commissions had been the traditional means of raising troops until they were replaced by the lieutenancy system in the reign of Elizabeth. They had been belatedly revived for the Scottish war in 1640.[3] The first to receive a commission of array in 1642 were a select group of Lancashire gentry at the end of May. On 12

---

1 *HMC Coke*, p. 320.
2 Clarendon II, 346.
3 A.H. Noyes, *The Military Obligation in Medieval England* (Columbus, Ohio, 1930), pp. 8–50, 61; Rushworth II, 1201, 1229, 1267; *CSPD 1640*, p. 642; Northamptonshire RO Isham correspondence, 235; Morrill, *Revolt*, p. 156.

June Charles announced his intention of establishing the scheme in every county.[4] The chronology of the commissions subsequently issued, with the Welsh ones trailing the rest in August, suggests that there was no coherent military plan.[5] They were seen essentially as a political instrument. The king's concern at this stage was to secure a loyal following among the most influential gentry of each county, so that wherever trouble came there would be men ready to use the trained bands or the ancient *posse comitatus*, specifically placed in the commissioners' hands, to suppress it and maintain order. Two or three great men were chosen as a quorum in each shire: his active support was expected in Northamptonshire, the aged Lord Montagu was told in a letter under the signet on 9 July, 'as far as your health will permit and by your power and interest'.[6]

The king's decision to raise commissions of array has been called a 'dreadful blunder'.[7] But it is fair to ask, assuming he could not ignore the defiance of the militia ordinance, what alternative presented itself. Hyde later argued that he would have done better with the well established lieutenancy system, yet parliament had effectively captured control of this. Many of the peers dismissed in March had surrendered their commissions.[8] Through the commissions of array Charles sought to consolidate or create royalist factions in the counties. But he intended that leadership should rest as far as possible with the nobility. Thus the power of leading the trained bands across shire boundaries against invaders or other enemies was reserved to the quorum. One of the best reasons for using the ancient commissions was surely that they offered a way of breaking with the assumptions of county defence that underlay the lieutenancy system. Mobility might be vital to a monarch faced with a rebellion that looked like being focused on certain towns such as London and Hull. It is also worth noting that the intention, however it was traduced, was to woo the gentry communities not to startle or terrify them: the king stressed his concern not 'to bring any unnecessary burden or charge . . . by augmenting the number of the trained bands'[9]

This approach was of a piece with every other aspect of the king's vigorous propaganda campaign during the summer. Those who showed generosity, like the Oxford academics for instance, were lavishly thanked.[10] Those who petitioned affectionately were warmly answered. The king's reply to the latest Lancashire petition was read to the crowd at

4 *CJ* II, 595, 635; *CSPD 1642–3*, p. 343.
5 Bodleian Tanner MS 63, fol. 84; Northamptonshire RO Finch Hatton MS 133; Rushworth III part I, 655–8; Hutton, p. 6.
6 *HMC Buccleuch* I, 307.
7 Morrill, *Revolt*, p. 40.
8 Clarendon II, 186, 201–5; J.C. Sainty, *Lieutenants of Counties 1585–1642* (BIHR, Special Supplements, 8, 1970), 10n.
9 *CJ* II, 633, 636; Rushworth III part I, 657–8, 661–9, 674–5; Bodleian Tanner MS 63, fol. 84.
10 BL E 108 (36): *His Majesty's Two Letters to the University of Oxford.*

an assembly of the gentry at Preston Moor on 20 June.[11] In September the corporation of Newcastle, following a loyal petition, was given a concession over the customs duties on goods sent abroad.[12] Those who were reprimanded were courted at the same time. In a letter to the corporation of Exeter on 2 July, about their failure to issue the royal proclamations, the king reminded the aldermen of the many charters given by the crown to enlarge their liberties and privileges.[13]

The royal recruiting campaign began in earnest during July. Activists were attempting to raise men to join the king's army in at least ten counties during that month: Cheshire, Dorset, Herefordshire, Kent, Lancashire, Leicestershire, Lincolnshire, Norfolk, Somerset and Yorkshire.[14] Sir Walter Earle, at home in Dorset, was so shocked at the news that a neighbour, John Digby, was raising a troop of horse for York that he rode at once to Westminster, arriving breathless with his report.[15] The king was seeking to collect arms from individual gentry, local militia bands and even the magazine at West Chester intended for Ireland.[16] He had already, since leaving Whitehall, received vast sums of money from the earl of Worcester and contributions from other sympathizers.[17] He now sought to extend the basis of his financial support with requests for loans to the universities and wealthy gentry.[18] In a few counties, like Herefordshire and Kent, systematic collections were begun during July.[19] First steps were also being taken towards the diversion of such monies due on the act for £400,000 as could be obtained to the king's coffers at York.[20] The king and his entourage, meanwhile, were almost continually on the move in Yorkshire and the north midlands. The siege of Hull was undertaken and subsequently abandoned; visits were made, among other towns, to Leicester, Lincoln and Nottingham.[21]

The king may have been accompanied by as many as 2000 horse when he set up his standard at Nottingham on 22 August. But he certainly had very few footsoldiers and those who were present were reported 'the scum of the country, being raised by beating drums for volunteers'.[22] The response so

11 HLRO, Main papers, 24 June 1642: Alexander Rigby to Speaker Lenthall; see also *Townshend*, pp. 76–7.
12 M.H. Doods, editor, *Extracts from Newcastle-upon-Tyne Council Minute Book 1639–56* (Newcastle-upon-Tyne Record Series I), 18–19.
13 BL Harl. MS 163, fol. 273r.
14 *CJ* II, 634, 676, 701;*LJ* II, 121; Hill, p. 107; BL Loan MS 29/174, fol. 266r; Harl. MS 163, fols. 196v, 289v; E 202 (33): *A True and Exact Diurnal*, 8–15 Aug., p. 1; Holmes, p. 56.
15 BL Harl. MS 163, fol. 273 v; E 202 (17): *A Perfect Diurnal*, 11–18 July, p.8.
16 *HMC Various Collections* VII, 427; BL E202 (37): *A Perfect Diurnal*, 8–15 Aug., p.2.
17 Gardiner x, 207.
18 E.g. *HMC Buccleuch*, p. 158; BL 669 f6 (64): *A Catalogue of Monies, Men and Horse Subscribed*.
19 *HMC Portland* III, 93–5;*LJ* v, 293; Everitt, p. 109.
20 Ormerod, p. 19.
21 Gardiner x, 210–14.
22 *HMC 5th Report*, p. 191; *LJ* v, 301.

far to an intensive recruiting campaign was meagre. The royalist army at this stage was an army of enthusiasts leading their tenantry. Its atmosphere is well captured by the troop of 30 horse under the command of a young cavalier seen on a Lincolnshire heath in late July: 'the rider every one in his buff coat and scarlet hose, rich scarves and feathers'.[23] The king had been giving out commissions by the dozen. Lincolnshire royalists for instance were rallying round Lord Willoughby of Eresby, given command of a regiment which was to include troops led by Sir Charles Boles, Sir John Monson and Sir William Pelham.[24] But this was one of several regiments that looked much more impressive on paper than in the field at Nottingham. Sir William Pennyman and Sir Ralph Dutton had brought in more complete regiments.[25] Lord Paget came with a regiment of Staffordshire foot armed at his own cost and with a month's pay in advance.[26] Gervase Holles led a company of just over 100 horse from his family's Nottinghamshire estates.[27] Some, like Sir Thomas Metham and Sir Robert Strickland, had based their troops on the old trained-band companies from their immediate neighbourhood.[28] On Tyneside meanwhile the earl of Newcastle had taken charge for the king, forcing his tenants to work for him. His chief ally there was Sir William Widdrington, whose steward was reported to have brought in a company of tenants in arms.[29]

The raising of the standard on the castle hill at Nottingham was a considerable anticlimax. A silk flag with the royal arms and the motto 'Give Caesar his due' hung from a long pole, 'like a maypole', dyed red at the upper end. The herald read a proclamation, which had been hurriedly corrected by Charles at the last minute. Though the courtiers and small crowd cried 'God save King Charles and hang up the roundheads', flinging up their caps, the standard blew down that night and, according to Hyde's account, 'a general sadness covered the whole town'.[30] The king's mood had already been swinging between optimism and apprehension. On 19 July he was very likely encouraged by watching his forces parading and skirmishing in practice for an encounter with the rebels in London. A Dutch engineer had the same day displayed his skill with a mortar.[31] In an intercepted letter to Henrietta Maria a few days later, Charles had spoken

23 BL E 202 (21): *A Diurnal and Particular of the last week's Daily Occurrences*, 16–26 July, p.2.
24 Lincolnshire RO Ancaster MS 12/A/5–6.
25 P. Young, 'King Charles I's Army of 1642', *Journal of the Society for Army Historical Research* XVII (1938), 102.
26 PRO SP 29/20/21. I am grateful to Mr John Sutton for this reference.
27 A.C. Wood, editor, *Memorials of the Holles Family* (Camden Society, third series, LV, 1937), 263.
28 *Slingsby*, p. 77; BL E 202 (12): *Some Special Passages*, 3–10 July, 669 f.6 (51): *Remarkable Passages from York*.
29 *LJ* v, 170; Hill, p. 109.
30 BL E 115 (4): *A True Relation of His Majesty's setting up his Standard*, 669 f.6 (75): *Remarkable Passages from Nottingham, Lichfield, Leicester and Cambridge*; Clarendon II, 290–1.
31 BL E 202 (21): *A Diurnal and Particular of the last week's Daily Occurrences*, 16–26 July, pp. 3–4.

of his confidence of gaining Hull and his assurance that he had won the hearts of his subjects in the north.[32] But things had not gone well during the following weeks and the storm that brought down the standard seemed a bad omen. The king's melancholy was obvious in the last days of August.

Everywhere Charles went on his summer travels he was full of promises and soft words. 'It is not in your power', he told his Lincoln audience, 'to name one particular, which might make you happy, that I have refused to grant.' 'I am come to you in a time when nothing could invite me to such a journey but my affection to and good esteem of you', he announced at Leicester. There were brave words also. 'I ask nothing of you', the Nottinghamshire populace were informed, 'but to preserve your own affections to the religion and laws established.' He would live and die with them in that quarrel. Your religion, your liberties, your laws are at stake, declared the king at Leicester, 'the concurrence and affection of my people with God's blessing will supply and recover all.'[33] Again and again Charles reiterated that he fought against arbitrary government and for the law. Moreover he was ready to match his protestations with proof. When he arrived at Leicester, he found a party of men guarding the county magazine, who refused to hand it over at his command. The cavaliers, we are told, were 'exceedingly offended and would have offered to take it by force but the king, perceiving the danger thereof, granted their petition.'[34]

The king must have found the contrast between the people's formal acclamations of joy and their failure to rally to his army perplexing and depressing. According to one report 30,000 of Lincolnshire's inhabitants came to the county town to see their monarch and hear the speeches of welcome, yet there were few Lincolnshiremen at the raising of the standard.[35] It was the same story elsewhere. On 4 August Charles again harangued the Yorkshire gentry, thanking them for such help as they had given him: for their sakes he had given up the siege of Hull, passing over 'considerations of honour'. But few answered his call to join the regiment formed 'for the guard of my person'.[36] At Coventry later in the month few appeared when the gates were shut in his face and Charles sent warrants to call out the county militia.[37] At his arrival at Nottingham for the auspicious ceremony less than a hundred people came in from the county to greet him.[38]

32 BL E 202 (28): *A Perfect Diurnal*, 28 July–1 Aug., p.8.
33 Bl 669 f.5 (63): *His Majesty's Speech at Leicester*, Guildhall Library, London: *His Majesty's two Speeches at Newark and Lincoln*.
34 BL E 202 (26): *A Perfect Diurnal*, 25 July–1 Aug., p.4.
35 E.g. *CSPD 1641–3*, p. 359; BL E 202 (21): *A Diurnal and Particular of the Last Week's Daily Occurrences*, 16–26 July, pp. 1, 7–8.
36 BL E 109 (26): *His Majesty's Speech to the Gentlemen of Yorkshire*; E 109 (31): *An Extract of Letters*.
37 BL E 202 (39): *An Exact and True Diurnal*, 22–29 Aug., p.2; Hughes, pp.250–2.
38 BL E 114 (23); *Certain Special and Remarkable Passages*, 22–26 Aug.

The royal propaganda was failing to provoke anything more than the unthinking loyalty and deference which expressed itself in cheers and cap waving. Charles's cause lacked ideological momentum. Indeed many were probably left wondering whom they were expected to fight against. The tale that there was a parliamentary design against the kingdom was simply not as persuasive as the contrary story that the nation's enemies were papists and their malignant friends at court. Besides the king's campaign went against the grain of localism. Leicestershire's determination to retain its magazine shows this. Time and again Charles was stymied by the people's attachment to the principle that the trained bands should not cross the county boundaries. There was a report from Northamptonshire, for example, that the militiamen utterly refused to go to the king's help outside Coventry despite the threats of the earl of Northampton.[39]

The Yorkshire gentry were put in a particularly harsh dilemma by the royal war offensive. They feared that the failure to take Hull would prolong the king's stay in the county, because he now had more men than arms. Most of them longed to be rid of him but they were determined not to give up their magazine or arms and be left defenceless.[40] The older families were incensed at the way men of little standing had been advanced and alienated by unsavoury gossip, such as the story of how a parliamentary messenger attempting to arrest a papist was thrown down the stairs by some of the king's officers. The parliamentarian faction had played hard on the cavaliers' ill reputation: they had neither 'interest in nor affections to the public good', declared the 3 June petition, 'their language and behaviour speaking nothing but division and war.' The behaviour of the cavaliers, besides intense localism, explains the county's refusal to lend their arms, despite Charles's heart-felt appeals.

It became apparent during August and September that the royalist offensive was shot through with contradictions. The king respected the Yorkshiremen's concern for their own defence but elsewhere, first in Leicestershire and Nottinghamshire, then in Derbyshire, he seized the militiamen's weapons. There was no other way he could provide enough arms for his mobile army. A single entry in the constables' accounts of the Nottinghamshire village of Thorpe thus carries great significance: 'our charges one day at Nottingham when we delivered up the corslet'.[41] After 18 months of incessant publicity about the popish threat, here was the king depriving men of their means of self-defence at a time when the political future had never looked so dangerous and uncertain. The decision to disarm the trained bands was disastrous for the king's reputation. The news of his actions spread quickly and when he reached Uttoxeter on 15

39 BL E 202 (40): *A Perfect Diurnal*, 22–29 Aug., sub 26 Aug.
40 *HMC 5th Report*, p. 191.
41 Nottinghamshire RO PR 5767.

September, instead of the dutiful welcomes to which he had become accustomed, he found a sullen group of knights and gentlemen ready to excuse the failure of the trained bands to appear on his summons. Some of the Lancashire hundreds likewise resolved not to appear in arms if the king came to the county.[42] The arbitrary way the king seized men's arms belied all his protestations of constitutionalism.

The royalists' plundering also made nonsense of the king's story that he merely sought to defend his crown and the law against a malicious faction. The king was said to be angry at the pillage of Yorkshire parliamentarians like Sir Henry Cholmley and George Marwood, but there was nothing he could do to control his followers. An account of the attack on Marwood's house at Nun Monkton reached Westminster on 18 August:

> It was done in the day-time and by 24 horse or thereabouts . . . they threatened Mrs Marwood and her servants with death to discover where her husband was and swore they would cut him in pieces before her face and called her Protestant whore and Puritan whore. They searched all the house and broke open 17 locks. They took away all his money, being about £120, and all his plate they could find.[46]

Prince Rupert made his first deliberate attack on a manor house at Caldecot in Warwickshire, the home of William Purefoy, towards the end of the month. He followed this by a tour of Northamptonshire, Nottinghamshire, Leicestershire and Lincolnshire, extracting money by threats of pillage and striking at the homes of men known or rumoured to be active parliamentarians like Bradgate Park, the Greys' mansion in Leicestershire.[47]

But there was another even more serious and embarrassing contradiction in the king's recruiting campaign. If the purpose of the royal army was really as Charles expressed it in the proclamation for raising the standard – defence of the Protestant religion, the laws of the land and privileges of parliament – why did papists, 'who hate them all', rejoice so much, show themselves so forward and resort to York in such numbers? This was the question that Protestant gentry asked each other and that one

42 J.L. Malcolm, 'A King in Search of Soldiers: Charles I in 1642', *Historical Journal* xxi (1978), 258, 266–8.
43 BL E 109 (26): *His Majesty's Speech to the Gentlemen of Yorkshire;* E 202 (37): *A Perfect Diurnal,* 8–15 Aug., p.2.
44 BL 669 f.6 (52): *Truths from York, Hull and other places.*
45 *LJ* v, 109–10, 169; BL Harl. MS 163. fol. 150.
46 *LJ* v, 302.
47 BL E 114 (34): *A Continuation of Certain Special and Remarkable Passages,* 25–30 Aug; E 114 (36): *Special Passages,* 23–30 Aug; E 202 (42): *An Exact and True Diurnal,* 29 Aug–5 Sept., p. 8; 669 f 6 (75): *Remarkable Passages from Nottingham, Lichfield, Leicester and Cambridge;* 669 f 5 (76): *The Examination of Joshua Hill;* Vicars, *Jehovah-Jireh,* p.155; E.W. Hensman, *Loughborough during the Great Civil War* (Loughborough, 1921), pp. 12–13; Gardiner, *Great Civil War* i, 15, 21.

of them put to friends in London on 13 August.[48] The king's dependence on massive support from his Catholic subjects first became blatant at the Yorkshire muster on 4 August. Although the general turnout of horse was poor, many Catholics were there bringing mounted soldiers. Next to the fear of losing their arms, wrote one observer, terror at the thought of papists in arms had 'caused so slender an appearance'. Charles made much of his requirement that those who served him should take the oaths of supremacy and allegiance, but a special dispensation may have been given at this time to English Catholics to subscribe. It was noted that 'many recusants, to make themselves capable of commands, do resort to Church.'[49]

The notion that the king was putting himself at the head of a papist army, exaggerated though it was, steadily gained ground during August. It was sustained by gossip and innuendo. A soldier in the earl of Lindsey's regiment, captured by some countrymen near Nottingham and taken before a JP at the beginning of September, 'confessed that he thought the greatest part of His Majesty's army are papists'.[50] When some cavaliers had tried to raise volunteers from the West Riding trained bands a few weeks previously the story got around, as the ten or twelve men persuaded to march to York were on the road, that the soldier employed to beat a drum was 'known to be a noted papist for 14 years past'. After a few miles, 'not relishing the behaviour of the cavaliers', the recruits all deserted.[51]

In the first fortnight of September 1642 the king was at his most vulnerable. There was no way he could match the parliamentarian forces now in the field not so many miles to the south of Nottingham. An engagement would surely have gone against him.[52] In a sense therefore the journey across country to Shrewsbury was a retreat, though a wise and timely one. The commission to Francis Ottley to raise 200 foot in Shropshire and conduct them to Shrewsbury, issued on 4 September, is the first indication that a decision to move the royal headquarters had been made. The journey, via Derby, Uttoxeter, Stafford and Wellington, took from 13 to 20 September.[53] If some incidents on the way, such as the Uttoxeter business, were discouraging, the welcome the royal party received in Shropshire fully compensated for them. The sheriff, John Weld, attended Charles from Wellington with 34 men in livery. At Shrewsbury three full trained-band companies and 100 horse awaited him, together with the mayor and aldermen 'all ranked in a very comely manner, they and all the

48   *LJ*, v, 301–2.
49   *Historical Journal* XXI (1978), 255, 259.
50   BL E 117 (7): *The Resolution of the Gentry of Nottinghamshire*, p.5.
51   BL E 202 (37): *A Perfect Diurnal*, 8–15 Aug., p.5.
52   Gardiner, *Great Civil War* I, 21n.
53   Phillips, *Civil War in Wales* I, 108–9.

people shouting with great joy throughout the whole town to the court gates'.[54] This was the most ecstatic reception the king had received anywhere for some months; it was more like what he expected from his people.

The period the king spent based at Shrewsbury, from 20 September to 12 October, was one of steady recruitment: the army more than doubled in size. 'All the country around within 12 or 14 miles of Shrewsbury is full of soldiers', reported a correspondent on 30 September.[55] In the end the royalists were able to face their foes without the handicap of a major disparity of men and arms and to leave strong garrisons at Shrewsbury and West Chester besides.[56] Hyde was content to ascribe this change in the king's fortunes to the workings of providence but more mundane reasons can be adduced.[57] The king had come into the heartland of royalism. Petitions suffused with loyalty and full of men's eagerness to defend the king's person, honour, estate and prerogative had come to him in August from Flintshire, Denbighshire and the rest of North Wales.[58] The earl of Worcester's estates in south Wales were a sure recruiting ground.[59] Herefordshire's royalist stamp has already been discussed. At the Shropshire and Worcestershire assizes enthusiastic responses to the king's letter declaring his policies had been initiated by the justices and readily signed by many present.[60]

The military potential of Wales, the Marches, Cheshire and Lancashire was enormous. How did the king exploit it? The ground was well prepared for his coming: in Shropshire Francis Ottley had worked tirelessly in the previous weeks. Lord Strange, who succeeded his father as earl of Derby on 29 September, had been recruiting in earnest in south Lancashire since mid August. His warrant to the high constables of Amounderness hundred referred to the 12 August proclamation about the king's plans to raise his standard and announced that he was appointed lieutenant general of the county. His scheme was to raise volunteers from the militia companies, relying on the pull of his name and leadership.[61] According to a report on 26 August, following his first muster at Preston, as many as 100 musketeers, 60 pikemen and 16 cavalry had agreed to enlist from a single

54 W. Phillips, editor, 'The Ottley Papers relating to the Civil War', *Shropshire Archaeological and Natural History Society Transactions* VII (1895), 246.
55 Phillips, *Civil War in Wales* I, 115, 126; II, 19; Hutton, p. 37.
56 *HMC 5th Report*, p. 142; BL E 202 (45): *A Perfect Diurnal*, 26 Sept–3 Oct; *HMC Various Manuscripts* IV, 435.
57 See the epigraph to this chapter.
58 BL E 109 (27): *Petition to the King from Denbigh, Anglesey, Glamorgan and the whole principality of Wales*; E 111 (3): *Petition of Flintshire*; *HMC Portland* I, 52.
59 *HMC Portland* III, 98.
60 Phillips, editor, *Ottley Papers*, pp. 241–4; *Townshend*, p. 68.
61 BL 669 f 6 (74): *A True Copy of the Lord Strange his Warrant*; Hutton, pp. 30–2.

hundred.[62] Royalist recruiting agents had been active in Cheshire in June and Orlando Bridgeman was working to get men to subscribe to Strange's forces there in August.[63] The royalist gentry, in other words, were poised ready for action and the king's visit to the capital of the county palatine from 23 to 27 September gave them their chance to mobilize support for the royal field army.

The welcome the king was given at Chester on 23 September must have raised his spirits. At Milton Green he was met by 600 musketeers, at Hatton Heath by Earl Rivers and Lord Cholmondeley with their tenantry in arms, at Rowton Heath by Sir Thomas Aston with his forces. By the time he came up Eastgate Street, with the mayor and aldermen marching before him in their scarlet gowns, there was a huge throng. According to one eye-witness, there was such great shouting for joy that Charles scarcely heard the recorder's speech. But this celebration was a painful moment for the county's leading parliamentarians, who were soon packed off to Shrewsbury in custody: Sir Richard Wilbraham, we are told, 'met His Majesty and fell down on his knees to him but His Majesty would not take notice of him.' Next day the king was presented with an adulatory petition at a review of the trained bands on Hoole Heath. Two regiments of foot, part of a regiment of horse and three companies for the royal lifeguard subsequently joined the royal army from Cheshire, probably around 2000 officers and men in all, serving under Aston, Rivers and Sir Edward Fitton. During the next few weeks Chester also became a rendezvous for the Lancashire men raised by Strange: the first troop of horse arrived while Charles was there. According to a report on 1 October 260 horseloads of arms in all had reached the city 'out of the north'.[64]

Whereas Lord Strange seems to have used a good deal of coercion in order to deliver three regiments of foot to Charles, Sir Edward Stradling and Thomas Salisbury were able to rely mainly on the deeply entrenched royalism of the Welsh shires for the enforcement of their recruiting drives.[65] It was a shrewd move on the king's part to send the prince of Wales on a short visit to Raglan, where he was bountifully feasted. When he stayed at Radnor Castle on the way there, the gentry of the district flocked in with presents as testimonies of their affection, 'everyone striving for the credit and glory of his country to exceed in several expressions of generous liberality'.[66] A few days later came the news that several thousand

62 BL E 114 (36): *Special Passages*, 23–30 Aug.
63 *CJ* II, 615; BL Harl. MS 163, fol. 152v; E 202 (6): *Diurnal Occurrences in Parliament*, 6–13 June, sub 7 June.
64 Phillips, *Civil War in Wales* I, 110–12; II, 10–15 17; M.D.G. Wanklyn, 'Landed Society and Allegiance in Cheshire and Shropshire in the First Civil War' (Manchester University, PhD thesis, 1976) pp. 227–9; BL 669 f 6(83): *The Gratulation of Cheshire*; Morrill, *Cheshire*, p. 65.
65 *Historical Journal* XXI (1978), 268–9.
66 Phillips, *Civil War in Wales* II, 26–9.

men were marching to the standard under Lord Herbert from Monmouth-shire and Glamorgan.[67] Salusbury's regiment, from Denbighshire and Flintshire, was another tenant band. Meeting in early August at Wrexham, the leading men agreed to levy £1500 for its expenses and they were soon writing round requesting 'half a score of lusty fellows' from each of their friends.[68]

There was 'scarce a family of any consideration' in north Wales, according to one observer, 'that was not engaged for the king'.[69] Yet it would be wrong to see the principality's good showing as entirely spontaneous. In letters from Derby on 15 September to the commissioners of array in the north Wales shires, the king announced a much more systematic approach to recruiting from the trained bands than he had attempted previously. He intended to appoint several regiments as 'a guard for our dearest son the prince' and the militiamen joining this guard would be received into pay on their arrival at Shrewsbury. This appeal was well received: 200 men were sent from Caernarvonshire, for instance, decently equipped and with money for their journey.[70]

Cash as well as ancient loyalty kept·the new levies at the king's side. Many royalist gentry in Wales and the Marches made generous donations at this stage of the campaign. By early October the mint was in business at Shrewsbury and there were reports of plate coming in daily. This was just as well since the border farmers were being offered good wages: Sir Paul Harris, recruiting on Myddle Hill, took on 20 volunteers at four shillings and fourpence a week.[71]

Although his military prospects improved once he was west of the Pennines, the king did not feel secure enough to resist the temptation to arm his Catholic subjects. He laid the ground for a public reversal of policy in his speech near Wellington on 19 September: 'there are divers protestations in it to keep the laws', summarized one newsbook, 'but an intimation that he intends to break them.' Four days later Charles wrote as follows to the earl of Newcastle:

> This rebellion is grown to that height that I must look not of what opinion men are who at this time are willing and able to serve me. Therefore I do not only

---

67 BL E 202 (45): *A Perfect Diurnal,* 10–17 Oct., pp. 2,8.

68 *Calendar of Wynn Papers,* p. 277; A.H. Dodd, 'The Civil War in East Denbighshire', *Denbighshire Historical Transactions* III (1954), 47–50.

69 BL E 144 (34): *A Continuation of Certain Special and Remarkable Passages,* 25–30 Aug.; see also A.H. Dodd, 'Flintshire Politics in the Seventeenth Century', *Flintshire Historical Society Publications* XIV (1953–4), 33–4.

70 P.B. Williams, *Tourists' Guide through the County of Caernarvon* (Caernarvon, 1821), appendix, xiii–vi; R. Williams, 'An Account of the Civil War in North Wales', *Archaeologia Cambrensis,* 1846, 33–4.

71 *HMC 12th Report,* appendix, part IX, p. 11; Staffordshire RO D 593/P/8/1/4; Phillips, *Civil War in Wales* I, 116–7; II, 30; Hutton, pp.37–8, 41.

permit but command you to make use of all my loving subjects' services, without examining their consciences – more than their loyalty to us – as you shall find most to conduce to the upholding of my just legal power.

He followed this on 27 September with an order to the leading Lancashire recusants to arm themselves, their servants and their tenants in the royal cause.[72] With these directives the papist conspiracy had at last become, in some sense, a self-fulfilling prophecy. Their impact remains to be fully assessed, but recent work on the north of England suggests that the Catholic presence in the royalist army may have been very much larger than some historians have suggested.[73]

'The king's personal efforts had been worse than disappointing', a recent study of his recruitment campaign has concluded: 'they were an embarrassment.'[74] This verdict may be too harsh, particularly with regard to the period from 19 September to the battle at Edgehill. During this time the king spoke personally to his army at least twice, near Wellington on 19 September and at Southam on 21 October, and to assemblies of gentry and countrymen at Shrewsbury, Chester and Wrexham. His speeches were quickly printed and widely distributed. It is hard of course to judge their impact, either on those who heard or read them, but they are such persuasive statements of the royalist case that it is unlikely to have been negligible.[75] Moreover the king constantly sought to check plunder and pillage and, though it was by no means eradicated, his words may have begun to have some effect. 'We hold it most necessary to advertise you since your hostility is in a righteous and religious cause', he declared at Southam,

> that you use no sinister action. Good causes never produce unrighteous effects, nor can truth be fortified with falsehood. Therefore we will and command you to march peaceably and quietly as a defending party not a provoking. Despoil not man's goods not in the least degree, abuse not their wives or servants or cattle . . . lest you make a breach in the law and liberty of the subject, the cause you stand to defend.[76]

The king's inspiration, even a certain magnetism, comes through in these speeches. He deserves some of the credit for the mobilization of a royalist army.

72 Ormerod, pp. 38–40; Gardiner, *Great Civil War* I, 35–6; *Historical Journal* XXI (1938), 270–1.
73 K.J. Lindley, 'The Part Played By the Catholics', in Manning, editor, *Politics, Religion and the English Civil War*, pp. 127–78; P.R. Newman, 'The Royalist Army in the North of England' (University of York PhD thesis, 1978); B.G. Blackwood, *The Lancashire Gentry and the Great Rebellion* (Manchester, 1978) pp. 63–5.
74 J. Malcolm in *Historical Journal* XXI (1978), 270.
75 Phillips, *Civil War in Wales* II, 20–22; *LJ* V; 376; BL 669 f 5 (83): *His Majesty's Speech at Shrewsbury*; E 119 (10): *His Majesty's Demands and Propositions to the City of Chester*; E 200 (67): *Three Speeches made by the King*.
76 Phillips, *Civil War in Wales* II, 30; Bodleian Ashmole MS 830, fol. 277.

Parliament, like the king, launched its war offensive in the midst of a barrage of propaganda. The enforcement of the militia ordinance was the centrepiece of this propaganda effort. The ordinance was seen as a defensive tactic and a political weapon, rather than as a means to wage war. The leadership envisaged musters organized by the new deputy lieutenants as demonstrations of solidarity and loyalty in the counties. The Lords were slow in establishing a formula for commissions to colonels and captains and some lieutenants delayed over appointing their deputies.[77] But training of the London militia began on 2 May, following a motion from Holles, seconded by Venn.[78] The review of it in Finsbury Fields on 10 May was explicitly intended 'as an example for the whole kingdom to imitate'.[79] The Commons only sat for two hours that morning before adjourning for the parade. Essex came 'in a new gilt coach', with other peers, including Holland and Northumberland: 'many great lords were there on horseback and in tents . . . and many gentry besides and the infinite shoal of people.' Estimates of the number of militiamen present varied from 8000 to 10,000 and their dexterity was much commended.[80]

The London muster was the signal for a sustained campaign for the enforcement of the militia ordinance. A committee of both Houses was appointed to manage the business: an initial plan for a single day for reviewing all the home counties bands was abandoned in favour of appointments for particular counties as the cooperation of lieutenants proved forthcoming.[81] In late May and early June, the Commons began to direct deputies to proceed on their own in counties near London where the lieutenant himself was still inert.[82]

Declarations, orders, ordinances, speeches, letters from the Speaker to sheriffs, congratulatory petitions and fast sermons all poured from the London presses during the summer. The parliamentary leadership looked for every piece of favourable publicity they could lay hands upon.[83] Early in the year they had left the circulation of propaganda largely to chance. MPs were expected to maintain contact with sheriffs and town councils but there was no systematic check on how thoroughly orders were distributed.[84] The report of a committee of MPs in Yorkshire in May about their difficulties in dispersing and enforcing parliamentary directions made the Commons aware of some of the difficulties. A committee was set

---

77 *CJ* II, 494, 519, 522, 531, 537, 555; *LJ* IV, 704; V, 4, 29, 33.
78 BL Harl. MS 163, fol. 100v; *CJ* II, 559.
79 *HMC 5th Report*, p. 178.
80 *LJ* V, 56, 60, 62, *CJ* II, 568, 570; *HMC Montagu*, p. 152; *HMC Buccleuch* I, 299–300; *HMC Coke*, pp. 314, 317; *HMC 3rd Report*, p. 85; *HMC 5th Report*, pp. 147, 178.
81 *CJ* II, 572, 583, 596, 606, 614, 651, 658.
82 BL Harl. MS 163, fols. 132v, 146v; *CJ* II, 590, 606, 609; *LJ* V, 137.
83 Fortescue, *Catalogue of the Thomson Collection*, pp. 57–175. For orders to print see e.g. *CJ* II, 557, 588; *LJ* V, 44; Clarendon I, 541.
84 *CJ* II, 377–8, 386, 403–4, 407, 578; *LJ* IV, 707.

up in this instance to pursue the matter.[85] As the king's propaganda campaign began to bite the seriousness of the paper battle became apparent. So on 4 June a new committee was established to investigate the standard of printing, the publication of votes and declarations throughout the kingdom and the execution of parliamentary orders.[86]

The scheme the new committee formulated was ambitious. The aim was no less than to get major printed items, spelling out parliament's case in detail, into the hands of every petty constable, head borough or tithingman in the land. Sheriffs and high constables were given responsibility for distributing the bundles of papers and their receipts were to be checked by the committee in London. MPs were given oversight of the smooth working of the plan. On 9 June five items were selected for this treatment: the Grand Remonstrance, the Remonstrance of 26 May concerning Hull, the Declaration concerning the three votes of 20 May, the Declaration of 27 May in reply to the king's proclamation against the militia ordinance and some recent accounts of the state's finances.[87] The order for 9000 copies of each of these items to be printed may have been based on an estimate of the approximate number of parishes in the country. On 4 July 9000 copies of the Declaration against the commissions of array were also ordered. By then dispersal of the propaganda was apparently in full swing.[88] The scheme was remarkably well conceived but how well it worked is largely guesswork. Even if it broke down in some places, it must have set a huge mass of publicity rolling through the localities.

The scale of parliament's propaganda campaign undoubtedly outdid the king's, for when it came to justifying a resort to arms, it certainly had the more difficult task. By March 1642 the arguments from precedents were of limited usefulness, though the leadership still sometimes employed them.[89] There was in fact no escape from a redefinition of the position of the monarch in relation to the state. This was where MPs' confidence in their representative function and conviction that they were engaged to save the country from its papist enemies stood them in good stead. When the king made war on it, parliament declared on 20 May, there was 'a breach of the trust reposed in him by his people, contrary to his oath, and tending to the dissolution of this government'. There was no flinching from the logical course of this argument. Though the king possessed a trust from his people, parliament was given a superior trust. For parliament was a council to provide for necessities, prevent imminent dangers and preserve the public peace and safety of the kingdom:

85   *CJ* II, 587, 590.
86   *CJ* II, 608.
87   *CJ* II, 613, 620, 648.
88   *CJ* II, 634, 654.
89   *Trevelyan Papers*, part III, 223; Kenyon, *Stuart Constitution*, p.197.

and what they do herein hath the stamp of royal authority, although His Majesty, seduced by evil counsel, do in his own person oppose or interrupt the same; for the king's supreme and royal pleasure is exercised and declared in this high court of law and council after a more eminent and obligatory manner than it can be by personal act or resolution of his own.[90]

Thus Pym and his allies found themselves severing the monarchical from the personal capacity of the king. Though reluctant to pursue radical courses, their distrust finally left them no choice but to claim sovereignty for parliament.[91]

'The ready having a strength of horse is now come into agitation', wrote Sir Edmund Moundeford to Sir John Potts on 7 June.[92] The war offensive proper began with the appointment the previous day of a new committee for the defence of the kingdom. The members included Fiennes, Hampden, Holles, Marten and Pym. There was to be no more hiding behind the declared need to relieve Ireland: the committee's remit was to bring propositions for raising horse, men and money.[93] The Propositions scheme which was presented two days later became the basis of the parliamentarian war effort. It was carefully thought out, coherent and daring, wholly characteristic, in other words, of Pym's mind. Subscriptions were invited of money and plate and offers to maintain horse, horsemen and arms to defend the kingdom against its enemies. In either case volunteers were promised interest at eight per cent, though some were quite rightly immediately sceptical about whether they would be repaid. Four aldermen of the City were established as a committee at Haberdashers Hall to oversee the scheme.[94]

On paper parliament now had the means to raise a national army. Deadlines for subscriptions were set two weeks ahead for the southeast and three weeks ahead for the west, midlands and north.[95] The boldness of the scheme reflects the confidence the petitions had given parliament's leaders that they could command support in every part of the land. It also reflects their confidence in their own men. It had come to be assumed that in any fiscal or administrative matter MPs themselves would act as parliament's agents. The core of members who had stuck by Pym's side, in other words, had gradually become the political supervisors of local government.[96] Much of this supervision had previously been exercised by

90 Gardiner, *Documents*, p. 257.
91 Gardiner x, 200–1; Zagorin, pp. 309–11, Ashton, *English Civil War*, pp. 179–80.
92 Bodleian Tanner MS 63, fol. 43v.
93 *CJ* II, 612–3; Pennington, pp. 183–4; L. Glow, 'The Committee of Safety', *EHR* LXXX (1965), 291.
94 *LJ* v, 121–2; Pearl, pp. 209–10; BL Harl. MS 163, fols. 153v, 154v.
95 *LJ* v, 121–2.
96 Pennington, pp. 169–70; *D'Ewes(C)*, pp.44, 108–9, 256–7, 334; Cheshire RO DCC 14/29; 47/26.

correspondence, but by March 1642 Pym had recognized that some men had to be encouraged to spend time in their own localities, even if the quorum was thereby endangered at Westminster. 'He would be able to do as much service there for settling the militia', he observed on 21 March, moving that Sir Edward Hungerford should be given leave to go down into Wiltshire.[97]

The Propositions scheme rested on twin hopes: that there really was mass enthusiasm for a war against the king in the provinces and that MPs would speedily go into action as promoters of subscriptions.[98] Neither of these hopes proved justified. The response of individual MPs was a warning of what might be expected from the country as a whole. According to information obtained by Secretary Nicholas, when the Commons was faced with this ultimate political test 70 members subscribed, 33 delayed their answer and 50 would lend nothing.[99] The plan was that the knights and burgesses should nominate suitable men as receivers in the counties, who would pay in the sums collected to the London treasurers.[100] But many of them were reluctant to take so blatantly divisive a move as imposing the scheme on their own neighbourhoods. The approach adopted by the Northamptonshire delegation is indicative of this. They merely compiled a list of gentry who they hoped might contribute and sent this down during July. 'I hope all men will consider', wrote Sir Gilbert Pickering to Sir Roland St John, 'that if the kingdom be asaulted it must defend itself and that cannot be without a stock of money and this must come voluntarily for there can be no compulsion without a law.'[101] Parliament's failure to mention the Propositions in the general instructions for several county committees during late July and early August, surely an obvious tactic, can probably be accounted for by this hesitancy.[102] Not until 18 August did Northamptonshire have a formally constituted committee for the Propositions and officially appointed receivers. About that time it became more normal to include enforcement of the Propositions in committee instructions and in a few other cases besides Northamptonshire, such as Huntingdonshire and Sussex, a special committee was established to deal with the matter.[103] In the long run, of course, the Propositions were a vital element in parliament's war machine and even tiny villages in some districts contributed impressively.[104] But this was because Propositions money came to be

97 BL Harl. MS 163, fol. 39v; *CJ* II, 490.
98 *CJ* II, 653–4, 673, 721.
99 BL Harl. MS 163, fols. 157r, 159v; *CSPD 1641–3*, p.340; Zagorin, p.323.
100 *LJ* v, 122.
101 Bedfordshire RO J 1410.
102 *CJ* II, 629, 655; *LJ* v, 140, 165–6, 177, 183–4, 260–1, 299–300.
103 *LJ* v, 250, 304, 311, 329–30, 338;*Sussex*, p.259.
104 See e.g. East Suffolk RO HD 224/1: William Heveningham's account book; M.V. Jones, 'The Political History of the Parliamentary Boroughs of Kent 1642–1662'(London D.Phil. thesis, 1967), pp. 353–4.

spent mainly on local defence. The scheme for creating a national army was diverted to localist aims, as Sir William Brereton had signified it would be when he told his Westminster colleagues in a letter of 8 August that the Cheshire gentry would not subscribe money, plate or horses until they were assured it might be used for the defence of their own shire.[105]

In any case events were moving much too fast for the leadership to wait upon the localities. It quickly became clear that the best chance of raising a parliamentary army lay in exploiting the eagerness and goodwill of the London citizens and of parliament's most enthusiastic supporters in the districts nearby.[106] Delegations from Westminster discussed the Propositions with leading aldermen on 11 and 17 June and on the 18th citizens were harangued by MPs at a Common Hall.[107] Abundant plate and money was already coming in by then.[108] Accounts for the wards of Bishopsgate, Cheapside and Farringdon Without show the large sums that were raised there before the end of August.[109]

Outside London the leadership concentrated on Buckinghamshire, Essex, Hertfordshire and Surrey. Arthur Goodwin, John Hampden, Bulstrode Whitelocke and Richard Winwood were sent down to advance the Propositions in Buckinghamshire on 5 July. Only a few days later £1000 was reported to be in hand.[110] A Propositions committee for Essex was constituted on 11 July and some of the deputy lieutenants went there to add the force of their presence a few days later.[111] Meetings to take subscriptions were held in towns such as Colchester and Saffron Walden around the end of the month.[112] Several of the Hertfordshire JPs attended the summer assizes with the purpose of forwarding the Propositions, after Watford had set an example to the county by raising £1250 and 50 horse towards a cavalry troop.[113] In mid July Surrey MPs undertook to propagate the scheme at a series of meetings.[114]

'We have the City and we have the hearts of the people who are ready whensoever we shall hold up our finger.' Henry Marten's boast on 23 July was soundly based.[115] At the first muster in Tuthill Fields on 2 July 800

105 BL Harl. MS 164, fol. 260r; Morrill, *Revolt*, pp. 54–5; D.H. Pennington and I.A. Roots, editors, *The Committee at Stafford 1643–1645* (Manchester, 1956), pp. xxxiii–iv.
106 *CJ* II, 614.
107 *CJ* II, 621, 633; *LJ* V, 147.
108 *Trevelyan Papers* III, 227.
109 PRO SP 16/491/130.
110 *CJ* II, 658, 664; *LJ* V, 207; BL E 202 (15): *A Perfect Diurnal*, 4–11 July, p. 9; Johnson, pp. 119–20.
111 *CJ* II, 670, 685.
112 Essex RO T/A 401/2: Saffron Walden Chamberlains Accounts, p. 294; Macfarlane, editor, *Diary of Ralph Josselin*, p. 12; Holmes, p. 35.
113 *CJ* II, 648, 650, 671, 675; *LJ* V, 207; BL 669 f 5 (52): *Petition of Watford*; E 202 (17): *A Perfect Diurnal*, 11–18 July, p. 6; E 202 (18): *A Perfect Diurnal or the Proceedings in Parliament*, 11–18 July, p. 5; Bodleian Dep C MS 165, no. 79; Holmes, p. 53.
114 *CJ* II. 671.
115 BL Add. MS 14827, fol. 169v.

horse with pistols and carbines had appeared.[116] On 9 July Pym carried a motion for raising 10,000 volunteers in the City by a majority of 80 votes.[117] Four weeks of hectic activity then preceded the departure of parliament's army from the capital.[118] Some of the first £7500 that the Propositions had yielded was spent on pistols and saddles; 500 horses were also purchased.[119] MPs were detailed to negotiate with carpenters and wheelwrights for carriages and carts for the army.[120] At a muster on 21 July, when neither House sat, 1000 men enlisted and Bedford and Essex rode among them, 'at whose presence the people gave a great shout and the troopers two or three volley of shot, which was done with great applause of all the spectators'.[121] Stepney apprentices and journeymen made their subscriptions after sermon the following Sunday.[122] More apprentices, with the consent of their masters, enlisted on 25 and 26 July, when Essex was present in the Artillery Garden. The people swarmed round his coach. On 27 July, when Essex was there again with Stamford and other peers, 3000 new recruits were reported.[123] On 28 July and again on 3 August neither House sat in the afternoon so MPs could attend the parades in Tuthill and Finsbury Fields.[124]

There were six bands of foot – about 4800 men – and eleven of horse in the army that set out for Warwickshire 'to secure those parts' on 8 August. Five hundred horse from Buckinghamshire and 300 from Essex had joined the massive citizen bands. The same day forces fanned out westwards to relieve Portsmouth, where George Goring had now declared for Charles, and to challenge the Marquis of Hertford, who was attempting to raise royalist troops in the west.[125] For those left behind in London the next weeks were ones of tense expectation. There were still soldiers in the streets and London turned to defensive preparations. 'We have him, we have him in a blue string', cried newly recruited troopers when the earl of Berkshire, arrested for enforcing the commission of array in Oxfordshire, was brought in on 16 August.[126] The City's militia in its complete arms appeared to see Essex take the road to the midlands in order to assume

116   BL E 202 (12): *Some Special Passages*, 3–10 July 1642.
117   *CJ* II, 667.
118   BL E 202 (16): *A Perfect Diurnal*, 11–18 July; Bodleian Tanner MS 63, fol. 101.
119   *CJ* II, 651, 658; BL E 202 (25): *Some Special Passages*, 18–26 July, sub 21 July.
120   BL E 202 (28): *A Perfect Diurnal*, 25 July–1 Aug. sub 29 July.
121   BL E 202 (24): *A Perfect Diurnal*, 18–25 July, sub 21 July.
122   BL E 202 (25): *Some Special Passages*, 18–26 July, sub 24 July.
123   BL E 200 (54): *The City of London's Resolution*; E 202 (26): *A Perfect Diurnal*, 25 July–1 Aug. pp. 2,4.
124   BL E 202 (28):*A Perfect Diurnal*, 25 July –1 Aug., p.6; E 202 (31): *A Perfect Diurnal*, 1–7 Aug; sub 3 Aug.
125   BL E 202 (25): *Some Special Passages*, 18–26 July, sub 21 July; E 202 (30): *A Perfect Diurnal*, 1–7 Aug., pp. 5,8; E 202 (33): *A True and Exact Diurnal*, 8–15 Aug., p. 4; *CJ* II, 724; Gardiner x, 216.
126   Bodleian Tanner MS 63, fol. 125. See the epigraph to this chapter.

his command on 9 September.[127]

The creation of the parliamentary army was a triumph of political manoeuvring, a considerable feat of organization and an expression of ideological commitment. We shall consider these three aspects of the matter in turn. In July and August 1642 Pym's dominance of the Commons was as secure as ever. So much so that when some of the fiercest war-party men were urging the expulsion of Sir John Culpepper, who had arrived with the king's plea for peace on 27 August, D'Ewes was shocked that the man whom everyone recognized as pre-eminent was for once almost brushed aside: 'some fiery spirits were so hot upon it as they would scarce permit Mr Pym himself to speak for Sir John Culpepper.'[128] Pym's general strategy had not changed since the spring. Whenever it really mattered, he supported the warmongers like Marten and Strode, trying to pull the rest of the House along in his wake. For instance when the king's reply to the petition sent to Beverley reached the Commons on 25 July and there were the predictable calls for accommodation, he insisted 'that the same jealousies still remain, that the king is still ruled by the same counsels, that we should go on with the levies we agreed.' Here was Marten's cue:

> That there be a declaration made to the people that we have petitioned for peace but 'tis denied us but upon conditions as is worse than war. That though the king be king of the people of England, yet he is not master of the people of England.

Once again Pym's words had brought respectability to the war party's uncompromising course of action. Walter Long at once supported Marten: he would 'as soon come with a halter about his neck as yield to those things that are propounded'. Even that quintessential moderate Sir John Holland took Marten's line. 'There is no security but in the actual going on with your preparation', he declared, adding that he wished parliament at the same time to 'give the world satisfaction that we desire peace'.[129]

The war offensive presupposed, so far as men like Marten and Strode were concerned, that all those who were not for parliament should be treated as incorrigibly against it. On 3 June Marten called for the immediate replacement of four lord lieutenants rumoured to be at York; on the 30th he declared that if the earl of Newcastle would not attend the Lords 'we should send the horse for him'. Strode was supported by Marten when he proposed a bill on 2 June to confiscate the lands of those peers who had gone to York as 'promoters of the differences'. A few days later he suggested the impeachment of nine peers who had refused to return to Westminster; on 14 July he demanded the expulsion of Hyde for the same

127 BL E 202 (44): *Remarkable Passages or a Perfect Diurnal*, 5–12 Sept., sub 9 Sept.
128 BL Harl. MS 163, fol. 303v.
129 BL Add. MS 14827, fols. 170v–171r.

reason.[130] Strode became increasingly merciless towards those whom he suspected of backsliding: 'Will Strode last day was so uncharitable to me as he moved to have me sent down after you in advancement of the peace of the county', Sir John Holland informed Sir John Potts on 4 August, at a time when he was under suspicion of using illness as an excuse for inaction.[131] The smallest hint of delinquency was enough to cause the war party to press for a man's expulsion. By the end of September 46 men in all had lost their places at Westminster.[132]

D'Ewes attributed the delay of half an hour before a quorum was reached on 10 August to the mastery of the 'hot fiery spirits', who 'carried all things now as they listed', leaving others with no incentive to make haste in the mornings.[133] Their ruthlessness was exhibited the next day in the imposition of the resolution in support of Essex, already referred to that week in one of the newsbooks as a covenant. Following the news of the king's proclamation declaring Essex a traitor, members had agreed that they would maintain him as their lord general with their lives and fortunes. The 'hotter spirits', noted D'Ewes, not content to pass the vote 'in a fair, ordinary and parliamentary way by one general question, . . . forced every man to answer particularly'. So when old William Jesson, an alderman of Coventry, refused to give his affirmative, Speaker Lenthall had no choice but to reprimand him. Other moderates like John Fettiplace and Sir Guy Palmes were apparently overawed by the treatment of Jesson into giving their assent; some coming back from dinner gave their approval without having time to ponder what they were doing.[134] In the next weeks the war party treated the resolution to follow Essex as a political test: 44 men who slipped back into their places before the end of September, having been absent on 11 August, were required to make their personal response.[135] When Sir Thomas Bowyer said he agreed with the declaration only 'so far as it might stand with the oaths of supremacy and allegiance' on 27 August, there were cries for him to withdraw, but he escaped his dilemma by a clever tactic invented by D'Ewes. He gave his assent to the resolution *in toto composito*, that is he would adhere to Essex 'for the maintenance of the true religion, the king's person, the laws of the land and the privileges of parliament'.[136] The war party in this case were hoist with their own disingenuous wording.

This then was the political context of parliament's war offensive.

130 BL Add. MS 14827, fols. 123v, 124v, 147r, 160r; Harl. MS 163, fols. 160v, 272v.
131 Ketton-Cremer, p. 146.
132 *HMC 5th Report*, p. 162.
133 BL Harl. MS 164, fol. 260v.
134 BL Harl. MS 164, fol. 261v; E 202 (37): *A Perfect Diurnal*, 8–15 Aug.; p.6; *CJ* II, 719; Gardiner x, 217.
135 *CJ* II, 744–5, 747, 759, 769, 778.
136 BL Harl. MS 163, fol. 304.

Dragging the moderates into line was a prerequisite for effective action. But how did parliament actually manage to put an army in the field? In the first place they enjoyed the wholehearted cooperation of the London Court of Common Council, which was intimately involved in the business of recruiting. The bonds of alliance between the City and the Commons, which had been so evident since the previous December, were drawn close by the practical business of organizing for war.[137] But as important as this was the creation on 4 July of the committee for safety. Both in terms of policy and of administration, this was the crucial instrument of parliament's war effort, as a recent article has shown: 'its indefinite powers, the breadth and variety of its activities and its taking over, however unevenly, of so many of the powers of the House itself, combine to distinguish it radically from the antecedent committees of defence'.[138]

About ten members of each house were regular attenders at the committee of safety in the first few months of its life. They included Fiennes, Holles, Marten and Pym from the Commons and Bedford, Essex and Northumberland from the Lords.[139] From the start it sat several times a week. Strode and others objected when letters from Hotham and the committee at Hull were read to MPs before the committee had seen them on 11 July. This procedure was soon reversed: the committee received and sifted all the news and reported to the Commons only what it thought fit.[140] It quickly became the main organ of military policy. It drafted the decision to appoint a general and raise an army; it put forward the names of the chief officers; it laid down the procedure for their taking the oath of allegiance. The committee employed its own messengers and quickly established its own intelligence system. It made the arrangements for the buying and delivery of war materials. It kept in close touch with Essex once he had left London on 9 September. It authorized almost all payments connected with the war.[141] Its first order book, which covers August and the first half of September, contains 148 warrants to Sir Gilbert Gerrard, the treasurer of the war funds.[142] By early August the committee of safety's control of policy and executive action was so complete that the Commons contemplated, but then abandoned, a plan for a recess leaving it together with a few subsidiary committees to carry on the war.[143]

There was never any question of parliament being able to pay for a military campaign from such Propositions money as was collected in July

137 BL E 202 (28): *A Perfect Diurnal*, 25 July–1 Aug., pp. 1,4; Ashton, *City and the Court*, pp. 206–7; Pearl, pp. 240–51.
138 Glow, *EHR* LXXX (1965), 298.
139 *CJ* II, 659, 661, 663; BL Add. Ms 14827, fols. 165v, 166v; Harl. MS 163, fol. 266v.
140 *CJ* II, 682; BL Harl. MS 163, fol. 263.
141 BL Add. Ms 14827, fols. 157r, 158r; *EHR* LXXX (1965), 291–5.
142 PRO SP 28/261/I.
143 *CJ* II, 707; *CSPV 1642–3*, p.123.

and August in London and neighbouring districts. But parliament was fortunate in having retained control of various fiscal measures established since November 1640. In so far as these could be activated, the money might be diverted to paying for the war against the king. The difficulty was enforcement. In theory £200,000, the first half of the act for £400,000 to relieve Ireland, should have been paid in by 20 June, but even by the end of July little of it had been received.[144] During June collection was still in its early stages in several counties: Berkshire, Flintshire, Wiltshire and Worcestershire for example.[145] Herefordshire and Surrey gentry were seeking abatements of the rates set on their counties.[146] Some of the Sussex commissioners did not settle their apportionments until mid July and in Devon the JPs gave the matter no attention at all until the quarter sessions that month.[147] In view of this situation, the Commons sought to extract what they could from the arrears of poll money, subsidy and the Irish Benevolence payments. Agents, who were awarded generous expenses, were given full powers on 26 July to harry the local commissioners for all these funds. There was a plan for 'discreet and able' men to inspect all the relevant papers in the localities and report how payments were being obstructed, but it is not clear whether it was implemented or what results it achieved.[148]

In any case parliament needed money quickly and could not wait on such schemes. On 11 June a deputation led by four peers – Essex, Holland, Northumberland and Pembroke – once more approached the City livery companies, but they were much less cooperative about the new loan proposed than about sparing London citizens to fight in the parliamentary army. Alderman Pennington suggested a sum of £100,000 but only two of the companies, the grocers and fishmongers, showed any enthusiasm and the money was very slow to materialize.[149] The only way of financing the army, it was plain, was by seizing resources intended for other purposes. A raid of £100,000 on the Irish Adventurers fund was agreed, according to D'Ewes, 'at a thin committee of the Adventurers, packed on purpose without the knowledge and to the great discontent of the rest and of many other in the House . . . there being only a colour pretended that it should be paid again out of the plate which had been brought in upon the Proposi-

---

144 *SR* v, 148; East Devon RO 1700A/CP24.
145 Guilding, editor, *Reading Records* IV, 45; *Calendar of Wynn Papers*, p. 277; Harrison,'Royalist Organisation in Wiltshire', pp.87–9; Birmingham Reference Library, Hanley Court MSS, Box 5, 398272–3.
146 *HMC Portland* III, 87; *CJ*, II, 550; BL Harl. MS 164, fol. 256.
147 *Sussex*, p.210; East Devon RO QS Order Book 1640–51, sub Midsummer 1642.
148 *CJ* II, 588, 649, 693, 695–7. For local examples see *HMC Portland*, I, 30; Essex RO, Q/SBa 2/46.
149 BL E 150 (24): *New Propositions to the Mayor and Common Council of the City*; Add. MS 14827, fol. 123v; *CJ* II, 626–8, 634; Pearl, pp. 208–9.

tions as soon as it could be coined.'[150] Many of the arms were supplied from the magazine previously held at Hull, which had been shipped to London in May.[151] Thus, though the training in Tuthill Fields gives an appearance of coherent planning, parliament's war effort was actually as hand to mouth as the king's. Posses of militiamen toured the capital in August searching private houses for plate and money.[152] One inestimable advantage parliament did possess from the start was the services of several able administrators with expertise in financial management and accountancy. MPs like Giles Green and John Trenchard from Dorset and the London property magnate William Wheeler were becoming trusted officials, whose reports were awaited in the Commons with bated breath.[153]

There was an intimate connection between the enthusiasm of many London citizens for the parliamentary cause and the long-established tradition of religious radicalism in the City, which had been so carefully nurtured since the Long Parliament opened by pulpit and pamphlet propaganda. During the first months of 1642 Pym's sometimes rather strained and uneasy relationship with men like Henry Burton was replaced by a close political compact with the London preachers. The celebrated fast-sermons programme had its origins in the king's proclamation of 8 January for a nationwide fast on the last Wednesday in each month, while the rebellion in Ireland persisted. Charles had 'put into the hands of his enemies a means of coordination and propaganda to which he himself had no parallel'.[154] The initial sermons on 23 February were an intoxicating occasion: MPs sat tight packed in St Margaret's from nine until four, joining in a psalm between the two orations. The preachers chosen, Edmund Calamy and Stephen Marshall, were both well known Puritan divines. Marshall's *Meroz Cursed* was the first of a long line of incendiary sermons. It cannot be read any other way than as a bloodthirsty call for total war: the Lord, Marshall explained, 'acknowledges no neuters'. Simeon Ashe, Thomas Goodwin, Joseph Caryll and William Sedgwick were among those who used fast sermons during the next months to offer a militant interpretation of current events. The godly might seem few in number, confessed Ashe, 'in comparison of the malignant party who oppose our hopes and welfare, yet may we pluck up our hearts from this consideration, that our help standeth in the name of the Lord who made heaven and earth'. The congregational New Jerusalem was close at hand, insisted Goodwin: parliament's role was to 'secure the land' against the royalists,

150 *CJ* II, 702; *LJ* v, 251; BL Harl. MS 164, fol. 262r.
151 *CJ* II, 598, 614, 641; *LJ* v, 70–1, 158, 215–6.
152 Gloucestershire RO D 2510/19.
153 *CJ* II, 298, 310, 344, 360, 620, 648; Pennington, pp. 164, 185; L. Glow, 'The Committee Men in the Long Parliament, August 1642–December 1643', *Historical Journal* VIII (1965), 4–5, 9, 11.
154 Trevor-Roper, *Religion, the Reformation and Social Change*, pp. 307–8.

and prepare the way for 'a perfect victory over the Beast'. Caryll painted parliament as the instrument of the saints, destined to demolish the forces hindering reformation. Sedgwick expected a direct divine intervention in the final stages of the struggle for the millennium: 'we hope by the help of Christ's hands the issue will be good. God seldom doth great things without commotion.'[155] The expectation that underlay many of these sermons was of the final overthrow of Antichrist and the early realization of Christ's kingdom.

The fast sermons were quickly printed and much reported. So they acted not only as a potent unifying force among MPs, but also as a means to keep parliament's ideology constantly in the forefront of Londoners' minds. The preachers built on the Foxeian tradition that the English were a nascent people of God who merely lacked a fully reformed Church in their midst. The point was plainly made by Thomas Hill in his sermon on 27 July *The Trade of Truth Advanced*:

> The stability of all our blessings must come by the true religion. God's presence is the best security, who is most powerfully present where there is most power and purity of religion. Would you have a flourishing kingdom, advance the kingdom of Christ in it. Let the state maintain religon and religion will bless the state.[156]

The excellence of Hill's sermon was noted in one of the newsbooks that week, 'both for the matter of it and the suitableness of it to the times and auditory'.[157]

A fortnight after Hill preached at Westminster the parliamentary army was on the road. The ideological atmosphere of the march to Coventry, which took two and a half weeks, is vividly conveyed by Nehemiah Wharton in his letters to a London friend. Altar rails and service books were burnt; surplices were cut up as handkerchiefs; marauding diversions were made to the estates of papists. At Aylesbury, where the army entered in triumph led by Hampden and a posse of Buckinghamshire gentry, sermons were heard from a pulpit hastily erected in the market place. It quickly became evident that the preachers who accompanied the troops would need to subdue and restrain them, while at the same time sustaining their militancy. Among those who marched were Stephen Marshall – 'that worthy champion of Christ' Wharton called him – Simeon Ashe and Obadiah Sedgwick. When the levies reached Southam on 22 August, they had no sooner begun to find quarters than a royalist alarm ran through the town: 'in half an hour all our soldiers, though dispersed, were

---

155 P. Christianson, *Reformers and Babylon* (Toronto, 1978), pp. 228–37; Wilson, *Pulpit in Parliament*, pp. 64–5, 257.
156 Wilson, *Pulpit in Parliament*, p. 173.
157 BL E 202 (26): *A Perfect Diurnal*, 25 July–1 Aug., pp. 4–5.

complete in arms ready to encounter the enemy, crying out for a dish of cavaliers to supper.'[158]

So just as the royalist clergy had recruited for the king so the Puritan divines did so for parliament. For example it was Cornelius Burges, their vicar, who was chiefly responsible for the energetic response of the inhabitants of Watford to the Propositions scheme and it was he who presented a petition of loyalty on their behalf on 1 July.[159] More work needs to be done on both gentry and popular allegiance at the start of the war before firm conclusions can be reached, but it seems probable that religious commitment of one kind or another was a decisive factor for many who fought in the first campaign. In a broad sense the armies that met at Edgehill were a citizen army led by Puritan gentry and an army of tenantry led by conservative squires. It was not so much men's belief in rival sets of political principles which distinguished the two armies as the sharp contrast between their religious attitudes.

158 *CSPD 1641–3*, pp. 371–3, 379–80; Gardiner, *Great Civil War* I, 27; Manning, pp. 249–50; Hughes, pp. 250–3.
159 Steele, no. 2206.

11

The Militia and the Array

That as it was no small comfort and settling to the well affected . . . when they understood the most excellent, necessary and reasonable ordinance . . . concerning the militia, so in special, we of this county, who did most earnestly petition for it, do desire to come short of none in this expression of our unfeigned thankfulness to them for the happy accomplishment thereof.

> The petition of the deputy-lieutenants, captains, officers, soldiers and volunteers of the Warwickshire trained bands to Lord Brooke,
> 9 July 1642[1]

The trained bands being come into Hereford, the drums beat up to call together the soldiers; then the commissioners read the commission of array . . . the captain and some other officers demanded, through the band, their willingness and reality to serve the king. Then they all threw up their hats and cried 'God save the king' and many of them again 'For the king, For the king'.

> A letter from Herefordshire,
> 14 July 1642[2]

Few wars can have broken out as untidily as the English civil war. Between the first musters in May and the meeting of the two armies in October, the incipient war in the localities was chaotic and uncoordinated. Not that the pattern of conflict became any neater after Edgehill. The nature of the war did not change with the first battle, which merely disappointed men's hopes of a quick and decisive outcome.[3] This chapter is concerned with the struggle within the counties between supporters of the militia ordinance and of the commissioners of array. Both focused their attention on the same makeshift military machine, the trained bands of the shires with their well stocked magazines which were usually kept under lock and key in the county capitals. The eagerness that both sides showed to grasp the militia was a matter of both political necessity and military sense. Its capacity had been enormously improved by the campaign since Charles I came to the

---

1 BL 669 f 5 (55).
2 *HMC Portland* III 90–1.
3 See e.g. *HMC Coke*, pp.323–4; Clarendon III, 460–1.

throne for an 'exact and perfect' militia.[4]

The enforcement of the militia ordinance began as a propaganda exercise. The check on muster rolls, inspection of arms and perfunctory training under the parliamentary lieutenant and his deputies could hardly be an effective means of securing more than token allegiance from ordinary countrymen, for whom the 1642 muster must have appeared little different from any other. What mattered more was that it involved many gentry, JPs besides deputy-lieutenants, in parliament's business and thus in defiance of the king. He and his deputies, wrote Lord Spencer to the Northamptonshire gentleman Sir Roland St John, had 'thought fit to summon the trained bands (and those others who will voluntarily come in) to be mustered'. St John's help by subscribing the lieutenant's warrants and dispensing them to constables would oblige Spencer to continue his 'faithful friend and servant'.[5] The courtesies of county society could be used to oil the wheels of parliamentary administration. The shift of allegiance that would be implied by St John's cooperation was barely perceptible unless he stopped and read the king's contrary propaganda.

Between late May and mid July the ordinance was executed in 14 counties (see Map 7, opposite). In many instances musters were held systematically throughout the shire, but in a few cases, like Cheshire and Lancashire, the business was never completed because it encountered such fierce resistance.[6] Buckinghamshire was first off the mark, though Lord Paget's desertion of his office after a triumphant first meeting at Beaconsfield delayed completion of the musters there until 17 June.[7] In the meantime the ordinance was fully executed in Essex, Lincolnshire, Middlesex and Northamptonshire. Five of the six Leicestershire hundreds showed their obedience to parliament's lieutenant between 14 and 20 June.[8] Bedfordshire and Hampshire mustered about the same time and Berkshire did so before the end of the month. The Warwickshire deputies completed the task by 5 July and the Wiltshire ones by the end of that month.[9] Some Sussex musters were almost certainly held in June, but it is not certain whether the deputies were able to take an account of the whole shire.[10] Only two out of all these counties – Bedfordshire and Middlesex – mustered at a single venue. The Leicestershire countrymen brought their arms to five traditional centres around the county,

---

4 A.Hassell Smith; 'Militia Rates and Militia Statutes 1558–1603' in Clark, Smith, Tyacke, editors, *The English Commonwealth*, pp. 93–109. See the references cited above note 123, p. 64.

5 Bedfordshire RO J 1400.

6 *CJ* II, 657; *HMC Portland* I, 46; Ormerod, p. 20.

7 *LJ* v, 82, 137; BL Harl. MS 163, fol. 160v.

8 *LJ* v, 117–8, 130, 139, 147, 155; *CJ* II, 594, 625; *HMC Buccleuch* I, 302; BL Add. MS 14827, fol. 135v; E 154(4): *A Relation of the Execution of the Militia in Leicestershire*.

9 *LJ* v, 156, 164, 170, 195.

10 *Sussex*, pp. 255–7.

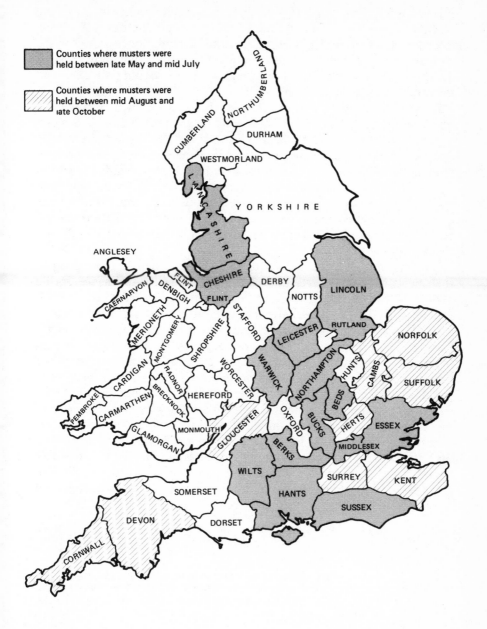

Map 7: The execution of the militia ordinance May–October 1642.

Northamptonshire mustered over three days at Northampton, Kettering and Oundle and the Warwickshire bands came in to Stratford, Warwick, Coventry and Coleshill.[11] In every case attention was concentrated on the footbands rather than the cavalry, whom Lord Willoughby excused altogether in Lincolnshire on the grounds that the warning was short and many of the horse were 'at soil'.[12]

Between mid August and late October the ordinance was executed in a further nine counties. Many of them were no great distance from London – Cambridgeshire, Hertfordshire, Suffolk and Surrey for instance – and there had been pressure on the lord lieutenant to act for two or three months beforehand. The Devon musters took place towards the end of August.[13] The Gloucestershire ones were held at Gloucester and Chipping Sodbury on 5 September, after Saye had replaced the royalist Lord Chandos as lord lieutenant.[14] The Kentish deputies met to make the necessary arrangements on 17 September.[15] In Norfolk the trained bands did not muster until late October.[16]

What accounts for the alacrity of 14 counties, when 10 more dragged their heels and some never mustered at all under the ordinance during 1642? Positive action by the lord lieutenant was needed to set the ball rolling. This did not necessarily mean vigorous personal involvement: a man like the earl of Northumberland, who already enjoyed well established and easy relations with his Sussex deputies, was able to leave them to manage the business.[17] Yet everyone knew how valuable an asset the personal presence of a nobleman with hereditary power in the county could be at such a critical time. The Essex deputies, 'doubting their own strength', procured a summons for the earl of Warwick to take leave from his duties as Lord Admiral in the Downs and come to 'animate his countrymen'. 'I doubt not but all will be of one piece in Essex', remarked Sir Edmund Moundeford, recounting this news to a friend.[18] In some cases the efficiency with which the task was performed owed much to the lead given by an energetic peer: Lord Brooke's energy in Warwickshire and

---

11   BL Harl. MS 163, fol. 163r; 669 f 6(50): *A True Relation of the Lord Brooke's settling of the Militia in Warwickshire*; *LJ* v, 195; J.F. Hollings, *The History of Leicester during the Great Civil War* (Leicester, 1840), p. 14.

12   *LJ* v, 155.

13   *CJ* II, 606, 651, 658, 664, 711, 716, 737; BL E 108(13): *His Majesty's Demands to Parliament*; E 114(34): *A Continuation of Certain Special and Remarkable Passages*; E 202(34): *A True and Exact Diurnal*, 8–15 Aug., p 4; Surrey RO (Guildford) Loseley MSS, correspondence, vol. VI, no. 133: Earl of Nottingham to the deputy lieutenants, 12 August 1642; Holmes, pp. 52–5; Andriette, pp. 56–8.

14   *CJ* II, 716, 723; *LJ* v, 291; Gloucestershire RO D 2510/20; *HMC Portland* I, 61–2.

15   *CJ* II, 728, 742, 769; Bodleian Dep C MS 153, no. 75; Everitt, pp. 107–116.

16   Holmes, pp. 51, 59.

17   *Sussex*, pp. 49, 176.

18   Bodleian Tanner MS 63, fol. 43r; Holmes, pp. 43–5; Ashton, *English Civil War*, p. 175.

Lord Willoughby of Parham's in Lincolnshire were notable in this respect. Yet in other instances, such as Buckinghamshire and Northamptonshire, execution of the ordinance was completed despite the waverings of lieutenants like Lord Paget and Lord Spencer.[19]

Leicestershire provides an instructive case study of the impact of the local aristocracy. The earl of Stamford was warmly welcomed at Leicester on 4 June: shouts of 'A Stamford, A Stamford' greeted him when he emerged from his discussions at an inn with the mayor about local defence. These led to part of the county magazine being lodged in the safety of his mansion at Bradgate Park.[20] His attendance at the musters held over the next fortnight did much to ensure their success. But before he had completed them, Henry Hastings, heir to the earldom of Huntingdon's vast Leicestershire estates, was challenging Stamford's supremacy. The whole course of the civil war in the county was to revolve around the long personal feud between the Grey and Hastings families. Stamford left a guard of 150 neighbours, tenants and servants at Bradgate when he returned to London at the end of June.[21] Nevertheless his departure was disastrous for his interest. Within days Hastings consolidated his hold on much of the county and was terrifying its villages with his bombastic proceedings. In a letter of 30 June Stamford heard that the sheriff no longer dared appear in public, but was fled to London, and that Hastings planned to besiege Bradgate. 'Such of the trained bands as lived thereabout', he was told, 'were unskilful and raw men and wanted a leader'.[22]

A forceful group of MPs could provide as much impetus as a vigorous and engaged peer. Fresh from the cockpit of the nation's politics, MPs suddenly enjoyed a special prestige among colleagues in local government. They could cajole those who hesitated and galvanize friends into action. In some cases a group of them formed a caucus in the deputy lieutenancy, taking on the responsibility of organizing the musters and attending themselves at each venue.[23] Six MPs signed the report from the Hampshire deputies that they had inspected the regiments commanded by two of their number, Sir Thomas Jervoise and Robert Wallop. The certificate from Warwickshire on 5 July contained the subscriptions of Sir Peter Wentworth, who had been sent down on 11 June, and his colleagues Godfrey Bosvile and John Barker, who had followed him a few days later.[24] The successful enforcement of the ordinance in Lincolnshire probably

---

19 *CJ* II, 627; *LJ* v, 115–6, 186, 190, 250; Bedfordshire RO J 1410; Hughes, pp. 230–8.
20 BL E 150(1): *Horrible News from Leicester.*
21 *HMC Buccleuch* I, 306; *LJ* v, 139; A. Everitt, *The Local Community and the Great Rebellion* (London, 1969), pp. 10–13, 15–20.
22 BL Harl. MS 163, fol. 252v.
23 *CJ* II, 583, 599, 622, 632, 668; BL Harl. MS 163, fol. 130v.
24 *CJ* II, 600, 633, 639; *LJ* v, 156, 195.

owed much to the competence of the seven MPs who were active, since few of those who were experienced local administrators were ready to take part. Four MPs were involved in Lancashire. Ralph Assheton, John Moore, Alexander Rigby and Richard Shuttleworth left London eager to do their duty by parliament on 9 June, but they were disconcerted when they arrived at Manchester by the evident might and boldness of the Stanley family, the hereditary overlords of the shire. It took an outsider, Sir William Brereton, to persuade them at least to attempt a muster in Salford hundred, the heartland of Lancashire Puritanism. More then 7000 men appeared 'well furnished with muskets and pikes'. A witness recorded that there was a great shout for half an hour 'For the king and parliament, For the king and parliament'.[25]

Cheshire was an unusual case in that the whole task of enforcing the militia ordinance fell upon one MP, Sir William Brereton, a man of exceptional vigour and determination. Saye played no active part as lord lieutenant and none of the other three members gave any help. The odds were against Brereton in a county where royalist sentiment was already showing itself and in a community of gentry rent by instability and dissension.[26] In sharp contrast to some other counties, Cheshire lacked a dominating small knot of families. Instead a group of about 20 jockeyed for place, with, as a recent commentator has put it, 'young ambitious men striking attitudes and trying to shake the tenuous hold of upstart peers and aged baronets, courtiers and time servers'.[27] Brereton's achievement was the more remarkable. He secured the active support of five men whose political views were more moderate than his own – Sir Richard Wilbraham, Roger Wilbraham, Sir Thomas Delves, Philip Mainwaring and Henry Birkenhead – but who saw in the militia ordinance a means to maintain local peace and order.[28] About the same time they were the leading sponsors of the Cheshire neutrality remonstrance that has already been discussed. Brereton's first reports on 2 and 5 July spoke of the good obedience he found in his first meeting with the trained bands: 'they having more appearance in one hundred than the commission of array had in four and they had more volunteers three to one than the commissioners of array had.' Three weeks later he related an equally satisfactory outcome in Northwich hundred, where 320 musketeers, 80 pikemen and nearly 600 volunteers appeared. He was only completely foiled in Nantwich hundred, where the gentry of the neighbourhood made a temporary truce that

25 *CJ* II, 619; *LJ* v, 128–9, 131–2, 174; Ormerod, p. 20. I am grateful to Professor Clive Holmes for information about Lincolnshire.
26 HLRO, Main Papers, 24 June 1642: Sir William Brereton to Speaker Lenthall; *CJ* II, 619; Morrill, *Cheshire*, pp. 42–4.
27 Wanklyn, Landed Society and Allegiance in Cheshire and Shropshire, p. 71.
28 T. Malbon, 'Memorials of the Civil War in Cheshire', *Lancashire and Cheshire Record Society Transactions* XIX (1889), 25–6; Phillips, *Civil War in Wales* II, 11.

enabled the royalists to triumph by false dealing.[29]

In two cases, Essex and Northamptonshire, the gentry on the spot were so competent that representatives from the parliamentary delegation could afford to arrive at the last minute, bringing a final stamp of authority and legitimacy to the mustering. The Northamptonshire MPs had been given plenty of warning that the review would begin on 14 June, but they only left London when prompted by the House: 'my Lord Spencer and Mr Tate go down this week in a coach together', wrote William Montagu to his father on 9 June, 'Mr Crew and Sir Gilbert Pickering go also.'[30] The representation was limited to four so as not to deprive the Commons of too much manpower.[31] Six MPs, all deputy-lieutenants for the county, who attended the Brentwood muster on 7 June had all been at work in the Commons three days previously.[32]

When due account has been taken of pressure and firm leadership, the sheer enthusiasm of the most forward counties, the 'cheerfulness and ready obedience' which was so much noted, remains to be explained. By and large the lieutenants reported militias up to scratch and well armed. Such deficiencies of arms as were discovered, in Essex and Lincolnshire for instance, were blamed on the demands of the crown for the Scots war. Here is further evidence that there may have been less slackening of standards in the 1630s than has been suspected. The turnout of volunteers up and down the county was also heartwarming for parliament as the map overleaf shows. At Brentwood, Warwick found that Sir William Masham's company was double its normal complement and he inspected a troop of nearly 500 volunteers under Sir Thomas Barrington's younger son.[33] 100 volunteers from Basingstoke joined 1800 militiamen at a Hampshire muster; around 400 volunteers attended in Leicestershire; 900 volunteers in Northamptonshire outnumbered the 740 enrolled men; 550 of the 600 trained bandsmen appeared together with 2850 volunteers in Warwickshire. Bedford, Lincoln and Marlborough were other places where volunteers showed themselves in force. At Boston on 10 June the volunteers, accompanied by the mayor and aldermen, led Lord Willoughby and his deputies into the town: they were 'handsome young men, well armed and every way well appointed and a captain in the head of them, who gave us divers vollies of shot and shewed themselves above an hour together upon the market place, performing very exactly all their

---

29 *CJ* II, 657; BL Add. MS 14827, fol. 155v; *HMC Portland* I, 44–6; HLRO, Main Papers, 22 June 1642: Sir Edward Fitton to Sir Thomas Aston; Wanklyn, 'Landed Society and Allegiance in Cheshire and Shropshire', pp. 235–6. Morrill, *Cheshire*, pp. 56–65 interprets these events rather differently.

30 *CJ* II, 606, 616; *HMC Buccleuch*, p. 304.

31 BL Harl. MS 163, fol. 153r.

32 CJ II, 609; BL E 150(6): *A Letter sent to Mr Speaker from the Commissioners in Essex.*

33 *LJ* v, 82, 117–8, 170.

Map 8: Towns that raised volunteers for parliament, June–September 1642.

postures and showing much readiness in the use of their arms.'[34]

In four cases – Buckinghamshire, Essex, Hampshire and Warwickshire – petitions were presented either to the lord lieutenant or direct to parliament in connection with the execution of the ordinance. Ten thousand it was said, supported the petition which Sir Thomas Barrington brought from Essex on 17 June; the Hampshire petition was subscribed on the drumhead at musters by soldiers as well as captains and colonels; the Warwickshire one was acclaimed by volunteers and militiamen amid scenes, according to one report, of weeping for joy. Essex's petition, greeted with tossing of hats and acclamation at the Dunmow muster on 10 June, was the most combative of this series:

> With our hands upon our swords, we stand ready at your command, to perform our vows to God and oaths of fidelity to His Majesty, in taking up arms against those false flatterers and traitors who abuse his royal favour, intending, under the glorious title of his name and standard, to fight against the peace and honour of their sovereign, against religion and the laws, and to make a prey and spoil of three flourishing kingdoms at once; and to spend our dearest blood in the defence of the lives and liberties of our countrymen, the laws which are the life of our liberty and peace, religion more precious than both, and the king and parliament.[35]

What Essex said so boldly the other petitions repeated more cautiously but no less plainly: the conspiracy against the king and kingdom, now more malignant than specifically popish, was still the mainspring of these men's political thinking. The enthusiasm expressed in the winter and spring petitions, in other words, was now being translated into offers of action. But that enthusiasm, we noted, had in no sense represented a war fever. There was probably a good deal of bravado in the statements which were drawn up by activists and publicized at a few of the summer musters. Most of the deputy lieutenants and the JPs who cooperated with parliament to the extent of calling out their local bands did so soberly, pursuing a traditional routine with a dawning understanding that they were involved in something different from a traditional muster but with no eagerness to fight in a war on parliament's behalf. By organizing these musters or attending them, many did not see themselves as having pledged their personal allegiance in a war against the king. Few had even come to terms with the fact that there was going to be some kind of military conflict. Yet the dangers and uncertainties of the political situation escaped no one who was at all well informed. In these circumstances, enforcing the militia ordinance, paradoxically, could make men feel more secure. They were

34 *LJ* v, 104, 132, 139, 155–6, 164, 195; *CJ* ii, 637; BL E 154(4).

35 *CJ* ii, 633, 651; Hill, p. 123; BL 669 f 5(50): *Petition of the Trained Bands of Buckinghamshire*; 669 f 5(53): *Declaration of the Trained Bands of Hampshire*; 669 f 6(33): *Resolution of the Trained Bands of Essex*; 669 f (55): *Petition of the Trained Bands of Warwickshire*.

performing a precautionary act, expressing a minimum gesture with regard to the defence of their own locality. The zeal of those who formulated the Essex petition was probably the exception rather than the rule.

The instructions sent to the commissioners of array made it quite clear what was required of them. They were to muster and train the county's militia, seeing that it was complete and well armed and that the officers were all 'persons of quality' with considerable local estates.[36] But the peers who received copies of their commission at York and carried them home or pondered them in their manor houses had a hard task. The gentry who had been nominated could not be blamed for reacting hesitantly to a form of authority that was at best unfamiliar and at worst highly dubious. Many of the JPs, and constables in their turn below them, who were used to receiving orders from lord lieutenants, had probably never heard of commissions of array.

The region which responded most positively to the commissioners of array was a long strip of western England, from Cornwall through Monmouthshire and the Marches of Wales to Cheshire and Lancashire, also the king's happiest recruiting ground for his field army. At the end of August 1642 six counties were more or less firmly under royalist control: Cheshire, Cornwall, Herefordshire, Monmouthshire, Shropshire and Worcestershire.

The solid foundations of Cornish royalism have already been discussed. Lord Mohun, the sheriff John Grills and John Arundel of Trerice were among those who responded enthusiastically to the commission the king sent them on 29 June.[37] They quickly drew in other influential squires: Sir Bevil Grenville, for instance, Sir Nicholas Slanning and Sir Richard Vyvyan. Thirteen commissioners in all signed the warrants for a muster of nearly 40 parishes at Bodmin Down on 17 August. The royalists had won a moral victory at the Launceston assizes a fortnight before. Judge Foster, studiously neutral, read parliament's declaration against the array but, as the six MPs present related dispiritedly, they had 'little respect': 'when my lord came to delare His Majesty's directions, he had vigour, voice and rhetoric to act that home.' In the evening, the MPs had no choice but to stand by helplessly while the sheriff read the king's proclamations to the assembled throng in the market place.[38] Yet the basis of the Cornish royalism was slender at this stage, as the Bodmin muster showed. The attendance was only 180. This was not so much a trained band review as an outing for the most loyal of the commissioners' tenantry: at least 80 men

---

36 Northamptonshire RO Finch Hatton MS 133; Steele, no. 2194; Rushworth III, part I, 657–8, 674–5.
37 Northamptonshire RO Finch Hatton MS 133.
38 *LJ* V, 275; *CJ* II, 714.

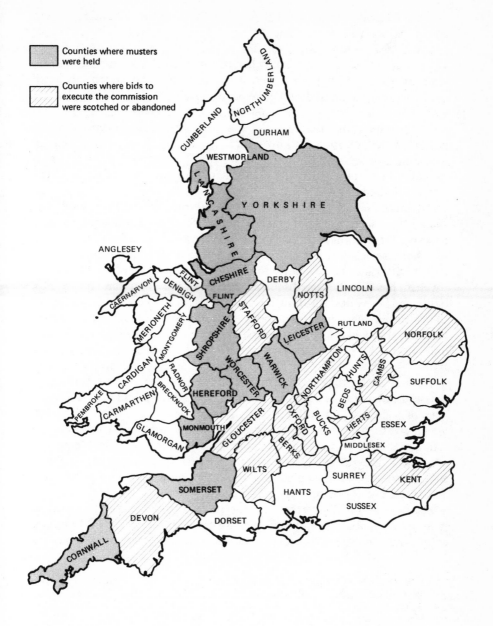

NORTHUMBERLAND

CUMBERLAND

DURHAM

WESTMORLAND

LANCASHIRE

Y O R K S H I R E

ANGLESEY

FLINT

CHESHIRE

DERBY

LINCOLN

CAERNARVON

DENBIGH

FLINT

NOTTS

MERIONETH

STAFFORD

RUTLAND

MONTGOMERY

SHROPSHIRE

LEICESTER

NORFOLK

CARDIGAN

RADNOR

WORCESTER

WARWICK

NORTHAMPTON

HUNTS

CAMBS

SUFFOLK

PEMBROKE

BRECKNOCK

HEREFORD

BEDS

CARMARTHEN

HERTS

ESSEX

GLAMORGAN

MONMOUTH

GLOUCESTER

OXFORD

BUCKS

MIDDLESEX

BERKS

SOMERSET

WILTS

SURREY

KENT

DEVON

DORSET

HANTS

SUSSEX

CORNWALL

Map 9: The execution of the commissions of array, July–October 1642.

carried Grenville's arms, 'very discernable for that the pikes and rests were all painted with white and blue'.[39]

There was no more loyal servant of the crown than the aged earl of Worcester, whose Catholic family had Monmouthshire at its bidding. The huge household at Raglan was quite exceptionally old fashioned in its style of life, maintaining a tradition of lavish hospitality which had been largely abandoned elsewhere.[40] Worcester's heir Lord Herbert played a clever double game during the summer of 1642, keeping on good terms with parliament whilst assisting the king with large sums of money. He seized the magazine and secured Monmouthshire for Charles, in September, with the aid of Protestant gentry like Sir William Morgan of Tredegar as well as Catholic dependents.[41]

In Herefordshire, Shropshire and Worcestershire, by contrast, power was shared by a select circle of wealthy gentry families. Royalism became a cohesive force in these three counties, holding the majority of the gentry together in such a way that they could comfortably combine a localist stance with cautious allegiance to the king. The genesis of Herefordshire royalism has already been discussed. In a letter to her husband on 15 July, Brilliana Harley described the burying of old scores which it involved: 'all the commissioners have tied themselves one to another by a deep protestation that what one does the other will do, so Sir William Croft, who once did not love Mr Coningsby nor Mr Scudamore, is now their mighty friend.'[42] The determination of many among the Shropshire and Worcester gentry to present a similarly united front is plain in their action at the summer assizes. In both cases they packed the grand jury and had it present a declaration suffused with constitutional royalism to Charles, which was then given the formal assent of the JPs, gentry and freeholders.[43] The Shropshire commissioners of array, according to one hostile report, acted 'as if they meant to set up a petty parliament among us, for whatsoever presentment they made they hold the county involved in the same and obliged to obey what they conclude.'[44]

Yet neither in Worcestershire nor in Shropshire were the royalists wholly unopposed. The Worcestershire commissioners got off to a false start when they were forced to abandon a muster fixed for the quarter

---

39 *LJ* v, 314–5; BL E 114(6): *The True Proceedings of the Counties of York, Coventry, Portsmouth and Cornwall*; Coate, *Cornwall in the Great Civil War*, pp. 30–8.

40 W.R.B. Robinson, 'Patronage and Hospitality in Early Tudor Wales: the Role of Henry, Earl of Worcester 1526–1549', *BIHR* LI (1978), 35; L. Stone, *The Crisis of the Aristocracy* (Oxford, 1966), pp. 209, 212–14; *LJ* v, 307; *HMC 12th Report*, appendix, part IX, pp. 10–11.

41 *Clarendon State Papers* II, 146; *LJ* v, 248; Hutton, pp. 18–19, 34.

42 *HMC Portland* III, 92.

43 BL Harl. MS 163, fol. 300r; 669 f 5(65): *The Declaration of the Grand Jury at Worcester*; 669 f 6(69): *The Declaration of the Grand Jury at the Shropshire Assizes*.

44 BL E, 114 (36): *Special Passages*, 23–30 Aug.

sessions on 13 July, because too few gentry appeared to see it through in face of a vigorous intervention by the knights of the shire. Humphrey Salway and John Wilde, hurrying home from Westminster at the news of the commissioners' activities, instigated a petition to the justices to execute the militia ordinance.[45] This was later followed by a petition of the freeholders in favour of parliament, which Judge Henden refused to accept at the assizes.[46] At the end of July three Shropshire MPs, similarly warned, hurried down to Shrewsbury. Their bid, in conjunction with a party of enthusiastic parliamentarians in the town, to foil the muster planned for 2 August produced a fracas in the market place and might easily have led to bloodshed had not moderate gentry like Sir Richard Newport intervened to pacify the contenders.[47] In both cases, though, the parliamentarian campaign was shortlived since the MPs found they could not sustain their cause in the gentry community.[48]

In a letter to the Warwickshire commission of array on 13 August, the Worcestershire commissioners spoke proudly of the evidence their musters had given that they were 'likely to make good the declaration published at the last assizes': 'the appearance of gentry and commons was very great and the acclamation very high for His Majesty's service, not a dissenting voice, but one and all like good subjects for the king's safety and honour.'[49] At Pitchcroft meadow outside Worcester the previous day, Lord Coventry and a solid phalanx of baronets and knights had reviewed the county's soldiery. This was another display of tenant loyalty, as one observer remarked. A motley collection of hedgebills, old calivers, pikes and clubs passed for arms among the yeomen and husbandmen cajoled from their fields in the midst of harvest.[50] The Herefordshire muster on 14 July had been a rather more impressive affair. Sir Robert Harley's enemies – Walter Brabazon, Fitzwilliam Coningsby, Sir William Croft and the Scudamores – were the organizers. There was a good appearance in all the footbands except Harley's own, 150 volunteers were present and 30 of the 92 listed horse. But the turnout in Harley's company was so meagre 'that it was not worth going into the field': his drummer and ancient were handed over to Coningsby who assumed the captaincy and set about reinforcing the band.[51] The most active commissioners of array in

---

45 Bodleian Tanner MS 63, fol. 88; *CJ* II, 661, 666; HLRO, Main Papers, 12 July 1642: Petition of the Worcestershire Grand Jury to the Bench; BL E 107(14): *A Letter from Mr Serjeant Wilde and Humphrey Salwey Esq*; *Townshend*, p. 68.

46 *CJ* II, 714; BL Harl. MS 164, fol. 260v.

47 *LJ* V, 233, 269–70; Wanklyn, 'Landed Society and Allegiance in Cheshire and Shropshire', pp. 248–9.

48 *HMC Coke*, p. 321; Bodleian Tanner MS 63, fol. 43v; R.H. Silcock, 'County Government in Worcestershire' (London PhD thesis, 1974), pp. 232–5.

49 *Townshend*, p. 73.

50 *HMC Portland* I, 53; BL E 239 (8): *A Perfect Diurnal*, 8–15 Aug.

51 *HMC Portland* III, 89–92; *CJ* II, 779.

Shropshire were Sir Vincent Corbet, Edward Cressett, Sir Paul Harris, Richard Lloyd, Francis Ottley and the sheriff John Weld. On 2 August Corbet and Lloyd trained their companies in the fields below the town, while Weld, together with the mayor, paraded an armed force up and down the streets.[52]

The struggle for control of the Cheshire trained bands was at its fiercest in July. Brereton, we have seen, held musters in several districts that month, but so did the royalists. Countrymen obeyed the commissioners' warrants in Bucklow hundred on 5 July and in Macclesfield hundred on 26 July.[53] The most active commissioners of array were Earl Rivers, Sir Edward Fitton, who had kissed the king's hands on a visit to York in June, and that obsessive defender of bishops and the liturgy Sir Thomas Aston.[54] By August their propaganda efforts, making full use of the pulpits, together with continuing rumours of the king's coming, were bringing the county's royalism into the open.[55] About this time old Sir George Booth abandoned his efforts to keep the local peace and retired from Dunham Massey on the Cheshire plain into the hill country towards Derbyshire, sending his son with friends, neighbours and tenants to the assistance of the parliamentarians in Manchester.[56] This retreat by one of the county's outstandingly influential families is an indication of the way things were going.

So successfully did the Manchester district resist Lord Strange throughout the summer that Lancashire cannot be included in the list of counties where a dominating royalist presence was established before Edgehill. Strange opened his campaign in the second half of June by seizing the magazines at Lancaster, Preston and Liverpool and his bid to take charge of the rest of the county's ordnance and powder, kept at Manchester, was only scotched by the swift action of some of the deputy-lieutenants living near the town. When he called a muster at Preston Moor on 20 June, the committee of four MPs sent down by parliament decided to attend in person. They sowed dissension in the crowd; they also tried to stop the reading of royal declarations and the king's reply to a county petition of loyalty. According to a parliamentarian sympathizer, when the sheriff, Sir John Girlington, called for 'all that are for the king' to follow him, 'about 400 persons, whereof the most part of them were popish recusants, went

52 Staffordshire RO D 593/P/8/1/1: John Weld to Sir Richard Leveson, 24 July 1642; LJ v, 269–70; Wanklyn, 'Landed Allegiance in Cheshire and Shropshire', pp. 247–9; Hutton, pp. 13–14.
53 *HMC Portland* I, 44–7; Ormerod, p. 21.
54 *LJ* v, 204; HLRO, Main Papers, 22 June 1642: Sir Edward Fitton to Sir Thomas Aston.
55 *HMC Portland* I, 51–2; BL E 239 (9): *A Perfect Diurnal*, 15–22 Aug., sub 20 Aug.; Hutton, pp. 8–9.
56 Wanklyn, 'Landed Society and Allegiance in Cheshire and Shropshire', p. 200; Morrill, *Cheshire*, pp. 51, 60.

with him and rode up and down the moor and cried "For the king, For the king" but far more in number stayed with the committee.' The failure of the MPs to repeat their divisive tactics at the next musters, however, suggests that this account gave an over-optimistic impression of their success. The Preston meeting on 8 July and the Bury one on the 15th were solid expressions of tenant loyalty to the ancestral overlords of Lancashire. A letter from a Preston parliamentarian to some London friends on 8 July captures the atmosphere of the day: 'the soldiers are all marched out of the town to the number of 4000 . . . and what this day will bring forth I cannot tell but they say they shout "For the king and Lord Strange" . . . we are beset with papists. I dare not go to the moor.'[57]

There were 12 counties where unsuccessful attempts were made to execute commissions of array in July or August. Parliament's superior intelligence and resources accounted for the collapse of several bids to propagate the royalist cause in counties near London. Thus Kent was seized for parliament just as knots of royalist gentry were beginning to take the commission in hand. Colonel Edwin Sandys's circular tour, securing castles and rooting out stores of cavalier arms, was a model of swift and decisive action.[58] The earl of Bedford drew up a troop of horse outside the Bell Inn at Hertford when a meeting of the county's commissioners, instigated by Sir John Boteler, was due to take place there.[59] The young earl of Carlisle, who headed the Essex and Cambridgeshire commissions, plucked up courage to act in the latter county at the end of August, only to find himself arrested by Oliver Cromwell, who had brought down a force of London dragoons.[60]

Lord Lovelace also came home from York with two commissions in his pocket, one for Berkshire, where his estates lay, and the other for Oxfordshire. He drew in the earl of Berkshire, one of those who had fought a rearguard action against Pym's allies in the Lords during April and May, and at a meeting in Oxford on 10 August plans were made to execute the two commissions successively. A number of prominent local gentry attended like Sir John Curson and Sir Robert Dormer.[61] But again parliament's information was too good for the royalists. The Oxfordshire countrymen gathered at Watlington on 15 August were watched from the Chiltern edge above the little market town by Bulstrode Whitelocke and a troop of parliamentary horse. When Whitelocke's scouts were spotted and

57 Ormerod, pp. 14, 16, 23–4, 29–30, 325–30; BL Add. MS 14827, fol. 147v; Ashton, *English Civil War*, p. 174.
58 *HMC 5th Report*, pp. 46–7; Everitt, pp. 111–16.
59 BL E 239(9): *A Perfect Diurnal*, 15–22 Aug.; Holmes, p. 53.
60 Northamptonshire RO Finch Hatton MS 133; Holmes, pp. 38, 55.
61 *HMC Portland* I, 56; *LJ* v, 286–7; BL E 239(9): *A Perfect Diurnal*, 15–22 Aug; Durston, pp. 33, 134–5.

news came of the approach of another 400 musketeers and 100 horse under Hampden's command, the meeting melted away. Berkshire, Curson and Dormer were all apprehended later in the day at Ascott, the Dormer manor near Wing.[62] Whitelocke related his dealings with the earl, whom he took home with him that evening to Henley, in his memoirs. He offered the courtesies due to a nobleman 'but, finding the lord very proud and peevish and sullen and empty in his discourse, I would not trouble myself any further to bear him company, but left him to the guards to be conveyed to London.'[63] Lovelace managed to escape implication in the Watlington muster and subsequently received pardon from the Lords for a long absence.[64]

In some cases commissioners of array saw their task primarily in terms of recruiting for the king's field army rather than securing the shire on his behalf. Lord Paget, uniquely, was involved in enforcing both the militia ordinance and a commission of array. After his defection in the middle of the Buckinghamshire parliamentary musters, he spent some weeks in the royal entourage. Later he called together the Staffordshire gentry who were joined with him in the commission, men like Sir Richard Dyott, Sir Richard Leveson and Sir Robert Wolseley. 'The execution of the commission is but to know what every person will willingly do or subscribe', related George Thorley, who was present at the meeting Paget summoned, to his friend Walter Wrottesley. Nothing more comprehensive appears to have been attempted.[65] The approach adopted by Lord Montagu and the earl of Westmorland in Northamptonshire was similar but rather more thoroughgoing. They drew sympathetic gentry into cooperating in a recruiting campaign and a muster was held for this purpose at Oundle on 22 August. The arrival of the parliamentarian army, however, soon scotched their efforts.[66] Montagu was subsequently arrested and sent up to London. The earl of Essex, riding out to take up his command, met Montagu's coach near Barnet and stopped it to pay his respects to the old man, but Montagu, so the story goes, would not speak to him and ordered the coachman to drive on.[67]

'The truth is', wrote Sir Robert Foster in a report to the king after riding the western assize circuit in July and August, 'the counties are much possessed with the illegality of the commissions of array and the unlimited power, as is alleged, in the commissioners and by reason thereof infinitely

62 *CSPD 1641–3*, p. 373; Wedgwood, *King's War*, p. 106; *LJ* v, 295.
63 BL Add. MS 37343, fols. 254v–255r.
64 Crummett, pp. 238, 248.
65 *HMC Buccleuch* I, 306; *HMC 5th Report*, p. 141; Staffordshire RO D 948/4/6/2; Crummett, pp. 344–5; Hutton, pp. 27–8.
66 Bodleian Dep C MS 165, no. 89; Tanner MS 63, fol. 157; *HMC Montagu*, pp. 156–8; BL Harl. MS 163, fol. 297v; *CSPD 1641–3*, pp. 383–6, 387–8, 391.
67 *HMC Portland* I, 60–1; Sir P. Warwick, *Memoirs* (1813), pp. 224–5.

averse thereunto.'[68] The commissions were a failure in the west because a massive propaganda campaign, as much localist in spirit as parliamentarian, was mounted against them. It was bad tactics of course to issue the commissions in Latin, which enabled their enemies to give them the translations they pleased. Countrymen were told that Charles had invented a newfangled device to extort crippling taxes and impose unheard-of burdens.[69]

The marquis of Hertford told the queen in a letter from Beverley on 11 July that the people's affections were breaking out and their eyes were being opened: they would no longer, he believed, 'be deluded with the imaginary fears and jealousies'. He was about to set out with commissions of array for Somerset and Wiltshire; on 2 August he was appointed lieutenant-general of the western parts of the kingdom.[70] Hertford was over confident. He expected his task would be easy, but the fact was that he was not loved in Somerset or Wiltshire as the earl of Warwick was in Essex or Lord Brooke was in the neighbourhood of his castle above the Avon. He did have considerable estates there but he simply did not enjoy their kind of hegemony. His experiences were thus baffling and disappointing. At Marlborough his bid to seize the magazine was forestalled by the townspeople.[71] The day he arrived at Bath the grand jury petitioned the king to cancel the commission of array. At the suggestion of the leading Somerset royalists, Wells was then chosen as a headquarters from which the marquis would rally the county. The story of the week he spent there and of his shamefaced retreat on 6 August to the security of Sherborne Castle has been well told and need not be repeated.[72]

The fierce reaction to Hertford's campaign could have been predicted. He had been given very wide powers and he made no secret of them. He came into Somerset, unlike other commissioners of array, with armed men at his side. Henry Lunsford had a commission to form a foot regiment; Sir Ralph Hopton, John Digby and Sir Francis Hawley were collecting troops of horse while Hertford was based at Wells. This was an intensive recruiting campaign, not a tentative one like Paget's in Staffordshire. The intention, as Hyde put it later, was 'to form an army if it should be found expedient'.[73] Hertford was bound to be seen as deliberately attempting to break the peace of the shire. The huge crowd of around 12,000 that assembled on the Mendips on 5 August was not brought there merely by

68 *CSPD 1641–3*, p. 376.
69 Clarendon II, 295–6; Underdown, pp. 31–2; BL E 118(31): *A Declaration by the Marquis of Hertford*, p. 1.
70 *LJ* v, 265; Clarendon II, 227.
71 BL E 109 (15): *Dreadful News from Wiltshire and Norfolk*.
72 Underdown, pp. 31–8. There is also a brief account in F.T.R. Edgar, *Sir Ralph Hopton* (Oxford, 1968), pp. 37–40.
73 Clarendon II, 227.

the skilful organization and propaganda of men like Sir John Horner and the clothier John Ashe. This was undoubtedly a genuine and quite exceptional popular movement, prompted by a mixture of local sentiment, fears of gentry tyranny, anti-Catholic hysteria and Puritan enthusiasm. Well drilled forces from north Somerset, Gloucestershire and Wiltshire were joined at this massive gathering by countrymen 'bringing pitchforks, dung picks and such like weapons not knowing (poor souls) whom to fight against'. Rumours were circulating that Lord Poulett, one of Hertford's party, had boasted he would see that no yeoman should have more than £10 a year once the tenantry had been put in their place. Hopton had been extolled by his Evercreech tenants as their knight of the shire in the Short Parliament. Now, it was reported, they came against him and cried him down. There was a sense of betrayal as well as fear in the vehement repulse the Somerset men gave their landlords when they came as part of Hertford's invading band.[74]

Neither of the peers who attempted to enforce the commissions of array in Gloucestershire and Devon had the countywide standing and personal prestige that the task required. The young Lord Chandos of Sudeley Castle sought to test the ground by a meeting with the gentry of the Cotswold hundreds, where his own estates lay. Its purpose, he told them disingenuously in a letter on 11 August, was 'to consider the course to be taken in the distracted state of the kingdom'.[75] Many guessed what he actually had in mind. The gentry and townsmen who met him at Cirencester refused to accept that his intentions were pacific until he had 'set it under his hand'. Even then he was given an exceedingly rough passage. After he had beaten a hasty retreat from the town, his coach, left behind in the market place, was torn in pieces by the townsmen.[76]

The earl of Bath was an ageing conservative whose memories harked back to Elizabethan England. He had a considerable following among the gentry who lived in the vicinity of his north Devon home at Tawstock outside Barnstaple. He also enjoyed some prestige in the county as a whole, as the assizes petitions to him show, but it was not sufficient to outweigh the aspersions parliamentarian propagandists had cast on his commission. In a petition on 12 August the Devon constables asked Sir Robert Foster to declare the commission of array illegal. Bath tried to counter the campaign against him by the publication of a statement that he had received no authority to levy taxes and impositions on the county and that he only sought to secure public safety. But his reception at South Molton, only ten miles from his own home, on 13 September shows how the county felt.

74 BL E 111(4): *Joyful News from Wells*; E 112(33): *A True and exact relation of the proceedings of the Marquis of Hertford*; *LJ* v, 278; Underdown, pp. 38–42.
75 *HMC 5th Report*, p. 346.
76 *CJ* II, 734; *LJ* v, 306; BL E 113(6): *A Letter concerning the Lord Chandos*.

Around 1000 people had gathered in the market place, 'some with muskets loaded, some with halberds and black bills, some with clubs, some with pikes'. The women had piled the steps of the cross with stones to hurl at the invaders; a butcher's wife 'came running with her lap full of ramshorns' to repel them. There was no point in attempting to read the king's proclamation in such a setting. Much the same happened when the sheriff tried to read the commission of array at Cullompton. The people resisted the royalists and many of the county's gentry, particularly from the south, hung back from Bath's meetings at Tawstock.[77] It was the same story from the Cotswolds down to the river Tamar: the commissions of array were seen as alien and intrusive, despite the backing they received from notable county families.

'The country is like a cockpit one spurring against another', remarked a reporter from the midlands in August 1642.[78] There were two counties in particular – Leicestershire and Warwickshire – which, having been initially secured for parliament by enforcement of the militia ordinance, were then vigorously disputed by the commissioners of array throughout the summer. The earl of Northampton began his campaign in Warwickshire on 25 June by seeking the coöperation of Coventry's mayor and aldermen, but he was publicly derided by the city's MP John Barker and he left in a huff.[79] He was not so easily dissuaded though. In August he seized the magazine at Banbury, just across the Oxfordshire border, and besieged Warwick Castle, which had been well fortified by Lord Brooke and was ably defended by Sir Edward Peto, who hung out a red flag, his winding sheet and a bible in defiance.[80]

Warwickshire was the first county after Yorkshire to learn the full wretchedness of civil war. 'Here is nothing but providing of arms', concluded one newsletter.[81] The unfortunate village militiamen, bewildered no doubt and reluctant to be dragged from their fields, were plagued by both the deputy-lieutenants and the commissioners for men and arms. The constable's accounts for Nether Whitacre record that within a few days men were sent to Brooke's training at Coleshill and Lord Compton's at Warwick.[82] Plunder was sanctioned by both sides. Royalist troops robbed carriers; parliamentarians were given a warrant by Brooke to search Lord

77 Andriette, pp. 60–3.
78 BL E 108 (26): *Terrible News from Leicestershire, Warwickshire and Staffordshire.*
79 *LJ* v, 164–5; *HMC Buccleuch* i, 306.
80 *CJ* ii, 682, 690, 693; *CSPD 1641–3*, p. 361; *HMC Coke*, p. 320; BL E 110 (8): *The Earl of Portland's Charge*; E 239(7): *True and New News*; *VCH Warwickshire*, viii, 459; D.F. Mosler, 'A Social and Religious History of the English Civil War in the County of Warwickshire' (Stanford University PhD thesis, 1975), pp. 17–23, 74–7; Hughes pp. 234–47.
81 BL E 109(3): *Some Special Passages from Warwickshire.*
82 Warwickshire RO DRB 27/9; see also BL Add. MS 28565: Stratford-upon-Avon constables accounts.

Dunsmore's home and park.[83] Prominent Puritan gentry were threatened or attacked by Northampton's men. The Purefoys stoutly held out at Caldecot; the Temples only escaped at Frankton because 40 tenants and friends came in to defend the manor house. Mary Temple's letter of 18 August, to her sister Anna Busbridge in Sussex, is full of pathos as she describes the death of her father at this critical time:

> We did see a special providence in it that the word should come in of our house as besetting that morning that my father departed and we for our joy have heard since that they had come, but they heard how well we were provided for them and that they came at their peril. They have disarmed since Kilsby and many other towns and killed three or four men there.[84]

The indecisive duel between Brooke and Northampton for control of Warwickshire was infinitely damaging to the unity of the gentry community. There was probably no other county where the pressure on the leading families to declare themselves was so intense at this stage. Sir William Dugdale, a fervent royalist who in his role at Blanch Lyon pursuivant proclaimed Peto a traitor at Warwick, recorded the state of the parties[85]: 92 gentlemen in all supported the commission of array and 36 the militia ordinance, while 50 'stood neuter neither appearing in the commission nor militia'.[86] At the summer assizes one of the JPs, Robert Leigh, preferred an indictment against Lord Brooke for executing the militia ordinance in the presence of the peer himself and friends of his such as William Purefoy. But it was too late in Warwickshire to contain the split in county society by legal arguments. On 18 July Judge Reeve found 'many about the hall with swords' in the crown court and had to read the statute of Northampton in order to quell the riot.[88] Violence was beginning to overlay customary standards of civilized behaviour.

The stalemate established in Leicestershire at the end of June persisted, with the advantage for the moment somewhat in favour of the royalists. Hastings held musters at Loughborough and Leicester on the two days immediately following the parliamentarian ones. He overawed the county with a skilful mixture of propaganda and menace, having the commission of array read in translation and bringing a force to the county town of 100 cavalry, 120 musketeers and 80 pikemen They gave the appearance, according to one account, of 'a great array, frightening everyone where

83   BL E 202(33): *A True and Exact Diurnal*, 8–15 Aug., p. 4.
84   East Sussex RO Dunn MS 51/56.
85   S.C. Ratcliff and H.C. Johnson, editors, *Warwick County Records* (Warwick, 1936) II, xxxi, xxxiv; Hughes pp. 270–1.
86   Warwickshire RO Z 237.
87   HLRO, Main Papers, 21 July 1642: Judge Reeve to Lord North; *LJ* v, 242.
88   *LJ* v, 147; BL Add. MS 14827, fol. 144v; E 202(15): *A Perfect Diurnal*, 4–11 July, p. 1; Hill, pp. 107–8; E.W. Hensman, *Loughborough during the Civil War*, pp. 7–8.

they came'. On at least one occasion they paraded through Leicester with drums beating, colours displayed and match charged and lighted.[89] The earl of Stamford's failure to go down again in person, as he was directed by parliament in early July, can possibly be explained by his doubts about whether he could raise the strength to dislodge Hastings.[90] In his absence the deputies' plan for a new muster in Sparkinlow hundred that month came to nothing.[91] But Stamford's men were at least able to hold on to the cache of arms and ammunition from the county magazine that had been placed at Bradgate during the lieutenant's visit. In August an indecisive skirmish of some kind between the opposing parties seems to have occurred near Loughborough.[92]

Finally there were some counties where the commission of array was talked of but where in the summer of 1642 it never got off the ground. Lord Mowbray, home at his ancestral mansion of Kenninghall in August, was persuaded to lay aside the Norfolk commission by two MPs who commanded great respect in the locality. He probably saved his own skin by listening to Sir John Holland and Sir John Potts.[93] Something very similar may have happened in Derbyshire, where the commission of array was headed by the young earl of Devonshire, not so long before Thomas Hobbes's pupil and in the late 1630s a fearsomely efficient lord lieutenant of the county.[94] He seems to have spent some time at Chatsworth during July where he probably had discussions with neighbouring gentry.[95] Sir William Lewis reported royalist murmurings in Hampshire on 22 July, but they came to nothing at this stage.[96] The array may have been abandoned in face of the parliamentary strength imported to besiege Portsmouth, where George Goring declared for the king early in August. When the port fell on 7 September parliament's control of the county was confirmed.[97] The leading Rutland commissioners of array were Viscount Camden, the head of the Noel family, and his eldest son Baptist Noel, who was a knight of the shire, a courtier and a Straffordian.[98] In a letter of 14 July to Speaker Lenthall, Sir Edward Harington and three other deputy-lieutenants expressed their fears that the commission, then in the hands of 'men of great power in the county', would soon be enforced, plunging its

89 BL Harl. MS 163, fol. 255v; *CJ* II, 653; *HMC Coke*, p. 320.
90 *LJ* v, 232.
91 BL E 112(20): *Exceeding Joyful News from Lincolnshire.*
92 BL E 202(33): *A True and Exact Diurnal*, 8–15 Aug., p. 5.
93 Holmes, pp. 56–8; Ketton-Cremer, pp. 135–7, 145–9.
94 L. Beats, 'Government and Politics in Derbyshire 1640–1660' (Sheffield PhD thesis, 1978), pp. 54–69.
95 *CJ* II, 666; *HMC Hastings MSS* II, 84–5.
96 *CJ* II, 690; BL Harl. MS 163, fol. 289r; E 112(18): *A Letter sent from Mr Parker at Upper Wallop.*
97 *HMC Portland* I, 54–6, 61; G.N. Godwin, *The Civil War in Hampshire* (1904), pp. 9–23.
98 *CJ* II, 469; Keeler, p. 286.

gentry into violent conflict.[99] But the Noels it seems lacked either the nerve or the inclination to act.

This then, so far as patchy documentation permits it to be told, is the story of the struggle between the militia and the array. It destroys any notion of a simple geographical division of the country into two camps. The most distinctly royalist counties are the ones we would expect from the factional pattern discussed in chapter 9. Almost all of them had produced petitions in defence of episcopacy and the liturgy. The most distinctly parliamentarian counties tended to be strongly represented among the active men at Westminster. In a number of cases, such as Buckinghamsire, Essex and Northamptonshire, a strong Puritan tradition among the gentry was also undoubtedly relevant to the positive responses displayed. The complex pattern of shire politics in the summer of 1642 indicated here must now be put in the broader context of attitudes to commitment and allegiance.

99 *HMC Portland* I, 43.

12

Activism and Neutralism

Such is the sad condition of these times as no man knows how to dispose himself, for now there is so much declared as makes all officers in the kingdom traitors of one side or the other, neither are standers-by in any better condition.

Thomas Knyvett to his wife,
24 May 1642[1]

What progress, Sir, you have made in what was entrusted in your hand touching the militia I desire to know and your intentions therein, for hereby I shall be better able to fashion my carriage here to the advantage of what becomes every honest man to endeavour – the peace of his country.

Sir John Holland to Sir John Potts,
18 August 1642[2]

The motives of those who took sides in the civil war will always to some extent remain inscrutable. There was no simple division between the activists and the neutrals since there were many degrees of commitment. Allegiance is much too large a problem to be tackled comprehensively in a book which is solely directed towards investigation of the outbreak of the war.[3] Nevertheless it demands attention. The discussion in this chapter is intended to put activist and neutralist responses during the period June to November 1642 in the context of men's hopes and fears as they watched the national political crisis turning into civil war, the worst possible outcome they can have imagined.

The struggle for control of the county militias raised the political temperature throughout the provinces. The atmosphere can be sensed from what has been said in the last chapter about counties like Cheshire, Cornwall, Lancashire and Warwickshire. Altercation and acrimony were common. In Lincolnshire, for instance, one of the lesser gentry, William Booth, took the opportunity to pursue an old enmity with Sir Christopher

---

1 *Knyvett*, p. 105.
2 Bodleian Tanner MS 63, fol. 126. The rest of this letter is quoted in Ketton-Cremer, p. 147.
3 For important recent work on allegiance, see Cliffe, pp. 336–62; B.G. Blackwood, *The Lancashire Gentry and the Great Rebellion 1640–1660* (Manchester, 1978), pp. 36–71; Wanklyn, 'Landed Society and Allegiance in Cheshire and Shropshire'; C.B. Phillips, 'The Royalist North: The Cumberland and Westmorland Gentry 1642–1660', *Northern History* XIV (1978), 169–92; J.S. Morrill, 'The Northern Gentry and the Great Rebellion', *Northern History* XV(1979), 66–87.

Wray, who was among the most energetic of the deputy-lieutenants. He tried to disrupt the muster at Caistor by reading Charles's proclamation against the militia ordinance to the assembled trained bands. 'Things would never go well', he declared, 'as long as King Pym governed.' Engaging the deputies in argument, he received support from Sir Gervase Scrope on a point of law, but was sharply told by Wray that 'they came hither neither to dispute the law nor to be taught the law, nor did value the law but must observe the orders of the House.'[4]

The sight of men in arms focused the tensions of small communities. In July some Waltham Abbey men were brought before a JP for calling their neighbours who went to train at Brentwood rebels.[5] At Rayleigh the same month a party of substantial Puritan householders met trouble when they returned from a military exercise nearby. An attempt to pull the ensign-bearer from his horse led to a general uproar: 'men and women striving and fighting promiscuously and confusedly together, few besides the affraiors themselves knowing the ground of the quarrel nor discerning their friends from their foes.' Each side stereotyped the other. The volunteers were slandered as 'roundheads, rogues and rascals'; their antagonists were sneered at as 'common enemies of religion and all peace and government of the town, drunkards and blasphemers'.[6] At Ashford in Kent volunteers who listed and went for training were discouraged and threatened by other inhabitants of the town.[7] A company of townsmen at Aylesbury sought to break up a training exercise with abuse and cries of 'God bless the king and devil take the parliament'. The minister of Southminster in Essex showered a soldier beating a drum in the street on 10 August with invective and swore to a woman who upbraided him 'by God we will cut the parliament's throats'.[8]

The affair of Isham Cross is a striking example of how enforcement of the militia ordinance could spark off factional conflict in a gentry community. The village cross in the village of Isham was destroyed on 28 June by a party of Northamptonshire volunteers, under the command of a zealous Puritan JP Captain Catesby. Some of the villagers informed Thomas Jenison, a seasoned magistrate living a few miles away at Irchester. He was a sober and conservative man and was probably approached because he was reputed as such. Somewhat hesitantly, for as he told Lord Montagu later 'I doubted I should be maligned', he agreed to

4 BL E 107(37): *A Declaration of the Commons in Vindication of Divers Members from the Petition of Captain Booth*; E 154(38): *The Petition of Captain William Booth of Killingholme*; E 202(23): *A Perfect Diurnal*, 18–25 July, sub 21 July.
5 BL Harl. MS 163, fol. 164v; *CJ* II, 632; Essex RO Q/SR 317.
6 HLRO, 8 August 1642: Petition of the captain and officers of the volunteer band of Rochford Hundred.
7 *CJ* II, 709.
8 Bodleian Dep C MS 165, nos. 78, 90; *CJ* II, 694.

take depositions, although he was not strictly the justice living nearest to the scene of the incident. He sought advice from the assize judge, who confirmed that if a riot was in question the matter should be dealt with by the two next justices at a special sessions. The difficulty was that both those who should have acted, Mr Sawyer and Mr Syers, were likely to be partisans of Catesby, who was himself a junior magistrate. On 6 July Jenison went to Wellingborough, where the Puritan JPs were dining with the ministers of the neighbourhood following the market-day lecture. He discovered that they had turned their meal at the Hind into a public disputation about the case, arguing 'that it was no riot' and accusing him for meddling unnecessarily. An angry dispute ensued. Sawyer related the gossip in Puritan circles that the death of Jenison's grandchild of the plague a few days before was a judgement of God for his having interfered in the business. But Jenison would not give way: a special sessions was summoned and Sir Roland St John, a senior JP, was called in as a mediator. Otherwise, Jenison told Lord Montagu, 'I think we should have gone together by the ears'.

At the sessions on 11 July 12 men were found guilty of causing a riot. Yet Jenison, who that night wrote his full account of the whole affair by candle-light, felt it had been a Pyrrhic victory. The foreman of the jury, a man who 'hangs on Mr Catesby's sleeves', had 'disheartened' the witnesses. Before the jury went out, Sawyer had lectured them about the superstitious nature of crosses and quoted the parliamentary order of 9 September 1641, which mentioned crucifixes but not crosses, as justification for the volunteers' action: 'I plainly and roundly told him that it was not fit for him to sit in that place which he possessed that would go about to pervert the jury, contrary to that which had been so plainly proved on the king's behalf.' Jenison felt cornered and abused. When he wrote to Montagu 'to prevent misreports', his house was still afflicted and he clung to his sense that social orders must be preserved despite innuendo and intimidation. His postscript summarizes the tensions of Northamptonshire society at this crucial moment: 'either procure Mr Catesby and Mr Sawyer out of the commission or I will petition to be dismissed.'[9]

Things were not everywhere as fraught as around Wellingborough, but the examples that have been quoted here indicate the atmosphere in the summer of 1642, an atmosphere of emerging strife but not yet of general violence and bloodshed. The civil war took such a long time to get started because in one place after another the gentry with whom the initiative lay avoided military confrontation. There were hasty retreats from towns when contenders approached: Lord Ruthven and Sir Arthur Haselrig

9 P. King and J. Wake, 'The Matter of Isham Cross', *Northamptonshire Past and Present* I, part 3 (1950), 17–21, 24; J.H. Gleason, *The Justices of the Peace in England 1558–1640* (Oxford, 1969), pp. 173, 179–80.

left Leicester on the news of the king's impending arrival at the end of July; Northampton escaped from the back door of the Black Bull at Coventry in August when Brooke was on his way; Brereton vanished from Cheshire on Charles's coming in September.[10] There were musters abandoned under challenge, such as Berkshire's abortive meeting at Watlington.

More remarkably there were the battles which were not fought. Somerset was on the brink of war on 1 August, when the parliamentarian and royalist forces glared at each other across the fields outside Shepton Mallet while the gentry parleyed angrily in the market place. Four days later there was a similar scene, involving much greater forces, at Wells when the parliamentarian throng, said to number 12,000, moved across the Mendips to the escarpment overlooking the cathedral city. Sir Ralph Hopton later described it:

> The horse and the dragoons and the gentlemen that were volunteers were drawn out of the town towards the enemy, where they faced then upon a little hill at the foot of the great hill where they were in batalia, and so after some time, and message sent between them, and the evening coming on, there was by the motion of the gentlemen that came from the disaffected party a truce agreed on for that night till next morning nine of the clock.[11]

Next day, deserted by many of the militiamen, Hertford drew away his troops.

Events in Warwickshire illustrate particularly clearly how anxious both sides were to avoid firing the first shot. Northampton massed a considerable force on Kineton Heath on 30 July to prevent Brooke's transfer of the ordnance at Banbury to Warwick Castle. Brooke brought his company to within musket shot and had them charge their arms while a parley took place. This began before ten and ended around five. Brooke would not deliver the ammunition, agree to desist from enforcing the militia ordinance or resign Warwick Castle as Northampton demanded, nor would he accept Northampton's challenge to a single combat or his suggestion that 20 men selected from each side should fight out the day's differences.[12]. While Brooke talked the countrymen came in to his assistance with bread, cheese and beer, so in the end the forces were much more equal than they had been at the start. The outcome was a compromise: Brooke returned the ordnance to Banbury and agreed to give three

10 BL 669 f 6(57): *Truths from Leicester and Nottingham*; Mosler, 'Civil War in Warwickshire', pp. 26–7; R.N. Dore, *The Civil Wars in Cheshire* (Chester, 1966), p. 15.
11 BL E 112 (13): *A Second Letter from John Ashe*; Underdown, p. 34; C.E.H. Chadwyck Healey, *Bellum Civile: Hopton's Narrative of his Campaign in the West* (Somerset Record Society XVIII, 1902), 4–5, 9–10.
12 BL E 109(19): *A Famous Victory obtained by the Lord Brooke*; E 110(8): *The Earl of Portland's Charge*.

days' warning before he removed it again.[13]

Later in the month Northampton's army faced the main parliamentary force which was marching towards Coventry. The desultory nature of the skirmish that occurred near Southam indicates that neither army was yet ready to engage in a pitched battle. 'After the cannon had played a while on both sides', reported Fiennes and Hampden to the Lord General that night, 'they retreated in some haste.' There were no more than a few on each side killed and injured, including one man who shot himself through the foot and another who had been shot by his fellow through the back.[14]

The only two engagements in the open field, besides this Southam one, before Edgehill, were both in a sense accidental. At Marshall's Elm in Somerset on 4 August, John Pyne, leading 500 militiamen along the road to Glastonbury, met a cavalier party of horse that had been cleverly disposed as an ambuscade on uneven ground which offered natural camouflage. Henry Lunsford, a seasoned professional, made the royalist dispositions, while Sir John Poulett and Sir John Stawell parleyed with Pyne: 'they spake very courteously', Pyne told his colleagues in the Commons later and told him 'how much they desired and should endeavour to preserve the peace of that county and so demanded whither he intended to go with those trained bands which he discovered.' If Pyne had realized that a hundred or so horse and dragoons waited for his men on the slope of the Poldens he would surely not have given an order to advance. The country levies were quickly routed. Pyne himself, terrified for his life when he heard some of the cavaliers were 'threatening to cut him in pieces', spurred his horse and rode straight to London 'in his doublet and hose without coat or cloak'.[15] The skirmish at Powick Bridge in Worcestershire on 23 September occurred because Prince Rupert seized an entirely fortuitous opportunity to attack a party of about 500 parliamentarian horse who were proceeding along a narrow lane, with no inkling that they would encounter the enemy at its end. Again the honours went to the king and the roundhead losses were this time rather higher than at Marshall's Elm, where Stawell quickly called off his men.[16]

The desire to stave off civil war, as the discussion in chapter 8 has shown, was widespread and deeply rooted. How far and how effectively was this desire expressed in neutrality or pacification schemes during the summer and autumn of 1642? Before considering this question, something must be

13 BL 669 f 6(58): *The Copy of a Letter*; E 202(30): *A Perfect Diurnal*, 1–7 Aug., p. 2; Hughes, pp. 245–6.
14 *LJ* v, 321; BL E 114(23): *Certain Special and Remarkable Passages*, 22–26 Aug., E 114(25): *A True Relation of the Skirmish in Southam Field*; E 114(27): *A True Relation of the state of Norwich*; Hughes, p. 253.
15 BL Harl. MS 164, fols. 259v–260r; *CJ* II, 712; Underdown, p. 26; Edgar, *Sir Ralph Hopton*, pp. 38–9.
16 Clarendon II, 323–4; *CSPD 1641–3*, pp. 396–7; Gardiner, *Great Civil War*, I, 30.

said about the nature of local society at this time. The county communities, by which term historians have largely meant the circles of gentry families that dominated the economic life and administration of a shire, were perhaps rather less introverted, rather more open to outside influences, than has sometimes been suggested.[17] The political awareness of country gentlemen by 1642 is amply demonstrated by the correspondence and petitions which have featured so prominently in this book. Moreover in some cases at least ideological differences had for several years before 1640 been working disruptive effects upon the harmony of county politics and administration. In Sussex, for example, the autonomy of the two magisterial divisions had become more complete because of the capture of the eastern Bench by a caucus of assertive Puritan JPs. A similar factional pattern seems to have applied in some other counties such as Gloucestershire and Suffolk.[18]

Yet, despite these developments, kinship remained the dominant principle of the gentry's lives and the leading families in most counties were still bound together by the rounds of hospitality and the chores of local administration.[19] There was still nothing that mattered so much for most of the leading gentry, particularly those with any kind of ambitions, than their standing in the charmed circle of the shire. Among the great families harmony, peace and good government were still everyone's chief desiderata. It would be hard to find a more committed supporter of parliament than Brilliana Harley but, because she recognized that trust was the only basis for peace in the locality, she urged her husband in August 1642 to appoint 'some of the other side' as deputy-lieutenants. Otherwise, she warned, Sir Robert Harley would 'mightly incense them': 'if you choose men of little estates you will make them odious to the country . . . if it be not so carried that they may see there is a respect showed to the gentry it will extremely inflame them.'[20]

It has been suggested that 'the central reality' for country gentlemen at this time was 'the increasing evidence of the collapse of order'.[21] But in one sense there was certainly no nationwide breakdown of order. The king's judges, we have seen, rode the assize circuits as usual in July and August 1642, bringing the majesty and authority of the central legal system to bear on the more complex problems of local justice.[22] Most JPs went about their tasks much as usual. Indeed the humdrum business of issuing

17 Professor Clive Holmes has explored this theme in 'The County Community in Stuart Historiography', *Journal of British Studies* XIX (1980), 54–73.
18 *Sussex*, pp. 89–90, 241–3.
19 *Sussex*, pp. 22–57, 127–227.
20 BL Loan MS 29/174, fol. 307r.
21 Morrill, *Revolt*, p. 34.
22 Cockburn, *History of English Assizes*, p. 272; J.S. Cockburn, *Western Circuit Assize Orders 1629–48* (Camden Society fourth series XVII, 1976), pp. 231–5.

recognizances, taking examinations and hearing cases at petty and quarter sessions probably had a certain reassuring quality at a time of such national uncertainty. Quarter sessions were held as usual almost everywhere in July and October. In Warwickshire admittedly two elderly JPs, who met at Michaelmas, found themselves deserted by their colleagues and were forced to adjourn the sessions before doing any business because 800 parliamentarian soldiers with trumpets blaring had just entered the town.[23] But this was not a typical case. Furthermore, though there were a few instances like Cheshire, East Sussex and Wiltshire of the control of the sessions by one party, by and large the quarterly meetings remained what JPs believed they should be, a genuinely representative forum of gentry opinion.[24] Attendances were adequate for the localities to be competently governed. In October there were sixteen on the Bench at Chelmsford, nine at Stafford, seven at Exeter; in Nottinghamshire, where the sessions were adjourned from town to town, three justices sat at Nottingham, four at Newark and three at Retford; in Suffolk, under the same system, eight sat at Beccles, five at Woodbridge and Ipswich and nine at Bury St Edmunds.[25]

Fear of disorder and social disintegration, which was certainly present but must have varied greatly in its intensity from place to place, rested on a mosaic of impressions and incidents. The main ingredients of this fear were economic dislocation, plunder and rapine, enclosure riots, anti-Catholic riots and evidence of class hostility. In the first place, the economic malaise evident in the winter became general and endemic during the summer months. Samuel Wood sent his master a long account of his difficulties in doing his master's business in north Wales, which he attributed to its having been 'all this year the hardest time to get in money, by reason that nothing gets any money but corn and victuals whereof few in these parts can spare any'. Men held back from dealing. 'No cattle will sell here but a special cow or such', Wood reported in May, 'the parks hang on me; they are dear and no man will meddle with them'.[26] 'Things stand in so ill a condition here', Margaret Eure wrote to Sir Ralph Verney from Yorkshire on 21 May, 'as we can make no money of our coalpits. If rents fail and those fail too we shall be in a hard case.' Down in Somerset, sales at the important Saint White Down fair near Chard in Whitsun week were about half their normal volume.[27]

23 Ratcliff and Johnson, editors, *Warwick County Records* II, xxv, 125–6.
24 Morrill, *Cheshire*, p. 60; *Sussex*, pp. 242–3, 255–8; B.C. Redwood, *Quarter Sessions Order Book 1642–1649* (Sussex Record Society LIV, 1954), pp. 15, 23; Harrison, 'Royalist Organisation in Wiltshire', p. 439.
25 Essex RO Q/SR 318/161; Staffordshire RO QO Book 1642, p. 142; Devon RO QS Order Book 1640–51; Nottinghamshire RO QSM 12, p. 152; East Suffolk RO B 105/2/1, fols. 50r–57r.
26 Clwyd RO Glynde MS 3275: Samuel Wood to Sir John Trevor, 16 May, 23 July 1642.
27 *Verney* II, 86; Underdown, p. 29.

In a letter to Sir Richard Buller on 5 August 1641 Sir William Courtenay reflected upon the misdeeds of the Cornish contingent on its way home from the Scottish war: 'I have seen the disposition of men that have arms and strength and sometimes officers suffer the soldiers to be their masters for their own ends.'[28] Predictably, once there were armies in the field, stories of plunder became common. The royalists' difficulties in checking it have already been mentioned. Speaker Lenthall explained to the Commons on 19 August how one particular device, the general warrant for stopping arms and money going to York, was being used to justify undiscriminating plunder: 'if they saw a house well furnished, though it were of never so honest a Protestant and a well-wisher to the parliament they would say he was a malignant person and so get his house to be rifled.'[29] In August Middlesex, Hertfordshire, Buckinghamshire, Northamptonshire and Warwickshire in turn felt the depradations of Essex's army and Yorkshire, Nottinghamshire and Leicestershire those of the king's.[30] In September there were reports of plunder in Cheshire, Dorset, Gloucestershire, Lancashire, Lincolnshire, Shropshire, Somerset and Worcestershire.[31] Yet for most men, of course, even in these counties, plunder was still a matter of news and gossip rather than personal experience.

The sporadic and localized enclosure rioting prompted by the reforming atmosphere of the Long Parliament continued during 1642. In March, for instance, crowds of several hundred people pulled down enclosures in Durham. In May Margaret Eure described a ritual hedge-breaking in Yorkshire: 'they had their pipe to go before them and their ale and cakes to make themselves merry when they had done their feats of activity.' In June ditches enclosing fenland at Holme in Norfolk were 'thrown down' and the men of Epworth in the Isle of Axholme destroyed the enclosures made as a result of drainage work by Cornelius Vermuyden. In September a crowd invaded the Great Park at Farnham in Surrey, pulling down the pales, killing cattle and taking 200 deer.[32]

The most disturbing feature of such incidents, from the gentry's viewpoint, was the atmosphere of defiance that accompanied them. There was a growing sense that, with king and parliament unable to settle their differences, the law was in disrepute. When some Essex poachers were threatened with legal penalties in May 1642, one replied 'that there was no law

---

28 *Buller*, p. 48.
29 BL Harl. MS 163, fol. 295v.
30 *CJ* II, 717, 729; *LJ* v, 302; BL Harl. MS 164, fol. 262v; E 202(42): *An Exact and True Diurnal*, 29 Aug–5 Sept, p. 4; *CSPD 1641–3*, pp. 314–5, 382–5; *HMC Coke*, p. 320.
31 *CSPD 1641–3*, pp. 387–8, 397; *HMC Portland* I, 65; BL E 202(41): *A Perfect Diurnal*, 29 Aug–5 Sept, p. 6; E 202(45): *A Perfect Diurnal*, 26 Sept.–3 Oct; Wallington II, 95–103; Phillips, *Civil War in Wales* II, 12, 15–16, 19, 30; *CJ* II, 731, 741–2; *HMC 5th Report*, p. 43.
32 *Verney* II, 86; *CJ* II, 409, 471; *LJ* v, 101; *HMC 5th Report*, p. 52; Manning, pp. 125, 134–5; Morrill, *Revolt*, p. 34.

settled at this time that he knew'. When the keeper at Farmham told some who chose a fast day to raid the Great Park that they should be at church according to parliament's directions, they said 'they cared not what parliament did or said'. The fishermen of Burnham in Essex laughed at an order of the Lords to secure the earl of Sussex's control of his oyster beds; the people of Balderton in Nottinghamshire defied the peers' order for the quiet possession of certain enclosed lands there by the queen's tenants.[33]

By the spring of 1642 the long-standing dispute between the commoners and the undertakers for the earl of Lindsey's drainage project had brought parts of south Lincolnshire close to anarchy. Numerous attempts to eject the local populace and restore the undertakers had failed. On 1 April the sheriff and JPs found themselves scorned by a crowd of 300 who pulled down houses and destroyed crops of cole and rape seed in the West Fen near Bolingbroke. Next day at Boston they managed to arrest two of the ringleaders but they were set upon by 'a mob of more than 1000 persons' while they were drawing up indictments for the riot. This crowd 'attacked the house where the sheriff and justices were, broke in the windows and having procured from the church the instruments used to pull down houses in case of fire threatened to pull the house down unless the prisoners were released'. The JPs were even pelted with dirt and stones as they rode away. Local juries refused to indict those who participated in these riots and before long the fenmen had regained possession of all their commons in the district.[34]

Whereas enclosure rioting affected a number of districts at one time or another in 1642, anti-Catholic rioting was confined to a small area on the borders of Essex and Suffolk during a few weeks in the late summer. The trouble began at Colchester where Sir John Lucas, whose family had been unpopular in the neighbourhood for some time, was suspected of collecting horses to serve the king. When he tried to slip away from his home at night he was caught and imprisoned at the insistence of the populace, who rifled his house and then moved on to raid the homes of two nearby Catholics, Sir Thomas Audley and Lady Rivers, at Beerchurch and St Osyth respectively.[35] The pillage then spread to Witham, Yeldham and the Sudbury district of Suffolk. The mob violence of these incidents horrified gentry who observed them: 'so monstrous is the beast when it holds the bridle in its teeth', observed the earl of Warwick's steward Arthur Wilson. But Sir Thomas Barrington and Harbottle Grimston, sent down by the Commons to appease the multitudes, found little difficulty in persuading

33 *HMC 5th Report*, pp. 19, 21; *LJ* v, 42; Manning, pp. 124, 126; Holmes, p. 44.
34 *HMC 5th Report*, p. 25; Manning, pp. 127–34. I am grateful to Professor Clive Holmes for making available his account of the Lincolnshire riots, which now appears in *Seventeenth-Century Lincolnshire*, pp. 152–6.
35 BL Harl. MS 163, fol. 297v; Holmes, pp. 35–6.

many of them to make restitution of goods they had taken, once they were persuaded that parliament had the nation's affairs firmly in hand. 'If the parliament were safe it was as much as they desired', the leaders of a crowd of 5000 or so told the MPs at Colchester. Barrington informed colleagues at Westminster on 29 August that some 40,000 would come to their assistance if need be 'all with pitchforks or some weapons.' The disturbances certainly owed much to political sensitivity based on the depression in the cloth trade. There was also well established anti-Catholic prejudice in the area. The trigger was rumour and dramatized gossip that parliament's security and existence was threatened. The Stour valley riots were a hard lesson for Pym in the perils of unbridled enthusiasm once the cause he had propagated caught the popular imagination.[36]

For a short time in the latter stages of the Stour valley panic the country-men became less discriminating in their targets and a bitter vein of class hostility emerged. Certain Protestant gentry were plundered because of their social status, and perhaps their personal unpopularity, rather than their religious leanings. The account written by Warwick's steward, Arthur Wilson, of his reception when he rode into Sudbury beside Lady Rivers's coach, which had her steward inside it, provides the best insight we have into the sheer confusion, terror and vulnerability of a small market town on the eve of the civil war. There were chains across the street ends and no one appeared till the coach was within them: 'then they began to run to their weapons and before we could get to the market place the streets swarmed with people.' The coach was quickly recognized and Wilson was taken for Lord Rivers himself, but luckily the town clerk, whose father was also a servant of Warwick's, recognized him. By insisting on Wilson's real identity, he was able to save him from being molested and to calm the people.[37]

Few gentry had so dramatic a personal experience, but a good many seem to have sensed an unusual degree of tension between the people and their landlords or masters. 'Many people grow bold, heady and audaciously violent hereabouts and spare not many of them to publish their minds in dangerous speeches', related Samuel Wood from north Wales on 23 July.[38] In September Thomas Gardiner told Sir Ralph Verney of the anarchic speeches he had heard were being uttered in Oxfordshire, such as that 'the gentry have been our masters a long time and now we chance to master them'. Words that could normally be dismissed as alehouse bravado were suddenly taken more seriously. 'Now they know their strength', reflected Gardiner, 'it shall go hard but they

---

36 BL Harl. MS 163, fols. 207v–308r; E 114(36): *Special Passages*, 23–30 Aug.; *HMC 5th Report*, p. 45; *CSPD 1641–3*, p. 377; *CJ* II, 740–1, 745; Holmes, pp. 43–4; Manning, pp. 171–7.
37 Holmes, p. 44; Manning, pp. 175–7.
38 Clwyd RO Glynde MS 3275.

will use it.'[39] It is difficult to say how many gentry had been prompted by
the various disorders mentioned here to ponder along these lines but there
were certainly some. In Norfolk Sir John Potts revealed his mind in a letter
to Sir Simonds D'Ewes on 19 August, that is before the Stour valley riots
occurred. There is no evidence of social unrest in his own neighbourhood
at this time. Yet he wrote as follows:

> I concur with you in the fears of an ungovernable multitude, from whence my
> thoughts always apprehended the most remediless dangers, which God avert
> . . . Whensoever necessity shall enforce us to make use of the multitude I do not
> promise myself safety.[40]

The previous month Sir Edmund Verney had urged his steward to look to
the defences of Claydon House, 'for I fear a time may come when rogues
may look for booty in such houses'.[41]

For all these reasons, then, the potential inherent in the national
situation for social disorder was plain for men to see. Many gentry, it seems
clear, asked themselves two separate sets of questions as the civil war broke
out and the answers they gave themselves did not necessarily produce a
consistent line of action. The first set of questions was about their
allegiance and political sympathies, the second was about the best interests
of themselves, their families and their locality. Sir George Booth, as we
have seen, sent his tenants to the parliamentarian stronghold of
Manchester. He also wrote to Thomas Legh, who lived not far away from
Dunham Massey at Adlington Hall, begging him to disband the forces he
was raising for the king or to use his troops to suppress forces raised in
Cheshire by either side.[42] Lord Montagu showed great vehemence in
recruiting for the king in Northamptonshire: for instance he threatened a
Lowick yeoman with the gaol if he did not send his two sons to
Nottingham. But in a conciliatory letter to the deputy lieutenants on 15
August he and the earl of Westmorland spoke of their hope 'that with joint
consent we may cherish the peace and quiet of the country'.[43] Localism, in
other words, was a crucial ingredient in men's thinking and actions. LOCALISM

What was localism? It can be defined as attachment to the interests of and
identification with units smaller than the state, such as regions, counties,
towns and neighbourhoods. Localism and neutralism were not the same
things. Indeed localism could appear in many guises and be exploited in
many ways, some of which are not at all obvious at first sight. But recent
work has shown how, in one way or another, the tension between local and
national interests was at the heart of many parliamentary elections in the

39 *HMC 7th Report*, p. 441.
40 BL Harl. MS 386, fol. 233.
41 *Verney* II, 94.
42 Morrill, *Cheshire*, p. 57; Wanklyn, 'Landed Society and Allegiance in Cheshire and Shropshire',
    pp. 200, 443.
43 *HMC Montagu*, p. 157-8; Bodleian Dep C MS 153, nos. 65, 66.

early seventeenth century, the parliamentary debates of the 1620s, the political problems raised by the making of war from 1643 to 1648 and the difficulties encountered by the Cromwellian regime in the 1650s.[44] Because the gentry communities believed that the Long Parliament had reform in hand and understood their concerns, this tension, normally so prominent, was latent in 1641. We have seen how the petitions of early 1642 indicate a quite remarkable degree of unanimity about the nation's problems. Localism, briefly, was largely superfluous, showing its head only in traditional grumbles about the weight of taxation and in the campaigns to remedy a few particular grievances like the billeting money due to Yorkshire, Durham and Northumberland. But in the summer of 1642 everything changed. When the king and parliament sought active support against each other, localism suddenly became a crucial determinant of the responses of both counties and towns to the national conflict. Activism and neutralism must now be put in this context.

Where the leading families of a county were virtually unanimous, the militia ordinance or the commission of array became a rallying point that fulfilled a double role. The most committed activists could see it as a local declaration of war against the other side; others cooperated because it fulfilled their localist aspirations. Thus in counties like Buckinghamshire and Essex the execution of the ordinance was a potent symbol both of loyalty to the representative institution of the state and of county unity and solidity. It was similar, though in a different sense, with the commission of array in counties like Herefordshire, Lancashire, Shropshire and Worcestershire. 'God bless the nine worthies of Herefordshire', shouted the volunteers who acclaimed the commissioners of array there on 14 July. At the Preston muster on 8 July the Lancashiremen who shouted 'For the king and Lord Strange' were expressing localist as well as surviving feudal sentiments.[45] There was also room under the same banner for both militancy and moderate constitutionalism.[46] Thus the grand jury at Shrewsbury stressed that it would obey the king 'in all lawful ways for the putting of the country in a posture of arms'.[47]

The possessiveness and tightfistedness of countrymen with regard to their arms, already noted in relation to Charles's recruiting campaign, and their insistence on the tradition that trained bands did not cross the shire boundaries, are striking manifestations of localism. In September 1642, for instance, the Cheshire militia under royalist command refused to cross

---

44 Hirst, pp. 132–188; Russell, *Parliaments*, particularly pp. 1–84; Morrill, *Revolt*, pp. 89–131; Ashton, *English Civil War*, pp. 255–87; D. Underdown, 'The Chalk and the Cheese: Contrasts among the English Clubmen', *Past and Present* XXXV(1979), 25–48; A. Hughes, 'Militancy and Localism: Warwickshire Politics and Westminster Politics, 1643–1647', *TRHS*, forthcoming.
45 *HMC Portland* III, 92; Ormerod, pp. 23–4.
46 Silcock, 'County Government in Worcestershire', pp. 232–5.
47 BL 669 f 6(69).

Stockport bridge to assist in the siege of Manchester.[48] Magazines had been stocked from resources raised by local taxation for local defensive purposes. Lancashire, perhaps exceptionally, had paid £7200 for ordnance and ammunition between 1638 and 1640.[49] No wonder counties clung to their own weapons. Lord Newark was balked by an angry crowd of townsmen when he tried to seize the gunpowder stocked in the Nottingham magazine for the king's use. They refused to have their arsenal raised 'when so many rude armed people' were daily passing through the county.[50] The Leicestershire grand jury, having suffered several weeks of the Grey-Hastings quarrel, decided that the presence of the major part of the county's weapons and powder in Leicester itself was too great a temptation to the contenders for the shire, so they petitioned the king on 22 July to distribute it on a proportional basis between the hundreds. It was to be 'dispersed to every town so near as we can equally'. This prescription, accepted by Charles, took local defensiveness, village by village, to its logical conclusion.[51]

In some places polarization went so far so quickly that the localist argument became mere rhetoric. So it must have looked, for example, to John Pyne when he parleyed with Sir John Poulett and Sir John Stawell at Marshall's Elm. Yet the search for isolation from the war was seriously pursued in a number of counties. The possibility of attaining it did not seem absurd when there was so much uncertainty about the nature and length of the emerging military conflict. There is a fascinating letter of 1 September from Sir Roland St John to Lord Montagu. Northamptonshire by this time was firmly under parliament's control and Montagu's chief ally, the earl of Westmorland, had abandoned his involvement in the commission of array. St John began by reminding Montagu that the array 'could have received no life in these parts if it had not been quickened' by Westmorland and himself. Therefore his activity, St John alleged, had brought 'the distractions of these times' to Northamptonshire, 'the sad effects whereof I am sure you cannot behold without extreme grief of heart'. Surely he was now ready to follow his colleague's magnanimous lead? St John pleaded 'from the grounds and bottom of my heart':

> You will not only preserve the amity of Northamptonshire but keep off the storms which as yet have been blown aside into other coasts . . . desisting from countenancing that commission will in all likelihood prevent the effusion of blood and much conduct to the peace of this country.[52]

In a few counties the gentry put social cohesion first and managed to keep

---

48 R.N. Dore, *The Great Civil War in the Manchester Area* (Manchester, 1972), p. 14.
49 HLRO, Main Papers, 5 Aug. 1642: Deposition of Sir Thomas Stanley; *Sussex*, pp. 188–92.
50 *Hutchinson*, pp. 54–6.
51 BL E 108(20): *Petition of Leicester to the King*; Hollings, *Leicestershire in the Civil War*, pp. 20–1.
52 Bedfordshire RO J 1384.

polarization in check by informal methods through June and July or even longer. The classic example of a gentry community which remained united and held to a neutralist stance is Derbyshire. This case is the more remarkable because Derbyshire's geographical position must have made it vulnerable to the heat of the controversy. The gentry's deference to both sides had been made plain in the moderate petitions formulated in February and March. Parliament's lord lieutenant, the earl of Rutland, was supine until 29 June, when he addressed a round-robin letter to JPs calling for a meeting to discuss the security of the county. He spoke of the 'manifold distempers of the times' and his 'indulgent and dutiful care of his sacred Majesty and safety of his parliament and this country'. Rutland made no attempt to enforce the militia ordinance; his pacific and defensive stance was clearly acceptable to most of the leading gentry families. The only energetic parliamentarian activist at this stage, Sir John Curzon, found his friends and neighbours determined to sit still. In the end Derbyshire had to be dragged into the war. In October Sir John Gell procured forces at Hull, recruited more at Chesterfield and garrisoned Derby, but he received a threatening letter from many of the great men of the shire challenging his disruption of the peace.[53]

The long delay before the militia ordinance was enforced in Suffolk can be attributed to an awareness among its MPs of the dangers inherent in their own political disunity. The Westminster delegation included two royalists and the neutralist Sir Robert Crane, who offered four horses under the Propositions 'for the defence of king and parliament not divided'. Sir Simonds D'Ewes was also the opposite of an activist. The key man was undoubtedly Sir Nathaniel Barnardiston, whose generous commitment upon the Propositions was matched by reluctance to see the harmony of his own community shattered. But JPs who were on the spot naturally reacted firmly to the riots in the Stour valley, calling out the militia and deluging constables with warrants for watch and ward and controls on the movement of the poor. These actions alarmed Barnardiston: he told a friend in West Suffolk on 1 September that the county's MPs thought them 'dangerous in these turbulent times'. He seems to have feared that any body of armed men, even if temporarily called together, might be taken over by the commissioners of array. The aim, he insisted, should be 'to labour to quiet the country with as little force as may be'. Back at his mansion in Kedington himself a few days later, his view of the local situation quickly changed. He recognized that it was no longer possible to keep Suffolk out of the armed conflict and by 14 September he was busy enforcing musters and the Propositions. Yet the rationale of the deputies' actions remained local security. It was this consideration quite plainly that had brought the county belatedly into line behind parliament. Directing constables that militiamen should be ready at an hour's warning on 26 October, Barnardiston and Sir Roger North explained that they had received complaints that 'divers lewd and disorderly people have assembled themselves in a tumultuous and riotous manner intending as is justly feared to enter into some desperate actions'. There was no reference to the civil war.[54]

The Norfolk delegation at Westminster took no action to assert parliamentary control of the shire until news reached them of royalist leanings among some of the gentry there at the end of July. This made the knights of the shire, Sir John Potts and Sir Edmund Moundeford, face the necessity of rousing the county, but Potts confessed to colleagues in the Commons on 1 August that he was nervous about the task. His soundings had not been encouraging and he had good reason to expect no cooperation from some deputy-lieutenants and captains. Several gentlemen, he believed, 'had been lately with His Majesty'. Since Sir John Hobart and others well affected to parliament had been dismissed from the Bench, he was informed, the papists 'who lately expressed much fear' grew 'very confident'.[55] Potts's delicate mission − he went down in early August − was to secure the best of both worlds: to ensure that the war was kept out of the county but that he could quickly take control of it if need be. Moundeford, delayed by illness on the way home, supported him to the hilt but signified his recognition that their policy was an activist one in a neutralist guise. 'If the event be not prosperous', he wrote to Potts, 'we are only passively accessory . . . I am confirmed that you dare do nothing but by the command of reason signed by a good conscience . . . I resolve never to give myself the lie by deserting the path you tread though bug-beared by all the neutrals in the county.'[56]

The policy Potts pursued during August, neutralization of the county by suspension of both the militia ordinance and the commission of array, was really Sir John Holland's notion. It was he, a man of great magnanimity, who set the tone of Norfolk politics in the summer of 1642.[57] 'Your presence will continue the country's peace, as your advice procured it', Potts told him on his arrival at Quidenham, 'I have not acted rashly so I shall not do anything without consulting you.'[58] In a letter to Sir Simonds D'Ewes on 11 August, Potts explained that he hoped to keep the shire

54 East Suffolk RO FB 19/12/1–2; Bodleian Tanner MS 63, fol. 146; *CJ* II, 764; M.A.E. Green, editor, *The Diary of John Rous* (Camden Society LXVI, 1856), p. 121; Holmes, pp. 48–51.
55 Bodleian Tanner MS 63, fol. 43: Sir Edmund Moundeford to Sir John Potts, 7 June 1642; BL Harl. MS 164, fol. 257v; Ketton-Cremer, p. 143.
56 Bodleian Tanner MS 63, fol. 116; *CJ* II, 695–6, 701; Ketton-Cremer, p. 145.
57 Ketton-Cremer, pp. 47–8, 108–13, 116–18, 146–7; Holmes, pp. 24–5.
58 Bodleian Tanner MS 63, fol. 117, incorrectly cited in Morrill, *Revolt*, p. 165 as a letter to a royalist commissioner of array.

quiet, while exploiting its resources 'by legal rates towards relief of Ireland and discharge of the Scots'.[59] For a short time his consensus politics worked, but by late August the war party at Westminster was questioning his loyalty and it became necessary for the deputy-lieutenants to implement the militia ordinance and the Propositions.[60] They fashioned a new policy to which we shall return.

The Staffordshire gentry's determination to preserve their neutrality is evident in the short shrift they gave both the militia ordinance and the commission of array and in their unenthusiastic response to the king's appeal for support at Uttoxeter.[61] The man the county looked to for a lead was Sir Richard Leveson. His equivocal course typifies the combination we have seen in other cases of a degree of commitment to the national cause, on one side or the other, with a strongly neutralist line at home. He had left Westminster in the spring and ignored summonses to attend; he also disregarded an approach in July from the Shropshire commissioners of array.[62] He promised ten horses for three months service in the royalist army at Lord Paget's recruiting meeting and supplied the king with some arms, but he obviously did not consider these actions compromised his independent stand in his own community, since he told Sir Richard Newport in September that he had never appeared either for the ordinance or the commission. 'That of which I have ever applied myself', he declared in this letter, 'is not to engage myself to any one side in occasions of differences, whereby I have ever stood an equal party to both and by that means able to compose great differences and not long since preserved the peace of this county when all had like to have fallen to blows.'[63] In a missive of 5 September, Leveson, together with his kinsman Thomas Crompton, George Digby and Ralph Sneyd, rejected an appeal for cooperation from the Shropshire commissioners of array, claiming that the commission was 'by special allowance of His Majesty' forborne in their county. 'Our shire being hitherto in peace', they announced, 'and many conceiving hopes of continuance therein, it is not thought safe for us, without supreme authority or greater motives of new demonstrable dangers, to raise the arms of our county.'[64]

Finally in this series of instances of neutralization mention must be made, although it was not strictly a county, of the Isle of Wight. Goring's

59 BL Harl. MS 383, fol. 206r.
60 Holmes, pp. 56–8.
61 D.H. Pennington, 'County and Country: Staffordshire in Civil War Politics 1640–1644', *North Staffordshire Journal of Field Studies* VI (1966), 16; Pennington and Roots. editors, *The Committee at Stafford*, p. lxi.
62 Staffordshire RO D 593/P/8/1/1; J.T. Pickles, 'Studies in Royalism in the English Civil War 1642–1646 with special reference to Staffordshire' (Manchester University MA thesis, 1968), pp. 69–71.
63 Staffordshire RO D 868/3/2; D 948/4/62.
64 Staffordshire RO D 593/P/8/1/7, 37.

declaration of allegiance to Charles at Portsmouth and the subsequent siege of the town predictably brought latent tensions into the open across the Solent. The townsmen of Newport clung to parliament, pleading to be sent some supplies of powder, whereas some royalist gentry briefly held Carisbrooke Castle, just outside the town, for the king.[65] But the gentry families of this tiny offshore community were long established and close-knit. They decided to bury political disagreements, and stand together on the sidelines of the war. On 18 August, striking a slightly more formal note, 22 of them signed a declaration of the island's neutrality:

> We will with our lives and estates be assistant to each other in the defence of the true Protestant religion established in the Church of England, against all papists or other ill-affected persons whatsoever. We will unanimously join the uttermost of our endeavours for the peace of this island, by protecting it by those forces already legally substituted amongst us and will admit no foreign power, or forces, or new government, except His Majesty by advice of his parliament upon occasions that may arise shall think it necessary to alter it in any particulars, for the good and safety of the kingdom.[66]

The logical conclusion of this kind of neutralism was the raising of a third force to keep both sides and all intruders out of the county. It has been suggested that this was attempted in three counties – Cheshire, Lincolnshire and Staffordshire – but the Cheshire case rests on a collation of the neutralist remonstrance of June 1642 with the articles of the West Riding pacification in September.[67] At a muster at Knutsford on 30 June there were shouts of approval when some of the deputies declared that their purpose was to arm 'for the joint defence of His Majesty and parliament together' and 'to confirm their fidelity and affection to both, that they may not be drawn away to any seditious course which tendeth to make division betwixt them'. But this seems to be as far as the matter went.[67] Lincolnshire and Staffordshire are the only authentic examples of counties raising a third force and Staffordshire's plan was the more coherent and specific of the two. It was promulgated at a special sessions of the Bench on 15 November. The JPs listed the actions 'contrary to the laws of this kingdom and liberty of the subject' that had occurred in the previous weeks: outrage and unlawful assemblies in 'warlike manner', imprisonment and fining of 'men of quality', robbery of horses and other goods. Their justification for intervention was their 'oaths and duties to His Majesty and the common safety of this county'. They decided to raise a

---

65 Bodleian Dep C MS 153, no. 50; *HMC Portland* I, 49, 55.
66 Herefordshire and Worcestershire RO 899/31 BA 3669/1(iv): *Three Declarations* (printed 17 Sept. 1642).
67 BL Harl. MS 2135, fol. 65v; Morrill, *Revolt*, pp. 37, 159–60 prints the collated documents, which are in Bodleian Ashmole MS 830, fols. 280–4. I am grateful to Dr John Morrill and Mr Richard Cust for valuable discussion of them.

force of 800 foot and 200 horse, 'together with such other volunteers as will willingly offer their service for the lawful defence of their country', which would be trained twice a week. The JPs envisaged an efficient mobile series of units, spread across the hundreds, ready to deal with trouble or incursions as they occurred, or at least to contain attacks on market towns until the 'power of the county' was raised to repel them. This was localism in its most formidable guise. The scheme was carefully constructed and it had the backing of the grand jury. Names that crop up in the list of captains, like Bagot, Bowyer, Littleton and Sneyd, indicate the active participation of the families that really mattered. Yet by January 1643 there were several royalist garrisons in the county and the scheme had collapsed. It was shortlived because a rising of the Moorlanders and the vulnerability of the country on all sides soon made it advisable to accept royalist help in the cause of local security.[68]

The Lincolnshire scheme is more surprising and remarkable than the Staffordshire one in the sense that the county was much more sharply divided in the summer of 1642. On the one hand the militia ordinance had been enforced without any great difficulty; on the other hand there was the strongly worded royalist petition of July. The county's enthusiastic welcome to the king on 13 July was hard for the parliamentarians to explain away: 'it stood not with their loyalties', pleaded one of them, 'to stand in flat opposition to His Majesty's commands.' The third-force scheme in this case did not represent consensus among all the leading gentry. It was rather a device by certain royalists like Sir John Monson, Sir Edward Heron, Sir Peregrine Bertie and Charles Dallison to hold a major part of the gentry community together by drawing upon their localist sentiments. The deputy-lieutenants stood aloof. Seventy-five gentry and high-ranking ecclesiastics personally subscribed a body of 168 cavalry to guard the county for three months. The intention that this force should be 'disposed of within the county' was made absolutely clear: a commentator spoke of securing the 'peace of the country' against overseas invasion, the marauding soldiers from Hotham's garrison on the Humber bank and internal insurrection by 'men of desperate fortunes'. Many of those who were involved were undoubtedly men who were reluctant to commit themselves to either party. The notion of a force that stood for the king, the Protestant religion, the laws of the realm and the privileges of parliament was immediately attractive to them. Sir Daniel Deligne, for example, who promised three cavalrymen, had been one of those insulted by the courtiers at York in March. A few months later he fled his house to avoid positive attachment to either side. Sir Robert Markham, who offered four horses,

---

68　Staffordshire RO QS Order Book, pp. 121, 142; Johnson and Vaisey, editors, *Staffordshire and the Great Rebellion*, pp. 28–9; *North Staffordshire Journal of Field Studies* VI (1966), 16; Pennington and Roots, editors, *The Committee at Stafford*, pp. xx, 341.

was also 'unwilling to declare himself on either side' and as a result he was later plundered by both.[69]

In the cases which have been discussed so far localism found expression in neutralization. There were other counties where precisely the same intention, of retreating behind county boundaries, lay behind defensive arrangements that were agreed by a broad spectrum of the gentry and put into effect under nominal allegiance to one side or the other. Gloucestershire and Norfolk are the two outstanding parliamentarian instances, Yorkshire and Worcestershire the two royalist ones. In these counties there were probably a good many gentry who, given a different local balance of power, would have been as ready to cooperate with the other side in schemes that were essentially county orientated.

Many Gloucestershire gentry attended a meeting called on 25 August by the parliamentary activists Edward Stephens, Nathaniel Stephens and Sir Robert Cooke. These men knew others were not all of their mind; they also knew that there was general unease about the vulnerability of the county on all sides and particularly towards south Wales, which was believed to habour hoards of papists. Their propositions, therefore, amounted to a comprehensive plan for the security of the shire, designed to unite the gentry. 'Voluntary submission' to the militia ordinance and enforcement of the Propositions, in order to raise money for local uses, were to be the limits of Gloucestershire's commitment to parliament. The stress throughout was on the role of 'the gentlemen in every division'. They were to propound the Propositions loans; they were to organize the troops of horse, making a body of 240 in all, which were to be ready to rendezvous with militiamen and volunteers at Huntley, Winchcombe, Cirencester or Chipping Sodbury 'upon all alarms'. The scheme was shot through with traditionalism: the most experienced captain, for instance, in the old trained-band manner would act as colonel in each division. The Gloucestershire scheme gives a strong sense of the rulers of a frontier region seeking to protect themselves. Militiamen and volunteers were to keep adequate powder, bullets and match from the magazine at their homes in readiness for emergencies. Every militiaman would have a horse at the county's expense to speed his passage to the rendezvous. Carts should be constantly available for transporting ammunition. No ferry boats which could be used for bringing across soldiers were to be left on the Welsh sides of the Wye or Severn.[70]

It is uncertain how fully the scheme was enforced but the horse were

69 BL E 112(20): *Exceeding Joyful News from Lincolnshire*; E 113(7): *True Intelligence from Lincolnshire*; 669 f 5(66): *The Resolution of the Gentry of Lincolnshire*; *CSPD 1641–3*, p. 355; Hill, *Tudor and Stuart Lincoln*, pp. 150–2; *Historical Journal* xxi (1978), 260–1; Holmes, *Seventeenth-Century Lincolnshire*, pp. 147–50.
70 BL E 116(15): *A Relation from Portsmouth; HMC Portland* i, 71, 98.

exercised weekly and an urgent appeal was sent to London for ordnance and petronels. The letters of the plan's proponents to John Smyth during September and October show how seriously they tried to rally all the gentry behind it. Smyth was urged to bear in mind the safety of 'ourselves and the country' and to bring in other gentry of the Berkeley neighbourhood to the fortnightly meetings at Gloucester. In November news of the movements of the armies led to a muster of the dragoons in Berkeley hundred to check upon their 'readiness for the safety of the county'.[71]

From September 1642 until early 1643 the Norfolk deputy-lieutenants consistently pursued moderate policies that were designed to maintain unity among the gentry. The principal slogan remained 'the peace of the country'. At a meeting on 5 September the deputies agreed that, should any tumult break out or intruders arrive, responsibility for suppression would lie with the militia band nearest the trouble spot. On 15 September 24 of the militia captains assembled at Norwich, including eight who were later to be sequestered, agreed to serve under Warwick 'for His Majesty, and both houses of parliament and for the peace of this county'. A larger group of gentry agreed to join with the deputies to defend the shire from 'all kinds of plunderers'. In the following weeks musters were held, arms were checked, inventories were made of the magazines and a force of volunteer dragoons was established to 'keep the county from plundering'. But there was never any reference to the campaign being fought elsewhere in England.[72]

The Propositions were enforced in Norfolk in the same localist manner. Sir William Paston, later a royalist, subscribed six cavalrymen 'for the defence of this county not to be sent out'. Thomas Windham, whose son took command of a troop of horse, offered two cavalrymen and two foot soldiers 'for the defence of this county within itself'. Those who proved intractable were treated leniently. Nicholas L'Estrange, whose family very likely hindered the Propositions in the Hunstanton district, was not replaced as a colonel in the militia until late October nor disarmed until March 1643. 'Quiet and connivance', the parliamentarian committee hoped, 'would keep these wasps from stinging'. Yet more and more, as time went on, Potts and Holland were playing a double game. They were open to accusations of bad faith. Sir John Spelman made the point in a moving letter to Potts in February 1643. Spelman was one of those who had been persuaded to lay aside the commission of array in the summer. If that policy had been as honestly pursued on the other side, he argued, Norfolk might have enjoyed immunity from 'the common calamity': 'to deal faithfully with you, Sir, how much soever your intention is the contrary, it is too much feared that the courses that are set on foot will

71 Gloucestershire RO D 2510/21, 22, 24; *HMC 5th Report*, p. 346.
72 Bodleian Tanner MS 63, fol. 152r; Holmes, pp. 58–9.

inevitably bring the war upon us.'[73] This of course was a realistic note, but the appeal to men like Potts and Holland, who could not wholly desert parliament, of isolating their own little corner of England in parliament's name is easy to understand.

The propositions foisted on the grand jury at the York assizes in August 1642 were royalist in origin but localist in intent. Their explicit purpose was 'the defence, peace and quiet of the county'. All the gentry charged with horse were to send in their cavalry to York on 24 August, provided with a month's pay. This force, under Sir Thomas Glemham, was responsible for checking the depredations of Hotham's men from Hull. The earl of Cumberland was given charge of the magazine and the assistance of a commission of oyer and terminer directed to the commissioners of array. The king agreed to the plan, although it meant excusing all those engaged in it from appearing at the raising of the standard, because he was anxious to settle Yorkshire before he embarked on his campaign. He even, as we have seen, agreed to spare the county its arms and ammunition and to leave it some ordnance and cannoneers. Once again we can detect men who felt varying degrees of commitment finding common ground on an isolationist platform. Those like Cumberland himself, Lord Fauconberg and Sir Thomas Glemham, who had thrown in their lot with Charles, were ready to listen to moderates whose chief concern was the removal of the cloud of war.[74] In fact there was probably little chance of quieting belligerence in Yorkshire, but the decision to leave the Fairfaxes in peace at Nun Appleton, when there was ample chance to take them prisoner, suggests that the royalists had not abandoned hope of doing so. The gentlemen of the county, Hyde later recorded, besought Charles to abandon a design to arrest the Fairfaxes: such action would be so 'ungracious and unpopular . . . that the disaffected would be so far from being weakened that their party would be increased thereby'.[75]

Worcestershire appeared immediately vulnerable during August to parliament's army marching into the midlands, so the commissioners of array established a body of horse 'to be disposed of within the county for three months'. The scheme was instigated by Lord Coventry, Sir William Russell, Sir Thomas Littleton and Sir John Packington. Their first appeal on 14 August was answered by 41 subscribers. Friends and neighbours who were roused subsequently bought the total of gentry contributors to 86. The mobile cavalry force was intended to maintain 'His Majesty's royal person and just prerogative, the Protestant religion as it is now established, the laws of the realm, the just privileges of parliament and the public peace against all opposition whatsoever'. But the narrowness of the

73 Ketton-Cremer, pp. 149–56; Holmes, pp. 59–61.
74 BL E 116 (31): *Articles of the Grand Jury of Yorkshire; Historical Journal* XXI (1978), 263.
75 Clarendon II, 285–7.

commissioners' horizons emerged in their correspondence with their Warwickshire colleagues, who were seeking active support against the parliamentarian forces there. They were ready to engage in the rhetoric of mutuality: 'the vicinity of counties involves the vicinity of interest.' But, as the Warwickshire commissioners soon discovered, they were not prepared to do anything, indeed they were unable to offer any assistance since their whole policy was based on localist intent. Most of those who gave the commissioners their trust, in the sense of sending cavalrymen into service, believed that it was their county's boundaries and no one else's territory that was at stake.[77]

Localism therefore manifested itself in various ways, was articulated more specifically in some cases than others and found more or less stable forms of expression. But a fundamental distinction can be made between the cases that have been discussed and the ephemeral pacts and truces, in the most fiercely disputed counties, that were merely bids to prevent excessive bloodshed and gain time. There are three outstanding examples: Yorkshire, Cornwall and Lancashire.

Yorkshire perhaps belongs more properly in this second category of counties than the first, since Cumberland was unpopular from the moment the king travelled south and the royalist administration's declared purpose of defending the shire was quickly shown to be specious. The parliamentarians' first reaction to the levy of contributions on the shire for the king's forces was a public protestation. Meeting at Otley at the end of August, 18 of them, led by Lord Fairfax, declared that their intention was 'to keep the peace of the county entire'. But during September the struggle for control of Yorkshire intensified. A regiment of Northumbrian horse passed through to the king unhampered, pillaging Sir Edward Rhodes's home near Barnsley on the way. West Riding parliamentarians under Fairfax took control of Rotherham, Sheffield and Bradford, while young Hotham brought companies of horse and foot from Hull to Doncaster. The royalists in turn settled garrisons at Knaresborough and Pontefract.[78]

The demilitarization treaty signed at Rothwell in the West Riding on 29 September followed a sharp engagement between some royalist horse and Fairfax's men at Lofthouse on the 26th. It was sensible enough on paper. The commission and ordinance would be suspended; hostile forces entering Yorkshire would be repelled as 'enemies against the peace'; goods for the king or queen's household would be given a safe convoy; there would

---

76 *CSPD 1641–3*, pp. 395, 397, 400, 416; *HMC Buccleuch* I, 306; *CJ* II, 613, 630; J.W. Willis-Bund, *The Civil War in Worcestershire* (Birmingham, 1905), p. 35.

77 *Townshend*, pp. 70–74, 77–8.

78 Bodleian Dep C MS 153, no. 82; Tanner MS 63, fols. 139–40; *CJ* II, 789. *LJ* v, 302, 373–4; BL E 114(12): *Intelligence from York*; E 202(42): *A Perfect Diurnal*, 26 Sept.–3 Oct.; Vicars, *Jehovah-Jireh*, pp. 154–5, 162; *Slingsby*, pp. 77–8; *Fairfax* II, 413–4; A.H. Woolrych, 'Yorkshire's Treaty of Neutrality', *History Today* VI (1956). 696–704.

be no pursuit of delinquents but the pillagers of Rhodes's property would be forced to make restitution; militiamen's arms would be restored to their rightful owners and Hotham would leave the ordnance he had commandeered at Doncaster and return to Hull. The spirit of the meeting was well summarized by the decision to impose a general amnesty among the gentry of the shire 'of all former unkindnesses and differences which have been bred by these distractions and we will hereafter be as one man to defend one another according to the law against all others'.[79]

Yet the West Riding treaty was essentially irrelevant to the military struggle that had developed in Yorkshire because the men who mattered most were left out. Those involved were powerful and respected locally. For parliament, Fairfax had at his side Sir Thomas Mauleverer, the MP for Boroughbridge and that energetic magistrate and correspondent Thomas Stockdale. Two MPs, Henry Bellasis and Sir William Saville, led the royalist delegation, which also included Sir Edward Osborne and Sir John Ramsden.[80] But Yorkshire's gentry community was vast and only one of those present lived outside the West Riding. Neither of the Hothams were there, nor was Cumberland or his right hand man Sir Thomas Glemham. None of these men apparently knew about the treaty or gave their assent. Indeed, Sir John Hotham, perhaps resentful at Fairfax's command of the Yorkshire parliamentarians, bitterly attacked it. Within a few days of it John Hotham moved up to Cawood on the Ouse, only seven miles from York. From there he issued a declaration explaining why he rejected the treaty. The royalists subsequently failed to take Bradford and were forced to abandon Knaresborough and Leeds, which they had briefly occupied. The struggle continued during October and November and the Rothwell truce was quickly forgotten.[81]

The Cornish truce agreed on 18 August between the commissioners and deputy-lieutenants was established because both sides saw the advantages of playing a waiting game. On the royalist side the keenest activists, Sir Bevil Grenville and Sir Nicholas Slanning, had just lost face through the poor turnout the day before on Bodmin Down. They gave way to the moderate councils of the earl of Bath. The deputies welcomed their propositions, reporting to parliament that the reputation of the militia ordinance was bound to be advanced by the previous day's events.[82] The agreement was that nothing would be done to execute either parliament's or the king's military directions unless a new command from one of them

79 BL E 119(29): *Fourteen Articles propounded by the County of York*.
80 Cliffe, pp. 97, 239, 250, 312, 319–20, 323, 359.
81 *Slingsby*, pp. 78–87; *HMC 5th Report*, p. 191; BL E 202(45): *A Perfect Diurnal*, 10–17 Oct.; E 280(30): *Reasons why Sir John Hotham cannot agree to the Treaty of Pacification; HMC Portland* I, 66–7; Manning, pp. 210–12.
82 *LJ* v, 314–5; BL E 114(6): *The True Proceedings of the counties of York, Coventry, Portsmouth and Cornwall*.

was received, in which case both parties agreed to give 14 days warning 'before they proceed any farther'. For a month it more or less worked, or at least both sides kept their preparations quiet, but the arrival of Sir Ralph Hopton in the county with a considerable force on 25 September spelt the end of the truce.[83]

Lacking strength to control the county, the Lancashire MPs sent down there in June tried to buy time by negotiation. Immediately after the royalist muster on Preston Moor, Alexander Rigby tackled the sheriff, Sir John Girlington, on the subject of the gunpowder and match in the town's armoury, showing him the parliamentary order of 10 May about disposal of magazines. Girlington told him he would defend the ammunition he had seized 'with the power of the county'.[84] However negotiation did bring a temporary respite to the tension in the Manchester area: after exhaustive discussions between Lord Strange, established with considerable forces at Bury, and some of the deputies on 23 and 24 June, the royalists abandoned their bid to take the Manchester magazine, even though the deputies would not accept their proposition that it should be returned to a property in the town belonging to Strange under mutual security.[85] The reluctance of some of the Lancashire MPs to execute the militia ordinance at this stage, which so irritated Sir William Brereton, seems to have been based on a sound appreciation of parliamentarian weakness outside the Manchester district and a forlorn hope that Strange could yet be won over. John Moore, one of those who talked to him at Bury, told MPs that he had agreed not to execute the array and declared he was 'loath to do anything to offend the parliament'. Ralph Assheton, still in Lancashire on 9 July, spoke of the possibility of Strange's being 'regained to our part' and made lord lieutenant.[86]

But religious distrust was poisoning social relationships in Lancashire. The acid test of a man's politics had become the company he kept: Alexander Rigby was horrified when in the midst of dinner with Sir Gilbert Houghton members of the Dalton and Tyldesley families 'came in as familiarly as if they had been hail fellow, well met'.[87] By 14 July, when Strange was back at Bury to execute the array, the Manchester townsmen were so terrified about their own vulnerability that they 'laboured an accommodation with his lordship', whereby they would entertain him and his chief dependents, such as Houghton and Girlington, to a banquet and

83 Edgar, *Sir Ralph Hopton*, pp. 46–60; Chadwyck Healey, editor, *Bellum Civile*, pp. 18–20. Coate, *Civil War in Cornwall*, p. 35 is incorrect in stating that the truce was only intended to last fifteen days.

84 HLRO, Main Papers, 24 June 1642: Alexander Rigby to Speaker Lenthall.

85 Ormerod, pp. 16–17; E. Broxap, *The Great Civil War in Lancashire* (Manchester, 1973), pp. 13–15.

86 *LJ* v, 174; BL Add. MS 14827, fol. 147v; Harl. MS 163, fol. 264v.

87 Ormerod, p. 21.

he would bring no forces into the town. But Strange did not keep his word and the fracas the next day ended the chance of peace in Lancashire.[88] A meeting arranged for 18 October at Bolton between six leaders of each side, which might possibly have heralded a new attempt at pacification, never took place because the parliamentarians retracted in response to a veto from Westminster.[89]

The English towns at this period included great provincial capitals like Exeter, Norwich and York, centres of county administration like Chester, Nottingham and Worcester and the scores of market towns that were dotted higgledy-piggledy across the countryside.[90] Most of the largest towns still had their ancient walls though they were not always in good repair. Such towns were bound to be a focus of the incipient military conflict since magazines were usually kept there. In any case it quickly became clear that the civil war was going to be fought from garrisons and, though castles and manor houses would obviously play their part, this meant that holding towns might be the key to control of large tracts of land.

If in some sense townsmen lived apart from the village populace they were nevertheless as deferential to the great men of the neighbourhood as any yeoman or husbandman. When Chipping Sodbury provided a gallon of sack to welcome Natheniel Stephens 'into the country at his coming down' in the summer of 1642 or Devizes was similarly liberal in greeting Sir Edward Hungerford these townsmen were doing more than performing a ritual courtesy.[91] Their bounty was an acknowledgement of dependence and trust. In the same way the king was loaded with traditional gifts by loyal mayors and aldermen as he toured the midlands.[92]

Corporations expected to treat the high and mighty but they also assumed they would fairly quickly go on their way. What was new as the war began to take its grip on the country was the fear of being occupied, exploited, drained of resources by one or other set of combatants. Those in authority began to face the problem of squaring their sense of duty with their steadfast attachment to the principle of local inviolability. The Bristol aldermen, for instance, felt it was only proper to offer accommodation to the Marquis of Hertford when the king sent him into the west in July, 'as other noblemen in the like kind have been and that his lordship be not driven to take up his lodging in an inn', but they were heartily relieved when the arrangements they proposed were declined. They

88 HLRO, Main Papers, 5 Aug. 1642: Deposition of Thomas Birch; Ormerod, pp. 30–5; Broxap, *Civil War in Lancashire*, pp. 15–19; Dore, *Civil War in the Manchester Area*, p. 10.
89 Morrill, *Cheshire*, p. 61; Blackwood, *Lancashire Gentry*, p. 49; Broxap, *Civil War in Lancashire*, pp. 55–6.
90 P. Clark and P. Slack, *English Towns in Transition 1500–1700* (Oxford, 1976); P. Clark and P. Slack, *Crisis and Order in English Towns* (London, 1972).
91 Gloucestershire RO D 2071/43, fol. 35v; B. Cunnington, *Annals of Devizes* I, 107.
92 E.g. W.T. Baker, editor, *Records of the Borough of Nottingham* (1900) v, 205.

refused to receive the cavalry Hertford wished to send into the city.[93] The corporation of Exeter told the captain on the gate on 9 August that if the earl of Bath came 'in an ordinary way unarmed' he should be received with all due respect, but if he was attended by more than 100 armed men the mayor and his brethren would consult before he was allowed to enter. When the king appeared before Coventry later in the month the town invited him to come inside the walls 'with a convenient attendance', on the condition that the cavaliers stayed behind with 'the mouth of the cannon turned upon them, that town being sensible of the rapine and pillage the cavaliers would commit there, if once they were in their mercy'.[94]

The nature of the royalist war effort often made the king's men appear as aggressors whereas parliament, so far from imposing a threat to urban autonomy, nurtured townsmen's localist aspirations by encouraging them to make defensive arrangements. It was also willing to indemnify companies of volunteers who wished to arm themselves and undergo training within the town's precincts. Permission to spend Proposition money collected locally for these purposes was readily given. Volunteer companies were formed in at least 34 towns during the summer and early autumn.[95] The first experience a number of towns had of the royalists, by contrast, was the arrival of a company of men, commanded by strangers, demanding food and lodging. No town welcomed the notion of such burdens. The inhabitants of Hull had been so hostile in January to Hotham's men, refusing at first to billet them, that he feared they would starve in the streets.[96]

The exclusion of intruders was always a popular rallying cry. This is how the royalists must have appeared at Bristol, Coventry, and Exeter. Denzil Holles was sent down to execute the militia ordinance at Bristol on 17 August in response to the citizens' reported fears about Hertford's 'wrongs and injuries' at Wells and of a Welsh army coming against them.[97] A long-standing feud in the Chester assembly was beginning to harden into a royalist-parliamentarian division when Lord Strange appeared before the gates in July intent on seizing the county magazine. In face of this threat the townsmen's localist spirit asserted itself: the city quickly armed itself and withstood his men from its high red walls.[98] Judge Foster found

93 Bristol RO Common Council Proceedings III, fol. 122r; Latimer, *Annals of Bristol*, p. 157.
94 East Devon RO Exeter Chamber Act Book, p. 276; *CSPD 1641–3*, pp. 375–6.
95 *LJ* v, 147, 156, 193, 228–9, 233, 281, 300, 309–10, 312, 318, 323, 374; *LJ* II, 601, 629, 648, 677, 683, 716, 719, 723–4, 727–8, 733, 735, 737, 765, 770, 793; Bodleian Tanner MS 63, fol. 43; BL E 114(15): *News from the City of Norwich*; E 116(5):*Resolution of the Salisbury Volunteers*; HMC Portland I, 49–50; Holmes, p. 56; see map 8, p. 354.
96 Bodleian Tanner MS 66, fol. 256r; BL Harl. MS 480, fol. 42r.
97 BL Harl. MS 164, fol. 262v; *CJ* II, 727.
98 E 202(12): *Some Special Passages*, 3–10 July; A.M. Johnson, 'Politics in Chester during the Civil Wars and Interregnum', in Clark and Slack, editors, *Crisis and Order in English Towns*, pp. 204–8.

Dorchester, when he reached there on his assize circuit, defended against marauders alleged to have intentions of burning the town. Hertford's royalist force was by then based nearby at Sherborne.[99] Other towns which resisted royalist forces that appeared out of the blue included Banbury, Brackley, Cardiff, King's Lynn, Poole and Windsor. At Brackley on 28 August the town and its surrounding villages reacted so quickly to the presence of Sir John Biron's troop, which was merely taking a well earned rest after marching without a break from Leicester, that the soldiers had 'to fly every man for his safety'.[100]

Hereford's reaction to forces that appeared before the city in September illustrates the confusions and unpredictability of mayoral behaviour. Two thousand Welshmen on the way to the king were reluctantly admitted, when they surprised the city, but were expelled the next day because they 'used themselves so inhumanly towards the townsmen and attempted to disarm them'.[101] A few days later, 900 parliamentarian foot and three troops of horse found the gates shut because the Marquis of Hertford had sent the mayor warning that they would prove plunderers and murderers. A parliamentarian alderman, however, spread a rumour that Essex was at hand with the whole army. After two hours standing outside the walls a gate was opened: 'the poor mayor, seeing he was so handsomely cozened was not a little angry'.[102]

Worcester provides a particularly informative case study in the politics of urban neutrality. The corporation was clearly divided in its sympathies. There was a Puritan element which sought to maintain godly standards: a company of players had been paid not to perform in the city in 1640. Two Arminian deans had been in trouble with Puritan aldermen over issues of status and ritual. But the royalist petition at the summer assizes on 3 August, professing readiness to attend the king 'in all lawful ways', attracted the support of the city's 13 grand jurors, the mayor and two alderman. Localism, in these circumstances, provided useful common ground. The corporation insisted it would have nothing to do with the commission of array, forcing the royalists to meet at the Talbot in the suburb of Sidbury which lay outside its jurisdiction. They resolved on 2 August to buy a private stock of arms 'for the general use and defence of the city and not to be employed but by consent of the chamber'. Three weeks later they undertook a review of the citizens' arms and set about buying

99 *CSPD 1641–3*, pp 375–6.
100 BL E 113(18): *Special Passages*, 13–18 Aug.; E 202(28): *A Perfect Diurnal*, 25 July–1 Aug., p. 3; E 202(33): *A True and Exact Diurnal*, 8–15 Aug., p. 2; E 202(35): *A Continuation of the True Diurnal*, 8–15 Aug., p. 4; *HMC Portland* I, 59; Phillips, *Civil War in Wales* II, 24.
101 BL E 202(45): A Perfect Diurnal, 26 Sept.–3 Oct., sub 26 Sept; Phillips, *Civil War in Wales* II, 24–5.
102 *CSPD 1641–3*, pp. 398–9.

powder, shot, match and ordnance.[103]

A series of propositions from the commissioners of array on 30 August, to induce the city of Worcester to work with the county, were rejected by the mayor after the chamber had received a forceful petition from the 'trained soldiers and commons of the city'. It expressed their fears of suffering cavalier atrocities, which were prompted by letters and printed papers circulating in the city, and their horror of other intruders:

> There are resorted to this city divers strangers, gentlemen and others whereof some of them are voted by the parliament to be delinquents and some other papists or popishly affected, whereby it is generally suspected and feared they have some design upon this city, or at leastwise may occasion the bringing an army upon this city to the ruin thereof and that we have been credibly informed that there is an intent to billet soldiers here which (we conceive) may be very dangerous to this city, in case they should overmaster the inhabitants.

We are back in other words, and we should not forget its pervasiveness even now, in the world of Pym's papist conspiracy. The petitioners requested that papists should be disarmed and expelled; that troopers 'which daily appear here to the terror of the citizens, the hindrance of our trade and market and tend to the dividing of the king and parliament' should be kept out; that no soldiers should be billeted under the pretence of the safety of the city; that some able men should be trained so that they could defend the whole community from sudden assault; and that there should be strict watch and ward at every gate and the quay head. The mayor accepted this charter of isolationism and Lord Lovelace, the chief delinquent who had taken refuge in Worcester, was at once asked to depart.[104]

There was undoubtedly sympathy for both sides among the Worcester populace as well as in the chamber. The parish of St Michael in Bedwardine was attached to its prayer-book services and traditional rituals. The church there was still normally decorated with rosemary and bays at Christmas and boughs at Rogationtide and the custom of bellringing on the king's accession day was strictly observed. It was in this part of the city that Richard Baxter was jeered, when he passed through about this time, with cries of 'Down with the roundheads'. Yet there was a good deal of positive support for parliament as well, which John Wilde, the recorder, was able to exploit and maintain.[105] On 13 September a petition from a group of the city's inhabitants to arm and train themselves as volunteers

103　P. Styles, 'The City of Worcester during the Civil Wars 1640–60', in *Studies in Seventeenth Century West Midlands History* (Kineton, 1978), 215–6, 221; Baker, editor, *The Church in Town and Countryside*, pp. 297–300; Bond, editor, *The Chamber Order Book of Worcester 1602–50*, pp. 354–5.

104　*Townshend*, pp. 87–9; Hutton, p. 13.

105　Styles, *Studies in West Midland History*, pp. 217, 221–2.

and put themselves in a posture of defence was granted by parliament.[106] But three days later Sir John Biron's dragoons entered the gates, only to be replaced as an occupying force a week after by Essex's army.[107] Neutralism could not be maintained under such intrusions, although for a good many weeks the city had managed to stand aloof from the polarization of the county. IMP ↓

By and large the urban response to the war was introverted and self-interested. Security was the main priority; faction so far as possible was contained. This was wholly consonant with the precautionary moves which, as we have seen, many towns had made in the aftermath of the five-members débâcle. Bristol's common council appointed a committee of aldermen to oversee the repair and strengthening of gates and walls and appointed gunners for its ordnance. Exeter's chamber prepared the city against a siege by buying in corn and ammunition, placing chains on the gates, mounting and checking the ordnance and removing all trees within 16 feet of the walls.[108] The Gloucester corporation paid particular attention to preventing a cavalry attack, putting chains on all the gates and placing 'turned pikes well bound and fitting' at lane ends and 'places most open for horse to enter'. In Northampton a special fund of £100 was raised for improving the town's defences. '500 men and 100 women have wrought all yesterday and this night carrying of earth to strengthen our walls', came a report on 20 August. At Salisbury an attempt was made to compensate for the vulnerability of a low-lying site by the construction of trenches under the walls. Some towns obtained professional advice about their fortifications; all those mentioned here established strong measures of watch and ward. From 29 July the Norwich city gates were locked at night and the keys left with the mayor; Gloucester adopted the same practice on 5 August, Dorchester on 7 October.[109]

The smaller market towns were hopelessly vulnerable to attack, as incidents such as Prince Rupert's pillage of Marlborough early in the war showed clearly.[110] Something was done in many such places to prepare for the worst. At Devizes in Wiltshire, for example, corslets, pikes, ordnance and gunpowder were purchased: on 25 October arms were issued to householders so they could be ready to resist an attack.[111] Yet many small towns

106 *CJ* II, 768.
107 Willis-Bund, *Worcestershire in the Civil War*, p. 49; Gardiner, *Great Civil War* I, 29–31.
108 Bristol RO Common Council Proceedings III, fol. 123r; East Devon RO Chamber Act Book 1634–47, fols. 277–85.
109 Gloucester RO GBR/B3/2 (Borough Minute Book 1632–56), pp. 220–8; Northamptonshire RO, Northampton Borough Book 1628–1744, p. 71; BL E 114(36): *Special Passages*, 23–30 Aug.; Norfolk RO, Norwich Court Book 1634–46, fols. 355v, 365v; C.H. Mayo, editor, *The Municipal Records of the Borough of Dorchester* (Exeter, 1908), p. 681; Salisbury District Council Muniment Room, ledger book D, fols. 8, 11r.
110 BL E 83(11): *Truth in Two Letters*; E 245(8): *Marlborough's Miseries*.
111 Cunnington, *Annals of Devizes* I, 103–6.

had no real choice but to bow to the predominant power of the neighbour-hood, even if this was one side this week and the other the next. Several of the Cornish boroughs entertained commissioners and deputies in turn as the gentry struggled for control of the militia there.[112] Most of the smaller towns that attempted a neutralist stance had little hope of maintaining it for long. Simon Patrick, a boy of 16 in 1642 living in Gainsborough, later described how the town 'thought it would be most for their security if they cast up some works round the town and got firearms . . . but they declared neither for king nor parliament, only intending to stand upon their guard against rovers.' The town soon had no choice but to surrender to the nearby royalist garrison at Newark.[113]

If townsmen basically wanted to be left alone it is easy to see why nominal parliamentarianism may have had more appeal then nominal royalism. Cavalier intruders, the examples quoted suggest, were more widely experienced and feared than roundhead ones. The initial strategic circumstances of the war thus favoured urban support for parliament; its policies also chimed more happily than those of the king with urban localism. Yet, for all this, there is reason to think that there was also a good deal of positive urban parliamentarianism, particularly in the ports and the growing industrial towns. Some of the East Anglian ports were decisive in their allegiance. Great Yarmouth's assembly faced the problem of dual commands quite squarely on 9 July. After three of the king's proclamations had been read, together with parliament's declaration of 6 July against publishing royal proclamations, the aldermen decided to accept parlia-ment's directions 'conceiving that to be the most fit way to preserve the public-peace both for king and kingdom'.[114] There was unanimous consent at the King's Lynn assembly on 19 September for immediate enforcement of parliament's order for the fortification of the town: an engineer working at Boston was summoned to help and plans were put in hand to make draw-bridges for the town gates.[115] On the south coast, Rye was the paradigm of a godly parliamentarian city set on a hill, while the mayor of Poole did not merely refuse to admit the earl of Hertford's drummer, but sent him with a message that he hoped to have the earl by force before parliament 'to be made an example' for his illegal execution of the commission of array.[116] In Devon ports like Dartmouth and Barnstaple vigorous defence measures, based on generous loans from leading townsmen, suggest something more positive than the cautious mood of self-preservation that was characteristic

112   Coate, *Cornwall in the Civil War*, p. 33.
113   S. Patrick, *Autobiography* (Oxford, 1839), pp. 7–11.
114   Great Yarmouth Town Hall, Assembly Book C19/6, fols. 509v–512v; BL E 202(44): *Remarkable Passages or a Perfect Diurnal*, 5–12 Sept.
115   King's Lynn Borough Records, Hall Book 8 (1637–58), fols. 97v, 103r.
116   BL E 113(18): *Special Passages*, 16–23 Aug; *CJ* II, 687.

of most market towns.[117] Inland, Birmingham quickly became a noted bulwark of the parliamentarian cause: Coventry's defiance of the king in July 1642 owed much to the stirring impact of Birmingham men in the city. The textile towns of Bradford, Halifax and Leeds likewise became the heartland of Yorkshire parliamentarianism[118].

A well established tradition of puritan piety was the surest foundation for allegiance to parliament. At Gloucester Baxter found a 'civil, courteous, and religious people, as different from Worcester as if they had lived under another government'.[119] Gloucester's Puritans may not have been quite as radical as a recent account suggests, but they were certainly committed.[120] Here, as elsewhere in the old cathedral cities, the godly aldermen were riding high after the defeat of Arminianism. Civil pride, identified with the Long Parliament's reform programme, was in the ascendant; the close was brought low. At Norwich a Puritan faction which had gained a majority in the Common Council, but did not yet control the Court of Aldermen, was asserting its hold on the city's affairs.[121] At Chichester a Puritan clique led by one of the city's MPs, William Cawley, together with the militia captain Henry Chitty, kept control of the magazine through the late summer, while royalists exercised menacingly in the close.[122] But the necessary leadership did not always come from inside the walls. So long as the ground was right, vigorous intervention by men of power living nearby could be instrumental in swinging a town parliament's way. Thus at Nottingham John Hutchinson, Henry Ireton and Francis Pierrepoint worked on the townsmen's fears of surprisal and organized a volunteer company to protect the magazine.[123] The establishment of a band of volunteers at Salisbury followed the arrival home at Wilton of the earl of Pembroke, whose armoury was provided for their use. The soldiers issued a resolution praising the earl in extravagant terms and promising their loyalty 'in defence of that cause your honour now stands to maintain'.[124]

When the king marched to Edgehill there were only three major towns — Chester, Newcastle and Shrewsbury — that he could call his own. The aldermen of York, dismayed by the experience of cavalier occupation, had fallen out with the earl of Cumberland during September and he had left the city. Informed by Hotham that no ill was intended against

---

117 East Devon RO Dartmouth MSS, DO 62701–8; R.W. Cotton, *Barnstaple during the Civil War* (1889), pp. 52–4, 78–84; Andriette, p. 64.

118 Manning, pp. 199–215; Hughes, pp. 255–7.

119 N.H. Keeble, editor, *Autobiography of Richard Baxter* (London, 1974), p. 39.

120 P. Clark, ' "The Ramoth-Gilead of the Good": Gloucester 1540–1640' in Clark, Smith, and Tyacke, editors, *The English Commonwealth*, pp. 167–89.

121 J.T. Evans. *Seventeenth-Century Norwich* (Oxford, 1979) pp. 105–24.

122 *Sussex*, pp. 258–9.

123 *CJ* II, 648; *LJ* v, 173; *CSPD 1641–3*, p. 368; Hutchinson, pp. 54–6, 70; Wood, *Nottinghamshire in the Civil War*, pp. 15–18.

124 BL E 116(5).

them from Hull, they adopted a guarded neutrality, locking even their postern gates at night and setting 80 citizens to patrol the walls.[125] Moreover the towns Charles did hold displayed little spontaneous royalism. Chester was manoeuvred onto the royalist side by Francis and William Gamull, two leading aldermen, but the magnificence of the official welcome given to the king in September reflected the fact that he came as a visitor not with an occupying force.[126] At Shrewsbury a dozen or so aldermen, supported by about 40 substantial citizens, had exercised as volunteers for parliament during July in defiance of a contrary faction led by the mayor. Shrewsbury had only buckled to the royalist cause under the impact of intervention by the county gentry.[127] The earl of Newcastle took control of Tyneside for the king in June and garrisoned Newcastle itself. His argument was force: the town had no choice but to do his bidding.[128] The corporation cooperated with him in August to the extent of lending money and arming its captains in 'His Majesty's service and the defence of the town'.[129]

This discussion of how towns and gentry communities reacted to the civil war emphasizes some of the difficulties in the way of discovering men's real allegiance in 1642. It is hard to believe, in view of everything that has been said in this book about the interaction of Westminster and the localities since November 1640, that many well informed men were pure neutrals at heart. The leading men in the shires, and to some extent the same goes for mayors and aldermen, had been too much involved in the political debate to avoid adopting their own standpoints. Few surely saw a precisely equal amount of right on both sides. Passion and argument had been aroused by petitioning and by numerous informal discussions. Yet at the same time everyone who was politically aware faced the dilemma that by being true to their deepest feelings they might increase polarization and destroy local peace. Thus commitment and activism were not the same things: on the one hand activism did not necessarily follow from commitment; on the other hand there was, as we have seen, a form of localist activism which did not imply confident or wholehearted commitment to one side or the other. Arguments from men's actions are thus full of pitfalls; intentions need to be interpreted with the utmost care. The terminology of allegiance is still confused, though recent work has made it clear that it is essential to distinguish between moderates and those who became more fiercely committed and between various kinds of

125 BL E 202(44): *Remarkable Passages or a Perfect Diurnal*, 5–12 Sept.; YPL House Books 36, fols. 740–77r.
126 Johnson in Clark and Slack, editors, *Crisis and Order in English Towns*, pp. 208–9.
127 HLRO, Main Papers, 16 July 1642: Petition of Shrewsbury; Phillips, *Civil War in Wales* I, 109.
128 Howell, *Newcastle-upon-Tyne and the Puritan Revolution*, pp. 144–6.
129 M.H. Dodds, editor, *Extracts from Newcastle-upon-Tyne Council Minute Book 1639–1656* (Newcastle Record Series I, 1920), pp. 15–16.

collaboration once the war was under way with the dominant party in a man's neighbourhood.[130]

Throughout the kingdom, asserted Hyde later, 'the number of these who desired to sit still was greater than of those who desired to engage in either party'.[131] His assessment was obviously correct with regard to the populace as a whole, or even with regard to the mass of lesser gentry who may have signed petitions but had played no part in formulating them. Even in so sharply divided a county as Warwickshire, we have seen that a substantial proportion of the gentry avoided showing any commitment to either the militia ordinance or the commission of array. No wonder the commanders of the parliamentarian army found things hard going in the west midlands. In a letter to the committee of safety on 12 October they bemoaned the narrow basis of their support: 'the parliament will be too wise to let them suffer who have freely offered themselves to support the commonwealth and to let such pass without any charge who seek to shroud themselves under a neutrality.'[132]

There was much to be said at the start of the war for playing a waiting game. By backing the wrong horse a landed family might irreparably weaken its power and status. The world now accounted it policy 'for the father to be on one side and the son on the other', wrote Cary Gardiner from Oxfordshire to Lady Verney on 5 September. Another of Lady Verney's correspondents speculated about how their divided family might fare when the war was over: 'I cannot see, if we have the better, how you will suffer, for sure your father will have power to save your husband, and if the king fail I believe my uncle will hardly come off with his life or any that are with them.'[133] There was a rumour in August that Sir William Russell had sent his son first to subscribe ten horses at York, then to subscribe ten more in London.[134]

Measures for personal self-defence could be an aspect of firm commitment or they could reflect indecision and neutrality. 'Most men in the country were affrighted with the news of the parliament's raising an army', recorded Bulstrode Whitelocke, 'and they begun in many places to arm and to provide for their own defence.' Many who went along with Pym at Westminster undoubtedly found it hard to accept that their own locality would become embroiled. But one after another MPs requested special permission to send down arms to their country estates: Charles Dymock to Lincolnshire, for instance, Sir Dudley North to Cambridgeshire, John

130 G.E. Aylmer, *The King's Servants*, pp. 379–421; J.S. Morrill and R. N. Dore, 'The Allegiance of the Cheshire Gentry in the Great Civil War', *Lancashire and Cheshire Antiquarian Society Transactions* LXXVII (1967), 44–76. See also references cited on page 369, note 3.
131 Clarendon II, 469.
132 Bodleian Dep C MS 159, no. 133b; Hughes, pp. 280–2.
133 *HMC 7th Report*, p. 440.
134 Bodleian Tanner MS 63, fol. 125r.

Hutchinson to Nottinghamshire, Sir John Curzon to Derbyshire. Whitelocke himself checked his defensive arrangements at Fawley Court.[135] At Gorhambury in Hertfordshire Lady Sussex had hidden away most of her plate by the end of June, though she was 'loath to eat in pewter yet'. Sir Edmund Verney badgered his steward at Claydon to have the carbines, powder and bullets in readiness.[136] Down in Gloucestershire and Herefordshire men like Benedict Hall, a Catholic dependent of the earl of Worcester, and Viscount Scudamore of Holme Lacy were raising earthworks round their homes and seeing to the repair of muskets, saddles and coats of mail[137].

Sooner or later many of those who sat tight were called upon to contribute arms, money or provisions to one side or the other. Whether they were more or less sympathetic to the party that put pressure on them was largely a matter of chance. But at this point sober calculation must often have defeated attachment on principle. Some felt this dilemma early. 'We be threatened because we give nothing to the parliament', Lady Sussex informed Sir Ralph Verney on 9 September.[138] Where disorder and lawlessness were rife some families abandoned their homes even during the first campaign. 'Many fly from the country into the city and take houses and carry their best goods hither', reported a Chester correspondent on 1 October, noting the plundering of Lord Grandison's troop in the shire.[139] The Petre family moved westwards along the coast of north Wales that month in order to live more securely. Thomas Hobson reported to a friend in London from the west country on 17 October that only a few gentry families were still at home in his district, since the 'rude and ungoverned multitude' threatened 'ruin and destruction to all whenever they can prevail'.[140]

Individual case studies suggest that among the most prominent county families neutralism often concealed a degree of sympathy one way or the other which was exhibited once the inexorable logic of war became apparent. After some pondering Bulstrode Whitelocke resolved his doubts about the militia ordinance and accepted deputy lieutenantships in both Buckinghamshire and Oxfordshire. Yet when Lord Wharton offered him the captaincy of a troop of Buckinghamshire volunteers in June he refused:

> I had not so much mind to the business as thus to engage at this time. I excused myself by my profession but that would not be admitted till I told some of my private friends that I looked upon it as a neglect and affront to me that my

---

135 BL Add. MS 37343, fols. 252v, 253r; *CJ* II, 625, 658, 660, 705.
136 *Verney* II, 94.
137 Webb, *Herefordshire in the Civil War*, pp. 106–7, 227–8.
138 *HMC 7th Report*, p. 440.
139 Phillips, *Civil War in Wales* II, 17.
140 *Calendar of Wynn Papers*, p. 278; PRO SP 16/492/38.

countryman Mr Goodwin and others should have the command of regiments and I thought worthy of no more but one single troop.

Whitelocke later recorded how by this tactic he kept himself uninvolved for 'a good time after'. Indeed he probably saw his preventive measures against the commissioners of array in August and against Sir John Biron at Oxford in September in the context of his obligation to defend the counties where he held office from disorder. This mild and moderate man, who had warned colleagues in July that they were plunging themselves into an 'ocean of troubles and miseries', was never likely to desert parliament altogether but he displayed all the sensitivity of one who attaches himself to a cause with the utmost reluctance and never blinds himself to its deficiencies.[141]

Another man whose neutralism was only skin deep, though in his case it was not until March 1643 that he showed his hand, was the Norfolk gentleman Thomas Knyvett. His letter to his wife on 18 May contains the classic vignette of a moderate's dilemma:

> Oh sweet heart I am now in a great straight what to do. Walking this other morning at Westminster, Sir John Potts, with commissary Muttford, saluted me with a commission from my lord of Warwick to take upon me (by virtue of an ordinance of parliament) my company and command again. I was surprised what to do, whether to take or refuse. 'Twas no place to dispute, so I took it and desired some time to advise upon it. I had not received this many hours, but I met with a declaration point-blank against it by the king. This distraction made me to advise with some understanding men what condition I stand in, which is no other than a great many men of quality do. . . . I hold it good wisdom and security to keep my company as close to me as I can in these dangerous times and to stay out of the way of my new masters till these first musterings be over.

Knyvett's royalism was not so compelling that he felt bound to join the king's army but his sympathy for Charles in the first months of the war is not in doubt. 'Poor king he grows still in more contempt and slight here every day', he wrote in May. He moved with circumspection while the situation in Norfolk clarified itself but then emerged as one of the ring-leaders of the royalist rising at Lowestoft.[142]

For MPs who in their heart of hearts felt attachment to the king rather than parliament neutralism could be a useful stopping point, while they disentangled themselves from the clutches of their colleagues. Sir Nicholas Slanning told the committee for the Propositions on 11 June that 'when the king and both houses of parliament shall command it he shall be ready to serve them with his life and fortune, till then he desires not to intermeddle'. Sir Richard Shuckburgh was another who refused to

141 BL Add. MS 37343, fol. 252v; R. Spalding, *The Improbable Puritan* (London, 1975), 82–5.
142 *Knyvett*, pp. 100–109; Ketton-Cremer, pp. 137–40, 179–81; Morrill, *Revolt*, pp. 136–7.

contribute, declaring that he had 'horses in readiness to defend the king, the commonwealth, the laws and parliament'.[143] Slanning subsequently raised a voluntary regiment for the king in Devon; Shuckburgh was given leave to go to his estates on 10 August and interrogated when he fell under suspicion in September. He finally threw in his lot with Charles when he met the royal army out with his hounds on 22 October.[144] The diarist Sir Thomas Peyton was an instinctive royalist with, it has been suggested, 'no real comprehension of the issues then dividing the politically conscious men of England'.[145] Yet he shrewdly kept his own council during the summer of 1642 and was still sufficiently trusted by Westminster colleagues in August to be made a deputy-lieutenant. His real feelings only came out when he was called upon to help execute the Propositions and take part in proceedings against Kentish delinquents the following month. He looked for the peace of Church and state, he told Captain Lee on 17 September, rejecting a paper he was required to sign as 'too large and indefinite a proposition for me to adhere unto'.[146]

Some men became tentative activists only because they saw a chance to preserve peace in their own locality, but changed course as the result of a chance incident or sober ponderings. Walter Wrottesley, for instance, was one of those involved in the Staffordshire neutrality efforts until he was swayed by an interview with the king at Uttoxeter on 15 September. The following week he accepted the baronetcy he had refused the previous year and sent in his arms to Charles. Yet a friend recalled later that showing his hand in this way 'seemed much to trouble him in that he feared his arms should be made use of to fight against parliament for whose happy proceedings he so much prayed'.[147] John Nanson acted in the Worcestershire commission of array because he saw the musters in a purely local context. Then on 26 September he wrote to the county's MPs explaining how much he regretted his involvement with the royalists: 'when the object of the design appeared to me at a nearest distance to be a war against the kingdom itself I abhorred it as monstrous.'[148]

It was much easier for the middling and minor country squires than for the men in the top ranks of county society to preserve a studied neutrality. They were less likely to come under the pressure of JPs, deputy-lieutenants or commissioners of array. John Fetherston of Packwood in Warwickshire was one such man. 'All my family are yet, I thank God,

143 *HMC 5th Report*, p. 28.
144 CJ II, 717, 779; P. Young, *The Cavalier Army* (London, 1974), p. 30; Gardiner, *Great Civil War* I, 41.
145 W.H. Coates in *D'Ewes (C)*, pp. xxxviii-xli.
146 *CJ* II, 724; BL Add. MS 44846, fol. 12v; Everitt, p. 116.
147 Staffordshire RO D 948/4/6/2; Pickles, Studies in Royalism in the English Civil War, pp. 55–7, 74.
148 Bodleian Dep C MS 153, no. 79.

well', he wrote to his brother in June, 'but we were lately very much affrighted by reason of a troop of horsemen that came to some of my neighbours' houses and did disarm them.' Fetherston was perplexed by the fact that he was obliged to provide a cavalryman for the Warwickshire militia in conjunction with Walleston Betham, a papist neighbour of his. Betham was responsible for the horse and man while he supplied the armour, petronels and saddle. The contradictory commands of king and parliament, he told his brother, left him unable to satisfy himself 'in point of judgement and conscience what to do': 'my Protestation puts me in mind that I am bound in conscience to serve both and yet there seems now a very great difference between them, which I humbly desire almighty God, if it be his will, may be peaceably and timely composed and settled for the good of His Church and kingdom.' The one aspect of the matter that was clear to Fetherston was that he should not deliver his arms to Betham, since both sides declared papists must be disarmed. His appearance in person at Lord Brooke's musters was probably merely a minimum gesture of compliance with the dominant party in his district of Warwickshire.[149]

Jonathan Langley, like Fetherston, simply wanted to be allowed to live at home without being pestered by either side. He had fled from his home, wife and children when Shropshire was overawed by the royalists at the start of the war. Some months later he explained his plight from his exile at Birmingham to the sheriff of the county. Like Fetherston, he believed the Protestation bound him to both sides. He perceptively described the absurdity of the war: 'there are two armies each seeking to destroy the other and by oath bound to preserve both, each challenging the protestant religion for their standard, yet one takes the papists and the other the schismatics for their adherents and (for my part) my conscience tells me they both intend the Protestant religion, what reason have I therefore to fall out with either'.[150]

Who then were the committed activists, the men who dragged the reluctant majority into war? Many of them on the parliamentarian side were undoubtedly militant Puritans who looked for an evangelical reformation in Church and state.[151] Sir Thomas Barrington was in this mould in Essex, Sir William Brereton in Cheshire, John Hutchinson in Nottinghamshire, Herbert Morley in Sussex, John Pyne in Somerset and Sir Anthony Weldon in Kent.[152] Such men were sustained by the same basic beliefs as Pym: that there was a popish conspiracy which had come to

---

149 M.W. Farr, *The Fetherstons of Packwood in the Seventeenth Century* (Dugdale Society Occasional Papers XVIII, 1968), pp. 6–7.
150 *Shropshire Archaeological Society Transactions* VII (1895), 263–4; Morrill, *Revolt*, p. 164.
151 Morrill, *Revolt*, pp. 47–51.
152 For Barrington see Holmes, p. 38; for Brereton, Morrill, *Cheshire* pp. 23–5, 45–56; Hutchinson, pp. 38–53; for Morley, *Sussex*, pp. 66, 113, 123, 264–6; for Pyne, Underdown, pp. 122, 143, 162, 187; for Weldon, Everitt, pp. 110, 134–5.

fruition, that they must secure the Protestant foundations of the state, that the king could not be trusted.

On the royalist side also religion was an important ingredient of activism. Many were drawn to the king by his staunch defence of the Church. Catholic gentry, particularly in the north, gave the king very substantial support.[153] The common denominators among committed royalists were probably dislike of Pym's methods and policies, particularly with regard to the Church, and the old-fashioned but still powerful concept of honour. Honour was the notion that inspired men like Richard Lloyd, the king's energetic agent in Denbighshire, Sir Bevil Grenville in Cornwall, Sir Edward Fitton in Cheshire and Sir John Digby in Nottinghamshire.[154] 'My conscience is only concerned in honour and gratitude to follow my master', Sir Edmund Verney explained to Hyde.[155] In a widely used metaphor, the gentry were bound to the king as a son was bound to his father. Thus in May 1640 Sir Thomas Peyton wrote of Charles's speech to the Short Parliament that it was 'the speech of a gracious and mild king . . . who resolved not upon their disrespects a revenge upon his people presently, but as a true father of his subjects would rather chose to stroke them still, till he had overcome their natures and assimilated them to his own goodness.'[156] At the heart of such men's concept of political obligation was a notion of personal service. 'If there could be an expedient found to solve the punctilio of honour I would not continue here an hour', wrote Lord Spencer from the royal court on 21 September.[157] It is easy to see how respect for their anointed king drew some to Charles's side just as intoxication with Puritan ideology made the choice equally straightforward for others. It is less easy to see how men in the thick of affairs could avoid feeling some kind of commitment, however shallow, when the struggle between the king and parliament became the absorbing preoccupation of political society.

153 P.R. Newman, 'Catholic Royalists of Northern England 1642–1645', *Northern History* XV (1979), 88–95.

154 M. James, *English Politics and the Concept of Honour 1485–1642* (Past and Present Supplements III, 1978). For Lloyd see *Denbighshire Historical Transactions* III (1954), 47–52; for Grenville, Coate, *Cornwall in the Civil War*, pp. 24–5, 30–1, 34–9; for Fitton, Morrill, *Cheshire*, p. 65; for Digby, Wood, *Nottinghamshire in the Civil War*, pp. 23, 29–30.

155 Cited in J.G. Marston, 'Gentry Honour and Royalism in Early Stuart England', *JBS* XIII (1974), 21–43.

156 *Oxinden*, p. 172.

157 Gardiner, *Great Civil War* I, 25.

Conclusion

I cannot more properly compare our case than to a man in perfect health, yet do fancy himself sick of a consumption.

> The Recorder of Lincoln in a speech to Charles I,
> 15 July 1642[1]

I am persuaded that conscience hath much to do on both sides which, though it may be erroneous, yet ought to be respected.

> Thomas Gardiner to Sir Ralph Verney,
> 19 September 1642[2]

Great events do not necessarily have great causes, thought it is natural for historians to seek them. Until recently early seventeenth-century parliamentary history has suffered from the straitjacket of the whig tradition, with its overriding but anachronistic concepts of 'government' and 'opposition'.[3] Now it is plain there was no high road to civil war. There was not bound to be a struggle between king and parliament in order that the balanced constitution of the eighteenth century could be its outcome.[4] Nor, it has been established, can the war be explained in terms of social revolution: the ultimate split was quite clearly a split within the governing class.[5] A new interpretation based on the notions of 'court' and 'country' is also unsatisfactory.[6] Most of those involved in the story told here did not think of themselves as belonging exclusively to either entity. No one who knows the Puritan world of lectures, fasts and exercises and who has also raised their eyes to Rubens's apotheosis of Stuart monarchy on the ceiling of Inigo Jones's Banqueting House in Whitehall can possibly doubt that there was a clash of cultures in the 1630s. Yet it takes more than a clash of cultures for a king and his subjects to go to war.

What then is the meaning of these events? A detailed step-by-step

1 BL E 200 (50): *A Speech delivered by the Recorder of Lincoln*.
2 *HMC 7th Report*, p. 441.
3 Russell, *Parliaments*, p. 4.
4 G.R. Elton, 'The Stuart Century' and 'The Unexplained Revolution', in *Studies in Tudor and Stuart Politics and Government* (Cambridge, 1974) II, 155–63, 183–9.
5 J.H. Hexter, 'Storm over the Gentry' in *Reappraisals in History* (London, 1961), pp. 117–62.
6 Zagorin, *passim*; Morrill, *Revolt*, pp. 14–31; Ashton, *English Civil War*, pp. 131–40; D. Hirst, Court, Country and Politics before 1629', in Sharpe, editor, *Faction and Parliament*, pp. 105–37.

account of an occurrence as important as the outbreak of civil war certainly reveals the complexity of any such political process, the concatenation of circumstances necessary to produce something so completely at odds with all men's assumptions about social and political relationships. But there is no need for political narrative to drain the story of all deep-seated meaning. The English civil war was in no sense merely accidental. Chance and coincidence played their part: things might have been very different, for example, if the Irish rebellion had not happened at the precise time it did. But the story is also full, as this book has tried to show, of personal idealism, collective emotion and ideological passion.[7]

Studies of parliaments and administration in the period 1603 to 1640 have shown that there was a functional breakdown in early Stuart government.[8] It became most obvious under the stress of war in the 1620s and again in 1640. But it is important to note that, superficially at least, the administrative problems brought into focus by the Scottish war were solved during 1641 by Pym's reform of the subsidy, the imposition of a poll tax, the peace treaty with Scotland and the disbandment of the armies. If there was a crisis of the constitution in 1640 and 1641, in other words, it was a crisis that was surmounted without recourse to civil war.

Some have seen the central interest of the period from 1640 to 1642 as residing in the need to explain the defection from the parliamentary cause of many of those who opposed Arminianism and ship money, wished Strafford removed from the scene and desired regular parliaments.[9] But this view begs the question of defining the 'parliamentary cause' at the opening of the Long Parliament. Most of those who rode up to Westminster in November 1640 had no concept of a parliamentary cause in their minds. Reconciliation and settlement were seen as the purposes of parliaments and the reforms that most MPs envisaged seemed perfectly compatible with such an end. Only Pym and a few close friends saw the matter in totally different terms: for them the parliamentary cause was the extirpation of a conspiracy that struck at the core of the nation's life. Their fundamental misconception of the political situation, relentlessly propagated and pursued over the next months, must surely be the starting point for an explanation of how war came about. The central problem is not so much why did some defect as why did so many, both at Westminster and beyond, hold fast to Pym and his associates despite their deluded and over-dramatized view of the nation's troubles?

The brilliance of Pym's leadership and the skill with which he mastered the devoted support of a core of sympathizers in both Houses has been

---

7   For a comment on recent work based on the same approach as this book see L. Stone, 'The Revival of Narrative', *Past and Present* LXXXV (1979), 20–1.

8   G.E. Aylmer in Lamont, editor, *Tudors and Stuarts*, p. 137; Russell, *Parliaments*, pp. 64–70.

9   Ashton, *City and the Court*, p. 201; Morrill, *Revolt*, p.13.

emphasized throughout this book. But one cannot fail to note the contrast between the shrewdness and practicality of Pym's tactics and the emotional basis of his policies. The policies themselves suggest the abnegation of reason. The parliamentary leaders were men who were in no position to distinguish between truth and rumour and had no desire to do so. From the start rhetoric was their trade. Distrust festered, faith was gradually broken and step by step the chances of restoring confidence in the king and those around him disappeared. External events and contingencies contributed to this process, bringing home to MPs the apparent substance of Pym's story and turning it into a self-fulfilling prophecy. The army plots, the Incident, the Irish Rebellion and the king's attempt to arrest the five members all played into Pym's hands. Each time something happened to make the plot more real, it also brought it closer to the person of the king himself. The skirmishes at Westminster and in Whitehall in December 1641 and the presence of the king in the chamber of the Commons a few days later appeared to be the logical culmination of everything that Pym and his associates had been saying since 7 November 1640. Richard Baxter, a man who later expounded Pym's interpretation of the war, must surely have been thinking of those days when he wrote that 'the war was begun in our streets before king or parliament had any armies'.[10]

Despite the wave of hostility he then suffered, Pym had acquired a powerful London following by the autumn of 1641. Secretary Nicholas reflected on the main obstacle to reassertion of royal authority: 'the noise of an intention to introduce popery was that which first brought into dislike with the people the government both of the Church and commonwealth.'[11] An indication of the mood of the capital is provided by a letter from Teige O'Brien, a Catholic resident of Covent Garden, to Sir Philip Percival. 'Though I am both their Majesties' sworn servant', he wrote, 'yet I dare not go out of doors, the persecution is so fearfully cruel and hot.'[12]

It naturally took the provinces rather longer to grasp Pym's message but the Grand Remonstrance, as we have seen, finally did the strick. An alert observer like Thomas Stockdale in Yorkshire was then quite ready to slot the accusation of the five members into place as a Jesuit plot.[13] Parliament's propaganda related every royal action between January and November 1642 to the papist conspiracy. The king's purging of the commissions of the peace, to take but one example, was alleged on 11 July to be a preparation to ease the 'great change in religion and government' intended.[14] The impact of this propaganda, evident in the spring petitions, remained

10 Cited in Lamont, *Richard Baxter,* p.188.
11 *Evelyn,* p.113.
12 *HMC Egmont,* p.142.
13 *Fairfax* I, 297.
14 *LJ* V, 201.

massive throughout the summer. New petitions renewed the parrot cries of February and March.[15] The outburst of anti-Catholicism in the Stour valley exemplified popular receptivity. So far from bringing reassurance, searches of recusants' homes in many counties revealed stores of money and arms, which, because they were well publicized, merely increased tension.[16]

Pym's triumph was that by imposing his own fears of popery so sweepingly on a susceptible populace he had many really believe that the papists were kindling a civil war. It was widely rumoured, not without foundation of course, that the papists were providing Charles with the money he needed. According to one report going the rounds in July he had already received £80,000 from the papists and clergy.[17] Time and again people attributed royalist aggression to the king's Catholic subjects. 'The papists are upon Lancashire and threaten some heavy doom to befall the Protestants in those parts', John Osborne informed Henry Oxinden on 27 July.[18] 'All the papists and Jesuits in England did conspire together to ruin him and his house', the earl of Stamford told MPs on 8 July, reporting events in Leicestershire.[19] 'Thou hast a rotten stinking heart within thee, for if thou wilt be for the king thou must be for the papists', an apothecary of Grantham had told a neighbour who confessed his royalism a few days earlier.[20] There was much gossip about papists who swarmed to the court at York. In a letter of 31 July a Monmouthshire gentleman confessed his fears that parliament's order for disarming separatists would be used locally to 'disarm the best Protestants and then leave them naked to the papists, who were not yet disarmed, to cut their throats.'[21] Goring held Portsmouth in early August, it was alleged, with the help of four or five hundred 'cavaliers and papists'. Sir Bevil Grenville, so that story went, visited most of the papist gentry of Cornwall and Devon in disguise during August to raise men and money for the king. Sir John Biron took control of Oxford with 'sundry papists and other desperate persons.'[22] The Kentish JPs reported to Speaker Lenthall on 23 November that the trained bands were troubled about papists finding favour after one had been released by the Lords from Maidstone goal: 'seeing all the declarations name them

15　E.g. BL E 107(33): *Supplication of Hull to the King; CSPD 1641–3*, pp. 307–1.
16　King's Lynn Town Hall, Hall Book 8(1637–58), fol. 96v; BL E 202 (41): *A Perfect Diurnal*, 29 Aug.–5 Sept. (Devon); E 202(42): *An Exact and True Diurnal*, 29 Aug.–5 Sept. (Northamptonshire); E 202(44): *Remarkable Passages or a Perfect Diurnal*, 5–12 Sept.(Essex); *HMC Portland* I, 64(Dorset).
17　Hill, p. 119.
18　BL Add. MS 28000, fol. 206.
19　BL E 202(12): *Some Special Passages*, 3–10 July.
20　BL Harl. MS 163, fol. 235r; *CJ* II, 645.
21　BL Harl. MS 163, fol. 93v; 164, fol. 260r; Wright, editor, *Autobiography of Joseph Lister*, p. 13.
22　BL E 202(30): *A Perfect Diurnal*, pp. 5–6, E 202 (40): *A Perfect Diurnal*, 22–29 Aug.; Bodleian Dep C MS 165, no. 129.

with the prelatical party the only causes of all miseries and distractions.'[23]

Pym's circle had never been so naive as to suppose that the papists could overturn English religion and government singlehanded. The potency of the Catholic design, the Grand Remonstrance stressed, rested on its enjoyment of the support of a band of fellow travellers consisting of the bishops, 'the corrupt part of the clergy' and councillors or courtiers working for private ends, which might include their own advancement through furthering the interests of foreign states.[24] The swift reaction to the bishops' protestation on 30 December 1641 reflected firmly held assumptions about their treasonable predilections. Once Strafford was removed many thought them 'the most suspected party of the kingdom.'[25] Rooting out dissolute clergy, as we have seen, was treated equally seriously, for as D'Ewes remarked on 21 July 1642, the House's investigations had proved that clergy who had brought in 'wicked tenets' such as Arminianism were 'for the most part men of most scandalous lives.'[26] Writing to the Committee of Safety on 12 October, the parliamentary command at Worcester recommended that the Michaelmas rents of all the bishops, deans and chapters should be sequestered, 'they being that generation of men who have showed themselves most active instruments in procuring of our present miseries.'[27]

The notion of a broadly constituted malignant party bent on the destruction of the nation was expounded increasingly persuasively as the events of late 1641 and 1642 unfolded. Individuals like Digby and Goring were easily drawn into the net. The latter was a 'loose and profane man', D'Ewes believed, working with the papists to make Portsmouth a royalist garrison.[28] It was impossible to miss the simple fact that the army officers who fought with the London citizens at Westminster and in Whitehall at the end of December 1641, attended Charles on 4 January and then caroused at Kingston, henceforward called the cavaliers, quickly became as important in their influence on the king as his well established counsellors. Sir John Hotham noted that many of those with the king at the gates of Hull on 24 April were men 'that were at the parliament door.'[29]

Thus the conspiracy made more sense than ever as its boldest protagonists revealed themselves: no one who was in the grip of Pym's propaganda doubted that papists lurked behind bishops, clergy and cavaliers. In a letter to Sir John Bankes on 31 May, the earl of Essex summarized the nation's enemies as 'delinquents, papists and men that desire to make their fortunes

23 HLRO, Main Papers, 23 Nov. 1642: JPs of Kent to Speaker Lenthall.
24 Gardiner, *Documents*, pp. 206–7.
25 BL Harl. MS 5047, fol. 62v; *CJ* II, 251; *D'Ewes(C)*, pp. 24–5, 47, 51, 133–6, 139–40, 237–41.
26 BL Harl. MS 163, fol. 284v.
27 Bodleian Dep C MS 159, no. 133b.
28 BL Harl. MS 164, fol. 259r.
29 Hill, p. 66.

by the troubles of the land'. Five months later, in his letters announcing a 'happy victory' at Edgehill, he dismissed the royalist army more succinctly as 'desperate persons ill affected to the state.'[30] There were a few like Henry Marten who scorned the fiction that the king was the innocent captive of his advisers, but most of the leading parliamentarians probably at least half believed their own propaganda.[31] 'I am persuaded that His Majesty would be graciously pleased to come to his parliament if those delinquents and cavaliers which are with him might be saved harmless, which he much desires', wrote Thomas Toll to his Norwich constituents on 10 September.[32] This is probably the note that most MPs would have struck. There is no reason to doubt the sincerity of Denzil Holles's letter to Bankes, hastily scribbled in the Commons chamber on 21 May. He was confident parliament would 'most readily cast itself at the king's feet with all faithful and loyal submission upon the first appearance of change in His Majesty, that he will forsake those counsels which carry him on to so high a dislike and opposition to their proceedings by mispossessing himself of them.'[33]

The strength of the parliamentary cause, both at Westminster and beyond, was its immediacy and indisputability. The nation's enemies appeared unquestionably evil and obviously implacable. Thus a sense of identification with and trust in parliament was a necessary defensive reaction. We have seen how strikingly this sense emerged in the petitions of early 1642 and how vigorously it was expressed in some of the summer musters under the militia ordinance. How much more powerfully must it have affected those who had actually toiled in the Commons for months on end. In a speech on 27 January 1642, Denzil Holles expressed his conviction that parliament preserved standards of probity and public duty which singled it out as the instrument called upon for the salvation of the state: 'whosoever shall for favour or affection or for hatred or by ends shall not freely deliver his mind here is not fit to sit within these walls and I am sure will never enter the kingdom of heaven.'[34] Sir Simonds D'Ewes spoke on 16 May of how he felt his own pride and dignity was bound up with the Long Parliament's achievement. 'For mine own part', he declared, 'I think they must have a wisdom beyond the moon that dream of any happiness to themselves after the ruin of this parliament, which I shall never desire to overlive.'[35]

30   Bankes, *Corfe Castle*, p. 126; Gloucestershire RO D 2510/25.
31   C.M. Williams, 'The Anatomy of a Radical Gentleman: Henry Marten', in D. Pennington and K.V. Thomas, editors, *Puritans and Revolutionaries* (Oxford, 1978), p. 133.
32   BL Add. MS 22619, fol. 38.
33   Bankes, *Corfe Castle*, pp. 124–6.
34   BL Harl. MS 480, fol. 68v.
35   BL Harl. MS 163, fol. 121v.

All this though is only one side of the picture. Charles I and his most intimate advisers lived in an equally closed mental world. His experience in the 1620s had given Charles a jaundiced view of parliaments and a strong sense of distrust of certain individuals who he believed were ready to challenge his monarchy for private and selfish ends. His troubles with the Scots had strengthened his belief that Puritans were inherently seditious, a view strongly pressed on him by Con in their conversations during 1638 and 1639 about the possibility of the pope coming to his aid. Con portrayed the Scottish rebellion as the product of greed and ambition cloaked by religion.[36] The king plainly saw the English one in the same terms. Parliament would put him and his children, he told the Yorkshire gentry on 4 August, 'into the hands of a few malignant persons who have entered into a combination to destroy us.'[37] 'You shall meet with no enemies', he declared to his army on 19 September, 'but traitors, most of them Brownists, Anabaptists and atheists, such who desire to destroy both Church and state.'[38] At Wrexham, in his speech to the inhabitants of Denbighshire on 27 September he summarized his case as follows: 'I have been dealt with by a powerful malignant party in this kingdom, whose designs are no less than to destroy my person and crown, the laws of the land and the present government both of Church and state.'[39]

Charles's strength of character was based on his enduring sense that he was answerable only to God. At the head of his army two days before the battle of Edgehill, he spoke of the 'inhuman and impious misbelief' of those who would not accept his word that he had no end but the kingdom's happiness and the defence of the Church, the law and the liberty of his subjects. 'Ambition which fills the veins of great ones to be greater', he insisted, 'must needs be free from us since we are greatest; envy and malice are as far since we have no competitor.'[40] The king's misunderstanding of his opponents' aims and motives would have been less serious if his character had been different. He was a man who magnified distrust even in the most loyal hearts. What men saw was the king's aloofness, his rigidity, his immersion in a cosmopolitan court culture they did not understand, his deep affection for his French wife who meant nothing to them.[41] What they suspected, quite correctly, was his deviousness and taste for intrigue. During a debate about execution of the recusancy laws in the 1625 parliament, an MP could say without fear of contradiction that the king's heart

---

36 Hibbard, pp. 190–2.
37 BL E 109(26): *The King's Speech to the Gentry of Yorkshire.*
38 *LJ* v, 376.
39 Phillips, *Civil War in Wales* II, 20.
40 Bodleian Ashmole MS 830, fol. 277.
41 Kenyon, *The Stuarts*, pp. 79–89; P.W. Thomas, 'Two Cultures? Court and Country under Charles I', in Russell, *Origins*, pp. 168–93.

was 'as right towards religion as we would desire it.'[42] No one would have dared to make such a statement in 1641.

Charles's wavering and indecisive policy during the first half of 1641 jolted men's confidence in him. His hard line thereafter seemed like proof that the papists had captured his mind. The king's blunders — above all the five-members débâcle — did much to make the political crisis insoluble. So did the general weakness of the Stuart monarchy at this particular moment. The specific grievances of the 1630s could be answered by new laws, but the disastrous loss of confidence brought about by the reversal of James I's foreign and religious policies and the introduction of an alien court culture could not quickly be restored.[43] Because the prestige of the monarchy was so low it was unusually vulnerable to a conspiracy story of the kind that Pym had to tell.

'Our sickness', the earl of Bristol observed in a speech to the Lords on 20 May 1642, 'is rather continued out of fancy and conceit (I mean fears and jealousies) than out of any real distemper or defect'. His analysis was perceptive: 'it is much easier to compose differences arising from reason, yea even from wrongs, than it is to satisfy jealousies, which arising out of diffidence and distrust, grow and are varied upon each occasion.'[44] The earl of Northumberland had offered an equally cool analysis in a letter to Sir John Bankes only the day before. 'It is too apparent that neither king nor parliament are without fears and jealousies', he wrote, 'the one of having his authority and just rights invaded, the other of losing that liberty which freeborn subjects ought to enjoy and the laws of the land do allow us.' 'The alteration of government', declared Northumberland harking back to the phrase first used in 1628, 'is apprehended on both sides.'[45] Some parliamentarians were quite explicit that their concern was to preserve their liberties. 'Peace and our liberties are the only things we aim at', wrote Sir Ralph Verney in June 1642, 'till we have peace I am sure we can enjoy no liberties and without liberties I shall not heartily desire peace.'[46] John Hutchinson, according to his wife, was satisfied that a conspiracy existed to introduce popery 'yet he did not think that so clear a ground of the war as the defence of the just English liberties.'[47] What Verney and Hutchinson seem to have been saying was that they could not trust the king to rule according to the law.

It is vitally important to distinguish between the issues raised by the political crisis of 1641 and 1642, such as the militia or appointment of

42 Russell, *Parliaments*, p. 230.
43 Kenyon, *Stuart England*, p.421; Ashton, *English Civil War*, pp.22–42.
44 Rushworth III, part I, 715; Zagorin, p. 320.
45 Bankes, *Corfe Castle*, p.122.
46 *Verney* II, 89.
47 *Hutchinson*, p. 53.

counsellors, and what it was actually about. The earls of Bristol and Northumberland surely saw the matter correctly. The civil war was based on mutual distrust. As early as 1626 two growing fears, of 'parity' on the one hand and 'popery' on the other, have been identified in English public life, fears which 'present a mirror image to each other and came to enjoy a curious interdependence, each being necessary to validate the other.'[48] What happened in 1641 and 1642 was that two groups of men became the prisoners of competing myths that fed on one another, so that events seemed to confirm two opposing interpretations of the political crisis that were both originally misconceived and erroneous. This may seem a frail foundation for civil war. But the war must be seen in the context of the imaginative poverty of the seventeenth century. This was a society in which people were made scapegoats for processes, which lacked the capacity to conceive of and weigh in the balance alternative political systems, which took a highly traditional view of the world as a place of 'limited good' where no one can prosper save at someone else's expense.[49]

For all this, any account of the origins of the civil war which fails to give due weight to its ideological content must be incomplete. If fear and distrust at the centre of the nation's affairs finally made war unavoidable, there was surely in addition something more positive which drove men to take up arms against their own countrymen. There were many on both sides in 1642 who believed they were fighting for a cause, not just to defend the state against a faction or a conspiracy. The civil war came about because of the coincidence of hopeless misunderstanding and irreconcilable distrust with fierce ideological conflict.

The royalists' ideology is the harder to define at the outbreak of the war because it was slow to crystallize. Generalized and amorphous conservative sentiment gave the king a good deal of his initial support. But it has been suggested here that royalism had its foundation in a critical attitude to the aims and tactics of the dominant clique at Westminster. The positive idealism which informed and sustained those royalists who were Protestants became apparent during 1642: its essence was attachment to a traditional and moderate concept of the role of the Church in society, emphasizing the importance of order both in worship and Church government.

The heart of parliamentarian ideology was the connection in men's minds between the struggle against popery and the preservation of true religion. The essence of the conflict with the king, as one historian has put it, was seen as a 'collision between true religion and popery.'[50] We can only understand the zeal of the parliamentarians at the start of the war if we appreciate the frustration many of them felt at the bizarre appearance of a

48 Russell in Clark, Smith, Tyacke, editors, *The English Commonwealth*, p. 164.
49 P. Burke, *Popular Culture in Early Modern Europe* (London, 1979), pp. 173, 176–7.
50 R. Clifton in Russell, *Origins*, p. 162.

Church half reformed, the inspiration afforded by the vision of a new Jerusalem and the shock created by the king's assault in the previous decade on the mainstream of moderate Puritan evangelicalism.[51] Protestants, as Holles put it in a speech on 22 June 1642, had seen the 'truth and substance' of religion 'eaten up with formality, vain pomp and unnecessary ceremonies; the gross errors of popery and Arminianism imposed upon us as the doctrine of our Church; a way opened to all licentiousness.'[52] Essex petitioners, we have seen, spoke of religion as more precious than their lives and liberties.[53] 'Our chief aim is to preserve religion', declared an MP in the debate about the king's reply to the propositions sent to Beverley on 25 July, 'now before the parliament the main design was to destroy religion.'[54]

What was really at stake at the deepest level of this crisis was not the issue of the militia or appointment of councillors, the immediate expressions of political distrust, but the future of the Church. The legislative priorities of the Commons in the summer of 1642 were the bills for summoning the assembly of divines, abolishing pluralities, extirpating Arminian innovations and removing scandalous ministers.[55] These were the bills that MPs were trying to hasten in the Lords, that they insisted upon in the Nineteen Propositions, that they kept in the forefront of the Treaty of Oxford negotiations in the first months of 1643.[56] In a speech on 6 July, D'Ewes argued that, whereas 'the liberty and propriety' of the subject had been clearly asserted, 'the main matter which yet remains to be secured to us in the reformation of religion.' He was one of those who believed parliament could simply not run the risk of a repetition of the Arminian attack on true religion: 'seeing those ceremonies which do give offence are no ways necessary, they are to be utterly abolished . . . and so we shall have no further trouble how to satisfy weak consciences in the use of them, which can scarcely stand without the abuse of them.' D'Ewes had emphasized a few days earlier that parliament did not wish to alter 'any fundamental or essential part of our religion established, but only to alter some things in the outward frame or government of the Church.'[57] It was ironic that, while royalists vilified parliament for condoning sectarianism, it was in fact taking repressive action: in September 1642, for instance, a feltmaker was imprisoned by order of the Commons for preaching publicly in Holborn.[58]

51   Kenyon, *Stuart England*, pp. 23–4; Russell, *Origins*, pp. 17–21.
52   Cited in Crawford, p.52.
53   Above, page 355.
54   East Devon RO 1700 A/CP 24.
55   *CJ* II, 510, 527, 560, 674, 677, 681, 695; *LJ* v, 151, 156, 210, 212, 214; BL Harl. MS 163, fol. 146v.
56   *LJ* v, 160; Gardiner, *Documents*, pp. 252, 263–4.
57   BL Harl. MS 163, fol. 259r; 164, fol. 257r.
58   BL E 202(45): *A Perfect Diurnal*, 26 Sept.–3 Oct.

The Puritan core of the parliamentarian party could not abandon their belief in the supremacy of truth and that belief had become incompatible with the Foxeian tradition of obedience to the godly prince.[59] Thus anti-Catholicism was turned against the court and even the monarch and the force of it carried men into rebellion. It was the king therefore who had opened the way for the call to apocalyptic warfare that thundered from the London pulpits in 1642 and who had forced a section of the gentry into an unnatural alliance with radical Puritans from further down the social scale. In this sense it is correct to state that the connection between Puritanism and the civil war was largely of Charles I's own making.[60]

At the start of the war popular support was crucial to the parliamentarians' strength. In a county like Sussex the entrenched Puritan oligarchy could surely not have fought parliament's battles without the spontaneous enthusiasm of the yeoman families of the weald and the eastern rapes, an enthusiasm that was nourished by decades of household piety and yearning for a godly commonwealth.[61] If men like Sir William Brereton, Herbert Morley and John Pyne offered the necessary leadership, men like the tradesman Nehemiah Wallington of London, the Yorkshire clothier Samuel Priestley and fervent townsman John Coulton of Rye sustained the parliamentarian cause in the field. Wharton's descriptions of the parliamentarian march to Worcester exemplify militant Puritanism in action. 'Though I and many thousands more may be cut off', he wrote after the reverse at Powick Bridge, 'yet I am confident the Lord of Hosts will in the end triumph gloriously.'[62] Priestley's brother left an account of how he went to war, against the entreaties of his family, insisting that he would rather die in the field in a good cause than see the same tragedy as had occurred in Ireland enacted in England.[63] Samuel Turner's letter to his brother in London about a cavalier raid on Henley in January 1643 radiates the same spirit: 'Certainly he was more than blind that could not see God manifestly in every particular of this fight, working deliverance for us and confusion to our enemies.'[64] Ralph Josselin, who defined his motives for contributing on the Propositions as 'my affection to God and his gospel', heard the news of Edgehill three days after the battle, as he was on his way to deliver a fast day sermon. He noted that the time it had been fought coincided with his prayers the previous Sunday, 'when I was earnest with God for mercy upon us against our enemies.'[65] There is a real sense in which the

59 Lamont, *Godly Rule*, pp. 17–105.
60 Russell, *Origins*, pp. 23–4; Russell, *Parliaments*, p. 432.
61 D. Underdown, *Past and Present* LXXXV (1979), 26; *Sussex*, pp. 61–75, 255–69. See also my forthcoming article 'Puritanism in Seventeenth Century Sussex' in M. Kitch, editor, *Studies in Sussex Church History*.
62 *CSPD 1641–3*, pp. 371–3, 379–80, 382–8, 391–4.
63 Manning, pp. 31–2, 211.
64 Vicars, *Jehovah-Jireh*, p. 260.
65 Macfarlane, editor, *Diary of Ralph Josselin*, pp. 12–13.

English civil war was a war of religion.

So war and bloodshed came to England, as no one could have foreseen or predicted they would two years previously. This was an unnatural war, as men recognized at the time.[66] Englishmen's sense of security in this period rested on ideas of balance, harmony and degree in civil society. Even their architecture and church monuments tell us how they clung to these notions. Men were not equipped to harmonize political change or upheaval with the fixed points of their mental world. Civil war made precedent irrelevant and forced a painful emancipation from the past.[67] If it was not inevitable, as this book has argued, then it was all the more tragic. A curious mixture of folly and idealism lies behind the events that have been described. At the outbreak of hostilities there was also a macabre element of farce: the royalists slew eight of their own men when a cannon split before Warwick Castle in August 1642; four soldiers in the earl of Bedford's regiment were blown up by 'careless looking to their powder' on the march to Sherborne a few weeks later.[68]

The final impression one is left with is of the pathos of the individual's dilemma, as men and women were caught up in a conflict that was not of their making yet in a sense was made by them all. For many in England's governing class it seemed that civilized life was at the brink of destruction. The sorrow men felt about the coming of war reaches out to us from their letters. In those euphoric early days of the Long Parliament, Thomas Knyvett had dreamed of a country cottage: 'I do fancy a little house by our-selves extremely well', he told his wife, 'where we may spend the remainder of our days in religious tranquil, for this parliament surely will settle all peace and quiet amongst us.' In the summer of 1642 he reflected sadly on the state of the nation: both sides strove for the maintenance of the laws 'and the question is not so much how to be governed by them as who shall be master and judge of them; a lamentable condition to consume the wealth and treasure of such a kingdom, perhaps the blood too, upon a few nice wilful quibbles.'[69]

The pain was worst for the genuine moderates, those who could not see the quarrel in black and white yet could not avoid joining one party or the other. The strain on deeply held friendships was acute. In his letters to Lady Temple in the autumn of 1642, Lord Saville expressed his bitterness at the way his reputation was being traduced at Westminster, but comforted himself with the thought that his friend Viscount Saye was probably as 'falsely represented' at court. 'Do your friend right against scandalous tongues which I hear blast me', wrote Sir John Potts to D'Ewes

---

66 E.g. Bodleian Dep C MS 164, no 24.
67 Thomas, *Religion and the Decline of Magic*, p. 425.
68 BL E 202(33): *A True and Exact Diurnal*, 8–15 Aug., p. 6; 669 f 6(77): *A Copy of a Letter sent from Sherborne.*
69 *Knyvett*, pp. 98, 107.

on 2 September, 'Sir, I assure you my conscience leads me to uphold the commonwealth to which I will prove no changeling.'[70]

So many of the gentry who were activists in the civil war could not envisage an outright victory for either side. 'I would not have the king trample on the parliament', declared Saville, 'nor the parliament lessen him so much as to make a way for the people to rule us all. . . . For as much as I love the king, I should not be glad be beat the parliament though they were in the wrong.'[71] Sir William Waller, whose letter to Sir Ralph Hopton is quoted at the start of this book, confessed afterwards that he abhorred the war though he acted in it, but it 'was ever with a wish . . . that the one party might not have the worse nor the other the better.'[72] John Hotham wrote as follows to the earl of Newcastle on 9 January 1643: 'I honour the king as much as any and love the parliament but do not desire to see either absolute conquerors; it is too great a temptation to courses of will and violence.'[73]

Civil war led the English gentry into the dark and they tried to maintain the courtesies of life as they knew it while the country was becoming consumed by strife. 'My Lord, I take it as a great favour that these differences that I hope God in his good time will make up again cause you not to forget ancient friendship', wrote John Hotham to Newcastle in a letter of 18 December 1642 about an exchange of prisoners.[74] There is perhaps no letter which expresses so well the poignancy of civil war as that written by Lady Brilliana Harley to Viscount Scudamore on 27 December 1642, about the treatment she was receiving from the Herefordshire royalists:

> My thoughts are in a labyrinth to find out the reason why they should be thus to me. When I look upon myself I can see nothing but love and respect arising out of my heart to them and when I look upon the many bonds by which most of the gentlemen in this country are tied to Sir Robert Harley, that of blood and some with alliance, and all with his long professed and real friendship and for myself that of common courtesy as to a stranger brought into their country, I know not how these who I believe to be so good should break all these obligations.[75]

The gentry could not know at this point that there would be no English revolution.

70 Cartwright, editor, 'Delinquency of Lord Saville', *Camden Miscellany* VIII, 5; BL Harl. MS 386, fol. 234.
71 Cartwright, editor, 'Delinquency of Lord Saville', *Camden Miscellany* VIII, 6.
72 Adair, *Roundhead General*, p.43.
73 *HMC Portland* I, 87.
74 Bodleian Dep C MS 153, no. 114.
75 PRO C 115/N2/8521. I am grateful to Mr Terry Smith for providing me with a transcript of this letter.

Appendix

Attendance and Voting in the House of Lords 17 January – 5 February 1642

	17 Jan.	24 Jan.	26 Jan.	1 Feb. a.m.	5 Feb.
Richmond	/	/	/	/	
Bath	/	/	/	/	
Bedford	/+	/+	/	/	/×
Berkshire	/	/	/	/	
Bolingbroke	/+	/+	/+	/+	/×
Bristol	/	/		/	
Caernarvon	/		/	/	/
Cambridge	/	/	/	/	/
Carlisle	/	/			
Clare	/	/+	/		/×
Cleveland	/		/	/	/*
Cumberland	/	/			
Denbigh	/	/	/	/	
Devon	/	/	/	/	/*
Dorset				/	/
Dover	/	/	/	/	/*
Essex	/	/+	/+	/+	/×
Holland	/+	/+	/+	/+	/×
Leicester	+	+	/+	/+	/×
Lincoln	/	/+	/+	/+	/×
Lindsey	/	/	/	/	/*
Manchester		/	/	/	/×
Monmouth	/	/	/		
Newcastle				/	
Newport	/	/		/	/*
Northampton	/	/	/	/	/*
Northumberland	/+		/+	/+	/×
Nottingham		/+			
Pembroke	/+	/+	/+	/+	/×

	17 Jan.	24 Jan.	26 Jan.	1 Feb. a.m.	5 Feb.
Peterbrough	/	/+	/		
Portland	/	/	/	/	/*
Rivers		/	/	/	
Rutland					/.
Salisbury	/+	/+		/	/×
Southampton	/	/	/	/	
Stamford	/+	/+	/+	/+	/
Suffolk	/		+		
Sussex	/				/
Thanet	/	/+	/	/	
Warwick	/+	/+	/+	/+	/×
Westmorland				/	/
Conway		/+	/+	/+	/×
Saye and Sele	/+	/+	/		/×
Brooke	/+	/+	+	/+	/×
Bruce		/+	/		
Capel		/	/		/*
Chandos		/+	/+		/×
Coventry	/	/	/	/	/
Craven	/	/	/	/	/
Cromwell		/	/	/+	/
Dacre		/+	/	/+	
Darcy and Conyers		/		/	/
Dunsmore	/	/	/	/	/*
Fauconberg	/	/	/		/
Goring	/	/	/	/	
Grey of Ruthin	/	/	/	/	
Grey of Wark	/+	/+	/+	/+	/×
Herbert of Cherbury	/	/	/	/	/
Howard of Charlton		/	/	/	/
Howard of Escrick	/+	/+	/+	/+	
Hunsdon	+	/+	/+		/×
Kimbolton (Mandeville)	/+	/+	/+	/+	/×
Littleton	/	/	/	/	
Lovelace	/	/			
Mohun		/	/		
Mowbray	/	/	/	/	/*
Newnham	/+	/+	/	/	/×
North	/+	+	/	/+	/×
Paget	/+	/+	/+	/+	/×

	17 Jan.	24 Jan.	26 Jan.	1 Feb. a.m.	5 Feb.
Pierrepoint	/	/	/	/	/
Rich	/	/	/	/	/*
Roberts	/+	/+	/+	/+	/×
St John of Bletsoe	/+	/+	/+	/+	/×
Saville	/	/		/	/*
Seymour	/	/	/	/	/*
Spencer	/+	/+	/+	/+	/×
Stanhope	/				
Strange					/×
Wentworth	/	/	/	/	/*
Wharton	+	/+	/+	/+	/×
Willoughby of Eresby	/	/	/	/	
Willoughby of Parham	/+	/+	/	/	/×
Chester	/		/		
London	/	/	/		
Rochester	/		/	/	/*
Winchester	/	/	/	/	/*
Worcester			/	/	/*

Notes on Appendix

Peers are listed alphabetically within the following categories: Dukes, Earls, Viscounts, Barons, Bishops.

/   Attendance recorded by the Clerk of the House
+   Entered protest after a division of the House
×   Probably voted for Bishops Exclusion
*   Probably voted against Bishops Exclusion

Decisions reached after a division:

17 Jan. Commons' petition to the king to remove Sir John Biron from the Lieutenancy of the Tower rejected.

24 Jan. Commons' petition to the king to put the forts and militia in the hands of parliamentary nominees rejected.

26 Jan. The Duke of Richmond's apology for moving that the House should adjourn for six months accepted as sufficient satisfaction.

1 Feb. The Commons' petition to the king to remove the Duke of Richmond from all his offices and forbid him to come to court rejected.

5 Feb. That the bill for taking away the votes of bishops out of the House should pass as a law.

Index

Where entries include sub-headings the listing of topics is alphabetical; in town entries places and buildings are listed alphabetically before topics.